CRIME AND PUNISHMENT IN
AMERICAN HISTORY

CRIME AND PUNISHMENT IN AMERICAN HISTORY

LAWRENCE M. FRIEDMAN

BasicBooks
A Division of HarperCollins*Publishers*

Designed by Craig Winer

Library of Congress Cataloging-in-Publication Data
Friedman, Lawrence Meir, 1930–
        Crime and punishment in American history / by
Lawrence Friedman.
                p.   cm.
        Includes bibliographical references and index.
        ISBN 0–465–01461–5 (cloth)
        ISBN 0–465–01487–9 (paper)
        1. Criminal justice, Administration of—United States—
History.
    I. Title.
    KF9223.F75 1993
    345.73′05—dc20
    [347.3055]   92–54517
                                                   CIP

94 95 96 97 ◆/CW 9 8 7 6 5 4 3 2 1

For Leah, Jane, Amy, Paul, and Sarah

CONTENTS

PART III
CRIMINAL JUSTICE IN THE TWENTIETH CENTURY

PREFACE

THE BOOK THAT FOLLOWS IS A GENERAL HISTORY OF AMERICAN CRIMINAL JUS-
tice, from its beginnings in the seventeenth century to the present time.
This is a vast subject, one that, frankly, has to be approached with a certain amount of fear and trembling. There is more to know about crime
and punishment in this society than any human being can possibly
know. The research on the subject, up to now, has been both thick and
thin: so thick in some parts of the subject that no one can cope with it,
certainly not I; in others so thin and wan that the intrepid storyteller is
reduced to guesswork, weaving great swatches of narrative from little
rags of data. Moreover, there is no way to tell it all, no way to make the
story complete. The author is forced to make choices, to throw the spotlight on some parts of the subject while others are left in the shadows.
In this day and age, this is bound to leave some readers frustrated or disappointed.

For many of the people who read this book, in a library or in the comfort of their homes, the world of crime and punishment may be something of a foreign country, one with strange customs, language, and
manners; they stumble about like tourists clutching a phrase book. It is
hard for the comfortable, the respectable, the solid middle class to imagine themselves in the shoes of the people on either side of the equa-
tion—those accused of crime, on the one hand; and the police, judges,
wardens, and prosecutors, who do the accusing and the judging and the
punishing, on the other.

I cannot pretend to be much better off myself, at least as far as the *present* is concerned. When I write about the past, I can make an honest attempt to bridge the chasm between what happened, and the reader's own experience; I can try to bring to life the dead and buried dramas that I find, pinned like dead butterflies, in the texts of old records. The beginnings of this story took place more than three centuries ago. The end of it—if it has an end—is only yesterday. This last is the delicate, dangerous part. As we get closer to our own times, the material swells obscenely in bulk. And the bodies are not all dead and buried. There are human witnesses, people who have been through it, or are going through it, people who experience the system in a way I can only guess at.

I have no real idea, no authentic gut feeling, about life in blasted, weed-choked vacant lots between crack houses, or in dark streets desecrated with graffiti; or what it is like to be behind the wheel of a patrol car, slowly penetrating "hostile territory," eyes groping to interpret shapes in an unfriendly darkness; or what it is like to sit on death row, or spend the night in a county jail, in a misery of moaning and vomit; or, for that matter, what it is like to be on trial as an inside trader or embezzler, or as a dumper of toxic wastes. Nor do I know the feelings that go through the mind of a public defender staggering under a stack of files, or a criminal lawyer picking a jury, or a judge in police court, or a juror trapped in a four-month murder case. Some of these experiences I can only guess at—and hope I guess right. Other parts of the story I am forced to omit, or leave for somebody else to do.

At times, working on this book, I found myself somewhat discouraged. The subject is fascinating—but also baffling and immense; fragmented into a thousand pieces; unwieldy, stubborn; hidden in dark places and inaccessible corners. It was easy to feel out of my depth.

But the sheer importance of crime and punishment, and their lurid attraction, won out at the end. Crime, in our decade, is a major political issue. Of course, people have always been concerned about crime. But there is reason to believe people are more upset about crime today than ever before—more worried, more fearful. They are most afraid of sudden violence or theft by strangers; they feel the cities are jungles; they are afraid to walk the streets at night. Millions of parents are afraid their children will turn into junkies. Millions see some sort of rot, some sort of decay infecting society, and crime is the pus oozing out from the wound.

These are not completely idle notions. Serious crime *has* skyrocketed in the second half of the twentieth century. We seem to be in the midst of a horrendous crime storm—a hurricane of crime. The homicide rate in American cities is simply appalling. It takes months or even years for

Helsinki or Tokyo to equal the *daily* harvest of rape, pillage, looting, and death in New York City. Why is this happening to us?

A history of criminal justice can, I think, help illuminate this question. It can tell us where we were, and why; and more or less where we are going. At least it can try. History does not give us *answers*; but it does sometimes dispel myths, and it can be like a flashlight shining in dark and deserted corners. Hence I felt the story needs to be told.

No author works completely alone. I have to take responsibility for shortcomings, but I also need to thank at least some of the people who helped me. There are, first of all, the scholars who made my job easier because of their own work in the field. There are too many to name, but I want to express admiration and gratitude for the historical work of Edward L. Ayers, Michael Hindus, Roger Lane, Erik Monkkonen, Mary Odem, and Samuel Walker, among others. I also want to acknowledge the help of John Bogart, Sarah Friedman, Joanna Grossman, Chris Guthrie, David Himelfarb, Leslye Obiora, Thomas Russell, Reid Schar, and Paul Tabor. Lynne Henderson made detailed comments on an earlier draft, which were enormously helpful. I also benefited from comments by Barbara A. Babcock and Robert Weisberg. Joy St. John, as usual, helped me greatly with the manuscript at various points; and I owe a debt, too, to the staff of the Stanford Law Library for their patience and cooperation in running down the odd sources I demanded from time to time.

Stanford, California
February 1993

INTRODUCTION

ABOUT THREE AND A HALF CENTURIES AGO, THERE WAS A STIR IN THE COLONY of New Haven, Connecticut. A sow had given birth to a "monstrous" piglet. In the minds of the colonists, this was no accident. Surely the misbirth was some sort of omen. Specifically, it had to be a sign of sin, a sign of a revolting, deadly crime: carnal intercourse with the mother pig.

Who could have done this horrendous act? The finger of suspicion pointed to Thomas Hogg (unfortunate name). Hogg insisted he was innocent. Was he telling the truth? The magistrates put him to the test: they took him to a pigsty, and forced him to scratch at two sows in the enclosure. One sow, the mother of the monster-piglet, reacted with a show of "lust" when Hogg touched her. The other sow made no reaction at all. Hogg's guilt was now crystal clear.[1]

Another scene: it is New York City, spring 1989. A group of young males in their teens, mostly black, sweep through the darkness of Central Park, in a mood of wild exuberance. First they chase a man on a bicycle. When he gives them the slip, they find and attack a young woman who, somewhat recklessly, has been jogging in the park. The woman fights back, but she is all alone; there are many of them, and they are much too strong for her. They rape her, beat her savagely, and leave her bleeding body in the bushes. The woman, who is white and works for a brokerage house, comes within an inch of death, yet somehow survives. The police find and arrest the young men who attacked her, and they go on trial in a blaze of publicity.

Still another image: it is a few years before the Central Park beating. Two wheeler-dealers issue stock to themselves in corporations that had, in fact, no assets at all. They sell this stock, unregistered, to suckers among the general public. They brag and boast about the company to brokers and investors; business is flourishing, the future is exceedingly bright. Everything they say is a lie. They sell more than two million shares and put millions of dollars in their pockets, before they run afoul of the Securities and Exchange Commission.[2]

And yet another vignette: in September 1900, George W. Howard married Helen Hawkes, age seventeen, daughter of a "rich Democratic politician of Brooklyn." The couple had first met at a dance. George was a civil engineer who hailed from Boston. After the marriage, George began to behave in a peculiar way. He kept returning to Boston on this or that excuse; so often, in fact, that Helen's brother became suspicious and hired a private detective to find out what was what. The truth was devastating. George was leading a double life. He had another wife in Boston—Anna Kay, the daughter of an Episcopalian clergyman—and a nine-year-old son to boot. George was put under arrest and charged with bigamy. In court, the prosecution piled on the evidence: twenty-eight witnesses and numerous exhibits, including a "piece of the wedding cake" from the Boston marriage. George was convicted of the crime.[3]

These four somewhat exotic or notorious or outrageous examples of criminal behavior are by no means unique. They were drawn from the past and (near) present. In every period of our national experience, thousands upon thousands of other crimes have been committed; countless numbers of crimes. A fair number have been lurid, gripping, unusual, emblematic. Most of them have not. Most have been ordinary crimes, dull crimes, crimes of deadly familiarity: shoplifting, wife-beatings, assaults, barroom brawls, drug offenses, forged checks, drunk driving, vagrancy, petty theft.

There are recurrent patterns. Among serious crimes, the overwhelming majority can be classified as one or more of the many forms of stealing—larceny, theft, burglary, embezzlement, and on and on. For much of our history, drunkenness was the single most frequently punished crime—the plankton of the criminal sea. Thousands of arrests and court appearances came out of the fighting and biting that drunkenness produces. In the colonial period, in some colonies, fornication, adultery, idleness, and lewd behavior filled the courtroom with sinners. However we measure and count, the historical record yields a rich, and somewhat depressing, harvest of crime.

This book is about the American experience of crime; more accurately, it is about the *social reaction* to crime. It is an attempt to sketch out the history of the criminal justice system in the United States, from its colonial beginnings right up to the present day. In this introduction, I put forward a few basic concepts and introduce some themes, which we will follow as they zig and zag through the centuries.

We begin, however, with a few attempts at definition. We have talked about *crime* and about *criminal justice*. But what do we mean by these terms?

CRIME

There is no real answer to the question, What is crime? There are popular ideas about crime: crime is bad behavior, antisocial behavior, blameworthy acts, and the like. But in a very basic sense, crime is a *legal* concept: what makes some conduct criminal, and other conduct not, is the fact that some, but not others, are "against the law."[4]

Crimes, then, are forbidden acts. But they are forbidden in a special way. We are not supposed to break contracts, drive carelessly, slander people, or infringe copyrights; but these are not (usually) criminal acts. The distinction between a *civil* and a *criminal* case is fundamental in our legal system. A civil case has a life cycle entirely different from that of a criminal case. If I slander somebody, I might be dragged into court, and I might have to open my checkbook and pay damages; but I cannot be put in prison or executed, and if I lose the case, I do not get a criminal "record." Also, in a slander case (or a negligence case, or a copyright-infringement case), the injured party pays for, runs, and manages the case herself. He or she makes the decisions and hires the lawyers. The case is entirely voluntary. Nobody forces anybody to sue. I can have a good claim, a valid claim, and simply forget it, if I want.

In a criminal case, in theory at least, society is the victim, along with the "real" victim—the person robbed or assaulted or cheated. The crime may be punished without the victim's approval (though, practically speaking, the complaining witness often has a crucial role to play). In "victimless crimes" (gambling, drug dealing, certain sex offenses), there is nobody to complain; both parties are equally guilty (or innocent). Here the machine most definitely has a mind of its own. In criminal cases, moreover, the state pays the bills.*

All sorts of nasty acts and evil deeds are not against the law, and thus not crimes. These include most of the daily events that anger or irritate

---

* It should be pointed out, however, that the further back in history one goes, the more this pat distinction between "civil" and "criminal" tends to blur. In some older cultures, the line between private vengeance and public prosecution was indistinct or completely absent. Even in our own history, we shall see some evidence that the cleavage between "public" and "private" enforcement was not always deep and pervasive: see, for example, the discussion of the vigilante movements of the Old West in chapter 8.

us, even those we might consider totally outrageous. Ordinary lying is not a crime; cheating on a wife or husband is not a crime in most states (at one time it was, almost everywhere); charging a huge markup at a restaurant or store is not, in general, a crime; psychological abuse is (mostly) not a crime.

Before some act can be isolated and labeled as a crime, there must be a special, solemn, social and *political* decision. In our society, Congress, a state legislature, or a city government has to pass a law or enact an ordinance adding the behavior to the list of crimes. Then this behavior, like a bottle of poison, carries the proper label and can be turned over to the heavy artillery of law for possible enforcement.

We repeat: crime is a *legal* concept. This point, however, can lead to a misunderstanding. The law, in a sense, "creates" the crimes it punishes; but what creates criminal law? Behind the law, and above it, enveloping it, is society; before the law made the crime a crime, some aspect of social reality transformed the behavior, culturally speaking, into a crime; and it is the social context that gives the act, and the legal responses, their real meaning. Justice is supposed to be blind, which is to say impartial. This may or may not be so, but justice *is* blind in one fundamental sense: justice is an abstraction. It cannot see or act on its own. It cannot generate its own norms, principles, and rules. Everything depends on society. Behind every *legal* judgment of criminality is a more powerful, more basic *social* judgment, a judgment that this behavior, whatever it is, deserves to be outlawed and punished. We will return to this point.

CRIMINAL JUSTICE

This is, if anything, an even vaguer term. It is not easy to describe or define this system. In fact, there is no single meaning; the criminal justice system is an umbrella label for certain people, roles, and institutions in society. What these have in common is this: they all deal in some significant way with crime—they define crime; or they detect crime; or they prosecute or defend people accused of crime; or they punish crime.

Of course, as we said, in a very real sense it is *society* that makes the decisions about what is and is not crime. "Society" is another abstraction; what we mean is that these are collective decisions. Not everybody is part of the collective that makes the decision. When we say "society" we really mean those who call the tunes and pay the piper; it would be worse than naïve to imagine that everybody's opinion counts the same, even in a country that is supposed to be democratic. To take one obvious example: the criminal law of slavery in the nineteenth-century South was a product of "society," but the slaves themselves had almost no say in the matter. This must be clearly understood. The rich and powerful, the articulate, the well positioned, have many more "votes" on matters of definition than the poor, the weak, the silent.

In any event, after "society," as it were, makes social judgments, the criminal justice system goes to work. It refines and transforms the list, interprets it according to its own lights, and does whatever is to be done about catching and punishing lawbreakers. Starting with a definition of, say, "armed robbery," the police and others do the dirty work. Enforcement, of course, is *always* selective; for all sorts of reasons, the system does not, cannot, and will not enforce the norms in any total way. Unenforcement is as vital a part of the story as enforcement.

The people inside the system of criminal justice include, among others, the experts who draft the criminal codes and tinker with the language, and the legislatures that make the codes into laws. But usually we think of a different cast of characters when we think of criminal justice. We think of police, detectives, narcotics agents, judges, juries grand and small, prosecutors and defenders, prison guards and wardens, probation officers, parole board members, and others of this stamp. These people are familiar to us from daily life (everybody has some contact with police), or from the mass media, or from popular (or unpopular) culture. People seem to have an insatiable appetite for reading about crime. They devour books and magazines about true crime; and even more so the imaginary crimes in Sherlock Holmes or Agatha Christie or Raymond Chandler. And where would movies be, or television, without crime and punishment?

Many in the cast of characters just mentioned are professionals, or semiprofessionals, whose lives revolve around matters of crime. Lay people, too, have a role—as jurors, for example. This is also, of course, the story of a much larger cohort of lay men and women: people accused of breaking the law; and their manifold victims. Their story is not, in the main, pleasant or uplifting; the lives caught up in the web are so often ruined, blasted, and wasted lives; through these pages parade example after example of foolishness, vice, self-destruction; selfishness, evil, and greed. It is a story with few, if any, heroes; and few, if any, happy endings. But it is important to the country; and it exerts a weird fascination.

Main Themes

As I have said, the story of American criminal justice is long and extremely complicated. The amount of detail is discouraging; the fifty states, and the three-plus centuries of time, add more complexity. But there is one grand, general *approach;* and a number of main themes run throughout the book. They do not tie everything together in a few neat packages—that would be a delusion—but they are crucial to the telling of the tale.

As to the approach: this is a *social* history of crime and punishment. The overarching thesis is that judgments about crime, and what to do about it, come out of a specific time and place. This seems so obvious it hardly needs stating. But the consequences are extremely important. This is not a history of "criminal law" as lawyers would conceive of it; it is not an intellectual history of penology or criminology; it is not about the philosophy of good and evil. It is about a working system and what makes it tick. And it is told from an outside perspective—from a perspective tinged with the viewpoint of the social sciences.

This means that I assume, at every step of the way, that the shape of the system, and what it does, is not accidental or random or "historical"—and is definitely not shaped by some intellectual or philosophical tradition. Rather, what makes the system is social *structure* (the way society is organized) and social *norms* (people's ideas, customs, habits, and attitudes). These interact chemically with the context, and with what is happening in the world—with specific events and situations; for example, the sheer size of the country, its climate and geography, its natural resources; plagues, depressions, and wars; and with human-made factors of change, like the invention of the telephone or the automobile.

If crime itself is a *social* concept, then the reaction to it is social squared. *Is* crime entirely a social construct? Are there acts that are *inherently* crimes? The older writers made a distinction between acts that were, as Blackstone put it, *mala in se,* that is, evils in themselves, "crimes against the laws of nature, as murder and the like," and *mala prohibita,* that is, mere offenses "against the laws of society."[5] These are sonorous Latin phrases, but hardly anybody takes the distinction seriously anymore. Certainly it is a fact that people consider some crimes more deep-dyed and horrible than others; cold-blooded murder is at one end of a pole of blameworthiness, and trivial regulatory crimes—taking the label off a mattress—are at the other.

But blameworthiness itself varies tremendously from society to society, and period to period. It is true that most (perhaps all?) societies have rules about murder and theft. It is hard to imagine a society—certainly no modern society—that would let people roam about killing each other to their heart's content, with no rules, limits, or controls. Even the Nazis had a concept of murder: anyone who killed a member of the party or an SS officer soon found this out.

On the other hand, no two societies have exactly the same definition of murder. Most modern societies outlaw blood feuds; other societies have allowed, or even fostered, revenge killing. Abortion, in the Republic of Ireland, is a crime, a killing; this used to be true in most American states. At this writing (1993), in the United States early abortion is not a crime at all but a woman's right, her free and open choice, by virtue of *Roe v. Wade.*

Crime definitions, then, are specific to specific societies. Social change is constantly at work on the criminal justice system, criminalizing, decriminalizing, recriminalizing. Heretics were burned at the stake in medieval Europe; there is no such crime today. Colonial Massachusetts put witches to death. In antebellum Virginia and Mississippi, two slave states, black runaways, and any whites who helped them, committed crimes. Selling liquor was a crime in the 1920s, during Prohibition. It was a crime during the Second World War to sell meat above the fixed, official price; or to rent an apartment at excessive rent. These are now extinct or obsolete crimes.

Every state, and the federal government, has a penal code: a list of crimes to be punished. In every state, too, and in the federal government, criminal provisions are scattered elsewhere among the statute books. This is particularly true of regulatory crimes. The modern criminal code, even after pruning, is still much bulkier than older codes. There were no such crimes as price-fixing, monopoly, insider trading, or false advertising in the Middle Ages. Many new crimes—wiretapping, for example—are specific to high-tech society. We live in a welfare and regulatory state. Such a state produces thousands of newfangled offenses: dumping toxic wastes, securities fraud, killing endangered species, making false Medicare claims, inserting a virus into computer programs, and so on.

Clearly, there are crimes and crimes. It is conventional to draw a line between property crimes, crimes against the person, morals offenses, offenses against public order, and regulatory crimes. Social reactions depend on the type of crime. Typologies are not very systematic; but they can be illuminating. For example, there are what we might call *predatory* crimes—committed for money and gain; usually, the victims are strangers. These are the robberies and muggings that plague the cities and inspire so much dread. There are also lesser and greater crimes of *gain:* shoplifting, minor embezzlements, confidence games, cheats, frauds, stock manipulations in infinite form. There are also what we might call *corollary* crimes, crimes that support or abet other crime—conspiracies, aiding and abetting, harboring criminals; also perjury, jail break, and the like. Much rarer are *political* crimes—treason, most notably; also, sedition, and, in a larger sense, all illegal acts motivated by hatred of the system, and which strike out against the constituted order. Then there are crimes of *desperation*—men or women who steal bread to keep from starving, addicts who steal or turn a trick to support their habit. Some crimes are *thrill* crimes—joyriding, shoplifting at times, acts of vandalism, and the like; some of these, too, can be little bursts of petty treason. There are crimes of *passion*—violence generated by thwarted love, jealousy, hatred that rises to the level of obsession. There are also crimes of addiction—crimes that arise from *failure of control*; crimes that stem from what some of us might consider flaws of character, or overwhelming temptation; this can be as minor as public drunkenness, or as horrific as rape. Lastly, there are what we might call *subcultural* crimes—acts that are defined as crimes by the big culture, yet validated in some smaller social grouping: Mormon polygamy in the nineteenth century, for example.

All crimes are acts that society, or at least some dominant elements in society, sees as threats. The threat may be physical (street crime) and affect the quality of life. Rape and sexual assault terrorize women and reinforce a rigid gender code. Morals crimes attack the way of life of "decent" people. Certain white-collar crimes—antitrust violations, securities fraud—strike a blow at the economy; regulatory crimes pollute the atmosphere, or the market. Traffic codes ration space on city streets and highways, and attempt to avoid strangulation; traffic crimes upset this public order. And so it goes. The sense of threat, and ideas about what to do about dangers, change prismatically from period to period, and are different in different social groupings.

THE FUNCTIONS OF CRIMINAL JUSTICE

Crime, as we have seen, is a slippery, variable, protean concept; and criminal justice is equally variable—mutable, time-dependent, culture-dependent. Criminal justice is a particular *kind* of reaction to crime; and it is worthwhile to say a word or two about its functions (or assumed functions) in society: What is it that this huge, unwieldy system is supposed to do for us?

The answer seems obvious: fight crime. Every society probably has some way to control and limit intolerable behavior. Even blood feuds and vengeance have to follow the rules, in societies that recognize vengeance and feuds. A community in which "anything goes" would tear itself apart in no time; it would make the Beirut of the 1980s look like a Sunday school picnic.

But criminal justice has no monopoly on the business of restraining evil inclinations. It isn't fear of jail that keeps most of us from robbing, pillaging, raping, murdering, and thieving. Powerful restraints, levers, and controls run the machinery of our selves; governors inside our brains and bodies, reinforced by messages from families, institutions, schools, churches, and communities. Even without police, courts, and jails, they work for most of us, most of the time.* Strong informal controls keep most people in line.

But not everybody. Very, very few social norms are *so* deeply rooted in the mind that they enforce themselves universally. In our own society, it is hard to think of a good example. If there is a crime on the books, we can be sure there are also violators; many, in fact. This is so, no matter how repulsive the crime—murder, rape, incest, and so on— and no matter how fierce the potential punishment. The taboo against cannibalism may be an exception. The idea of eating human flesh disgusts people; there are so few violators of this norm that cannibalism is not even *specifically* listed as a crime in the penal codes. When a case does crop up, we tend to assume that the person must be thoroughly unhinged. The rare exceptions are people driven half-mad with hunger— the Donner party, for example, in the nineteenth century. Yet some societies (it is said) allow members to eat human flesh. The taboo is cultural, not instinctual.[7]

No other norms, alas, seem quite so self-enforcing. Many need help from criminal justice. The help comes in the form of *sanctions*—rewards and punishments. The punishments are especially obvious. The burglar goes to prison. Embezzlers pay heavy fines. In a few extreme cases, people die in the electric chair or the gas chamber.

Punishments are a common, obvious element in our lives; we take punishment for granted. Parents punish children by yelling, scolding, spanking, taking away candy or toys, "grounding," revoking privileges. Teachers punish students; bosses punish workers. Punishment is unpleasant; it makes misbehavior costly. Punishment raises the price, so to speak, of the behavior that gets punished. In the case of a fine, it does this quite literally. But the risk of going to jail is also part of the "price" of a burglary. The system, by raising and lowering these "prices," influences the *amount* of this behavior—at least in theory.

This pricing or rationing function is one of the most obvious ways in which the criminal justice system works in society. It centralizes and socializes the punishment function; it supplements private punishment (ostracism, hitting, scolding). It acts as a substitute for private violence—for blood feuds and vengeance, for a dog-eat-dog society. In general, we do not let people "take the law into their own hands," although this idea still has romantic appeal. How well the system works, how effective it is, is another question.

---

* Nobody knows *how* effective these controls are. There have been, however, a few natural experiments—situations in which the law takes a holiday. Police strikes are one example. Another took place in Denmark, in 1944, when the Germans, who had occupied the country, arrested the entire police force. Generally speaking, crime rates go up during such episodes, but not through the roof.[6]

There is another, more subtle, function of criminal justice: symbolic, ideological, hortatory. Perhaps it is only a more sophisticated way of accomplishing the first function. When we punish children, we sometimes say we are "teaching them a lesson." The lesson is about what will happen if they don't mend their ways. Criminal justice "teaches a lesson" to the people it punishes; and also to the public at large. It is also a kind of banner or flag that announces the values and norms of society. By making burglary a crime, by chasing and arresting burglars, by putting them in prison, the system sends a message about burglary: burglary is wrong, is evil, is deserving of pain, incarceration, disgrace.

Thus criminal justice tells us where the moral boundaries are; where the line lies between good and bad. It patrols those boundary lines, day and night, rain or shine. It shows the rules directly, dramatically, visually, through asserting and enforcing them. (There are lessons from nonenforcement, too: from situations where the boundaries are indistinct, or the patrol corrupt or asleep; and society is quick to learn *these* lessons, too.)

The teaching function of criminal justice, its boundary-marking function, is exceedingly important.[8] Criminal justice is a kind of social drama, a living theater; all of us are the audience; we learn morals and morality, right from wrong, wrong from right, through watching, hearing, and absorbing. The sections of the penal code, written in crabbed legal language, harbor an unwritten subdocument, a subdocument of community morality. The penal code, after all, can be read as a kind of Sears Roebuck catalogue of norms; it lists things considered reprehensible, and tells us, by the degree of punishment, roughly—very roughly— *how* reprehensible they are. Groups that dominate society display their power most brutally and nakedly in the police patrols, riot squads, and prisons; but power expresses itself also in the penal codes and in the process of labeling some values and behaviors as deviant, abnormal, dangerous—criminal, in other words.

In short: criminal justice is not just an enumeration of forbidden acts, and what their punishments might be—a price list for disfavored behavior. It is also a guide book to right and wrong conduct, an ethical inventory. If the penal code announces that the punishment for burglary is five years in prison, that is not merely a statement about the (expected) *price* of burglary. It also pronounces the judgment of society (or some part of society) on burglary: and the punishment, when we compare it to other punishments for other crimes, tells us roughly *how* evil burglary is—again, as compared to other criminal acts.

This, then, is a second major theme: the history of criminal justice is not only the history of the forms of rewards and punishment; it is also a story about the dominant *morality*, and hence a history of power. Take burglary again: the rules against it are also rules of power. The system throws its arms of protection around people who own property; it strips away protection from people who try to seize that property "unlawfully." And the rules give tickets of authority to police officers, judges, wardens, and others, to carry out their jobs, to enforce these rules; in some cases, they are given the power of life or death itself.

There are some myths and ideals about criminal justice that most people accept without thinking. When men or women are put on trial, we assume the point is to find out whether the defendants are guilty, plain and simple. If they are innocent, they must go free. But the dramatic side, the teaching side, is not so concerned with guilt and innocence. Acts of injustice may send very powerful messages, too. If a white woman accused a black man of insolence or assault, in, say, Mississippi in 1900, his guilt or innocence almost did not matter. He had to be punished. The southern system of power and domination demanded that this message be sent. This, too, was American criminal justice doing its work.

CRIME, CRIMINAL JUSTICE, AND CULTURE

Crime is behavior; and its roots must lie somewhere in the personality, character, and culture of the people who do the acts we condemn. *People* commit crimes, not "the system." This much is obvious. It seems equally obvious that behavior reflects what society *makes* out of people, or fails to make. Committing a crime means that some message was aborted or ignored, some lesson unlearned, some order countermanded, or, at times, some small piece of social rebellion committed. But messages of deviance and misbehavior came from somewhere, too; they were not inborn. And much the same sort of thing can be said about *reactions* to crime; they, too, occur in individuals, though socially structured and shaped.

Hence the story of crime and punishment over the years is a story of social changes, character changes, personality changes; changes in culture; changes in the structure of society; and ultimately, changes in the economic, technological, and social orders. These changes are what this book is about. In Puritan Massachusetts, an unmarried man and woman, caught having sex in the barn, could be fined, or put in the stocks, or whipped. A few adulterers even swung from the gallows. In the 1990s, in most states, the couple having sex in the barn is not committing a crime at all, whether married or not. In many cities, a person who is curious can buy a ticket to a theater and watch people make love live, or on film. It is hard to imagine what Cotton Mather, or Thomas Jefferson, would have made of such goings-on.

This book is the story of *how* such amazing changes in norms took place; and what was in the background, and, if possible, *why*. This brings us to the third of our main themes: the relationship between crime, criminal justice, and American culture. Very roughly, we will describe three periods, three cultures, three ages of criminal justice: the colonial period, the nineteenth century, and our own times. These periods do not separate from each other neatly; and are of course impossible to sum up, even for our limited purposes, in a single formula. But it will help in organizing our thoughts, and in understanding the past, if we look at three states of culture, which correspond to three forms of freedom.

Freedom, as I use the word, is not a term of philosophy or political theory. It is a word that describes two things, one subjective, the other (relatively) objective. Nobody is free if she feels unfree. But objectively, *freedom* describes a specific social situation. It is a situation of rights; it is, moreover, a situation of loose ties, of light command, of strained authority; an attenuation of what is, after all, the more common human condition, historically speaking: tight societies, trying to control the thoughts and actions of their subjects.

Feeling and reality do not necessarily live in harmony. But they have an obvious relationship. American history is, in a way, a history of more and more freedom. I say this not to celebrate this country, only to describe it. Nobody could honestly call the colonial systems "democratic." They were little theocracies. They were free in certain senses, but they were also rigidly bound up in notions of hierarchy; leaders of the community believed deeply in a God-given, natural order or chain of command. A powerful, self-conscious religious ethos prescribed people's places in that order.

Revolution broke the ties to England, and gave the country political freedom. But the Revolution itself—the actual war—was in many ways not as important as the social revolution that began before the shooting and continued after the guns fell silent. By this I refer to the erosion of what was left of colonial autocracy. This happened not because Americans spent their time reading political philosophy, but because this was a big, open, mobile, expansive place, with land to burn, where the knots and constraints of the Old World—or of the Puritan divines—crumbled into dust. In the nineteenth century, society was reconstituted in terms of a culture of *mobility*.

Mobility has a social and a spatial meaning. This was a country of immigrants, a country of rolling stones; it was also a country in which it was possible to rise in society—and also to fall. The facts and the image of mobility drastically reshaped criminal justice. It made certain crimes possible—the confidence game, for one—and it made its influence felt in every corner of the system. The police and the penitentiary, for example, were new social inventions; they arose out of a painful awareness that the pathologies of a mobile society demanded new techniques of control. The chapters of part II will illustrate this thesis in detail.

The nineteenth century had broken open old cages of class, space, and place. But a good deal of traditional morality survived. The culture insisted (officially, at least) on self-discipline, control, moderation. Freedom did not mean shaping your own way of life. Mobility was economic and political; it was not a freedom to contrive a lifestyle; the body and mind still proceeded within narrow but invisible ruts.

It is important to recognize this limitation on that liberty that the nineteenth century so loved to boast about. And another limitation: in 1800, millions of Americans (including all the women) were voteless; most black Americans were slaves, without rights or a voice in the system. In 1900, women still lacked the vote, and the criminal justice system was insensitive to women's issues, their views on rape, and domestic violence. Blacks were virtual serfs in much of the South. Lynch mobs enforced a brutal code of white supremacy, killing with almost total impunity. Big city police forces were corrupt and brutal. Fornication, adultery, and sodomy were crimes almost everywhere; the way of the social deviant was hard.

Slowly, gradually, the twentieth century broke with the past. It became the century of the *self*, the century of expressive individualism. The old century thought it knew a thing or two about political and economic freedom. The new century redefined the terms, and added freedom to shape one's own life, expressive freedom, freedom of personality, freedom to spend a lifetime caressing and nurturing a unique, individual self. At least this was the ideal, the great concept that motivated millions of people. It was certainly not the social reality; but it was a powerful impetus to action.

This new concept of the self lies behind the women's movement, the civil rights movement, the sexual revolution. It has worked its will, once more, on crime and punishment. Old rules and arrangements fell like tenpins. The culture of individualism, paradoxically, worked a revolution in the law of groups, races, and classes. People were to be judged for themselves. Women and men had the same rights to be judge or jury. Native tribes had the right to run their own courts, defying majority culture. All this is probably for the good. There is a dark side to the era of the self. A great deal of twentieth-century crime can be explained, if at all, in terms of the exaltation of the self, a twentieth-century pathology. The explosion in violent crime must mean that our society is unable to teach enough people to submerge themselves in a higher morality. The family loses some of its grip; the peer group, the gang, the crowd takes over. Authority becomes horizontal, not vertical. The criminal justice system beats its feeble wings against this wall of glass. Part III is the story of *this* set of cultural changes, and their impact on criminal justice, from just yesterday to almost today.

Why all these changes took place is an interesting question; I hope this book gives at least some partial answers. The story told here—I want to make this point very clear—is not a story of "progress." Whether we are better off or worse off than before is for the reader to decide. I myself think we are considerably better off; but at a rather stiff price.

Beaumont and De Tocqueville, writing about juvenile reformatories (see chapter 7), used a striking phrase; the children in these institutions were not victims of persecution, they said; they were merely deprived of a "fatal liberty."⁹ *Fatal* is a strong word; probably too strong. But the phrase breathes a kind of cautious reminder: even freedom has its costs. This is not the best of all possible worlds; and not all changes are improvements. The shadow of crime haunts "respectable" society. Social pathology lays waste millions of urban lives. There is no free lunch. American liberty comes at a premium price. Total societies, traditional societies, disciplined societies, sometimes keep crime under firm control. After the Soviet Empire collapsed, we are told, street crime increased, along with general disorder. A well-run prison may have iron discipline and perfect order. Not many of us would prefer a well-run prison to the way we live. Yet this must be said (and it is the last of our major themes): a rich culture of liberty has evolved in the United States, but it casts a dark and dangerous shadow. The culture of mobility and the culture of the self are not costless. They have brought with them, like pests imported on exotic cargo, side effects of crime and social disorganization; and society, so far, has been unable to eradicate these pests, or bring them under control.

These, then, are the main themes of the book. Before we turn to the colonial period, I want to mention two points briefly. The first is about the *impact* of criminal justice on crime. Supposedly, the main function of the system is to control crime and punish it. Does it do this job?

For most of the period we cover—close to four centuries—we simply have no idea. Clearly, there must be *some* impact, some deterrent effect, some influence on morality and behavior. How much, is completely unknown. It is pretty certain that it is less than most people think; the constant clamor for more prisons, more executions, more police, assumes a potency that is almost surely a delusion.

On the other hand, this much can and must be said: the system may not do much, or as much as we would expect, about crime rates, but it is not unimportant. It impacts the lives of millions of people. It arrests and processes hundreds of thousands. It drags victims, bystanders, jurors, and witnesses by the thousands into its web; it spends billions and employs millions; its symbolic consequences, its remoter effect, must be enormous, even though there is no known or knowable yardstick.

The second point is about the politics of this book. I have tried to tell an honest story. It would be silly to claim total success. Bias is inevitable. History is not an exact science, with clear questions and right or wrong answers. Everybody who writes about the past is more or less a prisoner of the present, and of his own instincts and values. Crime and punishment are highly charged, emotional, political subjects; there is no way to wring prejudice, attitude, value, out of the text. It is impossible to shape a story without some guiding theories; and we do not choose our theories and approaches at random; they draw us to them, they suck us in.

There are many ways to look at the causes of crime, for example. Some people blame crime on poverty, on social disorganization, on injustice in society; others reject these theories. There are economic theories, psychological theories, psychoanalytical theories, cultural theories, genetic theories, and so on. We can label some of them right-wing or left-wing or middle-wing or multiwing. None of the theories can be proven (or disproven). Probably no one big, sweeping theory is ever going to work. Nobody is likely to discover *the* cause of "crime"; people are much too complicated for that.

All theories of crime are ultimately political. Most of them assume that crime is bad, that criminals are bad, and that crime is a disease in society. But most people would concede that all "crime" is not necessarily evil. Joan of Arc was burned at the stake; now she is a saint. George Washington, a national hero, was, of course, a traitor to the British; they might have hanged him had he lost the war. It was a crime in Nazi Germany to disobey Hitler, or to interfere with his extermination plans; dissidents and rebels were put to death. But these "criminals" seem like heroes to us. Some critics on the far left feel much the same way about rebels in *this* society. It is even a political statement to approve of sending burglars to jail. Most readers, of course, will be willing to make this kind of political statement. But very few of us approve of the *entire* system. After all, there have been and still are powerful movements to take things *off* the list of crimes—fornication, for one. One person's free speech is another's sedition. The ebb and flow of opinion on crime and punishment is an essential part of this history.

The following two chapters look at the first of our three main periods: colonial America.

I

TIGHT LITTLE ISLANDS: CRIMINAL JUSTICE IN THE COLONIAL PERIOD

I

THE SHAPE AND NATURE OF THE LAW

AMERICAN LEGAL HISTORY BEGINS, CONVENTIONALLY, IN THE EARLY SEVEN-teenth century, when English-speaking settlers first got a toehold on soil that is now part of the United States. The legal history of the continent, of course, actually began much earlier. There were Spanish-speaking settlements in the sixteenth century, in what is now Florida and Puerto Rico. And there were Dutch settlers in New York, in the seventeenth century.

And then, of course, the European settlers did not come to an empty land. They thought of themselves as "discoverers"; from their point of view, they had arrived in the unknown, and carved settlements out of "wilderness." But there were native societies in America, old, estab-lished societies—the peoples that Europeans called "Indians." Each In-dian society had its own law-ways, its own norms, its own way of pun-ishing deviants.

The native peoples did not, to be sure, have systems of writing. None of them has left behind a written record of their legal system as it was on the eve of European arrivals. But these systems were nonetheless real: vigorous, active, alive. We know something about the way they operated from the accounts of the settlers.[1] We know something about them, too, from oral histories taken in later years. Indeed, some of these systems (in modified form) survive to this day.

The settlers of the seventeenth century came at first in dribs and drabs, then in greater numbers; eventually, they overwhelmed the natives and their law. The "clash of legal cultures," as Kawashima has noted, was a one-way street: English settlers "had no intention of learning from the Indians"; rather, natives had to adjust to the white man's law.[2] Ultimately, the English buried their European rivals, too—the Dutch lost New Amsterdam; and the Spanish (much later) gave up Florida. Essentially, the story of English law in America is a winner's story: this is the law that prevailed, in modified form, along the Atlantic coast, and then, modified again, across the continent.

Criminal Justice: The Common-Law Background

What kind of beast was the law that the English settlers brought with them? It was the so-called "common law." Legal systems, of course, are tied to particular societies. They develop in their societies over time; they do not come from outer space. Legal systems change, but change is mostly piecemeal, gradual; certain structures, frameworks, skeletons persist over time. It is possible to compare these shapes and patterns, classify them, and divide legal systems into "families," or types.

The "common law" was, essentially, the law of England; and the common-law countries today are colonies of England, former colonies, and colonies of colonies: the family includes, among others, Canada (except for Quebec), Australia, New Zealand, Barbados, Jamaica, and quite a few African countries. In Europe in general, in Latin America, and (by adoption) in such countries as Japan, a different historical tradition prevails, the vast civil-law system.* (Civil law, by way of Spain and France, has been a major influence on the law of Louisiana, and has also made a mark, by way of Mexico, on such states as Texas and California.) The two systems differ in a number of large and small ways. The *jury*, for example, is a common-law institution; in some civil-law countries only trained judges decide on innocence or guilt.

There are other important traits that set common-law systems apart from other legal systems. Compared to continental systems, they put a great deal of emphasis on the spoken word. The heart of the criminal trial was and is oral testimony—examination and cross-examination— and the lawyers run the show. The judge sits on the bench as a kind of

---

* For a concise introduction to the civil-law system, see John H. Merryman, *The Civil Law Tradition* (2d. ed., 1984).

august, reverend umpire. On the European continent, a trial consists mostly of shuffling pieces of paper about. Lawyers have a less prominent role than judges, who investigate, develop evidence, and present it to other judges, who in turn decide the case.

Crime-handling in common-law England, on the eve of settlement, distinguished between serious crimes (felonies) and not so serious ones (misdemeanors). Serious crimes got serious treatment. It took a two-step process to convict a criminal. Before someone could be tried for, say, grand larceny, he had to be indicted by a grand jury. The grand jury, an ancient institution, was a panel of men drawn from the community who heard evidence about crimes. But the grand jury did not itself decide on guilt or innocence.[3] If the case seemed strong, the grand jury "indicted," or, as they put it, returned a "true bill" (in Latin, *billa vera*); if the evidence was weak, they returned a "no bill," and the accused went free. If the grand jury indicted, the case went to court, to be tried by an ordinary jury (or petit jury).

One striking aspect of trial was the system of private prosecution. English law had no district attorney, no public prosecutor. If you were a shopkeeper, and you caught a thief robbing your store, it was *your* responsibility to bring him to justice. A constable might help you chase and catch the thief; but that was all. In any event, the money for the prosecution would have to come out of *your* pocket.

So much for felony trials. Also under the umbrella of criminal justice were thousands upon thousands of smaller cases, cases of petty crimes. Local courts handled these, mostly without the drama of juries and the hurly-burly of a felony trial, and without the paraphernalia of the upper courts. In England, the local justice of the peace—a squire or gentleman who lived in the area—was in charge of these proceedings. Procedure and substance were as different from the world of the great courts of London as night from day. But both levels were important; and both had a profound effect on the system of criminal justice that developed in the colonies.

The colonial world is not easy to capture in a few short pages, and its criminal justice system is no less elusive. The further we look back in time, the dimmer the world gets, and the stranger. Individual years, decades, and centuries tend to blur into "periods." In our own lives, ten years is a long time, a whole *decade*, crowded with events and stamped with its own personality. Somehow, a century in the Middle Ages seems shorter and less consequential; and whole dynasties of ancient Egypt or China, centuries long, get telescoped into a few gnomic phrases, if we know anything about them at all.

Real time is thus not the same as social time, or historical time—the time measured by research, reminiscence, and memory. It is convenient to talk about the colonial years as a single "period." Yet this period lasted about 150 years, a span of many generations; people were born, grew old, died, were forgotten, all within this single "period." This was about as long a span as the time between the Declaration of Independence and the attack on Pearl Harbor; between the Continental Congress and the third term of Franklin Delano Roosevelt.

The world did not stand still during the colonial period; and certainly the colonies did not. They began as tiny settlements, crude and endangered, scratching a living from clods of earth; poor, isolated, ingrown. On the eve of the Revolution there were some three million people living in the colonies; there were cities, colleges, material culture. Puritan Massachusetts in 1650 was a different place from eighteenth-century Georgia; New York and Virginia contrasted in many ways; and so on. Life in New England, in the middle colonies, in the plantation South, formed part of a vast mosaic: thousands of tiny bits of colored stone. There *was* an overall pattern, which we can clearly see today; but the patterns dissolve the closer one gets—or the more carefully one looks at details. Each colony had its own character, its own law-ways.

Through this mass of detail, a few prime facts shine through. On the whole, life in colonial America was small-scale; it was life among neighbors, in small, tight communities. Moreover, it was life lived in the shadow of a few powerful, regnant ideas about God, punishment, the afterworld, religion, and the social order. In short, life in the colonies was village life, orderly life, religious life. It was also a life dominated by ideas about hierarchy and subordination; about obedience to fathers, ministers, masters. The colonies had no real aristocracy on the English model, but the leaders of the settlements were neither anarchists nor democrats; far from it. These facts of structure and ideology made the criminal justice system what it was; they shaped types of punishment and the very definitions of crime.

Criminal justice in the colonies was cobbled together from three basic elements. First, there was English law, or rather, as much of the law and customs as the colonists brought with them from England and remembered. The language of criminal justice was, as it had to be, plain English: terms like *judge, jury, defendant, felony, arrest.* Whatever jargon of law came to be used (not always accurately) also came over on the boat, so to speak, direct from England.

But the circumstances of colonial life bent the English patterns out of shape. The physical and social environment was the second of the three elements that made colonial law what it was. Life on this side produced problems that life in the mother country never had to face. English law had nothing to say about dealing with native tribes. It had no law concerning slavery. Native tribes and black slaves were part of the colonists' world.

Also, the colonies were small, struggling communities, especially in the early years. They were profoundly isolated, teetering on the brink of starvation, and at the edge of the wilderness. This sense of desperation was reflected in the early colonial law codes. The first Virginia code in 1611 ("Lawes Divine, Morall and Martiall"), usually called "Dale's laws," is famous for its draconian bite. Dale's laws were a kind of military justice; these were rules drawn up for a scared community, holding on to the tip of a continent by its fingernails.[4]

Law in Massachusetts did not show the same sort of autocratic desperation, even at the outset. Yet here, too, the brute facts of colonial life made English legal patterns and institutions wildly inappropriate, to say the least. English law was incredibly complicated on the institutional side; it was a crazy quilt of court systems. The whole fourth volume of Sir Edward Coke's *Institutes* (1628) is devoted to a description of English courts. He lists about a hundred different courts, with different powers and jurisdictions. Many of them were weirdly specialized.

Obviously, it made no sense to reproduce this mess in the New World. The English tangle of courts had evolved in the course of a long, tortured, and unique historical process. It could work—*if* it worked— only in an old, complex society. A store in New York City or Los Angeles today may make a living selling nothing but soap, or Chinese pottery, or shoes for people with big feet. A tiny town, a mere cluster of houses, will make do with a general store. Similarly, colonial institutions tended to be simple, undifferentiated, and humbly unspecialized— caterpillars where the English courts were gaudy butterflies.

The third factor also drew a line between legal worlds on the two sides of the Atlantic. This was the factor of ideology: the worldview of the colonists, or at least those who called the shots in the colonies. Massachusetts was dominated by the Puritans; Pennsylvania and, for a time, New Jersey, belonged to the Quakers. The laws and legal customs in the colonies were a mirror of what elites, magistrates, and leaders thought about the good, the true, and the right, about justice and order. And this was not the same as the ideas of the landed gentry of England.

Nor were these the same ideas and attitudes that animate criminal justice today, at the end of the twentieth century; or, for that matter, in the nineteenth century. Religion was a powerful influence on society on both sides of the Atlantic; probably more so in New England than in old England. Some of the colonies, too, were deliberate implants, grafted onto the body of an unfamiliar continent for reasons that were, at base, deeply religious. Many colonial leaders were not looking for land or fortune; especially in the Puritan colonies, they were looking for a way to serve God, the opportunity to build godly societies, societies governed by the word of God. They had clear ideas about what a godly society would look like, and they did their best; but circumstances beyond their control shattered the patterns they had worked so hard to build up. Social and technological change, as well as the brute physical facts of the continent, ultimately undid them. Forces stronger than hurricane winds swept their plans and their structures away.

These, then, are the main themes we will follow out: the role of religion and ideology in shaping criminal justice; how a system of paternalism and godly order developed and then declined; the rising force of new ideas and new facts, and the erosion of the colonial system. But first, we will take a brief look at the nuts and bolts of criminal justice in the colonial period.

Courts and Procedures

As we have seen, court systems were bound to be simpler in the colonies than in the mother country. To be sure, there was a good deal of variation from colony to colony, and a great deal of evolution over time. At the base of the system, typically, was a single magistrate, the justice of the peace, who handled cases of petty crime in his locality. The county court, as the basic trial court was called in many colonies, was a jack-of-all-trades, the workhorse of colonial government. It was an administrative body as well as a court; but criminal work was part of its business, too. Ultimately, in many colonies, there were higher courts that heard appeals, and specialized courts, particularly in cities and towns. In rare cases, a loser could appeal a case to the distant overlords in England.[5]

An English lawyer would recognize procedures and court jargon as English, but with a difference. Criminal procedure was rough and ready, in contrast to the fashion in London. The small scale of colonial life was responsible for some of the deviations, especially in the early years. Thus, early settlers in western Massachusetts did without a grand jury "because of the sparse population."[6] Generally speaking, procedure became more "English" as time went on; the grand jury, for example, took its place in Massachusetts well before the middle of the seventeenth century.[7]

Puritan justice had a strongly *inquisitorial* flavor, at least in the seventeenth century. That is, the judges, who were religious and political leaders, dominated the proceedings. They believed unswervingly in their right to rule in the name of God and according to the divine plan. They ran the show; juries rarely sat, except where the death penalty was possible; in colonial New Haven they *never* sat. The magistrates had a paternal-authoritarian aim: primarily they hoped to squeeze confession and repentance out of sinners. This was a task for elites, saints, not for lay juries. Indeed, if a defendant demanded a jury, this might be taken as a sign of obstinacy, a failure to feel and show remorse.[8]

Gail Marcus has given us a good description of criminal process in New Haven Colony in the seventeenth century.[9] Process began when a magistrate learned or heard that someone had committed an offense. He would send out the marshal or a deputy to haul in the offender. The magistrate would examine the suspect privately, often in his own home, but with other magistrates or deputies present. These examinations were "inquisitorial"; the magistrate was firmly in charge—he asked the questions and the suspect answered. There were no lawyers present, on either side.

If the magistrate felt the man was innocent, or the proof too weak, he could dismiss the case; if there was good evidence, or if the suspect confessed, the case was scheduled for trial. Until trial, the defendant was mostly free to go about daily life; in New Haven, no bail was required. This was a small town, a mere village, and apparently it was effective enough to warn a man or woman: appear or else. According to Marcus, only 4 defendants out of 201 did not show up after getting such a warning.

The trial itself took place soon, quickly, and without jurymen or lawyers. Witnesses appeared and gave whatever evidence they had. The magistrate was in firm control. Of course, the magistrate felt fairly sure of guilt before the trial even started; in all but 14 of the 201 criminal trials Marcus studied, the verdict was guilty on all counts. But the trial was no charade. At least the magistrates did not think so. It was, in fact, a ceremony of some importance. It was an occasion for repentance and reintegration: a ritual for reclaiming lost sheep and restoring them to the flock. The "more awesome the experience, the more valuable it could be as a means of humbling" the sinner. In addition, the trial "proved to God and men that New Haven was fulfilling its religious mission."[10] It was a public, open affirmation of the rules and their enforcement; a kind of divine social theater. It taught people about good and bad, and the wages of sin. It punished the guilty, and made justice and the law concrete.

This was a constant in colonial history: criminal justice as social drama. These were small communities, tightly organized and tightly run; the courts were at the very core of colonial governance. Here is Hoffer and Scott's description of Virginia justice in the middle of the eighteenth century:

Criminal courts met at the county courthouse. In Richmond, this was a small, square building at a crossroads two miles from the river. Administration of justice was a wholly public event. The courts' yards were open and crowded places, magnets for the commoner and the curious. Merchant, lawyer, and passerby mingled to do business, hear cases, and perhaps serve on a jury. The ceremonial of the courthouse, coupled with the colonists' interest in criminal cases involving neighbors, filled courthouses to overflowing. . . . The seating arrangement and placement of the bench in the courtroom gave visual emphasis to the power of the justices. The whipping post, to which many of the guilty were removed immediately after the justices had ruled, stood next to the courthouse. The gaol, with its yard, could be seen nearby. Whipping, branding, and pillory were public displays of the fruits of crime designed to warn the immoral. In a face-to-face society, public rituals of this nature strengthened the legitimacy of criminal proceedings.[11]

Theatrical elements came out with special force at hangings. The condemned were expected to play the role of the penitent sinner; it was best of all if they offered a final confession, a prayer, and affirmed their faith, in the very shadow of the gallows. Thus Esther Rogers, hanged for infanticide in 1701, had a "Radiant Countenance" as she went to her death; and her execution was a "deeply spiritual experience for all those who witnessed her final moments."[12]

Criminal process, of course, changed over time. One notable change was the increased use of the jury. Even in the seventeenth century the jury was a regular institution in Maryland trials; the Puritan colonies came to accept trial by jury as well. Practice, however, varied from colony to colony. Peter Hoffer's research on Richmond, Virginia, for the years 1711 to 1754 turned up relatively few jury trials: most defendants in minor criminal cases "either confessed or did not contest the charges"; only six of two hundred "put themselves upon the county" (that is, asked for a jury).

This may have been, in part, because a jury trial was costly and created a fuss. But Hoffer thinks something more basic was at work: that defendants avoided juries and submitted to the court itself because they expected the court, in return, to be "patient and lenient." Guilt or innocence was not the only point of criminal process; the judges were also concerned with "the willingness of the accused to submit to authority."[13] This trait, of course, runs like a scarlet thread throughout the story of American criminal justice.

The job of the jury has changed over time. The roots of the jury system go back to medieval England.[14] But the medieval jury was, in a way, the very opposite of the modern jury. Jurors were not supposed to be impartial, unaware, blank pages; but, rather, men (no women served) who knew their community inside and out, substantial men, men with a good sense of what was going on and a keen knowledge of the good and rotten apples in their barrel. It was not until much, much later that the jury came to be a panel of men chosen for complete cognitive virginity.

The jury today is a feisty, independent body. It works behind closed doors, and pretty much does as it pleases. In England in the seventeenth and eighteenth centuries, juries, and criminal trials in general, were a far cry from what they are today.[15] The judge dominated the proceedings; the jury was much more supine than its modern descendants. *Perry Mason* has affected our notions of the criminal trial; we think of trials as battles of wits between clever lawyers who use every trick in their repertoire, to convince (or befuddle) the jury. This image is *mostly* false as to the 1990s, and totally false with regard to trials in Stuart England.

In fact, most "trials," both in England and in America, were, if not nasty and brutish, certainly short. If you were transported back in time, to London, to the Old Bailey in, say, 1700 to watch criminal justice at work, a number of facts would immediately strike you. First of all, you would notice that the defendant had no lawyer. Most defendants could not afford one, of course; but this hardly mattered, since the accused was not *permitted* to have a lawyer. He had to face the court alone. The ban on defense lawyers did not break down until the eighteenth century; John Langbein dates the change to about 1730.[16]

The jury system in the colonies retained, not surprisingly, the flavor of its English models. An early Virginia law (1662) mentions the English practice of choosing juries from "the neighborhood" where the crime took place. In Virginia (the law went on), this was a bit troublesome, because of the "remotenesse of our habitations." But at least part of the jury *should* be drawn from "thence who by reason of their neere acquaintance with the busines may give information of diverse circumstances to the rest of the jury."[17] By the eighteenth century, however, the concept of the jury had moved closer to what it would be in our times. There was an emphasis on fair, random ways of picking the panel. In South Carolina, under an elaborate law of 1731, jury names were to be drawn out of a six-drawer box by a child under ten, and the names were to appear on pieces of paper of "equal size and bigness."[18]

The Organization of Justice: A System of Amateurs

Colonial justice was a business of amateurs. Amateurs ran and dominated the system. Today, professionals call the shots; men and women with special training, degrees, certificates, full-time positions—police,

prosecutors, defense lawyers, social workers, probation and parole officers, corrections specialists of various sorts. Even the criminals are
often, in a way, professionals.

Nothing of the sort existed in the seventeenth century. Lay magistrates decided most cases; the jurors, of course, were also lay. There
were no police in the modern sense. The local sheriff was in charge of
law enforcement; he also summoned the jurors. Constables made arrests, and night watchmen patrolled the streets of the bigger towns.

Constables and watchmen were, for the most part, ordinary citizens.
It was a man's civic duty to serve as constable or watchman. Not everybody had enough of a sense of obligation to make the system work. The
Dutch introduced a paid watch system in New York in 1648; in Boston
a similar plan took effect in 1663. Both towns later abandoned the
scheme because it was too expensive.[19] The night watch continued on
an amateur basis. A watchman's duty, in New York (1698), under English rule, was to go "round the Citty Each Hour in the Night with a
Bell," and "proclaime the season of the weather and the Hour of the
Night"; if the watchman met "Any people disturbing the peace or lurk-
ing about Any persons house or committing any theft," the watchman
was to "take the most prudent way . . . to Secure the said persons."[20]

Each colony had its own plan for getting an adequate supply of constables. In Georgia, under a law of 1759, they were recruited in a kind of
draft system. Free white males between twenty-one and sixty were liable to serve. The justices of the peace in each district were to meet "on
some day in Easter week"; the names of all eligible men were to be written down "on divers pieces of paper, and each rolled up by itself, and the
said pieces of paper so written and rolled up shall be put in a hat or box
[and] well shaken together." The justices were then to draw out names,
serve the lucky winners with a summons, and swear them in as constables; the term of service was one year. Ministers of the Church of England, of "dissenting congregations tolerated by the laws of *England*,
members of both houses of assembly, commissioned officers of the militia, licensed school-masters, physicians, appothecaries, sworn attornies,
madmen, ideots, and sick persons" were all exempt; and a man could
hire or induce a substitute to serve in his place.[21] In New York, too, it
was possible to hire a substitute to serve one's stint as a constable. Amateur constables could hardly be expected to do the job right. They were
sometimes no match for the lowlifes they wanted to arrest. Douglas
Greenberg found dozens of instances in eighteenth-century New York
in which men assaulted or resisted constables.[22]

The sheriff was a familiar figure in the various colonies. The governor
appointed a sheriff for each county, to enforce the law and act as the
chief agent of government in that county. He had a multiplicity of du-

ties. He was in charge of jury selection, as we have mentioned; he was also in charge of jails, prisoners, and the like. Like constables and night watchmen, sheriffs in New York were prone to neglect their business at times; some were reprimanded or prosecuted for malfeasance in office.[23] In Pennsylvania some sheriffs apparently exacted fees from prisoners, or sold liquor in the jails; statutes of 1730 prohibited sheriffs or under-sheriffs from extorting money from prisoners, and ordered them not to keep "any tavern, public house or alehouse," or to sell wine, rum, beer, ale, or other "strong liquors" to "any person or persons under arrest, or in prison."[24]

The office of the *coroner* was an ancient institution, brought over from England. The coroner conducted "inquests" in cases of violent or unexplained death. A special jury would view the body, under the coroner's direction, and decide whether it was a case of accident, suicide, or murder: whether, as the words of a New Hampshire statute put it, the person "dyed of Felony, or by Mischance and Accident? And if of Felony, whether of his own or anothers? And if by Mischance or Misfortune, Whether by the Act of God or Man? And if he dyed of Felony, Who were Principals, and who were Accessories?"[25]

A professional system tends to have clean, clear lines marking off the various "beats" from each other; the lay public is told to keep out. In the criminal justice system, there has been a long-term trend toward professionalism. The amateur world of the colonies drew no clear lines between public and private. The system depended on lay people, as Pauline Maier has pointed out, on traditional institutions, such as the "'hue and cry,' by which the community in general rose to apprehend felons." In other cases, magistrates would turn "to the posse comitatus . . . able-bodied men a sheriff might call upon to assist him."[26] As a result, "the difference between legal and illegal applications of mass force was distinct in theory, but sometimes indistinguishable in practice."[27] The very concept of the "mob" in the eighteenth century has to be taken with a grain of salt.

One American innovation in staffing criminal justice does deserve particular mention. In England, as we mentioned, there was no such thing as a "district attorney," that is, a paid official whose job was to prosecute crime on behalf of the state. People were supposed to prosecute on their own—and at their own expense. This was quite a burden for a simple shopkeeper, or a tenant farmer, to bear. The public prosecutor—a government officer in charge of prosecution—appeared quite early on this side of the Atlantic. He came to be called the district attorney, or county attorney, or the like. Where did the idea come from? Among the Dutch in New York, an officer known as the "*schout*" acted both as a kind of sheriff and as a prosecutor.[28] This, some scholars think, might be one crucial source of the American public prosecutor.[29] Perhaps; but nothing forced this institution down the throats of other colonies; and the idea of Dutch "influence" is both slippery and implausible. More likely, the concept of *public* responsibility for prosecuting criminals rang a bell in the colonial mind.*

Colonial society was certainly hierarchical—with a vengeance. Still, it was far less stratified than English society; and the people on top were not an aristocracy. Even in the seventeenth century, colonial society was far more fluid, more open (for white men, at least). Consequently, the law was in some ways more "popular" than in England. Ordinary people have an interest in protecting their bodies from assault, their property from thieves. These interests weighed more heavily in the colonies than in England. In addition, the leaders—magistrates, solid citizens, ministers—saw a sacred duty in enforcing the law. There was an obligation to find and punish bad behavior. The commandments of God's justice were too important to be left to the whims, and the pocketbooks, of individual victims.

---

* Public, of course, did not mean "professional." It did not mean that the district attorney worked full-time at this job and did nothing else.

2

THE LAW OF GOD
AND MAN

THE COLONIAL SYSTEM OF JUSTICE WAS PATRIARCHAL; AND TO A DEGREE, SUC-
cessfully so. Sinners were to be punished and brought back into the fold.
Every effort was made to bind people in righteousness to their community. The system was also strongly hierarchical. Magistrates and leaders
made the laws; the burden fell most heavily on the lower orders—servants, slaves, the young.

The colonies were certainly not democracies—they were, rather, au-
tocracies and theocracies—but the leading men did not think of themselves as dictators, and certainly not as aristocrats, born to lead. As we
have said, the law was in some respects profoundly popular. The thousands of pages of court records certainly breathe a popular flavor. Ordinary people *used* the courts, to get justice for themselves, vindication,
restitution; and in criminal as well as civil matters. As Bradley Chapin
has pointed out, the courts "acted as safety valves for society" with regard to "interpersonal relations." He refers here to cases of slander,
defamation, and assault; often, such cases did not end up with a final
judgment. A public "airing of the case" was enough; it "relieved
pressure."[1]

Colonial Religion and Criminal Justice

Nonetheless, it would be hard to overemphasize the influence of religion—the beliefs of magistrates and leaders—in shaping the criminal codes, in framing modes of enforcement, and, generally, in creating a distinctive legal culture. The criminal justice system was in many ways another arm of religious orthodoxy. This was true everywhere in the colonies; but most strikingly, perhaps, in the Puritan north.

A religious message leaps out of virtually every page of the early Puritan codes. Rules to buttress religious orthodoxy permeate the *Laws and Liberties of Massachusetts* (1648). The code condemned, for example, Anabaptists as "Incendiaries of Common-wealths & the Infectors of persons"; if these misguided creatures remained "obstinate" in their false beliefs, they were liable to "banishment." Heresy was also a crime in Massachusetts. The community had the right to banish believers in "damnable heresies, tending to the subversion of the Christian Faith and destruction of the soules of men." There was no welcome mat for Jesuits who entered Massachusetts (unless by "ship-wrack or other accident"); on the contrary, they were to be tossed out of the commonwealth. If an exiled Jesuit dared to come a second time, he could be put to death.

The laws against Quakers were particularly virulent in this colony. In 1658, the Massachusetts General Court allowed the death penalty for Quakers who returned after banishment. Quakers were particularly dangerous, since they aimed to "undermine & ruine" authority, making their heresy far worse than mere religious error. Two Quakers were hanged in 1659; in 1661, another Quaker, William Ledra, who had been banished and returned, died on the gallows.[2]

Blasphemy was another colonial crime. A New Hampshire law defined it as "Denying, Cursing or Reproaching the true God, his Creation or Government of the World," or "Denying, Cursing, or Reproaching the Holy Word of God, that is, the Canonical Scriptures, contained in the Books of the Old, and New Testament." Under this statute, a court in its discretion could put the blasphemer in the pillory, whip him, bore his tongue "with a red hot Iron," or make him stand on the gallows with a rope around his neck.[3] A Virginia law (1699), aimed at stamping out "horrid and Atheisticall principles greatly tending to the dishonour of Almighty God, and . . . destructive to the peace and wellfaire of this . . . collony," made it a crime to deny "the being of a God or the holy Trinity," or to "assert or maintaine there are more Gods then one," or deny the truth of Christianity, or the "divine authority" of Old and New Testaments.[4]

In the court records, however, blasphemy does not appear very often. A jury acquitted Gabriel Jones, of Kent County, Delaware, accused of saying, "with a lowd voice. . . 'Cursed be My God for Suffering me to live to be so old to be abused by Dennis Dyer.'"[5] Perhaps his words struck the jury as pathetic, rather than blasphemous.

Colonial law took the sabbath quite seriously. Sunday was for praying and churchgoing; almost everything else was against the law. Many colonists were taken to task for skipping services. In Salem, Massachusetts, John Smith and the wife of John Kitchin were fined in 1668 "for frequent absenting themselves from the public worship of God on the Lord's days."[6] In the province of Maine, in 1682, Andrew Searle paid a fine of five shillings "for not frequenting the publique worship of god" and instead "wandering from place to place upon the Lords days."[7] Virginia law (1662) required everyone who had "noe lawfull excuse" to resort "diligently to their parish church and chappell . . . and there to abide orderly and soberly" each Sunday, on pain of a fine of fifty pounds of tobacco (the currency of the colony); and there was to be no traveling on Sundays, "except in case of emergency."[8] Once in church, too, a person was supposed to behave. Young Abiel Wood, of Plymouth, was brought to court in 1758, accused of "irreverently behaving himself by chalking the back of one Hezekiah Purrington Jr. with Chalk, playing and recreating himself in the time of publick worship."[9]

Profaning the sabbath outside of church was also a definite offense. In 1656, a Boston man, Captain Kemble, sat in the stocks for two hours because of "lewd and unseemly behavior" on the sabbath. This consisted of kissing his wife; he had just returned from three years at sea. Thomas Thomson and John Horton, of western Massachusetts, were "admonished" and fined for making "a fray in the street in the Evening and about $1/2$ houre after sun sett" on the sabbath.[10] In 1712, a barber in Philadelphia was arrested for cutting hair on a Sunday.[11] The fervor to enforce these laws seemed to wane a bit in the eighteenth century, for example in Philadelphia; and some colonies were more zealous than others. But Sunday laws were a feature of all the colonies.

The colonies in general made little or no distinction between sin and crime; piety and religion especially dominated the lives of Puritan leaders and divines. Religion was the cornerstone of their community. It was the duty of law to uphold, encourage, and enforce true religion. Government was "the instrument of God on earth."[12] The core of the criminal code consisted of norms that were not man-made but the gift and command of God. This was the colonial ethos. The goal of legal authority, as David Flaherty put it, was "to translate the divine moral law into criminal statutes, in the interests of popular morality."[13]

In one part of the *Laws and Liberties of Massachusetts* this notion appeared quite graphically. The code contained a list of "capital laws." Each one came came equipped with citations to the Bible. So, for example: "If any person slayeth another suddenly in his ANGER, or CRU-ELTY of passion, he shall be put to death. *Levit.* 24.17. *Numb.* 35.20.21." Or: "If any man rise up by FALSE-WITNES wittingly, and of purpose to take away any mans life: he shal be put to death. *Deut.* 19. 16.18.16." The citations would serve to remind the people (if they needed the reminder) where in the end these rules really came from. It reminded them, too, that transgression meant more than punishment here below; it was a ticket to the fires of Hell, to eternal damnation.

Victimless Crime; Communal Punishment

Since crimes were sins, and sins crime, there was no sharp line between "victimless crimes" and crimes of predation or violence. The idea of a victimless crime is distinctly modern. An offense against God was an offense against society, and a positive threat to the social order. When Sodom and Gomorrah flouted God's will, his anger laid them waste.

Thus the codes, especially in Puritan New England, made crimes out of lying and idleness; they also punished fornication, adultery, sodomy and buggery;* general lewdness and bad behavior, and every sexual practice that stepped over the line of straight sex as the Bible approved it. The courts acted, in a way, as secular arms of the churches, which also punished these offenses, through reprimand, denial of privileges, and, in extreme cases, excommunication.[15] In court, the minor offenses earned minor punishments; but punishment for more serious sexual crimes could be very severe. A man guilty of buggery could, by law, be put to death.

The harsh statutes were not, by any means, dead letters, especially in the seventeenth century. William Paine was convicted of "unclean practices" in New Haven in 1646, and put to death. He was a "monster in human shape," an apparent sodomist in England before he came to the colony; and in New Haven he "corrupted a great part of the youth . . . by masturbations, which he had committed and provoked others to the like above a hundred times." Thomas Granger, of Plymouth, a boy of sixteen or seventeen, was indicted in 1642 for buggery "with a mare, a cow, two goats, five sheep, two calves and a turkey." Granger confessed and was required to identify the sheep he had buggered, in a kind of lineup. The

---

* The Puritan colonies usually applied the term *sodomy* to homosexual behavior, and *buggery* to bestiality.[14]

animals were killed;* then Granger himself was executed.[17] In Massachusetts, a man named Benjamin Goad, "instigated by the Divill" in 1673, one afternoon ("the sun being two howers high"), committed the "unnatural & horrid act of Bestiallitie on a mare in the highway or field." He was sentenced to die by hanging; the court also ordered "that the mare you abused before your execution in your sight shall be knockt on the head."[18] In the colony of West New Jersey, in 1692, one Harry, a "Negro man Servant," was convicted of "Buggering a Cow." This unlucky man had been caught in the act: Mary Myers, and some children, saw him "ride upon the Cow," which made the "usuall Motions of Cows when they had taken the Bull." A jury convicted him; and the judge was merciless; Harry would be "hanged by the neck till thy body bee dead, dead dead." The poor cow, too, was sentenced to death.[19]

In the eighteenth century, the death penalty was invoked less frequently for these crimes. Even in the seventeenth century, most sexual offenses were petty, and the punishments less than severe. Mild—but amazingly frequent. The smaller vices were punished by the hundreds. Indeed, in the seventeenth century, no crimes appear more often in the ancient pages of court records than fornication and other victimless crimes. Time after time, unmarried men and women who slept together were hauled into court, tried, and then fined, whipped, or put in the stocks. Women could be punished, too, for bearing illegitimate children—Hannah Dickens, of Kent County, Delaware, produced "One Bastard Male Child of Her Body" in 1702, and got twenty-one lashes in consequence.[20] In Massachusetts, in June of 1670, the Quarterly Court of Salem fined John Roapes and his wife for fornication before marriage, William Batt for drunkenness, and Daniell Salmon for excessive drinking.[21]

The thousands of cases of fornication and other offenses against morality point in two somewhat conflicting directions. In the first place, they seem to give the lie to a conventional picture of life in colonial times: sour, dour, obsessed with religion, drenched in an ethic of asceticism, treating all pleasures of the flesh with disgust. A frank and robust sexuality leaps from the pages of the record books. Still, our evidence of rampant sexuality comes from the proceedings of courts that were doing their best to punish and suppress that sexuality. And, on the whole, as Roger Thompson wrote of seventeenth-century Middlesex County, Massachusetts, most people probably did not transgress. The "great majority of men, women, and children" simply obeyed the rules

---

* The offending animal was a "deodand," that is, a chattel that caused a human death, and could be punished or forfeited along with the offending human. Under a law of New Hampshire, for example, the death penalty was prescribed for every man or woman "that shall have Carnal Copulation with any Beast or brute Creature," and the "Beast shall be slain and burned."[16]

of morals and law; the "silent majority behaved themselves and sustained the New England Way."[22]

That way was fairly austere. The leaders of the northern colonies were notoriously sour on games and on pleasures. The *Laws and Liberties of Massachusetts* decreed that "no person shall henceforth use the . . . game of Shuffle-board" in any "house of common entertainment," because "much pretious time is spent unfruitfully and much wast of wine and beer occasioned." No one was "at any time" to "play or game for any monie or monyworth." In western Massachusetts, in 1678, Philip Matoone was accused by several persons of "unseasonably Playing at Cards." Matoone, summoned to court, confessed that he played cards at night in the cellar of a house, secretly, with a group of men; he was fined five shillings for playing cards, five shillings "for being out at that Unlawfull Play . . . at unseasonable tyme of the Night"; the court threw in an extra five shillings, simply because Matoone had been "at so Nasty a busyness."[23] In the same place, and in the same year, Mary Crowfoot accused a soldier, John Norton, of "Lacivious and uncleane Cariage," that is, "takeing up her Coates and offering baseness to her." Norton claimed he was drunk and had no idea what he was doing; he was fined thirty shillings for lewdness, and ten for the drunkenness.[24]

The straitlaced Puritans of Massachusetts Bay were not the only colonial leaders who looked down their noses at vice, common or exotic. A Virginia law of 1657–58 directed local courts and parishes to use "all good meanes" to suppress "the odious sinnes of drunkenesse, blasphemous swearing and curseing," and "scandalous liveing in adultery and fornication."[25] The law was frequently amended, often with complaints about how ineffective prior laws had been. Virginia courts may have been a bit easier than their northern colleagues on such crimes as adultery, but they hardly ignored it. So, for example, in Richmond, in 1715, one Pavey was presented by the grand jury on suspicion of living in adultery, with Sarah Yeats; he was ordered to get her out of his house, to break off all relations with her, and to remain in custody until he could post bond for his good behavior.[26]

Colonial Corrections

The colonial frame of mind and the structure of colonial society influenced not only *what* was punished but also *how* crimes were punished. The early settlements were tiny places; the whole population of the American colonies in 1650 would not fill a good-sized baseball stadium today. In the early years, too, the settlements were little worlds on their own, cut off from each other and most definitely cut off from the mother country; it was a bit like life on a desert island (but with a tougher climate). It was also small-town life at its most communal—inbred and extremely gossipy. Nothing escaped the deadly eye of the collective. As Roger Thompson put it, writing about one Massachusetts county, the community was "well stocked with moral monitors who did not miss much in the goldfish-bowl existence of daily life."[27]

New England settlements of this sort had both the will and the ability to enforce laws against fornication, sins of the flesh, minor vices, and bad behavior. They punished these offenses the way autocratic fathers or mothers punish children; they made heavy use of shame and shaming. The aim was not just to punish, but to teach a lesson, so that the sinful sheep would want to get back to the flock. Punishment tended to be exceedingly public. The magistrates loved confessions of guilt, open expressions of remorse. They loved to enlist the community, the bystanders; their scorn, and the sinners' humiliation, were part of the process. Hundreds of colonial sinners were forced to sit in the stocks—in full public view. Punishment was sometimes tailored to fit the crime, to point up the moral more vividly. Samuel Powell, a servant, stole a pair of breeches in Accomack County, Virginia, in 1638. Part of his punishment was to "sitt in the stocks on the next Sabboth day . . . from the beginninge of morninge prayer until the end of the Sermon with a pair of breeches about his necke."[28]

Severity was not the point in punishing minor sins. The point was repentance and a good swift lesson. Warnings and fines were the punishment of choice for flirting, petting, and other small offenses. More aggravated sins led to the pillory and stocks, and more fines; for still worse cases, a sound whipping was inflicted. A servant, Daniel, in western Massachusetts (1654), had profaned the sabbath "in idle walkinge about and not comeinge to the Ordinances of the Lord"; his employer also complained of "grievous idleness in neglecting his busyness for Severall dayes." Daniel had been warned before; he promised "amendment; but grew worse and worse." At this point, he was sentenced to five lashes on his bare back, "well laid on," as the phrase commonly went.[29]

Whipping was an extremely common punishment throughout the colonies, especially for servants and slaves. In Charles County, Maryland, in 1664, the county court ordered Agnes Taylor to be whipped "at the whipping Post in the Publicke View of the People" twenty lashes "for having Played the whore"; Ann Cooper earned twelve lashes for "having had A Bastard." Three servants, Mathew Brown, Elizabeth Browne, and Joseph Fendemore, were brought to court as runaways; Matthew "impudently" alleged that he was abused, and not given enough "Vitualls"; but this, the court felt was a malicious lie. He was sentenced to twenty-seven lashes. Joseph Fendemore and Elizabeth Browne claimed they "went Along with him for company"; this brought from the court only sarcasm: they could join him "for Company sacke [sake]" at the whipping post, seven lashes for Elizabeth and nine for Joseph.[30]

It was a paternal society—a society built on the model of a patriarchal house. Like a stern father, the authorities did not believe in sparing the rod. The courts enforced *discipline*. In a way, it was a crime just to be a bad citizen: not to conform to standards of good virtue and respectability. The court could haul in a community nuisance and make him see the error of his ways. Or *her* ways: a Massachusetts law of 1672 denounced the "evil practice" of "Exorbitancy of the Tongue, in Railing and Scolding." Women were the target of this law; the punishment was to be "Gagged, or set in a Ducking-stool, and dipt over Head and Ears three times in some convenient place of fresh or saltwater."[31]

The colonial magistrates thought it made sense to humble a "scold" publicly, and in general to humiliate no-goods and other minor deviants. Shaming punishments were sometimes offered as alternatives to fines or other forms of punishment. In Maine, in 1671, Sarah Morgan, who had the effrontery to strike her husband, was ordered "to stand with a gagg in her Mouth halfe an houre at Kittery at a Publique Town meeteing & the cause of her offence writt upon her forhead, or pay 50 s[hillings] to the County."[32]

Shaming punishments were colorful; they were certainly used with great frequency. But the workaday fine, the drudge-horse of criminal justice, was probably the most common form of punishment. Not everybody had money, of course; runaway servants, who would be hard pressed to come up with cash, sometimes atoned for offenses in a much more appropriate way: by serving extra time. Under a law of New Jersey (1713), a servant who ran away would have to serve "Double the Time" he or she was absent.[33] Thieves were sometimes required to pay extra damages, or to make restitution; restitution was also a way of restoring the equilibrium the thief had disturbed. In Lancaster County, Pennsylvania, in 1736, Mary Roberts, who admitted stealing "worsted stuff" and other cloth from Stephen Adkinson, was ordered to "make restitution of the said goods stolen, to the owner." It was her third offense; she was also fined and whipped.[34]

The colonies made extensive use of bonds and recognizances: there was no such thing as probation, but courts commonly forced troublemakers and suspicious people to put up security, as a guarantee of good behavior. They were, after all, part of the community, for better or for worse. Jane Linch, convicted of stealing in Philadelphia (1760), was ordered "whipt on Wednesday next at the Carts tail round four Squares of the City," twenty-one lashes in all; she was also fined, told to make restitution, to pay the costs of the prosecution, to give security herself in the amount of fifty pounds, and to find two sureties for twenty-five pounds each "for her good Behaviour for twelve months."[35]

This "quasi-parole use of recognizances" was common in New York; bonds were used to make sure a defendant appeared at trial, as an alternative to trial and punishment, or as an addition to it. It was sometimes even used for an acquitted defendant.[36] In 1703, one Hannah Crosier was charged with stealing; she was found not guilty, but the court was not convinced; it forced her to put up a bond of twenty pounds to guarantee her good behavior for a year.[37] In Kent County, Delaware, in 1702, a jury acquitted Hannah Barnes, accused of committing adultery with Steven Nowell. Yet the court ordered her "to pay all Fees" of the case, to post security "for her good behavior and appearance at the next Court," and told her to keep away from Steven Nowell.[38] Recognizances were commonly used in Virginia: one man in Richmond County (1735), identified by the grand jury as a "Common Drunkard, a Common Prophane Swearer and Disturber of the Peace," and having "Nothing Material to Excuse himself," had to give "Good and Sufficient Security for His good behaviour during the Term of one year." He and a surety posted a bond of twenty pounds; the recognizance would be voided if he behaved for one full year.[39]

It is hard to say how well this system worked. Hoffer and Scott pronounce it a success; they found very few instances in Richmond, in the eighteenth century, in which bond was forfeited.[40] Everyone concerned lived in a tiny world, narrowly bounded and self-enclosed. More than 10 percent of the free men of property in Richmond County, Virginia, during the period 1710–54 or so were named as sureties on recognizances. "The whole community thus had a stake in keeping order," and thus "in supporting the authority of the courts." Recognizances created "a warn and watch system" in the county.[41] The people who posted bond were unlikely to lose their money, because there were enough watching eyes and listening ears to keep a miscreant in line. In 1696, for example, James Stoddart and Josias Towgood, sureties for Thomas Duley, in Prince Georges County, Maryland, reported a disturbing rumor. Duley, it was said, threatened to "Run away and Leave his Said Suretyes in the Lurch." The sureties "humbly" asked the court to let them out of their obligation; the court did so and turned Duley over to the Sheriff "untill he Should find other Suretyes" who would guarantee his behavior and his appearance in court.[42]

Confession and repentance were crucial aims of the criminal process. In Charles County, Maryland, in 1665, Mary Grub accused John Cage of fathering her child; the accusation turned out to be false. The court then forced her "in open Court to Aske him . . . upon her bended knees for-givnes Acknowledging that she hath maliciously wronged him."[43] The system assumed that most offenders would indeed repent and recant; that fines, humiliation, perhaps a good whipping, would bring most black sheep back into line. A New Hampshire statute against adultery (1701) neatly illustrates the theory, and suggests the practice. A man and woman convicted of adultery were to be "Sett upon the Gallows" for an hour "with a Rope about their necks and the other [end] . . . cast over the Gallows"; afterwards, they were to be "severely whipt." Moreover, the offenders would "for ever after weare a Capitall Letter :A: of two inches long and proportionable in Bignesse, cutt out in Cloath of a contrary Colour to their Cloaths and Sewed upon their Upper Garments, on the out Side of their Arme or on their Back in open View."[44] (Readers will remember Hawthorne's famous novel, *The Scarlet Letter*, in which Hester Prynne wore a scarlet letter A for her adultery.) *

Branding and letter-wearing were ways of marking an offender publicly—like sitting in the stocks, but far more permanently. The message was that *this* offender was not likely to mend his ways; disgrace would and should last until death. In 1773, in Fairfield County, Connecticut, one Alexander Graham, a "transient person" convicted of breaking into a shop and stealing goods, was ordered branded with a capital B on his forehead.[46] Mutilation was another form of bodily punishment. Graham, the Connecticut burglar, also lost an ear. In Richmond, Virginia, in 1729, Tony, "a Negro Man slave," was brought before the court to give evidence against two other slaves who were suspected of "hogg stealing." The court was convinced that Tony had "told Lyes and Given false Testimony"; it ordered the sheriff to "take him and Naile one of his Ears to the pillory and there to stand for the space of one hour and then cutt the said Ear off, and then to Naile the other Ear to the pillory and at the Expiration of one hour to cutt the said Ear off"; with thirty-nine lashes on top of that.[47] Dozens of detached ears, in fact, litter the record books.

Branding and mutilation labeled a man or woman a deep-dyed sinner. The next step was banishment: exclusion from the community altogether. A criminal could be banished because (as a heretic, for example) he was a permanent danger, or because of repeated criminality. Those who would not repent, those who could not be regathered into the bosom of society, had to be driven out.† Elizabeth Martin, of New York City, was a "very Low Notorious Wicked Woman" whose life and habits

---

* Under a Rhode Island statute of 1749, a person convicted of adultery would be "set publickly on the Gallows in the Day-time, with a rope about his or her Neck, for the Space of one Hour; and then be whipped."[45]
† The English, too, used banishment ("transportation") as a punishment; and here the colonies were on the receiving end: thousands of felons were shipped to the colonies in the eighteenth century. The colonists did not always greet them with open arms. In 1670, Virginia, for example, tried to prevent the landing of "jaile birds."[48]

were "evil," and who was "Reputed a Common Whore as with Negro Slaves as to others and a great Disturber of the Peace." She was ordered to get out of the city in 1738; when she refused, she was given thirty-one lashes and chased out forever.[49]

The Death Penalty

Of course, the ultimate form of banishment was death; from this, there was no danger of return. A death sentence meant the gallows; hanging was the usual way of carrying out the sentence. There is a fairly large literature on the death penalty during the colonial period. By the standards of the times, and by English standards, the colonies were far from bloody. By our lights, however, it seems barbaric to execute anyone for sodomy or adultery; but colonial leaders thought otherwise. And in a few regards, colonial law was more severe than England's. Adultery was not a capital offense in England; but it carried the death penalty in Massachusetts Bay. In 1644, Mary Latham and James Britton were executed for adultery; she had betrayed her elderly husband and boasted of it.[50]

This was, however, a rare event. Apparently the colonists had misgivings about executing adulterers. In some instances, juries simply would not convict, because they did not want the death penalty imposed.[51] After the mid-seventeenth century, there were no more executions for adultery;[52] after 1673, executions for buggery, too, came to an end in New England.[53]

Some of the other capital laws were also all bark and no bite. Under the *Laws and Liberties of Massachusetts* (1648), a "stubborn or REBELLIOUS SON" sixteen or over "which will not obey the voice of his Father, or the Voice of his Mother" and instead lived in "sundry notorious crimes" was to be put to death. (Apparently a daughter so rebellious was unthinkable.) Cursing or smiting a natural father or mother was also a capital offense. But nobody, it seems, was ever put to death for these crimes. Prosecutions were rare; and the punishments milder. In the 1660s, Joseph Porter, Jr., a very rebellious child indeed, called his father "theife, lyar, and simple ape, shittabed." He cut down his father's fence, set fire to a pile of wood near the house, and called his mother "Gammar Shithouse, Gammar Pissehouse, Gammar Two Shoes." He also "reviled Master Hauthorne, one of the magistrates, calling him base, corrupt fellow, and said he cared not a tird for him." Porter also challenged the power of the authorities to punish him. An English royal commission agreed with him; his conviction was not in accordance with English practice.[54]

On the whole, English law was more liberal with capital punishment than colonial law. In England, men and women swung from the gallows for theft, robbery, burglary; in the colonies, this was exceptionally rare. Property crimes were, on the whole, not capital. All things considered, too, the colonies used the death penalty pretty sparingly. Some capital laws were, as we have seen, dead letters. There were, it seems, only fifteen executions in Massachusetts Bay before 1660: four for murder, two for infanticide, three for sexual offenses, two for witchcraft; four Quakers were also put to death.[55] In Pennsylvania, there were apparently only about 170 convictions in capital cases up until the Revolution. And only 94 of these miserable wretches were actually executed; the rest were pardoned or reprieved.[56] The execution rate for this colony, in other words, was about one a year.

Pennsylvania was not the only colony where the pardoning power made a difference. By one estimate, the Governor and Council in Virginia pardoned or commuted the sentence of a quarter or more of those who were condemned to die in the eighteenth century.[57] In eighteenth-century New York, 51.7 percent of the condemned won some sort of mercy.[58] Some were pardoned on the condition that they leave the province, or, in a few cases, were forced to enlist in the army or navy.[59] In one special situation, a condemned person had a legal *right* to reprieve (though not pardon): a pregnant woman. In April 1736, for example, Margaret Grass, sentenced to death in New York, "pleaded her Belly and said she was with child." A "jury of matrons" was convened to examine her claim. This "jury" reported that Margaret was indeed pregnant, and she was spared until she should give birth; in August, she was given a pardon.[60]

Murder, of course, was a capital crime. So was rape. Rape was a violent crime; but, under English law, it was legally rape to have intercourse of any kind with a child under ten. Massachusetts Bay enacted a similar law, after an appalling incident in the 1640s: three servants of John Humfry had intercourse with his nine-year-old daughter. The General Court declined to impose the death penalty; there was no specific law on the subject, and it was not, biblically speaking, a capital crime. They fined the main villain, ordered his nostrils to be slit and seared, and made him wear a noose of rope around his neck. The other two culprits were fined and whipped. The General Court then made rape, including statutory rape, a capital offense.[61]

The death penalty was also imposed on persistent backsliders and incorrigibles. A Virginia statute of 1748 illustrates the point. For stealing a hog, the first offense was worth twenty-five lashes and a fine; the second offense meant two hours in the pillory, nailed by the ears, plus a fine. The third offense brought death.[62]

Nonetheless, it remains true that the colonies used the death penalty rather sparingly. In Massachusetts, one mitigating factor was evidentiary. No one was to be put to death in Massachusetts Bay "without the testimonie of two or three *witnesses*,"a rule that had biblical backing (Deuteronomy 17:6). This was yet another reason why colonial law so favored confessions: if the prisoner confessed, the two-witness rule was dispensed with.[63]

Another mitigating doctrine was that curious legal fiction, "benefit of clergy." This strange device neatly illustrates one of the quaintest habits of the common law: its skill at changing a rule while pretending not to. As the phrase implies, this was originally a doctrine only priests and monks could use. In the Middle Ages, if a priest was accused of, say, murder, he could claim the privilege of his status, and demand to be transferred for trial to the ecclesiastical courts. But how can we tell if someone is a priest or not? Simple: a priest can read, a layman cannot. A defendant proved his right to benefit of clergy by reading from a book; not any book, of course, but the Good Book.

By about 1600, this old device had been twisted into a wondrous new shape. In the first place, it protected anybody who could read at all, not just priests and monks; and, in the second place, a defendant who claimed the privilege did not go to a church court; he escaped the death penalty altogether. Instead, he received a milder punishment—usually branding on the thumb with a hot iron. The Bible "reading" also became quite stereotyped: the Bible was always opened to the very same passage, the first lines of Psalm 51: "Have mercy upon me, O God, according to thy loving-kindness: according unto the multitude of thy tender mercies blot out my transgressions." This passage came to be called the "neck verse." Its magic words delivered the defendant from the gallows.

Benefit of clergy was one of the legal customs that made it across the Atlantic; records in Virginia and Maryland are full of examples.[64] Thus, in 1664, in Maryland, a grand jury indicted Pope Alvey for killing his servant, Alice Sandford: he beat her to death with "Certaine Sticks . . . which hee . . . in his right hand then and there did hold." The petit jury found him guilty. At that point, the record states that Alvey "Craves Benefitt of Clergy, which was granted him, And the booke being given and demanded whither he read or not, Answere was made that hee read." The court then ordered Alvey to be "forthwith burnt in the brawne" of his right hand "with a red hott Iron. Which was by the Under Sherriffe immediately Executed."[65] In North Carolina, in 1702, Thomas Dereham was convicted of manslaughter; he beat William Hudson to death "with a Certain Weapon Comonly Called . . . a Catt of Nine tayles." But Dereham was "Savd by his Book"; his punishment was branding in the left thumb "with a hott Iron haveing the Letter M."[66]

The net effect, then, was to give another chance, and a minor punishment, to first offenders who committed "clergyable" offenses, even though the official punishment for their crimes was supposed to be death.[67] "Clergy" had become a total fiction. By about 1700 in England, women, too, were entitled to benefit of clergy; and, since any fool could memorize the "neck verse," literacy no longer made any difference.[68] These developments were followed in the colonies. In 1732 Virginia passed an act allowing women to claim benefit of clergy, and abolished the reading test.[69] In the eighteenth century, moreover, it became the practice in Virginia, in some cases at least, to use an "Iron scarcely heated," thus rendering the whole business a "Piece of absurd Pageantry," in the words of one contemporary.[70] After 1732, even slaves could claim benefit of clergy in Virginia; and in some cases they did.[71] By this time, "clergy" was so pervasive, that a legislature, when it wanted to show it meant business, added the phrase "without benefit of clergy" to a criminal statute; so, in 1730, a Virginia law assessed the punishment of death "without benefit of clergy" on anyone who maliciously burned a tobacco or grain warehouse, and in 1732 on anyone who stole a slave belonging to someone else.[72]

The Puritan colonies had little truck with benefit of clergy as a *form* (there are a few examples in Massachusetts, though only after 1730);[73] but the core idea, without the mummery, was very much alive in New England. For many crimes, only dyed-in-the-wool, repeat offenders were exposed to the death penalty. Under the *Laws and Liberties of Massachusetts*, a first-time burglar was to be branded on the forehead with the letter B; a second offender was to be branded and whipped; only for the third offense would he suffer death, "as being incorrigible."*

In the South, capital punishment was much more frequent than in the northern colonies; and the burden of it fell most frequently on slaves. In the period 1706–84, 555 slaves were sentenced to death in Virginia; this was a much higher death toll than in any northern state.[75] Yet one of the bloodiest episodes of capital punishment in the colonial period took place in New York, in 1741, not in the South; it, too, had a racial element. This concerned an alleged plot by blacks, in conspiracy with white devils, to rise up, pillage, and burn. A great conspiracy trial followed; more than 150 slaves, along with 20 whites, were tried. In the end, over 30 slaves were executed, along with 4 whites. The whites and 18 of the blacks were hung; 13 slaves were burned alive at the stake.[76]

Salem and Its Witches

Another bloody episode, also in the North, is perhaps the most famous (or infamous) aspect of colonial criminal justice. This is the Salem

---

* A burglar who did his dirty work on the sabbath was dealt with more harshly; in addition to the punishment listed, a first offender would lose an ear; a second offender lost his second ear.[74]

witchcraft trials. They have given rise to an enormous literature.[77] The "witch-hunt" in Salem was an eruption of the late seventeenth century. It was unusual, but not unique. Witchcraft was a recognized offense in England, and was also a crime in the colonies. *The Laws and Liberties of Massachusetts* of 1648 included witchcraft in its list of capital offenses: "If any man or woman be a WITCH, that is, hath or consulteth with a familiar spirit, they shall be put to death"—a proposition that, like the other capital laws, was generously peppered with biblical citations.

Witchcraft trials were rare in the southern colonies. In North Carolina there were apparently only three instances before 1730; in a few cases, an alleged witch sued her accusers for defamation. Nobody in North Carolina was, it seems, actually convicted of witchcraft. Grace Sherwood came the closest, in 1706: she underwent trial by water. Her right thumb was tied to a toe on her left foot, and her left thumb to a toe on her right foot; she was then tossed into the water. Supposedly, the innocent would sink, while Satan would buoy up the guilty. Grace Sherwood floated, which was a bad sign. Five old women then examined her body; they found "two things like titts on her private parts of a black coller, being blacker than the rest of her body." This was also a bad sign. Sherwood was thrown in jail; but there is reason to believe she escaped conviction in the end.[78]

The search for "witches' teats," which figured in Grace Sherwood's case, reflected a common belief that every witch had what was called a "familiar." This was a small creature, sometimes invisible, who helped the witch carry out her evil deeds. The witch suckled these creatures with her specially adapted teats. These teats, then, were excellent evidence of guilt. When Goody Knapp was executed for witchcraft in Fairfield, Connecticut, in 1653, local women "tumbled the corpse up and down," searching for marks of the devil.[79]

The Salem episode began in 1692. Some girls in Salem who had become friendly with a slave woman named Tituba began acting in a peculiar way—screaming, falling into convulsions, barking like dogs. Soon other girls in Salem caught this behavioral disease. Surely they must have been bewitched. They themselves testified that they were "bitten and pinched by invisible agents. . . . Sometimes they were taken dumb, their mouths stopped, their throats choked, their limbs wracked and tormented, so as might move an heart of stone."[80] The whole town was quickly seized with fear and horror: the devil must be at work in Salem. Three women, Tituba, Sarah Good, and Sarah Osborn, were promptly accused of witchcraft.

In the general atmosphere of hysteria, there was a chain reaction of accusations and confessions. William Allen saw a "strange and unusual beast" on the ground one night; when he came up to it, it vanished, and in its place two or three women sprang up and ran away. Sarah Good later appeared to him while he was lying in bed and "brought an unusual light in with her." She sat on his foot; he tried to kick her, but she disappeared. Sarah Bibber saw an "apparition of Sarah Good," that "did most grievously torment me by pressing my breath almost out of my body"; the witch later tortured her by "beating and pinching me and almost choking me to death, and pricking me with pins after a most dreadful manner."[81] Other villagers were drawn into the cycle of accusation and apparition. Salem mobilized to fight its terrible, invisible enemy.

News of the Salem problem spread; the governor appointed a special court of oyer and terminer* "for discovering what witchcraft might be at the bottome."[82] The deputy governor was named chief judge of the court. The court, mindful of the unusual, dangerous character of witchcraft, relaxed traditional rules of evidence and procedure. Instead, the court used special witch-trial procedures then current in the mother country. These included scouring the bodies of the accused in search of the elusive teats or marks. The court also accepted the evidence of "spectral sources"—visions seen by the townspeople.[83]

As David Konig has pointed out, it was the defiant, the hostile, the impudent who were put to death in Salem. Those who accepted the legitimacy of the court and humbly confessed their crimes were convicted, but their lives were spared.[84] In the end, nineteen people were executed, two people died in prison, and one man, Giles Corey, was pressed to death under rocks (the so-called *peine forte et dure*), because he stood mute and refused to plead or to testify.[85] No one was acquitted by the special court.

Presently, the hysteria subsided; people began to express doubts and second thoughts; the court was dismissed, and the governor directed the Superior Court of Judicature to handle any witchcraft cases left over. Most of the remaining suspects were acquitted; a few were condemned, but the governor released them. In less than a year the Salem witch-hunt had run its course.

There have been many attempts to explain the Salem episode. A number of factors were at work. Town rivalries and factions worked as irritants beneath the surface, perhaps. There was a gender aspect, too. Not all witches were women, but most of them were, and older women at that. In some subtle and not so subtle ways, the war against witches

---

* "Oyer and terminer" means, literally, "hear and determine." The phrase was used in some places as an ordinary name for certain criminal courts; but the phrase has sometimes been applied to a court specially commissioned to hear criminal cases arising out of some incident or disorder.

was also a war against women: or at least against disorderly, trouble-some, deviant women. In Puritan thought, order and hierarchy were "cherished values"; and those who rebelled against order "were the very embodiments of evil." The "subordination of women" was part of the natural order; the witch symbolized, or embodied, a kind of double re-bellion—of woman against man, and woman against the godly society. Like Eve in the Garden of Eden, she transmitted sin to man.[86]

Cotton Mather wrote an account of the Salem episode; he called it *Wonders of the Invisible World.* The colonists (at least those who com-mitted words to paper) firmly believed, like Mather, in the reality of this "invisible world," the world of angels and spirits, the world in which sin and the devil were not concepts but palpable reality; Satan, the eternal adversary, dominated the evil half of the invisible world. Indeed, the "invisible world" was a crucial aspect of the colonial theory of criminal-ity. Every period asks the question: Why is there evil in the world? Why do people do terrible crimes? Every period has its own conventional an-swers.

For most offenses, the colonial answer was: simple weakness and bad character. The basic punishments of colonial justice were aimed at those people who strayed. Some people were very bad, even incorrigible; some seemed to embrace evil boldly and with enormous relish. Witch-craft was one way to explain this mystery. It was a form of evil that came with a built-in account of its genesis. The witch was in league with the devil. She had sold out to the forces of darkness. She was human in form, but inhuman at heart.

In general, the world was full of signs, marks, omens, and portents; the invisible world imprinted itself on bodies living and dead. John Hughson, a white, and Caesar, a black slave, were among those who were put to death after the great conspiracy trial in New York in 1741. Their bodies were left hanging in chains for months. Then a "rumour" spread that Hughson had turned black, and Caesar white: that Hugh-son's "face, hands, neck and feet, were of a deep shining black . . . and the hair of Hughson's beard and neck . . . was curling like the wool of a negro's beard and head; and the features of his face were of the symme-try of a negro beauty; the nose broad and flat, the nostrils open and ex-tended, the mouth wide, lips full and thick, his body . . . swelled to a gi-gantic size." As for Caesar, "his face was at the same time somewhat bleached or turned whitish, insomuch that it occasioned a remark, that Hughson and he had changed colours." Moreover, Hughson's body "dripped and distilled . . . from the great fermentation and abundance of matter within him"; and eventually the body "burst and discharged pail fulls of blood and corruption," which some also "esteemed almost miraculous."[87]

Was it the sun, or poison, or some other "natural" cause? Or were these, in Hughson's case at least, "remarkable signs or tokens of his innocence"? Some of the curious "were ready to resolve" these facts "into miracles"; others were skeptical. But in general, there was a readiness to accept the idea of the supernatural. The public eagerly embraced the idea of the invisible world and believed, firmly, that that world trembled always on the brink of manifestation.

Imprisonment

We have discussed the colonial system of corrections. From our standpoint, what is most obviously missing, as a punishment, is imprisonment. And, in fact, loss of liberty was not a standard way of making criminals pay. It was not totally unknown: a proclamation in Maryland, for example, in 1661 prohibited the export of "any sort of Corne or graine out of this Province without expresse warrant . . . under the penalltie of twelve moneths Imprisonment."[88] But Douglas Greenberg found only nineteen cases in New York between 1691 and 1776 in which jail was the basic form of punishment applied.[89]

A society short on labor was reluctant to lock people up; but it would be wrong to suggest that the colonies made a deliberate decision not to use jails for punishment. That would be anachronistic. The penitentiary system was basically a nineteenth-century invention. Nobody in the colonial period had yet advanced the idea that it was good for the soul, and conductive to reform, to segregate people who committed crimes, and keep them behind bars. Quite the contrary: rubbing the noses of offenders in community context was an essential part of the process of ripping and healing, which criminal justice was supposed to embody.

In one interesting and revealing case, Charles Sheepey, of Burlington, in West New Jersey (1687), was convicted of raping Elizabeth Hutcheson. (Sheepey used a time-honored defense: "hee had Carnall knowledge of the body of the said Elizabeth severall tymes," but it was no rape— she "was always as willing as hee." The jury was not convinced.) The court sentenced him as follows: to be whipped, between the hours of two and three in the afternoon "upon thy naked Body at a Carts tayle," all the way from the house of one John Butcher, to the house of one Abraham Senior, and then down to the "Markett house," as many "stripes laid on as to the Magistrates . . . Shall be thought meet"; and then to be taken and kept "in Irons for the Space of three Moneths," and during that time, to be whipped three more times, on the seventh day of each month. During his three months' imprisonment, the prisoner was to work for his bread; after that period was up, he was to be brought out during every quarterly session of the court, for a year and nine months more, to be "whipt in manner and forme as afore is mentioned."[90]

Sheepey was one of the few who was sentenced to loss of liberty; but even for him, imprisonment was imbedded in a system of public, community sanctions.

There were, of course, colonial jails; and they were used. Jails had various functions. They held prisoners who were waiting for trial. They also housed debtors—imprisonment for debt was still the rule.[91] A thief who was ordered to make restitution, and failed to do so, was a kind of debtor; he, too, might be kept in jail. But under a New Hampshire law of 1718 no person "convicted and sentenced for committing of Theft" was to remain in prison "for and on account of Restitution or Damages" more than thirty days, unless the creditor was willing to pay or guarantee keeper's fees, up to two shillings and six pence a week. If the creditor failed to pay, the keeper could set the prisoner "at Liberty."[92]

Imprisonment for debt was certainly, from our standpoint, harsh; but the debtors who were "imprisoned" were not necessarily locked in cells. In many colonies, a debtor could more or less come and go as he pleased, so long as he stayed within a certain area (the "prison bounds"); he went back to jail at night, to sleep. These "bounds," or limits, could be liberal or severe, and they could grow or shrink, as the legislatures decreed. In 1774, debtors in the Hartford, Connecticut, jail pleaded to have the bounds extended to Main Street, "so that they could beg for alms and ask travelers to carry messages for them."[93] Debt prisoners were entitled to find food, clothing, and the like, for themselves, if they could; and some sheriffs, as we noted, were not above a bit of extortion at the expense of these prisoners.

There were also "houses of correction," or "workhouses." These were roughly halfway between a poorhouse and a jail. They housed the *lumpenproletariat:* people classified as vagrants, idlers, paupers. Pennsylvania's Great Law of 1682 provided for workhouses, one in each county. The houses were not to charge fees. Prisoners were to have "liberty to provide themselves bedding, food, and other necessaries."[94] A New Hampshire law tells a good deal of the tale about these houses. They were to be built for the "Keeping, Correcting and Setting to Work of Rogues, Vagabonds, and common Beggars, and other Lewd, Idle and Disorderly Persons." Other candidates for the house of correction included "Persons using any subtle Craft, Jugling, or unlawful Games, or Plays, or feigning themselves to have knowledge in Physiognomy, Palmestry, or pretending that they can tell Destinies, Fortunes, or discover where lost or stolen Goods may be found; Common Pipers, Fidlers, Runaways, Stubborn Servants, or Children, Common Drunkards, Common Night-walkers, Pilferers, Wanton, and Lascivious Persons, either in Speech, or Behavior"; also "Railers, or Brawlers [who] neglect their Callings, Mispend what they earn, and do not provide for themselves, or the support of their Families." The "Master" of the house could put these people to work; or punish them with "Fetters or Shackles," with "Moderate Whipping," or "abridge them of their Food," if they made trouble.[95]

The house of correction was thus a kind of heightened form of the normal mode of punishment; and a convenient *place* for "correcting"; significantly the New Hampshire act does not specify any particular length of time for vagabonds and the like to be incarcerated. Moreover, the workhouse did not interfere with the labor system; after all, inmates were people who did not figure in the work force anyway; and the workhouse was, as its name suggested, designed to cure this little disease. A Massachusetts Bay law of 1673, on the punishment of those who had the "Presumption" to run a "Whore House, or Brothel House," shows how aspects of the correctional system were interlaced in that colony. After thirty lashes "severely" administered "at the Carts-tayle," these convicts were committed to the House of Correction "to be kept with hard fare, and hard labour, by dayly Task, and in defect of their duty to be severely whipt every night with *Ten Stripes*"; at least once a week they were to be dressed in "hair Frocks and blew Caps," fastened to a hand-cart, and "forced along to draw all the filth laid up in the Cart, through the Streets, to the Sea side going to the Gallows in *Suffolk*, and in all other Counties where the Court of each Shire shall appoint, and so returned to the House of Correction, to be alike kept with hard Fare and Labour," for an indefinite term, that is, "during the Courts pleasure."[96]

Conditions in workhouses or jails were hardly luxurious, as one can imagine; but a prisoner with friends or family or connections did not have to eat swill or wear rags. For those who could not get things from outside, the jails were, at times, totally deplorable. The eighteenth-century jail in Charlestown, South Carolina, was described as "Close and Stinking." A person would be better off in the "French Kings Gallies, or the Prisons of Turkey or Barbary." The jail was small and had five or six rooms, each jammed to the gills with debtors. The summer heat was "intolerable"; prisoners often had no "Room to lye at length, but suceed each other to ley down—One was suffocated by the Heat of this Summer—and when a Coffin was sent for the Corps, there was no room to admit it. . . . Men and Women are crowded promiscuously—No Necessary Houses to retire too—The Necessities of Nature must be done by both Sexes in the presence of each other."[97]

Who Were the Criminals?

The answer is, primarily, men at the bottom of the heap. Women appear more rarely. The figures in Douglas Greenberg's study of New York crime in the eighteenth century are quite dramatic. Men were accused in 94.4 percent of the violent crimes, and 73.9 percent of the thefts.[98] In Massacchusetts, between 1673 and 1774, women committed 19.7 percent of the serious crimes, a somewhat higher proportion, but they nonetheless lagged far behind their brothers.[99]

There were, to be sure, a few crimes in which women predominated. Witchcraft was one. Women were also more likely to be charged with fornication, at least according to the records in Massachusetts.[100] One reason, of course, was that the evidence of fornication was often right there at hand, in the shape of a swollen belly. Some crimes in practice were specific to women. One was infanticide. Susanna Andrews, who killed her bastard twins, in Massachusetts in the 1690s, went to the gallows for this offense.[101] The women who killed their babies were mostly servants, and unmarried; they were tragic victims themselves of Puritan morality and the double standard.

Infanticide was a difficult crime to prove; unmarried women usually gave birth alone, in secret; and they killed in secret, too. A mother could always claim that the child was stillborn, certainly not a rare event. A Massachusetts statute of 1692, copying an English statute of 1624, referred to "Lewd Women . . . delivered of Bastard Children" and made it a crime to "conceal the Death" of a bastard, whether born alive or not; the punishment for concealment was death.[102] But eighteenth-century juries disliked this statute, and there was a tendency toward leniency in such cases and in cases of infanticide. Only one woman was convicted of infanticide in Massachusetts between 1730 and 1780, out of twenty charged with the crime.[103]

As we have suggested, most of the thousands punished for petty crimes, and for fornication, idleness, and other forms of misconduct, were people at the bottom of the ladder. Ministers of the gospel and substantial merchants were rarely whipped, put in the stocks, or branded. The Puritans in Massachusetts did, of course, punish some of the high and mighty for religious infractions, including heresy.[104] But the lash of the law, in all of the colonies, fell overwhelmingly on servants, apprentices, slaves, smallholders, and laborers. In Virginia, as in Massachusetts, the defendants were "day laborers, servants, and poor freeholders."[105]

The state's right to whip and punish servants (and slaves) was nothing but an extension of the right of the master or mistress. These people freely exercised their right to "correct" their servants, with a whip if necessary. Extreme cruelty was an offense; but it had to be extreme. In North Carolina, a law forbade "private Burialls of Servants and other persons." As the attorney general, Thomas Snowden, explained, this was to prevent a cover-up by masters who murdered servants, and to end the "barbarous Custom of Burying the Bodys of the Dead in Comon and Unfenced places to the prey of Hoggs or other Vermine." Every plantation had to have a place set aside for burying the dead; and neighbors were to be called in at burials, who would "in Case of Suspicion" view the corpse.[106]*

This was the dark side of colonial paternalism; and it was darkest with regard to black slaves, as we shall see. The silver lining of this paternalism, on the other hand, was the tendency to forgive and forget, provided the offense was not too gross; if the sinner repented, he was reabsorbed into the community. Eli Faber found a number of leading citizens in the Puritan colonies, officeholders in fact, who had once been punished for crime.[107] Colonial society was, as we have said, firmly hierarchical, and servants had to keep their place. Still, apprentices and indentured servants, people definitely on the bottom, were part of the community; they were supposed to share the norms and beliefs of their betters. Male servants, at least, would someday have a chance to climb the ladder of success. Today, a man (or woman) with "a record" is stigmatized far more indelibly. And, to be sure, "absorption" ended at the color line: an indentured servant could climb up the ladder of society at the end of his term of service; but slavery was forever.

Slavery and Political Justice

Criminal justice had at least one job in the colonies with no counterpart whatsoever in England: controlling slaves. Every colony also had a mass of indentured servants. In the northern colonies these servants far outnumbered slaves.

An indentured servant was, in some ways, a kind of temporary slave. It was a crime for a servant to run away from his or her master. There were also a fair number of slaves in the northern colonies; but already, by the eighteenth century, slavery was the "peculiar institution" of the South. In parts of that region, black slaves came to outnumber free whites, and by a considerable margin. Slaves were condemned to a lifetime of servitude; mothers handed down the condition to their children in the womb.

In the South, slavery was a prime concern of criminal justice. Masters and overseers had the basic job of controlling the slaves and policing slave society. They punished petty offenses quickly and summarily, on the plantation and in their homes. Slaves might therefore actually be

* At a session of July 29, 1707, the General Court of the colony fined Gabriel Newby for burying John Deal, "an Orphant Boy" who belonged to Newby, in violation of the statute. The punishment was hardly severe: six shillings, eight pence, and costs.

underrepresented in the regular courts; this was certainly true in Richmond, Virginia, in the mid-eighteenth century.[108]

The whip was the main tangible symbol of social control; masters, mistresses, and overseers used it quite liberally. William Byrd of Westover, Virginia, recorded the following in a dry, matter-of-fact tone in his diary: on November 30, 1709, Eugene, a house hand, "was whipped for pissing in bed." On December 3, Eugene repeated this offense, "for which I made him drink a pint of piss." On December 16, "Eugene was whipped for doing nothing yesterday." Three years later, on December 18, 1712, "I found Eugene asleep instead of being at work, for which I beat him severely."[109]

The slave had no defense, of course, against the whip; and punishment on the plantation could be brutal, even murderous. A Virginia law of 1669, on the "casuall killing of slaves" (casual means "accidental" here), recognized the right to punish "refractory servants," and, by implication, severely. If a slave resisted his master and was "corrected," and "by the extremity of the correction should chance to die," this was not murder or any other felony, since "it cannot be presumed" that the master really meant to kill and thus "destroy his owne estate."* Technically, killing a slave could be murder, if it was done maliciously. In Virginia, two men were executed in 1739 for whipping a slave to death; but this was highly unusual. When Andrew Burns, an overseer, killed a slave through whipping in Virginia in 1729, he was sentenced to death; but the governor pardoned him, because "the taking away the life of this man will, in all probability stir up the Negro's to a contempt of their Masters and Overseers."[111] And that, after all, was a cardinal legal and social principal.

The control of slaves was only one example of political justice in the period. In a larger sense, much of the religious regulation had a political bent or basis. The issue was godliness, to be sure; but beyond this was a more practical question: Who would run the colonies? Religious orthodoxy was the basis on which the authorities claimed the right to rule. There were high-level wrangles and disputes and theological debates and political debates. But there was also a low-level, nearly invisible struggle, a stuggle that also goes on in communities far less autocratic and paternalistic: on the one side, leaders trying to put down or control deviants, troublemakers, questioners of authority; on the other side, men and women trying to assert their individuality, or simply unable, for one reason or another, to behave the way society wants them to. Richard Gaskins, studying eighteenth-century Connecticut, found in-

* The statute actually says that what is not presumed is "prepensed malice," that is, malice aforethought, or, in plain English, a plan to kill; only with this sort of "malice" does a killing amount to the felony called murder.[110]

stances of bad behavior in and around church that were really expressions of religious dissent. In one case, a sabbath-breaker, dressed "in an indecent and unbecoming manner," positioned himself under a tree near the meetinghouse, "uttering profanities," and "scared the horses of those going to church."[112] Even in the strongholds of theocracy, rebellion found a way to take root and grow.

The Eighteenth Century

Research on the colonial legal system has been heavily slanted toward "origins," that is, the seventeenth century. There is, however, a growing body of research on the eighteenth century, a period of significant change and growth in which the tight reins of the theocracy loosened under pressure. William Nelson carefully examined prosecutions in seven counties in Massachusetts between 1760 and 1774. A fair number of cases (13 percent) were for religious offenses: profanity, nonattendance at church.[113] There were still many prosecutions for sexual offenses—fornication accounted for almost 38 percent of the cases in these counties. But almost all of these were brought against mothers of illegitimate children. There had been a crucial change in the *nature* of these prosecutions. They were no longer directed at sin as such; the point was to nail down responsibility for raising and supporting bastard children. Fornication prosecutions, then, had become a kind of welfare law; a prelude to paternity proceedings—a "kind of registration procedure whose purposes were only coincidentally related to the punitive assumptions of the criminal law."[114]

The change was only natural; colonial society itself had changed. Towns were bigger, more diverse; the population was growing; magistrates and divines had lost some of their control. The criminal justice system shifted focus, then, from victimless crimes to more conventional crimes—in particular, crimes against property. Figures for Virginia, too, suggest something of a shift away from morals crimes in the course of the eighteenth century.[115]

In addition, the criminal justice system became more "English," more concerned with legal niceties, more technically "correct," less rough and ready. It came to resemble more the law of the mother country, because *society* had drawn a bit closer to the overseas model. The small pioneer settlements had moved inland; places like Boston and Philadelphia were still a far cry from London, but they were nonetheless cities, centers of a kind of urban life.

The eighteenth century was the century of the American Revolution, a century of increasing strain between colonies and mother country, ending in war. There were a number of important political trials. One of the most notable was the trial of the printer John Peter Zenger in New York in 1735. Zenger had printed, in his newspaper, articles that attacked the royal governor. He was charged with seditious libel; but the jury refused to convict him.[116] The Zenger trial has gone down in history as a landmark on the road to a free press; and perhaps it deserves that fame. Zenger's lawyer, Andrew Hamilton, tried to argue that *truth* should be a defense to the charge of seditious libel. The judge felt otherwise; and he had the law on his side.

This strikes a modern reader as strange. But as far as authority was concerned, truth was irrelevant. The real crime was disorder, ridicule, disobedience, rocking the boat; the critique itself was the crime. Hamilton attacked this notion. When the judge refused to allow his point, Hamilton argued that the jury was the last word on law as well as on fact. In any event, Zenger walked out of the courtroom, free.[117]

The struggle over political justice grew more and more heated, until it ended in bloodshed and war. Behind the Stamp Act controversy, the writs of assistance controversy, the arguments over the acts of trade, the trials after the Boston Massacre (1770), were two sharply differing conceptions of political authority—and of the part that criminal justice was to play in the polity. British conceptions were in essence still autocratic. Autocracy, however, had decayed dramatically in the colonies. Something new was sprouting out of the rich dirt on this side of the Atlantic. What watered it and weeded this garden was not the subversive ideas of the Enlightenment so much as the physical and social world of America. King and bishops were far away; land was abundant; immigrants flooded in; the frontier was open. Under these conditions, stratification began to crumble; the little theocracies decayed. The colonists, like spoiled children, fell into bad thoughts and bad habits; their misbehavior became chronic, ingrained. Then the shooting started.

Evolution of Due Process

In criminal trials, some one man or woman stands in the dock, facing the raw and awesome power of the state. A democratic system acknowledges this fact, and is committed to some kind of balance. "Due process" is a basic concept of American law. It has many meanings. One of them, however, relates strongly to criminal justice. The scales must not tilt too much toward government. Arrests must be fair; trials must be fair; punishments must be fair. These are ideals (reality is another matter). The opposite of a democratic society is a police state. This is a state where the other side, the police side, the government side, always has the upper hand.

Fairness is a vague word; each generation defines fairness in its own terms. There has been a long, dynamic process of evolution in the meaning and practice of "due process." The following chapters tell, in part, the story of that evolution. The story has to be told on two very different levels. One is the level of theory. That level is interesting, and important. What the colonial laws said about due process; what the Constitution said, and state laws and constitutions; how courts and jurists squeezed meanings out of texts. This is significant, and undoubtedly makes *some* difference in the way the system works.

But consistent across time and space is the chasm between nice theories and grim practice. Criminal justice is more than mere words; it is patterns of behavior. The patterns *imply* ideas, ideologies, values, attitudes, but these are not the ones expressed in the higher culture, the official stories, the public propaganda. Police brutality, plea bargaining, and the third degree are just much a part of the fabric as decisions of the Supreme Court; and so, too, are thousands of unrecorded, tiny acts of minor clemency and petty tyranny at the level of the streets, station houses, courtrooms, and jails.

On both levels of the system, we can see developments that many people would label "progress": a more humane system, more attention to the rights of people accused of crime. Not that the story marches along in a clear, linear way; there are zigs and zags and lurches, like a drunk trying to walk a straight line. There was some sort of climax, perhaps, in the 1950s and 1960s. At this stage, as I write these words (January 1993), the system seems to be on pause. There is some impulse to cut back on defendants' rights, to speed up executions, to put more muscle into the system. How far this will go is a question. The public, on the whole, is quite disgusted with crime, horrified by crime; the *idea* of toughness is extremely popular. But, as we will see, it is much easier to talk tough than to put real toughness to work.

And we can and should question the concept of "progress" itself. The word is nothing but a label that we attach to change in a direction we like. There is a tendency to like what has actually happened. I doubt that many readers would want to go back to the whipping post, or the criminal law of slavery, or the lynch mob. We are not androids, with a built-in thought program, incapable of choice; but on the other hand, we are very much creatures of our time and place.

From where we stand, "due process" in the colonial period is apt to look weak and underdeveloped. As David Bodenhamer has put it, "the good order of society took precedence over the liberty of the individual."[118] This was true of the nineteenth century, and the twentieth, in many ways; but it was particularly true of the colonial period. Still, procedural justice was evolving; ideas were changing. Criminal process was not, for its time, particularly savage or bloody. Torture was avoided. As early as 1641, in the *Body of Liberties* in Massachusetts, it was laid down that no one should be "forced by Torture to confesse any Crime" except in a "Capitall case where he is first fullie convicted by cleare and suffitient evidence," and even then, "not with such Tortures as be Barbarous and inhumane."[119]

The system, all in all, aimed at honesty and fairness in the use of evidence; it made increasing use of juries of honest neighbors; it was, in general, not perverted by crass considerations of political expedience; it was fairly independent, within its own frame of mind. Colonial justice was not, on the whole, corrupt; judges and magistrates were mostly strong-minded men, not fawning tools of the crown.

But some aspects of the system seem strange to us, and distinctly unfair. Today it seems obvious that a person accused of crime had better get himself a lawyer; otherwise, he will be hopelessly outgunned. But England did not allow defendants to use lawyers. In theory, the judge would look after the legal rights of the defendant. Criminal justice in England before the days of the lawyers[120] was, in a sense, an act of state; it was part of the machinery of government, and the scales of justice were tilted accordingly. The system of private prosecution seemed to suggest a rather different message: a kind of indifference to the prosecution of criminals. Both the lawyerless trial, and the system of private prosecution, bent the administration of justice toward the interests of the rich and powerful.

The colonies, as we have seen, gave up on private prosecution in general; but colonial trials were at first as lawyerless as trials in England. Civil trials, in the early years, were almost as lawyerless as criminal trials. There were, after all, very few trained lawyers in the colonies before the eighteenth century. Judges, too, were for the most part not law-trained. Early colonial leaders tended to be, on the whole, rather hostile to lawyers. Change came about on a piecemeal basis. The eighteenth century saw a more plentiful supply of lawyers.[121] Under New York law, counsel could appear in felony cases, but only to help out on points of law. (In misdemeanor cases, oddly enough, the defendant could use a lawyer at any stage of the proceedings.[122]) In South Carolina, an act of 1731, after reciting that in criminal trials many innocent people might "suffer for want of knowledge in the laws how to make a just defense," gave defendants in felony cases the right to hire "so many counsel, not exceeding two, as the person . . . shall desire."[123] In Virginia, attorneys were taking part in criminal trials in the early eighteenth century; a statute of 1734 gave prisoners the right to "counsel" in "all trials for capital offenses"—if they could afford it, of course, which few could.[124]

The right to counsel was ultimately written into the Bill of Rights; this guarantee did not come completely out of the blue but was grounded in colonial experience. The revolutionary generation would give due process a push; and there would be a number of spurts and leaps in the next two centuries. But a certain amount of groundwork had been laid in the colonial years as well.

II

FROM THE REVOLUTION TO THE CLOSE OF THE NINETEENTH CENTURY

3

THE MECHANICS
OF POWER:
THE REPUBLICAN
PERIOD

IN 1776 THE COLONIES DECLARED THEMSELVES INDEPENDENT; AND FROM THAT time until 1781, they were engaged in a desperate war with England. It was a war for political independence, a civil war in which many residents had to choose sides, some of them reluctantly. The upheavals of war necessarily left marks on the criminal justice system.

But that system, on the whole, survived the Revolution, and fairly intact. War itself caused temporary local disruptions of process; but the criminal courts kept their basic structure, their methods and procedures. Here there was no revolution, at least not initially. In part this was because the real American Revolution was not the war itself, or independence, though these were, of course, important. In some ways, the real revolution was a silent revolution—silent and unintended. It was a cascade of cultural and economic changes in process long before anyone shot a gun or defied the king. Probably *evolution* is a better word than *revolution*: two societies had grown apart until they no longer talked to each other, understood each other, or saw each other's point of view.

Historians for a long time have argued about the nature of the American Revolution. Was it a revolution at all; and if so, in what sense? Did this "revolution" make deep changes—the French and Russian revolutions certainly did—or was it little more than a kind of palace coup, in which one set of elites shuffled off the stage, to be replaced by another?

Obviously, since men fought and died, they thought something fairly radical was at stake; but what was it? It does seem clear that the Revolution boiled up out of a ferment of new ideas, including ideas about the rights of man, and, not incidentally, about criminal justice. The American leaders were intelligent men who read books and discussed ideas. They were very much men of the Enlightenment. They read and absorbed the work of Cesare Beccaria, on criminal justice; they knew about Jeremy Bentham, John Howard, and other English writers on crime and criminal justice.[1]

Moreover, this was a huge continent, almost empty (from the colonists' standpoint); there was land to burn. A vast ocean lay between the American continent and the mother country; and the British government did not know at first how to run an empire. (How could it?) There emerged something resembling an imperial policy in the eighteenth century, but by then it was probably too late. The colonies had grown up; they were adults, not children; and they had minds of their own. American reality had formed those minds in rather un-British ways. British institutions could not and did not reproduce themselves, with their traditional strength, on the American side of the ocean.

British criminal justice was monarchic and authoritarian; American criminal justice was hardly democratic (in our terms), but it defined authority in a very different way. Power was, on the whole, quite local. In English legal theory, the king was the "fountain of justice," the source of all legal authority. But the colonies never bought this idea. For the Puritan leaders, God was the ultimate source of justice, and, in the course of the eighteenth century, more and more colonists apparently came to feel that the people themselves were the arbiters of justice; the king should himself be *bound* by law; he was not above and beyond it.

The Revolution swept away what was left of royal theories of justice. It did this literally: the king's name disappeared from legal forms and writs. That fact itself had a certain symbolism. Law was the locus of legitimate authority, and the people were the source of law. The new "fountain of justice" was the popular will. The old theories had been driven out by a century and a half of self-government, in an open, land-rich, new society.[2]

This chapter introduces the criminal justice system of the post-Revolutionary period. Three themes stand out: the impulse to *reform* the law, to make it conform to republican ideals; the evolution toward *professionalism*; and (running through all of these) the influence of American social conditions, in particular, the fantastic *mobility* of American life.

Reform and Reforming

The post-Revolutionary age was an age of reform in criminal justice. The Bill of Rights, as we will see, codified ideas about fair trials. Reform of criminal justice was in the air. Parts of the old system seemed chaotic and barbaric. The republic seemed to need a new system, more rational, more modern, more just and humane. Reformers, on the whole, hated the death penalty, and, to a lesser degree, other punishments of the body—whipping, torture, and the like. They hated naked authority. They hated boundless official discretion. They hated institutions of grace and mercy, insofar as they were not governed by principles of law. All these they associated with the defeated monarchy.

They had a point. English criminal justice was a patriarchal jumble, a peculiar mixture of extreme legalism and extreme discretion. The penal code seemed utterly pitiless; anybody who stole so much as a silver spoon or two could be sent to the gallows. But, as Douglas Hay has argued in a brilliant essay, there was an inner and perhaps subconscious logic to the system.[3] Many poor souls were indeed sentenced to death, and many ended up swinging from the gallows. But others escaped death, because some squire or noble put in a word for them, and evoked the king's mercy. This combination of mercy and terror, Hay argues, built a stronger, more efficient structure of social control than terror alone could have done.

This kind of system did not suit the American condition, or the American mind. It appeared (and was) autocratic. It depended on patronage, on the networks that tied together the big landowners in England, the crown, the nobility; on the dependency of poor tenants and farmers who rented or held land on great estates. That system was lacking in America.

A *republican* criminal justice system would look quite different. It would not tolerate cells of uncontrolled discretion, if at all possible. Popular government was supposed to be a government of *laws*, not of grace and favor. This meant that all crimes, and their punishments, should be embodied in a single, clear, definitive code.

Law had to be an open book. "Laws, to be obeyed and administered, must be known; to be known they must be read; to be administered they must be studied and compared. To know them is the right of the people." Edward Livingston wrote those words, introducing his proposed penal code for Louisiana in 1822.[4] In the event, Louisiana did not adopt the code; but the code idea made important conquests in many states, and a reform spirit pruned the criminal law of those features that looked the most irrational.

Codification and the republican idea, for example, were in conflict with the concept of the "common-law crime." This term had two rather different meanings. It referred, in the first place, to traditional crimes—acts recognized as crimes whether or not there was a specific law on the subject, because "everybody" simply *knew* these were crimes. Murder, in other words, was a common-law crime, whether or not some state had a formal text that prohibited murder. Of course, every state in fact did have a law against murder; this meaning of the term was therefore not very important.

The other sense of the term carried more weight. To put it bluntly, it referred to the power of courts to invent new crimes. A penal code, if it was (in theory) gapless and complete, would put an end to the power of judges to create new common-law crimes. In *United States v. Hudson and Goodwin,* decided in 1812, the defendants had been indicted for libeling the president and Congress (they had, in print, accused the president and Congress of "having in secret voted $2,000,000 as a present to Bonaparte, for leave to make a treaty with Spain").[5] The criminal laws passed by Congress did not cover this offense in so many words. The Supreme Court felt this was a crucial—and fatal—flaw. There was no such thing as a federal common-law crime. Unless Congress gave an explicit green light, by passing a law, the courts had no power to punish, no matter what a person may have done.

This was, of course, a federal case; the decision had strong overtones of states' rights. This was early nineteenth-century federalism—a niggardly view of the power of Washington, as compared to the power of the states. The states were, in fact, much slower to rid themselves of the concept of common-law crime. In a Maine case in 1821, defendant dropped the dead body of a child into the Kennebec River. No statute made this a crime as such; but the defendant was convicted, and the highest court of Maine affirmed. From childhood on, said the court, "we all have been accustomed to pay a reverential respect to the sepulchres of our fathers." There *was* a law forbidding people from digging up dead bodies. Therefore it should also be a crime to deprive a body "of a decent burial. . . . If a dead body may be thrown into a river it may be cast into a street:—if the body of a child—so, the body of an adult. . . . Good morals—decency—our best feelings—the law of the land—all forbid such proceedings."[6]

As late as 1881, the concept cropped up in a Pennsylvania court case. A man named McHale, along with some others, was indicted for stuffing ballot boxes. Nothing in the Pennsylvania code exactly fit the case. The court was willing to stretch a point, reaching into the grab bag of the common law. The issue was not "whether precedents can be found in the books," but whether the acts "injuriously affect the public." McHale's acts shook "the social fabric to its foundations"; the court could not let them go unpunished.[7]

These were, however, isolated cases. The concept of the common-law crime was in retreat throughout the nineteenth century. In Ohio, the high court stated flatly, in 1842, that "With us, there is no such thing as common law crimes."[8] In Indiana, the Revised Statutes of 1852 baldly laid down the rule that "Crimes and misdemeanors shall be defined, and punishment therefor fixed, by statutes of this State, and not otherwise."[9] In practice, too, the concept became less and less important, simply because more and more states passed comprehensive penal codes; by implication, anything not listed was simply not a crime. Judges had too much power, if they could invent new crimes, or extend old ones by analogy.[10]

Codification was only one aspect of (technical) law reform. In every state (and territory), there were attempts to smooth out the bumps and eliminate irrationalities. Benefit of clergy, for example, with its odor of archaism, its taint of legal fiction, was an early casualty. Also, the tide was running against bodily punishments, and benefit of clergy usually involved branding with a hot iron. In 1796, Virginia abolished benefit of clergy altogether; and in 1807, Maryland followed suit. The Maryland statute specifically replaced branding with imprisonment, which became, as we shall see, the republican punishment of choice.[11]

REFORM: THE LAW OF TREASON

One branch of law that called for immediate reform was the law of treason. The Revolutionary War created a rather delicate situation. It was, after all, a civil war; the people on both sides looked alike, acted alike, spoke the same language. "The enemy" was not just Great Britain; it was friends, relatives, and neighbors who took the loyalist side. And the colonists themselves were, in British eyes, traitors and rebels, guilty of treason.

The colonies, too, were engaged in defining treason—as one way of dealing with the enemy within.[12] The Continental Congress, meeting in 1776, recommended that each colony enact a treason law, aimed at people who would "levy war against any of the . . . colonies" or "be adherent" to the English crown, giving "aid and comfort" to the enemy. These were classic phrases drawn from the English statutes on treason.[13] Most of the colonies followed this advice.

Some of the statutes were harsh, extreme; the times were desperate. The Virginia law provided for fines and imprisonment for anyone who might "by . . . word, open deed, or act, advisedly and willingly maintain and defend the authority, jurisdiction, or power, of the king or parliament of Great Britain." Many states seized the property of loyalists: conviction for treason, under a New Jersey act of 1778, carried with it "a full and absolute Forfeiture" of the defendant's estate, "both Real and Personal."[14] A New York law of 1779 listed, by name, dozens of "enemies" of the state, beginning with "John Murray, earl of Dunmore, formerly governor of the colony of New York." The law declared these men "Ipso Facto, convicted and attainted"; all their property was forfeited and "vested in the people of this state." They themselves were "for ever banished"; if they came back to New York, they were "hereby adjudged and declared guilty of felony" and would be put to death "without benefit of clergy."[15] All this, of course, was by legislative fiat, without trial by jury or other niceties.

Silent leges inter arma, as the maxim goes: the laws fall silent during war. War is, after all, a serious business, a matter of life and death; and the roar of guns tends to drown out the song of civilization. There were executions for treason during the war; and instances of harshness and abuse, on both sides. In Philadelphia, David Dawson was executed for treason in 1780, along with Richard Chamberlain, whose crime was passing counterfeit money. The scene is described for us by a Quaker, himself in prison for "disloyalty": A "Crowd of Spectators" had gathered. The two men "walked after a Cart in which were two Coffins a Ladder &c, each had a Rope about his Neck & their Arms tied behind them." Dawson's brother and two sisters walked along with him; Chamberlain, too, was "accompanied by one of his Relatives." The two men were "hanged on the Commons" at about one o'clock.[16]

Dawson suffered the harsh fate of those who chose the wrong side. But when the war ended, and independence became a fact, the new nation rethought the problem of treason. The law of treason was thoroughly and decisively revamped. Indeed, the Constitution of 1787 defined treason narrowly. Treason was to consist only in "levying War" against the United States, or "adhering to their Enemies, giving them Aid and Comfort." This reduced the crime to a naked essence, and swept away large pieces of the traditional definition of treason, which (in England) included a number of other offenses we tend not to think of as treason—counterfeiting, for example, or killing a judge or high government official.[17]

The Constitution also put procedural restrictions on trials for treason. No one could be convicted of this crime "unless on the Testimony of two Witnesses to the same overt Act, or on Confession in open Court"; moreover, the punishment could not include "Corruption of Blood, or Forfeiture except during the life of the Person attainted" (Article III, section 3). Treason was the king of crimes; but the Constitution turned it into a constitutional monarch—indeed, conformed it to the requirements, as the framers saw it, of a democratic republic.

PROFESSIONALIZATION

Over the years, there were many crucial changes in the system of criminal justice. One of the most powerful and most marked was the drift toward professionalization. If we take a long-term view of the criminal justice system, from its beginnings in the colonial past to the end of the twentieth century, this is surely one of the master trends of the entire period. In the beginning, as we noted in chapter 1, there were no actors in the system who spent all their working lives in criminal justice. There were no police, professional prosecutors, public defenders, prison wardens, probation officers, detectives, social workers, and the like. There were also few full-time criminals. Laymen, amateurs, and ordinary judges (some of them without any training in law) ran the system, together with a few lawyers, and a ragbag of constables, night watchmen, and haphazard jailers.

The movement away from the amateurs has been strong and (apparently) irreversible. Still, if we compare the United States with other countries, American criminal justice retains a certain amateur flavor to this very day. The jury gives the lay person power at the very core of the system. The history of the jury shows a steady decline in the rate of use of this body; but the jury is still with us, a panel of twelve, picked up off the street, as it were, that holds the power of prison or freedom, sometimes the power of life or death. The right to a jury trial is engraved in the Constitution; there is no chance it will die out completely.

American judges, too, are in a way less professional than judges in most other countries. They are not trained as judges; only as lawyers (and in earlier years, sometimes not even that). Federal judges are appointed; and they serve during "good behavior," which means, in effect, for life or as long as they want. But in the states, in the nineteenth century, a strong and successful movement switched the state courts to elective systems. In most states, then, voters elect the judges who sit in criminal courts. Democratic principles seemed to demand this. But the result is more of a political than a professional ethos. The logic seems clear. After all, judges were part of the apparatus of government; they were policy-makers and (far too often) had been extensions of the executive. This, at least, is the way many voters read the book of American and British experience. An elected judge, on the other hand, would be responsible to the voters. In the first half of the nineteenth century, election of judges became the norm (Massachusetts was one of the few holdouts). The principle applied not only to judges. Under the Arkansas constitution of 1836, for example, every township was to elect a constable for a two-year term, and every county elected a coroner and a sheriff as well (Article VI, sections 16, 17).

THE POLICE

One of the major social inventions of the first half of the nineteenth century was the creation of police forces: full-time, night-and-day agencies whose job was to prevent crime, to keep the peace, and to capture criminals. The creation of police forces was another landmark on the road to professionalization, certainly a landmark in the long, slow retreat of lay justice.

Of course, society was not totally unpoliced before police forces were organized. In the cities, as we have seen, watchmen made their rounds at night, looking out for fires and disturbances. Constables were the day-time shift in the law-enforcement business. They guarded the city, arrested drunks and vagrants, hauled offenders before the grand jury, enforced local ordinances, and supervised the watch. In addition, able-bodied men could be called on to play a part. A New York law of 1787 laid out these duties. Whenever a serious crime was committed (murder, robbery, burglary, "burning of houses," theft, "or other felony"), "cries thereof shall be solemnly made immediately in all the towns, markets and places of public resort" near where the crime took place, "so that no man, by ignorance, may excuse himself." This makeshift force of "horsemen and footmen" would pursue the criminals "from town to town, and from county to county." All men were supposed to be "ready, and armed and accoutred" in order to carry out this duty.[18]

A system of this kind, assuming it worked at all, had obvious problems. It was loose and haphazard; it could hardly be expected to do the job right in a city like New York or Boston. There was a constant chorus of complaints about the constables and watchmen. In Boston, several burglaries were committed in August 1789, evoking a remark that it was "high time the watchmen were overhauled; they have been asleep since New Year's." The captains, it was said with a sneer, were "men in their prime, aged from ninety to one hundred years, and the crew only average about fourscore, and so we have the advantage of their age and experience, *at least the robbers do.*"[19] After 1800, complaints from the respectable citizens in the cities became more strident. The old system, it was said, simply could not cope.

The London Metropolitan Police, set up in 1829, preceded and helped inspire American experiments with a standing army of professional law-enforcers. In both England and the United States, one stimulus was fear: fear of the "dangerous classes," fear of riots and urban disorders. A metropolis was a place of danger; its twisted, narrow, darkened streets, its waterfront areas and slums were realms of vice and evil. In its impenetrable shadows lurked a tough, dangerous underworld, a sub-society of thieves, prostitutes, lowlifes, pickpockets, malcontents. It was, or could be, a "place of isolation and a breeding ground for the breakdown of moral sanctions."[20]

The cities were also violent places. A wave of riots swept the cities in the 1830s and 1840s—in Philadelphia, Baltimore, New York, Cincinnati, and St. Louis.[21] Some of these were race riots: vicious mobs ran wild in the black sections of town. Savage anti-Catholic mobs burned the Ursuline Convent near Boston in 1834. Group hatreds, insecurity, the abrasive, anomic conditions of city life all joined to produce a tense, dangerous atmosphere.[22] The urban mob no longer seemed a controllable aspect of city life. It was no longer an arm of justice; it was now an untamed beast.[23]

Reform and innovation often followed directly on the heels of a particularly vicious or frightening riot. In Philadelphia, there were major anti-Catholic riots in 1844. In July, when a mob laid siege to a Catholic church, militia troops came to the scene; they fired on the crowd, killing fourteen people. A grand jury called for a civilian solution: a police force of some hundreds of men. The force was established in 1845, and strengthened in 1850. By 1852 there were over seven hundred policemen in the county.[24] Boston established a day watch in 1838. Piecemeal reforms followed; then, in 1854, the old system of watch and police was finally consigned to the ash heap. What replaced it was a "Boston Police Department" of about two hundred and fifty men under a chief of police; the old brass badge was exchanged "for a silver octagon oval plate, little larger than a silver dollar, with a *'five-pointed star,'* on which was engraved BOSTON POLICE."[25] New Orleans and Cincinnati established police forces in 1852, Chicago in 1855, Baltimore in 1857.[26]

A badge was one thing, a uniform another. Men balked at the idea of a uniform, and the public was also wary. One newspaper questioned whether "an American freeman" would or should "strut about . . . in the livery furnished at the public expense." A uniform, however, represented visibility, control, and gave the police a smart, military flavor. In 1854, Philadelphia decided that officers should wear a black coat, a hat, and the badge; in 1858, the Boston police also adopted uniforms.[27] The departments began to issue rule books that stressed discipline, propriety, and uniformity.[28]

Wilbur Miller has drawn a sharp contrast between the "bobbies" of London and the police of New York. For its police, London recruited mostly country boys, strangers to London; this was a policy of "detachment from the citizens" and "professional impartiality." New York, on the other hand, stressed "closeness to the community"; the police were locals, city boys themselves. This was a policy that could and did slide easily into corruption. Also, it put the police in a position of dependence on politicians. Police discipline in New York was nowhere near as strict as in London, and patrolmen "looked to local politicans for appointment and promotion."[29]

The politicking went both ways; police, for their part, often worked to make sure "their" alderman got elected; the situation improved somewhat after reforms in 1853, but the unholy alliance between police and politics in New York did not vanish.[30] Other cities were no less politicized. Edward Savage, reminiscing romantically about the good old days in Boston, told how the police "very quietly dabbled a little (very little) in politics" in the election of fall 1858, when "things looked a little squally. . . . Our choice was successful."[31]

The American police, in other words, were less "professional" than their British counterparts from the very start; they dipped into local politics—indeed, they were drenched in it. They were full-time workers in the system, to be sure, but there was no job training, no requirements or prerequisites, and not much real control over behavior on the beat. Amateurism of a sort went all the way to the top of the force—a point illustrated by the antics of Francis Tukey, marshal of the Boston police after 1846. Tukey was only thirty-two when he was appointed; he was a lawyer, and a personal friend of the mayor. Tukey expanded the department, staged flamboyant raids on gambling dens, and showed a talent for publicity. In January 1848, the "police drew a crowd by mysteriously digging into Boston Common to uncover a cache of allegedly stolen money." In 1851, Tukey instituted a weekly "show-up of rogues"; this was "to identify suspicious persons for the benefit of both police and public." At the first "show-up," there were seventy-six "pickpockets, burglars, panel thieves, etc." When they left, they were "forced to run a gauntlet of crowing citizens who tore their clothing and marked their backs with chalk."[32]

Tukey's exhibition was an extreme case, of course; it blotted out the difference between the mob and the professionals. True distance came somewhat later. But the rise of the police was nonetheless an event of huge significance. The police interposed a constant, serious, full-time presence into the social spaces of the cities. They were a force for *order*; a patrol, trawling the urban areas for drunks, brawlers, mobs, disturbers of peace.

Under the police regime, too, law enforcement became much less random, less haphazard. Prosecution, in the past, had depended very much on victims who made complaints. This, of course, remained true for some crimes; but the police took over for others. They became the real complainants—the prosecuting witnesses. This was very notably the case for "victimless crimes," like gambling, where the participants were all equally guilty and nobody was minded to blow the whistle. Public drunkenness and prostitution fell into the same category.

This very fact exposed the police to the corrosion of money and corruption. The police could be a dangerous class themselves. The London bobbies carried truncheons—clubs. The Boston police, like those of most cities, did the same at first: they carried short clubs, tied to their wrists.* But by the middle of the century, the weaponry got more serious. In 1854, Philadelphia's mayor told the police to go out and buy guns.[34] In New York, in a fateful decision in 1857, the state armed the Metropolitan Police with pistols.[35] The police were thus a powerful agency for crime prevention and crime control, but also a powerful force, a weapon, an armed body that could be used for suppression and oppression as well. We will return several times to this theme.

The Federal Framework

One major change that the Revolution brought about was the federal system. The American republic, especially after the Constitution of 1787 was ratified, was a federal union. Thus a national criminal justice system was piled on top of the state systems. To be sure, the states—then and now—had the lion's share of the crime and punishment business. The federal government was a bit player, a spear carrier in the drama of criminal justice. The state courts were the exclusive venue for ordinary cases, ordinary offenses; the federal courts handled only special, "federal," crimes. Criminal justice in the territories and the District of Columbia was also "federal," of course.

In 1790, to be sure, Congress enacted a general Crimes Act, defining seventeen crimes against the national government. Some of these were simply ordinary crimes in a federal setting: for example, murder or other crimes "within any fort, arsenal, dock-yard, magazine," or other place under federal control; or "upon the high seas, or in any river, haven, basin or bay, out of the jurisdiction of any particular state." It was a crime to forge "any certificate, indent, or other public security of the United States"; or to commit perjury in a federal court. Other crimes—like treason, piracy, or violence to an ambassador—belonged more specifically to the federal sphere.[36]

In addition, several bits of constitutional text related directly to criminal justice. The Constitution gave Congress power to punish people for "counterfeiting the Securities and current Coin of the United States," and for committing "Piracies and Felonies . . . on the high Seas, and Offenses against the Law of Nations" (Article I, section 8). Federal and state governments were both forbidden to pass any "Bill of Attainder or ex post facto Law" (Article I, sections 9, 10). In federal courts, criminal trials were to be "by Jury" (Article III, section 2). The crime of treason, as we noted, was specifically defined. Another provision dealt with ex-

---

* Guns were not authorized for the Boston force until 1884; in that year, the City Council voted to provide arms, at public expense, and each patrolman got a Smith & Wesson .38-caliber revolver. Before that, in the period after the Civil War, most policemen carried guns, even though these were, strictly speaking, unauthorized.[33]

tradition: a person who "shall flee from Justice, and be found in another State, shall on demand . . . be delivered up, to be removed to the State having Jurisdiction of the Crime" (Article IV, section 2).

On the whole, though, criminal justice is hardly the main theme of the Constitution. But this could not be said of the Bill of Rights—that is, the first ten amendments to the Constitution, adopted in 1791. As the drafters saw it, the basic rights included rights to fair trials and fair procedures. The Fourth Amendment guaranteed the "right of the people to be secure . . . against unreasonable searches and seizures"; warrants were not to be issued except "upon probable cause." The Fifth Amendment provided that no one would be "held to answer for a capital, or otherwise infamous crime" unless indicted or presented by a grand jury. By the same amendment, double jeopardy was outlawed (that is, no one could be tried twice for the same offense); the defendant, moreover, had the privilege not to be "a witness against himself," in other words, the right to remain silent at trial, the right not to take the stand at all. The Sixth Amendment guaranteed a "speedy and public trial, by an impartial jury." The eighth outlawed "excessive" bail and "cruel and unusual punishments."

Thus about half the text of the Bill of Rights, by bulk, is concerned with criminal justice. Tyranny was, above all, an abuse of criminal justice: arbitrary cruelty, kangaroo courts, the use of massive power to crush dissent or terrify it into silence. The nightmare image was King George III, a despot sitting on a faraway throne, and the pathologies of English criminal justice. On these shores, a castle wall of law would guard citizens from abuse, and prevent the central state from oppressing its subjects.

The Bill of Rights applied, however, only to the national government, not to the states. The Supreme Court so held.[37] The states had their own bills of rights, often quite similar to the federal bill; issues of power, reform, tyranny, and fairness were state issues as well as national ones. The states, in fact, acted to protect fundamental rights before the national government did. Indeed, the Virginia Declaration of Rights, of 1776, contained the basic list: trial by jury, the privilege against self-incrimination, the ban on excessive bail, and on cruel and unusual punishments.[38] After 1791, federal models become heavy influences on state constitutions. Many states copied the very words of the Bill of Rights. But there was no system for *coordinating* the work of the states; no overall supervision by the federal courts. That was more than a century and a half away.

There was not that much to coordinate. In our times, there is a vast body of case law on the Bill of Rights: thousands of cases, some notable or hotly contested. But all through the nineteenth century, cases on the guarantees of the Bill of Rights were uncommon, both in state and federal courts; they were the merest whisper in ordinary trials. They were, in the main, taken for granted (or ignored). Not that trials were grossly unfair (in contemporary terms). But the cutting-edge disputes over criminal justice, so shrill in our own times, had not yet come to the surface.

DEFANGING DEATH

One very notable aspect of reform in the period of the republic was the movement to get rid of the hangman. This was by no means a total success; but it did reduce the use of the death penalty quite considerably. Pennsylvania, the Quaker state, played a leading role. In 1790, the legislature abolished the death penalty for robbery, burglary, and sodomy.[39] A statute of 1794 introduced an important innovation. This law divided murder into "degrees." Murder in the first degree ("perpetrated by means of poison, or by lying in wait, or by any other kind of wilful, deliberate, or premeditated killing, or . . . committed in the perpetration, or attempt to perpetrate, any arson, rape, robbery, or burglary") carried the death penalty; all other murder was second degree, and carried a lesser punishment (essentially imprisonment).[40] A number of states in the first part of the nineteenth century picked up on this general idea.[41] In New York, for example, only first-degree arson was a capital crime. This was the crime of setting fire, willfully, and at night (when arson was most treacherous and dangerous) to a "dwelling-house" with people in it. Everything else was arson in the second degree, and not a capital offense.[42]

In general, northern and midwestern states traveled down the same road as Pennsylvania: they sharply reduced the number of capital crimes. In Virginia, in 1779, Thomas Jefferson proposed eliminating the death penalty altogether, except for treason and murder. For rape and sodomy he proposed instead castration; for a woman who committed sodomy, he suggested drilling a hole at least one-half inch in diameter through the cartilage of her nose; for people who maimed or disfigured others, he proposed maiming and disfiguring in kind, "or if that cannot be for want of the same part, then as nearly as may be in some other part of at least equal value and estimation." Virginia never obliged its great man by adopting these curious suggestions; but in 1796, the state legislature got rid of the death penalty for all crimes except murder, and certain crimes committed by slaves.[43]

In the debate over the death penalty, a number of persistent themes were sounded. Both sides quoted scripture. The Old Testament recognized the death penalty, after all; hence, the Reverend John McLeod, a New York Presbyterian, could assert that abolition would be "most offensive to Jehovah."[44] The secular arguments were perhaps more telling.

Benjamin Rush, writing in the 1790s, equated the death penalty with monarchy, with tyranny, with irrationality. Republics, he wrote, "appreciate human life. . . . They consider human sacrifices . . . offensive."[45] Edward Livingston, a leading opponent, considered the death penalty barbarous and ineffective. The "infliction of death," he wrote, "if frequent, . . . loses its effect." Under such circumstances, he asserted, killing becomes "a spectacle, which must frequently be repeated to satisfy the ferocious taste it has formed."[46]

A serious attempt was made to abolish the death penalty in New York in 1841; petitions against the death penalty flooded the legislature, and capital punishment became the "subject of impassioned debate, fierce lobbying, ingenious maneuvering."[47] The death penalty survived, but for three crimes only: treason, murder, and (as we have seen) "arson in the first degree."[48] Somewhat unexpectedly, Michigan did, in fact, try full abolition in 1846; and Wisconsin and Rhode Island followed in the next few years.[49]

BODY AND SOUL

One strand in the movement against capital punishment is worth special mention. There was, in general, a revulsion against bodily punishments. Especially in the North, whipping and other means of mortifying the flesh fell into disrepute; in many states, corporal punishment was officially eliminated. The alternative (as we shall see) was the prison system. In Massachusetts, whipping, branding, the stocks, and the pillory were abolished in the 1804–5 session of the legislature—as Michael Hindus points out, roughly at the time that the Massachusetts State Prison opened for business.[50] In Indiana the legislature ordered a state prison to be built in 1821; when it was nearing completion, the legislature followed through by getting rid of whipping altogether.[51]

Reformers eagerly embraced the idea of locking up human beings for long periods of time; but they rejected quick and dirty punishment at the whipping post. Corporal punishment was "barbarous." In the antebellum period there were campaigns against whipping—not only as a legal means of punishment, but everywhere: in the schoolhouse, in the prison, and in the navy, where flogging was a familiar institution.[52]

Obviously "barbarism" is a social concept. Why reformers of the nineteenth century recoiled in such horror from direct, personal, physical punishment is not really obvious. But recoil they did. Somehow whipping was . . . unrepublican. It was an offense to the citizen's dignity. It thrived mostly in situations of private tyranny: the old-fashioned school, the prison, the navy—indeed, the family itself. Whipping was also the way slaves were punished; it was the dominant instrument of social control on southern plantations; it was, in short, "shameful," "humiliating."

Yet, as Myra Glenn has pointed out, whipping had its defenders; and they sometimes claimed it was anything *but* humiliating. Jefferson Davis insisted that sailors preferred to be whipped; it was a "manly" form of punishment; it tested a sailor's power to grit his teeth and take pain.[53] In 1839, naval officer Uriah P. Levy, commanding the *Vandalia*, tried to get rid of corporal punishment. Instead, he made drunken seamen wear a black wooden bottle around their necks; petty thieves wore a badge proclaiming their crime. One sixteen-year-old mess boy was strapped to a gun, and tar and parrot feathers were applied to his rear end. For these throwbacks to colonialism, Levy was charged with "scandalous and cruel conduct" and court-martialed.[54]

Whipping survived, then, in these small private despotism, and wherever the alternative (imprisonment) was inefficient or disruptive. After all, a sailor locked in the brig was of no use to the ship. It survived also in the more feudal, backward areas—the South, very notably. A slave in jail picked no cotton. It survived also, for some reason, in the tiny border state of Delaware—along with the ancient shaming modes of punishment. Thus, in the 1820s, a person found guilty of stealing a check or a bill of exchange in Delaware had to make restitution, suffer a public whipping, and, in addition, wear for six months a "Roman T, not less than four inches long and one inch wide, of a scarlet colour, on the outside of the outermost garment, upon the back, between the shoulders, so as at all times to be fully exposed to view, for a badge of his or her crime." A robber had to wear a scarlet R; and a forger, a scarlet F, "at least six inches long and two inches wide."[55] But where corporal punishment lacked support from the social context, it was denounced as barbaric and replaced by more impersonal, scientific, "modern" forms—notably, the great penitentiaries.

PRIVATIZING DEATH

In the nineteenth century, corrections went private. The walled-off penitentiary replaced the pillory and the whipping post; and most states abolished the public festival of hanging. The ideas that brought about this change were probably not unrelated to the ideas that, consciously or unconsciously, underlay the attack upon whipping.

Hanging, at the time of the Revolution, was a major spectacle, a dramatic show. When Bathsheba Spooner was hung in July 1778 in the town of Worcester, Massachusetts (she may have been the only woman ever executed in the state after independence), an "immense throng of people" gathered, "many of whom had come a great distance." The Reverend Thaddeus McCarty delivered a sermon in the presence of Mrs. Spooner and her fellow conspirators, who were also about to die. Mrs. Spooner was "carried in a chaise," in a solemn procession. A terrific thunderstorm "darkened the heavens." An "awful" half hour followed:

"The loud shouts of the officers . . . 'make way, make way,' the horses pressing upon those in front, the shrieks of women in the confusion and tumult; the malefactors slowly advancing to the fatal tree, preceded by the dismal coffins . . . fierce corruscations [sic] of lightning . . . loud peals of thunder . . . a dreadful scene of horror."[56] The crowd at an execution in Cooperstown, New York, in 1827 was so dense that a viewing stand gave way; two people were killed. In the same year, when Jesse Strang was hung in Albany, the crowd was estimated at between thirty and forty thousand.[57]

These spectacles were not, however, destined to last. Hangings, starting in the middle 1830s, were gradually withdrawn from the bloodshot eyes of the vulgar. The New York law of 1835 ordered executions to be "inflicted within the walls of the prison . . . or within a yard or enclosure adjoining," in the county where the prisoner had been tried.[58]* People from the "middle and upper classes" found public hangings "revolting."[59] Louis Masur connects the movement to the revulsion against "urban crowds."[60] There was, in the period, a new interest in privacy, seclusion, control of emotions, private space. Public hangings were considered too inflammatory; they excited base "animal" instincts. In earlier periods, periods of autocracy, public hangings may have been important outlets for these "animal" instincts, or may have served as dread warnings of the awesome power of the state. A republican society had different needs and demands: self-discipline, moderation, sobriety.[61]

This was, as we shall see, a persistent and recurrent theme in nineteenth-century legal culture; it affected whipping, too, and all forms of corporal punishment. People probably came to doubt that corporal punishment did a good job of chastening and reforming deviants. The "infliction of stripes," according to Edward Livingston, was "momentary" in its application, inimical to the very "idea of reformation," and when the whipping was finished, the sufferer, faced with "the alternative of starving," would immediately repeat his offense.[62] The aim of criminal justice had to be reformation; reformation meant instilling habits of discipline and strength of character into the guilty soul. Not only did bodily punishments fail this test, but they excited bloodlust and barbarism, encouraging the very behavior they were meant to punish. The remedy was the new path of punishment: the penitentiary system.

---

* New York's law directed the sheriff or under sheriff to be present at the execution and to invite in addition the judges, district attorney, clerk, and surrogate of the county, "together with two physicians and twelve reputable citizens," whom the sheriff or under sheriff would choose. There could also be up to two "ministers of the gospel," chosen by the condemned, and "any of the immediate relatives of the criminal" who wished, plus whatever prison officials the sheriff should think "expedient" to be present. But no one else would be permitted to come; and no person under age.

The Penitentiary System

Today, jails and prisons dominate the system of "corrections"; locking people up is the primary tool for punishing serious offenders. As we saw, this was by no means the case in the colonial period; jail was essentially a place to hold people for trial who could not make bail, and for debtors who could not pay debts. These primitive jails were not at all like the "big house" of gangster movies; they were dirty, undisciplined, unisex warehouses in which every form and shape of humanity was shoved in, helter-skelter.

All this changed in the republican period. Ultimately the prison became the centerpiece of correctional theory. Whipping, as we saw, fell into disrepute. In an age of rapid growth, impersonal cities, and rootless populations, public punishments (punishments of stigma and shame) seemed to lose their power. These tools worked best in small, closed communities.[63]*

New ideas about the *sources* of crime fed the urge to reform. People felt that bad company, vice-rotten cities, temptations, weaknesses in the family were producing waves of crime. They located the sources of deviant behavior in society itself, in the environment. This was, of course, quite different from the classic colonial view, which located the source of sin in individual weaknesses, or in the devil and his minions. But if society itself was corrupting, for some people, what was to be done? One solution was a kind of radical surgery: remove the deviant from his (weak and defective) family, his evil community, and put him in "an artificially created and therefore corruption-free environment."[65]

From these notions sprang the penitentiary system. Another root was the old house-of-correction idea.† The Pennsylvania constitution of 1776 called for the construction of "houses," to punish "by hard labour, those who shall be convicted of crimes not capital." This constitution still clung to the idea of shaming: the public, "at proper times" were to be "admitted to see the prisoners at their labour" (section 39). In Massachusetts, too, after the state prison was built in 1805, visitors were al-

---

* Of course, a prison was itself a small, closed community; and whipping survived as a punishment within the prison itself. Sometimes this was explicitly recognized. Virginia's penitentiary law prescribed that convicts guilty of "profanity, indecent behavior, idleness, neglect . . . of work, insubordination, . . . assault," or violation of rules "prescribed by the governor," could, "under orders of the superintendent," be punished by "lower and coarser diet, the iron mask or gag, solitary confinement in a cell or the dungeon, or . . . stripes."[64]

† Adam Hirsch argues that the penitentiary was neither so novel nor so American as some scholars, notably David J. Rothman, suggest; that the invention of the penitentiary was more evolution than revolution, and that the "new schemes of prison discipline . . . reflected no ideological break with previous strains of carceral theory." The house of correction is central to Hirsch's arguement.[66]

lowed in for a fee, "which put prisoners on display as if in a zoo"; this system lasted until 1853.[67]

But the prison of the late nineteenth century was not yet a true penitentiary. In Connecticut, a prison was improvised in 1773 out of certain copper mines at Simsbury. Called "Newgate" after the English prison, it became the state prison of Connecticut in 1790. This was, by all accounts, a horrendous dungeon, a dark cave of "horrid gloom." The "dripping water trickling like tears from its sides; the unearthly echoes, all conspired" to strike an observer "aghast with amazement and horror." The prisoners were "heavily ironed and secured by fetters"; they ate "pickled pork" for dinner, while working at forges; "a piece for each [was] thrown on the floor and left to be washed and boiled in the water used for cooling the iron wrought at the forges."[68]

There was no penal theory underlying a prison of this type, except the idea of instilling so much dread that no sane person would want to be in one. A new breed of prison began with the remodeling of the Walnut Street institution in Philadelphia in 1790; the remodeled prison contained a "penitentiary House," with sixteen separate cells, designed for solitary confinement. Pennsylvania had drastically reduced the number of capital crimes and decreed imprisonment in its place. Its constitution of 1776 ordered the legislature to make punishments less "sanguinary," setting up instead a system of "visible punishment of long duration." This meant, at first, that prisoners would work—and work hard—but in public, on the streets and highways. In other words, labor was to be a "form of public humiliation," like the old shaming punishments.[69] This system lasted only a short time. There were ugly scenes on the streets, as citizens and convicts taunted each other. The law of 1790, "to reform the penal laws of this state," recited that the prior acts had "failed of success" precisely because of the "exposure of the offenders . . . to public view" and their "communication with each other."[70]

The remedy was to add "unremitted solitude to laborious employment"; this would "reform" as well as "deter." The convicts were to be locked in cells that would "prevent all external communication." They would wear "habits of coarse materials, uniform in colour and make," which would mark them off "from the good citizens of this commonwealth"; they would shave their beards once a week; and they would eat "bread, Indian meal, or other inferior food," and one "meal of coarse meat in each week"; meanwhile, they would do labor "of the hardest and most servile kind, in which the work is least liable to be spoiled by ignorance, neglect or obstinacy." The prisoners were also to be "kept separate and apart from each other," as much as humanly possible.*

---

* The clauses about what to wear and to eat, and the clause about "servile" labor, were repealed in April 1795.[71]

Walnut Street was the beginning. Next came Auburn, in New York. Under the Auburn system, prisoners worked together during the day, and slept in solitary cells at night. The Massachusetts prison, opened at Charlestown in 1805, was at first nothing but a kind of county jail writ large, "with congregate living arrangements and individual piecework labor"; but by 1829, it was completely done over on the Auburn plan: the prisoners worked together by day, and slept in individual cells at night.[72]

The Cherry Hill prison in Philadelphia (1829) was another pioneer penitentiary.[73] This was a massive stone building, surrounded by mighty walls. Individual wings or cell blocks radiated out of a central core. Each individual cell was connected to a small walled courtyard. The prisoners were utterly alone, night and day. They wore hoods whenever they left their cells. In Cherry Hill there was a rule of absolute, total silence.[74] Gustave de Beaumont and Alexis de Tocqueville, who visited and wrote a report on the penitentiary system, found the night silence in these great houses of captivity especially awesome: it was almost the silence "of death. We have often trod during night those monotonous and dim galleries, where a lamp is always burning: we felt as if we traversed catacombs; there were a thousand living beings, and yet it was a desert solitude."[75]

Penologists debated the merits of two competing patterns: the Pennsylvania system, where the prisoners lived and worked in silence and alone; and the Auburn system, where prisoners worked together, though also in silence. Today these may seem like Tweedledum and Tweedledee, but in their day there was endless argument over which was better. Was *total* isolation inhumane? Did it drive prisoners mad? Everyone agreed that labor was a must. Solitude without work would drive anybody mad; where this experiment was tried (in New York, from 1821 to 1823) the results were horrific: one prisoner tried to kill himself by throwing himself "from the fourth gallery, upon the pavement"; another "beat and mangled his head against the walls of his cell, until he destroyed one of his eyes."[76] From then on, hard labor was the absolute rule.

All the new penitentiaries, whatever their differences, were committed to silence, to a certain amount of isolation; and, more fundamentally, to discipline and regimentation. When the prisoner entered the gate, the staff stripped him of his individuality and reduced him to a common fate. At the Eastern Penitentiary in Philadelphia, the new convict was undressed, his hair cut, and his body "cleansed in a warm bath." Then he put on the prison uniform; and a "cap or hood" to blindfold him; in this condition, he was led to his cell.[77] No one in the prison could speak. At Sing Sing in New York, officers wore mocassins, so that they could "approach the cells without the convicts being aware of their presence." The rule of silence was so well enforced that "for several years there has not been any case reported of a prisoner talking after he was locked up."[78]

During the long years of prison, all convicts dressed alike, gulped down the same food, woke, moved (often in lockstep), worked, ate, and slept to the same daily rhythm. At Auburn, summer's work began at five-thirty A.M. A bell rang; the cells were unlocked; then the men came out; they emptied their "night-tubs," washed them, and placed them in rows. They worked until breakfast, which took place at seven or eight A.M., "on the ringing of a large bell. . . . The convicts form in a line and are marched . . . across the yard. . . . On entering the mess-room they face round to their plates and stand in their places until all are assembled, when a signal being given, they instantly sit down to their meals. . . . The tables are narrow and the prisoners sit on one side only, and are never placed face to face, in order to avoid the exchange of looks." The rest of the day was equally regimented.[79] Unlike the corrupt, haphazard, filthy jails of the past, the penitentiary was a place of strict justice, a place of penitence and reformation.

Regimentation and uniformity: when Massachusetts converted its own state prison to the Auburn method, in the late 1820s, it specified detail after detail: each year a convict was to be allowed "one pair of thick pantaloons, one thick jacket, one pair of thin pantaloons, one thin jacket, two pairs of shoes, two pairs of socks, three shirts, and two blankets, all of a coarse kind." The law specified, too, the daily ration, down to an allowance of "two ounces of black pepper," for every hundred rations.[80] The daily allowance at Sing Sing was similarly specified; six pounds, nine ounces of food a day, beef and pork, flour, mush, molasses and potatoes.[81] Every detail, every item of discipline, every step of the daily regimen, was part of the plan of punishment and reformation.

Beaumont and De Tocqueville strongly believed in the system, as did almost all the prison reformers of the day. The prison was stern but effective medicine. Men turned to crime because of their defective background, their weak wills, their bad society. The prison cured these problems. It provided the missing training, the missing backbone. It was a caricature of the unyielding, disciplined, incorruptible family that the prisoners had never had for themselves.

There were dissenters, but they were not penologists. Charles Dickens, who visited the great Philadelphia prison in the early 1840s, was horrified by what he saw: "Those who devised this system . . . and those benevolent gentlemen who carry it into execution, do not know what . . . they are doing." Prison life was nothing but torture and agony. "I hold this slow and daily tampering with the mysteries of the brain, to be immeasurably worse than any torture of the body." The wounds it inflicted "are not upon the surface, and it extorts few cries that human ears can hear"; but there was a "depth of terrible endurance ... which none but the sufferers themselves can fathom, and which no man has a right to inflict upon his fellow-creature." The prisoners, who entered in black hoods, emblems of the "curtain dropped" between them "and the living world," were like men "buried alive; to be dug out in the slow round of years; and in the meantime dead to everything but torturing anxieties and horrible despair."[82]

The novelist's words ring truer today than De Tocqueville's, but it did not seem so at the time. The penitentiary system spread, though mostly in the North, and in fits and starts. What held it back was not humanity but stinginess and lethargy. When Beaumont and De Tocqueville observed the prison system in 1831, New York, with Auburn and Sing Sing, was very "advanced" in reform; but New Jersey, just across the river, had "retained all the vices of the ancient system." Ohio, despite a "mild" penal code, had "barbarous prisons." The two Frenchmen "deeply sighed" at the situation in Cincinnati; they found half of the prisoners chained in irons, "and the rest plunged into an infected dungeon." In New Orleans, men were locked "together with hogs, in the midst of all odors and nuisances," and chained "like ferocious beasts"; there was no attempt to make the criminals "better," but only to tame their "malice"; instead of "being corrected, they are rendered brutal."[83] In the Ohio prison, where "prisoners of every variety of character" were "indiscriminately associated," the prisoners, "as might naturally be expected," spent much of their time "in mutual contamination and in devising plans of escape."[84]

In the South, there was a fierce debate over the penitentiary system.[85] South Carolina, perhaps the most conservative state in the slave belt, never built one.* Whipping and shaming punishments (and the gallows) stayed on the books in South Carolina. The very arguments that made the prison seem preferable in the North, did not work in South Carolina, where "face-to-face contact remained important and where honor was accorded great protection."[87] The more "primitive" punishments, in other words, survived in this more primitive section of the country. Here were the fewest cities, factories, mines. Traditional punishment

---

* South Carolina kept, indeed, the old colonial system of "prison bounds." Some prisoners were allowed to leave the jail, provided they did not go too far, and provided they came back to their cells at night. Most misdemeanor convicts had this privilege by the 1830s; hence, a worker could keep his job, despite trouble with the law. A statute of 1828 extended the "Gaol bounds" for Charleston: on the west, the river at low-water mark; on the south, the south line of Broad Street; on the east, the east line of Meeting Street; on the north, the north line of Wentworth Street. A law of 1831 for the "Judicial District of Georgetown" extended the "prison bounds to the corporate limits of the town."[86]

suited this almost feudal social system: the honor code, shame and humiliation, corporal punishment. And for slaves, bodily punishment was considered most effective, and, in fact, downright indispensable.[88]

Of course, even in those states that had embraced the penitentiary system, the ancient jails survived, on the local or county level; and indeed they were infused with a new function. They were no longer merely holding pens but places of punishment; and this made their inadequacies stand out all the more: often they were filthy, degraded and degrading, poorly run, and cruel by omission or design. The city jail of Savannah, Georgia, according to a Superior Court grand jury, was "inhuman and demoralizing."[89] The jail in Coosawatchie, South Carolina, was so bad that a contemporary said it was not necessary to "try a criminal there . . . with a capital offense. All that was required was to put him in jail. . . . The State paid for a coffin, and saved the expenses of trial and execution."[90]

As for the penitentiaries themselves, the system, even in the North, despite the great hopes and the fanfare, ended up as a failure. The classic system melted away like winter snows. As a practical matter, it proved impossible to enforce the pure system of silence. It was gone in Massachusetts by about 1850.[91] Regimentation was probably also never quite so absolute as intended. Charles Dickens reported that one prisoner in Philadelphia "was allowed, as an indulgence, to keep rabbits," which was certainly not part of the original plan in all its purity.[92] By about the time of the Civil War, the penitentiary system as a whole had entered into a deep crisis. The dithyrambs of praise from Beaumont and De Tocqueville had come to seem utopian, naïve. The ideals of the penitentiary system could not be carried out in practice; or at least they could not be sustained. Thus the stage was set for the next phase of reform.

4

POWER AND
ITS VICTIMS

IN EVERY SOCIETY, PEOPLE ARE RANKED IN A KIND OF PYRAMID, WITH A MORE
or less clear top, middle, and bottom; probably in every society there are
more people on the bottom than on the top; in every society there are
definite rules about how and why one moves from bottom to top, or in
the other direction, or whether it is possible to make certain moves at
all. Every society, in short, has a structure, a system of stratification, a
way of sorting people out among positions and roles.

Laws and legal institutions are part of the system that keeps the
structure in place, or allows it to change only in approved and patterned
ways. The criminal justice system maintains the status quo. This may
sound more sinister and oppressive than it needs to be. Most people, in
most societies, *want* the status quo, or parts of it. However small and
pitiful their holdings, they want to keep what they have; they don't
want other people to take their "property" by force. They want some
kind of bodily security, too. But even if the legal system "neutrally" protects what people have, as well as their place on the pyramid, clearly
some people are higher up and have more than others. Law protects
power and property; it safeguards wealth; and, by the same token, it per-
petuates the subordinate status of the people on the bottom.

The American republic was supposed to be founded on justice, equality, opportunity. It had thrown off old yokes. Old types of authority were so many rotting corpses; the Americans buried them. Compared to much of the rest of the world, this was an amazing experiment in democracy—and in social mobility; these aspects of the social order affected every American institution, from top to bottom, not least of all criminal justice.

But when we look back from where we sit today, with the wise cynicism of hindsight, we see the warts and the failures more clearly. We see a republic created, on the whole, by and for white Protestant men; behind the flag-waving and the Fourth of July parades, we see the hideous grinning faces of inequality, oppression, biasses overt and covert, cruelty, lack of understanding, intolerance. This was no pure or ideal democracy; far from it. It was a democracy of assumptions—assumptions about race, class, gender, religion, and lifestyle—a democracy that rested on definite cultural postulates. If we put these postulates together, we can construct a more balanced picture of America: a half-democracy, an adolescent democracy, a smug democracy. Of course, people were aware of such blemishes as slavery (it was perfectly obvious); and it was a fact that women did not vote or take part in much of the system of American life. But most people probably thought these were natural, not artificial, hierarchies.

Natural or not, criminal justice followed, as it always did, the pattern of social norms. It fell, as it has always fallen, more heavily on the underclass, on the deviants, on the "outs." This is so almost by definition. Indeed, criminal law was (and is) part of the official process of labeling and identifying who is in and who is out, who is deviant and who is mainstream. Criminal justice was the strong arm of the stratification system. It was part of the process that made subordination real. And subordination was real, most notably, for American blacks; also for members of other minority races; and for the poor, the deviant, the unpopular.

Race

In the southern colonies, and in the southern states, a large mass of black slaves made up the bottom layer of society. Slaves were defined in law as chattels—items of property. They could be bought and sold like cattle, or mortgaged, or given away. They themselves could own nothing. They could not legally marry or exercise any civil rights. They were subject, too, to draconian laws. After all, the very essence of slavery, the pillar on which it rested, was the master's absolute control of the body and soul of the slave. Both custom and law shored up this system of control.

The criminal law of slavery was complex. As we have seen, each colony had developed a code of laws about master and slave. The northern codes, of course, came to an end when the northern states passed laws to abolish slavery, soon after the Revolution—Vermont already in 1777, Pennsylvania in 1780.[1] By the early nineteenth century, northern slave laws were dead or moribund. But in the South, no such development took place. The slave codes continued, they grew, they were discussed, added to, changed; they lasted in full flower until the end of the Civil War, when the abolition of slavery was forced down the throats of a beaten and disheartened Confederacy. The Thirteenth Amendment to the Constitution made the death of slavery official, part of our fundamental law. The racial reality, however, was not so easily reached by gallant words.

During the high noon of slavery, the slave codes were important documents. They varied in their details, from Florida to Arkansas to Texas; but the general outlines were, depressingly, much the same. To begin with, the law codified and expressed the basic theorem of slave law. This was the massive power of masters and mistresses, and the power of their agents and overseers. The concrete form of this power was the right to administer summary punishment or "correction." In plain, blunt English, it was the power to beat, to hit, to flog, to whip, to inflict quick and dirty punishment, on the spot and to the point.

Parents have this kind of power over small children; they are judge, jury, and enforcer, all rolled into one. Parents, of course, can abuse their power; and they often do. Power, for most parents, is tempered by great love. Apologists for slavery insisted that southern slave-owners were just like parents in this regard; they loved their slaves, cared for them, were anxious for their welfare. According to George Fitzhugh, one of the South's most articulate spokesmen, the slaveholder was "the least selfish of men," because he was "the head of the largest family"; there never was a man "who did not like his slaves"; the relation of master and slave was "one of mutual good will."[2] Perhaps Fitzhugh actually believed this tripe. In fact, many masters, mistresses, and overseers were vicious and cruel; the essential savagery of slavery ran very real and very deep.

Punishment on the plantation was, essentially, *physical* punishment. The whip was the correctional instrument of all purpose. Usually, the slave was stripped to the waist, hands tied, and flogged on the back. On James Henry Hammond's plantation in South Carolina, the overseer whipped eight slaves soundly for being slow in returning to work after the Christmas holidays. When the slaves "appealed to Hammond for sympathy, he responded by ordering them flogged again." Hammond believed in whipping, though not to exceed "100 lashes in one day & to that extent only in extreme cases. The whip lash must be one inch in width. In general 15 to 20 lashes will be a sufficient flogging."[3]

Whipping was thus a way of life on the plantation. The whip was "in constant use," according to Frederick Law Olmsted, who traveled through the "cotton kingdom." There were, he thought, "no rules on the subject"; overseers and drivers "punished the negroes whenever they deemed it necessary, and in such manner, and with such severity, as they thought fit." An overseer told Olmsted: "I wouldn't mind killng a nigger more than I would a dog"; this man also said that some slaves were "determined never to let a white man whip them, and will resist. . . . Of course you must kill them in that case." Olmsted saw a slave girl brutally whipped with a rawhide whip: first, the overseer gave her thirty or forty "blows across the shoulders . . . well laid on. . . . At every stroke the girl winced." Then he flogged her across her "naked loins and thighs, with as much strength as before. She now shrunk away from him, not rising, but writhing, grovelling, and screaming."[4]

On the Georgia plantation that Francis Kemble visited in 1838, the black slaves were divided "into troops or gangs"; on this plantation the driver of each troop was "allowed to inflict a dozen lashes upon any refractory slave in the field"; the overseer could give up to fifty lashes. And as "for the master himself, where is his limit? He may, if he likes, flog a slave to death, for the laws which pretend that he may not are a mere pretense." Under the laws of the slave states, no black could testify against a white; and on this particular plantation, the overseer (and the master's family) were the only whites.[5]

In a sense, any white man (or woman) ranked higher in society than any black, slave or free, in the states of the slave South; and, at least under certain conditions, the law permitted *any* white to punish a slave who stepped out of line. In Florida, it was illegal for more than seven male slaves to "travel in high road" without "having a white person with them." If "found in a body" these slaves could be "whipped, not exceeding twenty stripes each, *without reference to civil authority*" (emphasis added).[6] The owner of a home or a plantation in Alabama could give ten lashes to any slave who entered his premises without permission; in Tennessee, any person who found a slave hunting with dogs, could kill the dogs on the spot. The law, as Daniel Flanigan has pointed out, did not discourage summary justice on the plantation; on the contrary, summary justice was the cornerstone of the system. In Arkansas, for example, if a slave committed a minor offense against "the person or property of another person," the master was allowed to "compound with the injured person," that is, to make a settlement, and then "punish his own slave," without "any legal trial or proceeding."[7]

Black slavery was more than a form of labor or a system of property:

it was a crucial aspect of the structure of southern society, an institution that affected all of southern culture. Slavery was too important to be left entirely to slave-owners. Keeping slaves in check was, and had to be, a community effort as well.* In many slave states, there were slave patrols, made up of slave-owners and other white men, who enforced rules of order among the slaves: the Mississippi patrol laws authorized patrols to pick up runaways and "disorderly" slaves, and bring them before a justice of the peace; patrols were also told to be on the lookout for slaves "strolling without a pass"; patrols had specific power to "kill all dogs owned or kept by negroes."[9] Whether patrols were vigorous and effective seemed to vary from county to county, and from place to place. During times of restlessness, or when the whites were afraid of slave insurrection, their use could rise dramatically.[10]

Above the master himself, at the bottom rung of the official system of justice, was the local justice of the peace, the "jack-of-all-trades of county government." The justice tried slaves for minor offenses, and dispensed his own brand of summary justice, with few legal frills and (usually) no appeal. In some states, the justice did not work alone in slave cases; rather, he sat on a panel together with local slave-owners—four in Louisiana. In Alabama, a justice could order thirty-nine lashes on his own; for more serious punishment, he needed the concurrence of two freeholders.[11]

In big cases, for major crimes, the ordinary criminal courts had jurisdiction over slaves. In South Carolina, for example, a slave-owner had to bring his slave for trial in these courts for any offense that carried the death penalty. Cases in which more than one plantation figured also had to go to court, along with cases that involved control over the black population in general (gambling, illegal assembly). But the most common offenses were various forms of theft. Michael Hindus's figures for Anderson and Spartanburg districts of South Carolina between 1818 and 1860 show that 43.3 percent of the blacks tried were accused of crimes against property; only 12.3 percent were accused of crimes against persons (the opposite was true of whites); gambling, sabbath violation, and drinking made up another 10 percent; a mere 1.1 percent were for sexual offenses (rape or attempted rape of a white woman were very rare charges); 6 percent were prosecuted for harboring runaways; a few, but a significant few, 4.3 percent, were charged with crimes that threatened white authority—running away, insolence or impudence, insurrection.[12]

The courts, like slave-owners on their plantations, made liberal use of whipping and other forms of bodily punishment. The statutes, partic-

---

* For this reason, too, the law discouraged slave-owners from setting free their slaves and hedged manumission with all sorts of restrictions.[8]

ularly in the early years of the nineteenth century, prescribed such punishments richly: branding, cropping, or even pinning a slave's ears to
posts. This last, for example, was the punishment for false testimony in
Florida Territory; the slave had to stand this way for an hour.[13] More and
more, however, whipping became the punishment of choice. Imprisonment was not really an option. Slaves were supposed to work; and a
slave in prison was a dead loss to his owner. In some southern states,
there were virtually no slaves in the prisons. In South Carolina, 94.7
percent of the slaves convicted of crimes were whipped; 10 percent received some other or additional punishment.[14] As Thomas R. R. Cobb
put it, the slave "can be reached only through his body."[15] This meant
the whip—or, in extreme cases, the gallows.

The gallows was by no means sparingly used. In Virginia, between
1785 and 1831, thirty-nine slaves were executed for raping white
women; nineteen more were executed for this offense between 1832 and
1865. Rape was a serious crime in any event; but in the context of slavery and black-white relationships, it was something more: "an intolerable attack against slavery and white supremacy."[16] (Black-on-black rape,
or white-on-black, were obviously *not* "intolerable.") Capital punishment was an important pillar of the southern social-control system.
Hanging a slave from the gallows was a useful "ritual" to impress blacks
with the futility of violence against whites; at these hangings, whites
"made sure most blacks were in attendance."[17]

But slaves were pieces of property, and valuable ones; when a slave
swung from the gallows, a chunk of his master's investment swung
with him. Hence statutes in the South routinely provided for compensation to the owners of slaves put to death. Otherwise, owners would be
tempted to cover up for slaves. So, for example, in Louisiana, the "public treasury" would pay the appraised value of "slaves sentenced to
death or perpetual imprisonment," up to a maximum of $750 per
slave.[18] In South Carolina in the 1830s, the legislature's Committee on
Claims handled claims for compensation for slaves put to death. As a
rule, they recommended a standard $122.45 per slave.[19]

For what offenses could punishment be imposed on slaves? The answer is, basically, for all crimes whites could be punished for, and then
some. The extra crimes were those inherent in the status of slavery
(running away, insubordination, insurrection), and those necessary to
keep the slave population in its place. Any act of insolence, even the use
of "provoking language or menacing gestures to a white person," was a
crime.[20] A wide range of activities was forbidden to slaves. Under the
Georgia slave code, for example, slaves were not allowed to "enjoy the
privilege of laboring, or otherwise transacting business, for ... themselves, except on their own premises"; an *owner* who allowed violations

could be fined. Slaves could not rent houses or rooms; could not buy, sell, or trade any goods; could not keep "any boat, periagua or canoe," or raise any horses and cattle. "Any person" could seize these contraband items and take them to a justice of the peace for public sale.[21]

Moreover, slaves (and "negroes" generally) were not to "administer any medicine or pretended medicine to any other slaves," except at the "instance or direction of some white person," who owned or managed the slave; no slave could carry or use guns, or hunt, without special leave of an owner, and unless a white grown-up came along. There were restrictions on the "wandering and meeting of negroes and other slaves," especially on Saturday nights and Sundays and holidays, and on using "drums, horns, or other loud instruments, which may call together or give sign or notice to one another of their wicked designs and intentions."[22]

All this cruelty and suppression was not random; a pervasive fear of insolence, uprising, and rebellion underlay the slave codes; this tended to put a special spin even on "ordinary" crimes. Thus, one section of the Mississippi laws of 1840 lumped together the crime of rebellion and insurrection; and plotting or conspiring to murder "any free white person."[23] Whites who objected to slavery or worked against it were also criminalized. In Kentucky, a white who helped slaves escape, or who dared to "advise, counsel, or conspire with a negro, bond or free, and cause him to rebel or make insurrection against the authority of his master or the laws of the land," was guilty of a crime punishable by death.[24] It was even a crime to argue against slavery: under the Virginia Code, for example, if a "free person, by speaking or writing, maintain that owners have not right of property in their slaves," he could be punished by a jail sentence up to one year, and a fine up to $500.[25]

Free Blacks

There were also, in the southern states, blacks who were not slaves: the free black population. Southern white society detested these free blacks. (They were not exactly popular in the North, either, and the northern states, in general, granted them only second-class citizenship.) In the years leading up to the Civil War, defenders of slavery grew more tense and felt more threatened; many slaveholders were convinced it was bad for society to allow *any* blacks to be free. A free black population was an anomaly; moreover, it threatened the very institution of slavery. The destiny of the race was to serve whites, as slaves. Every slave state heaped disabilities on free blacks—to make the point, as a Georgia justice put it, that the "fancied freedom" of the emancipated black was nothing but "a delusion"; that the slave "who receives the care and protection of a tolerable master" was better off than the free black. Free blacks could never enjoy true civil freedom among the whites.[26]

Criminal law in the southern states tended to lump together all blacks, slave or free. The North Carolina Code of 1855 is full of instances: thus "Any slave, or free negro, or free person of color, convicted of . . . an assault with intent to commit a rape, upon the body of a white female, shall suffer death." The code looked with suspicion on fraternization between free and unfree blacks; it was a crime for a free black to marry or "cohabit" with a slave, or, for that matter, to play with any slave "at any game of cards, dice, or nine pins," or "at any game of chance, hazard, or skill, for money, liquor or any thing of value." Nor was any free black to "entertain any slave in his house, during Sunday, or in the night between sunset and sunrise." Free blacks were subject to many disabilities; they were not to "hawk or peddle" without a license; or carry a "shot-gun, musket, rifle, pistol, sword, dagger, or bowie-knife" without a license; or sell liquor.[27] The Virginia law that made it a crime to use "provoking language or menacing gestures" to a white person, applied to any "negro," not just a slave.[28]

Free blacks were subject to fines for many of these offenses, and often to whipping as well. Playing cards with a slave, for example, could earn a free black up to "thirty-nine lashes on his bare back" under the North Carolina Code. If a free black was unable to pay the fine," the sheriff could auction off his labor, for up to five years, "publicly at the court house door . . . to any person who will pay the fine;" and the hirer would have the same "rights to control the services of, such free negro, as masters have over free negro apprentices."[29] Newly freed slaves were supposed to leave the state (this requirement was sometimes waived), and there was definitely no welcome sign out for free blacks from other states. Tennessee law stated baldly: "No free person of color shall remove from any other State or territory of the Union into this State to reside here."[30] The so-called free blacks were, in fact, as John Hope Franklin put it, at best only "quasi-free."[31]

Black Victims

In theory, slaves were not completely without rights. Slave states had laws on their books forbidding the killing of slaves, or treating them cruelly. In North Carolina, in 1774, the punishment for killing a slave "wilfully and maliciously" was a year's imprisonment; and the murderer was required to pay the owner the value of the slave. In 1791, the state's legislature denounced this law as "disgraceful to humanity and degrading in the highest degree to the laws and principles of a free, christian and enlightened country" because it drew a "distinction of criminality between the murder of a white person and of one who is equally an human creature, but merely of a different complexion." Thereupon, by law, it was murder to kill a slave willfully and maliciously.[32] The Arkansas constitution of 1836 gave the General Assembly power "To oblige the owner of any slave to treat them with humanity"; and Mississippi law stated flatly that "No cruel or unusual punishment shall be inflicted upon any slaves."[33]

Were these laws dead letters? Not entirely. A search of cases reported from the slave states turns up quite a few instances of whites tried for killing or abusing slaves. These cases have convinced some scholars that the courts acquitted themselves honorably, even during the dark days of slavery.[34]

There is, in fact, not much reason for congratulation. Slaves were poor, mostly illiterate, and without resources or support in the white community. It was a rare black (in a rare case), who broke through to justice in the white man's court. Procedurally, the scales were tilted against the slave. No slave could testify against a master. No black could testify against a white man at all; yet witnesses, in most cases of cruelty, were bound to be black.[35]

Michael Hindus has examined the reported cases in South Carolina in which a white was convicted of murdering a slave; these cases suggest that "only the most atrocious or public murders, frequently committed by men of low standing, resulted in conviction."[36] Slaveholders wanted to believe that their system was just; these rare cases were valuable in that they reinforced those beliefs. A slaveholder could point to these cases as evidence of equal justice, for black and white. Indeed, blacks accused of major crimes did get a fair shake, procedurally, at the upper levels of the judiciary. But if the law, as Edward Ayers has argued, "protected slaves when they were on the highly visible stage of the courtroom," it did "little to protect slaves from their masters when both were out of the spotlight."[37] After all, the whole caste system, the whole system of subordination, was written into law, girded and buttressed by law; and it was law that put flesh on its bones. Rules that punished insolence or mutiny or any form of striking back were as much part of the southern way of law as the rules against cruelty by masters—and a much more vital and living portion of that law.

Thus, as one court put it, "in the nature of things," the "homicide of a slave may be extenuated by acts, which would not produce a legal provocation if done by a white person."[38] The year was 1820, the place North Carolina. Tackett, a journeyman carpenter, shot and killed Daniel, a slave; and a jury convicted him of murder. The appeals court reversed, because the jury had not been properly instructed. If the slave had been "turbulent and disorderly," if he offered "provocations," the crime might be "extenuated," even though, if the victim had been white, these would be no excuse or defense. Slavery altered the rules.

Total subordination of slaves was the very heart of the "peculiar institution": the duty to obey, and the right of the master, the mistress, and their deputies, to "correct" and discipline. If an overseer, or a slave-owner (or any white, under some circumstances) "corrected" a slave—that is, yelled at, swore at, hit a slave—it was the duty of the slave to put up with the punishment, humbly and contritely. Any act of insolence or defiance, as we have seen, was a serious offense.

An interesting Alabama case of 1847, *State v. Abram*, illustrates the point. Abram, a slave, was indicted for "biting off the ear of Isaac J. Kirkendall, a white man." Abram was convicted and sentenced to death. Kirkendall, an overseer, saw Abram "loitering about the negro cabins" and told him to get to work. Abram said he was too sick, "upon which the overseer felt his pulse, told him he was not sick, and again ordered him to his work." Abram moved slowly; Kirkendall struck him with his whip and kicked at him. The slave fought back and threw Kirkendall down. They fought; Kirkendall drew a pistol; Abram hit him with a stick. In the end, Abram "bit off a piece of the upper part, or rim of Kirkendall's ear, and received in his own side a severe cut from Kirkendall's knife."[39]

The first observation is that Abram was on trial, not Kirkendall: and on trial for his life. The appellate court, nevertheless, reversed his conviction: a slave is "bound to obedience, and forbidden to resist"; yet in the midst of "mortal strife," the slave may sometimes make use of self-defense. To hold otherwise would "reduce the slave, to a level with the brute creation." On one point, however, the court was quite firm: the defense had asked for an instruction that "if the prisoner was so sick as to be unable to work, he was not bound to obey the command of the overseer." No, said the court; such an idea is "untenable." The master, or his overseer, "must be the judge of the capacity of the slave to labor." Without such a rule, slavery itself simply "does not exist."[40]

The result in this case was unusual; few slaves ever successfully invoked the right of self-defense. In reality, slaves had no such right.[41] In Spartanburg, South Carolina, a court ordered a slave whipped because "under no circumstances a Negro ought to raise a stick at a white person." This was standard doctrine; what is fascinating about the case is the fact that the court admitted there was no proof the slave *had* raised the stick. The black man would be whipped anyway. In another case, the court acquitted a slave of theft but gave him eighteen lashes for "taking liberty a Negro ought not to take." Courts, in short, were "more concerned with preserving white dominance and control than with justice."[42]

In other ways, too, the criminal code (and southern practice) denied the essential humanity of the slave. In a Mississippi case, decided in 1859, a slave, George, stood charged with "carnal knowledge of a female slave, under ten years of age." Was it a crime to rape a little black girl? A trial court convicted the slave, but the appellate court reversed the conviction. Slaves had no rights under the common law, and no legal rights at all, except those that a legislature chose to give them. A few "humane judges and law writers" had talked about "civilization and Christian enlightenment," but this was "unmeaning twaddle." There was no statute on the books in Mississippi that made it a crime to rape a black; hence George had committed no crime.[43] This was apparently too cold-blooded even for the Mississippi legislature; a statute, enacted the next year, made it a crime for a black to rape, or attempt to rape, any "negro or mulatto female child" under the age of twelve.[44] One notes that rape of a black woman *over* twelve was still not a crime.

A Kind of Freedom

The controversy over slavery heated up steadily in the first half of the nineteenth century. It rubbed relationships raw on both sides of the great North-South fault line. As the political situation eroded, the South took more and more steps to protect slavery. Manumission became more difficult; abolitionists were persecuted. It was a crime in some states, as noted above, to stir up trouble among blacks; or to attack the institution of slavery itself. The slave states tried to quarantine themselves against the noxious germs of abolition. A Mississippi law in the 1850s made it a crime for any "vender of books, or other person" to bring in or sell "any book, periodical, pamphlet, newspaper, or other publication" that was "calculated or designed to promote insurrection or disaffection amongst the slave population of the State, or *advocated the abolition of slavery*" (emphasis added).[45]

The Civil War, which broke out in 1861, was long, bloody, and devastating. Much of it was fought in the South, and it ripped apart the whole social fabric of that region. When the war ended, large parts of the South lay in ruins, and the cemeteries were full of the bodies of young southern men. The slaves were free. The Thirteenth Amendment to the Constitution made this situation permanent.

What the war had not changed, and could not change, was the feelings of southern whites toward black people. As soon as the guns stopped shooting, the old slave states immediately began what Eric Foner has called a "search . . . for legal means of subordinating a volatile black population," and a search for ways to bring back as much of the *substance* of the slave-labor system as possible.[46]

White supremacy was anything but gone with the wind. The infamous "Black Codes" of Mississippi, South Carolina, and other southern states blatantly attempted to tie black workers to the soil, not as slaves (that was illegal), but as peons, or, to give the matter its best face, as contract laborers for white employers. Criminal provisions were a vital part of the codes. A black who quit his job while he was under contract to work was liable to arrest. It was a crime to "entice" a worker away from his job. In Mississippi, under a typical provision, all "freedmen, free negroes and mulattoes" who were over eighteen, and had "no lawful employment or business," were declared to be "vagrants." A vagrant could be fined up to fifty dollars—an enormous sum for a poor ex-slave—and imprisoned up to ten days; if a black could not pay the fine, the sheriff could hire him out to anybody willing to pay it, with a "preference" going to his employer, if he had one. The employer was then entitled to deduct these payments from the black's wages.[47] This was not slavery, of course, but dangerously close.

The Reconstruction governments, which the South had to accept, kicking and screaming, put an end to some of the most blatant aspects of the Black Codes; but a surprising number of the provisions lived on, even during the Reconstruction period, when blacks served in southern legislatures and had at least some measure of political power. It goes without saying that the white-supremacy governments, which gained power in the 1870s and held on to it tightly, made lush use of these instruments of suppression—vagrancy laws, enticement laws, and the rest.

Even before power devolved on these governments, the white South gained domination through the use of plain brute force. The Ku Klux Klan ravaged the South, killing and burning, intimidating blacks and any whites who dared oppose the Klan.* Congress passed acts that were supposed to safeguard the rights of blacks and put an end to the Klan: notably, the so-called Enforcement Act of 1870.[48] Supposedly, federal efforts help smash the Klan; but in a way the men in white sheets had the last laugh. The regime they established lasted for about a hundred years.

The Klan was hardly needed after the northern armies withdrew and southern whites were back in the saddle. During the long night of segregation and white supremacy, criminal justice systems in the southern states served as foot soldiers in the army of the dominant race. The black population was a kind of caste of untouchables. Keeping them in their place was a primary function of courts, laws, and police. Their place was on the land, working for white landowners, socially and economically at the bottom of the heap.[49] Of course, the criminal justice

---

* On the work of the Klan, see chapter 8.

system did not do this on its own; it echoed and reinforced the sturdy customs and ingrained prejudices that made up the "Southern way of life."

Particularly effective was the criminal-surety system, which had carried over from the bad days of the Black Codes. If a black was convicted of vagrancy, or some minor offense (petty larceny, drunkenness), and fined, he became (as we have seen) in effect a kind of slave; he was turned over to a white employer who paid the fine and got a laborer in return. For the black, moreover, there was no way out once he was forced to work. If a black signed a labor contract to get out of jail and then quit the job or ran away or otherwise failed to perform the work, many southern laws made this an offense in itself.[50] The cycle would start all over again, with the black deeper and deeper in trouble and debt.

The "ultimate sanction," the really heavy structure that propped up the labor system of the South, was the penal system. Typically, southern convicts (overwhelmingly black) were leased out for work on chain gangs or labor gangs. The lessees were worse than Simon Legree; they worked black bodies as hard as they could; they made use of "shackles, dogs, whips, and guns," and "created a living hell for the prisoners." The mortality rates on these chain gangs were staggering. Two hundred eighty-five convicts were sent to build the Greenwood and Augusta Railroad between 1877 and 1880. Almost 45 percent of them died—and these were young black men in the prime of their lives.[51] You can imagine what it would take, what cruelty, what conditions of work, to kill off almost half of these men.

Outright racial segregation began in the period after the Civil War. Before the war, segregation was taken for granted. Since that was no longer the case, the long arm of the law was needed. In November 1865, a Mississippi statute penalized railway officials who allowed "any freedman, negro, or mulatto, to ride on any first class passenger car . . . used by . . . white persons"; an exception was carved out solely for "negroes or mulattoes, traveling with their mistresses, in the capacity of nurses." A Florida law of the same year made it a crime for any "negro, mulatto, or other person of color" to "intrude himself . . . into any railroad car . . . set apart for the exclusive accommodation of white people." The punishment was whipping or the pillory.[52] Reconstruction swept away these particular laws, but later, in the 1880s, segregation laws began to appear once more.[53]

Was segregation legal? The question came before the United States Supreme Court in 1896, in the famous (or notorious) case of *Plessy v. Ferguson.*[54] Louisiana, in 1890, had passed a Jim Crow law dealing with railway carriages. Any passenger who insisted on "going into a coach or compartment to which by race he does not belong" was subject to a fine. Homer Plessy, a light-skinned black, bought and paid for a "first class passage on the East Louisiana Railway from New Orleans to Covington," took a vacant seat in a whites-only coach, and was "forcibly ejected" and thrown into the parish jail of New Orleans. His defense: the law was unconstitutional, a violation of his rights under the Thirteenth and Fourteenth amendments.[55]*

The Supreme Court turned a deaf ear, by an eight-to-one majority. Justice Henry B. Brown wrote the majority opinion. Brown saw nothing wrong with accommodations that were "equal but separate." (The genius of the English language, through some mysterious urge toward euphony, reversed the two adjectives; and the doctrine in *Plessy* came to be universally known as the "separate but equal" doctrine.) Brown's opinion was racist to the core. "Social prejudices," said Brown, may not be "overcome by legislation"; it was a "fallacy" to imagine that "equal rights cannot be secured to the negro except by an enforced commingling of the two races. . . . Legislation is powerless to eradicate racial instincts." Brown thought the relationship between the two races was part of the natural order, and any attempt to change it would only make things worse. "If one race be inferior to the other socially, the Constitution cannot put them upon the same plane."[56] The lone disagreeing voice was that of Justice John Marshall Harlan, whose somber and passionate dissent, in which he stated that "our Constitution is color blind," is justly famous. The *Plessy* doctrine held firm for over fifty years.

At about the same time, the South effectively disenfranchised its black citizens, through a mixture of legal tricks and violence. And the criminal justice system was lily-white: there were no black police, prosecutors, judges, or jurors. Even in ordinary cases—cases of theft or minor assault—and even when all the parties were black, color inevitably bent the processes of justice in southern criminal courts. A black defendant, uneducated and without a lawyer, entered a courtroom of whites who were convinced he was guilty, or that his rights, feelings, interests mattered less than that of whites, if they mattered at all. Edward Ayers's study of two southern counties found conviction rates for blacks much higher than for whites in the late nineteenth century; whites were convinced that blacks were congenital thieves, and this belief was deeply embedded in southern folklore. Blacks, for their part, mistrusted white justice, and for good reason. Ayers quotes a blues song:

---

* An interesting aspect of the case was Plessy's claim that he was not really black; that he was in fact an "octoroon," and the "mixture of colored blood" was "not discernible" in him. The Supreme Court, on this issue, said it would simply defer to state law.

White folks and nigger in great Co't house
Like Cat down Celler wit' no-hole mouse.[57]

White justice was most harsh, and lashed out most savagely, if a black offended against the system of white supremacy itself, or violated the "code" of the South. In these situations, a black man could expect no mercy whatsoever. The punishment, often enough, was death. The end of the nineteenth century was, we shall see, the golden age (as it were) of lynch law, in all its cynical brutality.*

The Other Americans

For most of American history, race law meant, above all else, the law of black and white. But there were other races and other minorities in America, and they, too, came into contact with the criminal justice system in ways that set them apart from the majority.

Historically, the most important of these groups were the many native tribes. They always occupied an anomalous position, legally speaking. There were Indians who lived among the whites and were subject to white laws;[58] and then there were tribal Indians who ran their own legal systems, and whose dealings with the whites were of an entirely different nature—often a relationship of war.

Formally, there were few norms that applied specifically to Indians within white communities, in peaceful relationships—except for the common provision that made it a crime to sell liquor to any Indian.[59] Where white settlers and native tribes collided, the results were often bloody; the history of the Native Americans in this country is a history of suffering, defeat, banishment, retreat, and, all too often, outright slaughter. White settlers, first oozing and then flooding into lands the natives lived in, sometimes met armed resistance; this almost invariably brought massive retaliation. In one unusual but revealing incident, in 1862, a military commission tried nearly four hundred men of the Dakota tribe for murder, rape, and robbery. The trial grew out of a small war between the Dakotas and white settlers in Minnesota, and later also between them and units of the U.S. Army. Three hundred and three of the defendants were convicted and condemned to die (about seventy defendants were acquitted). On December 2, 1862, thirty-eight Dakota men were hanged at Mankato, Minnesota. These proceedings were, to say the least, irregular.[60]

When the native tribes were no longer a military threat (and when most of the good land was in the hands of settlers, who had gotten it by

* See chapter 8.

hook or by crook), national policy made an abrupt turn. The goal of policy now became assimilation rather than destruction: the native peoples were to be absorbed into the bosom of American society. From this standpoint, the well-known case, *Ex parte Crow Dog* (1883), was something of an anomaly.[61] Crow Dog, a Sioux, had killed another Sioux. The killing took place on Sioux land, in Dakota Territory. A territorial (federal) court tried him and sentenced him to death. The Supreme Court reversed. The white man's courts could not try him; they had jurisdiction solely over crimes that crossed tribal lines and reached white society or property. The natives were "a dependent community . . . in a state of pupilage, advancing from the condition of a savage tribe" to a better status, "through the discipline of labor and by education." They were "members of a community separated by race, by tradition, by the instincts of a free though savage life"; it would be unfair to subject them to "the restraints of an external and unknown code . . . according to rules and penalties of which they could have no warning."[62]

The doctrine of the case did not stand for very long. Two years later, Congress gave the regular courts jurisdiction over murder, manslaughter, rape, assault with intent to kill, arson, burglary, and larceny, even when these were native-on-native crimes, and took place on reservation land.[63] Yet the goals of policy were the same as the goals expressed in Crow Dog's case: pupilage and assimilation. The noble savages were to be brought into the mainstream—kicking and screaming, if necessary. They were to become "regular" Americans. The only questions were when and how.

Assimilation was also the aim of the "allotment acts," the cornerstone of land policy; these laws aimed to break up reservations and turn them into little clusters of American farms, run by natives, but otherwise quite mainstream. In retrospect, all these policies seem vicious and disastrous: cultural genocide. But respect for native culture would be too much to ask for in the typical nineteenth-century mind. And the policy goal—"civilizing" the tribes, assimilation—stands in sharp contrast to the white man's law in the southern states. The black was *never* allowed to assimilate; he was segregated, suppressed, reduced to serfdom. There were, after all, millions of blacks; and they formed the basis of the labor system. The natives were relatively few and, when the guns fell silent, no threat.

In the far West, after the Civil War, there was virulent hatred against the Chinese population. Sometimes the hatred turned into bloodlust. In 1871, a mob in Los Angeles killed nineteen Chinese. In the 1880s, riots in Rock Springs, Wyoming, left twenty-eight Chinese dead; whites in Tacoma, Washington, put the torch to the Chinatown in that city; and there were outrages in Oregon, Colorado, and Nevada.[64]

California, which had the largest Chinese population—there were twelve thousand Chinese in San Francisco in the 1870s—was the focal point of this hate wave. There was a frenzy of punitive laws and ordinances. In the 1860s, "anti-coolie" clubs sprang up all over the state; members agitated for boycotts of firms that hired Chinese workers. The city fathers of Oakland and San Francisco turned the law-books against this pariah population.[65] The "Queue Ordinance" of San Francisco (1876) required the hair of every male prisoner in the county jail to be cut to within one inch of his scalp. The point of this was to inflict shame on Chinese prisoners.* The ordinance was declared unconstitutional in 1879.[67]

Another ordinance made it unlawful to run a laundry business without the "consent of the board of supervisors" except in a "building constructed either of brick or stone." Almost all laundries were, in fact, in wooden buildings; if a Caucasian owned the building, the supervisors gave their approval, but if a Chinese owned the laundry, the answer was invariably no. The Supreme Court struck down this discrimination as a "denial of equal protection" in the famous case of *Yick Wo v. Hopkins* in 1886.[68]

Such victories, alas, were rare. The Chinese minority continued to suffer under the lash of race hatred. Newspapers in California and elsewhere were, on the whole, racist to the core, reflecting majority opinion. The Chinese were associated with vice, opium, gambling, debauchery. Their districts were associated with nameless, unspeakable horror, and the seduction of innocent white girls.[69] The Chinese were often treated with sarcastic contempt. They were referred to, mockingly, as "celestials";† a typical account, in a San Diego newspaper, told about the trial of a Chinese for stealing forty-nine dollars from "a brother Chinaman"—the courtroom filled with "the Celestial and aromatic friends of both parties." The trial was "conducted through an interpreter" and provided "considerable amusement." The outcome was a hung jury.[70]

It was a constant theme of anti-Chinese agitation that the Chinese were impossibly different; that they were strange, alien, creatures; that they could eat less, work longer hours, survive in conditions that would kill a Caucasian. Above all, they could not be assimilated; they were simply too foreign. The blacks, too, were unassimilable, in racist theory; but there were many blacks, and they were needed, as we pointed out. There were only a few Chinese. Thus the goal of anti-Chinese policy

---

* The Chinese wore their hair in braided queues, and the mayor and other San Franciscans believed that this custom had some sort of religious significance. Forcing Chinese prisoners to cut their hair, then, would be a terrific insult, and humiliate them before their countrymen. Whether this was actually so is not at all clear.[66]
† This refers to the old nickname for China, the Celestial Empire.

was not suppression but expulsion. The keystone of black policy, in the South, was the criminal justice system: vagrancy laws, quasi-peonage, the chain gang. The keystone of Asian policy was immigration law, exclusion, and deportation.

Religious Minorities

The First Amendment, in the Bill of Rights, guarantees religious freedom; and independence brought in a period of (relative) religious tolerance. Nobody was hanged as a heretic in the new republic; and hardly a trace was left of the eagerness of the early colonies to punish dissenters. The law of blasphemy was one of the few surviving remnants. Blasphemy, the crime of ridiculing or defaming Christianity, had been a very serious offense in the colonial period, as we have seen. There were still some prosecutions for blasphemy in the nineteenth century. In a case from Delaware in 1837, Thomas Jefferson Chandler, "seduced by the instigation of the devil," declared that "the virgin Mary was a whore and Jesus Christ was a bastard." He was convicted, but the court was careful to explain that this was not a crime against religion; rather, it was a crime against public order. The law would protect the religion and sentiments of the majority, whatever that might be. Indeed, if the people of Delaware chose Islam, the blasphemy laws would protect *that* religion against blatant attack, said the judge (somewhat disingenuously), in the interests of preventing civil unrest.[71]

On the whole, blasphemy laws were withering away. Still, some minority religions remained outside the great American tent. These were religions that, for one reason or another, stretched public tolerance to the breaking point. The most important, perhaps, was the Mormon church. Their practice of polygamy evoked utter horror in the general population.[72] The Mormons, persecuted wherever they settled, retreated across the wilderness and founded a new home for themselves in Utah Territory. If they thought they were safe there, they were wrong; Congress passed a law prohibiting polygamy in the territories. The Supreme Court upheld that law, in the celebrated case of George Reynolds.[73]

Reynolds had been convicted and sentenced to two years at hard labor; he appealed, claiming his (two) marriages were "a religious duty" "enjoined upon the male members of [his Church] by the Almighty God." In its opinion, the Supreme Court refused to buy this argument. Polygamy, said the court, "has always been odious among the northern and western nations of Europe"; it was, rather, a "feature of the life of Asiatic and of African people." Religious duty was no excuse: suppose "human sacrifices" were part of one's religion, or the burning of widows. Of course, polygamy was if anything the opposite of burning widows, but the court was blind to this point. It also assumed, without discussion, that the standards of "Asiatic and . . . African people" were unacceptable in the American motherland. The moral *norms*, and thus the norms of criminal justice, were those of "the northern and western nations of Europe." Reynolds had to go to jail.

The Supreme Court, in *Reynolds*, merely reflected general sentiment against the "abominable" practice of polygamy. After the *Reynolds* case, the government stepped up the pace of prosecutions. Between 1884 and 1890, thirty men were convicted of polygamy in Utah Territory; 1,092 were convicted of "unlawful cohabitation."[74] The point of the Edmunds-Tucker Act, passed by Congress in 1887, was to destroy the Church altogether; among other things, it made proof of polygamy easier.[75] The campaign fizzled out only after the Church, bowing to the inevitable, recanted, receded from its polygamous doctrines, and began the long march to respectability.

The Poor

The best-known image or logo of justice is a blindfolded woman, holding in her hands the scales of neutrality. The law is not supposed to know rich or poor; everyone, popular or unpopular, favored or disfavored, is entitled to the equal protection of the laws. Of course, no society has ever lived up to any such ideal. Even more fundamentally, it is worth asking whether these really *are* the ideals of any society, whether they are anything *but* slogans. Law is a fabric of norms and practices in a particular society; the norms and practices are social judgments made concrete: the living, breathing embodiment of society's attitudes, prejudices, and values. Inevitably, and invariably, these are slanted in favor of the haves; the top-riders, the comfortable, respectable, well-to-do people. After all, articulate, powerful people *make* the laws; and even with the best will in the world, they do not feel moved to give themselves disadvantage.

Rules thus tend to favor people who own property, entrepreneurs, people with good position in society. The lash of criminal justice, conversely, tends to fall on the poor, the badly dressed, the maladroit, the deviant, the misunderstood, the shiftless, the unpopular.

Strictly speaking, the actual "poor laws" are not part of the criminal justice system, and the poorhouse was not a jail. But the parallels between the two are too striking to be overlooked. The poorhouse developed in the early nineteenth century; it became, like the jail, a dumping grounds for unfortunates. Indeed, jails often served as rough-and-ready shelters for desperate or homeless people. It seems cruel to lock up men and women in jail for no worse crime than poverty; but there was at least some kind of dim humanity in opening the jails on a bitter winter night for the detritus of society. In any event, respectable citizens of the nineteenth century did not always distinguish between paupers and criminals: the two together made up the "dangerous class" that threatened the very fabric of the social order.[76] Poverty, in the nineteenth century, came to be defined as "abnormal"; it was a social problem, something to be explained and, if possible, eliminated. This was supposedly a rich country, a land of opportunity. Economic failure, then, must be due to moral failure; pauperism was, in short, close kin to actual crime.[77]

It is not surprising, then, that the law was a scourge of unusual ferocity for drifters—the homeless poor, the vagabonds, tramps, hobos, the army of the unemployed. This was an incredibly mobile society, a society unlike all other prior societies: a society of rolling stones. Of course, human history is a history of great migrations. Nothing has been so formative in world experience as the movement of peoples: Huns sweeping out of the East, Angles, Jutes, and Saxons pouring into the British Isles; and, in the nineteenth century, immigrants with their pathetic bundles of belongings, coughed out of the holds of thousands of leaky boats. There were group movements, too, in America's history of immigration—whole towns that picked themselves up and moved to the Americas. Families brought families; cousins sent money for cousins; each individual immigrant was a hydraulic force, pulling in relatives, in-laws, friends from the old country. Yet, when all is said and done, mobility to and within America was, to a remarkable degree, a movement of individuals.

This was, then, a society based on mobility and immigration; but it was also a society suspicious of immigrants and strangers, especially those who were detached and alone, without community or social circle or family, without fixed setting. Fear and hatred of the deracinated is a theme that runs through much of the history of American law. This fear was, of course, not completely irrational. Most serious criminals, serial murderers, "bad hombres" in general, come out of the ranks of rootless men.

The hobo or tramp—that is, the unsettled, unattached male—crops up throughout the nineteenth century as an object of fear and scorn; people accused tramps of every conceivable crime or vice; they were probably the most common, most widespread of all nineteenth-century bogeymen.[78] Christopher Tiedman wrote in 1886 that the vagrant was "the chrysalis of every species of criminal. A wanderer through the land, without home ties, idle, and without apparent means of support, what but criminality is to be expected from such a person?"[79]

Yet, beyond a doubt, the vagrant, or tramp, was often more a victim than a predator. Under this heading people lumped together a wild miscellany of men. Certainly, there were roving thieves and lowlifes; a few were mentally disturbed; others were itinerant laborers, derelicts, the unemployed, the cast-off debris of capitalism, the casualties of an open and mobile society; some were men on the loose, seeking their fortune—or at least a living—far from home. Charles Sutton described the "tattered army of Vagrancy" in post–Civil War New York as a army of drunken, hopeless men, marching "to a pauper's grave under the same ragged banner"; they drifted in and out of station houses and jails; the police called them "Revolvers," and jails were "their only home."[80] What they had in common, if anything, was lack of family and home. This was the underlying problem. They represented a "deeply disrupted social order, a society without the stable nuclear family."[81]

The fear of tramps reminds us of the fear of "masterless men," from an earlier period, in England. In a tight, authoritarian society, such people were a tremendous threat to the established order. They were men out of place, men whose vibrations shook society like a house of cards. But nineteenth-century democracy, in its own way, was just as horrified by "masterless men," though for different reasons. The masterless men of the nineteenth century were men who were not part of the moral and social order. This order depended on family connections, above all. Rootless, normless people were a special threat to society because the whole grand experiment in self-rule depended on discipline and self-control. That is, a free country, a free society, a country with fluid class lines and freedom of movement assumed that people would play according to the rules; that they would put on, of their own free will, the yoke of conventional morality, the handcuffs of moderate behavior and self-discipline. And if they did not, they had to be punished.

Vagrancy laws are a case in point. These laws, to be sure, go back far into English history—to the Middle Ages, to be exact. They carried over to the colonies, and survived into the republican period. A law of Indiana Territory (1807) "concerning Vagrants," applied to gamblers, people loitering around without "wherewithal to maintain" themselves by some "visible property," and all "idle, vagrant and dissolute persons, rambling about without any visible means of subsistence." If the vagrant was under twenty-one, the sheriff could "bind him to some person of useful trade" until he reached twenty-one; if he was over twenty-one, the local justice could direct the sheriff to "hire him out for any term not exceeding nine months"; if nobody wanted to take the vagrant, the court could order him to be whipped on his bare back, up to thirty-nine lashes.[82]

This was not exceptional. The old settled states all had vagrancy laws. The laws also made the cross-country trip to the West: in 1855, in California, an act was passed against "Vagrants, Vagabonds, and Dangerous and Suspicious Persons." It covered "All persons except Digger Indians, who have no visible means of living," persons who do not "labor when employment is offered to them; all healthy beggars, who travel with written statements of their misfortunes; all persons who roam about from place to place without any lawful business." Any such pariahs could be "committed to jail" at hard labor for up to ninety days.[83] Vagrancy laws, too, as we have seen, were common in the South after the Civil War, and played a sinister role in the system of race oppression.

By the second half of the century, the police were in place as an army that could be mobilized in the struggle against the tramp. The police preserved the public peace; they monitored public spaces. They "trawled" the common areas of the city; and they tended to fasten their grip on drunken foreigners, on suspicious, vagrant men, homeless men, men who loitered, men who looked and dressed in a disreputable way; strangers, the unkempt, the unseemly. Thousands of arrests fell into the garbage-pail categories that made up the substance of vagrancy law.

The police also *used* vagrancy law, because of its very vagueness, as a way of harassing prostitutes or gamblers; or as a way to make preventive arrests. Thus, the Chicago police often hauled in "men whom they saw standing in the shadows on a street, or looking into store windows long after closing hours, or carrying bundles in commercial and residential areas after dark."[84] Nice clothes, community ties, and a middle-class manner were enough to buy immunity from these dragnets; if some innocent fish were caught in the nets of the law, the middle class was not likely to know or to care.

Industrial Labor

The police also played a role in the industrial wars that were waged in the late nineteenth century. They were an army of the status quo. They took the side of law and order, and this often meant the side of the employer, the factory owner, the boss. It would not exaggerate much to call the police, in some cases, strikebreakers plain and simple. In Detroit, three hundred special policemen were called out in 1877 during a strike at the Michigan Central Railroad.[85] In Milwaukee, in 1896, car men struck against the streetcar company, asking for higher wages. The company brought in scab labor to run the cars; and the police chief, after consulting with the mayor, mobilized a force of his men to protect these workers; police were assigned to every car barn. Lower-level streetcar officials were sworn in as deputies, patrolmen rode the cars (they were accused of actually running them), and many strikers were arrested. The strike was soon broken.[86] A similar tale could be told about strikes in many other American cities.

The police, in short, were invaluable agents of the employer side. The New York City police, according to one rapturous account of their role in late nineteenth-century strikes, "have held the mob in check and saved millions of property from destruction." The police "[have] a great antipathy to labor strikes and the disorder that accompanies them, and when they come in contact with a striking mob they are not tender in the ways of handling it." Strikes, after all, meant "long hours of duty and hard work."[87] But the main point, beyond a doubt, was more deeply ideological: the police ranged themselves on the side of the constituted order. They were the servants of power and wealth.

Criminal justice systems, on the whole, suffered from the same tilt; often enough, they looked suspiciously like so many strikebreaking cabals. Throughout much of the nineteenth century, it was a serious question whether the whole *concept* of organized labor was legal. If workmen gathered together, formed some kind of organization, and put collective pressure on an employer, was this some sort of "criminal conspiracy?" A few early court decisions answered with a resounding yes—for example, the famous trial of the Philadelphia Cordwainers, decided in 1806; the cordwainers (shoemakers) who had struck for higher wages were convicted and fined.[88] In 1842, however, in *Commonwealth v. Hunt*, Lemuel Shaw of Massachusetts reached the opposite conclusion; in this case workmen and journeymen bootmakers were indicted and convicted for "perniciously and deceitfully" conspiring to form an "unlawful club, society, and combination" to enforce what would now be called a closed shop.[89] Shaw's opinion, however, overturned the conviction and released the men.

The issue boiled up again in the 1870s; more and more, this was becoming an industrial nation, and the raw, jagged conflict between labor and capital moved to the center of the stage in the decades after the Civil War. The issue was not one-sided. Labor, after all, had the vote; and they had some clout in certain legislatures. Some states passed laws to defend unions and unionization; in Illinois, for example, under a law of 1893, it was an offense to prevent workers "from forming, joining and belonging to any lawful labor organization," or to coerce workers "by discharging or threatening to discharge" them because of union activity.[90]

Labor law, then, was part of a battle fought in part on the streets, in part in the courtroom, in part in the legislature. Some states passed laws to outlaw the blacklist, or the "yellow dog" contract, which forced employees to promise not to join a union.[91] But it would be a mistake to imagine that labor got its way, especially when the courts are factored into the operation. As the war heated up, some of the courts brought out heavy artillery. In the older conspiracy cases, punishments had been fairly mild. But now, at the end of the century, judges unveiled a new, very powerful tool to be used against strikers and unions: the labor injunction.[92] If management could get a court order "enjoining" (forbidding) a strike, or ordering the union to end it, then if workers or union leaders disobeyed, they were in contempt of court, and a judge had the power to throw them in prison—quickly and without any actual trial.

Strictly speaking, an injunction was a tool of civil, not criminal, law. But it was, in effect, a way to guarantee punishment of organized labor; and violators of injunctions were treated as if they were criminals. There were technical as well as political objections to the labor injunction, but from 1880 on, it proved itself in the war against organized labor. Injunctions were issued in Baltimore in 1883, in Iowa in 1884, and during the railroad strikes of 1886. From then on, as Felix Frankfurter and Nathan Greene put it, cases "grew in volume like a rolling snowball."[93]

The Supreme Court laid to rest any doubts about the labor injunction in 1895, in the famous case of *In re Debs*.[94] Traditionally, courts had no authority to enjoin commission of a crime. This was one of the technical objections to the use of the labor injunction. In *Debs*, the Court, speaking through Justice Brewer, swept this objection to one side. The injunction was "not simply to enjoin a mob and mob violence"; its "scope and purpose" was to restrain "forcible obstructions of the highway along which interstate commerce travels and the mails are carried." The message for the labor movement was unmistakable.

Nineteenth-century criminal justice was not, in short, blindfolded Justice. It was very definitely the servant of power, the protector of privilege. Probably this is the case in every society. In fact, the question is not: *Do* the scales tilt, but how much, and in what direction? If we tried to give a grade to nineteenth-century criminal justice in the United States, a lot would depend on what we were comparing it to, and through whose eyes we were observing it. The black judgment on the system would be far grimmer than the judgment of whites. Of course, taken all in all, American justice in the nineteenth century stands up fairly well, *if* measured against the standards of justice in tyrannies and dictatorships. But for us, looking backward, a century or two later, its blind spots, flaws, and rampant injustices are also painfully obvious.

5

SETTING THE PRICE: CRIMINAL JUSTICE AND THE ECONOMY

ALL RULES OF CRIMINAL JUSTICE ARE, IN A SENSE, POLICY RULES; THEY ALL have some purpose, some goal, some point, some notion of good and bad, of efficient and inefficient. If we enforce the rule, we do it in order to move an inch closer to the goal, whatever that may be. The penal code is not a random collection of rules; it is a catalogue of values, policies, attitudes, ideals—about property rights, the integrity of the body, morality, orderly behavior, and so on. Many of the rules and goals are "economic" in some obvious sense of the word. Securities fraud is a crime; it is also against the law for the butcher to put his thumb on the scale.

In fact, *all* criminal justice, whatever else can be said about it, is economic in one crude, primary sense: its rules are attempts to fix prices or ration behavior. Suppose it is a crime to shoot deer out of season; the punishment is a good stiff fine. One way to describe the law is to say that it tries to raise the price of shooting deer. If it succeeds, it rations, or controls, deer hunting. If the price is high enough, nobody will shoot deer (or almost nobody). Stiffening a penalty, then, is like raising a price.

As rationing gets tighter, control is greater—and demand for the behavior, other things being equal, falls off.*

We can apply the same analysis to the whole criminal code, even laws against murder and rape. In a sense, the codes set prices, and regulate the supply and demand of murder and rape. It seems cold-blooded to look at homicide law in this way; most people would say they want no murders at all, and if you asked them, they would say, vehemently, that they would *not* license murder, at any price. But in one sense that is exactly what the penal code does; it fixes a price. Certainly, there are other ways to understand why there are laws against murder and rape, and what makes them tick. But the price-rationing aspect is worth keeping in mind.

This chapter is not about murder or rape. It is about other aspects of the system, which are economic in a narrower, more literal sense. Criminal justice had a role, and an important role, in building a wall of protection for the economy, in regulating the market, and in safeguarding and encouraging a particular distribution of goods and services, and a particular form of economic life. Like the legal system in general, criminal justice did not simply protect an aged and creaking status quo; rather, it channeled and regulated change, so that change occurred only in certain approved ways, and not in others.

Economic law and economic regulation presupposed this particular society. They reflected the emphasis on individual property rights—but property rights valued for their dynamic potential, not as ancient, aristocratic, fixed markers of status. Economic law reflected the actual economy: growing, shifting from agriculture to manufacturing in the course of the century; and it reflected public fears of too much concentration at the top (the antitrust laws), and shiftless swindling at the bottom. At the beginning of the century, law reflected a boundless optimism, a sense of endless horizons; by the end of the century, themes of conservation, pinched resources, a shrinking pie, had crept into economic law. This chapter will explore some of these themes.

Theft

Perhaps the most primitive and basic rules in the criminal justice system were those that protected property rights. It is a crime to steal what belongs to somebody else. The laws against theft, larceny, embezzlement, and fraud are familiar friends. People may not know every techni-

---

* A penalty can be stiffened in two ways: by adding *severity*, which means jacking up a fine, say, from $100 to $200; or increasing the jail sentence for some act; or by adding *certainty*, that is, catching a higher percentage of violators, perhaps through putting more muscle into the enforcement effort.

cal detail, but they get the general point. Probably all human communities punish theft in one way or another; it is hard to imagine a society that does *not* have a concept of thievery, and some way to punish people who help themselves to things that "belong" to somebody else.

When we speak of "property" it is not a bad idea to put quotation marks around the word. This serves to remind us that property is not a thing, but a social concept. The definition changes with the times, and from place to place. Millions of black human beings, for example, were "property" in the American South before the Civil War; they were bought and sold and traded on the market; it was a crime to steal a slave. The Thirteenth Amendment, as we saw, made slavery unlawful; from then on, slavery was legally impossible, and, in fact, to enslave became a crime. There have been societies where wives were bought and sold; and others in which nobody could individually own land, since all land was held in common. And so it goes.

Theft and related acts were crimes, of course, from the very outset in this country. Certainly, colonial law punished theft in all its manifestations. What is interesting is how *dominant* theft and its cousins became in nineteenth-century criminal justice. To be sure, forms of punishment had changed—thieves in most states could not be sent to the gallows. Nonetheless, if we ask what the criminal justice system did in, say, the early nineteenth century, the best answer is: it protected property and punished stealing. It tried to safeguard what people owned, their money and goods, against nimble fingers, defrauders, and holdup men.

Property crimes were the most frequently punished crimes—or, at least, the most frequently punished *serious* crimes, disregarding the countless minor cases of liquor violation, drunkenness, disturbing the peace, vagrancy, and minor assault—the ordinary harvest of petty crime. Fifty-eight percent of the offenses punished in Boston's Municipal Court in 1830 were larceny cases, 71 percent of the cases that year in the Philadelphia Court of Quarter Sessions and the Court of Oyer and Terminer, 50.8 percent of the cases in the city courts of New York.[1]

The law distinguished between a number of crimes: simple larceny, or stealing, and two more serious versions of theft—burglary, which involved "breaking and entering," and robbery, that is, stealing "by assault or any violence, and putting in fear."[2] A holdup is the classical form of robbery. The lines between larceny, robbery, and burglary were legally significant, because the kinds of threat were different. Burglary and robbery were violations of body space or the sanctity of the home, and were thus more menacing than simple theft.

The essence of burglary is breaking and entering. If you enter a house through an unlocked door, this is no burglary—there is entering, but no breaking. An interesting North Carolina case, from 1849, drew a hairline but significant distinction. A clever slave, in the middle of the night, came dashing up to James McNatt's house and told him his mother's plantation was on fire. McNatt rushed off, leaving his door unlocked; his wife was alone in the house with a baby and a "small servant girl." The slave, Henry, waited a bit, walked into the house, demanded money, threatened the wife, and ran off with a tin trunk of notes and papers. He was caught, charged with burglary, and convicted; but the appellate court reversed. The unlocked door meant that the slave had not broken in.[3] In a somewhat later case, however, a slave entered a cabin through the chimney, with the purpose (unlike Santa Claus) of robbing the house. He was convicted of burglary. The court distinguished between a chimney, which cannot be locked, and a window or door, which can.[4] Courts were groping for a line between trickery and violence, between "simple" theft and a darker, more sinister kind.

Receiving stolen goods was an ancillary crime, apparently first singled out and labeled as a crime in the eighteenth century; the receiver was an "accessary" to the main crime. In the nineteenth century, "receiving" became an independent crime. "Every person," so ran the Illinois version, who "shall buy or receive stolen goods . . . knowing the same to have been so obtained," was guilty of a crime and could be imprisoned.[5] Receiving stolen goods was a city crime, and a crime that took on special importance where people did not know each other, where relationships were distant and impersonal, and under conditions where people moved about from place to place. It implied a certain kind of thief, as well: someone who stole valuable goods, not for consumption, but for resale; it implied a network of dishonest merchants and, later on, the infamous "fence," who dealt specifically in stolen goods, and who provided a market where the thief and the burglar could dump their goods and get cash.

In the course of the nineteenth century, penal codes tended to grow in bulk, and the number of crimes increased greatly. This was especially the case for property crimes. Simple, traditional crimes like larceny and theft tended to split off and divide like amoebas into a great number of daughter crimes: special rules for stealing this or that kind of goods. These split-offs were hardly random. They tended to reflect particular business sensitivities (or at least particular lobbying activities). The Texas Penal Code of the 1880s is a good illustration: in addition to the general rules punishing theft and larceny, article 746 was aimed at anyone who stole "any horse, ass, or mule"; article 747 applied to "cattle," and article 748 to "sheep, hogs, or goats." The punishments were different: five to fifteen years in the penitentiary for horse thieves; two to five for those who stole cattle; for sheep, hogs, or goats, it all depended on the value of what was stolen: if over twenty dollars in value, then two to five years in the penitentiary, and, if less, up to a year in the county jail, or a fine, or both.[6] Texas was a cattle state, of course. Definitions and punishments of forms of theft were clues to what was crucial to the polity.

Framing the Market

"Theft" can occur in any society; a market society, however, has certain specific institutions that need protection as much as simple "property." Money and banking undergird the whole economy. They generate a whole class of crimes. Counterfeiting, debasing the coinage, passing bad coins, and forging bank notes disrupt business and drag the economy down. Forgery is also generally destructive: the falsifying of public records—wills, deeds, leases, charters, and the like—can work great mischief. All these acts were quite generally criminalized. We have mentioned an early federal statute (1790) that made it a crime to forge any "certificate, indent, or other public security of the United States"; a law of 1798 added "any bill or note issued by the . . . Bank of the United States."[7] A New Hampshire law applied to "false and counterfeit coin made and forged in imitation and simulation of any gold or silver coin current within this state."[8]

Regulation of banks and banking was, for the time, both heavy and persistent. In New York's revised statutes of 1858 these regulations ran to over fifty pages bristling with prohibitions. In the later nineteenth century, there was equally heavy regulation of insurance companies, especially "foreign" (out of state) companies.[9] Usury was a old crime, with an ancient stigma attached. In the nineteenth century, there was a drumbeat of criticism of the usury laws, in the name of free enterprise. Some states went so far as to eliminate their usury laws, usually because of a strong social demand for capital at any price—for example, in order to finance the sale of public lands.[10] More commonly, statute law declared that a usurious contract was unenforceable; or attached a penalty—Illinois, in 1845, for example, specified that the lender would forfeit "three-fold the amount of the whole interest reserved, discounted or taken."[11] Strictly speaking, most of these usury laws were not criminal laws; but they did attach severe penalties to lending contracts that offended against the statutory law.

Government at all levels also took steps to protect its own revenues, not always successfully. One of the few sources of federal power and wealth was the treasure house of public land. Millions of acres were given away and sold for a song in a wild festival of bribery and corruption. There were, indeed, laws on the books intended to prevent the worst forms of corruption. Under a federal law of 1830, it was a crime for settlers to get together and "by intimidation, combination, or unfair management" prevent other people from bidding on or buying public lands.[12] But corruption proved far stronger than these laws.

Taxes were, of course, another source of money for the state. It was forbidden to cheat on taxes, or not to pay them at all. From the standpoint of the twentieth century, nineteenth-century taxes were as light as a feather. There were taxes on property, a ragbag of excise taxes, and not much else. Still, tax evasion was at least a minor issue. Under Missouri law, for example, anyone who delivered to the assessor a "fraudulent list of taxable property" would be "taxed triple," and could also be indicted and fined up to five hundred dollars.[13] After the Civil War, the federal excise tax on whiskey did become a serious issue in "moonshine" country, and the low, simmering war between the moonshiners and the "revenuers" went on for decades.[14]

A free market is supposed to be based on voluntary agreements between traders—contracts, in other words. But even a "free" market presupposes certain rules of the game. Traders can be sharp, but not too sharp. The law defines certain conduct as cheating, and outlaws it. There are also rules against false sales, bad weights and measures, and so on: these are designed to prevent corruption and keep trading honest; cheating destroys expectations, and is a drag on the economy. A typical provision, from Tennessee, set up standards—a bushel, for example, had to contain 2,150.42 cubic inches. Every storekeeper and warehouser had to have his weights and measures "sealed" each year, on penalty of a fine; if a person was defrauded through improper weights, that person could collect treble damages. Using false weights was a misdemeanor; and the false instruments were subject to seizure.[15] States had dozens of special weights-and-measures laws for particular commodities. Thus, in Rhode Island, when fish was sold "by measure" as manure, the standard measure was a barrel containing twenty-eight gallons, or a half-barrel with fourteen. These were to be "sealed by a sealer of weights and measures"; deviations were punishable by fine.[16]

Other rules struck at business fraud. Thus, under the Maryland code of 1878, it was a misdemeanor for a partner to commit "fraud in the management of the affairs of the partnership"; an officer or agent of a corporation was not to sign or "assent" to a fraudulent statement to the public or the shareholders with the intent "either to enhance or depress the market value of the shares."[17]

At the time, not much came of such laws. Today, there are elaborate regulatory structures to keep public corporations honest, and to prevent them from fleecing investors. There are massive federal agencies that are supposed to monitor the stock market. Nothing of the kind existed in the nineteenth century, and the great robber barons, market manipulators, stock waterers, and corporate malefactors had a field day. Some of these men died poor, some died rich; Congress investigated them, newspapers excoriated them; during their battles with each other, they made heavy use of injunctions, writs, civil suits of all kinds; but the sword of criminal justice never touched Jay Gould, Daniel Drew, James Fisk, and the others of their ilk.

Economic Regulation

"Economic regulation" is a hopelessly vague phrase. But we can use it to describe laws that try to set down rules that businesses (or particular kinds of business) have to live by. Nowadays, much of this regulatory work is done by administrative agencies. This was much less so in the past. Enforcement was either through private lawsuits, or through the criminal justice system.

In general, the regulatory arm of government, federal and state, was much shorter (by a country mile) and weaker in the nineteenth century than today. The federal government was especially weak. It was like the brain of a dinosaur: a tiny ganglion, in Washington, D.C., inside a huge and extensive body.

Most regulatory crimes, then, were state or local. Even in the colonial period, there were many of these. The local magistrates, in their little domains, enforced dozens of humdrum but vital rules and regulations. In colonial New York, justices of the peace were responsible for enforcing statutes on the sale of bricks, bar iron, leather, rawhides, flax, and bread; they were in charge of local roads and fences; they could punish people who repacked meat fraudulently, or sold unmerchantable flour, or violated acts about casks, weights, and measures for wine and flour.[18] There was pervasive regulation of the growing and marketing of tobacco, for example, in colonial Maryland and Virginia.[19] One aim was quality control, especially of products that were staples, or which were the basis of a rich export trade. In Pennsylvania, under a law of 1725, no flour could be exported unless it was inspected and adjudged good enough to go.[20]

There were also colonial fish and game laws; of course, the colonists were not environmentalists like their twentieth-century descendants; but still they realized that not every kind of tree, fish, fowl, and animal was in boundless supply, to be taken, shot, chopped, or destroyed at will. A Virginia law of 1699 made it an offense to shoot deer between February 1 and the last day of July; punishment was a fine of five hundred pounds of tobacco.[21] A New York law of 1715 made it unlawful to "gather, Rake, take up, or bring to the Market, any Oysters whatsoever" between May 1 and September 1.[22] And an interesting Massachusetts law of 1675, after reciting that raccoon fur was very good for making hats, forbade the "exportation" of "Raccoon furs or skinns . . . out of this Jurisdiction"; presumably, all such furs or skins were to be kept at home.[23]

All these general themes could be found in state laws of the nineteenth century—and then some. A visitor from another planet could tell a good deal about the economy of any state, just by reading the words of its regulatory laws. In Mississippi in the 1850s, for example, it was a crime to "fraudulently pack or bale any cotton."[24] In Rhode Island, the oyster is an important citizen; state law made it illegal to take any oysters from "free and common oyster fisheries" with "dredges, or with any other instrument . . . more destructive to oyster-beds than the usual method of taking them by oyster tongs." There was a commission to keep tabs on private oyster fisheries; still, the legislature saw fit to equip violations of the law (such as "taking and carrying away oysters from any private oyster ground") with criminal sanctions.[25] In the Minnesota statute books, there is nothing about oysters; but the laws of 1866 contain elaborate provisions on logging and lumbering; logging companies were to adopt distinctive marks for their logs and record them; and anybody who mutilated or rendered a mark illegible was guilty of a crime.[26] There were also many livestock and cattle crimes: butchering unmarked or unbranded animals; putting your brand on someone else's cattle; defacing a brand or mark. It was even a crime to milk someone else's cow.[27] In Maryland, it was a crime to "cut or destroy any tobacco plants belonging to any other person," or to counterfeit "any manifest or note of any inspector of tobacco."[28]

Many people think of the nineteenth century as the age of laissez-faire, a period in which government, on the whole, did rather little, and in which business had a fairly free hand to run its own show. In fact, there was more regulation than one might think, although admittedly it seems ludicrously light, by twentieth-century standards. A lot of the government intervention, besides, was promotional: ways to stimulate economic growth, to get business going, to encourage bridges, ferries, turnpikes, canals, railroads, banks, and the like; to promote the "release of energy"[29] rather than to tie ropes around business in the name of public health, safety, or welfare, or curb economic power before it got totally out of control.

Whatever the goals of regulation, criminal justice had a role to play as a soldier in the army of policy. On the statute books of the states, regulatory provisions, trailing along with them some criminal provision, are scattered about the pages. Their number, in the early years of the century, was not great; density increased as the years went on. This was a natural reflex of the increase in the density of economic life, the rise of big business, the explosion of city growth, mass production, the flowering of industry and commerce.

Any nineteenth-century statute book yields a fair sample of regulatory crimes. The Ohio statutes of 1841, for example, make it a crime to "exercise the trade or occupation of auctioneer" without a license; or to kill a muskrat between May 1 and October 15. An elaborate statute provided for the inspection of casks and barrels of flour, meal, beef, pork, lard and butter, pot and pearl ashes, liquor and linseed oil, among other products; any violation, by a packer or inspector, carried a penalty. Elaborate legal provisions provided for the protection of state canals: no one was to obstruct a canal or dig a ditch in such a way as to cause "earth, sand, gravel, or other material to be washed into any canal," or "wilfully put . . . any dead animal into any canal," among other things.[30]

Least visible, but no less important, were the countless municipal and local ordinances and rules that imposed fines (and sometimes jail sentences) for violations of rules and regulations. State statutes authorized these: for example, Massachusetts law (1855) gave the mayor and aldermen of any city, and the selectmen of any town, power to license pawnbrokers; anyone engaging in this noble business without a license was liable to a fine.[31] Every state had dozens of laws of this type.

It is easily to overlook these criminal provisions in the basement of the law—licensing laws; regulations of taverns and the liquor business; rules about sidewalks, buying and selling, and local markets—but they were often quite important in the life of the community. In one small city, Oakland, California, at the end of the century, the book of ordinances covered an astonishing range of topics. There were rules about the use of public spaces. There were rules about public health: it was "unlawful for any person to sleep or lodge in any room . . . unless said room contains at least five hundred cubic feet of air for each person sleeping or lodging therein." Contagious diseases had to be reported. Property owners were not to permit "any stagnant water or any nauseous or offensive substances" on their property. It was an offense to sell bad meat or "any diluted, impure, adulterated or unwholesome milk." No one was to dare to manufacture pickles in Oakland, except in a small district set aside for this perilous industry.[32]

There is very little information about enforcement of regulatory laws—at any level. Certainly, enforcement varied from time to time and from place to place. Most of the enforcement was local, most involved city and town ordinances, and most punishments were minor: small fines for obstructing sidewalks, peddling without a license, selling spoiled meat. Few men and women went to prison for regulatory offenses; no doubt a few were scattered among county jails. Embezzlement, forgery, and counterfeiting were more productive. The census of

1880, which reported 57,958 prisoners all told in prisons and jails, listed some 1,500 prisoners sent up for forgery and counterfeiting; 261 embezzlers; and a sprinkling of prisoners convicted of fraud, confidence games, or tax fraud.[33]

Quality Control

This was a classic theme of regulatory law: making sure that important goods for export or consumption measured up to standards of quality. Laws to protect the health of animals, for example, were obviously motivated by a desire to protect the domestic economy. The criminal code of Iowa in the 1870s included provisions against "knowingly" importing or driving into Iowa "sheep having any contagious disease," or any "horse, mule, or ass, affected by the diseases known as nasal gleet, glanders, or button-farcey." Cattle from Texas could not be brought into Iowa unless the cattle had been "wintered at least one winter north of the southern boundary of the state of Missouri or Kansas"; this was to prevent the spread of "Texas fever." It was also an offense to bring in or cultivate "hop roots" that were "diseased . . . or infected with lice or vermin"; and anybody who had "Canada thistles" on their lands and let the thistles "blossom or mature" was "guilty of a misdemeanor."[34]

In 1884, Congress entered the picture; it passed a law establishing a Bureau of Animal Industry under the Commissioner of Agriculture; the head of the bureau was to be a veterinarian. No railroad company or boat line was to accept or transport "any live stock affected with any contagious, infectious, or communicable disease, and especially . . . pleuro-pneumonia."[35] Quality control had become, more and more, a problem that spilled across state lines. No one state had the power to protect itself from infection. This simple fact eventually led to an enormous flow of power to Washington, D.C.

Curbing Economic Power

The flow of authority to the center was egregiously true of regulation whose point was curbing economic power—another theme that grew stronger in the latter part of the century. This had been a theme in the struggles over bank regulation, and over various issues in corporation law as well. The terms of the debate changed radically in the industrial age, when more and more people left the countryside to work as landless wage earners in big factories or mines; they were joined in the cities and in the mining and factory towns by hordes of new immigrants from abroad. Big business grew bigger; big fish swallowed little fish; and the result was the formation of huge agglomerations—the hated monopolies or "trusts." John D. Rockefeller's Standard Oil Company was the great exemplar, but there were trusts in cotton oil, sugar, and many other products; and the small merchant and farmer was as terrified and angry as the industrial worker, if not more so.

In the 1880s, there was a burst of legislative activity against these dreaded aggregations. The constitution of Washington State (1889) shouted out bravely that "monopolies and trusts shall never be allowed in this state"; and, more specifically, corporations were not to combine to fix prices or limit output (article 12, sections 18, 22). A Michigan statute of 1889 declared "illegal and void" any agreement or "combination" either to "limit, control, or . . . restrict" production of any "article or commodity," or to jack up its price, or in general to "prevent or restrict free competition in . . . production or sale." Any such agreement was a "criminal conspiracy."[36] The North Carolina law "to prohibit trusts," passed in the same year, made it a crime for any "merchant, broker, manufacturer or dealer in raw materials" to sell goods (raw or processed) "for less than actual cost for the purpose of breaking down competitors."[37]

What, if anything, these state laws accomplished is hard to say. They hardly laid a finger on the trusts. Some laws were poorly drawn; most were poorly enforced; and, most significant of all, the tentacles of the great trusts twisted and curled across the country, ignoring state boundaries—no North Carolina or Michigan by itself had the power to control them. Only a federal statute could do the trick. The center of attention shifted to Washington, D.C.

The famous Sherman Antitrust Law, passed in 1890, was what came out of the agitation; it laid the foundation stone of a whole branch of law (antitrust law). Senator James K. Jones of Arkansas sounded the main theme in debate: federal intervention was an absolute necessity. The miracles of steam and electricity had "well-nigh abolished time and distance"; the genie was out of the bottle, and the states were helpless to control it. The trusts were "commercial monsters," "sharks" that were fattening on the spoils they extracted from the public. If the "iron hand of the law" was not laid on them, and "heavily," the "boasted liberty of the citizen [would become a] myth."[38]

Only power, in other words, could fight (excessive) power; power that spanned the continent required countervailing force that also spanned the continent; and only *criminal* law could engage the full force of national will and national muscle. The Sherman Act was the result of this conjunction of attitudes. It is still in force today. The Sherman Act was (and is) in form a criminal statute.[39] It declared "illegal" any "contract, combination in the form of trust or otherwise, or conspiracy, in restraint of trade or commerce"; every person who "monopolized" or combined or conspired to monopolize "any part of the trade or commerce among the several States" was guilty of a misdemeanor.

For a law so famous and so important, the Sherman Act was surprisingly brief: less than two pages of text in the *Statutes at Large*. It was also exceedingly terse, not to say vague and ambiguous. Nowhere in the act was there any definition of key terms; "monopoly" and "restraint of trade" were left unexplained. The act set up no mechanism of enforcement—no administrative agency, no machinery at all. It was left to whatever energy the attorney general and his small staff might muster. The early years of enforcement were, to say the least, somewhat fitful and halfhearted; at the turn of the century there was little to show for all the fanfare and hooplah.[40] The courts were lukewarm themselves. A district judge in the Midwest, for example, smothered an indictment against lumber dealers who had conspired to raise lumber prices; and an attack on the cash register industry was also a failure.[41]

The Supreme Court delivered some serious setbacks to enforcements. One of the worst monopolies was the sugar trust; the American Sugar Refining Company dominated the business and was moving to absorb the last few independent sugar refiners. But the government's lawsuit, *U.S. v. E. C. Knight Co.* went down in flames.[42] This was a monopoly of "manufacture," and not of "commerce" said the Court; and the Sherman Act had nothing to do with making, only with trading and selling. In later cases, the Court showed more gumption; but on the whole, the Sherman Act's potential for trust-busting was still only a promise in 1900.

It is easy to be cynical about this whole exercise in prosecuting big business. Much of it was smoke and mirrors, or public relations. The public had been saying, in effect, *do* something. Congress did something: it passed a law. So, too, did the states. Two-thirds of them had little "Sherman Acts," or other antitrust laws, by 1900. For obvious reasons, the state laws were largely symbolic. The federal act itself was a promise, a hope, a statement of policy, and not much more. The net results were, almost certainly, microscopic. Ironically, antitrust law *was* used as a weapon against labor unions and as a strikebreaking tool; in 1894, Eugene V. Debs felt its lash in the midst of a railroad strike.[43] This was surely not what the clamoring citizens and small shopkeepers had in mind; but the *judges* had it in mind, and big business, too; and this is what counted at the time.

Corporate Crime

At one time, there had been technical doubts about whether the state could indict a corporation at all. Could an "artificial being," a corporation, commit a crime? By mid-century, the legal consensus was yes. Joel Bishop, who wrote a leading treatise on criminal law, could see "No reason . . . why a corporation, having by law the power to act, should not also have by law the power to intend to act; and mere intentional wrong acting . . . is all which is necessary in a class of criminal cases."[44]

This was, of course, not an academic question; at least not totally. Major regulatory laws applied to corporations and other business associations, sometimes explicitly. To pick one example, an Illinois law of 1891 made it "unlawful for any person, company, corporation or association" in the "mining or manufacturing business" to run a company store; another act required companies in the manufacturing, mining, "mercantile," utility, express, or water business to pay wages every week. By its very terms, this was a law for corporations only.[45] A contemporary Kansas law specified that all "private corporations doing business within this state . . . shall pay . . . wages earned each and every week in lawful money . . . not later than Friday of each week for all such wages earned the preceding week." "Steam surface railways" and corporations producing "farm and dairy products" were exempted.[46]

Bishop had spoken about "intentional wrong acting." But in some regulatory laws, intention was not particularly important, or not important at all. In one Massachusetts case, in 1875, a statute made it a crime to "sell, or keep, or offer for sale, naphtha, under any assumed name."[47] Wentworth, the defendant, claimed he had no idea the stuff he sold was actually naphtha. No matter, said the court: "guilty knowledge" was not essential to the offense. "It is like the statutes against the sale of intoxicating liquors, or adulterated milk, and many other police regulations: it prohibits the acts of selling . . . naphtha . . . not because of their moral turpitude, or the criminal intent . . . but because they are dangerous to the public." Obviously, then, it was unimportant what Wentworth thought, or knew. He was guilty all the same.

A case like this underscores what is distinctive about *some* regulatory crimes. They are not crimes at all, in the popular sense of dreadful, blameworthy deeds. Criminal justice here is merely a kind of unspecialized, all-purpose agency for carrying out regulations. Acts were classified as "crimes" so that authorities could enforce laws against them, at their leisure, and at their expense, without waiting for some aggrieved individual to sue.

The Public Health

Not all regulatory "crimes" have this neutral, bureaucratic flavor. One aim of economic law is to protect the public health. This was a motive, no doubt, in the background of the naphtha law. In general, any act "calculated to impair the public health" was at least potentially a crime.[48] And health offenses, if they were grievous enough, could easily cross the line into the domain of the truly blameworthy.

Health legislation did not make much of a mark in the first half of the nineteenth century. Quarantine laws, however, were common. If (under Virginia law) a ship should arrive in port "foul or infected" so as to "endanger the public health," it could be put under quarantine; a captain who hid information about "dangerous infectious disease" on shipboard or at a port of call, or who failed to "repair in proper time" to the "quarantine ground," or who left without authority, was liable to pay a fine.[49] Other health hazards were handled under nuisance law. In a Kentucky case of 1866, one Ashbrook was indicted for "keeping a common nuisance" in the city of Covington; the nuisance consisted of "sundry pens," in which he housed horses, mules, cattle, sheep, and hogs; these creatures of God produced "filthy excrements" and "unhealthy and pernicious smells," which "greatly corrupted and infected" the air. Ashbrook had kept, he said, animals in such pens for thirty years. But this was no excuse. A lot had happened in thirty years. Covington had grown from a village of "about five hundred souls" to a population of twenty thousand, and this kind of urban growth turned a lawful business into an unlawful nuisance.[50]

Covington's growth was nothing compared to that of New York, Chicago, Cincinnati, St. Louis, and other cities. Filthy tenements, smoke, crowded streets, and tons of horse droppings made cities pestilent and unhealthy. The march of science changed attitudes toward disease. It was no longer punishment for sin, or a mysterious scourge beyond explanation; disease was something concrete; it was carried in water or in dirt; it was a product of "germs"; and there were concrete steps that could be taken to alleviate or prevent it. These, more and more, came to be seen as *collective* steps. There were, by the end of the century, boards of health at the state, city, and county levels, issuing rules and enforcing ordinances.[51]

Criminal statutes relating to health were a miscellaneous lot. Some were simply reporting laws; doctors had a duty to tell local boards of health about a whole raft of contagious diseases. Doctors (and midwives) in New Jersey (1895), for example, had to report any newborns with swollen, inflamed, or reddened eyes.[52] Another group of laws regulated foods and drugs, either as to their ingredients or to their labeling. The same session of the New Jersey legislature just mentioned (1895) outlawed the sale of candy "adulterated by the admixture of terra alba, barytes, talc, or other mineral substance," or by "poisonous colors, flavors, fusil oil, intoxicants or other ingredients deleterious or detrimental to health." Another law made it unlawful to sell cakes or biscuits containing "yolka, yolkaline, turmeric, chrome yellow or any other substitute for eggs," unless the label said so.[53]

Labor and Management:
The Conditions of Labor

Public health was also often used as an excuse for regulation (in the struggle over oleomargarine, for example). This was egregiously true in the struggle between capital and labor. What workers wanted, after all, was more money and better conditions of labor. It is hard to draw the line between a pure "labor" law and a law about the health and safety of workers—if, indeed, there is any sense to drawing a line at all. Legally, however, there was a great difference: the state had plenary power to ensure public health and safety; but business vigorously denied the state's power to intervene in strictly economic disputes—and "redistribution of income" was a dirty phrase.[54]

Many states responded to pressure from organized labor by imposing duties on employers—to pay workmen in cash, for example, or at frequent intervals; or by outlawing company stores. We have already seen examples of these late nineteenth-century statutes. These were, as usual, criminal statutes in form—that is, they carried with them some sort of criminal penalty for violation, like a thorn on a rosebush.

The late nineteenth century was also the age of judicial review; the courts were flexing their muscles as never before. Some of the most famous court battles of this period turned on the validity of labor laws. In a few rather spectacular cases, courts struck down labor laws as unconstitutional. In New York, the state had prohibited the "manufacture of cigars and preparation of tobacco . . . in tenement-houses." The Court of Appeals, the highest court in New York, declared this statute void in 1885.[55] In California, a statute required employers to pay workers at least once a month. A quartz mine company appealed a conviction under the statute; the Supreme Court of California struck down the law in 1899. Such a law, the court said gravely, treats the intelligent workman as an "imbecile"; it takes away his "right" to make labor contracts for himself.[56]

It was this sort of attitude that encouraged legislatures to disguise labor laws as health laws, in the hope that courts would uphold them on that basis. The massive Illinois act on factories and workshops, passed in 1893, outlawed the manufacture of clothing (including "coats, vests, trousers, knee-pants, overalls, cloaks, shirts, ladies' waists"), purses, feathers, artificial flowers, or cigars, in any "tenement or dwelling house used for eating or sleeping purposes," except by the "immediate members of the family" who lived there. Factory inspectors would visit workshops to see that they were "in a cleanly condition and free from vermin and any matter of an infectious and contagious nature." No child under fourteen was to work in any factory; a child worker under sixteen needed an affidavit from parents or guardians. No "female" was to be "employed in any factory or workshop more than eight hours in any one day or forty-eight hours in any one week."[57]

But the statute was doomed. The Supreme Court of Illinois, in a strong if retrograde opinion, struck it down. It interfered with freedom of contract: "Labor is property, and the laborer has the same right to sell his labor, and to contract with reference thereto, as has any other property owner."[58] The law impaired this right, and the court could see no justification strong enough to balance the harm to the market. All phrased very logically and law-like, yet a product of conventional biases and attitudes nonetheless. The upper middle class—the judges, very notably—were afraid of the power of massed workers; afraid, too, that legislators, who needed votes, would cave in to demands that would harm society and its economic structure.

The usual view of the period, which seems quite plausible, is that courts were reactionary, legislatures more progressive. But this may be something of a distortion. Many labor laws were never tested in court at all; most of those that were, passed the test with flying colors. Nor were legislatures quite so "progressive" as they seemed on the surface. Legislatures rarely passed laws that seriously changed the balance of power, or redistributed income. A criminal law is cheap to pass, requires no tax money or civil servants, and passes the buck to local enforcement officials. Not all labor laws, of course, were of this kind; some laws established commissions, agencies, authorities, to carry out the work. But there were enough pure criminal laws to make us cautious in our general assessment of the impact of legislative intervention.

Rules of the Road

In this chapter, we have looked at rules of criminal justice as price-setting rules. Another way to put it is to think of these rules as devices that ration or control the supply of certain behaviors—through rewards and punishments, of course. Sometimes the system rations goods and services quite literally. During the Second World War, wages and prices were frozen and ration tickets issued for gasoline and sugar. Violation of regulations was a criminal offense.

Other legal rules ration in a less literal way. Probably no branch of law is bigger today and touches the lives of more people than traffic law;

a traffic offense is the only "crime" the average person is likely to be convicted of during his or her lifetime.* Traffic law is bulky and ubiquitous because traffic is bulky and ubiquitous; there are millions of cars, buses, and taxis on the road, and millions of drivers. Road space is a scarce commodity, especially in the cities. Clearly, if everybody drove as fast as they wanted, when they wanted, where they wanted, without regulation, the results would be total chaos. It is nearly that as it is.

Space, then, has to be rationed; it can't be treated as a free good, which everybody can grab for herself, first-come, first-served, like a park bench or space on the grass in the town square. The law is the instrument that carries out this rationing. Even in the nineteenth century there were rudimentary rules of the road; drivers of "carriages, sleighs, or sleds," as a New Jersey statute put it, had to "keep to the right," when they met another vehicle, and if "overtaken," the other vehicle must be allowed to pass "free and uninterrupted."[59] In Nebraska, a carriage owner could be fined if he hired a drunkard as a driver; no one was to ride or drive over a bridge "faster than a walk."[60]

Conservation laws are rationing laws as well. The preservation of wilderness is a distinctly modern goal. But the general idea of conservation goes back a stretch in time; we cited a Rhode Island statute on oysters, for example. As early as the colonial period, as we saw, there were restrictive fish and game laws. Every state in the nineteenth century had its own version. These laws, in general, were economic in the most baldly literal sense. They tried to protect a valuable commodity. At first, they carried out the dominant theme of economic development. Hardly anybody worried about "endangered species"; there was much more concern about *endangering* species. The New Hampshire statutes in 1851, which made it an offense to shoot or trap beaver, mink, otter, or muskrats between May 30 and November 1, also offered cash bounties for the killing of wolves, bear, or "any wildcat known by the name of Siberian lynx."[61]

Fish and game laws were recognitions, at least, that animal life was not without limit. A few laws also recognized that clear air and water, and an endless sky, could not be taken for granted any more than the supply of muskrats. Nuisance law, in cities, had something of this flavor. A New Jersey law of 1884 outlawed the "discharge ... of such refuse or residuum, resulting from the refining of petroleum, as is commonly called 'sludge acid,' into or upon any river, stream, ... pond or other body of water."[62] But these were still exceptional noises in a general symphony of growth and expansion.

Gradually, however, the conservation tones got louder. A sense of

---

* See chapter 14, below.

contraction, of limits, translated itself into positive rules. A Nebraska statute, for example, late in the century, made it unlawful to kill (except on one's own land) "any robin, lark, thrush, blue bird, king bird, sparrow, wren, jay, swallow, turtle dove, oriole, wood-pecker, yellow-hammer, cuckoo, yellow bird, bobolink, or other bird or birds of like nature": these birds, to be sure, "promote agriculture or horticulture by feeding on noxious worms and insects," but they are also "attractive in appearance or cheerful in song."[63] The fish and game laws—laws about what and where to hunt, when to hunt, how much to hunt—became more and more elaborate.

People came to feel, in other words, that horizons were *not* unlimited, resources *not* infinite. This was true in the crowded, urban East, but also in the empty, rural West. In Wyoming, by 1899, the "wanton destruction or the wasting of the game and fish of this state" was declared a misdemeanor. There were limits on game birds, ducks, geese, swans, deer, elk, mountain sheep, mountain goats, and beaver. No moose was to be killed until September 1902; and then only one male moose to a customer, and only during the season. And, most dramatically of all, there was a total ban on killing the buffalo; violation of *this* provision was a felony.[64] At one time there had been herds of these animals that seemed endless; and they were killed for their tongues, or for no reason at all.

6

MORALS, MORALITY, AND CRIMINAL JUSTICE

CHAPTER 5 EXPLORED THE ECONOMIC FACE OF CRIMINAL JUSTICE. THIS CHAPter looks at its other face, the moralistic face. Whatever else it does, the criminal code reflects, though perhaps at times as crudely as a funhouse mirror, some notion of the moral sense of the community—or, to be more accurate, the moral sense of the people who count, and who speak out, in the community. It never expressed, for example, the moral sense of slaves, and deliberately so; nor did it express, in any systematic way, the moral sense of women, except as refracted through the men in their lives.

In the previous chapter we said that all criminal law is economic, in some regard. But all criminal law is also moral law, again in some regard; every line in the penal code tags some behavior as wrong—either deeply and inherently wrong, or wrong because of its consequences. As we have seen, jurists once drew a distinction between crimes *mala in se* (evil in themselves) and crimes that are *mala prohibita* (evil only when we say they are, when we stick on a criminal label). Murder would be *malum in se*; most regulatory offenses, *mala prohibita*.

This is a shaky distinction, both historically and culturally. As we have said, ideas about what is right and wrong ebb and flow, in space and time; what is heinous in one period is shrugged off in another, or even lauded to the skies. In any particular community, however, the distinction has some meaning. To members of the community, some acts seem incomparably bad, some not so bad; some seem to ooze out from some darker, more primitive source of bone-deep, inescapable evil.

But "enforcement of morality" does not, on the whole, refer to the war against rape, murder, arson, and deadly assault. These are, of course, immoral acts; but "moral crimes" is used here and in the literature in a more restricted sense. It is one of three big, time-worn categories. (The other two are crimes against the person and crimes against property.)* Adultery fits in one box; assault with a deadly weapon in another; larceny and shoplifting in a third. Of course, in an important sense all of these are equally crimes "against persons"; and all, too, are crimes against morality.

It is not easy to corral in words what sets "crimes against morality" apart from other kinds of crime. The usual classification, weak as it is, does ask in a rough way some relevant questions: Who or what or which interests were hurt by whatever it was that the criminal did? Many crimes against morality are so-called "victimless crimes," that is, crimes about which nobody complains, or in which (arguably) nobody has been hurt. The crime, rather, damages us generally, rips the social fabric, or offends "public decency and order"—that is, Society with a capital S. Fornication was a good example; also sodomy, gambling, and drunkenness, public or private. Most of these acts, one notes, are behaviors of pleasure or leisure. People do not drink whiskey for a living. They do not (as a rule) fornicate for money. Rather, they do it because they like it, or want it, or can't help it.

These are offenses, then, against the "moral sense of the community," with or without an identifiable "victim," that is, somebody who feels hurt, or violated, or cheated in some way. But the "moral sense of the community" is a slippery and complex idea. As we have said, it is not everybody's moral sense; in our history (and this is more or less true everywhere), it is the moral sense of the people who count, the respectable middle and upper classes. Even so, it is not easy to measure or to sniff it out. Sometimes the penal code is the best evidence of what that moral sense might be; but of course that traps us in a circle. Moreover, people often say one thing and do another; the laws against morality certainly represent values people think they *ought* to have, but not at all necessarily what they (secretly) think or want.

And of course these values and ideas change over time. The ideas in

* There are other categories as well, which we often find in classifications of crime; for example, regulatory crimes and crimes against public order.

people's head reflect their experiences; and their experiences are distinctly time-bound and culture-bound. The moral sense of the tight, devout Puritan communities was in severe decay in the republican period. What shattered it, above all, was social and geographic mobility; the abundance of land, the rampant immigration, and the heady experiences of self-government fed this mobility. How these factors affected "crimes against morality" is the theme of this chapter.

The Victorian Compromise

One major way in which the law about morals crimes changed is that it lost something of its absolutist nature. This calls for a word of explanation. Moral crimes, like crimes in general, come in two forms, which, for want of a better way to put it, we might call the truly evil and the not quite so bad (or, bad in some but not all circumstances). State laws, for example, simply outlawed sodomy, which the codes described as totally evil, even unspeakable. Other moral prohibitions were more modulated. Take, for example, Sunday laws. Ohio law in 1831 did not allow anyone above the age of fourteen to engage in "sporting, rioting, quarreling, hunting, fishing, shooting, or . . . at common labor" on Sunday, except for "works of necessity and charity." It was also an offense for a tavernkeeper to sell liquor on Sunday, except to travelers.[1]

If it is an offense to fish on Sunday, or to sell liquor (or drink it, one supposes), it is hard to see why there should be any exceptions (say, for a thirteen-year-old, or for a traveler). The goal of the law, obviously, is not to stamp out all fishing on the sabbath, but to encourage a quiet, pious Sunday. It is a law, in other words, not about private sin, but about public surface and public order. Behind it lies a muddled but powerful theory of social control: a decent *official* moral framework is terribly important, not only to teach a lesson but also as a way of limiting bad behavior. Some bad acts, though they are going to happen anyway, get driven underground. This means there is less of them; and the bad behavior does not threaten the general fabric of society. Vice and crime stay in their place. We can call this arrangement, this double standard, the Victorian compromise.[2] It appeared strongest, and most obviously, in the law relating to sexual behavior, to which we now turn.

Control of Sexual Behavior

On the surface, the republican period carried on a rich, colonial tradition, committed to sexual control (or, more accurately, repression). There was no abrupt break with the past. By law, only married people were entitled to any kind of sex life at all, and only within narrow limits. Everything else was not only a sin, it was a crime. The laws of

Maine from around the middle of the nineteenth century were fairly typical.[3] Adultery was a crime, as were fornication, incest, and (of course) "the detestable crime against nature, committed with mankind or with a beast"—a crime so awful it was not even described, though presumably most people knew what was meant.* Any "open, gross lewdness and lascivious behavior" was also an offense. Similarly, it was a crime to cater to other people's lewdness—by keeping a house of ill fame, by "inveigling" or "enticing" a (previously "virtuous") woman into such a house, or by printing or selling obscene pictures or books. In the Illinois code of 1833, "public indecency, tending to debauch the public morals" was declared illegal.[5]

Reality was more complex. Take, for example, fornication. As we have seen, this crime was very commonly punished in some of the colonies. We have, of course, no way of knowing how many people got away with their dirty secret; we only know about those who were caught. There were literally thousands of these.

Harvesting fornicators required very precise social conditions, both cultural and structural. In the first place, enough people in the community had to find the act offensive. In modern California, fornication is not a crime at all; it has been relabeled and repackaged, and is, if anything, an esteemed, accepted way of life. In the second place, laws against fornication are hard to enforce except in small towns where everybody knows everybody else. In ports, big cities, communities of strangers, it is so much easier to hide your transgressions.

In the late eighteenth century and in the nineteenth, the criminal justice system paid less and less attention to victimless sex crimes. There were, as we saw, lots of prosecutions in the eighteenth century, but the point was not so much to make sinners squirm, as to squeeze money out of men who fathered bastards.[6] In the late eighteenth century, the numbers began to decline. Linda Kealey studied indictments in the Superior Court of Massachusetts between 1750 and 1796, a period that straddles the Revolution. Only 4.3 percent of the indictments were for "moral and sexual crimes," that is, fornication, adultery, incest, blasphemy, swearing, and sabbath violation.[7]

By the nineteenth century, the structural conditions had probably changed. Certainly, city growth and mobility made enforcement very chancy. Research on criminal justice in this period is skimpy, to say the least. The evidence, such as it is, suggests a fairly feeble level of enforcement. In Ohio County, Virginia, there were two hundred forty indictments for crimes and misdemeanors between 1801 and 1810; one was

---

* A few statutes were a bit more explicit. In late nineteenth-century Ohio, the crime of sodomy was defined as "carnal copulation in any opening of the body, except sexual parts, with another human being, or with a beast." The punishment was confinement in the penitentiary, for not more than twenty years.[4]

for sabbath breaking, four for bastardy, twenty-four for profanity; none were for fornication, adultery, or sodomy.[8] In Marion County, Indiana, during the period 1823–60, prosecutions for sexual offenses (mainly fornication and adultery) made up 2.4 percent of the prosecutions in the county.[9] This is a far cry from Puritan zeal.

Had the moral climate changed as well? Evidence here is even more slippery. Religious leaders, of course, had lost much of their grip. The statutes themselves, and the case law, provide indirect evidence of change in the inner meaning of laws against fornication and adultery. For the likes of Cotton Mather these were crimes because they went against the explicit word of God; of course they hurt society, but only because ungodliness hurt society, not for other, more instrumental reasons.

The nineteenth-century program had a different flavor altogether. To be sure, householders, churchgoers, the respectable citizenry, held fast to traditional morality. Sex outside marriage was wrong; and inside, too, for that matter, if the technique or the method was wrong. Indeed, orthodox science reinforced this view—from the standpoint of health. Moderation and self-control were the key to a healthy life. Sexual excess was ferociously damaging to body and soul. Sexual excitement, according to Sylvester Graham, who wrote in the 1830s, "rapidly exhausts the vital properties of the tissues, and impairs the functional powers of the organs."[10]

These ideas about sexuality, which seem ridiculous today, were not isolated quirks; they were part of a more general system of beliefs, the nineteenth-century obsession with social discipline and self-control, a horror of the bursting out of natural limits. Control, as Charles Rosenberg has put it, was "the basic building block of personality." The "passions" had to be repressed at all costs.[11]

Of course, such ideas did not come out of the blue. Perhaps it is not too farfetched to see a connection between the emphasis on self-control and the American experiment in individualism and self-government. This was a free country. The citizen had cast off his chains, so to speak; society encouraged men (I use this word deliberately, for obvious reasons) to let loose their own internal energies, their potencies. But the whole experiment *presumed* personal self-control; it assumed that citizens would not go wild, would use their energies in constructive ways, would not abuse the freedom that had been so painfully won.[12]

This was, to be sure, an ideal, and people have the inveterate habit of falling short of their ideals. Men were supposed to discipline themselves; and yet, and yet . . . what was to be done about those animal instincts, those terrifying drives, those bursts of passion? They could not be denied; a man's sexual "energies" had to find *some* outlet; and in fact, immoderate repression might even endanger his health.[13] As a practical matter, there was no getting rid of vice altogether—and who knows if it was even desirable. But it was crucially important to build dams and containments: structures of justice and social order that encouraged self-control, enthroned models of right behavior, and punished *extreme* deviance. This would drive vice into dark corners and back alleys, which was where it belonged—not extinct, by any means, but in a cage, with specific parameters. This is what we have called the Victorian compromise.

This point of view—rarely made explicit at the time, rarely formulated in coherent terms—helps to explain why, in a number of states, adultery was now a crime only when it was "open and notorious."[14] Adultery and fornication came to be treated more or less like the crime of "indecent exposure." There was nothing criminal about the naked body. Taking a bath was not against the law. But the body was private, for private use, and private eyes only. Public exposure could not be allowed.*

So, under Michigan law, it was a crime if a man and woman "lewdly and lasciviously associate or cohabit together, or if any man or woman, married or unmarried, shall be guilty of open and gross lewdness and lascivious behavior."[16] The word *open* was crucial here. In an Alabama case, decided in 1848, a man named Collins was arrested, tried, and convicted, for "living in adultery" with a woman named Polly Williams.[17] The evidence showed that Collins, a married man, spent one night a week at Polly's home; he "slept with her all night." These goings-on lasted about seven months. This was adultery, no question: but did the statute cover the case? An "occasional act of criminal intimacy," the judges admitted, was not a crime. But Collins and Polly were pursuing a "course of conduct"; it was "open and notorious," and thus "an outrage upon decency and morality." The conviction of Collins had to stand.

The lesson of the case, and of the statutes, was roughly this: sin itself was no crime—clandestine sin even less so. Of course, these were wrongful acts, but the evil had to be tolerated—up to a point. The contrast with colonial law is extremely sharp. The colonials make no distinction between just plain sin and open and notorious sin. If anything, they hated *concealed* sin more. What they wanted from criminals and sinners was exposure, confession, and contrition.[18] In the nineteenth century, the real crime was to act in such a way as to offend *public*

---

* Anthony Comstock, the famous bluenose, who campaigned tirelessly against obscenity, waged war on "the undraped female figure" in art. He explained his point of view as follows: "No one reveres the female form more than I do. In my opinion there is nothing else in the world so beautiful as the form of a beautiful maiden. . . . But the place for a woman's body to be—denuded—is in the privacy of her own apartment with the blinds drawn."[15]

morality. Hence vice won a certain grudging degree of toleration, or even acceptance—so long as it remained in the shadows.

This strikes the modern mind as hypocrisy; and no doubt it was hypocritical, to a degree. Men sat in legislatures and made up moral laws while pursuing, no doubt, their own hidden vices and pleasures. Nonetheless, a kind of implicit, and plausible, theory of social control underlay these laws. They gave the right *message:* they preached morality, and they strengthened the hand of respectable, God-fearing people. Barefaced defiance of morals and law were illegal. This was bound to have *some* impact on behavior. If open vice and open sex are crimes, there is bound to be less of them; their price, so to speak, has gone up, and the conditions of illegality mold the time, manner, and mode of violation. Speeding is illegal today; lots of people speed, but probably less than otherwise; and nobody speeds as the patrol car cruises by. It is almost always a mistake to dismiss the various American prohibitions (no matter what is prohibited) as utterly toothless and a waste of time.

The point was well put in a New York report on the "social evil" (prostitution), written much later, indeed at a time when the Victorian compromise was in the process of decay. The report urged steps to suppress every "flagrant" form of "incitement to debauch." Streetwalking, for example, should be utterly stamped out. "Haunts of vice" should be forced "to assume the appearance of decency"; the state should eradicate "every method of conspicuous advertising of vice." Much would be gained "if vice could be made relatively inconspicuous except to its votaries. . . . It is far better that prostitutes should be clandestine in fact as well as in name than that they should appear in their true colours."[19] Prostitution itself was an example of the Victorian compromise at work. In most cities, prostitution was a fact of life, a necessary evil, or, in the eyes of millions of men, no doubt a necessary non-evil, especially in western towns and other places where the supply of "decent" women was inadequate. In the big cities, nobody seriously thought of eliminating prostitution, even assuming most men wanted that. The goal, as we shall see, was only to keep it in its place—in the red-light areas, the tenderloins, the vice districts. We will return to this point, and to prostitution as a crime, in chapter 10.

The report we quoted one paragraph back drew a line between the "votaries" of vice, who were probably hopeless, and innocents who might be dragged down with them. This was another reason why vice laws needed to be passed, even if such laws were hard to enforce. Illegal vice would have to hide its face, and young folks would be less likely to come within its orbit of corruption. Obscenity laws, for example, were aimed at words and pictures that might "corrupt" the "morals of youth." Michigan law made it a crime to print, publish, sell, or introduce "into any family, school or place of education" any books, pamphlets, and so on, that used obscene language or carried obscene pictures prints, or figures.[20]

"Fill a clean, clear glass with distilled water," wrote Anthony Comstock, "and hold it to the light. . . . It will sparkle like a gem, seeming to rejoice in its purity, and dance in the sunlight, because of its freedom from pollution. So with a child." But if you "put a drop of ink into the glass of water, . . . at once it is discolored. Its purity cannot easily be restored." The "fountain of moral purity in our youth" is poisoned by bad literature, by obscenity. "A perpetual panorama of evil forms" will invade their minds. "Vile books and papers are branding-irons heated in the fires of hell."[21]

In 1848 in Massachusetts, a doctor with the interesting name of Walter Scott Tarbox was indicted (and convicted) for producing an offensive advertisement. It showed "an instrument for sale by him for the prevention of conception." He left this dreadful document on the doorsteps of respectable Boston households. Tarbox was convicted of violating the obscenity laws.[22] The message was clear. Sex and its mysteries had to be covered up and disguised, like the human body; even normal and laudable aspects of human life, such as pregnancy, childbirth, and giving mother's milk to babies retreated from public view. What was acceptable, even unavoidable, for adults, that is, adults with self-control, virtue, honor, respectability, would "corrupt" the young and the weak.

Gambling

Gambling had been punished in the colonial period, and it continued to be illegal in the nineteenth century. There were statutes against gambling in every state; often they banned a long list of habits and games, some of them still with us, some long gone. In Alabama, in 1807, the ban included "A.B.C." and "E. O." tables, faro, rouge-et-noir, and "rowley-powley."[23] Later in the century, the catalogue of forbidden games in Idaho included "French monte, three-card monte, E. O. or roulette, or the game commonly called the thimble game, or percentage stud-poker, or any other percentage game played with cards, dice, or any other device, for money . . . or any other representative of value."[24] The Illinois Code of 1833 authorized a fine on anyone who sold or imported for sale "any pack or packs of playing cards, or any dice, billiard table, billiard balls . . . or any obscene book"; it was similarly an offense to "play for money, or other valuable thing, any game with cards, dice, checks, or at billiards"; or to bet on any game.[25]

The statutes did not, of course, put an end to gambling; if anything, they testified to its continuing popularity. There were periodic crackdowns in various cities—no doubt without much long-term effect. But gambling was not exactly a victimless crime. The professional gambler was usually not, shall we say, an honorable man. The tricks of his trade included loaded dice and marked cards (introduced apparently in the 1830s); a shop on Liberty Street, in New York, sold various types of "advantage" playing cards and fine ivory loaded dice. Gamblers also sometimes wore special clothing, the better to hide high cards up their sleeve; or used such devices as mirrors and rods clipped under the table to conceal good cards.[26] In New York, gambling was big business in the middle of the century: according to one estimate, about 6 percent of the population made a living off gambling.[27] In 1872, a New York writer claimed that there were 200 gambling houses in the city, and from 350 to 400 lottery offices, "policy shops," and other places where people gambled.[28]

Yet the police made very few arrests. Only fifty-nine indictments were handed down in New York between 1845 and 1851; about half of those indicted paid fines; the rest got off.[29] The police in the 1870s, "for reasons best known to themselves," did nothing about the hundreds of gambling houses, all the way from first-class "Faro Banks," located in "magnificent" brownstone mansions, down to "policy offices" in "dingy little holes . . . in the most wretched quarters of the city," all of which did their business with "perfect openness."[30] Local government was feeble and corrupt, which explains why so little was done about gambling. Gamblers bought immunity from law enforcement with hard cash. But corruption is never random; it follows certain lines of demand. If there had not been a strong taste for gambling, gamblers would have failed to corrupt the local police. As it was, there were, in fact, periodic explosions of civic outrage, an expulsion of professional gamblers from this or that town now and then, an occasional episode of tarring and feathering. Sometimes these anti-gambling episodes turned ugly. In 1835, in Vicksburg, Mississippi, an anti-gambling mob gathered around the house of a gambler. Shots were fired, one citizen was killed, and then the mob seized the house and lynched five gamblers.[31]

There was more than a little trace of elitism in the war against gambling. At the New York constitutional convention of 1821, a constitutional ban on lotteries was proposed. One speaker, hotly in favor, cursed lotteries for their "tendency to promote and encourage a spirit of rash and wild speculation amongst the poor and labouring classes—to fill their minds with absurd and extravagant hopes"; these hopes "diverted" them "from the regular pursuits of industry." The lottery, in other words, like dirty books and pictures, had the effect of "debauching" the morals of the population.[32]

What was voiced here, too, was a classic American (and British) insecurity: a fear of work disincentives. This was a country that cultivated, encouraged, demanded, even thrived on "extravagant hopes"; but people were supposed to realize these hopes only in socially acceptable ways. Gambling was odious, then, because it was the wrong way to make money: it mocked the ideal of slow, steady progress through hard work. But the actual anti-gambling movement of the nineteenth century (or most of the century) was basically a form of the Victorian compromise.

Demon Rum

The liquor question deserves a special place in any discussion of the law of vice. Drunkenness had, of course, always been condemned; but there was, for the first time in the republic, a genuine temperance *movement*. How could a democracy govern itself, how could the people rule, unless the population was earnest, sober, disciplined? Hence drunkenness, like vice, threatened the very basis of a democratic order. As Lyman Beecher put it, in 1843, "When the laboring classes are contaminated, the right of suffrage becomes the engine of destruction."[33] As the country industrialized, liquor became an even more sinister enemy of order. A drunken farmer was one thing, a drunken factory hand another. Industrial discipline demanded punctual, orderly work habits. A man sloshed in liquor could hardly meet the test.

In the nineteenth century, drinking was blamed for almost every social evil: crime, pauperism, general decay. Intoxication destroyed religion, property rights, family life. When Irish and German immigrants poured into the country, strong drink also became associated with the foreign underclass. The temperance movement, which began as a movement of "moral suasion," moved into politics, and a drive began to pass restrictive laws.[34]

The most famous of these was the so-called Maine Law. That good Yankee state, in 1851, adopted a statute prohibiting the manufacture or sale of "any spirituous or intoxicating liquors, or any mixed liquors a part of which is spirituous or intoxicating."[35] Other states soon enacted their own versions of the "Maine Law." Most of New England was firmly in the temperance camp by 1856, when this particular spasm of temperance peaked. At that point a reaction set in; some laws were repealed, while others were weakened. The campaign heated up again, as we shall see, later in the century.

The Revolution of the Righteous

The Victorian compromise held firm, more or less, for most of the nineteenth century; or so it seemed. But in the years after 1870, it began to crumble. There was an outburst of new, more stringent legislation;

there were (apparently) stronger attempts at enforcement. The issue of victimless crime, of vice, of sexual propriety, ratcheted a bit higher on the national agenda. And it was the righteous, the respectable, the religious, who broke the (implicit) truce. Many moral leaders of society, in 1870 and afterward, were simply no longer satisfied with damning and damning; they smelled victory, and they wanted it. They demanded the elimination and prohibition of vice.

In the 1870s, societies for the "suppression of vice" became active in many cities. The Boston Watch and Ward Society was particularly notorious.[36] Elite society fostered the movement and gave it the money it needed. The list of contributors to the Watch and Ward Society was practically a "roll call of the Brahmin aristocracy," including the Cabots and the Lodges, who (according to the old joke) spoke only to each other, or to God.[37] In New York, the YMCA was an active focus for the crusade. One of its members, a dry-goods salesman from Connecticut named Anthony Comstock, became totally obsessed with the campaign, making it his life's work.[38] (We have already quoted his views on corrupting the young.) Comstock's ceaseless lobbying led to the first landmark achievement of the new movement, the so-called Comstock Law, which Congress enacted in 1873. Under this law it was a crime to send through the mails any "obscene, lewd, or lascivious" book, or any "article or thing designed or intended for the prevention of conception or procuring of abortion."[39]

The Comstock Law was, in a way, the opening shot in the new campaign, a new phase in the never-ending legal struggle against the forces of the devil. Many states strengthened their own laws against obscenity. In Oregon, for example, it was a crime to give or sell to a minor "any book, pamphlet, magazine, newspaper, or other printed paper devoted to the publication . . . of criminal news, police reports, or accounts of criminal deeds or pictures, and stories of deeds of bloodshed, lust, or crime." In Ohio, an obscenity statute passed in 1885 made it a crime to distribute a newspaper or periodical "devoted to the publication of criminal news or police reports, accounts or stories of deeds of lust, immorality or crime"; even adults in Ohio had to be protected from this trash.[40]

The Comstock Law, and its state counterparts, were not the only victories in the battle. Sex laws were tightened, on paper, at least. This occurred, for example, with regard to the crime usually known as "statutory rape." A man commits this crime when he has sex with a girl who, even though she says yes, is, legally speaking, too young for that sort of thing. The "age of consent" is the age that fixes the boundary between fornication and the much more serious crime of rape. The common law fixed the age (believe it or not) at ten. Toward the end of the century, the states began to raise the age; in California it went to fourteen in 1889, then to sixteen in 1897. The effect, of course, was to make teenage sex a serious crime.[41] Even more dramatic changes were to take place in the early twentieth century.*

There was also a renewed attack on gambling; this vice, like a deep-rooted garden weed, was hardy and could sprout back with amazing speed. The lottery was a particularly obnoxious form of weed: it was extremely "open and notorious," and indeed, unlike other forms of gambling, it had the stamp of official approval. At one time, state lotteries had been very popular. The war on lotteries began early, as we have seen. The lottery survived in only a handful of states by the time of the Civil War. But as late as the 1870s, New Yorkers, for example, flocked to buy tickets in the Havana Lottery, the Kentucky State Lottery, and the Missouri State Lottery.[42] In 1895, Congress took a decisive step against the lotteries: Congress made it illegal to sell lottery tickets across state lines, or through the mails, or to import lottery tickets from overseas; these provisions were a death blow to the (legal) lottery business.[43†]

This period, too, developed a more rigid attitude toward what is now known somewhat stuffily as substance abuse, which does not, of course, mean abusing the substance but abusing the body *with* substances (namely, liquor or narcotics). Prohibition movements flared up again in the latter part of the century. Kansas embraced prohibition in 1881, putting the ban on liquor into its constitution. An amendment (section 10) to Article 15 of Kansas's Constitution, adopted at a general election held on November 1, 1880, provided as follows: "The manufacture and sale of intoxicating liquors shall be forever prohibited in this state, except for medical, scientific and mechanical purposes."[45] Few states went that far; but in almost all states, the network of liquor regulation was dense and getting denser.[46]

In the Minnesota statutes of 1894, to take one example, there is page after page of regulation and prohibition. No one could sell liquor without a license. No one could sell liquor to a minor, or to any student or pupil, or to any habitual drunkard; or to *anybody* who was drunk, habitually or not; or on the sabbath; or to an Indian; or "within the capital buildings," if the legislature was in session; or within half a mile of the state fair; or within that distance from Hamline University; and so on.[47]

A number of states had "local option" laws; these permitted counties to decide whether or not to ban the sale of liquor altogether or permit it under conditions. Georgia and a number of other southern states were "local option" states.[48] Liquor control thus became enmeshed in local

---

* See chapter 15.
† Yet surprisingly few prisoners went to jail because of gambling or lottery offenses—at least according to the 1880 census. The figures are fifty and ten, respectively.[44]

politics; the result was a crazy quilt of bans and conditions, sometimes with small, puzzling variations. The 1872 session of the Mississippi legislature passed a law that made it illegal to sell liquor "in less quantities than five gallons" in or around Thomastown; druggists could sell liquor "for medicinal, culinary, or sacramental purposes, or for use in the arts" (whatever that meant). The buyer had to swear that this was the case. The ban in the town of Greensboro was on sales of less than *one* gallon; in Greenwood, in Leflore County, the bottom limit was twenty gallons, though "porter, ale and beer" were excepted. There was a total prohibition for two miles around Colfax Institute, in Choctaw County. The cordon around Tougaloo University extended for three miles.[49]

In 1880, Massachusetts passed a law to take the cover off the sale of liquor, so to speak. No licensed seller could block off his business with a "screen, blind, shutter, curtain, partition, or painted, ground, or stained glass window, or any other obstruction, which shall interfere with a view of the business."[50] Texas, too, in 1887, required taverns to be "open." No screen or similar device could obstruct "the view through the open door or place of entrance."[51] An "open" saloon, of course, would find it harder to sell liquor to minors; the law would throw saloons open to public scrutiny, driving out various forms of wickedness. The philosophy of these laws was diametrically opposed to the spirit of the Victorian compromise. The saloon was not to lock itself discreetly away from the eyes and ears of respectable people.

In the late nineteenth century, too, the first true drug laws were passed.[52] Generally speaking, narcotic addiction was no crime in the nineteenth century. It was considered an evil, a vice; but it did not carry a criminal label. There were scattered laws and ordinances against opium dens, which were associated with the Chinese. Newspapers spoke of "opium fiends," and "opium joints." Morphine addicts were objects of pity and horror. A California newspaper described the arrest of two "morphine fiends," a mother and son, in 1894, on a charge of battery. Young Eugene Sullivan had "pallid lips" that spit out "great flecks of foam." His mother was a picture of "loathesome degradation," "a grinning death's head" who "gibbered and raved."[53] But their sorry state of dependence did not, in itself, bring them under the sway of criminal justice.

The early drug laws struck out at opium, the Chinese, and their dens of iniquity. Idaho (1887) made it a crime for a "white person" to maintain "any house or place kept as a resort for purposes of smoking opium"; it was also an offense for a "white person" to be "found in any house, or place kept for use as a resort . . . for the purpose of smoking opium."[54] In California, in 1881, the penal code was amended to create a new misdemeanor: operating a place "where opium . . . is sold or given away, to be smoked at such place," or to "visit" or "resort" to "any such place for the purpose of smoking opium." In 1890, the city of Oakland enacted an ordinance to "Prevent the Abuse of Opium and Other Drugs"; druggists were to sell opium, morphine, or cocaine only on a doctor's prescription, and only for the "purpose of curing or alleviating disease." The ordinance also applied to morphine and cocaine.[55] An Illinois law of 1897 made it an offense to sell cocaine without a prescription.[56] General narcotics laws were a twentieth-century idea; but the foundations were laid in the nineteenth century. Here, too, the new law-making ethos was opposed to compromise; these drugs brought about corruption; they were contagious and addictive, and they had to be stamped out, if at all possible.

In short, there was a surge of interest in victimless crime, in vice, in sexual behavior, at the end of the nineteenth century. What brought it about? Why did so many people think it was important to try to eradicate vice? There were, to be sure, some practical reasons to worry: prostitution and promiscuity were indeed problems of public health. People had learned more about venereal diseases, how they spread, and the terrible toll they took.

But perhaps the causes lay deeper. One thesis is that there was a kind of moral struggle in America, between the old WASP elite and the new waves of immigrants. The old America felt under attack; it felt that its values were eroding. The rise of huge, hungry cities, the mobs of immigrants, the tempestuous pace of social change—all this profoundly unsettled the traditional elites. They smelled crisis, and were seized by the thought that, by God, something had to be done about it.[57] This is a plausible theory, and it helps to explain the death of the Victorian compromise, which rested on certain comfortable assumptions about the nature of American society.

In addition, criminal justice had become, in a peculiar way, more democratic. The social base of power was broader. All white men over twenty-one had the vote. The law responded, more and more, to a compact, middle-class mass of respectable citizens.[58] Tolerance for vice in the earlier part of the century had been, in a way, an elite attitude; an attitude, in part, of noblesse oblige. There was less of this in the United States than in England, because there was vastly less noblesse. Nonetheless, this was a factor to be recokoned with.

This was also a very mobile society, as we have many times observed. America was socially mobile as well as geographically mobile. There were no fixed classes (among whites). People rose; and people fell. In an elite society, with a stationary underclass, the top is not terribly interested in the sex lives of the bottom, or their vices. The poor are animals. In a mobile, industrial society, everybody is one class in the *moral* sense, because all the players can move from class to class. Respectable people believed in one society, one polity, one community—and a single universal moral code, which the legal code had to embody.

These are guesses—plausible or not. But whatever the reasons, the facts are clear: there was a strong move, successful in part, to tighten the laws against vice, sex, and victimless crime. Not everyone went along; and the backlash, as we will see, brought about a backlash of its own. But that story belongs to the twentieth century.

Enforcement

The new laws were obvious enough: they were printed in the books. But what about enforcement? That, as usual, was a far different matter.

Laws against adultery and fornication were certainly not rigorously enforced. Arrests were, at most, sporadic. In the Ohio Courts of Common Pleas, there were 28 indictments for adultery in 1875, and 7 for fornication (the population of the state was almost 3 million). And exactly 8 people in the state went to jail for these offenses in the year—6 for adultery, 2 for fornication. Yet in the same year, 304 divorces were granted on the grounds of the (crime of) adultery.[59]

Behind each instance was, no doubt, some particular story or incident. We catch a glimpse of the background here and there: the father of a young man, "prominent in society circles" in Philadelphia, has his own son arrested for adultery; the son, a married man, was carrying on in Reading, Pennsylvania, with a former servant, a "prepossessing young woman" who (it was said) received his "attentions without being aware that he was a married man."[60] In Alameda County, California, in the twenty years between 1880 and 1900, there was only one prosecution for adultery. The wife of Manuel Fritas, who ran a boardinghouse in San Rafael, ran off to San Francisco, became a prostitute, then left the sporting life and moved in with Nelson Tower, once a lodger in the boardinghouse. The outraged husband found them and filed a complaint. The wife went free; Tower was sentenced to two months in county jail.[61]

Most regulation of morality probably took place on the local level, and is almost invisible to researchers. An ordinance in Oakland, California, approved in 1879, made it unlawful "for any person to appear in a public place naked or in a dress not belonging to his or her sex, or in an indecent or lewd dress." An ordinance of 1897 forbade swimming in the harbor "unless clad in a bathing suit." If the swimmer was over twelve, he or she had to wear "trunks reaching from the waist to the thighs" and a "shirt or jersey . . . covering all the upper part of the body except the head and arms," or a "combination suit or a single garment" providing the same amount of coverage.[62] Whether the police arrested many people, or anybody, for these "crimes," is unknown.

Police reports do give some idea of the numbers of arrests for morals crimes; and the census of 1880 provides some data on prisoners. Out of some 58,000 prisoners in prisons and local jails, in the United States, a fair number (4,768) got there because of offenses "against public morals." But the overwhelming majority in this category had been arrested as "drunk and disorderly" (3,331). There were 121 prisoners charged with incest, 63 guilty of the "crime against nature," 257 bigamists or polygamists (only one of them in Utah), 161 jailed for adultery, 26 for seduction, 22 for "illicit cohabitation," 85 for "fornication," 88 for "open lewdness," 50 for indecent exposure, and 16 for obscenity.[63] These are hardly overwhelming numbers, but they are definitely greater than zero. What lies behind them, as we have said, is unknown territory; each case probably represented a separate tale, a separate incitement. In each case, *somebody* blew the whistle. There were no police "sweeps" for fornication, incest, or bigamy.

Enforcement of liquor laws was more complex. Millions of people thought liquor was a tool of the devil. Millions more liked to drink. It was an addiction to some; bread and butter to still others. No arrests in the nineteenth century were more common than drunkenness arrests; and on the local level, liquor violations, license offenses, and the like, were among the most common urban transgressions. In a situation of stalemate and opposition, corruption flourishes, on a small and large scale. The police and local officials were on the take in many American cities. Ida Bailey of San Diego, arrested in 1891 for selling liquor without a license, offered a "sensational" defense: she had paid an ex-councilman fifteen dollars for "immunity."[64] There were similar "sensations" elsewhere as well.

Every city, in other words, had its own special history of crackdowns, campaigns, arrests—and payoffs, immunities, and shoulder-shrugging toleration. In 1882, Cincinnati ordered its saloons to close on Sundays. Afterward, the police arrested 313 saloonkeepers for various violations; of these, only five were arraigned, and exactly one was convicted. The chief of police declared the law "a dead letter." And why? "Public sentiment does not sustain it."[65] He was almost certainly right; more precisely, there were two *kinds* of public sentiment, and they fought each other to a virtual standstill.[66]

Degenerate Man

Ideas about morality are ideas about people and their motives, not about conduct alone. The law punishes bad people who do bad things for bad reasons. A recurrent issue in criminal justice is the problem of defining *who* is bad. What makes the criminal tick, how do we recognize a criminal, what is the criminal personality (if there is such a thing)? The answers to these questions influence decisions about how to handle criminals and crime. Popular theories about the nature and causes of crime make a deep impress on the criminal justice system; scholarly theories also have an effect, though probably in a trickle-down way: by the time they reach the people who make and enforce law, it is probably in diluted and distorted form.

Roughly speaking, there are two general ideas about how criminal acts and criminal actors are related. Crime might be just one aspect of a person; or a quirk, a sport, a failing, a weakness, a temporary lapse. Or it might be something organic to the person—something total and all-consuming. Each period seemed to make a distinction of this kind; each period cut the cake in different ways. The colonists, as we saw, treated most criminals as plain sinners, people who fell from grace; their sins could be washed away or prayed away or whipped away. But there were also dyed-in-the-wool criminals, the incorrigibles. A witch was an extreme case, perhaps: a person who delivered herself body and soul to the devil. Beating and shaming did not work, of course, with such a person.

Vice laws, too, presupposed such a distinction. The law criminalized a good deal of what people did for kicks: gambling, sex, drinking. But the gambler and drinker, and the fallen woman's "john," were not thoroughgoing criminals; their indulgences were merely aspects of their lives, lapses, little weaknesses. The professional gambler and the prostitute, on the other hand, were steeped in criminality to the bone; vice was their way of life. Such was the judgment of society.

What was the difference between these two classes? The devil had apparently given up overt soul-seeking. By the end of the century, a genetic theory had become popular. Crime, for some people, was inherited; it was in the blood; degraded social behavior passed from father (and mother) to son. The great Italian penologist, Cesare Lombroso, had a kind of "revelation" in 1870, when he looked at the skull of a bandit and noticed "atavistic anomalies," such as the "enormous middle occipital fossa." He began (he thought) to understand at last the "irresistible craving for evil for its own sake."[67] The criminal, in other words, was a *type*; a throw-back, an atavism, a born degenerate.

In 1874, the New York Prison Association sent a man named Richard L. Dugdale to visit some of the county jails of the state. In one upstate jail, he found, to his surprise, a cluster of prisoners who were blood relatives. One man was "waiting trial for receiving stolen goods"; a daughter was a witness against him; her uncle was charged with burglary; two brothers from another branch of the family, nineteen and fourteen years old, had "maliciously pushed a child over a high cliff and nearly killed him." These were all members of the "Juke" family (a pseudonym), a rogue's gallery of thieves, brutes, prostitutes, vagrants and no-goods; they were all the descendants of a single line of rotten apples.[68]

This discovery opened Dugdale's eyes. It "brought seething to the surface" the idea that the "dangerous classes" were "not only a physical, but a *biological* threat—philoprogenitive, promiscuous, and irresponsible"; people who, "breeding like rats in their alleys and hovels, threatened . . . to overwhelm the well-bred classes of society."[69] Dugdale set about to trace the family back to its roots. Their "ancestral breeding-spot" was "along the forest-covered margin of five lakes," an area that was "one of the crime cradles" of New York State. Here squatters lived in rude log or stone houses, sleeping on floors of straw, in situations that "must often have evolved an atmosphere of suggestiveness fatal to habits of chastity."[70]

From a bastard son, the bad seed of the original "Mr. Juke" and one "Ada Juke," sprang "the distinctively criminal line"—a line of thievery, pauperism, harlotry, intemperance, syphilis. The lesson was clear; there was a class of hereditary trash, women and men, some of them criminal, in America. They settled at the bottom of society; the dregs, the garbage of the social order. Some were paupers—and a pauper, according to Dugdale, was an "idiotic adult unable to help himself, who may be justly called a living embodiment of death." Those with more vigor escaped from pauperdom—into crime.[71]

It is "established beyond controversy," wrote Henry Boies in 1893, that "criminals and paupers, both, are degenerates, the imperfect, knotty, knurly, worm-eaten, half-rotten fruit of the race."[72] But if this were so, if criminals were really these primitive, misformed subhumans, then how was the system of criminal justice to handle them? What, in short, was to be done?

The new eugenics movement provided one answer; it led to the idea that criminals should be sterilized. Society had to get rid of the "gangrened" members of the "body politic." "Discoveries" in "anesthetics and antiseptics," said Boies, "have rendered it possible to remove or sterilize the organs of reproduction of both sexes without pain or danger. This is the . . . most effectual solution."[73] In the 1890s, Dr. F. Hoyt Pilcher, an unsung hero of American history, superintendent of the Kansas State Home for the Feeble-Minded, castrated forty-four boys and unsexed fourteen girls who were under his wing—for eugenic purposes. Public disapproval put an end to this noble experiment; the development of vasectomy, for males, and salpingectomy (the cutting and tying of the fallopian tubes) for women made less drastic methods available.[74] This scientific weed came to full flower, however, in the twentieth century, as we shall see.*

* See chapter 15.

The Insanity Defense

In modern states, the criminal justice system punishes only those people who are "responsible" for committing a crime.[75] It is not only the result but the motive that makes a crime; simple carelessness or accident are not crimes, no matter what happens as a consequence. To commit a crime requires a certain minimum amount of mind; animals cannot be guilty of crimes, and the same is true of babies. Neither of these two propositions is the least bit controversial, or consequential. But there *are* problems at the borderland of adulthood (should a fifteen-year-old be held to the same standards as a twenty-year-old?); and also at the borderland of mental health.

It was established law, as Blackstone put it, that "idiots and lunatics are not chargable for their own acts, if committed when under these incapacities; no, not even for treason itself."[76] But how do we tell who is an idiot and who is not? The legal meaning of *insanity* became an important issue in the nineteenth century, particularly contested because "insanity" had become a *medical* question, a question of mental illness or disease, as well as a legal conundrum. The nineteenth century was an age of rampant science. Science was not unembattled (the fate of Darwinism is an obvious example); but science had prestige and persuasive power nonetheless.

The most important *legal* definition of insanity was the so-called right-or-wrong test. It was formulated by an English court in 1843. The test is often called the McNaghten test, commemorating one Daniel McNaghten, who shot and killed Edward Drummond, private secretary to the prime minister, Sir Robert Peel. According to the high court judges of England, ruling in the McNaghten case, a defendant was insane if and only if, at the time of the crime, he was "laboring under such a defect of reason, from disease of the mind, as not to know the nature and quality of the act he was doing; or, if he did know it, that he did not know he was doing what was wrong."[77]

This famous formulation, quite obviously, stressed cognition, the act of *knowing*. It tied in fairly well with other dominant themes of nineteenth-century thought (and law), notably the stress on discipline and self-control. If you were aware of what you were doing, and aware that it was terribly wrong, and did it anyway, then you were deliberately choosing crime or evil, and you ought to be punished.

The right-or-wrong test was formulated in England; but it corresponded to American notions˙, and it became standard in the United

* Thus, in the trial of one Lawrence Pienovi, "for biting off his wife's nose," in New York, 1818, the mayor of New York told the jury that the law does not regard "every slight degree of insanity—every trivial aberration from reason . . . as a defence." rather, the defense must be based on a "deep and total dementation . . . such as involves an inability to discriminate between right and wrong."[78]

States as well. In some states it was frozen into statute law. Thus, New York, in the penal code of 1881, laid down that no one was excused from criminal liability as "an idiot, imbecile, lunatic, or insane person," without proof that the person was "laboring under such a defect of mind" as not to know "the nature and quality of the act he was doing" or that the act was "wrong." A mere "morbid propensity to commit prohibited acts" was not a defense.[79]

There is little hard information about how the insanity defense played out at the level of the trial courts. The right-or-wrong test is, at bottom, nothing but words, which a judge can read or recite to a jury. What a jury made of these words in the nineteenth century is hard to tell. Folk concepts of sanity and insanity probably played more of a role than the official concepts. Some criminals, those who seemed obviously deranged, probably never reached the jury at all; they were let go at an earlier stage—or locked in an asylum.*

Almost from the start, there were those who criticized the right-or-wrong test as inadequate, or unscientific. In Kentucky, in 1845, Abner Baker, Jr., a doctor, killed his brother-in-law. The dead man had, Baker thought, debauched Baker's wife—a belief most people took to be completely lunatic. Baker was convicted, despite strong evidence of "monomania," that is, wildly irrational thought on one particular subject. Eight members of the jury signed a petition, requesting a pardon: "they believed that the prisoner labored under insane delusion . . . but . . . had capacity enough to determine between right and wrong generally." Baker went, nonetheless, to the gallows.[81]

In some states, a second formulation came to supplement McNaghten, by adding the concept of "irresistible impulse"; this test was sometimes called the "wild beast test." There was a medical basis for this test, too, which applied the concept of "moral mania"; some courts and doctors even spoke of "moral insanity." The idea was that certain conditions had the power to affect human emotions without necessarily destroying cognitive functions. The person is in the helpless grip of a force outside himself, borne along by a tornado of instinct or drive. As Joel Bishop put it, "a man may be conscious of what he is doing, and of its criminal character and consequences, while yet he is impelled onward by a power irresistible."[82]

---

* A minor incident, reported in San Diego in 1896, is suggestive. A young man, John B. Postema, was indicted for grand larceny: he stole a team of horses and a carriage. Postema's behavior was extremely peculiar. He could not stop laughing. He laughed "when he got up," and also "when he lay down to sleep—laugh, laugh, laugh." Sometimes, he even laughed in his sleep, in "one of the gloomy steel cells of the county jail." Finally, the sheriff called the county physician, Dr. Gochenauer, to examine the hysterical prisoner. Postema kept right on laughing. The doctor decided he was "an imbecile" who could not "distinguish right from wrong." The district attorney moved in court to set the indictment aside; this was done, and "the happy young fellow left the court room laughing."[80]

In *State v. Felter*, an Iowa case of 1868, Felter was on trial for killing his wife; his defense was "homicidal mania."[83] Felter was a farmer, about forty years old, married, and with a child. He smashed in his wife's skull, mutilated her, and tried to burn down the house. His little daughter saw the crime: "he struck [mother] . . . it was because she poured the buttermilk out; I left because he was going to kill me." Felter finally tried to slit his throat with a razor, but failed. The appellate court reversed his conviction, because the trial court had used the right-or-wrong test: medicine and law, the opinion said, "now recognize the existence of such a mental disease as homicidal insanity"; the trial court should have instructed the jury about the defense of "irresistible impulse." The jury, in other words, had to decide whether the crime was due to insanity or to mere "passion," the "outburst of violent, reckless and uncontrolled passion in a mind not diseased."

As this case suggests, the irresistible-impulse test, too, was consistent with the nineteenth-century theme of *control*. A defendant is insane if he lacks the ability to keep his impulses, his desires, his wild emotions under control, either because of some lesion in the brain or some deep-seated flaw in the neurons. The opposite of insanity is passion, that is, strong emotion. A human being has the duty to keep urges, drives, instincts under tight rein; whoever fails in this sacred obligation is a threat to society, and a danger to all fellow human beings.

The most "advanced" views of insanity were to be found, oddly enough, in the small state of New Hampshire. New Hampshire jurists, notably Justice Charles Doe, were attracted to the ideas of Dr. Isaac Ray, who was the leading expert on the "medical jurisprudence of insanity." In *State v. Pike* (1869)[84] the defendant, Josiah Pike, stood accused of murdering one Thomas Brown with an ax. He claimed to be suffering from "a species of insanity called dipsomania." Doe was one of the trial judges; when he instructed the jury, he told them they had the right to acquit Pike "by reason of insanity" if the killing was the "offspring or product of mental disease in the defendant." Doe also told the jury that there was no single rigid test of "mental disease," certainly not "knowledge of right and wrong"; rather, "all symptoms and all tests of mental disease are purely matters of fact," grist for the jury's mill.[85]

The jury convicted Pike anyway; but Doe's formulation continued to be cited. In his opinion in Pike's case, Charles Doe said that "insanity has been for the most part, a growth of the modern state of society. Like many other diseases, it is caused, in a great degree, by the habits and incidents of civilized life." He also felt that the law should abandon "old exploded medical theories" and embrace "facts established in the progress of scientific knowledge."[86] These two ideas were connected. Civilization was the wellspring of progress; it brought about democracy, science, medicine, technology; but it was, at the same time, a source of danger to society. Civilization was complex and stood in a delicate balance: modern life—rapid, unsettling, mobile—could drive certain persons insane.

Ideas about mental disease were rapidly evolving in the nineteenth century, and their progress can be marked in a series of notable trials. Perhaps the most famous of these was the trial of Charles Guiteau. Whether this trial represented any sort of "progress" is questionable. Guiteau, born in 1841, shot President James Garfield in Washington, D.C., on July 2, 1881, in the Baltimore and Potomac Train Station as the president was about to leave on a trip. Two months later, the president died of his wounds. Guiteau's trial was a long, drawn-out affair, a courtroom drama in which rival psychiatric schools battled for the attention of judge and jury. In fact, the jury deliberated only an hour or so, and the verdict was almost a foregone conclusion: guilty as charged. Guiteau was sentenced to death, and on June 30, 1882, the black cap was put over his face and he was hanged.[87]

To the modern eye, Charles Guiteau would seem completely deranged. His behavior throughout the trial was bizarre; as he stood in front of the gallows, he recited a "pathetic" hymn he had written hours before, in a high-pitched child's voice, beginning with the words, "I am going to the Lordy, I am so glad." Even some of his contemporaries remarked on his "obvious imbecility" and thought he would have escaped with his life if he had killed anyone but the President of the United States. Many psychiatrists were convinced he was a heredity degenerate; if so, it was as illogical to kill him, as one journalist put it, "as it is to kill a cave fish for not seeing."[88]

The Guiteau case represents, then, one extreme: the crime was such that the jury (and public opinion) would not accept the insanity defense; the rage to punish was too great. A small group of cases—they tended, however, to be quite notorious—stood at the other extreme. In these cases, the insanity defense was little better than a figleaf, an excuse for killing, hatched by desperate or inventive defense counsel. These were cases were the defendant was very sympathetic, or the victim very unsympathetic.

One such use of the insanity defense apparently made its debut in the sensational trial of Daniel Sickles, in Washington, D.C., in 1859. Sickles, a congressman from New York, shot and killed his wife's lover, Philip Barton Key. His lawyers argued a kind of temporary insanity—mixed in, to be sure, with other arguments about self-defense and (very significantly) fairly blatant suggestions that killing a foul adulterer was no reason to send a man to prison or the gallows. The jury came back with a verdict of not guilty.[89]

Or take, for example, the trial of Laura Fair, who shot and killed her lover, A. P. Crittenden, a San Francisco lawyer, on a crowded ferryboat sailing between Oakland and San Francisco. Her trial was the sensation of 1871. Since she had obviously pulled the trigger, she needed a fairly creative line of defense. Her lawyers tried temporary insanity: when she fired the shot, they argued, her mind was in a "state of semi-unconsciousness"; the act was "non-volitional," brought about by "hysterical mania," which was, in turn, occasioned by an "anteversion of the womb."[90] Whether the jury paid much attention to this mumbo jumbo is hard to know. The real issue, one suspects, was Laura's character: Was she a wronged, jilted woman, driven to violence by a philanderer; or was she a shameless hussy who killed a married man because he refused to abandon his wife and marry her? Insanity was merely the legal hook on which this dramatic choice was hung. In any event, Laura went free. *

In the twentieth century, these cases of "temporary insanity" might be called cases about the doctrine of diminished responsibility. In some cases, of course, "insanity" merely disguised one form of jury nullification; it was an excuse for upholding this or that "unwritten law." In another group of cases, the defendant's excuse (if you can call it that) was total drunkenness. But these cases, too, shed light on the social meaning of criminal responsibility. Was it a valid defense that the defendant was so dead drunk, so befuddled by liquor, that he had no idea what he was doing?

Strictly speaking, "voluntary intoxication" was "no excuse for crime committed under its influence."[92] This was standard doctrine in the law books. But—and this, too, was standard doctrine—the definition of many crimes included a requirement of some specific "intent," some particular frame of mind. Murder in the first degree, for example, was a crime of "malice." Malice was a difficult concept; it implied some kind of intent, or plan, or design—an impulsive, heat-of-passion murder did not qualify as murder with malice. Could you, then, be so far gone in liquor that you could not make the grade as a first-degree murderer?

Terrence Hammill was indicted for murdering his wife on New Year's Day, 1855 in New York. He was found in his house "in the act of stamping upon his wife," who died a few minutes later. Her body "exhibited marks of the most brutal violence, the head and chest being covered with bruises and blood." The prisoner, "who wore heavy iron-nailed shoes," had stamped her to death. Both of them were completely drunk at the time; an empty liquor bottle was found at the scene.[93]

The prosecution accused Hammill of cold-blooded murder; the de-

---

* Another example was the trial of Clara Fallmer, in Alameda County, California, in 1897. Clara was fifteen years old and pregnant; she shot her lover, Charles LaDue, who refused to marry her. The defense was that she shot her lover "during a state of emotional insanity." The jury acquitted her.[91]

fense urged a lesser charge, "manslaughter in the second degree." Hammill's lawyers tried to show that he was a man of "excellent character, unusually industrious and frugal," and "kind, attentive and affectionate to all of his family." Usually he was "strictly temperate." But when he did drink, what a difference: he became "infuriated and ungovernable, attacking any one who came in his way." The judge charged the jury that drunkenness as such was no excuse for a crime. But the drunkenness was not irrelevant. It bore on the question of intent: Did he mean to kill his wife? If his judgment was "in part obscured and his only intention was to severely beat his wife but with no thoughts of death," the jury might, if it wished, convict him of a lesser crime than murder. And so they did: they came back with a verdict of manslaughter in the second degree.[94]

These cases are still another reflex of the nineteenth-century emphasis on discipline and self-control. These traits were precious but fragile; when a person gave in to liquor, drugs, sex, and other forms of intemperance, he exposed body and soul to awful dangers. To indulge was, of course, blameworthy; but people were also ready and willing to believe that the liquor, drugs, and sex robbed you of your mind, your freedom, your very self. In an interesting case in Massachusetts, in 1827, a boy of thirteen was indicted for stealing a watch from a shopkeeper named Harvey McClenathan. McClenathan had sold the boy, Thaddeus French, a cigar; he also admitted selling the lad "three cents worth of *Tom and Jerry*"—a "liquor . . . composed of eggs and sugar, beaten together with ginger, allspice, nutmeg, and salaeratus, to which was added a portion of rum, brandy or gin to suit the purchaser." He sold this concoction "to all who wanted it, children as well as men."[95]

This was a serious admission. The judge, Peter Thacher, told the jury it was their duty to acquit if they believed the boy had been "put into a state of mental derangement" by virtue of the "noxious liquor" and the cigar. It was an "immoral act" to sell to children "such a vile composition, and it might well have happened that the combined influence of the liquor and cigar, on a child of so tender years, would produce a temporary insanity." The lesson was not lost on the jury; they dutifully came back with a verdict of acquittal.[96]

7

THE MECHANICS OF POWER II: PROFESSIONALIZATION AND REFORM IN THE LATE NINETEENTH CENTURY

THE POLICE, AS WE HAVE SEEN, WERE ESSENTIALLY AN INVENTION OF THE FIRST half of the century. In the latter half of the century, police departments were all over the map, and the old, more slipshod ways of patrolling urban (as well as rural) spaces were gone forever. Big cities had big forces; little cities had little forces. New York City was, naturally, the giant; according to the census of 1880, the city, with a population of about 1,200,000, had a force of 202 officers and 2,336 patrolmen; Kalamazoo, Michigan, with a population of 11,937, had one officer and two patrolmen (they made 175 arrests); Keokuk, Iowa, with a population of 12,117, had two officers and four patrolmen (who chalked up 1,276 arrests).[1] If we can believe the census figures, there were, all told, in 1880, 1,752 officers and 11,948 patrolmen in cities and towns with inhabitants of 5,000 or more.[2]

It was still the case—especially in big cities—that American police departments were more overtly political than, say, in England. In this country, police officers were "primarily tools of local politicians"; when the winds of politics changed, during or between elections, jobs and policy changed with it. In Cincinnati, for example, 219 of 295 patrolmen were dismissed after the election of 1880; six years later, after another election, 238 of 289 patrolmen, and 8 of the 16 lieutenants lost their jobs.[3]

Since local politics in many big cities meant, primarily, Democratic Party politics, the Republicans, who represented business and controlled more statehouses, found the idea of state control over the police unusually attractive. The state did take control over some cities (New York in 1857, Detroit in 1865, Cleveland in 1866, for example), but when the outs (the Democrats) regained office, they turned back the clock. Local control remained the general rule.[4]

That is, if there was any control at all. It would be a gross exaggeration to call the police "professionals." The job had no prerequisites and called for no formal training whatsoever. The man on the beat was, most of the time, entirely on his own; there was no real supervision. Nothing kept a patrolman from drinking in a tavern, or sleeping on the job. There was a long struggle to bring the policeman to heel. Rule books and codes of conduct sprouted. In 1861, the police commissioners of Chicago issued orders that "prohibited mustaches, prescribed the proper style for beards, and required that all patrolmen eat with forks."[5] A military model was the ideal: clean, disciplined, regimented. Some cities instituted military drill. City after city put their police in uniform—Jersey City (1856), Washington, D.C. (1858), New Orleans (1866), Kansas City, Missouri (1874). Every big city, and most middle-sized cities, followed suit. Terre Haute, Indiana, which made the move in 1897, was one of the last.[6]

The uniform symbolized discipline, military precision, and the like; but it had other functions. It made the police very much a *visible* presence in the community. This was in line with the basic function of the police: to keep order in public places, to deter crimes of disorder by patrolling urban spaces. People think of the police as crime-fighters; but order is, and probably was then, their prime goal.

Order is definitely the aim of the traffic cop today; and the thousands of arrests for vagrancy, drunkenness, and disturbing the peace are supposed to guarantee order and discipline on the streets, roads, and open spaces of the city. This can be rough work at times, and hardly fit the more refined notions of due process. That concept has changed a lot over the years, but even in the nineteenth century there was some grumbling about police behavior. A lawyer in Detroit, in 1880, told the press that "Men have for years been arrested . . . 'on suspicion,' confined for days and nights in a station house where nobody is allowed to . . . communicate with him, and finally . . . 'discharged' in the same arbitrary manner," while no police judge or court would take notice of the incident.[7] In Milwaukee, in the late nineteenth century, the police "maintained a rigid policy of arresting potential criminals on 'suspicion' and running them out of town." If the police suspected a man of some property crime but could not prove it, they locked him up, investigated, and then ordered the man out of town.[8]

One can be sure that it was not the wealthy or the powerful who were arrested "on suspicion" and thrown into jail cells. This was also true of some (but not all) arrests for drunkenness. Drunkenness was technically a minor crime or offense. The police did not treat drunks as threats to society; after all, most police got drunk themselves once in a while. But they cleared them off the streets, or dragged them out of bars where they were brawling—or even from their homes, when they made trouble for the family. When the drunken husband of Mrs. Annie Hules, of Alameda County, locked her and her baby out of the house in 1891, she, of course, called the police.[9]

The police tended to treat the ordinary drunkard with a kind of amused, vacant paternalism. It was important to arrest drunks, sober them up, and keep the streets in shape for respectable people. Often, the police infantilized drunks, who were mostly laborers, and often immigrants; they treated their offenses with malicious humor. This was also the attitude of the newspapers, when they reported the goings on in police court. It was, in a sense, a big joke. Laughing at drunks and skid row bums was one way to avoid taking the problem seriously.

The police also acted as a kind of catchall or residual welfare agency. This was a period in which the state (from a twentieth-century point of view) was lax and anemic. Besides, the civil service closes up shop at five o'clock and is nowhere to be found on weekends and holidays, or even at lunchtime. The eye of the police never closes. Even today, when in doubt about whom to call, people call the police. All the more so in the nineteenth century. Thus, in Oakland, California, in 1894, when people in a neighborhood fell into "a state of violent excitement" because a ghost appeared in an empty house, along with much shrieking, groaning, and clanking of chains, they called the police to get rid of it.[10]

Ghost-busting was not a common police function, of course. But the policeman's lot was a most miscellaneous one. The Boston police, during the fiscal year ending November 30, 1887, made (we are told) 30,681 arrests. But, in addition, there were

1,472 accidents reported; 2,461 buildings found open and made secure . . . 37 dangerous chimneys reported; 169 dead bodies cared for; 181 defective cesspools reported; 66 defective drains reported . . . 138 defective hydrants reported; 2,611 defective lamps reported; 4 defective sewers reported; 13,614 defective streets and walks reported . . . 148 intoxicated persons assisted; 1,572 lost children found; 269 insane persons taken in charge; 228

missing persons reported; 151 missing persons found . . . 7 persons rescued from drowning; 1,673 sick and injured persons assisted; 311 stray teams found; 51,302 street obstructions removed.[11]

It was common for police to run a sort of primitive welfare program. They collected and returned lost children; they gave shelter to the homeless.[12] How much the police did seemed to vary a good deal from city to city. In 1880, in New York City, there were 124,318 "lodgers" in the station houses; in Philadelphia, 109,673; Cincinnati, with about one-fifth the population of New York City, housed 47,658 of the homeless; St. Louis housed none.[13] In Philadelphia, the homeless usually got tea and crackers to sustain them. Not everybody was lucky enough to find a place in the station house, even in the generous cities; the "undeserving" could be simply turned away.

The crowd of ragged, hungry people "had a dreadful impact on the station houses"; they became filthy bedlams. There is a vivid description of tramps "crashing" in a Chicago station house in the winter of 1891: "an unventilated atmosphere of foulest pollution . . . the frowzy, ragged garments of unclean men. . . . Not a square foot of the dark, concrete floor is visible. The space is packed with men all lying on their right sides with their legs drawn up"; the men used newspapers for mattresses, wet jackets and boots for pillows; the whole place was crawling with lice.[14] Finally, toward the end of the century, cities began to build municipal lodging houses. Here conditions were often even worse; but at least it freed police stations from the job of serving as welfare hotels.[15]

Eric Monkkonen connects the end of the lodging-house era with a major overall shift in police function: from "class control" to "crime control." At first, the police had been mainly concerned "with the orderly functioning of cities"; next, with the control of "the dangerous class," which meant, not just criminals but a motley group of people from the lower orders, including the urban poor and tramps; then, finally, at the very end of the nineteenth and into the twentieth century, came the relative shift to "crime control." The police withdrew from their intimate *working* connection with the poor and their neighborhoods.[16] This change in the basic tasks of the police was, perhaps, a kind of side effect of one aspect of progressivism, the movement to make the police more rational, bureaucratic, and professional.

As the police gave up (hardly unwillingly) their dirty and repulsive role as landlords of the homeless, their relationship to the community became more complicated—and more ambivalent. Police and public, as Samuel Walker put it, were in a situation of "mutual disrespect and brutality."[17] The police were sometimes brutal on the streets; and they did not treat men in the station house with kid gloves, to put it mildly. Torture and brutality— the so-called third degree[18]—were common. The police had their ways of making people talk. We hear about the "sweat box," after the Civil War. This was "a cell in close proximity to a stove, in which a scorching fire was built and fed with old bones, pieces of rubber shoes, etc., all to make great heat and offensive smells, until the sickened and perspiring inmate of the cell confessed in order to get released."[19] The law books said nothing about sweat boxes; they were part of a police underground. There were even more direct methods of forcing and punishing: fists, blackjacks, clubs.

All this was only semisecret. The police were, in fact, proud of their physical directness. George Walling, a former chief of New York's police, called the force "the finest organization of its kind, . . . better trained, more athletic, more resolute and hardy"; it also enjoyed "unusual liberty of action." He sneered at the British police, hamstrung by legal niceties: "A band of pickpockets may rush through a crowd at Hyde Park . . . but the police are powerless. A howling mob of ten or twenty thousand rascals may gather in Trafalgar Square with the declared intention of sacking Buckingham Palace, but the police can only stand round, waiting for the commission of some illegal act." Not so in New York! A New York police officer "knows he has been sworn in to 'keep the peace,' and he keeps it. There's no 'shilly-shallying' with him. . . . He can and does arrest on suspicion." Moreover, "the men are given to understand that their actions, when governed by a desire for the public good, will be protected and upheld by the courts."[20]

Walling's instincts were probably sound. The respectable public, including the legal public, surely liked strong action, directness, force. Few members of the respectable middle class were arrested; hence few of them felt the blackjack or the fist of a patrolman—or suffered from police gunfire.[21] And the opinion was abroad, that evil was strong and ubiquitous, that fire had to be fought with fire. To be sure, there were limits to public tolerance. But the public chose, in general, not to know. Police tactics also varied a good deal from place to place. In Detroit, incidents of brutality were (apparently) not very common; although in 1874, a ward collector and his sons claimed they were beaten by police. There were only fifty-two claims of physical abuse over a twenty-year period in Detroit. But drunks and hoboes, as John Schneider points out, do not usually complain about brutality; and if they do, nobody pays attention.[22]

Many people, too, were willing to shut their eyes to a certain amount of police corruption. Again, only up to a point. In part, it depended on whose ox was goared. The party out of power was always more eager to expose corruption and brutality than the party in power. Politics was behind many police exposés, including the most famous, the so-called

Lexow investigation (1894). The target here was the police department of New York City.

Whatever its motivations, the special committee of the New York legislature turned over a lot of stones and brought to light a lot of creeping, crawling creatures. Election fraud, for one thing: the police had committed "almost every conceivable crime against the elective franchise" for the sake of Tammany Hall, that is, the "dominant Democratic organization of the city of New York." The police arrested and brutalized Republican voters; they stuffed ballot boxes, or let it happen; they wallowed in "oppression, fraud, trickery [and] crime."[23]

The Lexow Committee found widespread corruption, too, in law enforcement. In "most precincts of the city, houses of ill-repute, gambling houses, policy shops, pool rooms, and unlawful resorts of a similar character" were "openly conducted" under the noses of the police. The reason, of course, was a massive pattern of payoffs. Even "legitimate business" had to pay its toll. An illegal business, like that of "Mrs. Herreman, who had kept a number of houses of ill-repute in the fifteenth precinct," had to pay even more—some $30,000 over the years, which brought Mrs. Herreman "protection." In general, brothels were subject to "blackmail"; indeed, there was a systematic scale of payments, including "initiation fees" for start-ups, and a monthly rate based on the number of rooms or inmates. The police also tolerated poolrooms and and policy shops; they permitted "professional abortionists . . . to ply their awful trade"; they even collected from "boot-blacks, push-cart and fruit venders, as well as keepers of soda water stands, corner grocerymen, sailmakers with flag-poles extending a few feet beyond the place which they occupy," merchants who were "compelled to use the sidewalk and street"—small business that might be violating some minor ordinance, or who needed help or protection. All of them had to "contribute . . . to the vast amounts which flow into the station-houses, and which, after leaving something of the nature of a deposit, then flow on higher."[24]

Some policemen were incredibly brutal and callous. Victims paraded before the committee: "The eye of one man, punched out by a patrolman's club, hung on his cheek." One journalist had been "assaulted . . . with brass knuckles while he was a prisoner in the station-house." The police, it seems, "formed a separate and highly privileged class, armed with the authority and the machinery for oppression," and yet free themselves from any criminal responsibility. In some cases, the police combined extortion with brutality: there was the case, for example, of "Mrs. Urchittel, a humble Russian Jewess, ignorant of our tongue, an honest and impoverished widow with three small children." A detective "falsely accused" her of keeping a disorderly house; she was arrested, and dragged through the streets; when she did not come up with enough money for the detective's payoff, she was arrested again, and convicted on perjured testimony. She fell ill, her children were taken by the Society for the Prevention of Cruelty to Children, and she lost her home.[25]

Despite the scandals, the publicity, the headlines, the outrage, the exposés, police corruption and brutality had remarkable survival power. In city after city, the police were on the take. Saloonkeepers in Chicago and Boston were asked regularly for "contributions."[26] Everywhere, police were involved "in a systematic pattern of payoffs from drinking, gambling, and prostitution," and (as in New York City) voting fraud. The system of corruption, as Samuel Walker puts it, "was inherent in the fact that the police were largely a political institution."[27] It was inherent, too, in the Victorian compromise itself; and perhaps even more so after the breakdown of that compromise—the stakes became higher, the payoffs greater. The basic problem was the demand for vice. Cities were nests of vice, because vice had a huge clientele. Enough people lusted after gambling, hard liquor, and prostitution to support the cost of buying off the law.

The Decline of the Classic Penitentiary

Ultimately, the police were a success story of sorts; police departments probably played a role in reducing serious crime and disorder in the country, despite politics, oppression, incompetence, and corruption. The penitentiary system was another story.

The *idea* of the penitentiary—grim, total, silent; a monastery for criminals—gained many new converts; the idea spread from city to city, state to state. By the time of the Civil War, the newfangled penitentiary system was in place throughout the North and Midwest; the whipping post was only a memory, except in a few places (tiny Delaware was one holdout). The gallows remained, of course, but was used only for the most serious crimes. The convicted felon was simply thrown into prison; that was his fate. And the prison was modeled after the great eastern penitentiaries. Michigan Territory, for example, built a prison at Jackson in 1839, copied from the paragons in New York.* Even in the South, some states fell into line and built penitentiaries.[29]

But decay set in almost immediately in most prisons—almost as soon as the last brick was laid and the prison opened for business. The silent system, for example, had little staying power. Silence meant one-man

---

* In Wisconsin, the state at first could afford only a log structure at Waupun (1851); but it was equipped with individual cells, each with an iron door that could be transferred to a stone prison when such a prison might be built.[28]

one-cell; but solitary confinement was an expensive luxury. Men were sentenced to prison faster than the state built new cells and cellblocks. In the Massachusetts State Prison, the silent system, in its extreme form, was gone by the 1850s.[30] In Missouri, a prison opened in Jefferson City in 1836 with forty cells, which seemed enough at the time. By 1847, there were two and three men to a cell, and the governor was arguing that this posed no difficulty.[31] The silent system lingered in theory in many prisons; but its classic purity—and its effectiveness—was long since gone. When Hutchins Hapgood arrived in Sing Sing, late in the nineteenth century, prisoners still ate dinner "in dead silence. Silence, indeed, except on the sly, was the general rule of our day, until work was over, when we could whisper together until five o'clock, the hour to return to our cells."[32]

Money was the problem, or one of the problems. Austere, silent prisons were expensive; it was cheaper to let them get noisy and crowded. Even worse, states could not resist the temptation to make money off prisoners, which was difficult in the classic penitentiary. Illinois passed a law in 1845 leasing the penitentiary at Alton "and the labor of the convicts" to Samuel A. Buckmaster. Buckmaster was to pay a bonus of $5,100, the "usual fees of the inspectors," and furnish "at his own expense, the necessary guards and food, clothing, beds and bedding, and necessary bills of physicians for the convicts." He could use convicts to manufacture "hempen articles." Buckmaster continued as lessee until 1857, when he was replaced by S. A. Casey. Only in 1871 was the leasing system discontinued.[33] California tried a leasing system, too, in the 1850s;[34] and it became standard practice in the South.

There had been flirtations with leasing in the South before the Civil War; but the golden age of leasing came afterward. Before the Civil War, most prisoners in the South were white, not black; blacks were overwhelmingly slaves, and they were whipped and sent back to work (or hanged in more serious cases). After the war, the prisons filled with blacks—to be precise, young black men. In Virginia, in 1871, there were 828 prisoners in the state penitentiary; 609 of these were black men, 63 were black women; there were 152 white men, and 4 white women.[35] In Georgia, as of October 1, 1899, there were 2,201 state prisoners; no less than 1,885 of them were black men (68 were black women); only 3 white women were in prison, and 245 white men.[36] The ages of prisoners ranged from eleven to seventy-three—there were twelve boys and one girl under the age of fifteen—but the bulk of the prisoners were in their late teens and twenties. Half of the prisoners were completely illiterate.[37]

Racial facts powerfully influenced southern penal policy. In many parts of the South, it was not the prison that was put in private hands to manage, but the prisoners. Contractors got bodies, to be housed in work camps and made to slave away in mines, or swamps, or on the railroads. These prisoners were, of course, overwhelmingly black. Conditions were harsh and brutal. They slept at night in "filthy shacks. Men with capital, from the North as well as the South, bought these years of convicts' lives. The largest mining and railroad companies in the region as well as small-time businessmen scrambled to win the leases." In extreme cases, the "crumbling antebellum penitentiaries" were abandoned except for a few white murderers, black men too sick to work profitably, and women of both races.[38] Meanwhile, in the camps, men died like flies. In 1881, in Virginia, the death rate inside the penitentiary was 1.5 percent per year; in camps run by contractors for the Richmond and Allegheny Railroad, the death rate was 11 percent.[39] Even worse death rates, as we have seen (chapter 4), occurred on some southern chain gangs.

The leasing system was in local use as well. Throughout the South, prisoners convicted of petty crimes sweated their lives away in work gangs, laboring either for the county or municipality, or for private contractors. Crime, as Edward Ayers put it, became a kind of asset to the counties. They made money on the deal.[40] Conditions were, as usual, subhuman. One month in 1893, 160 black males (men and boys), along with 26 black women—and only 11 whites, 2 of them women—were working "from dawn to dark building a canal" for Chatham County, Alabama, slaving in the muck of the ditches, buried up to their knees. No wonder so many prisoners died; or that a young man (a white), who had been caught stealing a hat in a barroom, tried to cut his throat with "an old piece of iron barrel hoop" after three days on the chain gang.[41]

In the North and West, the prisons were still purveying, in theory, a stern, relentless system of discipline; they were supposed to be a kind of reformatory for the criminal class, severe but just. There was no thought of returning, officially, to the helter-skelter methods of the older jails. The ideology of stern but just reformation kept some of its zest. The South Dakota statute on prisons imposed on warden and officers the duty to treat their charges "uniformly" and with "kindness." This did not mean coddling. The convict was to eat "wholesome coarse food, with such proportions of meat and vegetables as the warden shall deem best." If a convict violated the rules, he could be sent to a "solitary cell" and "fed on bread and water"; on the other hand, no cruel or corporal punishment was (officially) allowed.[42] In Rhode Island, the law required an under keeper to inspect each cell daily to see that meals were "regularly furnished" and that the "cell and all its contents" were in "good order." Each prisoner was entitled to a "change of underclothing . . . at least once a week."[43]

Real life inside the walls was very different. In some instances, the regimen broke down, and discipline turned to flab. At Sing Sing, in the 1870s, corruption was rife; a prisoner could buy forbidden items from guards; convicts lolled about in the yard, which had "something of the atmosphere of a village."[44] More generally, real life meant filth and degradation. In the state prison of New Jersey, as described in 1867, prisoners lived as many as four to a cell, in cells measuring seven by twelve feet; the newer cells were only four feet wide and seven feet long. Real life was lived "in a room the size of a small bathroom, with a noisome bucket for a toilet and a cot narrower than a bathtub." A prisoner might bathe "occasionally" in a bathhouse in the yard, "which was closed in bad weather."[45] Wardens and guards, in many prisons, whipped prisoners liberally to keep them in line, regardless of what the statutes said.

There were other ways, too, to punish the convict's body. In New York, we hear about a practice called "bucking"; the convict sat with an iron bar between his legs and his wrists fastened down with chains. In Sing Sing, some inmates in the 1870s were hanged by the thumbs. In Ohio, there was the "humming-bird," an electric shock administered while a steam whistle blew. The cold-water bath was another trick of the trade in Ohio: the convict was tied to a chair or post, and buckets of ice water were poured over his head. Or the prisoner might be "blindfolded and lifted into a large vat filled with water."[46]

Prisoners were supposed to work; work was a tool of reformation. It was also a way to make prisons pay for themselves. The trick was to put prisoners to work on something the state could profitably sell. But this made prisoners direct competitors of organized labor; this provoked a bitter political struggle in state after state. The California constitution of 1879 included a clause against convict labor. The Illinois constitution was amended in 1866 to make it "unlawful . . . to let by contract . . . the labor of any convict." Under the Michigan Constitution of 1850, as amended, convicts were not to be taught any "mechanical trade" except the "manufacture of those articles of which the chief supply for home consumption is imported from other States or countries." A Pennsylvania statute of 1883 required convict-made goods to be branded as such, in "plain English lettering," and the brand had to be put "upon the most conspicuous place upon such article."[47] Some states tried to turn prison labor to political or economic advantage: in Minnesota, in the 1890s, prisons were directed to manufacture twine, to be sold to farmers. In this way, farmers would be helped in their struggle with the National Cordage Company, which the farmers considered one of the worst of the "trusts."[48]

Most often, however, it was out-and-out war between the unions and prison labor, which unions regarded as a vicious scab tactic, a strikebreaking, union-busting tool. In New Jersey, New York, and New England, prisoners manufactured hats, which made them economic enemies of hatters. In 1878, New Jersey banned hatmaking in state prison; and campaigns in New York, Connecticut, and Rhode Island in the next few years were successful in cutting down prison production.[49] Shoe manufacturers and workers, too, put aside their industrial differences to protest against the making of shoes in prisons.

Penology and Reform

The prison story, in general, was a story of failure; at any rate, it was *seen* as a failure. Yet there was no going back. Imprisonment was and remained the basic way to punish men and women convicted of serious crimes. The great penitentiaries were not pulled down. There they stood—corrupt and brutal; warehouses for convicts. Prisons did not seem to end crime, or cure criminals. A warden at the Auburn prison in New York told Zebulon Brockway, the penologist and prison reformer, "that in his opinion 60 per cent of his prisoners were as sure to resume crimes as they were sure to be discharged from prison; that another 30 per cent would in all probability do the same; and as to the remainder he could not form a confident opinion."[50] This did not leave many souls actually saved.

Whether this pessimism was justified or not is, in a way, beside the point. It attested to the wreckage of hopes. What was to be done? In the last third or so of the century, there was a fresh wave of penal reform. The basic aim of the reforms was to separate out, somehow, the men and women who could be detached from a life of crime. Correctional policy should punish the incorrigibles severely; but it should give those who could be salvaged a chance to start a new life.

The "good time" laws were one innovation. There was a law of this type in New York, as early as 1817; but most "good time" laws were passed after 1850; by 1869, twenty-three states had some version on their books.[51] A prisoner who behaved got "time off" for his good behavior. Under the Illinois law of 1872, a prisoner who kept his nose clean shaved a month off a one-year sentence; a two-year term shrank to one year and nine months, a ten-year term to six years and three months, and a twenty-year term to eleven years and three months.[52] Of course, this gave a powerful weapon of control to prison officials. To forfeit "good time" was a terrible penalty.

The indeterminate sentence was another, more striking device. This was the pet project of many penal reformers, especially those active in the National Prison Association, a kind of trade association of prison officials and penologists. The Association grew out of a meeting in

Cincinnati (October 12–18, 1870) of a "National Congress on Penitentiary and Reformatory Discipline." Zebulon Brockway and Reverend
E. C. Wines were among the leaders of the movement. The Association
became the mouthpiece for reform proposals. Sentencing methods were
an early object of its attention; at the Cincinnati meeting, Reverend
Wines put forward the "principle that imprisonment ought to be continued till reformation has been effected, and, if that happy consummation
is never attained, then during the prisoner's natural life." This, Wines
said, was the "conviction" of a large number of penologists.[53]

The indeterminate sentence carried out this simple idea. When a man
or woman was convicted of a crime, the judge should no longer fix the
sentence by himself. Rather, the criminal would go to prison for an indefinite period—until he was ready to be foisted back on the world. As
an anonymous prisoner wrote in 1911, the offender should stay behind
bars "until cured, just as a person suffering from physical disease or infection is sent to a hospital or asylum, to remain for such period as may
be necessary for his restoration to health."[54] It followed, of course, as Dr.
Wines put it, that if a man was truly incurable, criminally speaking, he
might as well stay in prison for the rest of his life. Definite sentences,
said Wines, "are never reformatory"; they are "founded on the character
of the act, which is past . . . and is therefore irrevocable. Reformatory
sentences can be based only upon the character of the actor, which it is
desired to correct." But the time "required to alter it cannot be estimated in advance, any more than we can tell how long it will take for a
lunatic to recover from an act of insanity."[55] Richard Dugdale, thinking
of the horrible example of the "Jukes," felt that "extinction" of the
criminal "race" was necessary "where we cannot accomplish individual
cure." Habitual criminals produce a "noisome progeny either by the
propagation or perversion of a coming generation." They must be
"sternly . . . cut off." In the old days, society tried to do this "by hanging; but for us it must be perpetual imprisonment, with certain mitiga-
tions to guard against barbarity."[56]

Of course, the indeterminate sentence never went to its theoretical
extreme. It was never completely indeterminate; it was never the law
that a criminal, so long as he seemed degenerate enough or incorrigible
enough, could be sentenced to a life in prison, even for stealing a
chicken. The indeterminate sentence was always tinged with compromise and nuance. Practically speaking, the first important law was New
York's, in 1877. Under this law, courts were no longer supposed to "fix
or limit the duration" of sentences for young offenders about to be sent
to the reformatory at Elmira. Rather, the board of managers of that institution were to grade the prisoners, as if they were schoolchildren. The
prisoners were to learn useful trades; and they were to be divided into

groups or classes. Prisoners who behaved themselves and showed promise were moved from lower to higher categories. If a prisoner amassed enough "marks or credits," it was a sign he was fit to leave the institution; the board had the power to set the young man free.[57]

Other states followed and expanded the idea. The typical indeterminate-sentence law prescribed a minimum sentence—usually one year—for serious crimes. The judge, however, did not fix a maximum; the prison board, at the end of the minimum term, would do that job. The decision would be based, in theory, on the way the prisoner behaved in prison, among other factors. The Illinois statute, passed in 1899, listed some factors the warden could take into account. They included "early social influences" relevant to the prisoner's "constitutional and acquired defects and tendencies." The warden was also supposed to take "minutes of observed improvement or deterioration of character." The state's attorney and the convicting judge had to furnish the board with whatever they knew about the "habits, associates, disposition and reputation" of the prisoner, and, in general, whatever facts might "throw any light on the question as to whether such prisoner is capable of again becoming a law-abiding citizen."[58] In 1901, New York made the indeterminate sentence mandatory for all first offenders.[59]

The indeterminate sentence pointed in two directions: leniency and rehabilitation for the savable; eternal damnation for the rest. "Habitual criminal" laws focused on the latter point. It was, in fact, a fairly old idea to heap additional punishment on two-time or many-time losers; even some colonial statutes had done so. There was a flurry of enactment in the last part of the nineteenth century. Penal reform was both carrot and stick, and "habitual criminal" laws were part of the stick. Under an Ohio law of 1885, a third felony conviction booted a convict into the category of "habitual criminal." After his regular sentence expired, instead of going free, he could be detained in prison "for and during his natural life."[60] In New York, if a first offense carried a possible term of more than five years, a second conviction would bring a prison term of not less than *ten* years.[61] In a few cases, habitual criminals argued that these rough sentences were illegal, unconstitutional—either as a kind of double jeopardy, or as cruel and unusual punishment. Appellate courts made short work of these arguments.[62]

Parole was another reform of the period. Parole is a form of conditional release; there were some traces of it early in the century; and the English "ticket-of-leave" was essentially the same idea. But parole blossomed only in the late nineteenth century, that is, the period after 1870.[63] The concept was discussed at the National Congress of Penitentiary and Reformatory Discipline (October 1870); it caught on, and more than half the states had some form of parole law by the end of the nineteenth century. The Ohio statute (1885) gave authority to the board of managers of the Ohio prison to set up a plan under which any prisoner (except a murderer) who had served his minimum term might be "allowed to go upon parole outside of the buildings and enclosures, but to remain, while on parole, in the legal custody and under the control of the board, and subject at any time to be taken back."[64]

Parole was a way to correct for inequities in sentencing. More important, it was still another way to sift worthy from unworthy prisoners, and give the worthy ones a chance to prove themselves.[65] Parole had some very discretionary features. The rules and regulations in Ohio limited parole to prisoners who had been "in the first grade continuously for a period of at least four months." A parolee had to have a job waiting for him. He could be put back in prison "for any reason that shall be satisfactory to the board of managers, and at their sole discretion." No lawyer (or anyone else, for that matter) was allowed to present "oral argument" at parole hearings; the prisoner could submit only written documents.[66]

Parole took some political heat off the governor, however, by reducing the (political) demand for clemency. Governors had previously held (and continued to hold) the power to pardon. In some states, governors used the power lavishly, so that a high percentage of prisoners went free early through this route. DeWitt Clinton, in his eight years as governor of New York (1817–22 and 1825–28), pardoned 2,289 prisoners.[67]

The pardon was a matter of grace and favor. No rules bound the governor; there were no guidelines. The governor might, and sometimes did, respond to appeals to his sympathy; or to whims; or to political pressures or cronyism. All in all, the process disfavored the "poor and friendless," or the "miserable foreigner." The executive ear never heard their "groans"; he pardoned, instead, "the rich, the intelligent, the powerful villains." These were the men who had friends, who employed "agents," and who made use of their "property, talents, and influence" to pry open the prison door.[68] Parole, on the other hand, was, in theory, controlled by professionals, using rational criteria. No doubt in practice it, too, worked against the poor and friendless, but more subtly.

Another correctional reform was *probation*. A convicted criminal who gets probation is released conditionally before he ever sets foot in a prison or jail. The pioneer in the history of probation was a Boston bootmaker named John Augustus. In August 1841, Augustus noted and took pity on a poor drunk who was desperate to avoid the House of Correction and swore he would go on the wagon. Augustus gave him that chance by posting bail. Augustus then began to act as a "private angel and guardian of men convicted of crime." Before he died, in 1859, he went bail for about two thousand convicts.[69] By that time, he was not alone: others had joined in the campaign. In 1878, Massachusetts formalized the system and provided for a paid probation officer in the criminal courts; in 1891, another statute authorized a statewide system. Several other states followed suit in the late nineteenth and early twentieth centuries. California, for example, passed its own version in 1903.[70]

Juvenile Justice

Young offenders were a special problem for the criminal justice system. At any rate, they were defined as such. It began to strike many people as barbarous to lock juveniles up in the same prisons as "hardened criminals"; or to lock them up at all. A prison was bound to be nothing but a school for learning vice.

To be sure, the law did not consider *very* young children capable of committing crime. There was a "conclusive" presumption that a child under seven could not have a criminal mind, and could not be put on trial. Between seven and fourteen, "the law also deems the child incapable, but only *prima facie* so, and evidence may be received to show a criminal capacity"—that is, the child could be tried for an offense if the state could show that he or she had, in fact, a "guilty knowledge of wrong doing."[71] From age fourteen on, the state could try children on a par with adults.

And try them it did, in a great many cases. In 1880, more than two thousand young people in the United States were listed as inmates in prisons and jails.[72] In 1895, Governor Atkinson of Georgia pardoned William Whitlock, who had been sentenced to twelve months in the chain gang; Whitlock was "about thirteen years of age," and "a simple, weak-minded boy." Hardy Bragg, convicted of arson and sentenced to three years, was "only twelve years of age," and had been "induced" to commit his crime "by an adult relative"; he, too, was pardoned.[73] In 1899, Cora Hicks, an eleven-year old black girl, was put on trial in Durham County, North Carolina; the charge was murder; the victim, a black infant who had been burnt to death. The jury convicted Cora Hicks of second-degree murder and she was sentenced to seven years in the state penitentiary.[74]

Institutional efforts to change the system of juvenile justice began in New York, Boston, and Philadelphia in the 1820s. New York State issued a charter in 1824 to a group of inhabitants "desirous of establishing a . . . house of refuge"; the courts had the power of committing to this house "all such children, who shall be taken up or committed as vagrants, or convicted of criminal offences."[75] These houses of refuge were curious hybrid institutions; a New York visitor, James Dixon, called the New York refuge "half prison and half school." The inmates were a mixed group—destitute and orphaned children, as well as children convicted of crime.[76] De Tocqueville and Beaumont, on their tour of American penal institutions, gave the houses a hearty stamp of approval. It did not bother them that some children had committed no crime but had been sent away "by way of precaution." Was this a violation of rights? They did not think so. It was, rather, a necessary evil. Outside the institution, the life these children led carried with it the seeds of their destruction. And these "boys and girls" were "dangerous to society and to themselves: orphans, who have been led by misery to vagrancy; children, abandoned by their parents and who lead a disordered life; all those, in one word, who . . . have fallen into a state bordering on crime." The houses "alleviated" the fate of these young unfortunates "instead of aggravating it." The children "brought into it without being convicted" were not "victims of persecution" at all; they were merely deprived of what the authors called, in a striking phrase we noted in the introduction, "a fatal liberty."[77]

Reformers were enthusiastic about the house; but we rarely hear what the customers thought. Hutchins Hapgood, who was sent to the New York House of Refuge late in the century, was blunt in his judgments: the House of Refuge was a "school for crime. Unspeakably bad habits were contracted there. The older boys wrecked the younger ones." It was especially hard on children "confined for the crime of being orphans." The boys, when they were not corrupting each other, slaved away making overalls; they were frequently beaten. "I say without hesitation that lads sent to an institution like the House of Refuge, the Catholic Protectory, or the Juvenile Asylum might better be taken out and shot."[78]

To outsiders, however, the houses of refuge seemed like a step in the right direction. Reform schools, as alternatives to prison, were the next stage. Massachusetts passed a law in 1847 creating a State Reform School for Boys. This was for boys under sixteen who had been convicted of any offense. They could be bound out as apprentices or servants, or kept in the school, to be instructed in "piety and morality," in "useful knowledge," and trained in "some regular course of labor."[79] In 1855, the state created a sister institution, the State Reform School for Girls, "for the instruction . . . and reformation, of exposed, helpless, evil disposed and vicious girls."[80] Other states set up similar establishments. New York law (1875) authorized "houses of detention" for women and juveniles (that is, boys and girls under sixteen); women, girls, and boys waiting for trial or held as witnesses could be committed to a house of detention rather than a jail.[81]

In other states, private "industrial schools" were authorized to take in children in need, or who had committed crimes. By 1887, there were four of these schools in Chicago, two for boys (one Protestant, one Catholic), and two for girls (one Protestant, one Catholic).[82]* As of 1889, the City and County Industrial School of San Francisco held 122 boys and 52 girls, most of them sent by Police Court judges. All but one of the girls had been adjudged guilty of something called "leading an idle and dissolute life"; fifty-two of the boys had committed the same offense. The rest had violated the criminal code; forty-seven boys, for example, had committed petty larceny.[84]

Despite all these institutional changes, children could still be arrested, detained, tried, and sent to prison in many states. In 1870, there were 2,029 minors in jail in Massachusetts; 231 of them were under fifteen.[85] And even in states with specialized institutions, houses of refuge, reform schools, industrial schools, and the like, the *trial* process for juveniles was the same as for adults.

Specialized criminal courts for juveniles attacked this problem. The pioneer was an Illinois law (1899), which applied to Cook County only (Chicago and its suburbs). The law covered "dependent, neglected and delinquent children": specifically, any child who "is destitute or homeless or abandoned," or who "habitually begs or receives alms," or who "is found living in any house of ill fame or with any vicious or disreputable person"; also, any "child under the age of 8 years who is found peddling or selling any article or singing or playing any musical instrument upon the street or giving any public entertainment"; and any child "whose home, by reason of neglect, cruelty or depravity on the part of its parents . . . is an unfit place for such a child."[86]

The law, in short, continued the trend of lumping bad and bad-off children together. Under its terms, a circuit-court judge would sit in a separate courtroom, and keep separate records. The judge had power to put the court's wards into the proper institution or to give them probation. Timothy Hurley, president of the Chicago Visitation and Aid Society, praised the act as a "return to paternalism," words that have a somewhat ironic ring today. But to him the "paternalism" was exceedingly welcome; it meant the "acknowledgment by the State of its relationship as the parent to every child within its borders." Civilization, Hurley felt, had lost sight of this relationship, and consequently faced "utter demoralization."[87] For him, then, the juvenile court movement was a form of interventionism—made necessary because the pillars on

---

* In *County of Cook v. Chicago Industrial School for Girls* (1888), the Illinois Supreme Court dealt the system a serious blow. The Chicago Industrial School, which had no building of its own, had been placing girls in institutions run by the Roman Catholic church; this, the court said, was a violation of the constitution of Illinois, which did not allow public money to go to "sectarian" institutions. After this, the system more or less collapsed. The juvenile court act was passed, as we will see, in 1899.[83]

which society rested, including the family, had weakened so in the late nineteenth century. The movement thus dovetailed neatly with the other reforms of the period, and with the upsurge in interest in traditional morality. The full story of the juvenile court movement, however, belongs to the twentieth century.

Local Jails

The newfangled devices and reform institutions were at the cutting edge of American penology. They were reforms that affected, on the whole, the great northern penitentiaries and certain special categories of offenders—notably, children. But they left virtually untouched the huge squalid mass of county and local prisons: the end of the line for thousands of men and women who were picked up for drunkenness or vagrancy, as well as brawlers, petty thieves, and countless others.

The local jails, in the aggregate, housed a considerable number of prisoners. The 1880 census counted 58,609 prisoners (not including juveniles in reformatories). Of these, 30,659 were found in penitentiaries, 7,865 in workhouses and houses of correction, 12,691 in county jails, 1,666 in city prisons, 499 in military prisons, 350 in hospitals for the insane, and 4,879 leased out to private parties as laborers.[88]

In the local jails, confusion was king, along with plain dirt and humiliation. These were the sewers and toilets of humanity. At best they were simply chaotic and neglected. In 1880, Enoch Wines described Michigan's jails as follows: "no work, no instruction, no discipline, no uniformity of structure." He pointed out, as so many had, that the innocent and the depraved were thrown together in "intimate and continuous association," the "old offender" boasting of his exploits to the "wayward youth," who drank in "the fatal poison, . . . burning with desire for similar adventures."[89] In rural Iowa, the local lockup, or jail—called the "calaboose"—was a tiny, simple building used to store drunks and tramps; offenders waited here to be dragged off to county jails, in the days before paved roads, when snow or mud made the long trip a torture. In Grand Mound, Iowa, the lockup was even used as a makeshift hotel, rented out to travelers as "an occasional low cost bed."[90]

In the cities, most people who were arrested never got further than a local jail; the "big house" was for serious crimes. If a person could not make bail, the first stop was a cell in a police station house. George Walling, writing in 1887 about New York, has vividly described the experience. Most of the men (and women) are hauled to the cells "in a state of beastly intoxication. They shout and scream and curse worse than any furies." Dumped in a "loathsome" room, cramped, with foul air, the prisoner has to spend the night on a "hard board," where "his limbs become lame and paralyzed" in a vain attempt to sleep. All around him, in other cells, are other objects of misery: a "howling Jezebel, . . . mad with liquor"; a "tender, refined, intelligent woman" who sinned out of "weakness" and who "moans and groans in her grief"; a "sobbing boy" spending his first night in jail, thinking of his mother; an old man, "half maniacal through the constant habit of drinking," tortured by "delirium tremens, and the strange creatures of his vision."[91]

The next stop for a convicted criminal in New York City might be the Ludlow Street Jail. This lacked the stern uniformity of the great prisons. One class of inmates, the "aristocrats of the jail," paid the warden fifteen dollars a week; this gave them a "respectable room" instead of a cell, and the privilege of sitting at the warden's table, "eating the luxuries of the market." A few rich prisoners paid between fifty and a hundred dollars a week; this bought a "nicely furnished room with all the luxuries"; their meals were served in their rooms and, in general, they lived "in royal style."[92]

The "non-paying boarder" was locked in a cell from seven-thirty at night, to six-thirty in the morning, when he "takes up his slop-pail and carries it down to the sink." Breakfast is brought to the cell: hunks of bread, which the prisoner grabs through the cell door as best he can, followed by coffee in a tin cup. Dinner is bread and a kind of soup, served at noon. Supper is tea and another hunk of bread.[93]

But the worst and most notorious of the jails in New York City was the prison usually known as "the Tombs." This massive building was finished in 1838, in a crazy style of architecture that vaguely resembled someone's idea of an Egyptian tomb. It had cells for both men and women. It, too, was divided into classes: there were five or six "comfortable cells," rooms with a view (of the street) for "aristocratic rogues" who could afford to "live in style."[94] Most of the prisoners, however, were far from "aristocratic"; they were, instead, members of the "disorderly or vagrant class." They appeared first in the police court, in the Tombs. Here they were, generally, found guilty and sentenced, in an "awful smelling court-room amid the dull and brutish stare of the assembled scum of the lower city wards." The cell that received them was small and damp, with a cement floor. The regimen was much the same as at Ludlow Street.

The Tombs was four stories high, and each floor was specialized. On the ground floor were "lunatics, *delirium tremens* cases, and . . . sentenced prisoners." The second tier was "Murderers' Row"; it also housed burglars, highway robbers, and "other desperate criminals." The third tier was for "prisoners arrested for grand larceny"; the fourth for "minor misdemeanors."[95]

The local jails in the South were scandalous in their own right. Here is the county "prison" of Cleveland County, North Carolina, as of 1870, as it appeared to a contemporary:

> The county prison is built of brick, and is thirty by twenty-six feet in size. It is three stories high, and has four cells for prisoners, including debtor's room; iron cage, etc. The iron cage is eight feet square and six feet high, the other part of the room twelve feet by fifteen. The other rooms for prisoners, fifteen by ten and fifteen by seven. There is one window in each room and cell, four and a half by three feet in size. There is no way of heating the prison except that of giving the prisoners in cold weather, a heated rock. There have been some of the prisoners frost-bitten during extremely cold weather. Each prisoner has allowed him, a straw bed and three blankets. The males and females are confined in different apartments. They have fresh water as often as they want it, and just as much food as they wish. The excrement is removed from the prison, and tar is often burned in the cells to take away the offensive smell.[96]

Even so, prisoners in such jails were lucky, compared to those in the work camps and chain gangs, where, as we have seen, the prisoners died like flies. In general, prison and jail conditions everywhere in the country were a scandal—hidden lesions and sores on society. They were also a lesson on the meaning of race, poverty, and lack of power—and the terrible indifference of respectable people to the miseries of life underneath their feet.

Capital Punishment in the
Late Nineteenth Century

The *formal* use of the death penalty continued to decline in the late nineteenth century. Michigan had abolished it, as a territory, in 1847, except for treason (not a major offense in Michigan); Maine got rid of it in 1876, restored it in 1883, then got rid of it for good in 1887.[97] Some states and localities continued to allow public executions, but a trend against it began in the 1830s, as we have noted. In California, public executions were banned in the 1850s; the hangman was supposed to do his dirty work discreetly, behind the sheltered walls of prisons and jails.

Executions still fascinated the public. Public executions, where they existed, were tremendous box-office hits. "Private" executions were also popular. The word *private* has to be taken with a grain of salt. These executions were, of course, not carried out in the public square, but neither were they well screened, at first, from the curious. The execution of Sam Steenburgh, on April 19, 1878, in the village of Fonda, New York, attracted about fifteen thousand visitors. "Two special trains from the east, aggregating 12 cars, and one of 7 cars, from the west" pulled in, jammed with "curiosity seekers" dressed in "holiday attire" whose ages ranged "from the . . . bent old man or woman of 70 to the child in arms"; the "sexes were quite evenly divided."[98]

Fonda had made elaborate preparations for this great event. The jail itself was a "small rectangular building of unhewn stone," located between the railroad track and the river. A high board fence had been built, enclosing a plot of turf 138 by 108 feet, on the western side of the jail. Inside this enclosure was the gallows, "a plain, upright structure . . . painted black." The condemned man was to be "jerked into the air by the fall of an iron weight of 310 pounds." The hanging "machine" had been built in 1871, and had been used in a number of New York executions. Near the river was a house with a peaked roof, and from here you could have "an excellent view of the scene." The owner, it was said, had rented out all the space, though "at fair rates."[99]

Steenburgh, a black man, had been convicted of the murder of a farmer named Jacob S. Parker; he confessed to this and many other crimes. On the morning of the execution, there was a scene of pandemonium outside the jail, beginning at nine o'clock. The weather was fine: a "gentle breeze tempered the rays of the sun." The area was "blackened with people. Stands had been erected for the sale of sandwiches, gingerbread, chewing gum and ginger-pop. . . . Hundreds of boys were dodging among the multitude crying out copies of the 'Confession.'"

Steenburgh had "slept soundly" until nine-thirty. After he dressed and "performed his ablutions," he said a prayer. His "mistress and their child" appeared at the gate; officials refused to let the woman in "for fear of unduly exciting the prisoner"; but "little Susie" did get to see her father one last time. For the execution, Steenburgh was given a "new suit of clothes and a linen shirt." At 12:50 P.M., a drum began beating and a "procession made its appearance around the corner of the jail." Soldiers marched on either side of the doomed man. At the scaffold, two priests prayed for Steenburgh's soul. Steenburgh's wrists, thighs, and ankles were bound by leather straps. Shouts and noises came from the "more disorderly of the mob" of onlookers. The sheriff asked Steenburgh if he wanted to make a last statement; Steenburgh spoke briefly, and said he was ready to die.

The noose was fitted around his neck and a black cap placed on his head. Steenburgh begged for five minutes' grace, then for ten. The crowd wanted blood. At one o'clock, the black cap was put on again; the sheriff's assistant touched "the lever with his foot," the iron weight fell with a crash, "and Steenburgh's body was jerked sideways and upward about five feet. . . . As he came down he swung and swayed from left to right for a few seconds." The newspaper lovingly recorded every twitch and contraction of the body, every detail of Steenburgh's pulse rate, until (after ten minutes) the doctors pronounced him dead. The body was lowered at 1:23 P.M. and placed in a coffin; the crowd pressed forward to look at the body.[100]

Crowds were present, in fact, at many "private" executions. Charles Guiteau, the assassin of President Garfield, went to the gallows on July 1, 1882; according to a newspaper account, the "representation of morbid sightseers was remarkably small"; yet over two hundred people crowded into the jail to watch, and hundreds more stood outside the jail, "staring."[101] When Lloyd Majors was executed in the jail yard in Oakland, California, in 1884, the streets were full of people who hoped to catch a glimpse of the show. Some of the spectators climbed on roofs; a few from atop the Sagehorn Building might have been actually able to see the event itself. The jail yard was jammed with viewers. Outside, "several boys had climbed into a tall poplar tree in front of the jail, in full view of the scaffold."[102] When an execution took place "in private" at the Tombs, in New York City, "the neighboring buildings are black with people, seeking to look down over the prison walls and witness the death agonies of the poor wretch who is paying the penalty of the law."[103]

Of course, when all is said and done, not many people could climb trees or roofs, or watch an execution with opera glasses; but millions could read all about it in the daily press. The newspapers of the late nineteenth century adored executions; they described the major executions in lip-smacking detail. When Nathan Sutton was hanged in California, in January 1888, the *Oakland Tribune* delivered to the breathless public a blow-by-blow account. People had climbed to the housetops in a desperate attempt to watch Sutton die an agonizing death. When Sutton was dropped, the rope cut deeply into his neck; his head almost separated from his body. According to the *Tribune* a "noise was heard ... like the gurgle of wind"; blood was "spurting from the left side of his neck ... bubbling from the right side ... welling from in front—rushing in a thick crimson torrent ... forming a sanguinary pool on the ground which sucked it voraciously.... The crowd stood spell-bound with horror."[104] At least the crowd was not bored; and neither, one guesses, were the *Tribune*'s readers. In a sense, then, the death penalty was perhaps as public as ever. Lynchings in the South, and vigilante executions in the West, were also often public events, where thousands watched people die.

Were executions even marginally more discreet, less primitive? It is hard to say. There was, however, a move to bring the methods up to date. New York pioneered in scientific death when it introduced the "electrical chair" in 1888, to replace the hangman, the gallows, and the noose. Experiments throughout the 1880s proved the awesome power of electricity; these experiments showed that electricity could kill animals swiftly and smoothly. Why not human beings as well?[105] The governor of New York sent a message to the legislature in 1885, proposing the use of electricity. Hanging, he said, was a remnant of the "dark ages"; now "science" showed the way to put criminals to death "in a less barbarous manner."[106] The law of 1888 provided that the "punishment of death must, in every case, be inflicted by causing to pass through the body of the convict a current of electricity of sufficient intensity to cause death."[107] The electric chair was also a step in the direction of true privacy; it was housed in a small chamber in the prison, and needed considerably less space than a good, old-fashioned hanging. But the coming of "the chair" did not, of course, dampen public curiosity; it only whetted the appetite of yellow journalists.

William Kemmler had the dubious honor of being first to die in "the chair." This was in 1890. The first woman executed by this "progressive" method was Mrs. Martha Place, in 1899. Her eyes closed, and clutching a Bible, she was guided into the chamber "dressed in a black gown with big sleeves and a few fancy frills at the bosom. . . . She wore russet slippers." Her hair was braided, but a spot had been clipped near the crown to make room for the electrode. Another electrode was fastened to her leg. A current of 1,760 volts went through her body. It was all over in a short time; the doctors pronounced her dead and took the Bible from her motionless hand. The execution, we are told, "had been successful in every way."[108]

8

LAWFUL LAW AND LAWLESS LAW: FORMS OF AMERICAN VIOLENCE

A PHRASE IN THE TITLE OF THIS CHAPTER—"LAWLESS LAW"—MUST STRIKE the reader as oddly contradictory. But it has a lot of concrete meaning. In this society, and in all modern societies, there is an ideal form or image of criminal justice. Only the state, the law, has the right to use force. The state is supposed to have a "monopoly of legitimate violence." And the only rightful use of force is against force; the only proper use of violence is against violence; the only proper use of law, is against the lawless.

The reality, of course, is another story. American history is rich in forms of lawlessness, and not all of them stand outside the legal system as enemies of "law and order." Many, in fact, take place "inside" the legal system itself, or are aspects of that system— police brutality, for example. There lawlessness masquerades as law, or acts as a secret supplement to law, or replaces law. Most forms of lawlessness are "private"; ordinary crime comprises the bulk of it. Other "private" forms of lawlessness have a collective aspect: urban riots, lynchings, vigilante movements. Sometimes these outbreaks of violence claim to be reactions against official neglect, corruption, or incompetence; sometimes they imitate law (holding "trials" and passing judgment); sometimes they set themselves up as rivals to the official system and its norms.

A Violent Society

Nobody seems to doubt that the United States is, comparatively speaking, a violent society. The murder rate, as I write this, is orders of magnitude higher than those of other developed countries. Violence, it is said, is as American as cherry pie. American cities are much more violent and dangerous places than European or African cities, on the whole. Cherry pie was not invented yesterday; and neither was the notion that American society is drenched with innocent blood. Most people who think about it at all seem convinced that America is a violent society by tradition, by inheritance, by ingrained habit. How far back can we trace this blot of blood?

In part, *violence* is a matter of definition, or at least of perspective. Even the definition of murder shifts over time: consider euthanasia, or abortion. Not many people today are willing to come out in favor of wife beating; battering a wife counts as violent (and illegal) behavior. But this was not always the case. (See chapter 10.) In many societies, vengeance and blood feuds are considered normal, possibly even a good thing.

Every society defines a sphere of legitimate *private* violence—spanking a child, for example. Of course, the boundary between lawful and unlawful spanking, between discipline and child abuse, is blurred; and it fluctuates. There were fathers in the past who were proud that they beat their children mercilessly—for the children's sake, of course; today these same fathers might be in danger of going to jail. A teacher who caned a third-grader would quickly lose her job.

Nonetheless, there is broad consensus about what is and what is not murder, so that we know how to label *most* violent deaths; and the same is true for robbery and assault. The small colonial settlements were not violent places, on the whole; there was rankling and quarreling, and *some* crime, but not very much of it was violent. The system, of course, used violence itself. Whipping was an ordinary weapon of government. These were authoritarian societies, and "correction" was an important part of the social structure. Slaveholders beat their slaves. Slavery was, in a sense, violence made into an institution; it rested, ultimately, on force. But then, so do all societies—to a degree.

The cities and towns of the nineteenth century had more raw violence than colonial settlements. The invention of the police was, in part, a response to the violence of cities—especially to urban rioting. Violence and brutality, as we have seen, were epidemic on southern plantations; after the Civil War, violence against blacks continued in another form. We will discuss this violence later in this chapter. In this country, apparently, there was also a good deal of random, sporadic violence, private violence, violence that was unorganized, individual, idiosyncratic.

What brought this violence about? Every human being is a private and unique story; every crime is one of a kind. But there are patterns and aggregates. In the aggregate sense, American violence must come from somewhere deep in the American personality. And the American personality—that is, the distinctive *patterns* of personality one finds in this country—cannot be accidental; nor can it be genetic. The specific facts of American life make it what it is. In this sense, crime has been perhaps part of the price of liberty; of a society that had loosened some of the strings, taken off the suffocating gag. When this happened, a small but important number of people ran wild. Put in another way, as autocracy loosened, as mobility increased, as rural life gave way to urban life, as community disintegrated, there were more and more unattached, normless men, men who were out of control. Loss of control, the failure of collective discipline, was the great social fear of the century. This fear explains many of the developments in the criminal justice system, as we have already seen. It cuts like a knife through the tangle of legal detail.

As we have noted, one of the great master-trends in the history of criminal justice is the shift from *private* to *public*; and from lay to professional. Pauline Maier, writing about riots and mobs in the colonial period, refers to the mob as the "extralegal arm of the community's interest." She points out that the line between public and private use of force was extremely fuzzy.[1] There was the old tradition of the "posse"—lay citizens scooped up ad hoc into law enforcement—and the tradition of the "hue and cry," in which ordinary citizens joined in the chase after criminals. There were occasional uses of the "posse" in eastern states, but as everyone who has seen "westerns" knows, the posse survived best on the frontier, that is, in places where law enforcement had not grown as professional as it had in the East.

In any event, in the eighteenth century, "disorder," as Maier puts it, "was seldom anarchic," and rioters often "acted to defend law and justice rather than to oppose them." Attitudes changed in the nineteenth century. The tolerance for mass action declined. There was a long, slow retreat from legitimate public participation in law enforcement. This was true symbolically as well as literally. Hangings, we recall, took place in open air, before crowds, in the eighteenth century and well into the nineteenth. Then they retreated, first to the courtyards of prisons, then to smaller, more secret rooms. Why did all of this happen? For many reasons: but surely one of them was the sense that society did not dare let loose the uncontrolled passions of the many. The "monopoly of violence" was the only way to keep violence scarce.

Or relatively scarce. Violence, like vice, never went away. American violence is still a historical puzzle. Other societies, as they modernized, lost much of their violent edge. There is some evidence that the police actually succeeded in taming, more or less, the slums of great cities like London. Economic growth, no doubt, helped. People who voted and had a bit of money and security were less prone to violent crime. This may have been the case in the United States as well. There is some evidence that serious crime did decline in the nineteenth century.[2] But the level of crime remained higher than in other countries. Perhaps (some people think) this was because the society was more mobile, more open; less bound to traditional ties of family, church, and town; or because of the frontier, or the "fatal liberty" of American society.

What makes the problem so intractable is the scarcity of facts. They were, of course, even scarcer in the nineteenth century itself. Still, it was commonplace, among conservatives of the time, that the radical democracy of America must, and did, lead to "anarchy and mass murder." In the 1830s, "thoughtful men were disturbed by a spirit of violence and brutality which seemed to be spreading across the nation."[3] The riots and disorders in the big cities were certainly an alarming fact of life in the first half of the century, as was labor unrest in the second. The New York City draft riots of July 1863, in the middle of the the Civil War, were perhaps the bloodiest riots ever experienced in the history of the country.[4] In 1850, a man who signed his name as "Veritas" wrote a letter to a newspaper, calling Philadelphia "The Murder City"; the homicide rates then were nothing compared to what they are now; but they were large enough to disturb respectable citizens.[5]

Violence and the Frontier Tradition

When people talk about the roots of American violence, they almost always invoke the frontier, or the frontier tradition.

There are, of course, frontiers and frontiers. After all, the Puritans in Boston, in 1650, were pioneers, and they lived on a frontier. Similarly, the Mormons in the "State of Deseret," beyond the reach of mainstream American law, were pioneers, living on the rim of society, or beyond it; but they ran a tight ship, and a nonviolent one, all things considered. John Philip Reid, in a remarkable study of behavior on the wagon trains of the overland trail in the middle of the nineteenth century—in absolute wilderness, in a place far outside the grasp of the long arm of the law—found very little violence and an enormous amount of respect for law and order.[6]

All this, however, does not do away completely with the image of a raw and lawless "frontier," or the romantic Wild West. The Wild West is, of course, interesting in its own right; it is the stuff of thousands of movies, books, and television shows. Americans seem to love the saga of sheriffs, gunfighters, badmen; Dodge City, Tombstone, Wyatt Earp, Billy the Kid, and the rest are part of American mythology. But is there really a *tradition* of violence? That is, did frontier life, frontier conditions, create or nourish a bloody way of life for which we still pay the price?

To begin with, it is not self-evident that the western frontier *was* violent. Scholars of the West are split on this issue. The West, in any event, was not a monolith. As Richard White has pointed out, no one contends that "Norwegian farmers in North Dakota habitually squared off with Colt .45s to settle the ownership of an ox . . . or that German Mennonites in Kansas regulated their farm boundaries by slicing each other with bowie knives."[7] The wild part of the West meant the mining and cattle towns.

Roger McGrath studied two such towns: Aurora, Nevada, and Bodie, California, both in the Sierras. These frontier towns, he feels, were "unmistakably violent and lawless, but only in special ways."[8] There were plenty of shoot-outs, but not much robbery or rape. The violence was "men fighting men," that is, fistfights and gunfights. The towns were crowded with "young, healthy, adventurous, single males who adhered to a code of conduct that required a man to stand and fight."[9] For the rest of the population, there was relative safety; women, unless they were prostitutes, were treated with respect; property was generally safe from depredations. (We shall return to this point.)

The frontier did attract some kinds of violence. The rootless killer was often a frontier killer, if only because the frontier, like the darkest slums of the cities, was full of places to lurk, to hide, and to flee. American mass murderers made good use of the country's frontiers. Starting about 1800, the Harpe brothers, "Big Harpe" (Micajah) and "Little Harpe" (Wiley), carved a trail of blood along the Wilderness Road, in Kentucky. They were robbers, but they also murdered, wantonly, sometimes almost without motive.[10] It is the twentieth century, of course, that has become the golden age of the "serial killer," but the Harpes can hold their own with most.

The point is that the frontier, as a place, is not to blame; neither is the frontier as a kind of settlement. The frontier did attract rootless, deracinated men; and *these* are the ones who carry the germ of violence.

What is to blame are situations in which uprooted men (and sometimes women) lose or lack control. Their gyroscopes gone haywire, their personalities bent out of shape, they suffer from profound character disorders, and no social force is strong enough to control or reshape them. Such people are the detritus of mobility. Individual acts of violence that come out of such a background can be sporadic, unpredictable. It may be sudden and senseless violence against strangers, though this kind of crime became far more common in the twentieth century. It is, perhaps, the kind of crime that criminal justice can do the least about.

Ritualized Violence: The Duel

Violence can also be patterned and ritualized. This is the case with the blood feud or the duel. It is an open question whether ritualized violence bears any relation to other kinds of violence. Is ritualized violence an *outlet* and a *substitute* for spontaneous violence? Or does it, in fact, breed more of it?

Dueling was an ancient custom, based on codes of male honor. At some point in the eighteenth century it crossed the Atlantic and found its way into American codes of honor as well. The most famous American duel took place on July 11, 1804, when Aaron Burr killed Alexander Hamilton on a field in Weehawken, New Jersey.

The official attitude, especially in the North, was one of horror and outrage: dueling was a crime. In 1784, Massachusetts enacted a strong statute against this "detestable and infamous practice." Anyone who engaged in a duel "with rapier or small sword, back-sword, pistol or any other dangerous weapon" was guilty of a crime, even if no one was killed. Dueling, according to the statute, expressed contempt for God, "the Supreme Giver and Disposer of life," and was based on "false notions of honour." The statutory punishment, therefore, maximized *dis*honor: the convict was to be "carried publickly in a cart to the gallows with a rope about his neck," to sit there for an hour, and then to go to jail for a year, or, "in lieu of the said imprisonment," to be publicly whipped, up to "thirty-nine stripes."[11]

Even more extreme were the provisions if death occurred: the body of the *victim* was to be buried "without a coffin, with a stake drove through the body at or near the usual place of execution"; or it might be delivered to any "surgeon ... to be dissected and anatomized." The killer was guilty of murder. If convicted and executed, his body, too, would either be dissected or buried coffinless, with a stake driven through it.

The statute has an archaic ring, but the point was to try to nullify the positive image of dueling as noble, honorable, and even aristocratic. In an interesting case in the mayor's court of New York City, in 1818, a man named George F. Norton had challenged one William Willis to a duel. His letter of challenge began: "I Expect You will give mee the satisfaction of a gentleman For the insult you have put upon Mee." The mayor told the jury that this "offence had hitherto been supposed to be confined to that class in society denominated gentlemen." Norton's case, he said, showed that "this fashionable crime was ... diffusing itself among the lower and, perhaps, the most useful classes in society." Though Norton "has assumed the character and etiquette of a gentleman, there is scarcely a word in his letters spelled right. Even the monosyllable *me* he had spelt *mee*." He exhorted the jury to nip this spread of dueling in the bud; Norton was convicted, sentenced to a month in jail, and ordered "to find security to keep the peace for one year from the expiration of his imprisonment."[12]

Dueling flourished in the southern states. Andrew Jackson's mother told him that law "affords no remedy that can satisfy the feelings of a true man."[13] In other words, a true man vindicated his honor outside the law. Dueling was illegal in the South as well as in the North—in Virginia as early as 1776, in Tennessee and North Carolina in 1802, in Georgia in 1809, in South Carolina in 1812. But these laws were totally ineffective.[14] Although officeholders in a number of states (Alabama and Kentucky, for example) had to swear that they had never fought a duel, in or out of the state, legislatures simply exempted, by resolution, those who could not take the oath without telling a lie. Many prominent men in the southern and border states had duels on their records. In January 1809, Henry Clay and Humphrey Marshall were on opposite sides of a heated debate in the Kentucky legislature. Clay called Marshall a demagogue; Marshall called Clay a liar. The result was a duel, fought with pistols at ten paces. Three rounds were fired; each man was "cool, determined and brave," and neither was seriously injured.[15]

Dueling had a specific place in the social structure of the South. In the South, only gentlemen fought duels, and one only fought a duel with a social equal. Dueling was thus one brick in a structure of stratification, an unwritten code, in which every member of society knew his or her place and stuck to it. It was part of the southern code of honor. This code "discouraged the growth of strong law enforcement agencies," and "lessened the effectiveness of the state courts."[16] It was, in short, prelegal, prerational, aristocratic. It was also tenacious. Dueling as an institution lasted in the South much longer than in the North; indeed, it persisted till the late nineteenth century. The end of the southern aristocracy and the rise of a new class, the white populists and smallholders, was perhaps the cause of its decline.

The code of honor, despite its aristocratic tang, was, at bottom, noth-

ing more than the common macho code in fancy dress. In the North, the
dominant ethos stressed rigid morality and self-control. This was the
message of the penal code, and the message from the pulpit. Working-
class culture had a different flavor. There was a kind of code of violence
and honor among unattached laborers and artisans—and also among
family men who left wives and children at home when they made the
rounds of saloons and gambling dens. Elliott Gorn, writing about the
culture of workingmen in mid-century New York City, described the
code as a "fighting cock's valor in the face of death, a bulldog's relentless charge into a bear's grasp, or a prizefighter's capacity to give and
take punishment." These men followed a "combative, physical" way of
life; they found "their deepest sense of individual identity" in the "strut
and swagger of leisure-time activities," centered on "saloons, theaters,
boxing matches, pleasure gardens, sporting houses, boardinghouses, and
brothels."[17]

One purpose of the criminal justice system was to control this energy, to keep this rampant physicality within limits, and to patrol, violently if necessary, the borders of respectability, protecting it from too
many of these eruptions. This kind of patrol was, for example, one of
the roles of the police. Unlike the South, the North never accepted or
condoned this macho code—at least, not offically.

The true blood feud crops up mainly in the mountain regions of the
South. The feud between the Hatfields and the McCoys has entered into
American legend. In Williamson County, Illinois ("Bloody Williamson"), between 1868 and 1876, a "bloody vendetta" broke out, initially
over a card game. The county had a history of violence and homicide.
Perhaps, as one contemporary thought, what festered in this county was
the contact between the "code of the South" and the "knock-down style
of the West."[18] Some of these feuds "rubbed nerves raw in animosities
bred by the Civil War, others in obscure conflicts whose precise origins
had long been forgotten."[19] The feuds seemed archaic in their adherence
to an ancient code of honor defined along precise family or clan lines.

The Vigilante Movement

This is one of the most familiar chapters in the history of American justice (or injustice). An enormous amount has been written about the vigilantes, some of it true. Despite all the books, novels, and movies (perhaps *because* of some of them), there are many issues about the history
and meaning of the movement that are still not resolved.

Richard Maxwell Brown, probably the leading expert on the subject,
has defined vigilantism as "organized, extralegal movements, the members of which take the law into their own hands."[20] This definition is as

good as any. Some eruptions that fit this definition occurred as early as the eighteenth century—notably, the South Carolina Regulator movement in the late 1760s—and in the early part of the nineteenth as well. It is no accident that the prime examples seem to come from the South. Formal law was weak in the South, and vigilantism flourishes in a culture where the formal law is flabby and where rival "codes" enjoy legitimacy. There was, for example, a vigilante group in Montgomery, Alabama, in the 1820s called the "Regulating Horn." Their specialty was to tar and feather "guilty" people and run them out of town.[21] In South Carolina, abolitionists were the main target of vigilantes in the 1840s.

By any measure, however, these were only curtain raisers. The golden age of the vigilante movement came later. It began in the 1850s and continued until roughly the turn of the century; and the dry and rocky states of the American West were the natural habitat of the movement. The two San Francisco "vigilance committees" of the 1850s were the most famous of them all, and were perhaps the immediate source of the term, *vigilante*. The vigilantes of Montana have earned themselves a solid second place.

San Francisco in 1851 was raw and new—a boom town, transformed from almost nothing to a big city in a few short years. When an American ship, the *Portsmouth*, entered the great harbor in 1846, during the Mexican War, the conquerors found a miserable little town of some two hundred residents, huddled in rude houses between the beach and the wilderness.[22] San Francisco had a magnificent setting and a magnificent location; the city was certain to grow under American rule. But the discovery of gold in 1848 stampeded the process. It let a jinni of fantastic size loose from its bottle. The city exploded.

San Francisco in the gold rush years was an exciting, strange, turbulent place, a city on the move in every way, growing, bursting at the seams, vibrant, alive. But was it also a festering center of crime? Historians have by no means made up their minds; but the local merchants had, along with many ordinary citizens. To them the city was in the grip of a colossal crime wave.

On February 19, 1851, C. J. Jansen's store on the corner of Montgomery and Washington streets, in the middle of the business district, was robbed. A man had demanded a dozen blankets, and as Jansen stooped down to get the blankets, he was beaten on the head and knocked unconscious. Two thousand dollars was later discovered missing from his desk.[23] The police arrested two suspects, both Australians. A great, angry crowd gathered in Portsmouth Square; a young merchant, William T. Coleman, got the crowd's attention and recommended that a popular court be set up immediately. The crowd held a "trial" of sorts, choosing three judges from among themselves. Coleman acted as prosecutor, and twelve citizens served as an ad hoc jury.

The two Australians were lucky; they escaped with their necks. At the "trial," some local lawyers defended them; they pointed out that Jansen could not really identify the robbers, and the "jury" deadlocked, voting nine to three for conviction. A few men "yelled out that the prisoners should be hanged anyway"; but most of the crowd "drifted off. The prisoners were returned to the legal authorities, who tried and convicted both of them."[24]

This was the prelude. In June of the same year, a "Committee of Vigilance" was formed. The committee was active for about a month before it disbanded, but it was a busy month indeed. It directed its attention to the "Sydney coves"—Australian criminals—and ended up hanging four of them. One of them was John Jenkins, a man of bad reputation who had been caught in the act of stealing a safe. He was given a "trial" at the vigilante headquarters and sentenced to death. Jenkins was marched to the Custom House, where the locals put a noose around his neck and hanged him on the spot.[25] The committee got rid of other bad characters in a less extreme way; twenty-eight of them were simply tossed out of town.[26]

For five years or so, there were no vigilantes at work in San Francisco. The second vigilance committee took form in 1856. In the background was an incident that occurred in November 1855: an "Italian gambler" named Charles Cora shot and killed a U.S. marshal by the name of Richardson. Cora was arrested and tried, but, as William T. Coleman (a prominent merchant, later a vigilante leader) put it, "all efforts to convict him . . . failed." Some elements in the city were outraged over the general lawlessness, as they saw it, and the "impotence" of the regular law courts. The straw that broke the camel's back was another dramatic incident: James P. Casey shot and killed a newspaper editor, James King of William, who had been "boldly assailing all evildoers." At this point, "the engine-bell on the Plaza was rung—the familiar signal of the old Vigilance Committee." According to an eyewitness report, the mob seized both Casey and Cora, and hanged the two of them from projecting beams rigged on the roof of a building on Sacramento Street.[27]

The second vigilance committee was a much bigger affair than the first; it had more than six thousand members. The leaders took aim not only at "lawlessness" but also at the local political machine, which was under the thumb of David Broderick, president of the California Senate and "boss" of the Democratic Party, which drew its strength from the Irish (and Catholic) workingmen of the city. Two more men were dispatched at the end of a rope, and thirty "rowdies" or so were forced out of the city. The committee entered politics, and its candidates defeated the men of the Broderick regime. It ended its work, in other words, by seeking official power for itself.

The political nature of these vigilance committees seems plain. "Taking the law into one's own hands" is a phrase that expresses two thoughts: first, that the action is *private*, the action of individuals or groups (or mobs) who seize for themselves the state's role as enforcer of law. But equally important is the second idea, that it is *law* that one is taking into one's hands—not vengeance, not whim, not personal opinion, but law. Thus the vigilantes came, as they saw it, not in defiance of law, but in fulfillment. The Vigilance Committee of Payette, Idaho, drew up a constitution and bylaws. It gave all accused persons the right to a trial by a jury of seven members; a majority could "render a verdict—which was final." Three punishments were allowed: banishment, horsewhipping ("to be publicly administered"), and capital punishment. Vigilantes, as we noted, sometimes ran "trials," heard witnesses, and reached verdicts. There were, to be sure, not many acquittals at these "trials."[28]

The vigilante movements enjoyed, in the main, rave reviews from those who wrote about them at the time; mixed to bad reviews in our day.[29] Hubert Bancroft, the nineteenth-century author of *Popular Tribunals*, was a devoted fan of the vigilantes; he called the movement a "keen knife in the hands of a skilful surgeon, removing the putrefaction"; he even dedicated one of the volumes of his work to William T. Coleman, leader of the San Francisco vigilantes. To Bancroft, the law had been "sick," and his "beloved rough-necks" had brought about a "speedy and almost bloodless cure."[30]

Another famous account of the vigilantes, Thomas Dimsdale's *Vigilantes of Montana* (1866) is another out-and-out apologia, written in a style that manages somehow to be both stilted and purple. Dimsdale was an Englishman who landed in Virginia City, Montana, in 1863. By the following year he had become superintendent of public instruction for Montana Territory. In Montana, "swift and terrible retribution was the only preventive of crime"—this was Dimsdale's faith. The vigilantes put an end to the "reign of terror" and restored law and order, which once had been "as powerless as a palsied arm." In the process, admittedly, more than a hundred lives were "pitilessly sacrificed and twenty-four miscreants . . . met a dog's doom."[31]

Dimsdale's book recounts these various "dooms" in detail. He gives us, for example, the arrest and execution of Captain J. A. Slade, a bad-tempered, foul-mouthed hell-raiser who made himself unpopular by galloping through the streets with his buddies, breaking up bars and using "insulting language to parties present." Once, Slade led his horse into a saloon, and, "buying a bottle of wine, he tried to make the animal drink it." The vigilance committee warned him to behave himself, but Captain Slade paid no attention. Finally, in a fit of foolish bravado, he threatened a prominent vigilante, cocking a derringer at his head.

This was too much for the committee. They "arrested" Slade, who realized, too late, what deep trouble he was in, begged for his life and invoked "his dear wife" in a plea for sympathy. A friendly messenger rode "at full speed" to Slade's ranch to warn his wife of what was about to happen. She sprang into the saddle and "urged her fleet charger over the twelve miles of rough and rocky ground." But it was too late: "stern necessity" had dictated the execution of Slade, and he was hanged. The body was carried to the Virginia Hotel and laid out "in a darkened room." At that point, Slade's wife arrived "at headlong speed, to find . . . that she was a widow." According to Dimsdale, the execution of Slade "had a most wonderful effect upon society. . . . Reason and civilization . . . drove brute force from Montana."[32]

John Clay, who wrote reminiscences of life on the range in Wyoming and Montana, had a similar reading of what "reason and civilization" required. He describes a rare event: the lynching of a woman, Ella Watson, also known as "Cattle Kate." This woman, who had appeared in Casper, Wyoming, "was a prostitute of the lowest type, . . . common property of the cowboys for miles around. If they could not pay her the price of virtue in cash, they agreed to brand a maverick or two for her behoof." This was cattle rustling, plain and simple, but it "was impossible to get a conviction." Finally, in summer 1889, after repeated warnings "that the objectionable class of business must stop," Cattle Kate and her henchman, Jim Averill, were hanged. "The man wilted and begged for mercy; the woman died game. This of course was a horrible piece of business, more especially the lynching of the woman, and in many ways indefensible, and yet what are you to do? Are you to sit still and see your property ruined with no redress in sight?"[33]

Modern historians, on the other hand, are not so sure about how to assess the vigilantes. They see much more ambiguity and diversity, a lot more dross among the gold. They see class conflict and elitism; they see the clash between law and "law and order." Vigilante movements were diverse, and had diverse motives, sought diverse ends.

Sometimes the good guys and the bad guys seem fairly obvious. In the days of the Klondike gold rush, the town of Skagway, in Alaska Territory, was terrorized by Jefferson ("Soapie") Smith. In 1898, Smith was murdered by vigilantes, who then, in a "frenzy of excitement," invaded "dive after dive, slugging, shooting, and intimidating." But the net result was law and order.[34] Vigilante groups typically complained of failure or corruption of the laws, or defects and holes in schemes of law enforcement. In Henderson County, Illinois, on the Mississippi River, the local vigilance committee attacked and burned a so-called gunboat in 1870. The "gunboat" was not a warship, but a "raft or flatboat with a cabin built on it, used as a floating gambling den, brothel, and drinking saloon." Both law officers and the inmates of the boats had acted as if the Mississippi River were "a sort of no-man's-land where state laws did not apply." The vigilance committee filled the vacuum of enforcement. Niceties of jurisdiction did not trouble them, and they got rid of this floating center of vice.[35]

Sometimes, then, vigilantes enforced the moral code in cases where the formal law did not seem strict enough or had fallen down on the job. According to a report in 1885, a man named Joseph White was arrested in Wallingford, Vermont, for abusing his foster daughter, who was thirteen. White had beaten the child mercilessly, pushed pins through her ears and needles through her tongue. His wife, not to be outdone, made the child stand on a hot stove until her poor feet were blistered. The Whites were arrested, but the justice merely assessed a five-dollar fine on Joseph and a ten-dollar fine on his wife, nothing more. The next night, "masked men caught White in his barn, and, after beating him, ordered him to leave the town."[36]

It would be hard to argue that White did not get what he deserved. The response of the vigilantes was, nonetheless, lawless. For some people, that in itself was damning enough. Besides, the vigilantes sometimes punished the innocent, and they often overpunished the guilty. Vigilante justice had its elite core and leadership, but it was always in tune with some deep strains of popular justice. Law did not allow a man to be banished or hanged because of his general behavior or past acts. Vigilante justice drew no such fine distinctions.

This was also the source of its worst abuses. Governor Thomas Ford of Illinois, an unusually astute observer, described a movement of "regulators" in Massac County, Illinois, in the 1840s. The "original purpose" of the movement was to clean out the bad guys, but soon this purpose was forgotten, "and instead of punishing horse-thieves and robbers those who drop the law and resort to force soon find themselves fiercely contending to revenge injuries and insults, and to maintain their assumed authority."[37]

Many vigilante outbursts cannot be labeled as spontaneous popular uprisings—or, for that matter, as mob action. Nor can their members be described generally as roughnecks, if this implies something about class origins. Some vigilante groups were, in fact, very much movements of elites, insofar as there were elites in their communities at all. The San Francisco vigilance committee of 1851, for example, was described at

the time as the "salt of San Francisco," a group of "first class men."
This was the judgment of contemporaries; modern research does not disagree. The movers and shakers were, for the most part, merchants. The
committee was, in fact, "a businessmen's club."[38] The 1856 committee,
too, was dominated by merchants and business interests. The *ordinary*
voter, the man on the street, had elected the political machine that the
1856 committee so bitterly opposed.

In his classic account, Dimsdale complained that the law had been
impotent, before the vigilantes got moving. "No matter what may be
the proof, if the criminal is well liked in the community, 'Not Guilty' is
almost certain to be the verdict of the jury."[39] Bancroft is even more explicit: "the establishing of courts tended to encourage crime rather than
to prevent it." He speaks of "demagogues" on the bench, court officers
who are "ruffians." "The juries of the interior," he says, were willing to
"hang a thief," but not to convict a murderer. But the jurors were "summoned from the hangers-on about courtroom, men fit for nothing else,
scarcely able to live by their wits, and yet too lazy to work." These "old
familiar faces" blossomed "under the genial influence of strong drink. . .
. They did nothing but sit in the jury box, the same person sometimes
serving several times in one day."[40] John Clay claimed that convictions
for rustling were impossible; and, to the "Eastern man or woman," who
"will exclaim 'Dreadful!'" with regard to vigilantes, he asked what *they*
would do if in their "quiet New England town," at home in their "vine-
clad or rose-covered cottage," burglars broke in and helped themselves,
yet no jury would convict. If the burglar returned, wouldn't you, as a
"man of spirit" simply "take down your shotgun and let him have it"?[41]

But when we are told that juries refused to convict, we are naturally
led to wonder: Who were these jurors, really, and why did they let defendants go? The answer is: they were members of the community, and
they had their own set of norms. But these were not elite norms. Thus
many of the vigilante movements were in fact elite revolts. They were
cases of culture conflict, and the winners, as is often the case, were the
men who wrote the history books as well.

Many of the vigilante leaders expressed what Richard Maxwell Brown
has described as the "loathing of upper-level men for the lower element—the contraculture—of the frontier."[42] The members made no attempt to hide their vigilance work. The vigilantes, in general, never
wore masks. Why should they? Some of them were, and others became,
extremely prominent in their states. William J. McConnell, "captain" of
the vigilantes in Payette, Idaho, became a U.S. senator and then a governor of Idaho.[43] Dr. John E. Osborne of Rawlins, Wyoming, who had
skinned the corpse of Big Nose George Parrott (a notorious outlaw

hanged by the vigilantes)—he tanned the skin and made it into objects, including a pair of shoes that were exhibited for years in a Rawlins bank—later became governor of Wyoming.[44]*

In the East, in the latter part of the nineteenth century, "law and order" had become at least partly professionalized. There were police forces and detective squads in all the cities. The engine of criminal justice, for all its creaking gears and rusty levers, did work, more or less, as a part of the general machinery of government.† In the West, justice was still a *community* matter—or, at least, a matter for the community of adult men. The regular sheriff "deputized" citizens when he needed reinforcements, and the "posse" was a recognized institution. The line between enforcement *inside* and *outside* the law was less distinct than in the East. This was not the cause of the vigilante movements, but it was the soil out of which these movements grew.

There was, to be sure, an eastern and mid-western variant, which showed a somewhat different face. This was "whitecapping," a "movement of violent moral regulation by local masked bands." It began in southern Indiana in 1887 and spread rapidly. Brown mentions 239 incidents before 1900. The whitecaps did not, for the most part, punish ordinary criminals, horse thieves, cattle rustlers. They went after "crimes" that were not against the law: people who offended the local moral code. They usually punished by whipping; and their victims were "wife beaters, drunkards, poor providers, immoral couples and individuals, lazy and shiftless men, and petty neighborhood thieves."[47]

The whitecaps in the South were a violent, secret group, something of a cross between the KKK and western vigilantes.[48] They were active in Mississippi, for example, where men in white masks rode at night in protest against the crop-lien system. In Georgia, they threatened merchants who would not wait for prices to go up before processing farmers' cotton. In some areas, they terrorized blacks; in others, they protected moonshiners. They whipped their enemies, and sometimes killed them. They were hard to prosecute because they intimidated witnesses and jurors; and because local officials were often whitecaps themselves. By

---

* Sometimes the transition from mass to elite movement was fairly obvious. In Montana, in 1863, a cool customer named George Ives had a number of killings to his credit; he was captured, and brought to Alder Gulch, where a crowd decided that his trial "should take place before the miners of the Gulch en masse." The trial was real enough—Ives even had a defense lawyer—but the upshot was conviction, and a hanging. It was after this event that a group of leading citizens decided to form a vigilance committee, to carry on the "heady struggle between order and crime."[45]
† One rusty area, however, was enforcing the laws against gambling and vice. Here, then we *do* find lay enforcement butting in and something like a "posse" appearing. For example, in the 1880s, Anthony Comstock, fighting the good fight against Satan, and with good reason not to trust the regular law-enforcers, raided gambling establishments in Long Island City with his own men, who had been appointed deputy sheriffs or peace officers for his specific purpose.[46]

1895, however, the movement had just about run its course in that particular area.

In its home bases, whitecapping, like the vigilante movement, was something of an elite movement, or at least it had elite elements. Enforcement of morality was its main function. But morals crusades, as we saw, were hindered by a number of factors: corruption, the indifference of much of the public, and, very significantly, by the fact that many people *wanted* "immoral" services and goods. The whitecaps operated in this vacuum of enforcement. Like all vigilantelike movements, whitecapping grew out of a situation of legal pluralism—a situation of clashing norms. There was, interestingly, at least one example of women who acted as whitecaps: twelve members of the Women's Christian Temperance Union, in Osceola, Nebraska, in 1893 (if the *National Police Gazette* is to be believed). These women were scandalized by the immoral activities of "certain young ladies." The avenging twelve put pillow cases over their heads, seized the shameless hussies, tied them up and gave them a thorough flogging. Eleven of the women were arrested; one of them was the wife of a local bank president, and all of them were "staunch church members and among the most charitable ladies of the city."[49]

Violent Resistance to Law

Somewhat comparable to the vigilante movement was the wave of "counterrevolutionary terror" that "swept over large parts of the South between 1868 and 1871" in the form of the Ku Klux Klan, the "invisible empire."[50] The Klan, too, had its elite element; and it acted to enforce a code that the official law did not or would not recognize: strict white supremacy.

The Klan was formed for one overriding purpose: to resist, violently if necessary, any attempt by southern blacks to gain a few crumbs of political and economic power. The Reconstruction North was nominally on the side of the black victims; but their backing was weak, sporadic, undependable. The Klan began in the late 1860s and spread like wildfire through the defeated South. The Klansmen wore bizarre disguises—both for secrecy and as an instrument of terror and mystification. The costume consisted, for the most part, of white sheets with cone-shaped white hats and masks. In some areas, the robes were red with white trim; in others, they were black.[51] The Klansmen rode at night, on horseback; they were the embodiment of white supremacy at its most extreme; they used menace, brutality, and intimidation to do their work. The Klan stopped at nothing; they whipped, burned and raped; they were willing, even eager, to kill. Black victims were usually innocent of any crime except upward mobility. The Klan murdered a black legislator in Sumter County, Alabama, in 1870 simply because he had become successful and was influential with "people of his color."[52] In Mississippi, Klansmen whipped a black man who dared to sue a white who owed him money; this was far too uppity.[53] A black who was making money and achieving some success was a natural target for Klan terror. Black people, in Klan ideology, belonged on white farms and plantations, as docile workers. The Klan was willing to beat or murder whites, too, if they sided with blacks or opposed the Klan.

Resistance was almost useless; local government was either supine, or helpless, or allied with the Klan. The local courts were little better. The stench from the Klan was too much for many northern Republicans; perhaps some of them wondered who, after all, had won the Civil War. In 1870 and 1871, Congress adopted a series of laws designed to curb the Klan. These acts, among other things, made it a felony for men "to band or conspire together, or go in disguise upon the public highway . . . with intent to . . . injure, oppress, threaten, or intimidate" citizens, and to prevent them from enjoying their constitutional rights.[54] This legislation moved the federal courts massively into law enforcement—a new and unaccustomed role. Enforcement was not an easy matter. The victims of the Klan were poor, frightened, and mostly black; and most of the white community was ranged on the side of the Klan.[55] In 1871 in Monroe County, Mississippi, twenty-eight whites went to the home of a black named Aleck Page, in disguise; they tied him, dragged him from his home, hanged him, and buried his body. An unusually zealous U.S. attorney indicted the Klansmen, for violating the federal Enforcement Act. The locals, however, treated the defendants like heroes, and the U.S. attorney, who saw the handwriting on the wall, agreed to drop most of the charges. The defendants entered pleas of guilty, and the judge fined them twenty-five dollars each and made them post a peace bond.[56] This, then, was the price for cold-blooded murder. In many districts of the South, it was impossible even to get this kind of pitiful result, or any conviction at all. There were thousands of indictments, but relatively few convictions; and hardly anything in the way of punishment. The federal effort perhaps succeeded in discouraging some of the worst excesses of the Klan, but it is hard to be sure.

After the 1870s, the Klan's reign of terror in the South petered out, but probably only because it was no longer needed. The Klan had gotten what it wanted. The South was white man's country. Segregation by law superseded the lawlessness of the Klan. But southern violence against blacks was by no means over. The horrors of lynch law, as we shall see, emerged from the swamp of southern racism toward the end of the century.

In the mountains of the South and the border states, another long struggle took place between the locals and the federal government in the last half of the century. It had quite a different character. This was the struggle between "revenuers" and "moonshiners."[57] The Civil War was fearfully expensive; it soaked up revenues like a sponge. Taxes increased enormously. Most of the tax laws expired after the war, but the federal government maintained its liquor tax, which it had come to depend on. In the almost inaccessible creeks and hollows of the Appalachian Mountains, "blockaders" made liquor in illegal, untaxed, unlicensed stills. The federal government meant to collect its tax and close down the moonshine operations. It sent agents to do the job, but they met bitter, often bloody resistance. Men died on both sides, and neither side could ever claim victory. Here, again, local authorities were indifferent or hostile to the general law of the land. Some local authorities even dared to arrest and try federal agents who had been especially zealous or who had used force, and inflamed local opinion.[58]

Lynching

Vigilantism still has its defenders; some modern self-help anticrime groups even call themselves (and proudly) vigilantes. But there is not much to be said for the southern version (or perversion) of do-it-yourself justice—lynch law. The very term is southern: it preserves the name of Colonel Charles Lynch, of Bedford County, Virginia. During the disturbed times of the 1780s, Lynch organized an extralegal group to catch and punish wrongdoers. Lynch conducted "regular though illegal trials," and punishment—whipping, mostly—was "inflicted under a large and locally famous walnut tree standing in Lynch's yard."[59]

But "lynching" came to have a much more sinister meaning: mob murder of men and women accused of crime, dragged from their cells and killed—or killed before the justice system could get any sort of grip on them. The line between some vigilante activity and out-and-out lynching was sometimes fuzzy at best. In a number of instances, sheriffs in Arizona unlocked the jail or simply skedaddled, and let the "vigilantes" do their work. In 1873, for example, Sheriff Oury of Tucson suddenly became ill from eating too much watermelon, and the Chief Justice decided it was just the day to visit San Xavier Cathedral; three men in jail fell victim to "vigilantes."[60]

Lynching, however, became more and more a part of the southern way of life. In Tampa, Florida, in 1882, a white drifter named Charles D. Owens broke into the home of John A. McKay, a leading businessman. He found Mrs. McKay's twenty-six-year-old sister, Ada McCarty, and assaulted her "with intent to rape," although he was frightened away before he could accomplish his "hellish purpose." Owens was caught and put in jail. An angry crowd gathered, almost immediately. The mob "marched on the jail, seized the prisoner . . . and carried him to a large oak tree across the street from the courthouse." Owens begged for mercy, but a noose was put around his neck and he was strung up on the tree. The rope slipped; Owens fell screaming to the ground, but six men grabbed the rope and pulled him up, and he died.[61]

The lynching of Owens was unlike many, if not most, vigilante actions. There is nothing to suggest that the courts of Tampa could not handle this case, could not dish out punishment. No one, in any event, waited to find out. Rather, the mob decided that honor *demanded* direct action—the honor of the white woman, her family, and the community. The lynching was part of an "unwritten code." Southerners distrusted the state, and preferred, in these cases, "personal justice." They "believed strongly that community justice included both statutory law and lynch law"; indeed, lynch law "was perceived as a legitimate extension of the formal legal system."[62]

The Owens lynching was by no means unique. One incident in New Orleans, in 1890, is important as an early example of fear of organized crime. The chief of police, David Hennessey, blamed a secret criminal society, the Mafia, for an outbreak of violence in the Italian community. Hennessey was subsequently murdered, but before he died, he accused the "Dagos" of responsibility. A roundup of Italians followed, and nine were put on trial. The jury found six of them not guilty, but could not decide what to do with the other three. In the meantime, an angry mob gathered outside the jail; soon some twenty men broke into the building and slaughtered all nine defendants.[63]

In one important sense, however, the Tampa incident and the New Orleans massacre were atypical. By far the majority of the victims were southern blacks murdered by gangs of whites. Lynching was hardly necessary as an instrument of terror and domination during slavery. But after the war lynching became a "crucial extralegal prop" of white supremacy. The Ku Klux Klan can be considered a kind of organized lynch mob. It was responsible for killing some four hundred blacks between 1868 and 1872. Blacks were lynched for murder or rape; they were also lynched for political reasons, as we have seen; some were brutally murdered for any behavior that "violated the prescribed system of racial etiquette."[64]

Bad as the Klan was, the worst was yet to come. The "golden age" of the lynch mob was in the years after 1880. Any threat to the ideology of white supremacy made a black man a candidate for lynching. The NAACP published a report on lynching in 1919, covering the thirty-year period in which lynching was rampant. The toll was awesome. More than a hundred blacks a year, on average, fell victim to the lynch mobs between 1889 and 1918. The count was 219 victims in the North, 2,834 in the South, 156 in the West; 78.2 percent of the victims were black.[65]

Lynch mobs were often savage and brutal beyond belief. In 1899, outside Newman, Georgia, a black man named Sam Holt was tortured, mutilated, and burned at the stake while two thousand people watched. He was accused of murdering a white man, Alfred Cranford, and raping Cranford's wife. None of the people involved wore masks or made any attempt at secrecy.[66] Some of the victims of mob violence were surely innocent—either falsely accused, or misidentified, or perhaps merely an outlet for the rage of a lynch mob. Some victims were castrated. Photographers sometimes sold picture postcards of the event; and there are reports of supposedly civilized southerners who collected souvenirs from the mutilated bodies of black victims. Local police almost never intervened; and it was practically unheard of to punish anybody for taking part in a lynching. A coroner's jury usually ended the matter with the solemn, hypocritical finding to the effect that parties unknown were responsible.

Lynching was a "ritual" that served to "give dramatic warning to all black inhabitants that the iron-clad system of white supremacy was not to be challenged by deed, word, or even thought."[67] More specifically, lynching warned blacks not to step over the *social* line; rape was a capital offense in the South, but whites in lynch mobs did not wish to take a chance on trial by jury; black-on-white rape (or suspicion of rape) was punished swiftly, brutally, unequivocally. A recent study of Georgia and North Carolina in the years 1882 to 1930 compared blacks who were lynched with those executed for crime. In Georgia, murder accounted for 88 percent of the executions of blacks, and rape only 12 percent; in North Carolina, the figures were 71 percent for murder, 22 percent for rape. The picture was quite different for "execution" by a lynch mob. Rape accounted for 41 percent of the lynch victims in Georgia—more than murder, which accounted for only 34 percent. In North Carolina, equal numbers were lynched for murder and rape (39 percent). The lynch mob, in short, showed an inordinate interest in stiffening the penalty for rape or suspected rape.[68]

Lynching, as the NAACP study showed, lasted well into the twentieth century. Most of the victims continued to be black, with some notable exceptions: for example, the 1913 lynching of Leo Frank, the Jewish victim of a Georgia mob, falsely accused of murdering Mary Phagan, a thirteen-year-old girl who worked for him in Atlanta.[69] The North, on the whole, was scandalized by lynching—not so much because people in the North believed in racial equality, but because they found lynching brutal, uncivilized, and bestial, as indeed it was. But despite long-term agitation against lynching, by blacks and some white allies, it was only the triumph of the civil rights movement and the passage of comprehensive civil rights laws in the 1960s that put an end, once and for all (one hopes), to this reign of racial terror.

In the previous chapter, we dealt briefly with the issue of police brutality; that, too, can be seen as a kind of lawless law. It would be a bit schematic to treat lynch law, the vigilantes, and police brutality as pieces of the same puzzle, neatly divided into regions: the vigilantes in the West, police brutality in the urban East, lynching in the South. For one thing, though all three phenomena had their "hubs," they all spilled over, at least somewhat, into other parts of the country. And they were very different in their origins and aims.

The three do share some common themes. When people talk about "taking the law into their hands," they mean taking action to make sure that the law has its effect. By *law* they mean the substance of the law, the marrow, the meat. Lawyers and judges are obsessed with procedures; they value orderly methods, "due process," almost for their own sake. Lay people certainly value fair trials and citizens' rights (especially when it applies to themselves), but they tend, as well, to be substance-minded, result-minded. Law is a code of behavior, a collection of rules of conduct; procedures are only means to an end. When the rules fail to work, or when they produce what people think of as "wrong" results, or "unjust" results, there is a temptation to go private and not endure the law's delay.

The "wrong" results in the nineteenth century came about because the *official* line stressed equality, fairness, classlessness. The norms of those whose voices counted wanted to suppress crime, never mind what it takes. This led people to wink at police brutality. The dualisms and compromises of enforcement of morality led to the whitecaps. The federal-state dualism led to the Ku Klux Klan. Lynching suppressed any movement, however small, that disturbed southern white supremacy, or southern "honor." Yet the myth of due process, of equality before the law, did have some strength. It was strong enough to preserve a basic fairnesss, in most aspects of *ordinary* trial. But it could not prevail against certain dark and passionate urges.

9

LEGAL CULTURE: CRIMES OF MOBILITY

A FUNDAMENTAL ASPECT OF AMERICAN SOCIETY IN THE NINETEENTH century was mobility—an amazing, unprecedented amount of social and physical mobility. American mobility affected every facet of society, and deeply.[1]

Of course, mobility is an aspect of the entire modern world—at least that part of the modern world which is actually modern; but it has always been especially true of America, and was especially true in America especially early. America was the land of mobility, above all other lands; a nation of emigrants, immigrants, migrants. Wanderers populated it; people who had uprooted themselves, shaken off clumps of their past along with chunks of their context, and moved to a new world.

There were, of course, instances of mass immigration into the country, and many examples of family immigration. Yet, on the whole, migration was and is an intensely individual experience, one that disturbs "community" at both ends of the trip. Mobility meant more than a flood of Irish and Germans and Italians and Swedes and Greeks; it was also the trek to the West, and a shuffling from one state to another, one town to another, one setting to another, one neighborhood to another—a general restlessness.

Moreover, American mobility meant more than just changing physical places; it meant climbing up or falling down the social ladder. People moved from rags to riches, and riches to rags; from narrow farm life to tumultuous city life, from working with their hands to working with their minds; from working for a boss to working for themselves; and back again. In this country, as De Toqueville noted, "great ones fall and the humble rise."[2] No formal barriers stood in the way.

The mobility of nineteenth-century America was not simply a matter of physical or social movement. Ideas and images traveled, too. In traditional society, the self was under the almost despotic rule of immediate, personal authority. The character of a boy or girl growing up in a European village, or perhaps in seventeenth-century Salem, was molded and formed inside a kind of protected cocoon. And when the self grew up and flew off into the world, it did not go very far, or look or feel very different from the people who had formed it. In a highly mobile society, even people who stay put are deeply affected: by the strangers who come and go, and by the messages that burst in, through newspapers or word of mouth.

The "modern" newspaper was a product of the nineteenth century. The early "gazettes" had few pages and small print; they discussed politics, ship arrivals, and commercial affairs. Later, the mass-circulation newspaper took center stage; it had pictures, bold headlines, more "features"—and a lot more news about crime and punishment. Railroads, telephone, and telegraph also transformed the world; then radio, movies, automobiles, jet airplanes, and television. These shrank even more radically old limits of space, isolation, and immobility.

In this process, which took perhaps a century to complete, the tight, face-to-face, vertical relations of authority, in small communities, weakened greatly; the horizontal authority of peer groups and the big world of the cities got stronger. The family, the village, the local church, no longer had the young in their exclusive grip. The media and mobility broke the monopoly on formative messages. The soul was now exposed, almost from birth, to the whole bursting, blooming, noisy world.

Mobility, real or imagined, had all sorts of effects on crime and punishment in the nineteenth century. A mobile society was just the right setting for certain crimes, which found their niche in this time and place. Big spaces, and the looseness of society, made it easy for a wanted criminal to get away. At the beginning of the century, there were still some crimes that were *literally* crimes of mobility, that is, crimes committed in the very act of physically moving on: slaves and indentured servants who ran away.[3] The savage labor laws of the South late in the century were laws designed to keep black workers in place. For the rest, mobility was not against the law; it was, in fact, the American dream.

Swindlers

American mobility created rich opportunities for crimes against trust. Swindlers, fakers, imposters, and con men swarmed about in the middle and late nineteenth century looking for (and finding) prey. Facts and figures are, of course, hard to come by; but there can be little doubt that swindling increased in the nineteenth century. Certainly, there was more talk about the various swindles and con games. Popular and semi-popular literature were full of accounts of swindlers and swindling. Swindling and fraud were very much crimes of mobility; these crimes depended on anonymity, ambiguity of identity, and the fluidity of lines that separated strata and classes in the population.

The Oxford English Dictionary traces the expression *confidence man* to 1849; it is American in origin. Herman Melville published a novel by that name in 1857. To be sure, trickery is as old as the human race; and state laws had long since criminalized fraud and related acts, including "obtaining money by false pretenses."[4] But confidence rackets positively blossomed in the nineteenth century. To a degree, the statute law reflected this rich pattern of growth by constantly defining new forms of cheating, imposture, and fraud. Thus South Dakota, to take one minor example, made it a crime to wear "the badge of the grand army of the republic," if you were "not entitled to the same."[5]

The point is not that a plague of special villainy infested the nineteenth century; rather, the conditions of American law and American society made types of swindling possible that had been difficult or impossible before. To begin with, there were new and efficient ways to *find* good victims to fleece. Mass media, a mass reading public, and the national postal system all helped in the search for suckers. As Anthony Comstock put it in 1880, swindling depended "upon two mighty agencies of our present civilization, the Newspaper and the United States Mail. By means of these two instruments for good or evil, it is possible to reach every household in the land."[6] There were, in fact, countless schemes of postal fraud. Other frauds made good use of the popular press. Newspapers were not, to say the least, fastidious about the advertisements they carried, just as they were not too finicky about making up or embroidering "news." Country newspapers, for example, were happy to print ads for incredibly cheap sewing machines—just send in your money. What you got in return was worthless, or almost so. One "scoundrel" pocketed the three dollars a woman sent him and shipped her "a large needle," telling her it was "the best sewing machine in the world."[7]

These and other frauds presupposed a mobile society. Investment frauds, of course, assumed a population of gulls with extra money and dreams of wealth. A mobile society is one in which people *have* such dreams. Mobility also means, above all, the ripping up of roots, the destruction of fixed, settled ways. This can happen literally when a person leaves his home, his place of birth, and moves to greener pastures. But, as we have pointed out, those who stayed put also experienced mobility in a psychological sense—their consciousness was changed under the influence of messages from the wider world, messages in the newspapers, books, and magazines they read, or brought by the U.S. Mail.

Many swindlers, to be sure, plied their trade in person. They were adept at face-to-face schemes. But these schemes often presupposed the anonymities of a mobile society. Con men slipped from place to place, geographically speaking; they also milked the fact of *social* ambiguity.

It was an age in which boundaries between classes (of every sort) were more porous than before. It was possible to pass oneself off as a lord, a professor, or a rich investor, which simply could not have been done in a tight, controlled, barnacled society where the markers of class are more obvious, if not indelible. Victorian society was a society of emulation. The respectable wealthy set the tone; and the middle classes and the respectable poor followed as best they could. Technology permitted the more obvious forms of emulation: cheap copies of hats or dresses; mass-produced artifacts and furniture. This made it possible for your humble parlor to resemble the parlor of your betters. But the drive to imitate was social and cultural; technology helped but did not create this drive.

The United States was, of course, a much more egalitarian society than England; but it was far from classless, and there were certainly rich, and very rich; and poor, and very poor. It was also easier here to imitate one's betters than in England—in voice, dress, and manner. This opened up rich opportunities for fleecing the gullible. Newspapers and crime literature are full of imposters, fake doctors, brokers, tycoons, foreign potentates, English lords, a Russian Count, and the like[8]—even imitation priests and nuns, men like James Crawford who, in 1902, dressed as a priest, went from house to house asking for money; or Mrs. Emma Meyer, whose disguise was the "garb of the Little Sisters of the Poor."[9] Charity collectors were frequently swindlers, and at the very bottom of the scale there were the "one-armed, or one-legged beggars, whose missing member, sound as your own, is strapped to their bodies . . . out of sight, [or] women wishing to bury their husbands or children, women with hired babies, and sundry other objects calculated to excite your pity."[10]

Many prominent swindlers aimed much, much higher in their impostures. A certain "Norman La Grange, Lieutenant Colonel of the Queen's Guards," swaggered about the Waldorf Hotel, in New York in 1894. This gentleman, who, of course, never paid his bill, was a confidence man who sometimes passed himself off as "Lord Ashburton."[11] George Walling, former police chief of New York, described Dr. Gabor Nephegyi, a great swindler, as someone who "lived gorgeously.... He was unmistakably a man of taste, education and refinement," with "extraordinary" powers of conversation.[12] Just as fleas and ticks tend to stick to a single species of animal, some con men preyed exclusively on one species of victim: hotel operators, or undertakers, or lawyers.[*]

Some swindlers came from good backgrounds; for these people, swindling was, perhaps, a form of downward mobility. Many other small or large-scale deceivers were simply cheating and pretending their way up the ladder. A fascinating little squib in the newspapers, in 1888, described the caper of a housemaid in Reading, Pennsylvania. When the mistress went away, the maid put on her employer's "best dress," and called on "ladies" in the city. These visits were, apparently, a success; the ladies returned the visit, and the maid entertained them handsomely. If she had been able to resist the temptation to steal goods as well as status, she might have gotten by.[15]

Too Many Weddings

Another reflex of mobility was the apparent rise in the incidence of bigamy in the late nineteenth century. We have already met one of these bigamists, in the introduction. Bigamy, of course, was not a new crime in the nineteenth century. The common law had disapproved of bigamy for a very long time. In colonial Maryland, for example, we read about a certain Anne Thompson, who was "burnt in the hand for having two husbands."[16] Sarah Forland suffered the same punishment for the same crime in 1756.[17]

---

[*] One check-raising scam was practiced mostly on small-town undertakers. The con man told the undertaker his dear brother had just passed on; he needed a cheap coffin. He paid the undertaker in cash with a large banknote but insisted on a check for his change, so that it could be sent by mail to the grieving family. The con man raised the amount on the (genuine) check, cashed it, and immediately moved on.[13]

In another scam aimed mainly at lawyers, a young man who passed himself off as the nephew of a prominent lawyer and an agent for the *Minneapolis Journal* "victimized practically all the lawyers in Watertown, S.D., and a number in Brookings, S.D." He claimed to be tubercular and in need of money to travel to Arizona for his health.[14]

Every state code made bigamy a crime. In Tennessee, for example: "If any person, being married, shall marry another person, the former husband or wife then living, or continue to cohabit with such second husband or wife in this State, such person shall be imprisoned in the penitentiary not less than two nor more than twenty-one years."[18] Comparative figures are difficult to come by, but there seemed to be a growth spurt in bigamy prosecutions in the nineteenth century, especially the last part of the century and into the early twentieth century. It was never a particularly common crime, as far as we can tell, compared to ordinary property offenses; but there is a constant drumbeat of newspaper accounts, and a small but definite number of arrests: twelve in Philadelphia in 1897, sixty in New York in 1913, seventeen in Los Angeles in 1914–15.[19]

Bigamists can be divided into two broad categories. The first is a group of swindlers, plain and simple—men like the bounder J. Aldrich Brown, who (according to detectives) had a rich career as a serial husband in the 1880s. He married at least seventeen times, staying no more than ten days with each wife. Brown was forty-five, "handsome, intelligent-appearing," and six feet, two inches tall. He specialized in "sewing girls in wealthy families"; he robbed them of "their little savings, their valuables and wearing apparel," which he sold before disappearing.[20] A less flamboyant example of this type was James Dougherty, who in 1869 married a young "domestic" in Darby, Pennsylvania. She had a nest egg of about six hundred dollars. Dougherty wormed most of it out of her, claiming he needed the money to buy a house; then he eloped to New Castle, Delaware, with another woman.[21]

Another group consisted of men who were not swindlers so much as restless or faithless husbands. These men found marriage number one unfulfilling for one reason or another; so they decamped without bothering to get a divorce and started over again, often in a different locale. Philip A. Mitchell, said to be a "leading clothier" of Bridgeport, Connecticut, fled his home in September of 1888 when a woman arrived from New York claiming to be his real wife. She produced photographs and a marriage certificate. He had dumped her after nine days of marriage.[22] John Wilgen had a wife and two children in Minneapolis, where he worked for a printer. He corresponded with Rena Mead of Bradford, Pennsylvania. Wilgen married Mead on August 18, 1897, in Limestone, New York. He passed himself off as a "man of wealth and position" and told people he had to go to Minneapolis "on important business." Mead's family ultimately became suspicious and began to investigate; Wilgen's double life fell to pieces.[23]

Dr. John W. Hughes, whose trial for murder was one of the sensations of 1865, had been born in the Isle of Man. He emigrated with his first wife to the United States in 1862, served as a doctor in the Union Army, and then settled in Cleveland, where he practiced medicine. There he met young Tamzen Parsons. The doctor described what happened in these words: "a wild mad love took possession of me, such an one as I had never experienced before." He pretended he was divorced, and married Tamzen; for this he was arrested for bigamy and adultery, convicted, and jailed. When he was released, he went back to his family; but the "wild mad love" never left him. One night, after a "drunken revel," he went to see Tamzen. She tried to avoid him and rushed away; he shouted at her to stop and fired two shots from his revolver; Tamzen died. Hughes was arrested, tried, and convicted; in February of 1866, he was hanged in the yard of the Cleveland jail.[24]

Why did the second wives marry the men in these cases—often men who were almost total strangers to them, who told wild stories about their businesses, their fortunes, their families? Certainly, some of these women were extremely naïve or rash or gullible. Rena Mead, the second wife of John Wilgen, "had fallen in love with his picture, which he had caused to be published by a matrimonial agency."[25] But this is not the whole story. The key is the social role of nineteenth-century women. Women were not free to roam; or hardly ever. Their mobility was the mobility of their men: fathers, husbands.

Bigamy, as a crime, illustrates the primacy of *choice* in personal relationships: the unraveling of ascriptive, traditional ties. Mobility and choice, however, meant one thing to men, another to women. Men could be and often were rolling stones; women never had the privilege. Nineteenth-century women did choose their husbands; or had veto power, at least. But a woman's place was still very much in the home. If the male ideal was ambition and hard work, the female ideal was service and obedience. Her function was marriage and childcare. A woman's world was the sphere of domesticity.[26]

For women, there were only two respectable patterns of life: marriage and chastity. Chastity had its drawbacks, to say the least. It was a virtue for young women, but it lost its luster over the years. Nobody wanted to be an "old maid," or a spinster. These were pathetic and useless creatures, in men's estimation at least. Into this void, stepped the handsome, mysterious stranger. Sometimes he promised money and success. Women could hardly achieve these on their own; at the very least, the stranger promised a way out of a lonely, useless life. Some women leaped to the bait. Some of these women got what they bargained for, or a reasonable approximation. Some did not. Among these were the unfortunate victims of bigamy.

For women, then, victimization by bigamists was part of a system of truncated mobility, and a reflex of their limited social role. But bigamy was also a sign of emancipation. It is a crime of exogamy. As we said, the age of arranged marriages was over. There is no bigamy where parents choose mates for their children; or where marriages only take place inside tight groups, clans, villages, family groups. The women who married bigamists were "modern" in the sense that they chose their own husbands. To be sure, they "fell for a line"; they agreed to share their life with a man with no authenticated past. They said "I do" without getting a real picture of their husband's family, or his background, without immersing themselves in their husband's world, his circle of friends.

Bigamy tells us a lot about American society, as well as about gender roles. The handsome stranger, the rich stranger, was not an object of suspicion—not necessarily. The whole country was awash with strangers. It was no crime to be a rolling stone. It was also a period in which missing people were hard to trace. A husband who walked out, a wife who disappeared—who was to say they were still alive? People died all the time—of accidents, disease. After years of silence, perhaps we can assume they *were* dead. *Some* men and women who committed bigamy must have honestly believed their spouse had passed on. Or wanted to believe.*

A few women turned the tables on men and committed bigamy themselves. Catherine and Rocco Fennelle were married in Italy in 1875; the marriage disintegrated some time after they emigrated to the United States. In 1896, Catherine met Pasquale Corino. He had $20,000 in gold, and she married him without bothering to shed Rocco legally.[28] More commonly, women were victims. They were lied to, betrayed, defrauded. Worst of all, they lost something almost beyond price: their chastity, their respectability.

This last point is probably the key to the horror that bigamy evoked. Victims of bigamy were, in the language of the times, "ruined" women; that is, women who had lost their virginity, their ticket to respectable matrimony. Even worse, the second wife was living in sin. She was committing a legal and social crime—through treachery. This was an impossible situation. When the American wife of Theodore Foens, a "big, handsome man" who had emigrated from Denmark, found out that he had a wife back home in Copenhagen, she promptly turned him in to the police. She felt "like a Judas," but she had no choice: "I had to protect my good name."[29]

Laws punishing bigamy were, in other words, part of a dense system of social norms about chastity and respectability. The law protected these goods, for the sake of "decent" women, and for the sake of the

---

* Courts and legal scholars were unclear whether a person accused of bigamy could use good-faith belief as a defense.[27]

men in their lives as well. Bigamy laws were only a small part of this system, which included laws against seduction, against statutory rape, and similar offenses (see chapter 10), not to mention the civil action for breach of promise of marriage.

Bigamy seems to have gone into decline in the 20th century. Published, reported cases are not a very reliable gauge of what the criminal justice system is up to. Still, for what it is worth, I note that the digests of reported cases for 1870 to 1910 list dozens of appellate cases about bigamy; the *Decennial Digest* for 1966–76 lists only two. There are still, to be sure, occasional cases of bigamy; but fewer than in the past. There are a number of reasons why. Divorce is easier to get, relatively cheap, and carries much less stigma. Gender roles, too, have changed considerably; women are more mobile, less dependent on marriage (to a degree). Chastity is certainly not what it used to be. A little sex here and there does not "ruin" a woman forever or destroy her chances of getting married—not, at least, in most circles of society. Swindling is still a growth industry; and there are surely men who are eager to separate women from their money. But the drastic step of marriage is no longer central to the scheme.

Mobility and Murder

Mobility was the soil in which bigamists and swindlers thrived; in it grew rich crops of victims as well. These crimes were also *threats* to mobility. They were perversions of it, misuses of it, and hence attacks on the very basis of American society.

When a man left home to seek his fortune, he was playing a classic American game; but the game had rules. Bigamists and swindlers abused the rules, took advantage of them. This is why they were condemned, hounded, punished. America was full of towns and communities peopled by strangers. Strangers were ambivalent figures at best. It is hard to trust a stranger. But a society of strangers, like all societies, depends on trust, shared norms, on common understandings, on basic expectations.

At the very core of the system of criminal justice was a profound distrust of men without settled connections. As we have seen, the laws and norms weighed heavily against hoboes, vagrants, tramps. These were the debris of mobility, the failures at the game of seeking one's fortunes, those whose habits of life mocked American ideals. They were not out looking for opportunities, they were looking for handouts, rummaging in garbage cans, begging, stealing, hanging around. No greater affront to respectability can possibly be imagined.

Mobility affected crime and punishment in a deeper, more pervasive way. It worked on the motivations of men (and, to a degree, women) in society. It held out opportunities that not everybody could take; it offered hopes that were frequently dashed. For some people, crime was a shortcut to money and position. For others, it was a consequence of rootlessness and anomie. Of course, mobility had different meanings for different classes of the population. It had, as we have seen, different meanings for men and women; men and women stood on a different footing in society. Mobility and gender relations were interlaced in many "ordinary" crimes, not only in bigamy. Any crime could be a crime of mobility. Even murder.

The celebrated trial of Chester Gillette, which inspired Theodore Dreiser's novel, *An American Tragedy*, is a good example. Dreiser's version was not far from the "real life" drama in its essential outline. Gillette was accused of murdering Grace Brown at Big Moose Lake, New York, early in the twentieth century. Gillette was an ambitious young man; he was poor, but he had wealthy relatives. Unfortunately, he was burdened with a plain, working-class girlfriend. She became pregnant; he killed her, because she stood in his way. A jury convicted Gillette, and he was put to death.[30]

Dreiser's choice of title was extremely apt. This *was* an American tragedy, American to the core. It was a tragedy of upward mobility, of a young man's climb up the ladder. What thwarted Gillette were the rules of gender relations in respectable society. On the one hand, the blurring of class lines made the tragedy possible. What Gillette dreamed of achieving was certainly not impossible. Far from it; the goal seemed just within reach. But Grace Brown held him back. On the other hand, Grace, too, had aspirations. In England, thousands of servant girls were seduced and abandoned by the men they worked for: sons of merchants, young baronets, doctors, members of the bar. But these victims never had Grace's chance. They could never hope to force a man of higher rank into marriage. Grace's hopes were real, and they led to her death.

Nineteenth-century America was a land of opportunity—for some. Opportunity means, in part, the chance to change identities. All the crimes discussed in this chapter were crimes that turned on false identity, or false position in society. The great virtue of a traditional community is that nobody ever has to ask: Who am I? Its great vice is that one is stuck forever with the answer. In this country, men (and, to some extent, women)* were allowed to choose who they were; allowed to discover and create an identity. But this game had rules, and breaking the rules was a

---

* It goes without saying that these statements refer primarily to *white* men and women; the law paid little respect to chastity, respectability, and choice of identity among blacks; and, especially in the South, the law positively hindered black mobility. *Within* black society, however, many of the same social norms that ruled white society applied as well.

crime. In the twentieth century, as we shall see, the rules changed once more, and the criminal justice system changed along with it.

The crimes discussed in this chapter also concern another core concept of nineteenth-century culture: *respectability*. This is a quality that can inhere in anybody, regardless of wealth, or class. Not everybody can become rich or famous. In this society, failure is just as common as success, probably more common. Respectability is a kind of consolation prize. Anybody who really wants it can achieve it; and the status that goes with it. But what *is* respectability? Essentially, it is a way of life, a code of conduct. And there is nothing standing in the way (formally at least). Anyone can lead a respectable life; anyone can be honest, virtuous, clean-living, just, and humane.

Respectability is an inner quality; but like a lot of inner qualities, it is judged by outward appearances: the way a person dresses, walks, talks, comports herself. It is the community, the public, common reputation, and the like, that confer "respectable" status on people. In communities made up of strangers, or in which lots of people come and go, community reputation is not a safeguide. The bigamist and swindler took advantage of this structural flaw. They imitated respectable behavior; they were imposters of respectability. This was among the worst aspects of their crimes.

The nineteenth century, as we have seen, put great value on appearances. Secret vice was not condemned as much as open vice; this was the essence of what I called the "Victorian compromise" (see chapter 6). In this regard, too, there was a great divide between the nineteenth and the twentieth centuries. If the theme of the nineteenth century was mobility, the theme of the twentieth, as we shall see, was self-expression. Both themes went to the very heart of the criminal justice system.

The Rise of the Detective

American society was a society of strangers, not all of them honest men. Some of the bad eggs were swindlers of various stripes, who assumed and reassumed identities, mostly false ones. Of course, most criminals were, as always, members of the "dangerous classes." It was pretty obvious, from the way these people walked, talked, dressed, and behaved that they were not part of respectable society. In small, old communities, everybody knew (or thought they knew) all the good-for-nothings, the violent people, the lopsided. This same knowledge was difficult to obtain in a city, or in a new community of whatever size. Swindlers did not advertise themselves as swindlers; on the contrary, they imitated polite society; they could succeed only if they kept their criminal identity secret.

It took new and different techniques to fight this kind of crime. The man who used these techniques occupied a new social role: the detective. The nineteenth century invented the detective along with the policeman. Detective squads, or divisions, were organized in Boston in 1846, New York in 1857, Philadelphia in 1859, and Chicago in 1861.[31]

The detective, in some ways, has a fairly old lineage. One strand in his history goes back to the "thief-takers" in England or America. These were constables who had connections in the underworld; they were skilled at getting stolen property back, though usually at a price. The most notorious "thief-taker" was Jonathan Wild, who became rich and famous in England in the eighteenth century, before ending up on the gallows.[32] There were constables who acted more or less like "thief-takers" in Boston and New York as early as 1820.[33] Many victims of theft were glad to pay to get their goods back, no questions asked. Of course, this was a source of corruption and scandal. In New York in the 1870s we hear about dishonest detectives who "deliberately divide with thieves." The owners regained about two-thirds of the "plunder"; the thief and the detective split the rest. "This business enables some of the force to wear big diamonds, and own and live in brown stone fronts, on a salary of $1,200 a year."[34] A number of Boston detectives were also out-and-out go-betweens; they were adept at getting back stolen bonds, cash, gold watches—but, again, the victim had to pay. Some noisome scandals were the result.[35]

In order to succeed, the "thief-taker" had to be well known in the underworld. But there was also his opposite number: the undercover detective—stealthy, sometimes in disguise, often worming his way into criminal circles through trickery. He was, in short, a kind of reverse con man. The detective, wrote George Walling in 1887, "must have, at times, histrionic traits, and must be able not only to wear a disguise, but to enact the personage he assumes to be."[36]

The uniformed police were obvious, overt, extremely visible. They patrolled social space, keeping order, preventing or squashing riots, arresting public drunks and brawlers. The detective was covert, sly, masked, underground—his domain was the secret crimes, the crimes of simulated identity, the swindles, the mysterious and the unsolved, the behavior in the shadows of great cities. The uniformed patrols, as Gary Marx points out, protected "concrete property rights" and policed "visible offenses." But the "more abstract property rights and invisible offenses called forth invisible police and deception," in short, the detective.[37]

The detective, then, was the counterfoil to society's hidden crimes and deceits. One of the most interesting accounts of the detective is a book called *Knots Untied*, an exploration of the "hidden life of American detectives," published in 1873 and attributed to a New York detective, George McWatters. Much of the book is devoted to the exploits of McWatters, his triumphs, his amazing feats of detection. But in an interesting final chapter, McWatters paints a grim, cynical picture of American capitalism. There are, he says, only two "great classes in civilization—the oppressed and the oppressors, the trampled upon and the tramplers." The detective is, and has to be, one of the tramplers. "He is dishonest, crafty, unscrupulous, when necessary to be so. He tells black lies when he cannot avoid it; and white lying, at least, is his chief stock in trade." He is, in short, "a satire upon society. He is a miserable snake, not in a paradise, but in the social hell."[38]

But the detective has "one palliative to his conscience"; the lies, the trickery, the falseness, the betrayal are all in the interests of "justice." When all is said and done, he can stand erect as a "public benefactor." The detective is the answer society gives to the problem of secret, mobile, complex crime. Only lies and shams can counter shams and lies. The detective is a master of unmasking. McWatters "can tell a rascal by a sort of instinct. A stranger to him is like a piece of coin in the hand of the skilful medallist."[39]

The book gives many examples of this skill. New York was full of young men "of large appetite and small conscience," who specialized in eating free at hotels. McWatters enters the dining room of the Metropolitan Hotel. He glances about the room with his "penetrative optics." Aha! He sees Jack Vinton, "that most notable and audacious of non-paying hotel diners," whose "brassy impudence" had "enabled him to pass muster, as a guest of the hotel." Vinton, at twenty-three, is a "master swindler" with "the manners of a polished gentlemen." But McWatters ("who, by the way, was in citizen's dress") saunters over and asks him, politely, if he was "stopping at this hotel," and "Is your name registered?" "Registered? I never heard of such a name...." "You misunderstand me. Is your name on the hotel books?" They play cat and mouse, but Jack soon sees that the game is up. In desperation, he offers to pay for the meal, but McWatters is not to be put off. He "conveys" Jack to the Second District Police Court, "to answer this and other graver offences of swindling."[40]

The incident shows the "histrionic" skill of the master detective. He had to be able to disguise himself, and to play many roles. Just as the thief "ingratiates himself among honest men in order to plunder them, so the honest man associates with thieves in order to frustrate their plans."[41] He can "read a man at a glance. He knows a bogus story from a real one."[42] But this, of course, was only part of the work of the detective. Much of it was less glamorous, and more scientific. The detective was also the official who used "scientific" methods in fighting crime.

His acts of detection and unmasking were accomplished not only on the streets but, increasingly, through patient "detective" work—sifting clues, following leads, and (finally) making use of the fancy findings of the lab.*

The nineteenth century also invented a new form of literature: the mystery, or detective story.[44] In the 1840s, Edgar Allan Poe wrote "The Murders in the Rue Morgue" and two other short stories, which (in hindsight at least) gave birth to countless thousands of "mysteries."[45] In England, Wilkie Collins published *The Moonstone* in 1868, and Arthur Conan Doyle launched the greatest of all fictional detectives, Sherlock Holmes, in *A Study in Scarlet* in 1887.[46] In the United States, Anna K. Green published *The Leavenworth Case* in 1878, sold an enormous number of copies, and launched a fabulous writing career for herself. By the end of the century, this form of writing was already amazingly popular—as it is to this day.

Each mystery story is unique, of course, but the form does observe certain conventions and regularities. In the classic format, the criminal (usually a murderer) is not exposed until the last chapter; up to that point, no one, including the reader, knows who he or she is. If, in fact, the reader has guessed who "did it," the book has probably failed. The ending should be, if possible, a total surprise. The criminal, in other words, cannot be obvious; the dastardly villain must turn out to be someone masquerading as a noncriminal, as an ordinary person. It must be someone harboring secret identities and motives.

These characteristics are already present in *The Moonstone*, Collins's masterpiece. The crime was the theft of a fabulous diamond. The real villain's name comes out only in the last few pages; he turns out to be an upper-class character in the novel who had been leading a double life for years.[47] One character in *The Moonstone* is an actual detective, Sergeant Cuff. In the "detective-story" the person who ferrets out the crime and uncovers the secrets may be a genuine crime-worker or a cunning amateur. In later years, the "detective" in such stories could be anyone imaginable—a lord or lady, a village spinster, like Agatha Christie's Miss Marple; a priest; a rabbi; a stockbroker; a blind man; heaps of lawyers; men, women, and children; the list is endless. I am not aware of a dentist detective, but there must be one somewhere. Through all this, however, the essence of the story remains nonetheless the dif-

---

* Besides public detectives, there were also private detectives. The most successful and famous of these in the nineteenth century was Allan Pinkerton, who founded the detective agency whose logo was an open staring eye. The private detectives worked for private companies (sometimes providing them with strikebreakers) as well as for individuals, investigating crimes (such as embezzlement) or grubbing about in the muck of divorce and infidelity.[43]

ference between the surface world and the hidden world, and the ability of some men and women to glide noiselessly in between.

Thus the "double life," the hidden identity, is at the heart of the detective story, just as it is at the heart of crimes of mobility in general. In this sense, popular literature, like criminal justice, reflected the norms of the general society, the context of daily life. In modern, anonymous, anomic society, one cannot rely on appearance, on social markers, on accent, on anything, to tell good from evil, human from subhuman, saint from murderer.

The detective story, then, is the fictional version of the work of the real-life detective—very stylized, very formulaic, but related, nonetheless. Both reflect a fluid, restless, mobile social system, with endless possibilities for false identity, mysterious origins, strange secrets. The detective (amateur or professional) cuts through to the hidden core. His or her skill consists of reading tiny clues to sniff out identities. Sherlock Holmes was the ultimate master. In *The Hound of the Baskervilles* (1902), a man calls on Holmes while he is out and leaves behind his walking stick. Holmes returns and deduces that his caller was a country doctor, "under thirty, amiable, unambitious, absent-minded, and the possessor of a favourite dog, which I should describe roughly as being larger than a terrier and smaller than a mastiff." In *The Leavenworth Case*, Ebenezer Gryce, a much dimmer American detective, looks at the way a gun was wiped clean and decides the killer could not have been a woman; he thus rules out the two beautiful Leavenworth cousins, who were prime suspects in the killing of their uncle.

These are heightened and exaggerated forms of the feats of a man like McWatters, a true detective of New York. Class and character were easily imposed and disguised; but they did leave behind a residue, as fragile as an ash or a smudge. The clever detective was able to decipher the code, peel away the outer covering, find the telltale marks, and reveal the underlying reality. As we have already noted, the idea of "born criminals" became popular toward the end of the century, along with a "science" of criminal anthropology and anthropometry, which claimed that the born criminal could be identified through physical signs, shapes of the skull, and the like (see, further, chapter 15). But these were low, vulgar, atavistic brutes, who committed crimes because it was in their blood. The higher class of criminal gave off a more subtle kind of signal: these were men and women of good family whose character had curdled—the confidence men, the forgers and imposters, the swindlers and rogues. They were people of misused, perverted talent. Among the criminal class, according to Allan Pinkerton, were "men of powerful minds, of strong will, and of educational advantages which, if correctly applied would have enabled them to make their mark in the professional and business circles of the community."[48] Here was, of course, the natural quarry of the detective.

Forensic Science

Crime has always been clandestine, but in the nineteenth century it had become clandestine in new and different ways. There were more mysterious crimes: dead bodies nobody could identify, thefts where the thieves skipped from town to town, and city to city—this in addition to the crimes already discussed in which identity also was an issue. The problems of secrecy, identity, and mobility set off a search for countermeasures, for new ways to find and label criminals. This was the century, then, of forensic science. It took all the ingenuity and technology of the century to keep up with the consequences of mobility. New York's detectives, we are told, were "in constant telegraphic communication with other cities," exchanging information about crimes and criminals. By the 1870s New York's detectives were using photographs of criminals for purposes of identification, collecting them in a "rogues' gallery."[49]

Another advance was the "Bertillon method," which was the rage in police departments at the end of the century. The system was named after Alphonse Bertillon, a Frenchman who worked for the Paris police, in the 1880s. Bertillon, a "young man with pale, thin, dismal face, slow movements, and an expressionless voice," who "suffered from bad digestion, nosebleeds, and terrible headaches," became obsessed with the problem of identifying criminals precisely.[50] The Bertillon method called for very exact physical measurements (length and width of the head, the dimensions of the feet, and so on), and very exact notations about scars and other features. Bertillon eventually devised a scheme that used eleven physical dimensions of body and limbs. This scheme, along with the use of photographs, made identification of criminals much more rigorous.[51] In the 1890s the Bertillon method became standard in police departments. Fingerprinting at first supplemented it, then later supplanted it.

The need for scientific rigor also affected the ancient office of the coroner, who held "inquests" when nobody was sure exactly how a particular body had become a corpse. In big cities, the coroner was something of a throwback. The coroner was a layman, often an undertaker, usually an elected official. Coroners and lay juries of inquest were all well and good in an old village, but big-time mysterious death required something better. As early as 1858, a committee of the American Medical Association suggested giving the coroner's job only to a "competent and respectable doctor in medicine."[52] Massachusetts abolished the office of coroner in 1877. Instead, each county was to designate "able and discreet men, learned in the science of medicine, to be medical examiners."[53]*

Mobility and Crime

In the nineteenth century, the culture of mobility and the culture of criminal justice were deeply intertwined and deeply interinvolved. Amateur justice does not work well in a society of cities, a society of people constantly moving about. Professionals are needed. The community cannot rely on gossips, on posses, on lay people in the halls of justice and in the correctional system. Hence the need for police, detectives, prison officials, medical examiners, forensic scientsts, and, in general, a growing army of criminal justice workers.

The relationship between the mobile society and criminality itself is tough and elusive. Serious crime, however defined, is related to rootlessness—to shifting and moving about—in various ways. To begin with, the shifting and moving creates special opportunities for crime; it encourages some kinds of crime. Swindling and bigamy were given as examples; there are certainly others. For example, the "fence," who deals in stolen property and makes markets for stolen goods, became an important figure in large cities, where goods are fungible and anonymous.[55] In the second place, the rootless and mobile fill the ranks of the criminal class—those who take advantage of the new opportunities. But these people also fill the ranks of victims of criminal (in)justice: they are the ones whom the system most persecutes, stigmatizes, and bedevils.

The traits we have discussed obviously increased in the course of the nineteenth century. Did *crime* itself increase? It is hard to tell. The statistical data is poor, and such as it is, it points in two directions at once. There is, on the one hand, some evidence for "crime waves," bulges in the curve, in this period. One notable wave occurred, apparently, a few years after the Civil War.[56] It would be no surprise if the war produced a crop of criminals. War could make soldiers callous about blood and guts, even comfortable with violence and death. War puts guns in the hands of young men. The war jerked men and boys out of their homes, disrupted social systems, and raped familiar landscapes. At the end of the war, military discipline was relaxed. The same young males were discharged, their inner selves disrupted and loose, rattling about inside a broken box of norms. The war, in other words, accelerated and exagger-

---

* New York did not get around to this reform until 1915; and Milwaukee, Wisconsin, got a medical examiner in 1942. As of 1942, however, the seventy other counties of Wisconsin still had coroners, thirty-three of them "persons directly engaged in the undertaking and funeral business." Only twenty were doctors.[54]

ated a state of mobile normlessness for the most crime-prone elements of the American population.

But this was a short-term trend. The long-term trend is exactly the opposite: crime almost certainly declined in the late nineteenth century, serious crime most notably. Most studies of arrest data and most guesses about crime rates show a *decline* in the late nineteenth century: arrests appear to go down, and as far as one can tell, so does serious crime. What was true for violence and "serious" crime was not necessarily true of "crime" in general. Still, homicide, the most easily measured crime, reached some sort of trough by about 1890, after which it began to rise again.[57] Most of the studies of crime rates, for all their flaws, do point in the same direction, as we have seen: a falling crime rate in the latter part of the century.

It is certainly not easy to explain what was happening. Why had the country become more civil, or indeed more *civilized* (for want of a better word)? Policing was not as haphazard as it had been before the organization of police forces; perhaps this accounts for some of the change. But on the whole, it is a puzzle. And an even greater puzzle lies ahead, in the twentieth century. After the middle of the century—after 1950, say—the trend reversed itself with a vengeance. The dam went smash in the night and dark waters of crime flooded the country. When we discuss the late twentieth century, this question will be in the front of our minds: What was it that let down the barriers? What, in short, brought about a collapse of civility, and sent the curve of violent crime through the roof?

10

WOMEN AND CRIMINAL JUSTICE TO THE END OF THE NINETEENTH CENTURY

IN THE DRAMA OF CRIMINAL JUSTICE, MOST LEADING PLAYERS HAVE BEEN MEN; heroes, villains, stagehands, hangers-on. Throughout most of our history, women have been shut out of key roles in criminal justice. There were no women lawyers before the 1870s, no judges or jurors to speak of until the twentieth century. Policewomen and women detectives came late to the scene, and remained uncommon. Women, of course, took the witness stand; and they contributed their share to the great roster of suffering victims. Women in large numbers were robbed, murdered, beaten (often by their husbands), seduced, cheated, and raped.

Women *criminals* were always in short supply. There were, of course, exceptions, some quite notable. "Mother Mandelbaum," the "queen of fences," handled stolen goods on an enormous scale. Her specialty was silk, but she dealt in every kind of stolen property. She had a good reputation as a businesswoman "whose honesty in criminal matters was absolute." When the police closed in on her, she fled to Canada.[1] "Madame Restell"—her actual name was Ann Lohman—was a notorious abortionist who began her work in the 1830s. She was arrested numerous times, and founded branches of her New York business in

Boston and Philadelphia.[2] Her career lasted until the 1870s; facing prosecution and disgrace, she slit her own throat with an ebony-handled carving knife in the bathtub of her mansion. In the Wild West there was Flora Quick, a horse thief of Oklahoma Territory with "hair as black as a raven's wing and eyes like sloes," who did her dirty work dressed as a man and calling herself Tom King. Probably no other western horse thief ever broke out of jail by seducing a sheriff's deputy and eloping with him.[3] There was also the occasional woman charged with murder: Lizzie Borden, who either did or did not give her father and stepmother forty whacks with an ax, was probably the most famous of these.

The criminal masses, of course, committed property crimes of staggering banality; and women were no exception. But the patterns of criminality among women were not the same as those among men. Women shied away from burglary. By some accounts they were underrepresented in the pickpocket business, perhaps because of the "manner in which women dress, and from the fact that females are nearly always more observed than men."[4]* But their clothing may, in fact, have given them an edge in shoplifting. This was particularly true, according to one detective in the 1880s, for the higher-class shoplifter. He described her as a woman who lived in a "fashionable private boarding-house" and never came home from a shopping foray "without a good haul." "Under their rich and costly silk dresses are thick, heavy skirts, in which are huge bags or pockets. Cleverly concealed slits in the dresses communicate with these pockets." A man had no such chance to hide goods.[6] According to another account, young women, "modest in demeanor," posing as flower girls, were the worst blackmailers in New York City. These women gained access to the "offices and counting rooms of professional men and merchants, and then, if the gentleman is alone, close the door, and threaten to scream and accuse him of taking improper liberties" unless he paid up.[7]

Most women who were arrested were probably none of the above. They were, instead, part of the underclass of great cities: neglected and destitute girls of the streets. There were women hoboes, vagrants, and tramps. When they turned to crime, women were not violent, as a rule. Sometimes, however, they formed gangs of petty thieves, and many of them turned to prostitution. No one, said George Templeton Strong, the New York lawyer and diarist, writing in 1851, could "walk the length of Broadway without meeting some hideous troop of ragged girls, from twelve years old down, brutalized already almost beyond redemption by premature vice, clad in the filthy refuse of the rag-picker's collections,

---

* There were, of course, exceptions, such as Mabel Keating, the "pickpocket queen," the "most adept and dangerous of all the women in her class." This striking woman with hazel eyes was twenty-six years old when scooped up by the police in San Francisco in 1896.[5]

obscene of speech"; there was "foulness on their lips"; they had "thief written in their cunning eyes and whore on their depraved faces, though so unnatural, foul and repulsive in every look and gesture, that that last profession seems utterly beyond their aspirations."[8]

Yet the weak showing of women, particularly in crimes of violence, is constant, throughout American history; every study of the subject shows it, as does every state, city, or region that has figures for arrests, trials, and convictions. To take one example, in a sample of New York criminal cases in the latter part of the nineteenth century, less than 10 percent of defendants were women.[9] The percentages may vary a bit up and down; but women never have their "fair share"; and the more serious the crime, the less likely it is that women commit it. American women, on the whole, have simply never been a violent lot.

Indeed, the official line was that committing crimes was almost unthinkable for women, especially married women. "If a woman commit theft, burglary, or other civil offense," wrote Blackstone in the middle of the eighteenth century, "by the coercion of her husband, *or even in his company*, which the law construes a coercion, she is not guilty of any crime, being considered as acting by compulsion, and not of her own free will" (emphasis added).[10] In theory, then, a married woman ("feme covert" in legal jargon) was not guilty of a crime she seemed to be committing, if her husband was with her at the time, because the law treated him as the perpetrator and the wife as a helpless tool in his hands. It was this notion that led Mr. Bumble to his famous outburst, in Charles Dickens's *Oliver Twist*, that if the law believed any such thing, then the law "is a ass—a idiot."*

The doctrine of coverture, like many others, was English in origin and respectably old. The treatise writers felt that it was part of American law as well. The case law talks about it, and so do the scholars, well into the nineteenth century. Joel Bishop treated it seriously in 1858: the "feme covert" (married woman) is, he wrote, "under certain obligations of obedience, affection, and confidence" toward her husband. In return for this, the law "allows her this indulgence, that, if through constraint of his will she carries her duty of obedience to the excess of doing unlawful acts, she shall not suffer for them criminally."[12]

Very few reported cases actually seem to turn on the doctrine. Was it ever part of the living law? One careful study of colonial Pennsylvania turned up precious little evidence that courts took it seriously. In Pennsylvania, at least, a "woman seemed almost never to be the recipient of

---

* Mrs. Bumble had admitted stealing a locket and a ring. Mr. Bumble said "It was all Mrs. Bumble. She would do it"; only to be told that "the law supposes that your wife acts under your direction." This was the statement that evoked Bumble's famous reply. He continued by saying, "If that's the eye of the law, the law's a bachelor; and the worst I wish the law is, that his eye may be opened by experience."[11]

leniency because of her alleged legal subservience to her mate."[13] The doctrine was codified in a few states in the nineteenth century.[14] But most likely there was not much enthusiasm for applying it in practice.

Sally Freel was convicted of murder in the second degree in Arkansas in 1860. She had (allegedly) aided and abetted her husband in the killing. In her appeal she invoked the doctrine of coverture. An Arkansas statute excused married women "acting under the threats, commands or coercion of their husbands." But this did not save her. Upholding her conviction, the Arkansas court said that "Marriage does not deprive the wife of the legal capacity of committing crime," and "the mere presence of her husband does not excuse her."[15] The doctrine was a two-edged sword. In *Mulvey v. State*[16] James Mulvey was convicted of selling liquor without a license. Mulvey was a policeman; his wife owned a grocery store in Mobile. Two men went into the store and asked for whiskey. Mulvey "directed his wife, who was then behind the counter," to give the men what they wanted. They drank and paid twenty cents. The court upheld Mulvey's conviction. "As a general principle, when the wife acts under the coercion of the husband . . . she is not responsible. . . . Criminally, she is not guilty." Mulvey, "by his conduct . . . made his wife's act his own."*

By mid-century probably, and certainly by the century's end, the doctrine was crumbling to dust. Men and women stood equal in the eyes of the criminal law. Subordination of wives was not a *legal* dogma anymore. Signs of this change had been visible in earlier case law. In 1854 in Pennsylvania, a woman named Samantha Hutchinson was indicted "as a common scold." She was convicted, but the appellate court threw the case out. How could there be behavior, the court wondered, that was criminal "when acted by a woman, and innocent and lawful when acted by a man"? In the age of "barbarism" women were regarded "as the slave and not the companion of man." That was the age "when women were burnt as witches, and men had their ears nailed to a pillory." Under "Christian civilization" women were entitled to "equality of right and consideration."[18]†

---

* In a Massachusetts case of 1873, the defendant, Jason Reynolds, was·charged with "illegal sale of intoxicating liquor." The evidence was this: two men twice went to Reynolds's house and bought whiskey from his wife in the kitchen. The defendant was not "present" but came in "while the witnesses were there," and said nothing to them at all about the liquor. Was Reynolds guilty of a crime? The judge instructed the jury that he was, *if* his wife was acting as "his agent or servant." It was legally significant that they were together in the house, "in the usual relations of marriage." The jury convicted, and a higher court affirmed. The case, obviously, rested on an idea *like* coverture: the subordination of wives to their husbands.[17]

† Of course, the societies that burnt women at the stake and nailed men to the pillory considered themselves Christian civilizations, too—indeed, very Christian and very civilized. But legal memories are short.

The Woman Victim

Whatever this Pennsylvania judge may have thought, and however the formal law put it, the "companion of man" was very far from equality with her companion in actual fact. Women were, for one thing, disproportionately victimized, as we have said. Men raped, abused, and beat thousands of women. Domestic violence was an everyday matter, and overwhelmingly it ran in one direction, that is, from man to woman, not the other way around. The formal law, of course, condemned brutality toward women, although its attitude toward wife-beating, as we shall see, was a shade ambivalent. Rape was a felony, and penal codes took it very, very seriously. In many states it carried that dread sign of seriousness, the death penalty.[19] Brutality and assault were crimes, too. But women had almost no voice in defining these crimes or in shaping the law of rape or domestic violence. They had little or no voice in enforcement strategies or policy. There was a women's rights movement in the nineteenth century, but it was fighting an uphill battle, and on the whole a losing one. Men who beat women, who harassed them, who raped them, were arrested by men, tried by men, sentenced by men; and in many ways, the system looked at the whole process through men's eyes, using men's standards and men's consciousness.

Nowhere was this as clear as in the law of rape. The flat, legalistic words of the law books covered over male biases and assumptions. For one thing, the law really protected only "respectable" white women (and their menfolk). Women who were not "respectable," or who were black, or Native American, were effectively outside the circle of protection. Of course, the words of the statutes never *said* as much, but that was the practical result; it was rare for poor or black women to seek or get justice after rape.[20] In general, too, men and women had, on the whole, different ideas about what constituted force, violence, unfair coercion; and women's ideas were not the ones translated into law, or taken into account there.

Rape was a classic crime, with a long history behind it. Every state had its own statute, from early on. Rape was violent, nonconsensual intercourse: it was a crime to "ravish," as a New York law of 1787 put it, "a married woman, or maid, or any other woman." Other acts, too, were labeled rape. The New York statute made it rape to "know and abuse any woman child, under the age of ten years ... unlawfully and carnally." This was so-called statutory rape: sex with a child was taboo, and "consent" was no defense at all. A special provision applied to rich women, women with "substance," either in "goods moveable" or "in lands and tenements" or who were "heirs apparent unto their ancestors." If some villain wanted their "lucre," took them against their will, and either married them or "defiled" them, this, too, was a felony, and, like rape, was punishable by death.[21] The language of the rape laws became less archaic over time, but the formal law did not change very much before 1900.[22] The southern states retained the death penalty for rape. In Alabama, for example, the jury had discretion to decide between death or life imprisonment.[23]

We have already seen the role of rape on the southern racial code. To *convict* of rape, North or South, the law required proof of "penetration." Nothing short of this would do.* (Southern lynch mobs were less fussy.) And penetration had to be violent. Consent was a defense to rape, since the law required the "carnal knowledge" to occur "forcibly and against her will."[25] But the yardstick, in practice, was what the average male *considered* consent; and there is no reason to think that this was the same as what the average woman might think. "Just say no" was not official doctrine. The law required the woman to put up a real fight; anything less was considered a kind of grudging consent. Popular culture glorified the woman who defended her honor—even to the death. Thus, in 1894 Clara Casper, a seventeen-year-old of Fort Lee, New Jersey, "fought for her release until her strength gave way, finally fainting"; and Minnie Rauhauser, also seventeen, of New York City, fought off the advances of William Miller, a toolmaker. He cut her throat "from ear to ear," and thus she died, according to the *New York Times*, "bravely in defense of her honor."[26] A woman who yielded, even under pressure, had really no right to complain. A woman was supposed to resist with every ounce of her strength.

The reported rape cases underscore this point. Charles Dohring, of New York, was convicted of raping Frederica Brussow, a servant, fourteen years old, in 1874. He trapped her (she said) in the barn, fastened the door, and threw her down on the ground; she started to cry, and he promised to "buy her a new dress" if she let him have his way. She told him she was afraid of getting "in the family way"; no problem, he said, he was "an old man." She "cried out and tried to get away but could not, as he held her down."[27]

Had she resisted enough? A woman must use (said the court) the "utmost resistance," the "greatest effort of which she is capable . . . to preserve the sanctity of her person." Resistance must go to the point "of being overpowered by actual force, or of inability from loss of strength

---

* On penetration, see, for example, *Davis v. State*.[24] The victim's mother found the victim, a white child, on the ground with defendant, a black adult male, "in the act of copulation." The victim had red, swollen "private parts," but no blood or lacerations. A doctor, testifying for defendant, claimed that a "man of his dimensions" could not have penetrated without lacerations. The appeals court reversed because there was insufficient evidence of penetration.

longer to resist, or from the number of persons attacking resistance must be dangerous or absolutely useless, or there must be duress or fear of death." After all, this was what one had a right to expect; what woman (said the judges) would *not* be so "revoltingly unwilling" to be raped that she would not "resist so hard and so long as she was able"?[28]*

In theory, violating any woman, even a prostitute, was rape; but, as we have said, the practice was rather different. At least one southern court flatly rejected the idea that there could be such a thing as the rape of a black slave. After slavery died, southern courts (and lynch mobs) wreaked horrible revenge on black men accused of "defiling" white women; white-on-black rape was, apparently, rarely if ever prosecuted. But white or black, if a woman was not "chaste," not respectable, she had little hope of bringing a rapist to the bar of justice. The statutes did not, of course, make this point. Technically, it was a question of evidence, and a question of convincing a jury. But in actuality, the law protected "the unsullied virgin and the revered, loved and virtuous mother." One could hardly expect it to defend the "lewd and loose prostitute . . . whose arms are open to the embraces of every coarse brute who has money."[30]

It is very hard to get accurate figures on rape. This is true today, but even more hopeless for the past. The law was tilted away from the concerns of women victims, which discouraged these victims from coming forward.[†] "Respectable" women were very reluctant to report rapes, because of shame, prudery, the trauma of the legal process, and the stigma that attached itself to the victim. And women who were not "respectable" were in no position to complain. What does seem clear is that rape was always among the least-reported, least-prosecuted, and least-punished of the major crimes.

Virtue and Seduction

Rape was a violent crime, but the core of the crime was not violence; it was defilement. As a Georgia court put it, the "citadel" of a woman's

---

* Despite this language, the court affirmed Dohring's conviction, saying that, while the victim "may or may not have done all that she could do," it was for the jury to judge.

A few courts seemed to allow women to be a bit less heroic in their resistance and still claim rape; one such was *State v. Shields*.[29] This case was also unusual in that the victim, who suffered a gang rape, was not exactly a pillar of the community; in fact, there was testimony she had once lived in a "house of ill-fame." Presumably, as a married woman, she had mended her ways.

† Male fear that women might blackmail them or accuse them falsely of rape was an important factor in shaping the working law of rape. No doubt there *were* some instances of blackmail. And certainly the accusations were false in some of the southern cases where white women accused blacks of rape or attempted rape.

character was "virtue; when that is lost, all is gone . . . She esteems herself as put to the ban of society, and as incapable of deeper degradation."[31] Sex except with her husband "ruined" a woman, destroyed her life's chances, made her unfit for polite society. "Virtue" meant chastity for an unmarried woman, total fidelity for a married one. Loss of virtue was an unparalleled catastrophe—the worst thing that could befall a respectable woman. Whether these women themselves thought so, of course, is another question; basically, nobody asked them.

Themes of virtue and ruin underlie the statutes on rape. So, if a man "wilfully and maliciously" has "carnal knowledge of a married woman," by "pretending to be her husband," the act must be punished as if it were rape (according to a Tennessee law). This statute also contained a clause, quite typical, that made it a crime to have "carnal knowledge" of a woman by "administering to her any substance, or by any other means producing such stupor, imbecility of mind, or weakness of body, as to prevent effectual resistance."[32]

Men's attitudes toward loss of virtue seem somewhat hysterical to us in retrospect. Occasional cases of sexual trickery probably reinforced these attitudes. In an interesting Michigan case, the defendant Moran "violated" a girl of sixteen, who had been delivered to him for treatment for consumption, a disease Moran claimed to be "skilled" at handling. He told her a wild story about her condition; her uterus was "inverted," which was a most perilous situation. He could either operate, he said, which would probably kill her, or he could fix everything through the less dangerous method of "sexual connection."[33] In a Massachusetts case, Charles Stratton gave a young woman figs to eat; they contained "a large quantity of cantharides" and made her very sick. Charles did not deny doping up the figs but said, in his defense, that he thought the drugs were "love powders" and "perfectly harmless."[34]

These were not the standard ways to seduce a woman. A more humdrum sort of trickery and artifice underlay the crime of seduction—a criminal code entry that supplemented civil suits for seduction, and for breach of promise of marriage, and gave these added bite. Under a New York statute of 1848, any man who "under promise of marriage" seduced or had "illicit connexion with any unmarried female of previous chaste character" could be sentenced up to five years in prison.[35] A Georgia statute expressed almost poetic wrath: a man was guilty if "by persuasion and promises of marriage, or other false and fraudulent means" he was able to "seduce a virtuous unmarried female, and induce her to yield to his lustful embraces, and allow him to have carnal knowledge of her."[36]

These laws were not dead letters; there is a decent sprinkling of cases among the law reports, some of them of unusual interest. Walter Clark was convicted of seducing Alice J. Morey "under . . . a promise of marriage" in Michigan in the 1870s. The state tried to show three separate acts of "illicit intercourse." But, said the appellate court, sex acts numbers two and three could not be considered seduction, since after sex act number one, Alice was obviously no longer "chaste."* Walter also argued that Alice and her parents were plotting to "inveigle" him into marriage. He also disputed her account of the events. One of the acts of "illicit intercourse" took place, supposedly, in a buggy; Walter tried to show, by medical evidence, that sex in a buggy was "highly improbable if not impossible." He succeeded in winning a new trial.[37]

The core idea of the seduction statutes pops up elsewhere in criminal codes as well. An Ohio statute, passed in 1886, applied to any "male person over twenty-one years of age" who was a "superintendent, tutor or teacher in a private, parochial or public school, or a seminary . . . or instructor of any female in music, dancing, roller skating, athletic exercise, or any branch of learning." It was a crime for this "male person" to have "sexual intercourse, at any time or place," with a "female" who was "under his instruction," even though the intercourse was "with her consent." A lustful tutor could serve from two to ten years in the penitentiary.[38] The law, in effect, conclusively presumed that the tutor was a vile seducer, the pupil an innocent victim. Men were, after all, politically and socially dominant. And, in an age of double standards, women suffered far more than men from loss of innocence.

Men could, in short, be sent to jail for seduction, and some few men were. But this was hardly the real point of the laws. A woman could use seduction laws as a crude crowbar to force a man to marry her. This was hardly the way to begin a lifelong romance, but it was sometimes effective, especially if the woman was pregnant and faced social disaster. In 1867, an instructive account in the *Police Gazette* ran under the heading ALL'S WELL THAT ENDS WELL.[39] The story was as follows. People in Troy, New York, were "shocked" to learn that young James B. Hoyt had "been playing fast and loose with the affections of a charming young lady, a Miss Law." Law had allowed herself to be "overcome," perhaps because of "specious promises of marriage." The young man "refused to fulfil his promise"; there was nothing left to do but "apply to the young libertine the screws of the law." He was indicted and put on trial.

The trial, in a crowded courtroom, went badly for Hoyt. In desperation, he proposed "an offer of marriage." The young lady thought it

---

* Of course, the court admitted, a woman could repent and reform, and presumably become (more or less) chaste again; but there was such a short interval here between "illicit" acts that this theory did not hold water.

over—her sisters advised against it—and then said yes. Love "won the victory over reason." The courtroom cheered when the Reverend Dr. Baldwin arrived "to perform the marriage ceremony." The reverend did his stuff, the "prison gates" flew open, Hoyt was free, and the lovebirds "left the courtroom arm in arm."

This cautionary tale was not unique. In a Michigan case in 1888, Kate Morrow, of Shiawasee County, accused William Gould of "seducing and debauching her." On the day scheduled for trial, Gould married Kate during the court's lunchtime recess before a justice of the peace. But at seven o'clock that evening, he took "the east-bound train for Port Huron," deserting his wife. Gould was caught, arrested, tried, and convicted. But his conviction was reversed on appeal: the marriage, fleeting and loveless though it might have been, was enough to remove the criminal taint from Gould.[40]

These public soap operas, and the law behind them, told an important moral story. They also reflected an image of the respectable woman. She was pure, chaste, delicate, a precious flower to be protected from the buffeting of a rude and masculine world, a tropical bird in a silver cage. Society, through its legal system, had taken on the duty of protecting her honor and her sensibilities. Virtue and chastity were pearls of inestimable value.

These themes ran particularly deep in the legislation of the southern states. It was an offense under the law of Alabama to use "abusive, insulting, or obscene language" in the "presence or hearing of any female," or to "wilfully disturb" any women "at a public assembly, met for instruction or recreation, or in a railroad car, steamboat, or in any other public conveyance, or at a depot [or] landing" by "rude or indecent behavior, or by profane or obscene language."[41] Indeed, in Alabama the high court upheld the conviction of a man named Weaver, who, when asked to get out of his ex-wife's home, flashed back, in a rude and angry voice, "I'll go when I God damn please."[42]

Dillard v. Georgia (1870) was a more telling case.[43] The accused, James T. Dillard, asked Mary S. Sanders (a married woman) to "go to bed" with him. He was fined one hundred dollars. An appeals court upheld his conviction. The statute "is intended to protect females from insult." And what "higher insult to a virtuous woman can be conceived of than the language used in this case"? The statute also had another function. Friends and relatives of a woman who had been "unlawfully shocked, or whose feelings have been wounded" would feel an almost instinctual urge to avenge her honor: the law gave them a nonviolent alternative.

The Unwritten Law

The violent alternative was also possible. Adultery and seduction were evils, and the wages of these sins were ruination and, very possibly, death. Adultery and seduction were also, of course, highly attractive. The popular press, especially the lower levels of it, fed the public stories of seduction, elopement, and attempted rape; also murders and assaults with themes of sexual jealousy and revenge. The *National Police Gazette*, from the mid-1840s on, was a potent vehicle for such stories—stronger stuff than usually appeared in print, told luridly with pictures and a thinly disguised prurient leer. A typical headline (from 1878) read as follows: TERRIBLE TALE. ILLICIT LOVE AND ITS DIREFUL CONSEQUENCES. . . . A HUSBAND'S JEALOUSY. . . . MURDER OF HIS WIFE AND HER PARAMOUR."[44]

The so-called "unwritten law" decreed that a man had the right to avenge the sexual dishonor of a wife, mother, daughter, or sister. It is hard to pin a starting date onto so elusive an object as an "unwritten law," but this one apparently crept into criminal practice around 1840. The notorious trial of Congressman Daniel Sickles in 1859 for killing Philip Barton Key gave it a dramatic push forward. Key was the lover of Sickles's young wife. A jury acquitted Sickles, and the unwritten law was undoubtedly the primary reason.[45]

In the later years of the century, dozens of men were acquitted in more or less similar cases. Their lawyers used various legal approaches: self-defense, temporary insanity, and other dodges, but the real defense, sometimes made explicit in passionate speeches to juries, was the unwritten law.[46] Many of these indignant and outraged husbands were notorious philanderers themselves (it was certainly true of Sickles), but this seemed to make little or no difference to the (all-male) juries, since, after all, boys will be boys.

The unwritten law was thus a law for men only, on the whole. Women were not supposed to avenge themselves on husbands, kill mistresses, or that sort of thing. What a woman's husband did behind her back (or even flagrantly) did not destroy her sense of personal honor. She was supposed to grin and bear it. It was only when her own sexual virtue was at stake that violence might *possibly* be in order. Most women who killed former lovers were, in fact, convicted.[47] Kate Southern, a Georgia wife, stabbed her husband's mistress to death; she was convicted and sentenced to death.[48] By way of contrast, a different fate was in store for an "intelligent-looking young lady" who turned herself in to the Boston police in 1858. Her "suitor" had made her "a solemn promise of marriage, had accomplished her ruin," and then, in her "misfortune" (that is, her pregnancy), abandoned her. Desperate, she made ready a "double-barrelled pistol," loaded both barrels (his and hers), and shot him. She

succeeded only in wounding him. On these facts, the grand jury refused
to indict. The poor girl was discharged, taking refuge under the roof of
her "kind father," while the villainous lover carried in his body a
"leaden memento of his perfidy."[49]

The women who were "protected" by seduction laws, and whose
honor was the subject of the unwritten law, were white and middle
class. They were not chattels; nobody could "own" them. But the laws
against insulting or victimizing these women did carry a whiff of the
property idea about them. Such an odor, almost overpowering, rises
from the words of a Texas law that made homicide "justifiable" if a husband killed someone caught red-handed (so to speak) "in the act of adultery with the wife."[50] This statute stayed on the books in Texas until
the 1970s.[51]

Domestic Violence

The odor of property is also strong in the laws relating to wife-beating.
Aggravated assault was a crime in every state, but wife-beating was
taken much less seriously. Judges, particularly in the first half of the
nineteenth century, tended to think of this as a mere personal or domestic matter. The law should stay out, so long as the beating was "moderate," that is, only a matter of discipline, something more or less on a par
with "correcting" a child.[52] A writer in 1838 suggested, somewhat face-
tiously, that "the punishment of death" ought to be meted out "for all
persons who interfered in the quarrels of man and wife. Experience, that
tutor of us all, has taught us, that judges, jurors, and other officers of the
court, are the only sufferers from such accusations."[53] Ball Fenner, writing about the Boston courts around 1850, noted that a "brute in human
form" who undertook to "chastise a vicious horse" would end up in
prison, but, he added, not "one out of a hundred" of the men who
abused or beat their wives (unless the "brute" maimed or blinded her)
was made to answer for his crime; and if he was, in fact, brought to
court, "he is sure of getting off by the payment of a small fine," say,
three dollars and costs.[54]

In the course of the century, there was a certain shift in doctrine. In
the later years, courts were less likely to laugh the matter off or find excuses for wife-beating. Ultimately, a number of states passed statutes
that made wife-beating a crime.[55] The old attitudes seemed barbarous;
this sense was perhaps connected to the growing revulsion against punishing the *body*, which was a strong aspect of nineteenth-century law
reform. (See chapter 3.) Paradoxically, however, some people in the anti-
wife-beating movement voiced a demand to bring back the whipping
post. Perhaps the crime seemed primitive—the punishment should be

equally primitive. At any rate, Nevada passed a law in 1877 that ordered every county to erect "in some public locality at the county seat" a "substantial wooden post or stone pillar." Any "male person" above eighteen "who shall willfully and violently strike, beat, or torture the body of any maiden or woman" sixteen or older was to be "lashed in a standing posture to the post or pillar" for at least two hours (but not more than ten), wearing on his chest "a placard bearing in large Roman characters the words 'Woman beater' or 'Wife beater' as the case may be."[56] There is no evidence this law was actually enforced. Other states went further and called for actual flogging of men who beat their wives.[57]

Wife-beating, then, could not be condoned, and *was* not condoned; but it was quite another thing to see it as a serious social problem. Laws forbidding violence against women expressed an idea and an ideal; in practice it is not clear if these laws accomplished very much. Some men did go to jail. A study in Pennsylvania in the 1880s identified 211 wife-beaters who were put away for an average of three months each behind bars.[58] But the police were notoriously reluctant to make arrests in what they considered family squabbles. Some wives were reluctant to complain, or ashamed, or simply terrified of their brutal husbands. Sometimes it was outsiders—friends, relatives, church groups—who brought about enforcement; sometimes even vigilante groups, like the whitecaps.

Most of those arrested for this crime were immigrants and blacks. "Nice people" apparently did not wash their dirty linen in public. A man who beat his wife was supposed to be a brutal aberration. The popular image of the wife-beater was a lower-class drunk, an undisciplined beast with stubble on his chin. It was not often admitted that "nice" men beat wives, too; that wife-beating was epidemic and a sign of something rotten in the relationship between men and women in this culture. It was twentieth-century feminists who put forward the theory that male dominance itself was the problem, that is, "chronic battering of a person of inferior power" by the lord and master.[59] Wife-beating was, by and large, a secret vice, which makes it hard to chart its ebbs and flows. Did the general mobility and weakening of authority lead to more wife-beating or less? Was it more, because of some sort of crisis within the family and some men's loss of restraint? Was it less as women became, over time, relatively more empowered?

Women's Crimes

A few crimes were specific to women, or dominated by women. Prostitution is the best example: the oldest profession, as the phrase goes. Other old professions gained legitimacy and prestige over time, but not this one. It was never accepted as a way to earn an honest dollar. It was always a crime to keep a "disorderly house." We have already met Elizabeth Martin, "a very Low Notorious Wicked Woman ... and Reputed a Common Whore" who consorted even with "Negro Slaves" and was ordered out of New York City.[60] There was no change after independence: the business of prostitution remained outside the law in every state and every city.

For much of the century, some states lacked laws that *explicitly* criminalized prostitution. Too much should not be made of this. It was a crime to own and operate a brothel; and there were laws against "nightwalkers" and "vagrants," and against "lewd and lascivious" behavior, all of which provided more than enough ammunition for sweeping prostitutes into the nets of the law—whenever the law cared to do so. An ordinance of Milledgeville, Georgia, ordered the arrest of "women of disreputable character, commonly known as 'street walkers,' who may be found standing or loitering about the streets or stores of this city at night, and who cannot prove that they are on unavoidable business." One woman arrested in Milledgeville had the effrontery to appeal her conviction to the Georgia Supreme Court, which labeled her as "one of the most shameless of the class of depraved women." The state had no statute against "nightwalking," but, said the court, "such practices were inhibited by the common law," and in any event, they "tend strongly to vagrancy, lewdness and other offenses." The court also held that the trial court could admit evidence of the woman's "general character"—that is to say, she could be convicted on the basis of gossip, rumor, and public understanding.[61]

St. Louis, Missouri, between 1870 and 1874 was a single and somewhat instructive exception to the general rule. During those years the city ran an experiment in legalization.[62] In 1865, St. Louis had a total population of about 300,000; by police estimate, the city's prostitute population was 2,500. There were the usual raids on whorehouses, but they did little more than scatter the inmates, who "took private rooms, paraded the streets, and openly plied their infamous trade." These were the words of Dr. William L. Barrett, the city's chief health officer. Moreover, according to Barrett, when the brothels were closed, men were encouraged to vent their lust on innocent women instead.[63]

It all seemed so futile. Perhaps—just perhaps—regulation might be better than an outright ban. There was the somewhat dubious example of France, which had a licensing system for prostitutes. But Americans were hardly impressed by what went on in such a wicked country. On the other hand, people were coming to see prostitution as a problem of public health, and not just a problem of sin or vice. In the 1860s and 1870s, police and public officials in some cities had made some favorable noises about mandatory medical examinations for prostitutes. Bills to license prostitution in New York City were proposed in 1867, 1868, and 1871, but Albany said no. St. Louis, however, got a new state charter in 1870; the health and police boards of the city persuaded the state to give the city a flock of new powers. These included the power to "suppress prize fighting, coon fights, dog fights, chick and cock fights, gaming and gambling houses"—and the power to "regulate," as well as suppress, "bawdy or disorderly houses, houses of ill-fame, or assignation."[64]

The city moved promptly to make use of this power. An ordinance was passed, giving the police licensing authority over brothels. The Board of Health was given the right to examine prostitutes for venereal disease. From the clergy came warnings about opening the "floodgates of pent-up lust," warnings that St. Louis was in danger of importing the "deplorable standards of Parisian morals." But the public, by and large, seemed willing to try the experiment—at first. The authorities went busily to work: they registered 1,284 prostitutes and licensed 136 brothels, 9 houses of assignation, and 243 single rooms.

Yet three years later the law was dead—killed in Jefferson City, Missouri; the legislature amended the charter of St. Louis to destroy this noble experiment. What had gone wrong? Enforcement, to begin with, proved difficult, especially with the "lower" prostitutes. Politically, trouble soon developed. Women's rights leaders denounced the system, which they felt was extremely unfair; it bore down on promiscuous women and did nothing about promiscuous men. The clergy roused themselves and kept up a drumbeat of criticism. The local newspapers switched sides: "regulating social vice," as one of them put it, "has shocked the moral sense of the people."[65]

Regulation, in other words, failed because it looked too much like a bargain with the devil; such bargains have never been popular on the overt, official level, in this country. Regulation was really another example of the Victorian compromise, but without the subtlety and indirection America seemed to prefer. The living law of prostitution, of course, was nothing but a complex web of bargains with the devil. Covert, under-the-table recognition was one thing, *formal* recognition was another. The St. Louis experiment came too late in the century; it coincided, unfortunately, with the beginning of a new outburst of militant morality. The ordinance was doomed from the start; it was swimming against the tide.

The dirty little secret of the century was not prostitution itself, but the *business* of prostitution. Men (and women) ran houses as a business; policemen, from patrolmen to captains, were on the take. Most shocking of all (to some) was that many of the women looked on prostitution as simply a job. They chose prostitution over starvation, or grueling factory work at starvation wages. John H. Warren, Jr., a self-described reformer and detective, writing in the 1870s, put part of the blame on "love of ease and luxurious living." He wagged his finger at the "system of female education which fosters a contempt for the mother that delves among the pots and kettles in the kitchen, while the accomplished daughter just home from school, armed with her diploma, thumps away at the piano in the drawing room."[66] On one level, this is nothing but a piece of Neanderthal moralizing. Behind it, though, are hints of a complex web of contradictions: between the cult of success and the cult of female domesticity and subservience; between economic reality—women's need to earn their bread—and the myths of morality.

Prostitution, like all illegal activities, was a precarious business, since its survival depended so much on informal bargains and corruptions. Its relationship with criminal justice was necessarily jagged and stormy. There were sporadic spasms of enforcement, usually stimulated from outside the police department: sometimes it came from the top-down (from city officials, at the demands of moral leaders); sometimes it was the voice of the poeple, or, to put it simply, the mob. In Boston in August 1823, Mayor Josiah Quincy led a posse of volunteers against the vice center of Boston, known as "the Hill," in the West End. Mass arrests of prostitutes continued through the fall of 1823. Two years later, a mob of hundreds of men in blackface, carrying pitchforks, tin pans, drums, and whistles, attacked brothels in the North End, beginning with "the Beehive," a three-story building on North Margin Street, where a widow, Marm Cooper, ran a house of prostitution.[67]

In Detroit, Michigan, in the 1860s, the police made frequent raids, particularly on lower-class houses. Sometimes the superintendent of police himself led the attack. In 1866, there was a raid on twenty houses; more than fifty arrests were made. A state law of 1869 specified three years in the Detroit House of Correction for convicted prostitutes over the age of fifteen.[68]

Despite these bursts of moral energy, enforcement officials adopted, for the most part, what one author has called a policy of "maintenance." After all, large numbers of respectable citizens had no real interest in rooting out this evil weed, or did not think it possible. They wished merely to control it, which could mean "driving prostitution underground, confining it to specific areas, or prosecuting only its most disorderly or lowly haunts."[69]

A newspaper editorial published in 1892 put the point rather precisely. Prostitution, the writer said, "is ineradicable." But, "if handled properly, it can be curtailed." "Houses of illfame" were tolerable, "so long as they are not located in respectable neighborhoods." The writer also made the "delicate" point that "such places" were "a necessary evil." What was "necessary" about the evil? Well, they ministered to the "passions of men who otherwise would be tempted to seduce young ladies of their acquaintance."[70] Thus, prostitution helped maintain the "hydraulic" system of self-control and (male) discipline; it provided an outlet for overheated men. The flesh was weak, the sex drive strong. Prostitution helped maintain a system in which *nice* women could be put on a pedestal, could be required to stay chaste, virtuous, virginal, and fairly sexless, at least before marriage—and not all that different thereafter.[71]

This theory was not often aired in public. And, of course, there were always those who wanted to stamp vice out absolutely. They never had the muscle to prevail. By the middle of the 1870s, the police in Detroit had lapsed again into peaceful coexistence. They raided disorderly houses only when they became truly disorderly. The vice district had achieved stable borders. It was confined to parts of the city where its go-ings-on neither threatened nor offended the sensibilities of "the re-spectable." At this point, everyone (well, almost everyone) was happy with the arrangement.[72]

In city after city, there were "red-light districts," mostly immune from crackdowns. Prostitution was an extensive business. In 1866, it was said, there were 615 houses of prostitution in New York City, plus ninety-nine "houses of assignation, seventy-five concert saloons of bad repute, two thousand six hundred and ninety prostitutes, six hundred and twenty waiter girls of . . . bad character, and one hundred and twenty-seven bar maids" who were "vile" in their habits and inclina-tions. Bishop Simpson, of the Methodist church, gave a fire-and-brimstone speech at Cooper Institute; he claimed, somewhat hysteri-cally, that there were as many prostitutes as Methodists in the city. For him, one supposes, this was a reversal of the natural order. In any event, the police (said Bishop Simpson) did nothing to quell all this vice: "All the public houses of prostitution are known to the authorities"; but the authorities were doing next to nothing.[73]

In reality, the authorities in many cities were doing something, but not what the Bishop would have liked. They were actually *regulating* the "social evil," despite the incongruity of regulating a business that was not supposed to exist. In New Orleans, for example, the Common Council set the boundaries of the red-light district by ordinance. No "public prostitute or woman notoriously abandoned to lewdness" was allowed to "occupy, inhabit, live or sleep in any house, room or closet" *except* within the district. The ordinance meticulously detailed where the district began and ended: "South side of Custom House street from Basin to Robertson street . . . " and so on. Outside those boundaries, no one could lawfully rent space to such a woman; and it was illegal to "es-tablish or carry on a house of prostitution or assignation" except in the zone. Of course, to carry on *inside* the district was just as illegal, but the Common Council ignored that troublesome fact.*

The vice-district system had its darker side: police corruption, shakedowns, and payoffs. The police and the politicians could manipulate crackdowns so as to punish women, madams, and houses that were behind in their payments, or did not pay enough, or who backed the wrong political horse. Toleration was also riddled with class bias. The more genteel figures of the sporting life had much more immunity than the poor women of the streets. Streetwalkers were treated like vermin. But the police winked at the fashionable houses. The New Orleans ordinance plainly revealed a class distinction. Prostitutes were not to stand on the sidewalk near where they worked, or lurk about alleyways, or "accost, call or stop any person passing by," or "stroll about the city streets indecently attired." In general, they were not to behave in public in such a way as "to occasion scandal, or disturb and offend the peace and good morals of the people." These rules obviously bore down heavily on streetwalkers, and left the fancier houses untouched.

The poorer women fared the worst, but all prostitutes suffered from social stigma. "Revolving door" arrests of prostitutes were common in the last part of the century. Paraded through the streets or riding in patrol wagons, prostitutes were jeered, beaten, harassed by onlookers. They were herded into filthy, degrading lockups to wait for trial in the morning. In court, the prostitute was either released or fined; if she could not pay the fine, she went to the workhouse, or to a home for fallen women. Sooner or later, the woman was back on the streets; one prostitute in St. Louis, arrested in 1882, had already been arrested 103 times.

The situation was worse during cleanup campaigns. In New York City, between 1894 and 1898, the "fly squad," a plainclothes police unit, swept through the vice district, arresting women who solicited for prostitution. The amazing Clara Foltz, California's first woman lawyer, was one of those who attacked the policy. She objected to the double standard; she also claimed that the police were arresting respectable women on trumped-up charges.[75] Cleanup campaigns always died down in time, but the double standard survived.

---

* This ordinance so outraged a certain L'Hote, of New Orleans, that he fought it all the way to the U.S. Supreme Court. L'Hote's problem was that his home was perilously close to the edge of the district. *His* neighborhood (he said) was made up of "moral, virtuous, sober, law abiding and peaceable" citizens. The ordinance, he felt, would attract "lewd and abandoned women," and people coming to the area "to gratify their depraved appetites." The ordinance thus amounted to a "taking" of his property, for which he demanded compensation. But the Supreme Court brushed his objections aside.[74]

Abortion and Infanticide

In the last half of the nineteenth century, there were dramatic changes in the laws relating to abortion.[76] Before 1860, some states did not regulate abortion at all. In 1821, Connecticut made it a crime to administer "any deadly poison, or other noxious and destructive substance, with an intention . . . to murder, or thereby to cause or procure the miscarriage of any woman, then being quick with child."[77] This was essentially a murder statute; moreover, it applied only to the period after quickening—the time when the mother feels the baby stirring inside her. New York's statute of 1827 went further; here it was a crime to "wilfully administer to any pregnant woman any medicine, drug, substance or thing whatever, or . . . use or employ any instrument" to "procure the miscarriage of any such woman," except "to preserve the life of such woman" or if "advised by two physicians to be necessary for that purpose."[78]

Between 1840 and 1880, the number of abortions apparently increased. Women eagerly bought Madame Drunette's Lunar Pills, Dr. Monroe's French Periodical Pills, and countless other nostrums, which supposedly would get rid of an unwanted fetus. This was the period of the great, famous, rich abortionists—most notably "Madame Restell" (Ann Lohman), whom we have already met. Madame Restell sold "female monthly pills" to induce miscarriage and spent a fortune discreetly advertising her wares and services. She kept in her employ a force of salesmen who peddled her pills. Her establishment was the height of luxury. There were many of these private "female" clinics. George Ellington, writing in 1869, describes one house on New York's Fifth Avenue as "magnificently furnished"; five floors of statues, paintings, rare bronzes, objets d'art, all "chosen with unexceptionable taste." In this house, women engaged rooms "at enormous rates." Here, of course, the customers were not poor women; they were pregnant women from middle- and upper-class society.[79]

Abortion laws after 1860 were broader and more drastic. Between 1860 and 1880, states passed more than forty antiabortion laws. Over a dozen states banned abortion for the first time; others tightened their existing legislation. Organized medicine led the crusade against abortion.[80] There were a number of reasons for their zeal. One was certainly professional, connected to a general campaign against "quacks." The new abortion laws put power in the hands of doctors. Doctors fought hard to medicalize childbirth. They aimed to drive abortionists (many of them women), midwives, and other rivals out of business.

But there were probably deeper social reasons for the campaign against abortion. Many women who wanted abortions were married. This was, to some observers, a most alarming fact. A woman's highest duty was to bear children, not to snuff out their lives. When middle-class white women killed the life they were carrying, they were not only perverting their own natures and denying their God-given role, they were also helping America commit racial and genetic suicide. Marriage, as one clergyman put it rather hysterically, had not been instituted so that "the husband may live in legal fornication and the wife in legal prostitution"; marriage was, instead, a baby-making machine, and by express "command of the Bible."[81] Charles Sutton, warden of the Tombs, wrote in 1874 that "It is no longer the *mode* to bear children—they are out of style, like last season's bonnet. At least it is getting to be so among the butterfly people of the world—those who prefer to look at life as if it were an immense carnival." Only the "lower classes" still wanted to "hear the sweet lullaby sung."[82] James Whitmire, in an 1874 article on "Criminal Abortion," blamed abortion for the fact that there were so few "native-born children of American parents. . . . We are fast losing our national characteristics, and slowly merging into those of our foreign population."[83]

Thus a woman who went to the abortionist and got rid of her baby was committing a terrible sin against society. She also sinned against womanhood, domesticity, humility, motherhood, and obedience, and against the general image of moderation and self-control so crucial to the nineteenth-century mind-set. Jonas B. Phillips, an assistant district attorney around the middle of the century, cried out at one of Madame Restell's trials that "Nature" was "appalled that woman, the last and fairest of her works, could so unsex herself as to perpetrate such fiend-like enormities." (Phillips apparently had a direct line to mother nature.) "The gardener," he went on, "watches with jealous care the seed he casts into the fertile earth. . . . But this defendant destroys the germ," and "all for the sake of . . . base lucre."[84] The battle against abortion was tied into the general eugenic madness, the sense of contracting horizons and the image of threatened values so prominent an aspect of the late nineteenth-century cultural scene.

Infanticide was another crime more or less specific to women. Men, of course, are perfectly capable of killing babies, including newborn babies; but, practically speaking, this was a felony of women. And the killer was almost always the mother of the child. There has been infanticide in every period of American history—the colonial period provides some startling examples (see chapter 2). Indeed, abandonment and infanticide have never gone extinct.* It seems likely, however, that the inci-

---

* Thus, to take one of, no doubt, many countless examples, a Brooklyn newspaper reported in December of 1918 that the "body of an unknown infant about four weeks old" was found "wrapped in a newspaper" in a lot at the rear of a cemetery.[85]

dence of infanticide reached its peak in the nineteenth century, and then went into something of a decline; but precise figures are hard to come by.*

In England, in the late nineteenth century, there was a positive epidemic of infanticide, which gave rise to a good deal of public discussion. Hundreds of tiny bodies were found floating in the Thames every year.[87] Most of these dead babies were never identified, and thus no one could be arrested or prosecuted for the crime of killing them. Infanticide was hard to prove in the best of circumstances. The act was done in secret; the mother, when caught, invariably argued that the child was stillborn or had died quickly of some disease. These events were, alas, all too common. As we have seen, English law, out of a kind of frustration, made it an independent crime to conceal the birth and death of a child; the idea was, the murdering mother could at least be convicted of *something*. The states had similar laws: it was a crime in New Jersey, for example, for a woman to "endeavor privately, by drowning or secret burying, or in any other way ... to conceal the birth of any ... issue of her body, which, if it were born alive, would by law be a bastard."[88]

Whether infanticide was as much a problem in the United States as it was in England is not entirely clear. There is some evidence of regional variation. The cases in England conformed, in general, to a single depressing pattern. The defendant was a domestic servant, incredibly poor, who became pregnant without benefit of a husband (or any male willing to help shoulder the burden). Somehow she manages to hide her condition. Economically, the child's birth was bound to be a disaster; she would lose her job and be thrown out on the streets. For many women caught on the horns of this dilemma—sick, impoverished, at the end of their tether, abandoned—the only way out was to strangle the baby, or poison it, or drown it in a bucket. There were American examples, too. Mary Gardner was a servant girl in New York City who gave birth secretly and hid the baby in a chest, "wrapped in rags." The child died, either accidentally or (more likely) after a beating. At her trial, in 1819, the jury showed mercy and acquitted.[89]

How often did women kill their babies in the United States? There are, of course, no precise figures. *Abandoned* children were certainly common enough. According to Edward Crapsey, writing in 1872, there

---

* The homicide rate for children less than one year old, according to a study published in 1983, was 5.3 per 100,000 live births in the United States—slightly below England and Wales (5.5), much below Japan (8.6), but much higher than most other countries in a group of developed countries (for example, the rate in Israel was 1.4, in France 1.9, in Norway and Sweden 0). But there is no indication that these killings were infanticide in the sense used here: killed by a mother at birth. Most were probably cases of child abuse. And there is absolutely no way of knowing whether this is more or less than the rates in the nineteenth century.[86]

had been 939 foundlings in New York in the decade before he wrote—"waifs on the sea of sin." These "castaway babes" were picked up off the streets and placed in public asylums "where most of them speedily, and as a matter of course, died."[90] John H. Warren, Jr., also writing in New York at about the same time, had harsh words to say about "baby farming," or, as he put it, "in plain English, baby destruction." These "farms" destroyed babies through starvation. The babies were unwanted, illegitimate children, delivered "into the hands of the baby farming mid-wife, the modern butcher of our surplus infant population." Once in a baby farm, these children "never give their mothers, fathers, or anybody else . . . any trouble." They die of marasmus; that is, they waste away, and that is the end of them.[91] In Boston, in 1890, a private "lying-in hospital and nursery" apparently charged mothers twenty-five dollars to leave their babies; what happened next is suggested by the fact that thirty dead infants were found in the neighborhood.[92]

What Crapsey and Warren discussed was not quite the same as raw, unadulterated killing of infants.[93] Indeed, "baby-farming" was a kind of fig leaf, a veneer of legality. Plain murder, too, was not unknown. Roger Lane found forty-one cases that went to trial for infanticide between 1860 and 1900 in Philadelphia. Twelve of the defendants were black. In one notorious case, in 1881, a woman named Lizzie Aarons had been found walking "ragged, nearly barefoot, without stockings in the snow," and extremely pregnant. She was taken in to a lodging home by a sympathetic woman; the baby was born, heard to cry, but the next morning "its tiny body was discovered in the courtyard below." In this case, too, the jury, obviously sympathetic, let the defendant go.[94]

This crime took place in Philadelphia, a great eastern city. Friedman and Percival studied criminal justice at the other end of the country, in Alameda County, California, for the years 1870 to 1910.[95] Their research in court records and coroners' reports turned up not a single unmistakable case of infanticide. They could hardly help concluding that infanticide was extremely rare in this moderately urban county. Was infanticide in fact rare in the West? And if so, why? Was the West less moralistic, less oppressive on unmarried mothers? Was the key factor mobility and (relative) affluence? In this country, as compared with, say, England, it was easy to pick up and drop identities. Women trapped in a system of poverty and shame, women who saw no way out, no hope, were the ones who were driven to kill. Where it was easier to change names, start a new life, pass oneself off as a widow, make a living, even remarry, the infanticide rate, one suspects, would be low.

Women Behind Bars

As we have seen, women committed few crimes, and were arrested less often than men. Naturally, then, they were poorly represented in prisons and jails. In 1850, women made up less than 4 percent of the inmates in thirty-four state and county prisons. The figures varied somewhat: 5.6 percent of the prisoners in New York's penitentiaries were women, but women were rare sights in penitentiaries in the antebellum South. The governor of Virginia, William Giles, boasted to the "whole civilized world" in 1858 that "for the last four years, but one white woman has been convicted of a Penitentiary offense."[96]

Women were mostly arrested for petty crimes; hence, there were more women in local jails than in the big house. Massachusetts had no women in the state prison, but the state put its women convicts in county jails and houses of correction, where they made up almost 20 percent of the inmates. Drunkenness, prostitution, and petty larceny were among the most common of their crimes.[97] In Philadelphia, in 1860, the county jail held 309 white men and 66 black men, as compared to 57 white women, and 24 black women—a female population of about 18 percent.[98]

There were no freestanding, independent prisons built solely for women before the 1870s; in 1835, New York established the Mount Pleasant Female Prison at Ossining, which was "administratively dependent" on Sing Sing. It opened for business in 1839. Despite the "dependence" on Sing Sing, Mount Pleasant was a significant milestone: women ran its day-to-day operations.[99] Indiana had the honor of building the first penal institution for women that was not an appendage of something built for men. This was the Female Prison and Reformatory Institution for Girls and Women, which opened its doors in Indianapolis in 1874. Number two in this category was the Reformatory Prison for Women, built in Massachusetts, under a law of 1875.[100]

On the male side in Massachusetts, there were two prisons: a penitentiary and a reformatory. The women's institution, as its name suggests, combined both features. Most of the women, not surprisingly, had committed reformatory-type crimes, not prison-type crimes. In 1895, when there were 336 women in the Female Prison and Reformatory, only 39 of them had been sentenced for crimes against persons and property (larceny accounted for 26 of these). Eighty-three had committed crimes "against Chastity," which included 13 women sentenced for adultery, 34 "common night-walkers," 6 convicted of fornication, and 23 sent up for "lewd cohabitation" or just plain "lewdness." The bulk of the women inmates had committed offenses against "public order":

drunkenness (144), and being "idle and disorderly" (47).[101] Twelve women were imprisoned for "stubbornness."*

As the roster of prisoners indicates, the double standard was in full flower. Far fewer men were imprisoned for crimes against chastity—in 1895, there were only three men sentenced to the reformatory for adultery, two for incest, one for indecent exposure, one for lewd cohabitation, and one for an "unnatural act."[104] Also, under the law, women could serve longer terms than men for certain petty offenses. The excuse was that they would do time in a more benign institution. As Isabel Barrows put it, in 1900, although it might seem a "hardship" to send a woman drunkard to the reformatory for two years, the imprisonment was *for reformation*; and two years was not "too long a time to be under wise and strict guardianship." In fact, she regretted that "judges did not at first take advantage of this law"; as a consequence, "women were sentenced for such short terms that the best results could not be secured."[105]

Whether the reformatory was actually so benign remains a question. But there was one aspect, certainly, in which it was strikingly different from the men's institution. In the year ending September 30, 1895, convicted women entered the prison with eleven infants, and seventeen more were born within prison walls.[106]

---

* The Massachusetts law on rogues, vagabonds, idlers, "night-walkers," and the like, included "stubborn children" in the list of ne'er-do-wells.[102] When Massachusetts authorized a woman's reformatory prison, the statute was amended to allow a judge, at his discretion, to send a female offender to the "reformatory prison for women for not more than two years."[103] There were some men, too, in the men's reformatory whose crime was "stubbornness."

11

THE EVOLUTION OF CRIMINAL PROCESS: TRIALS AND ERRORS

The Criminal Trial in the Republic

In American history, dramatic changes in criminal justice took place in the nineteenth-century. Dramatic changes took place in society, too: from the America of John Adams to the America of William McKinley is a quantum leap indeed.

Yet in many ways, the basic shape of the criminal trial stayed the same throughout the century. There were changes, of course, some subtle, some fairly obvious. One constant was the sheer diversity of criminal process. There was not, and never had been, one single system. A full-blown murder trial and the "trial" of a drunk or a vagrant never had more than a vague family resemblance, if that.

In real life, the criminal justice system was composed of levels, or strata, arranged, as it were, like the layers of a cake. At the bottom was a summary layer, the layer of the petty courts, called police courts or justice courts or municipal courts, depending on time and place. On top of this was the layer of ordinary but serious crimes: felonies mostly, thousands of cases of burglary, larceny, assault with a deadly weapon, arson, embezzlement, and the like. At the very top of the cake was a crown of sensational cases, a handful of big, celebrated cases, cases that filled the courtroom with spectators, that aroused the public to fever pitch.[1] Even this picture does not do justice to the complexity of the system; in some states the boundaries between layers were blurred, courts straddled layers, and, arguably, there were crucial sublayers as well.[2]*

Curiously enough, not much is known about the day-to-day work of the courtroom in, say, 1800. Trial work and ordinary criminal process of the period are like a buried city, covered with the silt and garbage of time. Newspaper accounts, and a few trial transcripts (mostly of sensational cases), lift the curtain a bit. Reported cases, statutes, and official documents add something to the story.

People v. Weeks, the so-called Manhattan Well Mystery, gives us a glimpse of criminal justice at the beginning of the nineteenth century. On January 2, 1800, the body of a young woman, Gulielma Sands, was found in a well in New York. Miss Sands had lived with her cousin, Catherine Ring, in a boardinghouse on upper Greenwich Street. She was engaged to be married to Levi Weeks, another boarder. After her body was found, the finger of suspicion pointed, naturally, toward Weeks. A coroner's inquest ended with a finding of willful murder, and the grand jury indicted Weeks. He made bail; the trial began on March 31, 1800. Alexander Hamilton appeared as counsel for the defense, along with Aaron Burr and Brockholst Livingston.[3]

It was a long and hotly contested case, for its time. About seventy-five witnesses appeared. The trial ended on April 2, 1800, at around three in the morning. Weeks had put up a vigorous defense, which included strong evidence of an alibi. The defense must have been powerfully persuasive; the jury took all of five minutes to bring in a verdict: not guilty.

Much of what we see in the pages of the transcript would be familiar to a modern lawyer—and indeed, fairly familiar to anyone who watches trial dramas on TV or in the movies. A panel of thirty-four prospective jurors was called. The defendant's lawyer challenged some members of the panel. Some were excused for one reason or another; the Quakers on the panel "had scruples of conscience," which prevented them from sitting on "a case of life and death."† After a certain amount of jockeying,

---

* Thus, in Massachusetts, police courts and justices of the peace could hear, in addition to the petty cases that were the staple of such courts, all other criminal cases except the most serious felonies. These crimes could also be tried in the Court of Common Pleas (after 1859, the Superior Court). And the highest court, the Supreme Judicial Court, sat as a trial court in capital cases. For the organization of Massachusetts courts, see Laws of Massachusetts 1859, chapter 196, page 339.
† In Rhode Island, it was "local legal tradition" to ask prospective jurors in a capital case three questions: Was the juror a relative of one of the principals in the case? Did he have "scruples about convicting a man of a capital crime"? And: "Had he already formed an opinion of the merits of the case?"[4]

twelve men were seated in the jury box. The jury heard the words of the indictment; prosecutor and defense made opening statements; witnesses for both sides testified and were cross-examined. The presiding judge then charged the jury—he "instructed" them on the law that applied to the case. After that, the jury "went out" and reached their (extremely rapid) verdict.

A major trial today might be fairly similar, in bold outline. The roles of judge and jury, the rhythm of witness and cross-examination—these have remained fundamentally unaltered. There were, no doubt, some local variations, local trial customs, local differences in codes of criminal procedure, nuances of selecting and charging a jury, and in carrying on a trial. The details tend to be, as we said, obscure. Some state courts were more formal than others. In South Carolina, the sessions courts, which handled serious crime, started off each term of court with a kind of parade to the courthouse, led by a sheriff, in a cocked hat and long coat, carrying a sword. A local parson read a sermon; the judge wore a black gown; and proceedings began with a cry of "Oyez! Oyez!"[5] In Illinois, around 1818, on the other hand, judges held court "in log-houses, or in the barrooms of taverns"; in one circuit court, where the judge's name was John Reynolds, court opened when the sheriff went into the courtyard and announced "Boys, come in, our John is going to hold court."[6]

In *People v. Weeks*, all the jurors were men, and every one with an official role in the courtroom was male. This was true in every state. Witnesses apparently had a good deal of leeway to tell their stories uninterrupted; there was less fussing over minor points of evidence than would be true today, less shadowboxing over rules of procedure; the judge's charge was looser, freer, more colloquial, more tailored to the particular case. One small but surprising difference: the court ignored the clock. In most courtrooms today, five o'clock is quitting time, and this is held sacred. But the Manhattan trial went on to half past one in the morning; on the second (and last) day, the assistant attorney general begged (at two twenty-five) for an adjournment, claiming he had been "without repose forty-four hours" and was "sinking under his fatigue." The judge said no, and the trial went on until three.[7]

This was, of course, a big, famous case. It received the full treatment. In 1800, just as today, big, famous cases existed in a different world, procedurally speaking, from the small, routine case. It is much harder to get to know the ordinary case, the small fry wriggling in the sea of criminal justice. We know, though, that most of these cases, early in the century, actually went to some sort of trial. Most of these "trials" were short; most of the defendants had no lawyer, and had to cobble together whatever they could say or do in their own defense; and there was not much quibbling about niceties of evidence.

What was the quality of justice in these courts, and in these cases? It is hard to be sure. We will take a single example, one of hundreds of its type, no doubt—a trial of an ordinary, but serious crime. The year was 1816; the defendant, a "young female" named Eliza Perkins; the place is the Court of Sessions in New York. Perkins is accused of stealing Nathaniel Hopping's pocketbook, with $140 inside. This is grand larceny; $140 was a good deal of money at the time. Hopping, a married man, came over from New Jersey one evening and went to the house of a certain Mrs. Daniel. Perkins was there, dancing. She "manifested much fondness" for Hopping and even "hung round him." They danced, and Hopping bought her some gin. Then she "absented herself." Hopping stepped outside and saw her there, but "she fled from him." A little while later, he realized his pocketbook was gone. When he managed to get hold of Perkins the next morning, she begged him "not to send her to Bridewell"; she promised to "restore the money." She gave him back twenty-eight dollars. She had paid off some debts with the money.

Eliza Perkins was in deep trouble, but she knew enough to get herself a lawyer. He went on the attack—rather clevely, too. How do we know, he asked, that there was "an actual felonious taking"? What if Perkins had found the pocketbook on the floor? Perhaps Hopping, he said, making fun of the man's name, "in *hopping* about right merrily at the sound of the viol, with these Cyprian damsels," "dropped it inadvertently." Nice try; but the jury was not convinced. They "immediately pronounced her *guilty*, but recommended her to mercy, by reason of her youth." Her sentence was "suspended until the next term."[8]

The defendant in this case was young, and a woman, and on the fringes of respectable society, or worse; and in debt. She was convicted of the crime. But the few lines of the report strongly suggest that this was not a foregone conclusion. Her case had not been hopeless from the start. She had an advocate; she had a chance to win—and a chance for mercy, if nothing else. In the event, she did get a suspended sentence rather than a jail term. It is easy to be cynical about the myths and ideologies of justice. The scales of justice were undoubtedly tilted; there were so many ways in which the powerful and the comfortable were better off than the lowly poor. Tilted, yes; but not completely fallen on their side.

Rough Justice

The bottom layer of the system is, in many ways, the most obscure. Here we find literally thousands and thousands of sub-planktonic cases, cases of vagrancy, petty assault, drunkenness, and disorderly conduct. In some places, the judge was a justice of the peace; he disposed of his docket in a quick-and-dirty way, a bit paternalistically, without a jury, and almost always without lawyers. The justice himself was usually not a lawyer, either. These lower courts were often the locus of homespun, rough-and-ready justice for the masses, a form of what Max Weber called *khadi* justice.* In Philadelphia, hundreds of ordinary people brought their gripes and their quarrels to the local alderman, who dispensed justice (for a fee). A constant parade of troubled and mismanaged lives passed before the bench in these and other lower courts. Allen Steinberg, in his study of Philadelphia, has called the system in the early part of the century a system of private prosecutions:[10] complaints that ordinary people brought to their aldermen. The aldermanic courts were an outlet for grievances and troubles, a neighborhood forum; in these courts, the line between civil and criminal cases was blurred. In some ways, a (minor) criminal case was not much more than a civil suit with a government subsidy; people could use the threat of prosecution to wrench out a civil settlement from an unfriendly, irascible, or dishonest opponent. This kind of genteel blackmail had some statutory basis in some states. In New York, for example, when a person was charged with "assault and battery or other misdemeanor, for which the injured party shall have a remedy by civil action," the victim could appear before a judge, attesting "in writing" that "he has received satisfaction for such injury and damage," and the judge, "in his discretion," could then drop the case, with costs.[11]

In the Philadelphia courts, cases of assault and battery were particularly common. Because the criminal law was "so accessible and pliable," people used it to "influence the outcome of a private squabble." The Philadelphia courts acted as a kind of agency of domestic relations. Many of the assault complaints came from battered wives. Some were less serious: Henry Blake's wife prosecuted him "for refusing to come to bed and making too much noise, preventing her from sleeping." John Fort's mother complained that he destroyed the furniture during his drunken binges.[12]

Even later in the century, when court reform ended the age of private

---

* A *khadi* is a Moslem judge; Weber used the expression "khadi justice" to describe a system in which the judge decides cases not according to formal doctrines but on the basis of ethical ideas, common sense, or religious notions.[9]

prosecutions in Philadelphia, the petty courts of the city continued to handle hundreds of these domestic quarrels, local feuds, and minor property disputes. But these were not as much "people's courts" (users' courts) as they had been; they became more of an instrument of social control, more top-down in their behavior and consequences, more under the thumb of local politicians. One sign of this change was that the proportion of assault and battery cases fell while the number of larceny cases rose.[13]

Even before these changes, there were grave pockets of injustice in these courts; and, as always, the top-down aspect of the system was toughest on outsiders, nonconformists, the unattached, the poor, the defenseless. Nobody should confuse America in 1800 or 1825 with, say, a modern totalitarian state; the sins of the times were sins of ignorance and blindness, for the most part. But empathy for the downtrodden was often in short supply.

The Oakland police court of the late nineteenth century was not a "place where the ritual and majesty of law hung heavy in the air. The court often did its business in a hurry and with little fuss."[14] Drunks and vagrants, its staples, usually pleaded guilty, or forfeited bail, or were convicted after a short and snappy hearing. In 1881, over 70 percent of all cases were disposed of without trial. No one, or hardly anyone, went scot-free; over the period 1872 to 1910, only 1 percent of the defendants were acquitted in the police court.[15] The *Oakland Tribune* reported in 1884 that Judge Allen "broke a record. . . . At 9 o'clock the court met. At 9:06 the thirteen cases on the docket had been disposed of and one minute after the Judge was on a car bound for Haywards."[16]

Occasionally, of course, a defendant pleaded not guilty in the Oakland Police Court. This gave rise to a bench trial. But these trials were perfunctory, to put it mildly. They were little more than a contest between a policeman and the defendant, each swearing to tell the truth. The defendant rarely won. Here is a "case" from 1895, as reported by the *Oakland Tribune:*

> "I didn't think I was drunk, your Honor," said Gus Harland this morning.
> "Not drunk?" said the court.
> "Not very drunk."
> "How drunk?"
> "Well—I could see the moon."
> "It was raining hard Sunday night when I arrested that man," said the officer.
> "Six dollars or three days. Next."[17]

Perhaps not all lower courts were quite so slapdash. The quality of the justice was variable. So was the quality of the justices. Many basement courts were staffed by laymen. In many states, they got their money from fees, which made some of them rapacious. In a number of jurisdictions, there were persistent rumors and complaints about justices who were ignorant and grasping. The justices in the West, by common repute, were "new, young, restive residents"; but John Wunder's study of the justices of the peace of Washington Territory found, on the contrary, that they formed a rather "stable, established, contented group." Most of them were "well-to-do property owners."[18] Peter Oxenbridge Thacher, judge of Municipal Court in Boston between 1823 and 1843, was "distinguished for his earnest study and thorough knowledge of the criminal law," for his "fidelity and devotion to the arduous duties of his office," for his integrity, and for "fearless administration of justice."[19]

Everywhere, however, the justices and petty court judges paid less attention to legal niceties than their more august colleagues. It would be an exaggeration to say that they did as they pleased; but they had a measure of discretion that came not from the law but from the fact that they dealt, on the whole, with the little man, the little woman, and, most often, with the unwanted and unwashed. One can search the statute books in vain to find banishment listed as a punishment. Nonetheless, magistrates frequently told vagrants, hoboes, petty thieves, and prostitutes simply to get out of town.[20]

Steinberg's picture of the Philadelphia courts in the first half of the century and the picture of the Oakland courts in the last half are, on the surface, discordant. Was this because of the time factor? What seems more likely is that the bottom courts had a double aspect. They were an arm of the state, a part of the social control apparatus bearing down heavily on the poor, the deviant, the unattached. But they were also, at the same time, a kind of makeshift social service agency, a resource that common people could and did use to strike back at bad neighbors. A worker—or farmer, or shopkeeper—swearing out a complaint for assault and battery, or some other petty crime, in front of a police court judge, was looking for popular justice. "Petty" was not petty for him—or for the accused.[21]

The Middle Layer

Felony cases were, of course, handled with more care and treated more seriously than cases in the bottom courts. For these cases—burglary, robbery, arson, major fraud, manslaughter, assault, rape, and murder, among others—the law prescribed a two-stage process. First a grand jury had to indict; then a petty jury had to convict. But over the course of the century, there evolved significant deviations from this pattern. The grand jury held its ground in most states—New York, for example. In 1900, 4,473 arrested men and women were presented to the New York County grand jury, which returned 3,674 indictments.[22] Twenty-three men served on the grand jury, and a new group was chosen each month. A bit of simple arithmetic shows that in this county each grand jury indicted, on average, about 300 women and men.

But in other states, the grand jury went into eclipse. Those states changed to the so-called system of *informations*. This was also a two-stage process. In the first stage, charges and accusations went to a "magistrate," that is, a lower court judge, and not to a grand jury. This judge held what was called a "preliminary hearing." He listened to what there was in the way of evidence; if he thought there was enough of a case to justify a trial, he would so hold and "bind over" the defendant to the trial court. Otherwise, the magistrate would let the defendant go. California authorized such a system in its constitution of 1879; the state did not abolish the grand jury, but after 1880, indictments were used only in exceptional cases.*

A defendant waiting for trial was either locked up or set free on bail. Bail was an old institution; the Eighth Amendment to the Constitution mentions it specifically and forbids "excessive" bail. State constitutions had similar provisions. Under the Alabama Constitution of 1875, it was provided that "all persons shall, before conviction, be bailable by sufficient sureties." The exception was "capital offenses, when the proof is evident, or the presumption great."[24]

Bail cost money. The point was to make sure the defendant showed up for trial. Courts had wide discretion in setting bail. To "make bail," the defendant usually filed a bail bond, which was signed or vouched for by family or friends, respectable citizens. If the defendant skipped town, bail was forfeited.[25] Toward the end of the century, professional bail bondsmen begin to appear: individuals or firms in the business of financing bail.[26]

State and federal constitutions guaranteed the right of trial by jury. Jurors were, of course, always men; and they were, practically speaking, always white. Even after the Civil War, blacks were generally excluded from juries. In *Strauder v. West Virginia* (1879),[27] the U.S. Supreme Court struck down a statute that restricted jury service to "white male persons." There was a certain irony here: West Virginia was a state made up of breakaway, Unionists counties that refused to join Virginia in seceding. The southern states learned a lesson from *Strauder:* open,

---

* In *Hurtado v. California* (1884), the U.S. Supreme Court upheld this change in California law; the due-process clause of the Fourteenth Amendment did not force states to stick to the method of indictment by grand jury.[23]

formal exclusion of blacks would not work. They found more sinister ways to keep blacks off their juries. The proud words of the *Strauder* case, boasting that the law would be "the same for the black as for the white," were written on the wind.

Jurors were supposed to be average citizens (or at least average white men) chosen at random. In Massachusetts, their names were "drawn by lot from boxes, in which are deposited the names of all citizens who are qualified for the service."[28] State laws listed classes of people who were excluded, or entitled to wriggle out of this duty. Attorneys and judges were quite generally excused; so were senior citizens (those over sixty or sixty-five, depending on the statute), plus a motley assortment of others. In Florida in the 1890s, these included "officers of colleges," teachers of various sorts, doctors and pharmacists, "ministers of the gospel, one miller to each grist mill, one ferryman to each licensed ferry, telegraph operators," train engineers, "ten active members of any hand fire company, six active members of any hose company, twenty active members of any hook and ladder company."[29]

There was, then as now, considerable fidgeting and squirming to get out of jury service. People claimed to be suddenly sick, or indispensable, or pleaded dreadful personal hardship. In the end, there were always enough fish caught in the net. The canonical number was twelve.[30] To serve, however, a juror also had to survive the *voir dire* process. Lawyers for either side could "challenge" jurors. They had a certain number of "peremptory challenges"—this was the privilege of excusing a prospect for no explicit reason. If the defendant's lawyer thought a man looked too sour, or if he thought Swedish-Americans were too prone to convict, he could use one of his precious stock of peremptory challenges. In California, the prosecution had five of these, the defendant ten, except in capital cases, where the numbers were doubled. In Colorado, each side had fifteen in a capital case, ten in cases where the defendant could wind up in the penitentiary, three in all other cases.[31]

The lawyers also had at their disposal an unlimited number of challenges "for cause." This eliminates people likely to be biased: relatives of the defendant, for example. In Ohio, kin of the victim or defendant could be challenged up to the "fifth degree" (for example, the children of first cousins). Lawyers could also challenge, for cause, "habitual" drunkards, and anybody who had "formed and expressed an opinion as to the guilt or innocence of the accused."[32] The judge had the discretion to allow a prospect to serve even though he had formed an opinion, if, after questioning, the judge felt that the juror was capable of coming to an impartial judgment. In a capital case, the prosecution could also challenge anybody who was opposed to the death penalty and might for that reason refuse to convict.

To the layman, voir dire often seemed a pointless ordeal, a ritual of ridiculous questions. The *Oakland Tribune* mocked the process in 1875: "How long since your youngest child had the whooping-cough?" or "How would you prefer to die—with the jaundice, or to fall off a church?"[33] It was, nonetheless, a serious business, especially in hotly contested and sensational cases. A person's life could depend on who served and who did not. In the famous trial of eight radicals in Chicago, for (allegedly) throwing a bomb and killing policemen in Haymarket Square, it took twenty-one days to pick a jury; and 981 men were processed before a jury of twelve was finally seated. At that, the court had to use heroic measures. The first eight days yielded not a single juror. A special bailiff was appointed to get potential jurors by hook or by crook; and he did his job, though in a fairly high-handed way. The problem was that, in the atmosphere of frenzy and hysteria over the "anarchists," it was almost impossible to find anyone without *some* opinion. In the event, the "unbiased" jury did not seem that unbiased; seven out of eight defendants were sentenced to death.[34]

As we have said, the dramatic shape of a trial, in broad outline, remained much the same during the century. The role of the lawyers, if there were lawyers, was to produce evidence, to cross-examine, and, at the end of the case, to sum up their case to the jury. Their speeches, especially in the great cases, were often flamboyant flights of purple prose. Some lawyers pulled out all the stops. The prosecution hoped to rouse the jury to rage and indignation, with tears of pity for the victim; the defender, calling loudly for sympathy and mercy, heaped scorn on the prosecution's case.

There are countless examples. To take just one—the trial of Ann K. Simpson, a young woman of Fayetteville, North Carolina, on trial for murdering her rich old husband. She was accused of slipping arsenic into his coffee and his "syllabub." The evidence was strong, but circumstantial, and her lawyers rose to heights of purple eloquence: she was a young innocent, "almost a child, fair and beautiful," "shivering amidst the pitiless peltings of the storm of adversity," a "poor simple-hearted girl," with a "guileless heart," a "lamb in its innocent gambols." They spoke of Ann's "devoted mother," who "pillows her head upon her bosom as she lies almost lifeless in the prisoner's box." The very idea of the crime was a slander, too, on North Carolina: a "crime so monstrous, so revolting, so unnatural" seemed almost impossible in that fair state. "Instances . . . may have occurred in other lands, doubtless they have . . . but, thank God, hitherto in North Carolina . . . the land of morality, whose whole scope of country is dotted with the temples of a pure religion . . . hitherto in North Carolina it has been accused against no one." The prosecution had its own rhetorical turns; but in this case at least, it was hopelessly outemoted. The jury acquitted.[35]

In the course of the century, there were important changes in trial procedure that affected the balance of power between state and defendant, judge and jury. For one thing, the defendant became, for the first time, a courtroom player at his own trial. In England, a defendant could neither act as a witness nor take the stand in his own defense. This was doctrine in the United States as well. No defendant was permitted to testify under oath,* although he could give an unsworn statement to the jury without cross-examination. In the latter part of the century, the law was "revolutionized."[36] Beginning with Maine, in 1864, the federal government and every state (except Georgia) conceded to a defendant the right to testify under oath.[37]

Most defendants were arrested, tried, and sentenced (or acquitted) without a lawyer. This was almost always true in the petty courts and for small cases. Felonies were another matter. Many felony defendants, of course, hired attorneys; but many—perhaps most—could not afford this luxury. In many states, in the late nineteenth-century (California, for example, from 1872 on) there was a right to free counsel at a felony trial.† (In other states, including Florida, there was no such right.) New York had a system of assigned counsel; the attorneys were not entitled to a fee except in murder cases. Assigned lawyers, we are told, always tried to wheedle some cash from the defendant or his friends. "If unsuccessful in this attempt they pay little attention to the case."[39] The modern system of public defenders is, essentially, a product of this century.

At the beginning of the century, trials tended to be quite short. They rarely lasted a day, and most were probably much shorter. Trials probably got longer and more complex over time, as more and more of them were conducted by lawyers. But they still went forward at what would be considered today a very snappy pace. In Alameda County, California, in the decade of the 1880s, the average length of trial was 1.5 days; the median length was 1.2.[40] In other parts of the country, trials may have been even shorter. In Leon County, Florida (Tallahassee is the county seat), the Circuit Court sometimes handled up to six complete "trials" per day. The same jury sat for all of them. Most of these "trials" must have taken less than an hour.[41]

Over the years, there were subtle shifts in the relative powers of judge and jury. At the beginning of the century, jury instructions were really instructions: the judge often wrote them himself, and he tried to set out, as clearly as he could manage, what the law of the case was re-

---

* Nor could the *state* call him to the stand against his will. This was because of the privilege against incrimination guaranteed by the Fifth Amendment and its state counterparts.
† Between 1880 and 1899, at least one-quarter of the defendants in felony cases in Alameda County, California, had appointed counsel. These lawyers received no money for their pains; many of them were apparently young lawyers who were hanging around the courtroom anyway, hoping to pick up a crumb or two of business.[38]

ally all about. The language was often vivid and colloquial; the judge took care to show the jury how the law should or could apply to the concrete facts of the case. This continued to be the practice in some states. In the Lizzie Borden case, the judge's charge to the jury took about an hour and a half. The judge, who commented freely on the evidence, seems to have written the instructions himself, though undoubtedly the attorneys made suggestions.[42]

These charges were useful and instructive. They were also dangerous. A judge was tempted to try to sway the jury, to bring in thoughts and ideas which were, to say the least, irrelevant. In the trial of Ann K. Simpson, the judge gave his view that the prosecution was overzealous, and had failed to prove a motive. The state had painted a dark picture of defendant, "but, when we examine its various features, they . . . fade away, one by one, and scarcely any color [is] . . . left on canvas." A few minutes later, the judge delivered this peroration: "The heart of woman is a well-spring of kindness. It sends forth its streams over this parched and withered earth, and causes it to bud and blossom and put forth the fruit of good works. Woman is by far the better portion of our race, and if our sex were only like her, different, far different, would be the condition of the world." This had nothing to do with the case, of course, except for the fact that the defendant was a member of that "better portion."[43]

In other states, practice changed rather radically, perhaps in response to a sense of abuse and browbeating of juries. The judge lost his right to comment on the evidence. In Mississippi, he could only tell the jury about "principles" of law, and his instructions had to be in writing.[44] In states like Mississippi, an upper court could reverse a lower court if the judge even dared to add or change anything *orally* in these instructions.[45] In California, another state in this camp, instructions became crabbed, gnomic, abstract.[46] Plaintiff and defendant each submitted lists of suggested instructions. The judge chose the instructions he found legally most correct—which, of course, had nothing to do with which one might best enlighten a jury. Case files are full of drafts of such instructions with marginal notes in the judge's hand: "given" or "refused."

In any event, these California instructions certainly did not instruct. One can only guess what the poor jury made of them. In the case of William Butts, on trial for manslaughter in 1895, the instructions ran to thirteen legal-size, double-spaced pages. Nowhere in these pages is there any reference to the particular fact of the Butts case. One instruction defined manslaughter: "[It is] the unlawful killing of a human being without malice. It is of two kinds: voluntary, upon a sudden quarrel or heat of passion; involuntary, in the commission of an unlawful act which might produce death in an unlawful manner, or without due caution or circumspection." The judge offered the jury no hint of how to apply this dreary verbiage to the case of William Butts. Nor did the judge say anything at all about the evidence. That would have been "eminently improper."

The jury went out, talked the case over for three hours, then sent a message that they needed "further instructions." The judge brought them back into the courtroom and asked what was up. The foreman asked for "some further instruction [as to] what is the nature of self-defense." They wanted enlightenment. They never got it. The judge reread the page and a half of jargon on the subject: "It must be an imperious necessity, or such an apparent necessity as would impress a reasonably prudent man that it existed." He flat-out refused to step out of his formalism, and give them some honest answers.

Of what earthly use was (and is) this kind of "instruction"? It shifts some power away from the judge, who can no longer insinuate as much to the jury as he once could. It has, of course, some advantages for the judge as well. It puts less of a work burden on him. It also cuts down (he hopes) the chance that an upper court will set aside the case because of an "error" in the instructions; and judges do not like to be reversed for any reason.

What the jury makes of the judge's instructions, or, indeed, what the jury thinks and does in other regards remains a mystery. The jury does its work behind closed doors, and its deliberations are, on the whole, mysterious.[47] Occasionally, like a flash of lightning on a dark night, a rare piece of information bursts into view. In *Crabtree v. State*, a Tennessee case decided in 1855, the defendant, William Crabtree, was on trial for murder.[48] The jury found him guilty of manslaughter, and fixed his punishment at six years in the penitentiary. On appeal, Crabtree produced affidavits about some goings-on in the jury room. Each juror, it seems, had written down on a piece of paper how many years he wanted Crabtree imprisoned. The numbers were added up, divided by twelve, and that was the verdict. The Tennessee court reversed the conviction, because it was not "the deliberate judgment of the jury, produced by argument and reflection." This kind of trick was, apparently, jury custom in Tennessee and some neighboring states.*

Nobody should be surprised to learn that jurors are human beings, and that they make deals, compromises, and arrangements inside the jury room. Indeed, the whole point of the jury system is to let human

---

* In a later case in Tennessee, whose facts were amazingly similar, a juror said, inside the jury room, that "he had been on criminal juries before, and it was usual and the custom" to do it that way and to "return the result" of this adding and dividing as the "verdict of the jury." The appeals court reversed the conviction.[49]

beings decide, on a human basis. The doctrine of the *Crabtree* case seems to open up a Pandora's box: If a defendant could convince a juror or two to lift the curtain on what went on in the jury room, he might have a crack at overturning his conviction. In *Glidewell v. State*, in 1885, the Tennessee court found a way to get around the *Crabtree* case. It was all right, said the court, for the jury to add and divide if there was "no agreement or understanding, expressed or implied, tacit or otherwise," to be actually *bound* by the results of the arithmetic. They could use the technique, so long as they independently decided, after the magic number appeared, that the number was really what they wanted their verdict to be.[50]

What is involved here is a fundamental ambiguity about the role of the jury. The jury had enormous power. It held life and death, freedom or imprisonment, within its hands. The state could not appeal an acquittal—if the jury acquitted, its word was absolutely final. But there were also rules of criminal evidence, a body of law of bewildering complexity. No country in the world has such a Byzantine effloresence of doctrines about evidence: a jungle of rules, counterrules, subrules, exceptions to rules—and exceptions to exceptions of exceptions. The law of hearsay, the law of privileges, and other branches of evidence law—all had their greatest growth spurt in the nineteenth century. The net result was to suppress great chunks of truth. The point of this gigantic system—Wigmore's treatise of 1904, which summed it up, took five thick volumes—was to preserve the sacred innocence and neutrality of the jury. The point was to make sure the jury saw, smelled, and heard only the most carefully examined and predigested pablum of evidence.*

All this completed a process, which over the centuries had turned the jury on its head. It was no longer a wise panel of neighbors, men who understood the context of the crime and maybe even knew something of the crime itself. It was now supposed to be a totally sanitized panel, people who knew nothing, had heard nothing, suspected nothing, understood nothing. The defendant was "presumed" to be innocent. The jury was supposed to treat him as if he was a complete stranger: a blank slate as to personality, character, and prior life.

This was a concept appropriate to mobile societies and big cities,

---

* In theory, this was supposed to be entirely for the defendant's benefit. As Francis Wharton put it, "in a criminal prosecution, the State is arrayed against the subject; it enters the contest with a prior inculpatory finding of a grand jury in its hands; with unlimited command of means; with counsel usually of authority and capacity, who are regarded as public officers, and therefore as speaking semi-judicially; and with an attitude of tranquil majesty, often in striking contrast to that of a defendant engaged in a perturbed and distracting struggle for liberty if not for life."[51] Of course, like so much else in criminal law and procedure, the full beauty of the law of evidence was only unfurled in big trials, felony trials, trials in which lawyers took part.

where it was easy to be unknown and anonymous. In small towns, and in traditional societies, the idea was ludicrous. In sensational trials, too, this virgin-juryman was hard to find. Mark Twain, talking about juries in Virginia City, Nevada, was characteristically acerbic: trial by jury "puts a ban upon intelligence and honesty, and a premium upon ignorance, stupidity and perjury." In one trial, in which a "desperado" killed a "good citizen," twelve men were finally chosen who swore "they had neither heard, read, talked about, nor expressed an opinion concerning a murder which the very cattle in the corrals, the Indians in the sagebrush, and the stones in the streets were cognizant of." The jury was "composed of two desperadoes, two low beer-house politicians, three barkeepers, two ranchmen who could not read, and three dull, stupid, human donkeys!" The verdict was "Not Guilty. What else could we expect?"[52]

Juries were, on the one hand, supposed to reflect popular norms; but, on the other, they were not supposed to indulge in popular stereotypes. On the one hand, they were lionized; on the other, mistrusted. Mark Twain was not the only critic of the typical jury.[53] In some ways jurors were also positively forbidden to use their common sense. Why else treat so many obviously relevant facts as *legally* irrelevant? If the state put a man on trial for some crime—burglary, for example—it could not show he had committed some *other* crime, or the same crime in a different place, or in a different way. In Pennsylvania in 1872, Emanuel Shaffner was indicted for poisoning his wife, Nancy. Shaffner had had "improper intimacy" with another woman, Susan Sharlock, whose husband had also died of poison; Shaffner's first wife, Sarah, died of this same suspicious cause. The state managed to put in evidence that Mr. Sharlock came to his death through poisoning; but when the jury convicted Shaffner, the high court reversed: "A distinct crime, unconnected with that laid in the indictment, cannot be given in evidence against a prisoner."[54]

Most people (myself included) would smell a very large rat in this situation. Coincidences do occur, but the epidemic of poisonings in and around Emanuel Shaffner stretches the notion of coincidence to the breaking point. Not many of us would be willing to have a meal at Shaffner's house without bringing a taster along. The law did not exclude evidence of the wave of poisonings because it proves nothing, but rather because it proves too much—too much for the *theory* of a trial system tilted toward the defendant and insisting on a jury of virgins. An old-time jury would have known all about the other poisonings, of course; the whole town would have been abuzz with the news. (And, to be sure, that could still be the case; but the law did not want to know it or admit it.)

A pure jury was also, ideally, an isolated jury, a jury that did not listen to rumors and noise from the outside world. Jurors were not to read about the case, talk about the case, dream about the case. A conviction for manslaughter was reversed in Tennessee in 1882 because an article about the case, published in the *Chattanooga Times*, reached the eyes of some members of the jury.[55]* To keep the jury pure, they had to be treated like monks, or perhaps like lepers. Under the Texas code of the 1870s, in all felony cases the jury was not "permitted to separate until they have returned a verdict"; the sheriff was to provide "a suitable room" for them to deliberate in, along with "necessary food and lodging" (but no liquor of any kind); and no one was to "converse with a juryman" once the juror was impaneled.[57] In Connecticut, in capital and life-sentence cases, the court had discretion to "require the jury to be and remain together" under the sheriff's wing.[58]

In long, drawn-out cases, the juror's lot was probably not a happy one. A law of Washington Territory (1877) provided that no justice of the peace could deprive a retired jury of food for more than six hours at any one time, which suggests that justices at least occasionally tried to "starve juries into submission."[59] In the sensational trial of Laura Fair in San Francisco (1871), the jurors were locked up at night in hotel rooms. The trial dragged on for weeks. The judge allowed them to go to church, to the theater, and to the race track; but family life was out of the question. One Sunday, the judge kindly let the jurors visit their homes: all twelve went together, in carriages, with a deputy; each juror had the chance to kiss his wife and children, while eleven other men and a deputy looked on. One of the jurors was a bachelor, and the whole entourage trooped over to see his girlfriend. She was "not enchanted by this unexpected visit by a dozen strange men, most of them middle-aged and all enveloped in the warm and heady aroma of good cigars and good wine." This visit was particularly awkward, as one can easily imagine.[60] Afterwards, the carriages took the jurors back to their dreaded hotel.

The Decline of Trial by Jury

Another duality in the heart of the legal system was even more fundamental: the gap between theory and practice. The average burgher and his wife, if they heard a speech about defendants' rights, about the pre-

---

* In a Georgia case, decided in 1892, the jury reached a verdict at night and sealed it up. To escape the sweltering Georgia heat, jurymen went out on the veranda, where some of them ate watermelon—guarded by two strict bailiffs who "prevented all intercourse by others . . . during the night." The defendant, who was convicted, appealed on the point (among others) that the jury had left its isolation-chamber; but to no avail. What saved the day, of course, was the lack of "intercourse" with the outside world.[56]

sumption of innocence, about the wonders and the fairness of the system, would no doubt nod in solemn agreement. This was America, by God! But the same pair also wanted an efficient, effective system; they wanted to sleep soundly at night; they wanted security, law and order; they wanted the police to sweep vagrants and tramps off the street, to get rid of the scruffy, disgusting human flotsam that disfigured their cities; they wanted the police to catch dangerous criminals who robbed and stole and assaulted; they wanted the system to convict these men and put them away. The system, in real life, was equally ambivalent; it bounced from one pole to the other.

The official theory exalted trial by jury; this was a vital safeguard of liberty, a "palladium" of liberty no decent system of justice could do without.* When the United States gobbled up land (Louisiana, Florida, Texas, the Southwest) once part of the civil law world, whose French and Spanish and Mexican roots were juryless, the conquerors immediately swept away the old methods of handling criminals and imposed trial by jury instead. The Louisiana Constitution provided for a "speedy public trial by an impartial jury of the vicinage." Although the clash of legal cultures was an issue in Louisiana, generally speaking, the introduction of the *criminal* jury went smoothly and without any noticeable opposition.[62]

But, in fact, in the nineteenth century trial by jury was in process of slow decline. What tended to replace it, more and more, was the guilty plea. This trend began fairly early in the century, and snowballed. By 1900, in New York County, there were more than three times as many convictions in felony cases because of guilty pleas than there were convictions by judge or by jury.[63]

At least some of these pleas of guilty were not driven by remorse or hopelessness; some, beyond a doubt, reflected a "deal." Plea bargaining would become pervasive in the twentieth century, but it certainly existed in the late nineteenth century, and perhaps even earlier. Plea bargaining has many shapes, but the essence is a deal between the defendant (with this lawyer, if he has one) and the prosecution team; occasionally the judge too plays a role. What exactly is the deal? The defendant pleads guilty. In return, the prosecution drops some charges, or knocks some down from felony to misdemeanor, or the prosecution promises to recommend probation, or a lighter sentence; it all depends. In any event, plea bargaining shifts the focus from the courtroom, and the lay jury, to lawyers and prosecutors. It is part of the trend to professionalize and rationalize criminal justice, which we have noted so frequently before.

* Mark Twain said, on this subject, "I do not know what a palladium is, having never seen a palladium, but it is a good thing no doubt at any rate."[61]

Evidence of plea bargaining in the late nineteenth century is quite unmistakable.* For example, in Alameda County, California, in 1880, Albert McKenzie was charged with embezzlement. He was an agent for a sewing-machine company, who collected $52.50 in gold coin, and pocketed the money. He pleaded not guilty. The judge fixed a date for the trial: February 6, 1881. On that day, McKenzie, his lawyer, and the district attorney met. McKenzie withdrew his plea and pleaded guilty to a misdemeanor—embezzling an amount less than fifty dollars. The district attorney, instead of shouting that this was nonsense, that McKenzie either stole *more* than fifty dollars or nothing at all, simply voiced his agreement, and the deal became official.[65]

In general, Friedman and Percival found that 14 percent of all defendants in this county between 1880 and 1910 changed their pleas from not guilty to guilty. Half of these pleaded guilty to a lesser charge, or fewer charges—unmistakably the sign of a deal. Almost certainly, these figures understate the actual amount of plea bargaining. There was also, beyond a doubt, a great deal of "implicit" bargaining.[66] Defendants sometimes plead guilty without an actual overt agreement; they expect the state will reward them for saving the trouble and expense of a trial; no words need to be spoken. In the late 1880s, prisoners at Folsom Prison, in California, were asked why they had pleaded guilty, if they did. Out of a group of 330 who had so pleaded, 120 said they wanted to "mitigate the penalty"—a little more than one out of three, if we can believe what they said.[67]

The Theater of the Law

At the top of the pyramid of trials stood a few select cases of great drama and great theater. Some were famous and important because the crime was especially heinous, lurid, or extreme: the great murder trials, the headline-making trials, the sensations of the courtroom. We have mentioned quite a few, for example, the 1871 trial in San Francisco of Laura Fair, charged with killing her lover, A. P. Crittenden.[68] In other instances, what set the case apart was the identity of victim or defendant. There was, for example, the trial of Charles Guiteau, the deranged office-seeker who shot President Garfield in 1881.[69]

It was in those cases that lawyers outdid themselves in oratory and in maneuvering; these were the trials where the art of cross-examination

---

* There is some evidence for the earlier part of the century, too. Theodore Ferdinand's data for Boston's police court show a rise in guilty pleas between 1826 and 1850 from 9.3 to 51.3 percent in public drunkenness cases; in larceny cases, from 10 to 22.2 percent; in violations of city ordinances from 20 to 65.6 percent. Ferdinand argues that in some classes of cases, plea bargaining accounts for the swelling rate of guilty pleas.[64]

was at its height. These were the trials where witnesses sobbed and women fainted on the stand. These were trials of high drama. Most were cases of murder, the queen of crimes. Death was in the air, the victim's ghost and the shadow of the gallows falling across the face of the prisoner. These were the only cases that were truly *individual* in treatment; every potential juror was screened, every fact sifted, every point contested. At the end of the century, the development of "yellow journalism" placed even greater emphasis on these trials. They were good copy; they were mighty engines for selling newspapers—better than anything else, perhaps, except war or a good execution. The papers often vied with each other for the fullest, most sensational coverage of great criminal trials.

In some of these cases, the line between justice and show business became quite fuzzy. Hordes of people tried to force their way into the courtroom. They lined up early in the morning to get seats. In the days before movies and TV, a good trial was a great spectator sport. The newspapers of the 1880s and 1890s, of course, reported the show for the curious millions who were not lucky enough to squeeze into the courtroom.

No case in the history of American criminal justice was as famous as the trial of Lizzie Borden, rising out of the tragedy in Fall River, Massachusetts.[70] This mystery tantalized its contemporaries, and still exercises a kind of eerie fascination a century later. On the outside, nothing appeared more normal than the comfortable house in Fall River, where Andrew J. Borden, a rich man from an old family, lived with his second wife, Abby. Borden's first wife had died long before, leaving him two daughters, Emma and Lizzie, both unmarried. There was also an Irish servant-girl. It was a close, churchgoing, modest family, and from the outside, a model of propriety and American respectability.

But something was radically wrong behind the lace curtains. The murders took place on a day that was hot, stifling, unbearable; not a breath of air was stirring. In that close atmosphere, Lizzie, choked and strangling with repressed hatred, perhaps reached her breaking point. At any rate, somebody, on that still morning, savagely murdered Abby Borden with an ax and left her body in an upstairs room while the blood congealed. An hour or so later, Andrew returned from business in town. He lay down on a sofa, took off his shoes, and, as he rested, the ax descended again and cracked open his skull. Emma was out of town; only Lizzie and Bridget, the maid, were about the house—as far as anybody knows.

Lizzie was arrested and charged with the crime. Armies of reporters descended on the scene. The press made a martyr out of Lizzie. She must have been falsely accused. She was a woman, a daughter, a spinster. She came to symbolize, in a way, American innocence. The jury chose to believe in the symbol. Such a person was simply incapable of violent crime. It must have been a stranger, or the maid, or *somebody*, some alien force, some tramp, some foreigner with a hatchet—anybody but the stiffly buttoned, silent woman sitting demurely in the courtroom. The charge to the jury was, to say the least, tilted in Lizzie's favor. The jury found her not guilty and sent her home. The trial passed into legend, and there it remains.

Crime and punishment, as we have said, are unique social indicators, mirrors of society—distorted mirrors, perhaps, funhouse mirrors, or cracked mirrors; but even the distortions are symptomatic and systematic. Major courtroom trials, even though they are posed, hypocritical, stage-managed, even though they sift and twist facts, and distort evidence for the sake of making points, are nonetheless extremely telling; at times they can lay bare the soul of a given society.

The great cases served a number of functions. Since they *were* theater, they helped underscore and teach the rules of the game. They presented in dramatic form the norms of community life. These were crude popular norms; the rhetoric was shrill, exaggerated, the quality of the theater was often very low; much of it was too melodramatic for our current tastes. But these shows were messengers, preachers; they carried tales of conventional morality, stories of evil and good, to the audience inside and outside the courtroom.[71] Conventional morality, too, defined and limited the quality of the courtroom drama. The Lizzie Borden case, for example, speaks volumes about conventional ideas on the nature of women and their social roles.

Clara Fallmer, age sixteen, was on trial for murder in Oakland in 1897. The case was a local sensation. Clara came to court every day veiled, dressed all in blue, her gloved hands clutching a bouquet of violets. Clara had shot and killed her lover, who had refused to marry her. Her hope lay in projecting an image of wounded innocence. The victim's mother also appeared in the courtroom, "in deep mourning," her voice "frequently broken with emotion." All this tomfoolery, crafted by the lawyers, was designed to shape the case in terms of what people wanted to believe. In the event, Clara won: the jury acquitted her.[72]

It was from cases like this, too, that the average person absorbed what he or she knew about criminal justice. But what message did these cases broadcast? It was a curiously two-faced message. On the one hand, people learned about due process, about the rights of the defendant. They saw how carefully each stage of the case was prepared. They watched the lawyers battle each other like gladiators before the eyes of judge and jury. Nothing was hidden, secret, Star Chamber–like. The state seemed to have no great advantage over the defendant at the bar of justice; on the contrary, the rules seemed delicately balanced, scrupulous, rigidly fair.

This, at any rate, was what they thought they saw. Of course, it was only an illusion. The real work of the system was obscure, quiet, hidden from view; what they saw was a grotesque exception, a caricature. They saw something like the huge, bloated shapes, garishly colored, that one might see at a Mardi Gras, a carnival, an outdoor show. People saw that justice was real; but they also saw it as absurd.[73]

In short, they saw both more and less justice than the system actually provides. More in that the other face of justice—heartless, dry, efficient, uncaring—never reached their consciousness. Less in that the tricks, the tomfoolery, the loopholes, the lawyers' machinations, had nothing to do with the staple work of the courts: the thousands of cases of larceny, assault, or drunkenness. They saw justice as a ham, a mountebank, a fool; the other face of justice, swift, callous, crude, was lost in the shadows.

Criminal Appeals

If the jury comes in with a verdict of not guilty, or if the judge dismisses the case, that ends the affair. The defendant "walks"—that is, he strolls out of the courtroom, free as the breeze. In the Anglo-American system, the prosecution has no right to appeal an acquittal, no matter how ludicrous it might seem, or how much it went against the weight of the evidence.* Nor can the defendant ever be tried again for the same offense. That would be "double jeopardy"; federal and state constitutions specifically forbid this.†

If the verdict at a trial is guilty, however, the defendant (through his lawyer) can file a motion asking for a new trial. The defendant may also ask the judge to set aside the verdict; once in a while, the judge obliges. Most of the time, of course, the judge sticks to his guns. At this point, the defendant has, and had, in every state, the right to appeal.

In some legal systems (but not ours), an appeals court goes over

---

* Historically, neither side had the right to appeal. The modern system developed in a piecemeal, ragged way. But, in essence, one way of looking at the way appeal developed is simply to say that states started to give defendants the right to have review in appeals court, but left the prosecution essentially where it was before.[74]
† Exactly what constituted double jeopardy was an issue the courts wrestled with occasionally. In one interesting Massachusetts case, a man named Hodgdon delivered cloth, velvet, flannel, and other materials to the defendant; the defendant was supposed to make overcoats out of these materials. Hodgdon returned the first few coats as unsatisfactory. Then defendant supposedly made off with the materials and the coats. He was tried for embezzling the cloth, the velvet, and so on, and was acquitted. Then he was indicted for embezzling the coats. The Supreme Judicial Court allowed the second trial; it represented a distinct, separate offense.[75]

everything—facts, testimony—in effect, retrying the case. In American law, an appeals court only corrects "errors"; it does not rehash everything that went on at the trial. The convicted defendant (or his lawyer), on appeal,* must be able to point out some technical flaw in the indictment, in the procedures followed, or in the way the trial was run. Did the judge allow forbidden bits of evidence? Did he keep proper evidence out? Did he give the jury erroneous instructions?

The law of criminal appeals was very complicated and technical. Some cases early in the nineteenth century, reflecting English practice, refused to hear complaints except about errors on the face of the record, which pretty much barred anything that went wrong at the trial itself. But it soon became established practice to allow review of all sorts of errors, including mistakes at the trial itself, as long as the defendant (or his lawyer) had raised an objection at the time and had "reserved" an "exception," laying the basis for an appeal.

Only a small percentage of criminal cases were ever appealed. Arguably, these cases, which crawled or clawed their way to the top level of the judicial system, were the most important. These were the cases, to be sure, that become the source of official legal doctrine. Only appellate courts, by and large, *publish*; a treatise on criminal law, therefore, is mostly a synthesis of gems laid down and propositions enunciated by appellate courts, assembled into a rich display of doctrine. These reported cases, for all their importance, are not a reliable guide to what happens at the trial court level. We learn *something* about trials; but what we learn is subject to distortion, since appellate cases are not and cannot be typical. And as far as the petty courts are concerned, they might as well be dead and buried. Reported cases have nothing at all to say about them. For these we have to rely on other historical sources.

Appellate-court rulings, however, often showed an extreme fussiness about procedures and pleadings. Some appeals courts seemed to be saying about indictments: FRAGILE—HANDLE WITH CARE. The least little mistake could be fatal. In the last part of the nineteenth century, we hear complaints of hypertechnicality, of too much reversing for piddling, technical reasons. Texas was supposed to be the horrible example. In 1877, a case was reversed because the jury wrote, "We, the jury, the defendant guilty," omitting the word *find*.[76] In a later case (1886), a defendant had been tried for receiving stolen cattle. The jury returned a verdict of "guity," omitting the letter *l*. This was grounds for reversal,[77] even though in 1879 a conviction of "guily," missing a *t*, withstood attack.[78]

* Originally, the word *appeal* referred to certain kinds of civil appeals, in cases of equity. But it is the common word for the process of taking a case to a higher court; and by now it is technically quite correct to use the term for all such cases.

No wonder, then, that someone should remark caustically in 1887, that the Texas Court of Appeals was apparently "organized to overrule and reverse." The writer claimed that during a twelve-year period the court had reversed twice as many cases as it affirmed: 1,604 to 882. In one volume of cases, the ratio was supposedly five to one.[79] If the writer wanted a fearful example of technicality gone wild, he could have cited *Taylor v. State* (1887).[80] Charles Taylor was indicted for the crime of breaking and entering, and taking the property of J. W. Bilgen and R. Y. Holman "without *their* consent." This indictment, said the appeals court, was "fatally defective." Why on earth? "When there are more owners than one, an indictment for theft must allege that the taking was without the consent of *either* of said owners." To say "without *their* consent" would not do.

Was Texas an extreme case or not? Only an array of quantitative studies, which we do not have, would tell us if the problem of excess reversal and hypertechnicality was specific to Texas, or a national problem. Perhaps even for Texas it was exaggerated. In 1893, the Texas court affirmed 110 criminal cases on appeal and reversed 61.[81]* This is hardly a disastrous ratio. The law literature tells horror stories but is short on rigor and analysis. Of course, there are examples of hypertechnicality in other states, too, that match anything Texas could come up with, and suggest that bad habits were at least sporadically national. Perhaps some sort of high (or low) point was reached in a Missouri case in 1908. One Campbell was indicted for rape; the indictment ended with the words "against the peace and dignity of State, " leaving out the word *the* before the word "State." This was a fatal flaw:

> While it may be conceded that the word "the" is a small one, . . . we see no escape from the conclusion that the definite article . . . is absolutely essential in order to designate the particular State against which the offense is charged to have been committed. . . . The omission of this word not only changes the sense but the very substance of the clause.[82]

What was the point of a decision like this? Perhaps the point lay in the ideology of judges and lawyers. The profession believed in strict procedural justice. Hypertrophic appeals gave the *appearance* of meticulous justice. Like the great show trials, and the trials in which an underdog won, there was perhaps some propaganda value in cases of reversal of conviction on technical grounds. These cases were trying, in their own clumsy way, to send a message to the profession, and to the outside

---

* Most cases were decided on technical points of procedure: ninety-seven cases turned on procedural points and only seventy-nine on matters of substance (although the line between these two is not always clear).

world. The message was this: our system is dedicated to fairness; it is absolutely obsessed with the rights of defendants. This was, of course, a matter of pride, and an answer to people who said the system was biased or unfair. Lawyers themselves may have liked to hear this message. For the larger public, such a message legitimated and defended the system by parading an exaggerated image of justice. Did the message, in fact, get through? Did it affect behavior? Very doubtful. The public never knew, or cared, about the technical work of high courts.

III

CRIMINAL JUSTICE IN THE TWENTIETH CENTURY

12

A NATIONAL SYSTEM

BEFORE THE TWENTIETH CENTURY, CRIMINAL JUSTICE WAS OVERWHELMINGLY the business of the states, not the federal government. Of course, the federal government did have its responsibilities; the District of Columbia had a full-scale penal code, all the trappings of city law enforcement, and a prison system as well.[1] All the states outside of the original ones had had their larval periods as "territories," and territorial law was federal; territorial courts were federal courts. These territories had their criminal codes and their systems of criminal justice. Moreover, by the twentieth century, the United States had become something of an empire; and the federal government was ultimately responsible for its colonies and dependencies, wherever they were.

The federal sphere also included a certain number of cases coming out of the armed services, handled through courts-martial.[2] Murder and other crimes on the high seas, aboard ships, were subject to national jurisdiction, as were crimes committed on navigable waters (and, later, on airplanes), in national parks, and in odd bits of federal property inside the states, such as forts, magazines, arsenals, dockyards, and the like.[3]

All this was certainly not insignificant; but when all is said and done, the federal government was not a major player in criminal justice. The list of specifically *federal* crimes was not very long: immigration offenses, customs violations, tax fraud, crimes on the high seas, smuggling, and a few others. In the Northern District of California between 1851 and 1891, district judge Ogden Hoffman handled about 2,800 criminal matters, or roughly 70 a year, and they were quite a miscellaneous lot. Some came out of admiralty: there were 30 cases of desertion at sea, and 199 in which sailors claimed they were beaten. The biggest bulge was made by the 1,066 prosecutions for offenses relating to business taxes or licenses. There were also 272 federal liquor violations, 71 cases of selling liquor to Indians, 142 cases of smuggling opium, 313 cases of naturalization fraud, 102 mail offenses, 96 cases of counterfeiting, 94 cases of false voter registration, and 49 cases of cutting federal timber.[4]

For the fiscal year that ended in June 1889, the federal district courts in the country as a whole handled 14,588 criminal cases. Over 5,600 of these were "internal revenue cases"; and the bulk of these were most likely cases of moonshining and other violations of the national laws that taxed liquor. According to the report of the U.S. attorney general, exactly twelve cases, in the entire federal system, fell under the heading of "civil rights."[5]

There is no easy way to compare these federal figures with figures on state criminal justice, but, obviously, the federal contribution was a drop in the bucket. The situation changed dramatically in the twentieth century. The states, to be sure, remain primarily responsible for most matters of crime and punishment. The important, basic crimes are all exclusively state crimes, or nearly so—murder, armed robbery, theft, rape, larceny, arson. The policeman prowling the streets on foot or in a car works for the city, the county, or the state; the vast majority of men and women behind bars are locked up in local jails or in prisons run by the state. The federal government, however, is no longer a distant outsider, with nothing much to say or do about local crime. It casts an important shadow. There are significant federal crimes—tax evasion, drug offenses, securities fraud, heaps of regulatory crimes. The federal government also gives money to support local law enforcement; and it has a voice in setting crime policy. Its role in the system has grown to impressive size, starting from a baseline of close to zero. Politically, too, crime has become a *national* issue.

Some sort of shift toward the center was probably inevitable in the twentieth century, when we consider what the country became, compared to what it was. The United States is vast, sprawling, diverse. It stretches from the Arctic wastelands of northern Alaska to the tropical islands that dribble off the tip of southern Florida, and from Maine to Hawaii, with some outlying islands thrown into the bargain. Today the population is over 250 million, of every race and national background imaginable.

The millions of immigrants have, in general, homogenized. Whether they jumped into the melting pot or were pushed hardly matters. Even African-Americans, not wanted in the mainstream, became very much a part of the culture, whether they intended to or not. Today, for the most part, Americans speak the same language, watch the same TV programs, dress and sing and talk along similar lines. People talk about roots and the old country, but it is mostly just talk. They have, in general, shucked off their ancestries like outworn shoes. Movies and radio and TV act as a giant cultural blender, and most people cannot or will not resist.

There are, of course, cultural and geographic dialects; the fault line of race is still jagged and not to be bridged; there is a powerful Hispanic presence, especially along the southern borders; there are Polynesian and Inuit and Chinese and Navajo enclaves, among others. How much real cultural diversity there is, or ought to be, in the United States, is sharply controverted.

American diversity is obvious: a rainbow of colors, shapes, habits, and human designs. The homogeneity is just as real. In parts of the Old World, in the past, every valley had its own dialect, every village was an island; few people traveled outside a short radius of distance. Villages, groups, and towns grew more and more different over time, like the beaks of Darwin's finches. But America in the 1990s is one country in a blindingly literal sense. Satellite communication and jet airplanes make a mockery of distance and time. Even those too poor or sick or stuck in their rut to move about themselves have a window on the whole country (and the world) through the nearest television set.

One of the most profound trends in the history of government, law, and society in this century is the drift or pull or rush toward the center. The national government has become more and more powerful, has done more and more, matters more and more, fills more and more of our political and social consciousness. Yet the states have by no means withered away. Their governments are more important than ever in an *absolute* sense—they do more, tax more, spend more. But compared to the federal government, they have consistently lost power and influence. Schemes to revitalize the states, the periodic "new federalisms" and the like, are always dead on arrival. The big show, the main show, is now Washington, D.C.; and the big gun is the president, not the governor or the mayor.

In the twentieth century, the state boundaries have become increasingly porous. They are more or less arbitrary boundaries, to begin with; there is no big culture difference between North and South Dakota, or, for that matter, between Maine and Florida. Even the differences in culture between regions—the South, New England, the West—are slacking off, because of migration from region to region, and, more important, the transmission of sounds, pictures, people, and bytes across space. Cars stream freely across state lines; they hardly even slow down. There are no border guards, no customs declarations. Yet one point has to be made. *Jurisdiction* stops at the border: the boundary between North and South Dakota is a fine mesh that lets everything flow through except one: the law. The penal code of North Dakota means nothing once you cross the frontier into South Dakota.

In the nineteenth century, there was less traffic across the lines; and it was slower. We have stressed American mobility in the nineteenth century. Still, there were physical limits. It took months to get from Missouri to Oregon in, say, 1850; the trip was grueling and dangerous. Eventually, the railroad cut the trip to about a week. Cars were soon as fast, and more convenient. Then the airplane made distance meaningless. Jet travel eliminated, for all practical purposes, the places in between. When you fly from coast to coast, you don't go *through* the midwest; you just fly over it.

This is physical travel. Ideas and pictures travel even faster. The whole country watches the president on TV—simultaneously. This is new. Technology makes this one country, with one capital, one primary center of power.

Federal Crimes

These facts of twentieth-century life do not automatically translate into changes in criminal justice. But if the central government swells and bloats, that must have consequences. In our century, federal laws have piled one on top of the other, and then some: laws about taxation, welfare, business regulation, and the like. The Internal Revenue Code is perhaps the most awesome and convoluted of all federal statutes. The income tax dates from 1913.[6] The tax code is not, of course, a criminal code, but cheating on taxes is most definitely a crime, including failure to file a return or filing a "false or fraudulent return."[7] The Internal Revenue Service makes some startling arrests of prominent people; countless millions were and are aware of the shadow of the IRS, looking over their shoulders.

The federal leviathan grew and grew in the twentieth century, and this expanded the sheer *number* of federal crimes, big and small. In the same session that enacted the income-tax law, Congress made it a crime to take commercial sponges "measuring when wet less than five inches in their maximum diameter" from the Gulf of Mexico or the Straits of

Florida; it became a crime also to violate the Cotton Futures Act.[8] Each session of Congress peppered the statute books with regulatory crimes. The New Deal accelerated the process; and there was no letup in the post–New Deal world.

In the nineteenth century, Congress was a caged tiger. But the tiger burst out of its cage in the twentieth century. The Mann Act (the so-called White Slave Law), passed in 1911, was a remarkable instance of the tiger on the loose.[9] This law put the federal government squarely into a life-area (sex), which had been as purely state and local a concern as anything in the whole legal system. And this was only the beginning; next came tougher drug laws—the start of a long, unhappy marriage—and then Prohibition, which came and went.

Congress took another giant step in 1919, when it passed the so-called Dyer Act, the National Motor Vehicle Theft Act. This law, in essence, made it a crime to drive a stolen car across state lines, or to deal in stolen cars that had moved across state lines.[10] In *Brooks v. United States* (1925), the Supreme Court unanimously upheld the law, even though it seemed to stretch the power of Congress under the "interstate commerce" clause of the Constitution. Chief Justice Taft cited the Mann Act, "the radical change in transportation" brought about by the automobile, and "the ease with which evil-minded persons can avoid capture." The Chief Justice spoke darkly, too, of "elaborately organized conspiracies" to steal cars and spirit them away into other states. It was this situation that had "roused Congress to devise some method for defeating the success of these widely spread schemes of larceny."[11] In short, new technology, with its lightning speed and crushing power, was beyond the reach of the thin arms of local government; the federal government alone could save the day.

Leviathan grows especially fat during wartime. The First World War, no exception to this rule, stretched the powers and capacities of the federal government. The war brought with it still more federal crimes, though mostly temporary ones: evicting the family of a soldier or sailor, or repossessing goods sold to a serviceman on the installment plan.[12] The war also revived treason and espionage as issues. The great Red Scare, right after the end of the war, plunged the federal government into the dirty and dubious business of sniffing out dissenters, squashing left-wing opinion, looking hysterically for wild-eyed anarchists and bushy Bolsheviks, and generally trampling on the right of free speech (see chapter 16.)

Probably nothing in the first half of the twentieth century matched Prohibition in expanding the federal crime effort. The Prohibition Amendment, which outlawed the liquor trade, was followed by the Volstead Act (1919), which provided the teeth and the mechanism for carrying this out (see also chapter 15.) Prohibition is often described as a dead letter, but it was an extremely lively corpse. The assistant attorney general in charge of Prohibition, Mabel Willebrandt, reported in 1924 that the federal courts were "staggering" under a load of liquor cases—over 22,000 cases were pending at the end of the fiscal year.[13] The federal war against demon rum used some newfangled weapons, such as wiretapping; for this and other reasons, many important constitutional cases, on such issues as illegal searches and seizures, came out of a Prohibition background.*

Prohibition sputtered to an inglorious end at the beginning of the New Deal period in the thirties. In general, the New Deal sucked power away from the states and into the federal government, in response to the crisis of the Great Depression. The crime role of the central government also increased. In March 1932, a great crime horrified the country: the kidnapping of Charles Lindbergh's baby. Lindbergh was, of course, an American hero, the first person to fly solo across the Atlantic Ocean. The Lindberghs paid the ransom, but the baby boy had, in fact, been murdered the day he was kidnapped. Bruno Hauptmann, an immigrant carpenter, was arrested, tried, and executed for the crime. Meanwhile, Congress reacted to the uproar by passing the so-called Lindbergh Act, which made it a federal crime to take across state lines anybody who had been "unlawfully seized, confined, inveigled, decoyed, kidnaped, abducted or carried away ... and held for ransom or reward."[16] Walter Weisenberger, president of the St. Louis Chamber of Commerce, argued before the House Judiciary Committee that if federal force could follow prostitutes and stolen cars, why not the fiend who stole a child "from the mother's breast."[17] In 1934, the Lindbergh Law was tightened: the death penalty was added. If the victim was missing for seven days, a *presumption* arose that some state line had been crossed and the FBI could enter the picture.[18]

Lindbergh Act cases were never much of a burden on the courts, of course. But the law reflected a national mood, a feeling that the federal government and its agencies had a role to play in crime-fighting. Crime had become interstate. Crime was not just a few evil men, skulking in local corners. Twentieth-century criminals had wheels and wings.

---

* In *Olmstead v. United States*,[14] the defendants were a big-time operation, with about fifty employees, including salesmen, bookkeepers, an attorney, and a fleet of boats to bring liquor from Canada to Washington. Yearly sales were on the order of $2 million. The government used wiretapping to smash this nefarious ring. The issue before the Supreme Court was whether the government could use this evidence to convict; the Taft Court said yes. Wiretapping did not "amount to a search or seizure within the meaning of the Fourth Amendment." Four justices dissented, including Oliver Wendell Holmes, Jr., who said he felt that it was "less evil that some criminals should escape than that the Government should play an ignoble part."[15]

Moreover, like big business, crime was no longer a mom-and-pop, small-time affair. Now there was *organized* crime as well. Organized crime was run along the lines of a business, with "capital investment, a regular payroll, and problems of manufacture, distribution, and retailing." Some kinds of crime cried out for scale, for "coordination" or "consolidation." For example, bookmaking needed a wire service. Small-time gamblers lacked enough capital to cover their losses on an unlucky day. Larger organizations thus had a competitive edge.[19] The FBI grew big and strong on the basis of the idea and the reality of large-scale crime, as we shall see.

In 1934, Congress passed a flock of new penal laws. One of these made it a crime to rob a national bank; another criminalized "extortion by means of telephone, telegraph, radio"; another, the National Stolen Property Act, made it a crime to transport "any goods, wares, or merchandise, securities or money" worth $5,000 or more across state lines, or to receive this kind of stolen property, knowing it to be stolen.[20] Still another act made it a crime to flee from one state to another to avoid prosecution for murder, kidnapping, burglary, robbery, mayhem, rape, assault with a deadly weapon, or extortion accompanied by threats of violence, or to flee across state lines to avoid giving testimony in criminal proceedings.[21] That same year, Congress passed a National Firearms Act, which taxed and regulated the sale of guns, including machine guns. Violations of the act were, of course, federal offenses.[22]

The Federal Courts

These laws, and later criminal statutes passed by Congress, had a cumulative effect on the federal courts. At the beginning of the century, as we have seen, the federal courts handled few criminal cases. The number rose with the number of federal crimes. For example, for the year 1915, the U.S. attorney general reported that 135 people were convicted of violating federal meat inspection laws; and there were even three convictions (with fines) for violating a migratory bird law.[23] In the Prohibition years, vast numbers of liquor cases poured into the federal courts. In the fiscal year 1924, in addition, no less than 590 cases were "disposed of by the imposition of fines" under the migratory bird law. There were also 264 food-and-drug cases in that year, and 183 of these resulted in fines.[24]

In the fiscal year ending June 30, 1940, there were 48,856 criminal cases in the federal district courts of the forty-eight states. Prohibition was over, but even so, almost half of these (23,448) were liquor cases, mostly for violations of liquor tax laws. There were 3,504 immigration act violations; the Motor Vehicle Theft Act contributed 2,309 cases; narcotics laws, 3,572; postal law violations (including postal frauds), 3,195.

The Mann Act contributed a healthy 663 cases; and there were 2,587 cases of counterfeiting and forgery. The rest was a miscellaneous, and somewhat surprising lot—890 violations, for example, of the Migratory Bird Act, which is quite a flock of birds.[25]

Criminal caseloads in federal courts do not show constant, linear growth. In 1961, the number of cases had declined to 28,460. Liquor cases had largely disappeared from the dockets. Auto theft, with 5,098 cases, was the largest single category, and there were 1,524 narcotics cases. By fiscal year 1973, the federal criminal docket had climbed back up to 40,367. Auto theft cases were down to a mere 1,960, but there had been a huge jump in narcotics cases (to 8,817), and there was a significant number of cases under other federal statutes, including 136 criminal cases involving civil rights.*

The federal criminal docket continued to grow in the 1980s. In 1985, 53,060 men and women were tried in federal court on criminal charges;[27] in 1990, the total was 65,359. Of these, 23,193 were drug defendants. The next largest category was fraud, with 9,685 defendants. There were 8,662 cases of drunk driving, which seems surprising; but these were drunks who drove in national parks and other federal enclaves. The old liquor tax offenses had shriveled to a mere 13 defendants, and auto thefts were down to 363.[28]

What is most noteworthy about this catalogue of cases is its somewhat erratic quality. State dockets fluctuate, too, but there is a fairly steady and predictable diet of assault, burglary, theft of various forms, and the like. The federal docket is all fits and starts. Prohibition came and went. The effort to catch auto thieves came and went. The Mann Act came and went. Today, drug offenses have taken over these empty nests. The progress of regulatory offenses has been somewhat steadier, though here, too, there are peaks and troughs. Federal criminal justice, then, has been more subject to the changing winds of politics, to fashions and movements, than the state systems; it has been more ancillary, less fundamental in its focus.

It is still true today that the sum of the state systems completely dwarfs the federal system. Felony prosecutions in federal courts amount to less than 2 percent of the national total. In the 1980s, according to one estimate, there were about one million felony filings in state courts; if misdemeanors, traffic cases, and the like, are thrown in, the total goes over ten million.[29] In 1990, there were said to be 1,790,428 criminal filings in Texas alone.[30] Federal filings, quantitatively at least, are a spit in the ocean.

---

* This was a sizable jump for civil rights; in 1961, there had been only eight cases. There were 3,043 cases under the Selective Service Act in 1973, although this was a declining category.[26]

One other factor must be mentioned. In the twentieth century, the *standards* of criminal procedure have been nationalized to a considerable degree. This was most blatantly the work of the Supreme Court under Earl Warren, and it reached its climax in the fifties (see chapter 14.) States can no longer ignore what the federal courts say about the Bill of Rights. They must pay attention to federal standards.

Law Enforcement and Corrections

The federal government was such a bit player in criminal justice in the nineteenth century that it did not even have a prison it could call its own before 1891, except for soldiers and sailors.[31] It boarded out its other prisoners in state and local jails. In January 1877, twenty-five of the fifty inmates in the Alameda County, California, jail were federal prisoners. Most of them were Chinese, sentenced for "peddling or selling unstamped matches or cigars," a federal tax crime. In 1887, Congress made it illegal for states to "hire or contract out the labor" of federal criminals housed in their prisons and jails.[32] Up to this point, the prisoners had cost the states little or nothing; now they began to charge by the head for putting up these prisoners.[33] In 1905 in California, the federal government was paying forty cents per day per prisoner.[34]

In 1891, Congress authorized construction of three federal prisons. The first one open for business was Fort Leavenworth, in Kansas. It had originally been a military fort. The Department of Justice took it over in 1895. A second prison opened in Atlanta in 1902; the third prison was a converted territorial jail on McNeil Island in Puget Sound.[35] These three were the only federal prisons until 1925. By 1930, there were five, one of them a women's prison, the Federal Industrial Institution for Women, which opened in 1927 at Alderson, West Virginia (see chapter 18). In 1930, Congress passed an act creating a federal Bureau of Prisons within the Department of Justice. The attorney general under this act had power to "establish and conduct industries, farms, and other activities; to classify the inmates, and to provide for their proper treatment, care, rehabilitation, and reformation."[36]

The federal prison system, like most state systems, came to consist of specialized institutions. They have ranged from the more relaxed, "country club" prisons, to the grim steel-and-concrete dungeons of ultra-maximum security, reserved for the most desperate or despised of prisoners. This was the role of "The Rock," the notorious prison at Alcatraz Island, a wind-swept and jagged bit of land in San Francisco Bay, which began its career in 1934.

Alcatraz is on a hill, looking out deceptively at the lights and towers of San Francisco, shimmering across a narrow but treacherous body of water. No one, as far as is known, ever made good an escape from Alcatraz, except in the movies. Alcatraz housed Al Capone and dozens of other hardened criminals or plain lost souls. It shut its doors in 1963, rotted for a while, was occupied for a spell by a group of militant Native Americans, then restored somewhat. It is now a major tourist attraction. Every day, hundreds of Americans and foreign visitors take the ferry from San Francisco, scurry up from the dock, poke their noses into the bare, metallic cells, stare at the naked walls, laugh at the jokes of the guides, and buy souvenir T-shirts to remember their visit.

Alcatraz is "history," but the federal prison system is far from quaint and historical. It shows no signs of turning into Disneyland, or a theme park of yesterday's crime. The number of federal prisoners has grown steadily over the years. In 1890, there were fewer than 2,000 federal prisoners; in 1915, there were about 3,000;[37] by 1930, the numbers had reached 26,000 (half of these, however, were military prisoners);[38] on January 1, 1940, there were 20,000 nonmilitary prisoners; in 1980, slightly under 25,000; the drug wars boosted the figures so that by the mid-1980s the number of prisoners ranged between 35,000 and 40,000.[39] On December 31, 1989, the system housed 53,347 men and women—86.6 percent of them sentenced, 13.4 percent awaiting sentence.[40] The Bureau of Prisons controlled some forty-seven institutions in various parts of the country.[41]

Of course, there are vastly more state than federal prisoners, in 1992 as in 1900. But the federal system is slowly catching up. In 1910, there were 66,831 prisoners in state institutions as compared to 1,904 in federal prisons—thirty-five times more. In 1940, the figures were 146,325 and 19,260, respectively; by then the state totals were only seven and a half times as great. In 1980, 261,292 men and women were in state prisons, 41,085 in federal prisons, a ratio of about six to one.[42] But there are still, today, about twice as many prisoners in California's prisons (about 100,000) as in the whole federal system. It remains to be seen what the future will bring.

As the federal law of crimes has grown, so, too, has federal law enforcement, which did not amount to much before 1900. In 1908, a Bureau of Investigation was created inside the Justice Department. This was the rather Napoleonic brainchild of Attorney General Charles J. Bonaparte (who was, in fact, a relative of Napoleon). Bonaparte had asked for authority to hire investigators. When Congress failed to give him what he wanted, he struck out on his own. He issued an order organizing a small investigating staff. The president, Theodore Roosevelt, who had Napoleonic tendencies of his own, transferred eight agents from the Secret Service to this brand-new bureau.[43] President Taft's attorney general, George W. Wickersham, ratified the action.[44]

Out of this bureau, and these modest beginnings, grew the famous (and sometimes notorious) Federal Bureau of Investigation (FBI). In 1921,

J. Edgar Hoover became assistant director of the agency, and in 1924 he took over as director. Hoover dominated the agency from then until his death in 1972, a period of some forty-eight years. During that time, presidents came and went, but Hoover stayed. He exercised immense power, surviving the gyrations and perturbations of politics. He became, in the words of one critic, "the greatest untouchable in American history."[45]

Franklin Roosevelt's administration must shoulder some of the responsibility for boosting the FBI's power. When Congress created a flock of new federal offenses in 1934, the FBI was given the job of enforcement.[46] Hoover, a master of publicity, made full use of his authority; he "skillfully manipulated the media," turning a number of "otherwise ordinary criminals" into "public enemies."[47] When, in the thirties, the FBI caught dangerous crooks on the order of John Dillinger (or took credit for catching them), its reputation and mystique grew to heroic size. The FBI was fearless, incorruptible, efficient, bold—a magnificent army in the war against crime. Or so it seemed.

Hoover ran a tight ship. His own views were xenophobic and reactionary. The FBI was a most reluctant ally, if it was an ally at all, in the battle for civil rights. It is true that Hoover was an early opponent of the Nazi regime, and he was against interning Japanese-Americans in camps during World War II.[48] But whenever it was a question of "communism," "leftism," or "subversion," Hoover was like a man obsessed. He came to see a communist under every bush. His right-wing paranoia poisoned much of the work of the FBI: its vendetta against Martin Luther King, Jr., is a good example.[49] In the fifties and sixties, the FBI, more and more, turned into a kind of "political police," an "independent security state within the state."[50] The FBI was, in many ways, a law unto itself. It was widely believed, too, that Hoover's secret dossiers, filled with "dirt" on politicians and other leaders, gave him vast power and made him impregnable in office.

The FBI did come to stand for the latest in forensic science, blood tests, fingerprinting—in short, professionalism. It preached this gospel of crime detection to local law-enforcement officials.[51] It also got involved in some mundane but useful tasks. One of these was the gathering of crime statistics. The Uniform Crime Reporting (UCR) program, run by the bureau, goes back to the 1920s. A committee of the International Association of Chiefs of Police prepared a plan for gathering uniform crime statistics in 1929. Seven crimes (the "index" crimes) were listed: murder and manslaughter, rape, robbery, aggravated assault, larceny, burglary, and motor vehicle theft. Arson was added in 1979. The FBI set out standardized definitions for these crimes; and from 1930 on, the UCR has produced the most widely used index of American criminality.[52]

Whether these figures are good enough, however, has come to be questioned. Not all crimes are reported to the police, after all. "Victimization" studies turn up figures quite different (and higher) than those of the UCR. These studies start from the other end—that is, by asking people if they have been victims of crime. Nonetheless, the federal role in putting together some useful *numbers* is not to be sneezed at.

The Syndicate

One factor that fed the movement toward federal involvement was fear of organized crime, "the syndicate," or the "Mafia." The Mafia was supposed to be a giant criminal conspiracy made up of Italian gangsters (Sicilians, to be specific). The Mafia was blamed for the murder of the police chief of New Orleans, in 1890.[53] Prohibition was an era of crime syndicates, an age of celebrity gangsters, men like Al Capone—many of them Italian. When Prohibition died, there were plenty of other lines of illegal work to replace it—gambling, vice, extortion. People found it easy to believe that some sinister web united crime factions in the various cities.

The Mafia flared up again as an issue in the 1950s. Senator Estes Kefauver of Tennessee headed a special committee of Congress to investigate racketeering and organized crime.[54] The Kefauver Committee claimed it uncovered a lot of dirty linen, and it made superb use of publicity in the process. The committee's message was that the Mafia had its tentacles in every major city; it was growing rich and powerful on the spoils of vice and crime. The eye of the television cameras covered the work of Kefauver's committee; the hearings were one of the earlier demonstrations of the sinister power of *this* medium, whose tentacles were in the process of spreading everywhere, too. One especially dramatic moment came during the testimony of the gangster Frank Costello: the camera avoided Costello's face, focusing instead on his hands "as he crumpled a handkerchief, interlocked and picked at his fingers, grasped for a glass of water, stroked his eyeglasses" and "rolled a little ball of paper between his thumb and index finger." The TV images suggested a faceless, hidden man, a man of "immense conspiratorial power."[55] Viewed in the cold light of hindsight, Kefauver seems to have produced little in the way of hard evidence. But he produced a lot in terms of images and headlines, which to Kefauver and others on his committee were far more important.

The FBI, somewhat reluctantly, formed a special unit to fight "racketeers" and interstate syndicates in the 1950s. In the early sixties, the Justice Department under Attorney General Robert Kennedy also paid special attention to crime families and their networks.[56] Whether any of *this* burst of activity did much good is also doubtful. But the Mafia theme was endlessly fascinating to the general public.

Was there a *national* Mafia, connected by ties of blood and sacred oaths? The evidence was, in fact, rather slim (or at least controversial); but the media hardly cared. The Mafia made good reading—good fodder for movies, books, and magazine articles. The mystique of the gangster, a theme of the silver screen in the thirties and forties, was perhaps a throwback to the theme of the beloved outlaw and the western gunfighter. Western movies were even more popular than gangster movies, in this period. Perhaps Jesse James, Billy the Kid and Wyatt Earp paved the way for James Cagney and Scarface, and *The Godfather*. There is and has been a good deal of romance connected with the outlaw—at least with certain outlaws. Then, too, the twentieth century is the age of the celebrity and celebrity culture. It hardly mattered who the celebrities were: they could be boxers, presidents, rock-and-roll stars—or notorious criminals. John Gotti, on trial in New York in 1992 for racketeering and murder, had what amounted to an adoring claque at his trial. His autograph, after all, was as good as a movie star's.

The notion of a vast, hydra-headed crime syndicate had other values, too. It was a simple and satisfying explanation for at least *some* of the crime that plagued the nation. It put the blame on a single monster, an identifiable presence, a defeatable enemy—and a foreign enemy, at that. This belief was much more comforting than the main competing theory: that crime was a diffuse, poisonous substance that came, as it were, from nowhere, an invisible enemy, subtle and mysterious. Or the idea that crime had deep, difficult social and economic roots. Moreover, if the Mafia was a reality, who better to fight this vast interstate octopus than the federal government, the only entity capable of fighting and winning the war against crime? Only *national* power had any hope of destroying organized crime.

Crime as a National Issue

Neither George Washington nor Abraham Lincoln mentioned crime on the streets in their messages to Congress or in their inaugural addresses. President Herbert Hoover was the one to break the long silence, in 1929. "Crime is increasing," he said in his inaugural address. He proposed a federal commission to study the problem. This became the famous Wickersham Commission, the National Commission on Law Observance and Enforcement. It was chaired by George W. Wickersham, who had been Taft's attorney general.[57]

The commission did a massive job. It published fourteen reports in 1931, on a variety of issues: police behavior, penal institutions, the causes of crime.[58] The reports were hardly a whitewash; the commission excoriated and threatened and pointed out and exposed; it accused the criminal justice system of brutality, corruption, and inefficiency. Morris

Ploscowe, writing for the commission, asked whether the sorry state of crime and criminal justice did not suggest something fundamentally wrong in "the very heart of . . . government and social policy in America."[59] But in the end, the reports sat on the shelf; not much came of the commission's many recommendations.

Crime popped out again as a major national issue after World War II, and nobody was able to put the jinni back in the bottle after that. Most presidential candidates did not try. In the campaign of 1964, the Republican candidate, Barry Goldwater, made a great fuss over law and order; when he accepted the nomination at the Republic convention, Goldwater spoke of "violence in the streets" and the "growing menace [of crime] to personal safety, to life, to limb and to property."[60] Presumably the federal government ought to do something about the problem. Goldwater lost the election; but the winner, Lyndon Johnson, picked up this issue, which was obviously dynamite.

In 1965, Congress passed the Law Enforcement Assistance Act (LEAA). Under this law, the attorney general could make grants to improve local law enforcement. The Office of Law Enforcement Assistance administered the program. Johnson also established a Commission on Law Enforcement and the Administration of Justice; his mandate to the commission sounded a somber message: "Crime is a sore on the face of America. It is a menace on our streets. . . . It is a corruptor of our youth. . . . We must bring it under control. . . . We have taken a pledge not only to reduce crime but to banish it."[61]

Of course, Johnson's war on crime did not banish crime any more than his war on poverty abolished poverty. The year 1968 was another election year. It was also a year of serious rioting, the year in which Robert Kennedy and Martin Luther King, Jr., were assassinated; and in which George Wallace, roaring up out of the white South, frightened mainstream politicians with his blatant appeals to racism—and his shouts about law and order. Richard Nixon, the Republican candidate, for his part blasted away at the decisions of the Supreme Court, which (he said) coddled criminals and worse. Partly in response to these rumblings, Congress passed the Omnibus Crime Control and Safe Streets Act.[62] This law set up a separate body, the Law Enforcement Assistance Administration, within the Department of Justice, to handle the new war on crime.[63]

Mostly, the weapon of this war was money. The LEAA during its ten years or so of vigorous life was mostly a tube for siphoning money out of the federal government and funneling it to the states, in the form of grants. The strategy of the act was to "establish the federal government as a source of money and technical assistance to state and local agencies." These agencies would "use this assistance to support planning, self-study, and new and innovative projects."[64] Billions of dollars flowed out of Washington. The grants to local agencies were supposed to foster innovation, to stimulate research on issues of law enforcement. Whether they ever accomplished much is doubtful. Ultimately, LEAA faded out of the picture. But crime has stubbornly remained an issue, a rude, insistent item on the national agenda. Candidates run for federal office on anticrime platforms; they accuse each other of being soft on crime, and they promise, once in office, to do *something* (not usually specified) about the terrible problems of violence and corruption.

It is easy for people to vent their anger on crime. The anger is justified after all. But it is also a way to vent feelings against poverty, race, and other issues for which crime is a convenient stand-in. Politicians pick up these fears and emotions on their antennae and broadcast what they think their people want to hear.

In general, today, the public, or at least some large part of it, has gotten the message. It holds the federal government responsible for a good deal of what it finds wrong with criminal justice. The narcotics nightmare is a good example. The federal government, as we shall see, has been in this quagmire since 1914. It digs itself in deeper and deeper; it spends more and more, flailing about madly, fighting, spending, arresting. The programs, state and federal, have been, on the whole, exercises in futility; but frustration only fuels a desperate determination to get tougher.

The federal government, in fact, may be helpless to do anything about drugs. Drugs flood into the country; there are millions of people buying, selling, sniffing, snorting, shooting up, smoking, and the like. Still, the federal government has the muscle and the jurisdiction to make a big noise, to mount campaigns, to wage "wars," with airplanes, Coast Guard cutters, and all sorts of paraphernalia. After all, there is precious little that Michigan or the city of Omaha can do to keep heroin and cocaine away from their streets and houses. And the American public, by and large, refuses to believe that some problems simply do not have current solutions, at least not workable ones. (This is true of crime in general, not merely the drug dilemma; we will come back to this theme in chapter 20.)

When all is said and done, despite all the hoopla, the federal role in criminal justice is limited, and will stay limited in the foreseeable future. The irony is that recent conservative presidents, who have long mouthed slogans about states' rights and local government, have been more zealous than the liberals in denouncing crime, drug use, and the like. They have thus helped keep alive the myth that the federal government can actually do something about the problem. In fact, there is not much the federal government *can* do, at least under present laws and jurisdictional arrangements. Of course, the federal government could *pay* state and local governments—could support criminal justice systems, police systems, prisons, and the like. But the federal government is loath to put its money where its mouth is.

Very few national politicians dare to say this out loud. Most of them seem anxious to make political hay out of criminal justice. In his State of the Union Address on January 28, 1992, President George Bush declared in ringing terms that "we must do something about crime," especially "violent street crime." A "tired woman on her way to work at six in the morning on a subway deserves the right to get there safely," he said. "Congress," he begged, "pass my comprehensive crime bill. . . . Help your country."[65]

But the comprehensive crime bill he referred to, which was then languishing in Congress, was anything *but* comprehensive, as the president must have known. It would do nothing much for the woman on the subway. It would have, at best, microscopic influence on crime. The national government was not and is not in control of criminal justice. At best, it has been a kind of Broadway angel, handing out money but never running the show. And even here it has mostly been a tightwad.

The truth is, national politicians never *wanted* to be in charge. They wanted no part of the real system of criminal justice. The real system is complicated, dirty, and a mess. Whoever touches pitch, gets defiled, or at least entrapped, and criminal justice is a tarpit of colossal proportions.

13

CRIME ON THE STREETS; CRIME IN THE SUITES

MOST CITIZENS—CERTAINLY MOST MEMBERS OF THE MIDDLE CLASS—WILL probably go through life without running afoul of the more serious parts of the criminal justice system. Many will be victims of crime—robbed, burglarized, assaulted. A great many will be called up for jury service; some will wriggle out of this duty, but a fair number will actually serve, though perhaps not at a criminal trial. Only a minority will ever be tried for a felony or spend time in prison or jail. Yet there is one part of the system that almost everybody will have to deal with, and probably more than once. That part is traffic law.

Traffic Law

This vast system is almost entirely a development of the twentieth century. Traffic law existed in the nineteenth century, in the horse-and-buggy era, but only in a rudimentary way (see chapter 5). Today, in the age of the automobile, traffic law processes an incredible volume of petty offenses and transgressions, and a good sprinkling of more serious offenses.

Almost everybody who drives—and that means, by now, almost

every healthy adult—is bound to be "guilty" of some traffic or auto sin; even the best drivers. In cities, it is hard to avoid getting a parking ticket every once in a while. The smaller traffic offenses, on the whole, carry very little moral intensity or bite. People who would immediately call the police to report a thief or a shoplifter would never do the same for a speeder, or someone they saw making an illegal U-turn. Spurned lovers expose some "victimless crimes"; irate ex-employees turn in tax evaders; but almost nobody snitches on people who violate traffic laws. Enforcement depends on the traffic police, and on them alone. And, to be sure, the police car, prowling up and down the streets, or roaring down the highway with sirens blasting and lights flashing, is a familiar part of the landscape.

The automobile made its first appearance on the streets, for all practical purposes, in the first decade of this century. It was, at the outset, a toy of the rich. But it was an exciting and dangerous toy, and it evoked regulation and police activity early on. In the last three months of 1906, the New York City police made 646 arrests for violations of laws and ordinances relating to motor vehicles.[1] As early as 1905 in California, driving an unregistered vehicle was a misdemeanor. Soon afterward, driving without a license became another. In 1925, the minimum age for a driver's license was fixed at fourteen; and habitual drinkers, drug addicts, and the "feeble-minded" were barred from licensure.[2] In 1931, the minimum age was raised to sixteen.[3] In New York in 1910, the law required all drivers to drive "in a careful and prudent manner and at a rate of speed so as not to endanger . . . property . . . or . . . life or limb"; any speed over thirty miles an hour, if persisted in for a quarter-mile or more, was "presumptive evidence" of careless, imprudent driving.[4] This statute also made hit-and-run driving a felony.[5]

By 1940, the United States had became an automobile society. The volume of traffic offenses was astronomical: traffic offenses had replaced drunkenness and loitering as the basic fodder of justice. At the beginning of the 1940s, 212 cities with a combined population of 45,420,696 reported more than 6,000,000 violations of traffic and motor vehicle laws.[6] Of course, most of these violations were small potatoes. But in California, in the first six months of 1950, 6,407 jail sentences were handed down in motor vehicle cases, 2,377 combinations of fines and jail, 232,079 fines, and 299,214 instances of "forfeitures" (practically speaking, the same as a minor fine).[7]

The numbers have continued to rise, as automobiles choke the roads and highways, and millions of people, living in the land of suburban sprawl, use the automobile as their lifeline—connecting them to work, shopping, and the outside world in general. Everybody, as we have said, even the most timid and correct of souls, breaks *some* traffic rules. But there are rules and there are rules. At the bottom end, many traffic offenses are not even treated as criminal; they are handled administratively, and their criminal-law aspects have shriveled to a vestige.

Thus, a person who parks overtime and gets a "ticket" will get an order to appear in court and face the music. But this is not a serious threat: if the car-owner chooses not to contest, she can "forfeit" the "bail" and send in a check instead. This "bail," of course, is nothing but a small fine masquerading as something else. In Massachusetts, starting in 1965, traffic violators could plead guilty by mail, waive trial, and send in a fine based on a fixed catalogue of penalties.[8] In some states, the minor offenses are not called crimes at all but "infractions." These "infractions," along with other minor traffic offenses, are staggeringly common. In North Carolina, in one twelve-month period (1989–1990), there were 1,200,000 motor vehicle crimes and infractions in the district courts; this was double the number of all other criminal cases.[9] In 1988, in the district courts of Michigan (the base of the judicial system), 633,979 cases of traffic misdemeanor were filed—about twice as many as all other felony and nontraffic misdemeanor put together.[10]

In many localities, traffic matters got handled by municipal courts, police courts, justices of the peace, and sometimes by specialized departments of municipal court. Large cities often had separate traffic courts.[11] By whatever name, such courts were the absolute bottom of the judicial system. Society never saw fit to equip its traffic courts with the trappings of majesty. American courts in general do not go in for ritual and pomp, but traffic courts are the extreme case. Physical conditions in these courts could be quite primitive. In one large southern city, around 1940, the traffic court shared a converted basement with the local jail. The courtroom was "filthy. A terrible odor prevails and on a humid, summer day the place is almost unbearable." Of sixty courtrooms inspected at that time in various cities, nine were rated "inexcusable," and more than half were declared fit to be condemned.[12]

The traffic court judge, as one would expect, did not have the prestige and dignity of higher-grade judges. A study of South Carolina in the 1960s found a "distressing lack of formality and dignity." The judges "conducted court in street attire or workclothes, rather than judicial robes."[13] George Warren, who studied traffic courts around 1940, reported that some judges seemed to treat "the proceedings in these courts as a joke. . . . Instances of familiarity and light by-play with defendants, of pleasantries with women violators and of the use of good-natured profanity were observed."[14] As a result, the defendant "leaves the traffic court without . . . a heightened consciousness as to safety problems" and without "a feeling of respect."[15]

The root of this evil was, perhaps, the fact that defendants did not—and do not—see themselves as criminals, but rather as unlucky people who got caught breaking a rule that everybody breaks once in a while.

The judges probably felt no different. Traffic crime is middle-class crime. For much of the century, the poor did not own cars, and even now, most car-owners (like most people in general) are solid members of the solid middle class. A "crime" that everybody in this group commits is unlikely to carry much of a stigma.

This attitude came to the surface in a 1958 American Bar Association report on traffic matters in Oklahoma. The report concluded that traffic cases should be treated differently from other police court cases, because "traffic offenders are of a different class of people than drunks, thieves, prostitutes, and similar offenders and should not be compelled to mingle with the latter when summoned into a court of justice."[16] Most people would probably concede the need for traffic laws, and for enforcing them. But they think of their own "punishment" as a kind of traffic tax, and an unfair tax at that, because its incidence is so random and irregular.

Drunk Driving

Attitudes toward drunk driving are generally much less cavalier. The formal legal system takes driving "under the influence" fairly seriously. In 1910, in New York, it was a misdemeanor to operate a motor vehicle "while in an intoxicated condition"; the second offense was a felony and could bring a prison term. Violators were in danger of losing their licenses; and owners of vehicles driven by drunks could lose their "certificate of registration" as well.[17] In 1926, New York created a new felony: causing serious bodily injury by driving while intoxicated. In 1941, a further statute on drunk driving allowed courts to "admit evidence of the amount of alcohol in the defendant's blood," as "shown by a medical or chemical analysis of his breath, blood, urine, or saliva." The statute also laid down the rule that a blood-alcohol level of more than 1.5 percent was "prima facie evidence" of intoxication.[18]

In 1953, New York took a further step; it enacted an "implied consent" law. Any driver with a license was "deemed" to have allowed the police to run a "chemical test of his breath, blood, urine or saliva" to see how much alcohol he had in his system. Of course, this "consent" was pretty much coerced. If a driver decided to be unreasonable and withhold consent, or refused to allow the tests to be given when stopped on the road, the state could use this stubbornness as an excuse to revoke his license.[19] Interestingly, this provision bypasses the courts (potentially at least), in favor of an administrative process. If a drunk driver refuses the test, he may lose his license, but he does not go on trial for the offense.[20]

On the books, then, drunk driving is a major crime, with heavy penalties. The reality—the law in action—is, as usual, a good deal more complicated. Large segments of the population are ambivalent, or worse, with regard to drunk driving. Thousands of drunk drivers, unlike drunk walkers or common drunkards—or burglars, for that matter—are members of the middle class. This gives them more clout in the system and certainly evokes more empathy from judges, jurors, and prosecutors. Kalven and Zeisel, in their study of the American jury (published in 1966), found evidence of this ambivalence in drunk driving cases. Many jury members sitting in judgment seemed to say to themselves, "There but for the grace of God go I," or some equivalent. One judge told the researchers that jurors who drank were "inclined to be sympathetic," and wanted "more proof of alcoholic influence than the law requires."[21]

Attempts to put money and effort into the fight against drunk driving were usually ephemeral. Congress passed a Highway Safety Act in 1966. This law set up a National Highway Safety Bureau, later called the National Highway Traffic Safety Administration. NHTSA made grants to support anti–drunk driving projects in various cities. But the program dribbled out in 1977. A Vermont report, covering the year 1969, expressed pessimism about the chances of tough enforcement of laws against drunk driving. Any increase in penalties was likely to be "counterproductive"; the public simply did not care. Putting drunk drivers in jail was a terrible idea; "reasonably clean and decent jail facilities" were unavailable; in any event, jailing caused "disruption" in the lives of those put in jail.[22] Of course, jail was just as dirty and disruptive if you were a burglar or mugger. It was the *class* aspect of drunk driving that insulated drunk drivers from the fate of burglars and muggers.

The wheel began to turn in the seventies. An "extraordinary grass roots anti–drunk driving movement" sprang up at about this time. After a drunk driver killed a teenager in Schenectady, New York, in 1979, a woman named Doris Aiken founded Remove Intoxicated Drivers (RID). A similar and very active organization, Mothers Against Drunk Driving (MADD), was founded by Candy Lightner in 1980 in Sacramento, California. A drunk driver had killed Mrs. Lightner's daughter.[23]

Drunk driving is, in some ways, an odd crime. James Jacobs has called it an "inchoate offense," meaning that the crime is committed when you drink and drive even if nobody gets hurt at all.[24] (It is not, of course, the only example of this kind of crime: carrying a concealed weapon is just as "inchoate," and so, perhaps, is possession of drugs.) In any event, the social movements directed against drunk driving have, in a way, recriminalized it. In part, MADD is an aspect of a more general movement to assert the rights of victims. It is also, in some ways, a women's crusade, a crusade of mothers on behalf of their children, against a macho ethos of reckless and drunken driving.

Nobody defends drunk driving or recklessness, of course, but a few scholars (Joseph Gusfield among them) feel that the whole business has been blown up out of all proportion. Drunk driving, they argue, is not a major social problem in the first place, and severe new penalties and crackdowns will, in the end, accomplish nothing. A much larger (silent) group no doubt agrees. These are the people who drink and drive, and their numbers probably include people in all walks of life, even judges, lawyers, and members of juries. Hence the campaign against drunk driving tends to make more of a mark on paper than it does in terms of real deterrence, or even in terms of severity of punishment.

No doubt educational drives and tighter rules have *some* effect; the question is how much. Two researchers, Ross and Voas, studied a crackdown that took place in the 1980s in New Philadelphia, Ohio. A judge there, Edward E. O'Farrell, had announced his intention to get tough. Plea bargaining would not be tolerated, and every convicted drunk driver would go to jail for ten days. Judge O'Farrell won honors, and was invited to appear on talk shows, but the remorseless facts of Ross and Voas showed that the impact on driver behavior was pitifully small. Drivers knew about the policy; they were aware that they faced tougher sentencing. But the risk was somehow not great enough to get them to change their way of life.[25] No doubt boiling drunk drivers in oil, on the spot, would put the fear of God into likely offenders; but here, too, as elsewhere in the system, the *practical* limits of severity are soon reached, and at a point that yields a meager harvest of deterrence. Thus drunk driving joins speeding, prostitution, and vice in general among the ranks of double-standard crimes.

Regulatory Crime

There have always been regulatory crimes, from the colonial period onward, as we have noted (see chapter 5.) But the vast expansion of the regulatory state in the twentieth century meant a vast expansion of regulatory crimes as well. Each statute on health and safety, on conservation, on finance, on environmental protection, carried with it some form of criminal sanction for violation. Sometimes a criminal charge was at the very heart of the statute. The very first words of the Food and Drug Act of 1906 declared it "unlawful" to manufacture "any article of food or drug which is adulterated or misbranded" and to sell that article in "interstate commerce."[26] Legislators would attach a criminal tail to every important regulatory law. So, for example, the National Labor Relations Act of 1935, passed during the high days of the New Deal, created various categories of "unfair labor practice," and gave to an administrative agency, the National Labor Relations Board, the power to define, regulate, and enforce the rules through administrative action. Still, at the end of the act, there was a doorway into the criminal justice system. It was a crime for anyone "wilfully" to "resist, prevent, impede or interfere with any member of the Board or any of its agents or agencies in the performance of their duties."[27]

The twentieth-century Leviathan, in short, does not shrink from the use of criminal sanctions. Its main regulatory weapons, of course, are administrative; technically these remedies are not "punishment" in the criminal sense. Take, for example, occupational licensing. Sam B. Warner and Henry B. Cabot, of Harvard Law School, writing in 1937, found that fifty-eight jobs or activities required a license in Massachusetts (up from seventeen in 1886): driving a car or an airplane, practicing law and medicine; working as an embalmer, nurse, or dentist; selling securities, running a lodging house, hunting and trapping animals; operating a Turkish bath.[28] Losing your driver's license, or your license to practice dentistry, was a serious detriment, regardless of whether you called it "punishment" or gave it some other name.

The vast expansion of the *federal* regulatory apparatus is the most obvious source of the new regulatory crimes—violations of antitrust laws, securities fraud, civil rights violations, polluting the air or water, and so on. But state governments have not been bashful, either, about rushing headlong into the administrative era. Most states have literally hundreds of regulatory laws, and more are passed every year in every state. The general effect of all this activity seems to be cumulative. Wholesale extinction may be going on in the animal kingdom, but it does not seem to be much of a problem among regulatory laws. These now exist in staggering numbers, at all levels. They are as grains of sand on the beach.

Offenses against state laws, often in fifty separate versions, run parallel to federal offenses in some instances; in others, the states go their own way. There are state food laws, health laws, sanitary laws, antitrust laws, and so on. Other laws (occupational licensing, for example) mostly lack federal equivalents. In Ohio, in 1911 alone, forty-nine criminal statutes were passed. The overwhelming majority of these made or amended regulatory statutes. One act required manufacturers to report serious work accidents, on pain of a fine. Another forbade certain banks from using the word *state* in their name or title. Another regulated the sale of commercial fertilizer, and punished noncompliance; still another amended an act "pertaining to the guarding of machinery"; failure to comply with an order of the chief inspector resulted in a fine, the proceeds to "inure to the benefit of the county hospital for tuberculosis."[29] One extremely elaborate law created a building code for Ohio; it contained detailed rules about building standards for theaters, assembly halls, churches, school buildings, asylums, hospitals, hotels, club and lodge buildings, workshops, factories, and "mercantile establish-ments"—all in the interests of safety and fire protection. The statute was more than 140 pages long. As usual, there was criminal icing on this cake: it was "unlawful" for owners and builders to violate the law.[30] In addition to all these state laws, there are thousands upon thousands of local ordinances, in New York City and in Keokuk alike, concerning liquor sales, land use, the obstructing or cleaning of sidewalks, weights and measures, dry cleaners, taxicabs, and almost every imaginable activ-ity of urban life.

Most specialists in "criminal law" or "criminal justice" know very little about these laws, or about their enforcement. Police officers do not concern themselves with price-fixing or violations of the Securities and Exchange acts. To be sure, some local ordinances are vigorously policed. In New York City in 1907, nearly 6,000 people were arrested for violat-ing health laws; and there were scattered arrests under factory laws, laws about steam boilers, pure food laws, tenement house laws—even thirty-five arrests for violating the city's Game and Forest Law![31] But most regulatory crimes, including most of the *major* ones, exist in a kind of shadow-land between crime and noncrime.

Moral views about the quality of acts, of course, are not timeless and unchanging. Regulatory laws and their criminal provisions are generally pinned to a particular period. They do not represent inelastic judgments about good and evil. Indeed, sometimes they are quite specific responses to emergencies. Rent control, for example, was imposed during both of the world wars of this century, and was largely repealed at war's end.

During the Second World War, moreover, there was an elaborate sys-tem of price control, which meant, of course, a huge black market—and black market crime.[32] Meat and gasoline were rationed; prices and rents were fixed. There were countless violations. The Office of Price Admin-istration (OPA) and the Justice Department imposed 259,966 sanctions between 1942 and 1947; and there were 13,999 cases of criminal prose-cution. The government won 93 percent of the cases it brought to trial, but judges imposed "extremely mild sentences": 74.4 percent of those convicted were fined or put on probation; only a quarter got any impris-onment.[33]

A black market cannot survive without customers, without support from the general public; but it also cannot survive without support from inside business itself. A study by the sociologist Marshall Clinard showed that many wholesale dealers in meat, during the war, were con-vinced that the laws were unfair, the regulations ridiculous. These of-fenders refused to think of themselves as real criminals. The OPA, in the opinion of these meat wholesalers, "just made a bunch of crooks out of honest men."[34] No doubt people differentiated *among* violations: gouging on rents was worse than fiddling a bit with extra meat rations.

Dealing in black-market gas was a temporary crime, and violation did not seem terribly harmful to most people.

Of course, a meat dealer who broke the law would have a strong need, psychologically, to defend himself, to convince himself he was not a "crook." So, too, the customer who wanted extra meat, or the steak-house that needed the meat to stay in business. The wartime controls were sudden laws—they made crimes out of behaviors that had been perfectly legal before. It was a complicated—perhaps impossible—job to regulate the prices of absolutely everything and the rents of millions of apartments. To be sure, a patriotic glow surrounded the war effort. This surely kept the rate of violation lower than it might have been. But violations were nonetheless as common as bees among flowers.

Anti-Trust

Naturally, there are vast differences *among* regulatory crimes in their moral status within society. There is a huge gulf between what people feel about a corporation that pours tons of poison into a river and how they feel about someone who pulls the tag off a mattress. Yet many regulatory rules are so technical, so hard to understand, so legalistic—or on the contrary, so enmeshed in microeconomic theory—that it seems wildly inappropriate to use *criminal* law to enforce them.

Yet exactly this choice was made when the Sherman Act was passed in 1890 (see chapter 5). The Sherman Act was, in some ways, a special case; it created no federal agency, leaving enforcement to the tender mercies of the attorney general and his staff—and, of course, to the courts. In the twentieth century, the federal courts built up a substantial body of antitrust law putting meat on the bones of the statutes (or, in some cases, sucking out the marrow).

There was precious little "trust-busting" in the early years of this century. Indeed, government seemed more interested in harassing labor leaders for Sherman Act violations than big businessmen— the sort of irony that warms the heart of the corporate giant and leads radicals to say, "I told you so." Apparently, not a single violator of the Sherman Act actually went to jail until 1921, when jail was the fate of some men in the wall-tile business found guilty of price-fixing. This was more than thirty years after passage of the act. Enforcement ebbed and flowed (mostly ebbed), until the New Deal ushered in a period of relative vigor, in the thirties. Thurman Arnold, head of the Antitrust Division, filed fifty-eight criminal cases in 1940 alone.[35] Later administrations were less zealous, to say the least.

The Sherman Act was the only major federal law on the subject of antitrust for twenty-four years. In 1914, Congress passed the Clayton Act and the Federal Trade Commission Act; these did not push the

Sherman Act aside; rather, they supplemented it. They represented, on the whole, a turn toward *administrative* law, instead of criminal law, in dealing with problems of unfair competition. In later years, too, other federal (and state) laws were passed regulating competition, competitive and anticompetitive practices, and such topics as resale price maintenance.[36]

Antitrust law has been controversial from the start; economists, lawyers, and regulators do not agree on what the Sherman Act originally meant, what it ought to mean, of what use it is, or what it accomplishes. National competition policy is plagued by ambiguity and doubt. The doubts surround economic questions, moral questions (how shall we punish violators?), and even the most basic goals. For every strong law promoting competition and the free market, there is an equally strong law intended to protect some industry or type of business *from* competition—small stores versus chain stores, big versus little, product versus product.

The policy issues are not our concern here, except for the policy of using criminal justice. The case of *U.S. v. Hilton Hotels Corp.* (1972) illustrates one of the basic dilemmas.[37] The manager of Hilton's hotel in Portland, Oregon, made deals with other hotels, restaurants, and supply companies; all agreed to kick in money to attract convention business. They also agreed to give "preferential treatment to suppliers who paid their assessments." This was a clear violation of the Sherman Act.

Hilton's defense was that the manager had acted entirely on his own; in fact, what he did was "contrary to the policy of the corporation," according to management.[38] But the court held that this was no defense. There was nothing wrong with making a business criminally liable for something its "agents" did "within the scope of their employment." The Sherman Act, said the court, was not concerned with "intent" to commit crimes; it "aimed at consequences." Otherwise, top management could give a secret wink or signal, preserve its own "deniability," and put the blame on underlings. The act, in other words, stuck the criminal label on certain conduct because it wanted to get rid of that conduct, and the criminal sanction was an effective way. Obviously, if Hilton's bosses were telling the truth, they themselves had done nothing wrong. But to hold them liable nonetheless was a blow against price-fixing, and that was the point.

The Public Health

One major theme of regulatory law is, of course, public safety and health. There were laws on this subject, in a somewhat rudimentary way, going back to the very beginnings of American legal history. The sheer amount grew steadily over the years, mostly in the states. Thus, Louisiana passed a law about the slaughter of diseased cattle in 1880; a general law against the sale of "adulterated" food and drugs in 1882; an elaborate general food and drug law in 1914. Other laws were more specific: the state passed a law in 1910 against selling watered or adulterated milk, skimmed milk (unless frankly labeled as such), "milk produced by diseased cows," or milk "produced, stored, handled or transported in an improper, unlawful, unclean or unsanitary manner."[39] Still another law, passed around the turn of the century, forbade the adulteration of sugar and molasses, or of candy, "by the admixture of terra alba, baryter, talc or other mineral substance, by poisonous colors or flavors or other ingredients deleterious or detrimental to health."[40]

These laws, of course, had decidedly mixed motives. Some of them were basically protectionist; the health motive was a sham. A notorious example was the epic struggle of dairy interests against their worst enemy, "butterine," or oleomargarine. Oleo had been invented in the 1860s. The first state statute aimed against it was New York's, in 1877. By 1886, thirty-four states and territories had passed labeling laws, and nine others had gone as far as enacting some form or other of prohibition. In striking its blow against this intruder, New Hampshire passed a bizarre law in 1885 outlawing "imitation butter" if it were any color "other . . . than pink."[41]

State laws did not work well enough for the dairy interests, so in 1886, Congress enacted a tax and regulatory act to fight this dreaded substance.[42] The battle continued in the twentieth century; as late as 1931, Congress imposed a crushing tax on the sale of any margarine that was colored yellow (specifically, as measured on the "Lovibond tintometer scale").[43] But the power of farmers was receding in this urban, industrial nation. The federal law was repealed in 1950, and state laws subsequently went into oblivion one by one. The last holdout was Wisconsin, "the dairy state," whose dairy farmers had enough muscle to fight on. Colored oleo was not fully legalized in Wisconsin until 1967.[44]

Oleo had become a federal issue because no one state in this economic union could keep unwelcome products from streaming across its borders. This was one factor that lay behind the passage of the Pure Food Act, which got through Congress in 1906. The politics of this law were interesting. There had been a pure food movement for some time in the United States, but the food industries had managed to block any federal legislation. Then Upton Sinclair published his sensational novel *The Jungle*. A horrified public read about moldy meat products, contaminated sausage, and putrefied goods put in cans and marketed. One disgusting passage described how a worker fell into a vat and was processed as lard. Sinclair's point in writing the book, he said, was to improve the lot of the "wage slaves" who toiled away for the "beef trust" in Chicago. But, as he put it later, "I aimed at the public's heart . . . and I hit . . . the stomach."[45] Indeed, after Sinclair's novel was published and made headlines, sales of meat products plummeted. For business, regulation turned out to be better than bankruptcy. *Anything* to restore public confidence. The Pure Food Act sailed through Congress.

This was not the only time that scandal helped push along some piece of legislation; the Sherman Act itself comes to mind. Scandal was particularly important in supporting the *criminal* aspects of this and other regulatory laws. Scandal has a way of throwing motives into high relief—motives of greed and immorality; and scandal highlights, too, the consequences of those motives.

The Elixir of Sulfanilamide scandal of 1937 was another important event in the history of food and drug legislation; it strengthened the hand of the Food and Drug Administration (FDA), which administered the act. "Sulfa" was the great wonder drug of its day, the first true antibiotic, an amazing cure for many diseases. But some people had trouble swallowing pills. A drug company, the Massengill Company, wanted to sell the drug in liquid form. The drug, it turned out, could be dissolved in diethylene glycol, without ruining its taste and appearance. Unfortunately, as tests would have shown, this "elixir" had one small drawback: it was a deadly poison. More than a hundred people died before the FDA managed to pull the "elixir" off the market. But the law, as it then stood, did not allow for criminal prosecution, despite the deaths. The FDA could only fine the company for mislabeling. Congress, aroused by the scandal, gave the FDA much greater power. After 1938, no one could market any new drug without prior approval from that agency.[46]

FDA, the federal agency, became the dominant force in controlling the marketing of food, drugs, and cosmetics, and in protecting the public from dangerous products. But the states did not leave off legislating. They created their own little FDAs. By the late forties, some twenty-two states had adopted acts more or less patterned after the federal law.[47] A model state act, coordinated with the federal version, was drafted; and Indiana adopted it in 1939.[48] Every state had food laws, usually many of them, covering food in general, or particular foods, or some combination. Hardly a session went by in any state, without some fresh contributions. In 1929, Wyoming outlawed the sale of eggs "unfit for human food," eggs that were "addled or mouldy" or containing "black spot, black rot, white rot, or blood ring; or . . . a stuck yolk or a bloody or green white (albumin)," or eggs that consisted "in whole or in part of a filthy, decomposed, or putrid substance."[49] Milk and dairy products were particular favorites of legislation; meat and meat products were others.

Many of the hundreds of health and safety laws, like the oleo laws, were far from pure in their motivations. But this is not to deny genuine concern about health and safety. This country was enormous; society was complex and technologically advanced. There was a heightened sense of danger; we were all at the mercy of strangers: the people who made our food, built our cars, flew the airplanes or drove the buses we rode on, poured the concrete for the buildings we worked in, installed elevators, boilers, furnaces, machinery of all types. What controls were there over their behavior? We never saw these people face to face—the builders, the workmen, the designers. We relied on *law* to keep them honest and true; we relied on *law* to protect our own hides.

But dependence on strangers was only half of the story. The other half was popular faith in the magic of science and technology. Unlike our ancestors, we came to believe that there *was* a way to cure or prevent disease, avoid accidents, save lives—a technological fix. Not surprisingly, there were swindlers who took advantage of this faith—men like William J. A. Bailey, who sold "radium water," a nostrum that put an end to medical problems permanently by killing the drinkers. Bailey, who was arrested in 1915, and again in 1927, also sold a belt that would "ionize the adrenal glands" by its "biopositive radiation," along with similar devices.[50] The naïve people who bought radioactive belts and quack nostrums were more gullible than most; but the whole population, by and large, shared a core belief in the wonders of a scientific age. Out of this belief came a demand for more law, more rules, more control, so that these wonders of science, medicine, and technology could become generally and uniformly available. The result was a huge tower of regulation.

Regulatory crimes are nonviolent; they are not street crimes. Some regulatory criminals are despicable and shadowy figures—the purveyors of quack medicines, for example—but others are members of the middle class, or may even come from the ranks of the rich and the powerful. This is, of course, more typical of finance crimes, rather than in crimes that rape the consumer. There are also violators in the upper ranks of corporations whose crimes are more lethal; who dump toxic wastes or hide the news that their products can kill people. Many acts become regulatory crimes, as we pointed out, for administrative reasons, rather than because that they involve "real" criminality—that is, what we define as evil, guilt, blameworthiness. But the line is hard to draw.

And getting harder. People in our times feel themselves dancing on the deck of a doomed ship. They hear that the air is poisoned, the water full of muck, resources shrinking, forests shriveling, the planet collapsing from consumer debauchery and wanton material waste. In this climate, some regulatory crimes—polluting water and air—get redefined as *real* crimes, as crimes against the human race. What started out as *malum prohibitum* ends up as *malum in se.*

White-Collar Crime

The sociologist Edwin Sutherland was apparently the first to coin the phrase "white-collar crime," which was the title of his book that appeared in 1949.[51] The phrase is hard to define precisely. It refers, at core, to "nonviolent, economic crimes that involve some level of fraud, collusion, or deception" committed by "persons in traditionally 'white-collar' jobs."[52] The first part of this definition is probably more reliable than the second; income tax fraud, for example, is on the usual list of white-collar crimes; but anybody with an income can commit it, including truck drivers, baseball players, and nurses.

White-collar offenses include, conventionally, some important regulatory crimes (price-fixing, violations of the Sherman Act, violations of the Securities and Exchange Act), along with such old and well-known crimes as embezzlement. Some white-collar crimes—various mail frauds and con games—are committed by individuals acting alone or with a henchman or two; some (embezzlement) are committed by individuals within organizations; some are crimes *by* organizations (price-fixing agreements between major corporations, for example).[53]

The first three decades of the twentieth century were not notable for enforcement of laws against white-collar criminals. The small-fry—embezzlers, counterfeiters, writers of bad checks—were prosecuted as before, and there was always *some* enforcement of laws against regulatory crimes. A few prosecutions of wealthy crooks did occur—stock manipulators, and so on—and there were spasms of trust-busting by the federal government. The Teapot Dome scandal, during the presidency of Warren Harding, produced some high-profile trials all the way to the threshold of the White House.[54]* But the business of America was business; there was a certain lack of zeal for punishing business behavior, even sharp and shady practices.

The stock market crash of 1929 was more than a financial shock. The prestige of Wall Street and big business also came tumbling down. One strand of the New Deal fed on popular disgust with "malefactors of great wealth." The crash also resulted in some attempts to punish finan-

---

* Harding's Secretary of the Interior, Albert Fall, was charged with conspiracy to defraud the United States and with bribery. He was convicted of bribery in 1929. Harry Sinclair and Edward Doheny, oil executives who were involved in the scandal, were never convicted for their part in this sordid affair.

cial jugglers. Samuel Insull, a Chicago tycoon in the public utility business, was charged with mail fraud and embezzlement in October 1932. He was, however, acquitted at the trial, which took place in 1934. This acquittal apparently so outraged and disgusted Edwin Sutherland that it helped stimulate his work on white-collar crime.[55] The Securities and Exchange Act, passed in 1934, created a whole new cluster of white-collar crimes. It also set up a mechanism, the Securities and Exchange Commission (SEC), which was responsible for enforcing the law.[56]

The SEC is still a pillar of the regulatory state. But its history has been, in some ways, "cyclical," that is, "dotted with periods of vigor and vitality . . . [as well as] lethargy, passivity, and ineffectiveness."[57] The New Deal period (the thirties) and the sixties and seventies were active periods; the forties and fifties and the Reagan years (the eighties) were apparently periods of cutback. Attitudes relaxed, and regulation was laid on with a kinder, gentler hand. What seems to determine the ups and downs of this cycle is not sunspots, or chance, but American politics—and, perhaps even more so, general trends in social attitudes toward wealth. In boom times, when "anything goes," when "lifestyles of the rich and famous" stand as models, there is less impetus to pin the criminal label on people who are making a lot of money, no matter how the money is made.

But the Reagan years ended, and the antics of the period left something of a sour taste in the mouths of many people. The savings and loan scandal of the eighties was a kind of "collective embezzlement" epidemic.[58] When the scandal broke, it carried with it a price tag in the megabillions, which the public will have to pay. Jail seemed too good for the people who looted this industry; yet few of them actually went to jail. The fuss over Ivan Boesky, insider trading, and Michael Milken have also generated miles of publicity, all of which must have *some* impact on public attitudes. Exactly what Ivan Boesky did in the 1980s to get himself a jail sentence is wholly mysterious to 99.9 percent of the population; these are arcane crimes of paper-pushing and computer-blipping. Probably the public sees only that men of vast wealth have committed strange, unknown, incredibly harmful acts, which have rotted out the economy and made the whole financial structure totter. But how and why and what are totally arcane, beyond the grasp of most good citizens (the author included).

There is much less mystery about what it means to dump toxic wastes into the water source, or to spew killer fumes into the air. The future of the ozone layer is as technical and mysterious as the ways and habits of the futures market. But the awful consequences that will or may occur are pretty easy to grasp: skin cancer, for one. In any event, not many people play the stock market, but everybody has to breathe and drink water. The publicity over some pollution scandals has been as great as that about piracy in the savings and loan business or insider trading. Here, too, there must be some impact on the public.

The issue of corporate criminality, and of crimes of the rich and famous, has a distinctly political flavor. Sutherland was a scathing critic of the "apparent disregard" of the legal system "for the serious harm that white-collar crimes caused."[59] He argued that these high and mighty malefactors did far more harm to society, and deserved more punishment, than some poor wretch who stole a loaf of bread or held up a dimestore. He was disappointed that the legal system would not criminalize even high-class plunder; the criminal justice system, he felt, treated business people and the well-off with kid gloves.

Moral indignation is one thing; objective research is another. Does the legal system, in fact, go easy on white-collar criminals? This is not a simple question to answer. Sutherland felt that the system ignores a lot of extremely reprehensible behavior—certain rapacious business tactics, for example, are simply not to be found in the statute books. The scales, in short, are tilted before we even begin to consider enforcement policy.

But even if we put this point to one side, we can still ask: Does the white-collar criminal do better in court than the street criminal, other things being equal? Of course, other things never *are* equal. And there are white-collar crimes and white-collar crimes. The most elaborate recent study found that about the same percentage of white-collar criminals went to prison as did those who committed ordinary crimes in a sample of cases in federal court (46.4 and 49.7 percent, respectively). But there were wide variations: 66 percent of those convicted of securities fraud did time, as compared to 19 percent of the antitrust violators; and the sentences for antitrust violators were absurdly short. Generally speaking, "common criminals" served longer prison terms than the white-collar offenders.[60]

White-collar criminals, after all, are typically richer than the average street criminal. They can hire better lawyers; they are more sophisticated and articulate. All this surely helps. What may help even more is the general perception that they are "not really criminals," that their acts are "not really crimes." Severity of sentence, then, depends on what society as a whole—*and* judges, juries, and enforcers—think about the moral quality of defendant's acts.

"White-collar crime" is, in some ways, a garbage-can category; it is too varied for any single generalization. Some of these offenses are very salient; others are not. Boesky and his travails made headlines; so did the tax fraud indictment of Leona Helmsley, the "queen of mean," a woman who owned or controlled (with her husband) posh hotels and prime real estate. She, too, went to jail.[61] Most white-collar crimes are obscure. Some are enormously common. A little bit of tax fiddling is probably as common as hay fever. Apparently, millions of people cheat on their taxes without losing a wink of sleep.

It seems also quite normal to cheat insurance companies (many of them cheat back). According to a newspaper report published in 1992, fraud against these companies is so common and so blatant in Massachusetts that, by one estimate, 40 percent of all auto insurance claims in that state have a bogus element. A recent study estimated, too, that as many as 90 percent of the injury claims in Lawrence, Massachusetts, in the 1990s involved "either fraud or severe abuse."[62] Some people even dump their cars in rivers and report them stolen to collect on their insurance. Not many of these cheaters get caught. Those who do, get off with a small fine or a slap on the wrist.

The report gives the impression that insurance fraud, which is certainly nothing new, is now growing by leaps and bounds. There is, of course, no reason to think that Massachusetts is a unique den of thieves. Anecdotal evidence seems to confirm the fears of insurance companies; so do skyrocketing insurance rates. This may reflect a massive increase in the number of people who think it is okay to cheat an insurance company.

The police do not, in general, bother themselves with white-collar crime—they have other things to do. Insurance companies have an interest, of course, but they find it cheaper and easier just to raise premiums. And the public is obviously not outraged about the problem—it is the public, after all, that does the cheating.

Beyond a doubt, old norms—thou shalt not steal, for one—have gotten weaker in the late twentieth century. A kind of double standard seems to be developing. Many people who would not dream of cheating the people next door—or lifting their friend's wallet, or mugging a stranger—apparently have much less scruples about filching something from Sears Roebuck, or from city hall or the federal government. These very large entities seem to be endlessly rich. Taking a bit of the cream from them does not seem so very terrible. This makes large organizations especially vulnerable to certain kinds of crime. Plain, ordinary theft is part of the picture: billions of dollars leak out of inventories and storehouses. White-collar crime is the corresponding leakage in the office. Where protection is weak, detection unlikely, and enforcement sporadic and unreliable, all sorts of crimes proliferate. The twentieth century seems to be the golden age of crime, and white-collar crime is no exception.

14

REALIGNMENT AND REFORM

STARTLING CHANGES HAVE TAKEN PLACE IN CRIMINAL JUSTICE IN THE COURSE of the twentieth century. These changes have affected substantive law, procedural law, and the law of corrections. In many ways, however, state penal codes in the 1990s do not look very different from those of 1900. The classic crimes—murder, arson, burglary, and the like—remain much as they were. The growth has been in crimes *not* listed in the penal codes: economic and regulatory crimes. There has also been some tinkering with this or that definition, of this or that crime, sometimes in significant ways. The law of rape may be one example.

In the twentieth century, procedural rules have been reformed and rationalized. This has happened for rules of criminal procedure as well. Criminal procedure in the federal courts had once had been something of an incoherent mess. The rules had been moving in a piecemeal way toward the ideal: a simple, limpid, transparent system, fair to defendants, efficient, and free from the old, crabbed, hypertrophic rules. In 1940, Congress gave the Supreme Court authority to prescribe "rules of pleading, practice, and procedure" for the federal district courts in the states and territories.[1] The Court appointed an advisory committee that met, drafted, wrangled, published preliminary versions, then a final version of rules. The attorney general submitted them to Congress on January 3, 1945, and they went into effect on March 23, 1946. The federal rules have been an important model to the states, which were also intent on cleaning up their procedural systems. Some, indeed, simply swallowed the federal rules as a whole.

Change and reform are themes of every chapter in part III of this book, but this chapter singles out a few topics for special treatment: the "constitutionalization" of criminal justice; punishment and corrections; and the death penalty. In each case, an interesting pattern of development is apparent. There is periodic "reform" throughout the first half of the century, but after World War II the curve shoots up dramatically. A climax comes in the 1950s and 1960s, after which the curve flattens out or actually dips—and this is the situation today. By *reform* we refer, generally, to changes that emphasize due process, rather than crime control.[2] There are considerable differences in detail, from topic to topic, but the pattern is so similar that it obviously reflects gross cultural changes. Later on, we will try to piece together some notions of what these might be.

The Twentieth-Century Constitution

One development of great importance was what we might call *constitutionalization*. In the twentieth century, constitutional principles—doctrines and ideas rooted in the texts of the federal and state bills of rights—began to play a larger and larger role in criminal law. Constitutional law and criminal procedure came together with a bang, like the *Titanic* and its iceberg, in this century.

The U.S. Constitution celebrated its two-hundredth birthday in the late 1980s in a burst of hoopla and publicity. There was a loud chorus of celebration and praise. It was a grand old Constitution, noble of thought and praiseworthy above all for its marvelous stability. In a world of revolution, upheaval, juntas, coups, wars, and epic dislocations, it stood (so people said) like a rock. No other national constitution had lasted two hundred years. Between 1800 and 1987, it had been amended less than twenty times.*

But the praise is a bit deceptive, to say the least. The Constitution, as a living system, as a web of meanings rather than as a piece of parchment with words scribbled on it, has been a good deal less immutable.

---

* The Constitution might well be contrasted with the *state* constitutions, which have been, on the whole, considerably less stable, and certainly less sacrosanct. Many states have gone through three, four, or even more constitutions. Louisiana seems to be the champion, with nine or ten, depending on how one figures.

In fact, the Constitution had been turned upside down and inside out over the years—and not merely once. In many ways we are not living under the same Constitution as George Washington at all. The bare, abstract *frame* of government, the two houses of Congress, the presidency, and the like—these are still with us. But the power of the institutions, what they do, their meaning in society—all these are completely different from what the founders had in mind, and necessarily so.

A Jefferson or Hamilton or Madison, brought back from the grave, would not even vaguely recognize constitutional *law*, the body of doctrine built up by the Supreme Court and other federal courts. There was a kind of constitutional revolution just after the Civil War, when the Thirteenth, Fourteenth, and Fifteenth amendments were adopted, and there have been several mini-revolutions since then. The public understanding of the Constitution, the body of rules and decisions, and the very attitude of the courts—all of these have been totally transformed.[3]

This transformation has been quite marked in the field of criminal justice. Inside the Bill of Rights, as we pointed out, was a kind of mini-code of criminal procedure, rules to guarantee trials against unfairness, against the tyranny and power of the state. Of course, the revolutionary generation, when they thought about the "state," thought about George III, a tyrant from their point of view, and his autocratic government in Westminster. They wanted at all costs to avoid something similar here at home. In the twentieth century, George III was a distant and unimportant memory; after all, this was government of the people, by the people, for the people, or so we thought. The focus of attention had shifted. Government was not the enemy, at least not in *this* area of life; the enemy was the bad people, the criminals, the "dangerous classes."

It would be misleading to say that there was some sort of general consensus about rights of defendants, due process, and the like, in the nineteenth century. It would be more accurate to say that underdogs and losers rarely challenged the power of the law, and even more rarely succeeded. The case law, both federal and state, on constitutional rights of defendants was fairly skimpy.[4] This continued to be true well into the twentieth century. The Illinois Supreme Court, for example, in the decade between 1917 and 1927, reversed 394 criminal cases on appeal; in only eleven of these cases (roughly one a year) did the reversal hinge on a *constitutional* reason, that is, some violation of the defendant's basic rights.[5]

All this changed dramatically later on. Between 1940 and 1970, no less than 31 percent of the business of the Illinois Supreme Court was criminal, and in a third of these cases some issue of procedural due process came up. Of course, there was considerable state variation: for the same period, 25 percent of the cases before the supreme court of

Nevada were criminal, and a quarter of these had due process issues; in Alabama, 11.9 percent were criminal, but only 6.7 percent of these raised such issues.[6] But, on the whole, the states concerned themselves more and more with issues of fairness at trial in criminal cases, at the highest level of their judicial pyramids.

After 1950, this was, in part at least, a reaction to pressure coming from the *federal* courts. This was a dramatic, new development. It meant that for the first time there would be *national* standards of criminal procedure, at least formally; since federal law trumped local law, federal courts could and would ram these standards down the throats of state courts. The technical vehicle for this development was the Fourteenth Amendment to the Constitution (1868), and what is known as the "incorporation" doctrine. This calls for a word of explanation.

The words of the Bill of Rights, as the Supreme Court read them, did not, in themselves, create a national standard. They applied only to the federal government, and not to the states. The Supreme Court so held in 1833 in *Barron v. Mayor of Baltimore*.[7] Criminal justice was, overwhelmingly, the business of the states; thus the *Barron* decision read the national courts out of the business of monitoring criminal justice.

Not that this made much difference in the nineteenth century. Both state and federal courts stayed within fairly solid, well-respected, and traditional lines, on questions of fair trials and due process. Not many cases even raised such issues. There were cases about double jeopardy, about searches and seizure, but almost never were they at the cutting edge of legal development. Undoubtedly, there were regional variations; but the doctrinal gap between retrograde and progressive states probably became wide only in the twentieth century.

Around the turn of the century, a few federal cases revealed a new attitude toward criminal justice. In 1893, in *Wilson v. United States*,[8] the facts were these: George E. Wilson, a bookseller and publisher in Chicago, was indicted for sending obscene materials through the mails. He remained silent at his trial. The district attorney said to the jury: "They say Wilson is a man of good character . . . but I want to say to you, gentlemen of the jury, that if I am ever charged with a crime . . . I will go upon the stand and hold up my hand before high Heaven and testify to my innocence." The trial judge made some mild comment on this but did not "condemn the language" in strong terms. Wilson was convicted and sentenced to two years in prison. The Supreme Court reversed the conviction; the trial court should have told the jury, "in emphatic terms," that counsel was "forbidden" to make any statement that would cause the jury to think failure to testify was a suspicious fact.[9]

This was a federal case, and the Supreme Court was not only

supreme arbiter of constitutional meanings, it was also the supreme head of the federal system.* It had the power to lay down rules that all federal courts had to follow. So, in *McNabb v. United States*[11] defendants were members of a "clan of Tennessee mountaineers" living outside Chattanooga; they made and sold moonshine. During a raid on the still, a revenue agent was shot and killed. Defendants were arrested and held incommunicado in a "detention room" for about fourteen hours, a violation of federal procedures. They confessed and were convicted, but the Supreme Court reversed. Courts, said Justice Frankfurter, could not become "accomplices in willful disobedience of law." He did not need to invoke the constitutional issue at all: only the power of the Court, as overseer of the federal system, to impose rules on lower courts.

What about the states? The Fourteenth Amendment said nothing explicit about criminal justice or the Bill of Rights. But it did speak of rights of due process and equal protection—slippery, open-ended, protean concepts. It imposed the "due process" obligation on the states. States, then, had a constitutional duty to run fair trials. But by whose standards? Were federal standards now a yoke on the necks of state courts?

There was no simple and immediate answer. The doctrines did not spring into life full-blown; rather, they evolved. In *Twining v. New Jersey* (1908),[12] the issue was the privilege against self-incrimination, a part of the Fifth Amendment. The facts were a bit like *Wilson*. Albert Twining and David Cornell were bank directors who had been convicted of bank fraud. They did not testify at their trial, and the judge pointed this out to the jury: "Neither . . . has gone upon the stand. . . . [This] fact . . . is sometimes a matter of significance." The significance depended on the facts. One witness had made a direct, flat-out accusation against Cornell. Cornell said nothing. The jury, said the judge, had a "right to consider" the fact that Cornell just "sat there" and did not go on the stand to deny the accusations.

The trial had taken place in New Jersey, and the judge's charge was good law in New Jersey. Did the Fourteenth Amendment now impose a

---

* *Bram v. United States* (1897) arose out of a trial for murder on the high seas. Bram was a ship's officer accused of killing the captain, the captain's wife, and the second mate. Bram was in custody in Halifax, Nova Scotia; he was stripped, searched, then questioned by detectives. They told him that another suspect, Brown, had seen him do the killings. Bram's reaction was to say that Brown "could not see me" from where he was—a statement that was at least *somewhat* incriminating. At the trial, Bram's lawyer struggled to keep this statement out of evidence but failed, and Bram was convicted. Bram appealed, and the Supreme Court reversed the conviction. The statement was tainted. If a person confessed, or made an incriminating statement, it had to be "wholly voluntary and in no manner influenced by the force of hope or fear." Bram's words did not meet this test.[10]

higher standard on that state? The Supreme Court was hesitant. It was "possible" that some "personal rights safeguarded by the first eight Amendments . . . may also be safeguarded against state action," because they were essential to the concept of "due process of law."[13] But after nagging at the issue like a dog gnawing at a bone, the court came down on the side of the state. The judge's words did not go beyond the standards of "due process."[14]

The worm turned later in the century. In a bold series of decisions, the Supreme Court took up the suggestion casually made in *Twining*. It held that many (though not all) of the guarantees in the Bill of Rights had been "incorporated" into the Fourteenth Amendment. This was because they were "fundamental" or "basic." They were part of the very definition of a fair trial. They thus became part of a national standard.

One landmark along the way was *Powell v. Alabama*, decided in 1932.[15] This arose out of the notorious Scottsboro case (see chapter 16). Nine poor young black men had been sentenced to death after a trial in rural Alabama. They had been accused of gang-raping two white girls. The charge was a complete fabrication. The Scottsboro defendants were lucky to escape the lynch mob. The trial itself (the first of several) was a scandal; it was quick and slapdash; the air was thick with race prejudice. The jury, of course, was all white, and the defendants, practically speaking, had no help at all from their lawyers. Until the actual morning of the trial, in fact, no lawyer had been "named or definitely designated to represent the defendants." And the actual defense was weak and flabby.

Justices of the Supreme Court read the newspapers; they must have known something about the background of this notorious case. In any event, the Court reversed the convictions. A trial without a lawyer, or without good legal help, in a case as serious as this just could not be fair. The due process clause, in other words, swallowed up or presupposed the right to counsel mentioned in the Sixth Amendment, at least under some conditions. The "Scottsboro boys" were young, illiterate, surrounded by a hostile public, far from home, and in "deadly peril of their lives." In "light of the facts," the "failure of the trial court to give them reasonable time and opportunity to secure counsel was a clear denial of due process."[16]*

On the whole, though, the Supreme Court was fairly timid about "incorporation" in the thirties and forties. Yes, the due process clause

---

* The Supreme Court decision did not end the matter, which dragged on for over a decade—the local officials stonewalled and kept retrying the defendants; the Alabama Supreme Court invariably affirmed the convictions.[17]

meant a national right to a fair and decent trial. But the states had the right to decide for themselves, within limits, what fair and decent meant. The Court interfered only in egregious cases.

The decades of the fifties and sixties were dramatically different. Under Earl Warren, the Supreme Court moved boldly, using the incorporation doctrine as a sword to slash through state practices that the Court felt were retrograde and unfair. After all, the incorporation doctrine would have done very little in itself if the Supreme Court read the *meaning* of the Bill of Rights in the anemic fashion of the nineteenth century. But instead, the Court struck out on a new path. It condemned police practices and trial practices that once had been accepted and condoned. It showed a new, strong concern for the rights of men and women put on trial.

In form, the cases decided by the Supreme Court were often about procedures, due process, and so on; but on a deeper level they were about substance, content. They were, in form, *interpretations* of what the Fourteenth Amendment meant. But of course, what really decided these cases were the postulates of modern legal culture. In nineteenth-century legal culture, courts (and the public) cared very little for prisoners, criminal defendants, and the like. They accepted the idea of broad zones of immunity and discretion—zones of unquestioned authority. Wardens and police officers were the petty sovereigns of such zones. There were, to be sure, limits, but these were fairly elastic. This was emphatically no longer the case with the doctrines that emerged in the second half of the twentieth century.[18]

Very striking was the way the Supreme Court laid down rules to control police behavior: rules about arrests, interrogation, searches. The Bill of Rights forbids illegal searchs and seizures. One recurring, nasty issue was left unresolved: namely, if the police make an illegal search and find incriminating evidence, can the prosecution use it in a trial? In 1914, in *Weeks v. United States*, the Supreme Court said no as to *federal* trials.[19] A U.S. Marshall had searched Weeks's apartment, without a warrant, and discovered some incriminating documents. These documents were produced at the trial, and helped to convict Weeks of promoting an illegal lottery through the mails. The Supreme Court reversed the conviction. The poisoned fruit had to be excluded. If the search was bad, the evidence was tainted.

But most of the states rejected the "exclusionary rule," and let in tainted evidence. Search and seizure was a particularly salient issue during Prohibition. As late as 1949, in *Wolf v. Colorado*,[20] the Supreme Court agreed that the states were free to ignore *Weeks*. But eleven years later, the Warren court swept *Wolf* away in the landmark case of *Mapp v. Ohio* (1961).[21] This was a particularly striking example of "incorporation." Three Cleveland police officers had burst into the house of Dolly Mapp. They searched a dresser, a chest of drawers, a closet, some suit-cases; they poked through all the rooms until they found some "obscene materials." They had no proper search warrant. In its decision, the Supreme Court firmly asserted its power to control and discipline the squabbling, disagreeing state courts. It made the "exclusionary rule" ab-solutely binding on the states, replacing all state rules to the contrary. Anything else would be an "ignoble shortcut to conviction," liable to "destroy the entire system of constitutional restraints" and open up the courts to "brutish means of coercing evidence."

In *Griffin v. California* (1965), the question was, did the prosecution have the right to make something of the fact that the defendant kept silent?[22] Since 1893, the answer had been no in federal court; such com-ments undermined the privilege against self-incrimination.[23] The states were split on the question. California allowed judge and prosecutor to comment, if they wished, on defendant's silence; indeed, this rule was enshrined in the California Constitution (Article I, section 13). Griffin had been tried for murdering a woman. He was with the women the night she died. Well, said the prosecutor, in that case he should know "how the blood got on the bottom of the concrete steps. . . . He would know how her wig got off. . . . If anybody would know, this defendant would know. Essie Mae is dead, she can't tell you her side of the story. The defendant won't." The Supreme Court reversed the conviction (and death penalty). The federal *no* became a national *no*.

Another in this line of notable cases was *Miranda v. Arizona*, decided in 1966.[24] Ernest Miranda, the defendant, had been arrested for rape and questioned by the police. After less than two hours of interrogation, Mi-randa confessed. The detectives and police claimed at his trial that they had made no promises and used no force. On appeal, the Supreme Court reversed Miranda's conviction. In his opinion, Chief Justice Warren quoted liberally from police manuals, which described various tricks of the trade, ways to get defendants to confess. For example, fake winesses may identify defendant in a lineup as a man who had committed "differ-ent offenses"; when this happens, the prisoner may "become desperate and confess to the offense under investigation in order to escape from the false accusations."

Clearly, police procedures of the day did not meet Earl Warren's stan-dards of fairness. The Constitution gives criminal defendants the right to stand mute. In Warren's view, that right would be a very empty ves-sel, if police could use these tricks and coercive practices, as was their habit. The Court reached out for a rule, a principle, to put flesh on the bones of the Fifth Amendment right. They came up with what is now called the "Miranda warning." If a person is "held for interrogation," he has to be "clearly informed" of his rights: the right to be silent and the "right to consult with a lawyer and to have the lawyer with him during interrogation."*

Gideon v. Wainwright may be the most famous of all the Warren Court cases on the rights of the accused.[26] Here the Supreme Court held that the states, at their own expense, had to provide a lawyer to help in the defense of anyone accused of a serious crime, if the defendant could not afford to pay. Clarence Gideon was a classic poor defendant: a shiftless loner, a loser, constantly in trouble, a man without resources or attachments. He had been charged with breaking into a poolroom, in Florida. Gideon said he was innocent. Nobody believed him. He insisted on a lawyer. In Florida, he was told, he had no such right; if he could not pay, that was that. Gideon was convicted, and tried to appeal on his own, writing arguments in pencil on lined sheets of paper. The Supreme Court agreed to hear his case; Abe Fortas, a prominent Washington lawyer (later a Supreme Court justice) argued for Gideon.[27] He argued well; but more important, it was a receptive court. In the event, Gideon won his case. The Supreme Court overruled its older line of cases, and greatly expanded the "right to counsel." Lawyers, wrote Justice Black, "are necessities, not luxuries." The "noble ideal" of a fair trial "cannot be realized if the poor man charged with crime has to face his accusers without a lawyer to assist him."

These dramatic decisions of the Warren Court proved to be quite controversial. The decisions got a lot of publicity; for courts, unlike Broadway, not all publicity is good publicity. The Court was criticized, sometimes hysterically, on the grounds that it was perverting the meaning of the Constitution, tilting the scales too far in the criminal's direction. These decisions (and the Court's decisions on race) so incensed some conservatives that they talked about impeaching Earl Warren. Nothing came of this.

There have been many turns of the wheel since the 1950s, but these decisions have proved to be durable, perhaps surprisingly durable. The Burger and Rehnquist Courts have refused to extend them, to be sure; and they have nibbled about on the edges. There is controversy about how far the nibbling has gone. No landmark decision, however, has been actually overruled—at least not yet.

Scapegoating of the courts continues. It is easy to dump the blame for

---

* Miranda's life ended with irony. In 1976, when he was thirty-four, Miranda got into a fight with two illegal immigrants. One of them stabbed him twice, and he died on the way to the hospital. The killer escaped, but the other man was caught. The Phoenix police, as they arrested this man, dutifully read him the Miranda warning, in both Spanish and English: "You have the right to remain silent. . . . You have the right to the presence of an attorney. . . . Do you understand these rights?"[25]

the crime explosion on liberal courts like the Supreme Court of Earl
Warren. Court-blaming was by no means a new idea. In 1937, Sam B.
Warner and Harry Cabot, of the Harvard Law School, referred to the
"widely held" opinion that "trial procedure gives the criminal defendant an unfair advantage over the prosecution."[28] The howls of outrage
became much more strident in the fifties; by then the crime problem
had certainly gotten worse. But the dogs were, in a way, baying at the
wrong moon. Certainly, the Supreme Court took a bold stance. But it is
good to remember that there were parallel movements in the state
courts, too; and even state legislatures played a part. The *Gideon* case
made very little difference in the vast majority of the states. They were
already providing free counsel—some of them for almost a century. (See
chapter 11.)

After Warren Burger replaced Earl Warren, in 1969, and the Supreme
Court seemed to be standing still, or moving backwards (from the liberal
viewpoint), a number of state high courts charged boldly ahead on their
own. In some cases, they outdid the federal courts. If a state court could
find an "independent state ground" for a decision (its own constitution,
for example), it could, in effect, ignore federal doctrine. The story of
state developments underscores the point, if underscoring is needed,
that social change—slow, glacial movement in the normative climate—
was the real shaper of legal doctrine, not particular personalities on the
bench; least of all technical legal argument. The roots of changes can be
found in the broader "rights revolution," whose fulcrum lay outside the
courtroom door.

There is an enormous literature, of praise and invective alike, about
Gideon, *Miranda*, and the other landmark decisions of the Warren era.
In some ways, the debate over *Miranda* and like cases has a kind of
chicken-or-egg flavor. Thousands of nineteenth-century tramps and
thieves were beaten, coerced, arrested, thrown into jail, all without
lawyers. They confessed after long stretches of the third degree, and almost nobody uttered a murmur of protest—certainly not the tramps and
thieves; but neither did their advocates, if they had any. The legal culture has profoundly changed in the course of the twentieth century.
There is hardly any group so downtrodden that its members do not have
some organization, some people who speak up for them. The culture of
rights is an outgrowth of American individualism, which in turn has
evolved in a particular direction.[29] The culture of rights created *Miranda*
and the other cases which in turn embodied those rights.

But there is a further question. Did *Miranda* (and similar decisions)
make much of a difference to the police, or to the people they arrested?
What was the actual impact—on the streets and in station houses, jails,
and interrogation rooms? There is a small but suggestive literature.[30]

Certainly, people are now more aware of their "rights," including a lot of people who, in the past, would have been aware of no such things. In a sense, there was nothing much for them to know. The police did more or less as they pleased.

Is *Miranda* more than a routine gesture, more than just a "piece of station house furniture"? The quote is from David Simon's book, which tracks the work of the Baltimore homicide squad in 1988. *Miranda* does not mean very much in Baltimore. Most defendants sign a piece of paper and waive their rights. They do this, even though it is hard to see what advantage it gives them. The detectives con and manipulate them. Perhaps it has to be that way. *Miranda* requires, in Simon's words, a kind of "institutional schizophrenia." It is like "a referee introducing a barroom brawl: The stern warnings to hit above the waist and take no cheap shots have nothing to do with the mayhem that follows."[31] The Supreme Court, obviously, has no power to micro-manage the police. How far its power *does* reach, and by what mechanism, remains mostly an open question.

Punishment and Corrections

In the early years of this century, the reforms of the late nineteenth century came into full flower: parole, probation, the indeterminate sentence. States that had not yet adopted them, now did so. Thus California enacted an indeterminate sentence law in 1917.

During the twenties in the Massachusetts Reformatory, the "Elmira system" came into full use. When the doors first closed on an inmate, he was classified as a prisoner of the second grade. If he earned 750 credit marks within five consecutive months, he graduated to the first grade. "Perfect conduct, industry and labor, and diligence in study" earned five credits a day. Misconduct, of course, cost credits; and a second-grade inmate who failed to earn 125 marks a month for two months in a row dropped into the hell of the third grade—a rare condition, which at one time meant the convict was forced to wear a uniform of "flaming, cardinal red." First grade, on the other hand, meant a uniform with yellow chevrons; for a perfect record, a diamond was added to the chevrons.[32]

Parole came into its own in the twentieth century. By 1925, forty-six out of the forty-eight states of the union had parole laws (the exceptions being, as one might expect, two southern states: Mississippi and Virginia).[33] Even these two states fell in line by 1942.[34]

Parole, like the indeterminate sentence, was part of the process of making criminal justice better suited to the *individual* case. And this was, in theory, profoundly humanizing. In practice, the results were somewhat checkered. In Illinois, which adopted a parole system in 1897, prison sentences actually grew *longer* rather than shorter after the law was passed: men sentenced to the penitentiary at Joliet were serving an average of 2.1 years by the mid-1920s, as opposed to 1.5 years before parole was introduced. Moreover, parole in Illinois tended to replace pardons and commutations, which had shriveled almost to zero by 1926.[35] Parole and the indeterminate sentence were deeply discretionary; but they were also powerful instruments of control. A 1925 Pennsylvania report put the matter succinctly: "Parole is not leniency. On the contrary, parole really increases the state's period of control." If the prisoner is "liberated by any other means," he goes out of prison "a free man." The state has "lost its control. Society is no longer safe."[36] Parole, however, kept the convict on a string, even after release.

The report had a point. In the 1940s, a man on parole was subject to a tremendous range of conditions. In Illinois, it was a parole violation to drink or use drugs; in Minnesota, to go into debt or to buy goods on the installment plan; in Connecticut, a parolee had to file monthly financial reports; in California, "public speaking" or political activity were forbidden; in Massachusetts, a parolee could not "live with any woman not [his] lawful wife."[37] Prison discipline, in a sense, went with the man onto the streets.*

The Age of Backlash

In retrospect, the fifties and sixties represented a peak, or high point, in a movement to make criminal justice more humane, to tilt the balance away from the state, the police, and the prosecutors. In time, a reaction set in. A wave of conservatism swept the country. It had its roots, perhaps, in the great fear and hatred of crime. This wave led to the collapse of the campaign against the death penalty, which we will deal with later in this chapter. The crime rate had increased catastrophically. Politically speaking, crime and punishment were suddenly like an exposed nerve. The public put enormous pressure on politicians to do something about the problem.

In the light of this pressure, the system did a kind of about-face. There was a backlash against those institutions that seemed too lenient. These included both parole and the indeterminate sentence. In periods of high crime, at times when the articulate public is scared to death of crime, the American system tends to shift its emphasis from the *of-*

---

* Most who were returned to prison for parole violations were in fact accused of crime, suspected of crime, or arrested of a crime, rather than one of the minor offenses. And no doubt many of them were guilty of the crime they were charged with. But the process was quick and summary, lacking in due process.

fender to the *offense*. When fear of crime is reduced from a boil to a slow simmer, professionals can put through programs of reform and rehabilitation. This was the case in the late nineteenth century and in the first part of the twentieth. The political system accepted the various plans to separate sheep from goats; criminal justice shifted its stress toward fairness for the individuals who stood in the dock. But in an age of paralyzing fear, middle class gives off as it were a great shout: "We don't care *who* these people are, and what excuses they give, or what their backgrounds are. We want them caught, convicted, and put away!"

After long service, the indeterminate sentence came under attack from all sides.[38] In the 1970s, many states began tinkering with sentencing structure; much of this tinkering was directed against indeterminate sentencing. The idea was to replace it with a firmer, tighter system: a "flat-time" system."[39]

Both wings of public opinion seemed to favor such a move. What we might call the soldiers of due process—the left—were also disenchanted with the indeterminate sentence. It was arbitrary and unfair; a prisoner's fate was in the hands of some faceless board, not a court, not a judge, not a jury of one's peers. It was a highly discretionary system, whose "covert practices" tended to discriminate against the weak and the unpopular, and particulary against blacks.[40]

Liberal critics are a dime a dozen and are usually ineffectual—unless they are sitting judges. California was one of the states that got rid of the indeterminate sentence in the seventies. This move had a complex historical background. But one clear factor, certainly, was an attack centered in the California Supreme Court itself. One important case, in 1972, concerned the trials and tribulations of a man named John Lynch. Lynch had been convicted of indecent exposure.[41] A woman who worked nights as a carhop at a drive-in restaurant, told the following story: Lynch drove up and ordered a cup of coffee. After enough time had gone by so that the first cup must have gotten cold, he asked the carhop to bring him another cup. Dutifully, she got him his coffee. When she arrived with it, there was Lynch, with "the fly of his pants open, his hand on his erect penis and a 'pin-up' magazine open on the front seat next to him." He saw her and said "Oops." She beat a hasty retreat, but about fifteen minutes later, she looked at him "through a rearview mirror on his car and saw he was still exposed." At that point, she called the police.

This took place in 1967. Unfortunately for Lynch, he had been convicted of this same offense back in 1958. At that time he got off with two years' probation. Now he was a second offender; the California Penal Code (section 314) ratcheted the crime up to a felony. The punishment was imprisonment "for not less than one year." This was an indeterminate sentence; there was no maximum. In theory, Lynch could rot in prison for the rest of his life. In fact, when the U.S. Supreme Court finally heard his case, Lynch had been in prison for more than five long years. More than three of them had been spent in a maximum security prison (Folsom). The Adult Authority had four times denied him parole.

The justices obviously found this story profoundly disturbing. The "theory" of the indeterminate sentence was that it permitted "the *shortening* of a defendant's sentence upon a showing of rehabilitation." Here, for a fairly trivial crime, Lynch was liable to be jailed for life, and, in fact, had already served an appalling stretch of time. This was "so disproportionate to the crime . . . that it shocks the conscience and offends fundamental notions of human dignity."

This was the seventies. The so-called sexual revolution was in full flower. The Court was not terribly shocked by Lynch's crime. It was not, of course, "victimless," but "any harm it may cause appears to be minimal at most." The "victims" of flashers run "no danger of physical injury," and there was no "convincing" evidence of "long-term or significant psychological damage." In many cases, it was simply an "annoyance." The indeterminate sentence, in the Court's judgment, had to meet standards of decency and fairness, and in Lynch's case, it did not.*

The Lynch case, which was followed by other cases along the same lines in California,† illustrates dramatically what the critics from the left felt was wrong with the indeterminate sentence, if not with the criminal justice system altogether: arbitrary, heartless, unfeeling, subject to random outbursts of scapegoating rage. These critics wanted to eliminate the indeterminate sentence and replace it with definite *short* sentences. What we might call the law-and-order crowd—the right wing—felt, for its part, that the indeterminate sentence was too soft a device for hardened malefactors. For them, the real problem was leniency; they did not trust judges and parole officers, who (for whatever reason) let dangerous hoodlums back on the streets far too early. Like their liberal colleagues, they wanted certainty in sentencing, but they wanted definite *long* sentences.

What emerged was a kind of compromise: definite *medium* sentences. A number of states besides California (they included Maine and

---

* The Court also felt that the punishment not only failed to fit the crime, but failed to "fit the criminal." Lynch was not "an exhibitionist" who "forced himself on large numbers of the public by cavorting naked on a busy street at high noon." The violation was fairly technical; it was not 100 percent clear that Lynch actually *intended* to expose himself to the carhop.[42]

† For example, in 1957, Robert Nathan Foss was convicted of possession of heroin.[43] Fourteen years later, he was convicted again, this time of selling heroin. For a second conviction in a narcotics case, Foss received a punishment of ten years to life; that is, he was not eligible for parole until ten years were up. This, too, was declared cruel and unusual.

Illinois) simply abolished the indeterminate sentence. Under the Illinois scheme, felonies were divided into seven classes. Murder was in a class by itself. Another class was for "habitual criminals," those convicted three times or more of a violent offense. A third was class X, which covered rape, armed robbery, and aggravated kidnapping. Then there were classes 1, 2, 3, and 4, in descending order of gravity. The judge *had* to imprison felons convicted of murder, class-X felonies, and some of the more serious offenses. The statute set a fairly narrow band of prison terms from which the judge had to pick. For example, burglary, a class-2 felony, called for a sentence of between three and seven years. The statute provided for extra time if the offense was "exceptionally brutal" or showed "wanton cruelty."[44]

What was the actual impact of this change? Judicial discretion was of course not totally eliminated. Did determinate sentencing affect fairness? Did it change the way prisoners felt about the system—reducing cynicism and encouraging rehabilitation? One study tried to measure the impact of the system on the attitudes or behaviors of prisoners.[45] The study found no impact at all. The powerful "prison environment" was "to a great extent, immune from the effects of determinate sentencing reform."[46] But, like so much else in criminal justice history, nobody seemed to care about the practical effect; once the political passion had spent itself on *getting* the change, the polity somehow lost interest.

A parallel movement, with the same general motives and aims, leveled heavy artillery at the parole system as well. Here was another institution that looked terribly unfair. The prisoner had no real say, no due process. The parole board could use whatever criteria it liked, and its decisions were beyond review. The law-and-order people (and much of the general public), on the other hand, let out a howl every time somebody out on parole committed a crime. Illinois, for example, abolished parole in 1977, at the same time that it eliminated the indeterminate sentence.[47]

The movement for "victims' rights" was another symptom of backlash against the due process revolution in a period of high crime and high concern.[48] Its message was: the system cares more for criminals and their rights than it does for the poor damaged victims. A "victims' bill of rights" was adopted in Oklahoma in 1981; California, by popular vote, adopted a victims' bill of rights in 1982. The movement was distinctly conservative, distinctly "law and order." It invoked the image of a person "preyed upon by strangers . . . an elderly person robbed of her life savings, an 'innocent bystander' injured or killed during a holdup, or a brutally ravaged rape victim"—in short, a "blameless, pure stereotype, with whom all can identify."[49] The "rights" of victims included the right to play a role during the sentencing proceedings. More significantly, there were provisions in the California law aimed at dismantling some of the more liberal "improvements" added on to the house of due process; the purpose was to make the system tougher on defendants. But these provisions were wrapped in a mantle of victims' rights. Law-and-order people expected good results from giving victims a voice in the system. Victims, after all, rarely turn the other cheek; on the contrary, they become (understandably) bitter and frustrated. As an old joke put it, a neoconservative is a liberal whose pocket has been picked. The outrage and pain expressed by victims would counterbalance the tendency to wax sentimental about the defendant and *his* hard knocks.*

Prisons and Prisoners' Rights

In the first few decades of the twentieth century, conditions in prisons, and in local jails, continued to be absolutely abominable. Overcrowding was epidemic. In the Eastern Penitentiary of Pennsylvania, in the early 1920s, 1,700 inmates were crammed three and four to a tiny cell: "There is less room per prisoner in some of the cells than a dead man has in his coffin."[53] When Lewis Lawes, later to be warden of Sing Sing, arrived in 1905 as a rookie guard at Clinton Prison, in Dannemora, New York, he found the prison still run "on the silent system." Prisoners "were allowed very little recreation outside their cells. . . . Just aimless treading across a barren waste of ground." Lawes was transferred to Auburn, supposedly an innovative prison, in 1906. But here, too, silence reigned: "It was the hush of repression." In this "city of silent men," clubs and guns were used to enforce obedience of the rules.[54]

From all over the country, with monotonous regularity, came reports of inhuman conditions. In 1913, a grand jury in Westchester County, New York, censured Sing Sing: the cells were "unfit for the housing of animals, much less human beings"; there were no toilet facilities in cells, only the infamous slop buckets; there was no running water; the cell blocks were "infested with vermin"; prisoners were jammed to-

---

* In some states, too, legislatures created modest programs of compensation for victims. California passed a law in 1965 providing for aid, in case of "need," to "the family of any person killed" or to the victim and his family if "incapacitated as the result of a crime of violence."[50] The statute also provided that the defendant could be ordered to pay a fine "commensurate in amount with the offense committed," to go into the state's fund for aid payments. But no fine was to be imposed if "such action will cause the family of the defendant to be dependent on public welfare." In the following years, almost every state passed some sort of compensation law, almost always similarly modest. The federal government established its own program for federal crimes in 1984.[51] These programs rested, of course, on a much different cultural base than the "victims' rights" laws. They were part of the general expectation of justice so pervasive in contemporary American law, to the effect that compensation ought to be forthcoming from *some* source for every calamity.[52]

gether, "healthy men ... subjected to the nightly companionship of syphilitics"; hardened criminals were put together with first offenders; young boys were "condemned to room with ... creatures who make a practice of sodomy"; and (this from New York, mind you) "negroes and whites have shared the same cells."[55]

Joseph F. Fishman, who visited (he said) 1,500 jails in the United States in the years before 1920, painted an appalling picture of disease, filth, muck, and neglect. The jails were "human dumping grounds"; a sentence of thirty days in jail was a sentence to "wallow in a putrid mire demoralizing to body, mind and soul." In the jail in Phoenix, Arizona, up to a hundred prisoners were packed in a "foul cage" supposed to house forty people at most, and crawling with vermin. Men slept in hammocks, or "helter-skelter on the hard steel" in indescribable heat. In state after state, Fishman reported on unsanitary conditions, disease, and immorality. In Princeton, West Virginia, he "saw a prisoner with the worst case of syphilis that I have ever seen.... Part of his tongue was gone, and his mouth was literally half eaten away"; yet this man used the same drinking glass, tub, and toilet as the other prisoners. "Homo-sexuality," he reported, was "the invariable concomitant" of the jails, both for men and women.[56]

Exposés of this sort occurred with monotonous regularity. In 1908, Kate Barnard, Oklahoma's Commissioner of Charities and Corrections, visited the Kansas Penitentiary to explore the fate of prisoners from Oklahoma who were housed in the Kansas prison.[57] Her investigations, and those of others, blew the lid off conditions of massive brutality—floggings, water torture, confinement in a chamber called the "crib." "Sodomists and masturbators" were dealt with by "a minor surgical operation during which a brass ring was inserted through the foreskin of an offender's penis." There were sometimes short-term improvements after some particularly dramatic exposé; or perhaps a head or two rolled. But, also with monotonous regularity, the situation soon returned to abnormal.[58]

Southern prisons and jails were especially bad. Robert E. Burns, sent to prison in Georgia in 1922, expected to see a large stone building "surrounded by a huge wall." What he found in Bellwood, Fulton County, Georgia, at the "so-called penitentiary" was a "few old dilapidated low wooden buildings." He was put in "stripes" and sent to the blacksmith's shop, where a "heavy steel shackle was riveted on each ankle, and a heavy chain ... permanently fixed to connect the shackles." On the chain gang, permanently chained, he worked long, brutal hours under subhuman conditions.[59]

In the winter and spring of 1910–11, Oscar Dowling, president of the Louisiana State Board of Health, inspected "every jail, lock-up and police station in Louisiana." He described them, on the whole, as "relics of barbarism." County jails were "ill-ventilated, foul-smelling structures with no room for exercise and scant, if any provision and no incentive to personal cleanliness." One prisoner wrote: "the Bedding Hav not Ben changed nor aired" in his jail, and "the Bed Bugs is geting a Start"; the water closets did not work and "the odor is something Terible"; the flies by day and "the mosquoitos at night Dount allow no Sleeping"; the food was monotonous and made for a "volum of Gas in my Stomach tel it causes me to suffer most all the time."[60]

Most southern prisoners were black; they had no power, no voice in the system. Uproar over chain gangs often occurred after exposés that featured *white* prisoners. But times were changing. In 1943, a black man named Leon Johnson escaped from a Georgia chain gang and fled to Pennsylvania. The governor of Georgia demanded extradition; and Pennsylvania complied. Johnson invoked the shelter of the federal courts. He asked for a writ of habeas corpus, claiming that the situation in Georgia was so intolerable that it deprived him of his constitutional rights. The third circuit court agreed. Life on a Georgia chain gang was so debased, said the court, that it amounted to "cruel and unusual punishment."[61]

The Supreme Court, in a terse, technical decision, reversed this decision.[62] But Georgia, meanwhile, had been embarrassed by chain-gang horror stories. The state made changes in the system. A constitutional provision (Article V, section 5, adopted August 7, 1945) set up a State Board of Corrections. The legislature directed the board in 1946 to provide "wise, humane, and intelligent prison administration." Whipping, shackles, leg irons, and chains were abolished; the board also had authority to do away with the "county public works camps."[63]

The picture was not universally bad. There were people inside the system who worked hard to make it better. Probably the most remarkable of these was Thomas Mott Osborne of New York. Osborne was chairman of the New York State Commission on Prison Reform, in 1913. He was a hands-on person; to see what prison was like, he had himself admitted to prison as "Tom Brown" and spent a week behind bars. Later, in 1914, he became warden of Sing Sing. His most dramatic move was to give the convicts a large dose of self-government; the Mutual Welfare League, which he organized, let the prisoners play a significant role in runing their own institution.[64]

But Osborne was forced out at Sing Sing; and the status quo soon reasserted itself. The underlying problem of prisons, of course, was political and social: the men and women locked up were the lumpenproletariat; many of them were black; and the general public neither knew nor cared what happened to them. Indeed, people *wanted* prisoners to be treated harshly. Anything halfway decent was sneered at as a "country club." Governor Haskell's reaction to Kate Barnard's charges were typical: "Kate would like to see the prisoners kept in rooms and fed and treated as if they were guests at the Waldorf Astoria."[65]

When change did occur, it was partly because the system was becoming more professional—and more differentiated. There are maximum-, medium-, and minimum-security prisons, prisons for men, and prisons for women, and juvenile institutions of various sorts. There is no point to a minimum-security prison, of course, unless it is different from the hard-boiled prisons for hard-boiled prisoners. But even the "big house" changed over the years. The civil rights movement, an increased sensitivity toward minorities, and the general rights-consciousness of society: these forces and influences scaled the walls of the prison, or whatever substituted for walls. The prison was more a microcosm of the outside world, than an island, hermetically sealed.

Illinois's Stateville Prison, built in 1925, was a "big house" of the classic type. From 1935 on, a tough, strong warden, Joseph Ragen, ran the prison as an absolute dictatorship. Ragen's reign was severe but efficient; he imposed order and maintained it.[66] But the Ragen years could not last forever; when Ragen left, no autocrat of the same dominant power replaced him. In part this was a matter of personality; Ragen was a strong authority with an iron will and great energy. But, more important, the ferments of the late twentieth century swept over Stateville and engulfed it. The age of iron discipline passed into history; prisons lost their autonomy; the civil rights revolution made its mark on these institutions as well.

Prison riots took place in Ohio in 1968. Ysabel Rennie, of Columbus, Ohio, wrote a report on prison life, after the riots. She found the usual situation of inhumanity. Not a single institution in Ohio failed to "degrade, corrupt, pervert, and dehumanize the men committed to its charge," she reported. "Men can stand only so much abuse." The "wonderful programs of rehabilitation, education, vocational training" were mere charades. In one incident, guards at Chillecothe Correctional Institute collected prisoners' pet cats, including six newborn kittens, and "dashed their brains out in sight of the whole prison population." This aroused a storm of indignation: "irate cat-lovers all over the country must have taken pen to paper to protest against the cat massacre." But the "murders and beatings of prisoners" went almost unnoticed.[67]

Almost, but not quite. Two prisoners went to federal court, asking for an injunction against the horrors of prison life, which amounted, they said, to "cruel and unusual punishment." These cases represented a new wrinkle in prison law: the prisoners' rights movement. Prisoners had always had (in theory) certain rights; but courts had been extremely reluctant to get involved in the reality of prison life. A minor Pennsylvania case, from a district court in Allegheny County in 1912, tells the story. The plaintiff, in jail, refused to go to religious services on a Sunday. The keeper threw him in the dungeon; later, he was forced to attend "religious exercises." Plaintiff went to court, claiming his rights had been violated. The court brushed his complaint aside. The warden, said the court, had the kind of power and control over an inmate that parents have over their children. If a parent wants a child to go to church, the child has to go.[68]

To this judge, and to most judges in general (and, no doubt, the general public), it was sheer *chutzpah* for a convict to whine and complain about prison conditions. A prisoner, as one nineteenth-century court put it, was a "slave of the state."[69] The prison, in short, was a zone of power and immunity from law in which warden and guards could do as they pleased—except in very extreme cases. But, starting in the 1960s, a series of decisions, reflecting a new form of activism, changed the legal situation dramatically.

Talley v. Stephens was an Arkansas case, decided in 1965. Three convicts complained that prisoners were savagely whipped for "infractions of discipline," and for not working hard enough in the fields.[70] The federal court listened, and acted: it issued an order. Arkansas prisons, for example, were forbidden to use corporal punishment, until there were "appropriate safeguards" to keep whipping fair and under control.[71] A wave of scandals and investigations followed. The Arkansas legislature created a Penitentiary Study Commission in 1967; heads rolled; changes were made. But prisoners wanted more. More lawsuits followed, and in 1970, in *Holt v. Sarver*, a federal court declared the whole state system to be one giant violation of the Constitution, one giant act of cruel and unusual punishment.[72] Conditions and practices in Arkansas were "so bad as to be shocking to the conscience of reasonably civilized people." They had to be changed.

In the 1960s, Arkansas ran its prisons on the basis of the "trusty" system; this system, used in Arkansas, Louisiana, and Mississippi, gave great power to convict favorites ("trusties"). In Cummins prison, in Arkansas, for example, there were "only 35 free world employees" for "slightly less than 1,000 men."[73] This was a cheap way to run a prison, but hardly enlightened penology. The effect of prisoners' rights cases in Arkansas was to force the state to hire a more professional (and costly) staff.

In other regards, the situation in Arkansas was cruel, but (alas) hardly unusual, especially for the South. In the years after *Holt*, dozens of lawsuits were filed, and the courts in many states put their prison systems under a kind of tutelage. The classic prison was what Erving Goffman has called a "total institution."[74] The classic prison was (or was supposed to be) a model of discipline; the prisoner was silent, isolated, cut off from the world, helpless but not hopeless—raw matter, which the prison tried to mold. The prison controlled every aspect of the prisoner's life, the clothes he wore, the books he read, the mail he wrote, when he got up and when he went to sleep, what he ate, even the way he cut his hair. But prisoners were now demanding an end to this situation. They demanded that the total institution give up some of its totality.

Prisoners won some notable victories. Regulations in California made it a "privilege," not a right, for a prisoner to send and get mail. A prisoner could not get or send "inflammatory," "inappropriate," or obscene letters, or letters about "criminal activity."[75] In *Procunier v. Martinez* (1974), the Supreme Court struck down those California regulations.[76] The Court also struck down an administrative rule that, in effect, did not let prisoners (and their lawyers) use law students and paralegals as investigators. This was, the Court felt, "an unjustifiable restriction on the right of access to the courts."[77]*

It is hard to tell exactly how much effect the prisoners' rights movement actually had on prisons and jails. It was surely greater than zero. Prison life became, in some ways, more humane, though it is difficult to say that the court cases *caused* these changes, except in the most obvious ways. Still, progress is easy to see in some ways: better general conditions, better health care; more recreation, education, and religious freedom. Prisoners today can play baseball, write letters, watch TV, go to school, and do all kinds of normal things. In some prisons, male inmates can even have sex with their wives from time to time. These are the so-called conjugal visits. Our times have a horror of sexual repression; celibacy seems downright abnormal. At any rate, the state is aware that sex *does* occur in prison, only not the right sort. Mississippi formalized conjugal visits in 1963, and a number of states followed this rather odd leader.[79]

And yet, many prisons are domains of fear; they combine despotism and anarchy. The strong brutalize and terrorize the weak. A Philadelphia study found thousands of incidents of rape of male prisoners in Philadelphia jails, in a period of about two years (1966–68).[80] In some prisons, the murder rate is as high as on the mean streets of the most desperate cities. Gangs, organized by race or otherwise, dominate the prison yard. Drugs and weapons are freely available. In the movie *Escape from New York*, which came out in 1981, Manhattan Island had been converted into a giant penal colony. The state dumped convicted felons into the city, and simply left them there. No one was allowed to escape,

---

* In *Johnson v. Avery*,[78] the Court voided a prison regulation that did not allow prisoners to help each other prepare writs of habeas corpus and other legal documents.

but no one patrolled or controlled the island. Manhattan grew its own Hobbesian regime, with the most ruthless and vicious at the top of the heap. Are some American prisons heading in this direction?*

Despite the guards with their guns, the walls, the rules and regulations, the prison of today is a far cry from the penitentiary that Dickens and De Tocqueville described. Of course, corrections do not exist in a social vacuum. A society does not randomly pick ways of punishing people; methods of punishment are always related to what is happening in the larger world. They are related to ideas about the causes and cures of crime that rattle about in the heads of good citizens. How afraid are people of crime? How high on the agenda is crime and punishment?

Some systems of corrections are offender-minded, some offense-minded. That is, some focus more on *who* the criminal is, while others focus more on *what* he did. Of course, there is always a mixture of both of these considerations; it is the proportions that change. As we saw, corrections shifted direction in the late nineteenth century. It moved somewhat from the *what* to the *who*. Indeterminate sentencing, parole, probation, juvenile justice—all had this in common. Who was born bad? Who could still be rescued? There was lacking the overwhelming, obsessive fright, the fear of crime that is everywhere today.

A strong strain in the literature, up to around 1950, describes criminals as typically weak, disjointed, and unconnected to family and economic life, but not, generally speaking, vicious and depraved beyond redemption. "Stanley," the "jack-roller"† whose story was taken down by Clifford Shaw in the late twenties, had come from an unhappy family. His mother was dead, his stepmother wanted to get rid of him. "Stanley" throws away chance after chance in favor of adventure, fun, immediate gratification, false bravado. He describes other criminals as essentially the same as he was—not evil so much as reckless and short-term in their thinking: "Consequences didn't concern them much. They thought only of getting by."[83] "Stanley's" story has a happy ending: he gets married, has a child, and holds down a good job as a salesman. Similarly, Thomas Mott Osborne described prisoners as regular fellows; men of honor and talent; if you trust them, "they will show themselves worthy of trust"; if you "place responsibility upon them they will rise to it."[84]

---

* Anarchy probably had been the rule in some local jails for a considerable period. Fishman, writing in 1923, reports on the "kangaroo courts" in the jails of Kentucky (the institution was, in fact, much older). A kangaroo court was an organization run by the prisoners, who "make the rules and enforce them, and . . . in the majority of cases . . . do not temper justice with mercy." In most jails, "the kangaroo court itself is composed of the lowest class of prisoners," and they tyrannize outsiders "with brutality and callous indifference."[81]

† A "jack-roller" was a man "who robs his fellows, while they are drunk or asleep."[82]

Some people still sound these themes, but on the whole the system has shifted in the other direction. The overwhelming fear of crime, the anger, the frustration, must surely be the main underlying cause. Screams of rage drown out the milder voices. The prison system bulges with prisoners.[85] The rate goes up and up. As of 1988, there were over 600,000 men and women (mostly men) in state and federal prisons—the number had tripled in about fifteen years.[86] In California, there had been "extraordinary growth" in the prison population. At the beginning of the 1980s, there were 22,500 prisoners; eleven years later there were over 100,000.[87] We throw people into prison at an astonishing rate. There has never been anything like it in American history. Penology is overwhelmed by the sheer pressure of bodies. The general public is not interested in rehabilitation, not interested in what happens inside the prisons, not interested in reform or alternatives. It wants only to get these creatures off the streets.

No one is satisfied. No one has real answers. Conditions in the prisons may be better than in the nineteenth century, but the prisoners are twentieth-century prisoners. They are sullen and resentful. Terrible riots still occur: Attica (New York), in 1971, was one of the worst; but far from the only one. And riots continue to erupt.[88] Despotism and anarchy turn out to be a dangerous, explosive combination.

The Death Penalty

The Supreme Court has handed down many dramatic and consequential decisions in this century; but *Furman v. Georgia* (1972) would have to rank high on any list. *Furman* swept away every death penalty statute in the country; and spared the lives of every man and woman on death row in one grand gesture.[89]

Furman did not come up out of nowhere. It was the climax of a long campaign against the death penalty. Among the campaigners was the NAACP, keenly aware that blacks were put to death out of all proportion to their numbers. Blacks may be a minority in the population, but over half of the people put to death were black, and death for rape was practically a black monopoly.[90] Generally speaking, too, public opinion had turned against the death penalty. In 1936, according to the Gallup poll, 62 percent of the population supported the death penalty; by 1966, the number had fallen to 42 percent.[91]

Fewer and fewer people were actually put to death: 199 in 1933; 82 in 1950; only 2 in 1967. Alaska and Hawaii (in 1957), Oregon (in 1964), and Iowa and West Virginia (in 1965) did away with the death penalty, joining Michigan, Maine, and Wisconsin, which made the move in the nineteenth century. From 1967 to *Furman*, when the issue was finally adjudicated in the Supreme Court, no one was executed at all.[92]

The *Furman* court was, to be sure, deeply divided. Every single one of the nine justices wrote a separate opinion. *Furman,* said Robert Weisberg, was not "a case" at all; it was a "badly orchestrated opera, with nine characters taking turns to offer their own arias."[93] The so-called majority of five was itself deeply split on the central issue: Was the death penalty inherently unconstitutional, or was it only that *existing* laws had some correctable flaw? Justice Brennan thought the death penalty was "cruel and unusual" in all cases, a "denial of the executed person's humanity" and "uniquely degrading to human dignity." Only Thurgood Marshall agreed. Three other justices joined the majority, but rested their case on less global condemnations. Death sentences under the current laws, said Potter Stewart, were "cruel and unusual in the same way that being struck by lightning is cruel and unusual." Only "a capriciously selected random handful" get sentenced to death. The four dissenters pointed out, correctly, that the Constitution itself mentions the death penalty. How, then, could it violate the Constitution? Yes, the death penalty was comparatively rare; but this was a sign, according to Chief Justice Burger, that juries were "meticulous," not that they were arbitrary. Capital punishment, moreover, did not offend "the conscience of society"; it was not like "burning at the stake"; it was not "repugnant to all civilized standards."

In this welter of words, there was certainly no "bright line" standard. No one knew exactly what *Furman* really meant. Obviously, existing statutes were invalid. Was it possible to write better laws—better in the sense that the Supreme Court would buy them? Legislatures in many states clearly intended to try. They scratched and pecked through the text of the opinions in *Furman* like chickens, looking for hints. They came up with two main types of statute. The Supreme Court had obviously been troubled because the process seemed random and arbitrary. One group of states, then, passed statutes that made the death penalty *mandatory* for certain crimes. A second group tried a different tack. They tried to cure the ills of the laws by making them more cautious and elaborate. This batch of statutes, as it turned out, had the right stuff to bring the Supreme Court around.

In 1976, the Court decided a new cluster of death penalty cases, from five different states. The mandatory laws failed the test; the Supreme Court struck them down. The North Carolina law, for example, under which *everyone* found guilty of first-degree murder had to die, was "unduly harsh and unworkably rigid"; it did not meet "evolving standards of decency."[94] At least this is what five justices thought, out of nine; and that was enough. In *Roberts v. Louisiana*[95] the Supreme Court reversed the death sentence imposed on the killer of a police officer on duty; Louisiana law made the death penalty mandatory in this case, and that too was found to be unacceptable.

On the other hand, in *Gregg v. Georgia*, the Supreme Court accepted a new Georgia death law.[96] The Georgia law set up elaborate procedures. After a defendant was convicted of a capital crime,* the judge had to consider any mitigating and aggravating evidence. The Supreme Court of Georgia had to review all death cases to see whether "passion, prejudice, or any other arbitrary factor" had influenced the sentence, or whether the sentence was "excessive or disproportionate to the penalty imposed in similar cases." The message of *Gregg* was still far from crystalline, but the general approach was clear enough. Life and death could not be left to the unbridled discretion of the jury. There had to be guidance, there had to be extra steps.

Many states lost no time taking up the hint. In California, for example, the death penalty could only be imposed for murder in the first degree, and only if the jury certified that it found one or more "special" circumstances. Killing "for financial gain" was a special circumstance; so was killing a police officer, a fire fighter, a prosecutor, or a judge, or sealing the lips of a witness to a crime by murder. It was a "special circumstance" to kill somebody with a bomb or by poison, or with "the infliction of torture," or "while lying in wait." Race-hate killings, too, could bring the death penalty.[97]†

Gregg v. Georgia did not, of course, end the controversy over the death penalty. But the tide had turned. Public opinion began to favor the death penalty. Somewhere in the 1970s, those who said yes to death became the majority once more, and that majority solidified over the years. By 1988, 79 percent of the general public favored putting murderers to death.[99] Abolitionists became a shrinking minority; but they have guts and persistence, and they do not give up. Executions themselves began again in 1977, when a firing squad in Utah put Gary Gilmore to death. At this writing (1993), there have been more than 150 executions. Almost all of them cluster in a handful of southern states. Outside the South, although hundreds of convicts sit on death row, only a handful have walked the final mile, and, in some states, none. Many prisoners have come within a whisker of execution, but last-minute writs or stays have held off the northern or western angel of death in almost every case.

More conservative than before, the Supreme Court stuck to its guns

---

* There were six of these: murder, kidnapping for ransom or where the victim was harmed, armed robbery, rape, treason, and aircraft hijacking.
† Also on the list: multiple murder, or a previous conviction for murder; and situations in which the murder was "especially heinous, atrocious, or cruel, manifesting exceptional depravity." In *People v. Superior Court of Santa Clara County*,[98] the California Supreme Court declared this particular clause unconstitutional. It was too vague; its terms did not meet "the standards of precision and certainty required" for a death-penalty statute.

in the 1970s, at least in the sense that it did not go back to *Furman*. It was impossible to cobble together an anti–death-penalty majority. Some cases did chip away a bit at the death penalty. In 1977, in *Coker v. Georgia*[100] the Court struck rape from the list of capital crimes. It was a heinous offense, to be sure, but death was a "grossly disproportionate and excessive" punishment for rape, and could not stand.[101] But later news was bad for the abolition movement, however, and kept getting worse.

The situation today is fairly bleak. The most recent general attempt, in a way, to attack the death penalty broadly was *McCleskey v. Kemp* (1987).[102] Warren McCleskey, a black man, had taken part in a robbery of a furniture store in 1978 in Georgia. A police officer, answering a silent alarm, entered the store during the robbery. He was shot and killed. McCleskey was convicted of murder and sentenced to death. McCleskey's central claim was that "the Georgia capital sentencing process is administered in a racially discriminatory manner." This argument rested on an elaborate statistical study: an analysis of over 2,000 murder cases in Georgia, conducted by a team headed by Professor David C. Baldus. "Sophisticated" statistics tended to show that someone in Georgia who killed a white was much more likely to get the death penalty than someone who killed a black. But McCleskey lost, by a bare majority. The study, five justices thought, did not prove that race was a significant factor in McCleskey's particular trial. It merely showed a "discrepancy that appears to correlate with race."[103]

Nobody can read the justices' minds, but it is hard not to wonder what the majority justices were really thinking about. Baldus's statistics were impressive, and even the present conservative Court tends to be somewhat sensitive to issues of race. Perhaps the majority was worried about the consequences of letting McCleskey off. Would that mean that *no* southern black could ever get the death penalty? Or perhaps no black in any state? If so, then the whole structure would collapse: the Court was not about to create a system in which only white people were eligible to die. And the current Court, like most Americans, believes in the death penalty; it is clearly unwilling to get rid of it, directly or indirectly.[104]

The most recent cases have, on the whole, gone badly for the men on death row. Kevin Stanford was sentenced to death for murder and other crimes committed when he was seventeen. His lawyers argued strenuously that the death penalty was "cruel and unusual" for a lad of such tender years. The Court affirmed his conviction in 1989, in *Stanford v. Kentucky*.[105]

Most of the current justices, in fact, want to change the system: they want more executions, and they want them to come more quickly. This sounds more callous than it is. It comes out of a sense of frustration—or restlessness, impatience, disgust—a sense the public shares, unless every sounding of popular opinion is grossly off base. The march to the death chamber is simply too slow. The constant appeals, writs, pleas, the endless legal maneuvering, the setting and resetting of dates, the last-minute stays—all this disturbs and angers people. Why can't we just put these terrible people to death and be done with it?

The Supreme Court does what it can, but the process speeds up, if at all, only a little.[106] Death on death row is still a lingering death. The march to the death chamber is a torturous crawl. It takes so long, that in the process it converts into martyrs of sorts men and women whom *nobody* would otherwise sympathize with. The slow pace is a fairly recent development. To be sure, there have been complaints about delay for almost a century. The Tucker case, early in the century, was regarded as a horrible example. Tucker killed Mabel Page, in Weston, Massachusetts, on March 31, 1904. He was arrested, tried, convicted, and sentenced to death. But he actually went to the chair in June 1906, two years and three months after his arrest.[107] Today, this would be considered lightning speed; in fact, it would be almost impossible to accomplish. On February 15, 1933, Giuseppe Zangara tried to shoot president-elect Franklin D. Roosevelt in Miami, Florida. Zangara did not hit Roosevelt, but he wounded Anton Cermak, the mayor of Chicago, who was with Roosevelt. When Cermak later died, on March 6, 1933, Zangara was indicted, arraigned, pleaded guilty, was sentenced to death—and died in the electric chair, all in an incredible rush. The execution day was March 20, 1933—a little more than a month after the shooting, and less than two weeks after Zangara's victim died.[108] Such speed, even with a guilty plea, would be unthinkable today.

Even in the years before *Furman v. Georgia*, the process had shown signs of slowing down. It became as expensive and protracted as building a nuclear power plant. No case was as notorious as Caryl Chessman's. Chessman was sentenced to death in California on June 25, 1948. He had been convicted under the state's "little Lindbergh" law. He spent almost twelve years on death row. Chessman fought like a tiger for his wasted, unhappy life. He wrote three books on death row, won stay after stay, attracted the support and attention of such movie stars as Marlon Brando and Shirley MacLaine, and became a national symbol of resistance to the death penalty. In the end, he lost. He went to his death on May 2, 1960.

The death penalty, as we have said, has became vastly more popular since Chessman's execution, as far as the general public is concerned. Today, hardly any politician dares oppose it. Yet popularity does not translate itself into speed. Chessman was considered an unusual case, in his day. But long delay is now the rule, not the exception. Death penalty cases bounce back and forth endlessly between state and federal courts. The defendant has absolutely nothing to lose, and there is a small but devoted corps of lawyers and activists who loath the death penalty and fight it every inch of the way. Jerry Joe Bird died in Texas on June 17, 1991, at 12:21 A.M., of a lethal injection. He was number forty to be executed in Texas (number 147 in the country) since the Supreme Court had resurrected the death penalty. Bird was executed for a crime he had committed in 1974; he had been a resident of death row for seventeen years. Some men have been under the shadow of execution even longer.[109]

The Supreme Court gets the most headlines; but the death penalty and its case law are an issue in many of the states as well. In California, the voters threw Chief Justice Rose Bird out of office in 1986; one reason, probably the main reason, was the charge that she was undermining the death penalty. The Chief Justice denied the charge; she said (they always do) that she was only following the law. In point of fact, the California Supreme Court had a suspicious habit of reversing death sentence cases—some sixty-four out of sixty-eight, between 1979 and 1986.

After Chief Justice Bird and two colleagues were handed their walking papers, the Republican governor, George Deukmejian, was able to replace them with new judges more likely, he thought, to send evildoers to the gas chamber.* Yet, for six more years California put nobody to death. Finally, on April 21, 1992, Robert Alton Harris died in the "apple-green gas chamber" while the father of a boy he murdered in 1978 watched him through the glass, six feet away. It took Harris about a minute and a half to die from the gas, but the struggle over his own doomed life had lasted thirteen years.[110] On the day that Robert Harris died, the clock was ticking away for 2,500 men and women on death rows across the country—329 of them in California, 315 in Florida, 349 in Texas.[111]

California was not the only state where a stubborn court thwarted the public clamor for blood. More than a dozen states that have the death penalty have yet to use it, among them New Jersey, Kentucky, and Nebraska. In August 1991, the New Jersey Supreme Court, by a vote of four to three, threw out the death sentence of one Richard Biegenwald, who had killed a woman in Camden in 1982 (nine years earlier). This was Biegenwald's third conviction for murder. The court, rather surprisingly, said prospective jurors should have been told this fact, to

---

* In California, Supreme Court judges run for office unopposed; the issue for voters is yes or no for continuing them in their positions. When the voters did say no, vacancies were created that the governor could fill by appointment.

"weed out those who might have felt unable to judge him objectively." The defendant "has killed twice before," said Justice Robert L. Clifford. "We are not sure, under these circumstances, how many people could fairly sit on a jury in this case." But of course this horrendous information, about Biegenwald's habit of killing people, is *verboten* as evidence in the *guilt* phase of a trial. Thus the New Jersey court was, practically speaking, requiring *two* separate juries for all capital cases.[112] This was the thirtieth time (out of thirty-one cases) that the New Jersey high court had reversed a sentence of death. In January 1992, the court made it thirty-two out of thirty-three when it set aside the death sentence of Braynard Purnell.[113]

The Massachusetts story is just as dramatic. The state's highest court declared the death penalty unconstitutional on the grounds that it was cruel and unusual punishment, in violation of the Bill of Rights of Massachusetts. Of course, on this point the state and federal constitutions were practically identical; the U.S. Supreme Court had upheld a very similar law, specifically ruling that the death penalty was *not* "cruel and unusual." No matter; the English words *cruel and unusual* meant something different in Boston than they did in Washington, D.C.[114]

The legislature in Massachusetts found this decision hard to swallow. It was also unpopular with the voters. The legislature proposed a constitutional amendment, which read: "No provision of the Constitution . . . shall be construed as prohibiting the imposition of the punishment of death." That seemed plain enough. The public voted yes on this proposed amendment in November 1982. Thereupon the legislature adopted a new death-penalty act, sat back, and waited.

But the Massachusetts court had another trick up its sleeve. In 1984, the court struck down this new law. How could they do this? The court explained, a little disingenuously, that they were not construing anything as "prohibiting" the death penalty altogether; the new amendment did not mean they were not entitled to strike down some *particular* death-penalty law, if it did not measure up to constitutional standards.[115]

Massachusetts and New Jersey judges, it seems plain, could barely conceal their distaste for the electric chair and the gas chamber and the whole death-penalty apparatus. The New Jersey and Massachusetts decisions are as convoluted, as hypertechnical, as distant from common-sense logic as any nineteenth-century examples of legal "hypertrophy." The judges claimed they were only deciding the "law," but this was a fairly transparent fig leaf. There seems to be, in short, a sharp conflict between, on the one hand, the general public, which wants the death penalty (though how much? and under what circumstances?), and, on the other hand, a minority that finds it repellent, and a tiny band of zealots who would move heaven and earth to get rid of it. Any field of law so embattled, so locked between strong, irreconcilable groups, will develop certain pathologies. It will become complex, Byzantine, its pace will slow down, its behavior will become jerky and erratic. This is not because of any technical reasons, but because social conflict *produces* erratic, unpredictable behavior as the combatants rain blows on each other and the legal system gets buffeted this way and that.

Thus Robert Weisberg has a point when he speaks about a "culturally optimal number of executions." What number is that? It would be the resultant of a sort of "logical, if crude compromise between the extreme groups who want either no executions or as many as possible." The compromise takes the form of having "some executions, but not very many." One can imagine "a socially stabilizing design for the death penalty which leads to just the right number of executions to keep the art form alive, but not so many as to cause excessive social cost."[116] No political institution would be cynical enough, and clever enough, to devise such a scheme, but social evolution can be as ruthless and clever as Mother Nature herself.

This does not mean, of course, that there cannot be, or will not be, another turn of the wheel. The judiciary of 1993 is, on the whole, more conservative than before, and a kind of collective patience is running out. (The Clinton administration, to be sure, may slow or reverse the trend.) The federal courts, as we have seen, have gone some way toward washing their hands of the whole matter. The pace of executions is rising. State after state is losing its virginity; the death penalty is no longer a monopoly of the deep South. California broke the ice in spring of 1992. Delaware put a man to death. Arizona followed soon in its footsteps.[117] The long wait on death row seems to be getting shorter.

15

LAW, MORALS, AND VICTIMLESS CRIME

IN CHAPTER 6, WE LOOKED AT HOW THE SYSTEM TREATED VICE, SEXUAL BEHAVior, and "victimless crime"—how the current of lawmaking and law enforcement ebbed and flowed. In the last three decades of the nineteenth century, there was, as we saw, an upsurge of energy, a born-again war against vice and sin. The Victorian compromise grew tattered and worn, and the fabric began to give way. In the first third of the twentieth century, the war raged, with more and more success. Then it came to a halt, and the counterattack began. In the last part of this century, victimless crimes were more and more decriminalized; the war against vice, with some egregious exceptions, seemed lost. How and why all this happened is the theme of this chapter.

Morality Enthroned

The first three decades of the twentieth century were the peak period, the climax, in the battle against vice and moral decay. It was a period of fresh legislation and spasms of zeal in enforcement.

This was, for example, notably true of gambling, though with rather meager results. Gambling entered the twentieth century an illegal vice, and stayed that way for decades. There were periodic crackdowns in city after city. Yet, despite an occasional burst of arrests, it is doubtful that police took the gambling laws very seriously. When they did, the courts treated gambling with a yawn.

Thus, in San Diego, California, in November 1908, thirteen men (twelve players and the proprietor) were arrested in "the wee hours" as they played draw poker in the rear of the "Eureka cigar store." Unknown to them, a detective, disguised as a farmer, had had the place under surveillance. The men were hauled down to the police station, where they each put up ten dollars' bail. The newspaper dryly recounted that none of the men appeared when their case was called; bail was forfeited, and that was the end of the affair. It was nothing worse than a parking ticket today.[1]

In Alameda County, the police made occasional gambling raids in the early years of the century. In 163 raids between 1906 and 1910, they arrested 4,159 people. In the town of Alameda, the local Civic League hired private detectives to ferret out gambling, bookie joints, and illegal liquor sellers. In Berkeley, Chief August Vollmer moved against the cigar stores that harbored illegal poker games.[2]

But the truth was, the public was indifferent, except for the occasional reverend and members of civil leagues; and the police, sad to say, were corrupt or uninterested. In Alameda, complained Reverend MacFarlane of the Civic League, men gambled openly and notoriously, and the police officer on the beat winked at it. Perhaps, said the reverend, sarcastically, the police thought this was "a prayer meeting," and "the rattle of the chips was the taking up of a collection for the poor, the blind, and the deaf."[3] Alameda was, alas, no doubt typical. Generally speaking, a dual system persisted throughout the early decades of the century. Gambling was illegal, and commonly tolerated. The crusaders never reached the Holy Land.

The Mann Act

The crusade against sexual misbehavior, on the other hand, achieved some spectacular successes—or so it appeared. This crusade reached a climax of sorts, a kind of high-water mark, in 1910, when Congress passed the Mann Act, the famous "White Slave Traffic Act."[4] The title of the law (putting aside its obvious racism) tersely expressed one of the ruling ideas, or assumptions, that lay behind its passage. It was this: a life of immorality and prostitution for women is a fate worse than death, a form of slavery. The point of the law was to stamp out the business of vice, the enslavement and sale of women's bodies. The language of the text was, however, quite a bit broader, and it gave courts an opening to read the law more expansively, which, as we will see, they seized on.

The background was an excited campaign against "white slavery." It had, in its brew, a fairly strong dash of nativism. Foreign prostitutes, flocking into America, with a repertoire of exotic sexual ways, threatened the national morals. Congress set up a commission in 1907, headed by Senator William P. Dillingham of Vermont, to look at how immigration affected vice and crime, among other things. The commission's report claimed that "The vilest practices are brought here from continental Europe"; "imported women and their men" were corrupting this innocent land with "the most bestial refinements of depravity." The "continental races," apparently, could somehow tolerate these evils, but these unspeakable acts were sure to bring about "moral degradation" in America.[5]

There was already a federal law against importing "women for the purposes of prostitution."[6] The Mann Act strengthened this principle; one section of the act specifically applied to people who "harbored" any "alien" prostitute who had entered the country within the previous three years.[7] But there was another image, too, behind the Mann Act, and it pushed its way forward during the debates. This was the horrific image of the simple country girl lured by the glitter of city life, enticed and seduced to her ruin by dark, evil men. These were the true white slaves: blond, blue-eyed girls in "dens of infamy"—"drugged, debauched and ruined," reduced to a life so abject that even murder "would be a mercy after such treatment."[8]

Historians have tended to be skeptical about "white slavery;" the evidence, such as it was, dredged up by vice commissions and congressional committees seems, on examination, skimpy and overblown. Did sexual bondage really exist? Reformers of the time had rigid, inflexible ideas about women and their sex lives. They refused to believe that any healthy young girl would ever choose "the sporting life" unless some devil drugged her, kidnapped her, and held her a prisoner of vice. Sally Stanford, who wrote a book about her life as a madam (although at a somewhat later period), sneered at the very idea: "Personally, I never met a white slave in my life. . . . If captive females were sold, drugged, or slugged into prostitution, I never knew a case." On the contrary, Stanford wrote, it was a "continual nuisance" to her how many women arrived "at my various front doors" begging for a job in her house; and most of them, she writes, were far from destitute.[9]

Sally Stanford no doubt reported on life as she experienced it. Exaggeration and hysteria were obvious in the Mann Act crusade. But if we peel these away, along with the racism, sexism, and general phobic behavior of the time, a solid residue of sexual oppression remains that, if we wish, we can call a form of slavery: women were recruited into the business of sex; some were even bought and sold, or forced to live lives in which they traded their bodies for money.[10] Maude E. Miner, writing in 1916, attached the label of "white slaves" to any "unprotected girls" who were drawn into the life either by promises or by force. She tells the story of two girls, sixteen and seventeen, who came from their small city in Massachusetts to New York "on a lark" with two men. In New York, threats and beatings forced them into prostitution; they were held prisoner in a "parlor house," and only after some days were they able to escape.[11] There were probably many different patterns, and many different stories, in the business of sex.

Whatever the underlying reality, the Mann Act had become law. From 1910 on, it was a federal crime, on the statute books in black and white, to "transport . . . any woman or girl" across state lines "for the purpose of prostitution or debauchery, or for any other immoral purpose." What, however, were these "other" immoral purposes? The debates in Congress were mostly about prostitution, venal sex, sexual commerce. But the "crime" that underlay the famous case of *Caminetti v. United States,* decided by the Supreme Court in 1917, was of an entirely different order.[12] Two young men, Drew Caminetti and Maury Diggs, both married, had gone gallivanting about California with their young girlfriends. Their adventures took them across the border to Reno, Nevada, as well.

Commercialized vice had no role whatsoever in these doings, but Caminetti and Diggs were nonetheless arrested, tried, and convicted of "debauchery" and transporting women across state lines "for an immoral purpose." The Supreme Court brushed aside the argument that the Mann Act had nothing to do with amateur, unpaid sex. What the two men did was "immoral," and thus fell squarely under the act.

This decision alarmed at least one commentator, who said, a bit hyperbolically, that *Caminetti* would empower federal courts to act as "censor of the nation's sexual morals." There were, in fact, some startling prosecutions and convictions. In one case, the Mann Act was used to prosecute someone who transported a woman across state lines to work as a chorus girl, in a theater where smoking, drinking, and cursing went on; in another case, the villain was a dentist who had a rendezvous with his young love in another state, shared a hotel room with her, and talked about her pregnancy; in yet another case, two students at the University of Puerto Rico had sex on the way home from a date; in still another, a man and woman lived together for years as man and wife and roamed around the country while the man sold securities.[13] Cases like these unquestionably stretched the words of the statute and inserted the national government into people's intimate affairs.* Still, these were not typical cases. People crossed borders for "immoral purposes" every day by the thousands, or committed their immoral purposes in the territories or in Washington, D.C.; but only a handful were ever prosecuted. Critics (and the dissenting opinion in the *Caminetti* case) claimed that the unscrupulous would use the Mann Act to blackmail people. No doubt this sometimes happened.

The Mann Act was also used for other unsavory purposes. In one notorious instance, Jack Johnson, heavyweight champion of the world and a black man, was arrested for crossing *color* lines, not state lines. Johnson lived with a white woman, Belle Schreiber. He sent her seventy-five dollars to travel from Pittsburgh to Chicago, where she would meet up with him. Johnson was convicted and sentenced to a year in jail. The verdict, said the district attorney, "will go around the world" as a warning against "miscegenation."[15]

Between 1910 and 1915, more than a thousand defendants were convicted of white slavery in the United States.[16] Most of the defendants were men. But women, too, were sometimes caught in the Mann Act web. A study of 156 women sent to prison in this way, between 1927 and 1937, found a fair number (23 percent) who were not prostitutes at all, and were totally unconnected with commercial vice. Many of them were unmarried women traveling with married men—men they loved and wanted to marry. They ran afoul of the law when an enraged and scandalized wife complained to authorities.[17] The Mann Act, in short, was used as a blunt instrument of conventional morality. Not until later in the century, as we shall see, did it loose its grip.

Red-Light Abatement

The age of the Mann Act was also the climax of the so-called Red-Light Abatement Movement. The point was to put teeth into vice laws; to

---

* Some states passed their own versions of the white slave laws. In Montana, there was the so-called Donlan White Slave Act which prohibited the "importation" of women into Montana, or their "exportation," for "immoral purposes." In 1915, the Donlan act snared one J. E. Reed, who ran an employment agency in Butte, Montana. He had offered Dorothy Burger, aged seventeen, a job as a waitress in a hotel in Diamondville, Wyoming, for thirty dollars a month, plus room and board. Diamondville, according to the court, was a "mining camp consisting largely of Italians and Austrians." Reed bought a ticket for Dorothy, and told her "the place was a sporting-house, and that her duties would be to dance, play cards, drink beer, and entertain men." She told this to a woman friend, who went right to the chief of police. At the trial, there was evidence that "the place was not one where a girl could live for any length of time and be respectable." The defendant knew that the "chief desideratum" at the hotel was "good-lookers" rather than "efficient cooks and waitresses." Reed was convicted, but the conviction was reversed because the judge had given the jury too broad a definition of "immoral".[14]

close down red-light districts, smash the brothel trade, and end the cozy system of police protection. A survey of seventy-two cities, carried out in 1910, showed that forms of proto-zoning for vice were common, along with other sorts of unofficial regulation. No less than thirty-three of the cities—including Detroit, Galveston, Milwaukee, Nashville, Pittsburgh, Richmond, Salt Lake City, and Tacoma—had segregated vice zones. In a few cities—Atlantic City, New Jersey; and Cheyenne, Wyoming—vice was "licensed in fact, though not in law." In Cheyenne, prostitutes had to pay a fee for an examination to see if they had any "communicable diseases"; they were checked for "personal cleanliness and the sanitary condition of persons and premises." If they passed the test, a certificate was issued to them.[18]

No more symbiosis; no more prostitution and gambling under the noses of the city leaders: this was the message of more and more moral leaders. The Reverend James Ely of Philadelphia, speaking in 1910, had a novel plan, which would, in effect, convert a vice district into a kind of giant reformatory. He proposed drawing a line around the district from Arch Street to Spring Garden, and from Eleventh Street to the Delaware River, making the line "so clear by police and glittering signs that no one could mistake it." At every entrance to the vice district a large sign, suspended across the street, would announce that "The Wages of Sin Is Death." In the middle of the district would be a "non-sectarian Christian mission, with restaurant, baths, reading rooms, and auditorium." On top of the building, in letters of gold, would appear the words "God Is Love," and "This Is the Way Home." The district would be flooded with religious workers. The way into the section would be "very difficult, and the way out very easy. . . . No tourist or curiosity seeker should be any more allowed to visit this place than to visit a smallpox camp."[19]

Needless to say, nothing came of this plan. The enemies of the "social evil" preferred blunter and more direct ways. The basic idea was simple: enforce the laws and stamp out vice. In October 1909, Rodney Smith, an evangelist (they called him "Gipsy"), led "a band of 12,000 Christian men and women" through the red-light district of Twenty-second Street in Chicago "in an attempt, like the crusaders of old, to reclaim the region to Christianity." In 1912, 10,000 people paraded in a Chicago rainstorm, demanding the destruction of the kingdom of vice. The authorities, who were sensitive to this kind of pressure, closed down the district—for a while.[20]

The movement gained strength, and information, from vice commission reports. City after city, in the early part of the century, created vice commissions that met, investigated, reported. Between 1910 and 1917, no less than forty-three cities probed and poked about in their subworlds of vice and prostitution; most commissions published reports of what they found.[21] The Chicago report was one of the best and most sober. Prostitution, it said, was an unmitigated evil; it was the source of loathesome disease, more horrible than a "leprous plague," which struck down the "innocent wife and child" along with the guilty sinner. The conclusion was obvious: the city must not condone or tolerate the "Social Evil"; Chicago had to stamp it out. The "honor" of Chicago, and the "physical and moral integrity of the future generation" demanded no less.[22]

This was a common theme of the vice reports. No compromise was possible or desirable. Physical health was an important issue, but the main issue was moral health. Medical examination of prostitutes? Absolutely not; this would be a terrible mistake, according to New York's "Committee of Fifteen." Such a plan would fatally reduce the *moral* onus on prostitution, it would put the "social evil" on an ethical par with regulations of "the weight of the loaf of bread, or the size and quality of the yard of woollens." Making prostitution medically safe would be "pretty sure to increase the patronage of the prostitute." A growing boy would have an "almost irresistible impulse to experience" this evil pleasure. Brothels should also not sell liquor or provide other forms of "amusement." If they do, then men looking for "harmless" amusement will be drawn into the net, "subject to temptations which they do not have the strength to resist."[23]

The militants used every available forum. They agitated in city halls and lobbied in legislatures. As a result, some states passed severe "abatement" laws, beginning with Iowa in 1909. By 1917, thirty-one states had their own versions.[24] The Michigan law of 1915, for example, gave the state's attorney general and "any citizen" the right to bring an action in court to abate a house of prostitution. Evidence of "the general reputation of the place" was admissible to prove this "nuisance."[25]*

Mass action on the streets and pressure on station houses were probably more effective than laws and court actions. Enthusiasm for red-light abatement spread like a virus, from city to city. In San Diego, the red-light district, called the "Stingaree," was located between the wharf and the main business district and catered to sailors and businessmen. A local Vice Suppression Committee put pressure on the police in 1912 to do something, and in November of that year the police launched a massive raid. They arrested 138 women. All but two of the women agreed to get out of town; and the district was (theoretically) shut down.[26] In

---

* Note that this is a *civil* rather than a *criminal* statute. Its goal, of course, was punitive; and since the whole area of vice regulation and suppression has historically been within the domain of criminal justice, the statute must be mentioned here.

Houston, bawdy houses and taverns were congregated downtown in an area nicknamed "Happy Hollow." Despite tough state laws and some local agitation, the district survived until 1917, when it was closed down under extreme public pressure: on Friday, June 15, Happy Hollow ceased to exist. The night before, sightseers toured the area, and the pianos were going "at full blast"; it was a farewell party for Happy Hollow. By dawn, the noise had died down and the streets were crowded with moving vans. The district became a "deserted village."[27]

A wave of crackdowns took place all across the country. There were loud war cries, and high hopes among the militants. Yet, almost without exception, the crusades dribbled out after a while, and what they accomplished proved superficial, temporary. Vice always bounced back. Some famous red-light districts were indeed destroyed—Storyville in New Orleans had been one of the most celebrated—but the women simply relocated, leaving town or merely changing neighborhoods. And there were always fresh recruits. In Chicago, by 1916, "the ghost of the levee" was "stalking about the streets and alleys of the south side, manifesting unmistakable desires for resurrection." Now there was "vice in all of the 'Loop' hotels and in many of the cabarets and dance halls."[28] In the twenties, vice was flourishing in Chicago as if abatement had only been a dream; and it was (so people said) now under the control of organized crime. In San Diego, too, the "social evil" never actually got out of town; it simply changed its address. For example, in 1915, Julia Barton, who had run the Yellow Canary Cottage in the red-light district, was now working out of the Milan Hotel. Arrests for prostitution *increased* in San Diego. In 1917, the city went so far as to adopt an ordinance outlawing fornication in hotels or apartments: only married people had the right to make love in such places. This ordinance had (no surprise) "little effect, except for adding a new law to arrest prostitutes."[29] In some cities, when the red-light district was destroyed, arrests for streetwalking rose. Prostitution merely went out of doors.[30]

In any event, the red-light abatement movement was yet another battle in the great cultural war that began, as we have seen, in the period of the Comstock laws, reached its climax with Prohibition, and has been ebbing more or less ever since Prohibition ended. The key principle was a refusal to compromise with vice, debauchery, and sin. But the subterranean demand for vice was too great for victory. Nobody publicly *defended* the social evil, but the customers were not creatures from outer space. They were real people, men in all walks of life, from blue-collar workers to doctors, lawyers, and politicians. This silent army had no pulpits, but it was enormously resilient, and its silent power first dulled and then bent the law out of shape. Ultimately, too, "vice" would come out of the closet to fight openly with the armies of the righteous and set them to rout. But all this lay in the future.

Fornication and "Statutory Rape"

In most states, adultery and fornication laws were still part of the penal code in 1900—either in pure form or of the "open and notorious" variety. Enforcement, to be sure, was patchy and sporadic. In 1910, the New York City police arrested twenty-three men and eleven women for adultery; six were convicted. This was out of a citywide total of 108,000 misdemeanor arrests.[31] In Chicago, in 1926, ninety-five men and women were convicted of adultery; most of them were fined or put on probation, but four were sent to the county jail, and twenty to the house of correction.[32]

For one reason or another, there seems to have been a good deal of local variation in enforcement. Boston, for example, was apparently more serious about fornication and adultery than New York or Chicago. In the first six months of 1920, seventy-seven men and eighty-one women were arraigned in Municipal Court for "fornication"; twenty-five men and twenty women for "adultery"; and forty-six men and forty-nine women for "lewd and lascivious co-habitation." A "white couple," for example, was charged with this last particular offense: "their history showed that they had lived together for eight years" without bothering with wedding ring or license. Even in stern, bluenose Boston, the punishments for these offenses were light; cohabiters were encouraged to get married, and given probation. A "colored couple" convicted of adultery was sentenced to three months in jail but released on probation.[33]*

Still, there was not much call for removing laws against fornication, adultery, and the like from the statute books. In some regards, the states strengthened their sex laws considerably, especially in the early part of the century. The most dramatic move was to raise the so-called age of consent. The age of consent was a crucial aspect of the law of rape. A man was not guilty of rape, of course, if the woman "consented." But consent was meaningless, legally speaking, unless the woman was old enough to say yes.

A trend set in, in the late nineteenth century, to raise the threshhold age (it had been, originally, ten; see chapter 6). This trend continued

---

* In Philadelphia, in 1915, the Municipal Court heard 640 complaints concerning fornication and bastardy. But there was a simple reason for this: in order to get child support, an "unmarried mother" had to bring a criminal suit against the father, "and establish his legal identity as a violator of the law against fornication and bastardy." If the father was a married man, the charge was adultery. But the men were, in fact, almost never prosecuted for this offense. The penalty for adultery was imprisonment, which "would defeat the purpose of the bastardy proceedings."[34]

well into the twentieth century. Indiana raised the age of consent from fourteen to sixteen in 1907.[35] In 1913, California raised the age from sixteen to eighteen.[36] So did a flock of other states, including Arizona, Colorado, Florida, New York (1895), South Dakota, and Wyoming. Tennessee went the furthest: under Tennessee law, it was a felony to have sex with any woman under twenty-one. The age of the male made no difference in these statutes; if two sixteen-year-olds rolled in the hay, the boy was guilty of rape, and the girl was officially an innocent victim. It was legally the same regardless of whether she was, in fact, a victim or a willing and eager partner in crime.[37] The laws, in short, made teenage sex a serious crime—for males. It was a crime to take a woman's chastity, even if she gave it away.

Again, it is not easy to know exactly how often these laws were enforced. Certainly, there never was (nor could be) any systematic crackdown on young lust. But the statutes were hardly dead letters. There were enough angry or disgruntled whistle-blowers to see to that. In 1895, Andrew Di Santos, a black man of Alameda County, California, made love to fifteen-year-old Jennie Petranick, the girl next door. He went to Jennie's mother, admitted he had "used" her daughter, and asked for permission to get married. The answer he got was prosecution for rape.[38]* George Brown, a candy dealer of Cincinnati, was sentenced to fifteen years for statutory rape in 1891. He supposedly managed to entice "about twenty young girls to his place, where he succeeded in accomplishing their ruin."[39] In 1925, in Santa Clara County, California, Roy White was accused of plying a young girl, fourteen years old, with drink and then having sex with her; he pleaded guilty and was put on probation.[40]

Mary Odem studied prosecutions for statutory rape in Alameda County, California. In the decade 1910–20, there were 112 prosecutions in this county, which had a population of roughly 250,000. Fourteen male defendants were between fifteen and nineteen years of age; thirty were between twenty and twenty-four. Over 70 percent of the young women admitted they were willing partners. When the age of consent went up to eighteen, there was a wave of prosecutions. Police and probation officers made some arrests on their own; but parents and other family members accounted for most of the prosecutions. Working-class and immigrant families "used the law as a way of regulating male sexual behavior." One mother, for example, discovered (and read) a letter written by her darling daughter and learned she was sexually active. The mother

---

* Jennie's mother first claimed Jennie had been raped while unconscious; this charge was groundless, and she shifted to the assertion that Jennie was "weak-minded." Di Santos went free, but only after a long and costly ordeal.

beat the daughter, reported her to juvenile authorities, and had the boyfriend arrested for statutory rape. The brothers of another "victim" chased the boyfriend and threatened to shoot him after they found him in their sister's bedroom.[41]

Today, most of this would hardly be criminal at all; there are plenty of people who decry young lust, but they do not call it rape. Up to half or three-quarters of the young male population would qualify for jail if such laws were vital and enforced. On the other hand, *some* "victims" were, in fact, awfully young; and the line between "real" rape—violent, unwanted sex—and the behaviors that touched off some of these cases is murky at best.

In the 1930s, Jacob and Rosamond Goldberg studied 1,400 young girls who were victims of "rape" (both kinds) in New York City. They had trouble drawing the line between consensual and forcible rape of young girls: "considerably more than one half of the girls were violated despite every effort on their part to escape. . . . Of those who were classified as giving their consent, many were . . . too young to comprehend."[42] This seems entirely plausible. The "statutory rape" cases came out of very different types of situation. In many instances, the "victim" was truly coerced or manipulated, or was too young to give intelligent consent. In others, she and her partner were *both* victims—victims of parents or of a prudish and repressive society.

The statutory rape laws rested on certain obvious assumptions about what women were like, what their sex lives were or ought to be, and about the value of modesty and chastity. Well into this century, Victorian standards remained the official line. Many people—perhaps most people—assumed the state had the right, if not the duty, to enforce this code, so that at least the surface of society conformed to the standards of decency. There was probably considerable local variation. Some towns and cities pursued public decency with a vengeance. Thus, in 1930, in nine suburban township courts in Franklin County, Ohio, as many as 38.3 percent of the criminal cases were for "indecent exposure," and 8.7 percent for "parking without lights," an offense "made up largely of cases of indiscreet young couples out to enjoy a warm summer evening, in quiet spots on little travelled roads." Most justices of the peace and constables ignored "petting parties," but others felt "impelled to search the byroads and hedges" looking for couples who displayed too much "ardor."[43]

But all the while, behind the bushes, so to speak, the old standards were rotting away, probably even in Ohio. Culture and behavior were conspiring underground to create the "sexual revolution," which would first weaken and then destroy the Victorian fabric of sexual order.

Degenerate Man

The first few decades of the twentieth century were the high-water mark of eugenics, the genetic theory of crime, and the pseudoscience of criminal anthropology. Conceptually and socially, these tendencies went hand-in-glove with the struggle for sexual purity and the battle against vice. They were part and parcel of a battle to save the American soul from rot, disease, and decay: our moral traditions could not survive unless society protected its germ plasm.

The nineteenth century had read in horror about the "Juke" family. Their twentieth-century equivalent was the pseudonymous "Kallikak" family, a cautionary tale of bad blood, told by Henry Herbert Goddard, director of research at a New Jersey institution for the feeble-minded.[44] The family descended from Martin Kallikak, a soldier in the Revolutionary War. Martin fathered a bastard, a "feeble-minded" son; the mother was a "feeble-minded" woman he had met at a tavern. This encounter produced a miserable line of 480 descendants; 143 of these were "feeble-minded," forty-six were "normal." (As to the rest, who knows?) There were thirty-six illegitimate children, thirty-three "sexually immoral persons, mostly prostitutes," along with alcoholics, epileptics, criminals, and keepers of "houses of ill fame." Kallikak, after his tavern fling, met and married a respectable woman; this union produced a "good family." The Kallikak family tree was a kind of "natural experiment." It proved, Goddard thought, that mental weakness and other undesirable traits were handed down from father and mother to daughter and son, according to the very laws that Gregor Mendel discovered in his work "on the propagation of the ordinary garden pea."[45]

What was to be done? Goddard asked. Defectives and degenerates were breeding like rabbits, with appalling consequences. Sterilization had to be the answer: "The operation itself is almost as simple in males as having a tooth pulled. In females it is not much more serious."[46] Indeed, by the time Goddard wrote these words, eugenic sterilization was no mere theory; some states had written it into law.

Even in the late nineteenth century, there were some tentative experiments (see chapter 6). Indiana has the honor of passing the first law (1907) that made sterilization official policy. The law solemnly recited that "Heredity plays a most important part in the transmission of crime, idiocy and imbecility." Every institution in Indiana that housed "confirmed criminals, idiots, rapists and imbeciles" was to add two "skilled surgeons" to its staff. The regular doctor and the board of managers of the institution would recommend inmates to the surgeons for examination. If this "committee of experts," together with the board of managers, decided that "procreation is inadvisable," and if there was "no probability of the improvement of the mental condition of the inmate," the surgeon might "perform such operation for the prevention of procreation as shall be decided safest and most effective."[47]

This was only the beginning. California, in 1909, passed a law on the "asexualization" of prisoners—convicts committed twice for sexual offenses, three times for any other crime, or serving a life sentence—if any such inmate gave "evidence while . . . in a . . . prison in this state that he is a moral and sexual pervert."[48] Within a generation, about half of the states had some sort of eugenics statute; many of them, like Indiana, indiscriminately mixed together criminals and "idiots."

Some states sterilized with a vengeance. In Indiana, the aptly named Dr. Harry Sharp, a doctor at the Indiana Reformatory in Jeffersonville, was a pioneer in vasectomy. He began in 1899, when a nineteen-year-old patient who masturbated between four and ten times a day asked the doctor to castrate him so that he could rid himself of this horrible habit. Sharp performed a vasectomy instead; this (he claimed) did the trick. Later, he sterilized some three hundred inmates.[49]

Behind the fear of hereditary crime and degeneracy was, perhaps, another source of uneasiness for old-line Americans: the influx of riffraff from various parts of the world who threatened to swamp the good old Americans and bury their values in rubble. The stupid and feebleminded masses would engulf the intelligent elites. Who were these new "dangerous classes"? They were "tramps, poor farmers, slum dwellers, unskilled laborers, Negroes, and immigrants."[50] And the way they reproduced! The mentally incompetent had "astonishing fecundity." And when "a criminal father" begot a child, it was a "foregone conclusion" that the child was "predestined to criminality."[51] Many contemporaries lumped together the feebleminded and the criminal class. Some members of the army of the "degenerate," as one writer put it, were "entirely helpless—slobbering idiots or hopeless imbeciles"; others, "the criminal insane, sexual perverts and confirmed drug addicts," were "dangerous to the public welfare." Since most of the "causes of social inadequacy" were "largely and positively the results of heredity," and since "most types of degenerates are entirely potent sexually and many are over sexed," responding to "the purely animal instincts," these creatures should be "rendered incapable of reproducing."[52]

The gospel of eugenics affected criminal justice even in its ordinary course. It fed the panic over victimless crime, since it accentuated the social dangers of "vice" and "debauchery." It affected sentencing and the way convicted criminals were judged: woe unto him whose family background revealed signs of weakness or degeneracy.* Any such person

---

* In 1922, Mrs. Nellie Stermer-Koulik was indicted for mass poisoning in Chicago. Justice Harry Olson of the Municipal Court was horrified to read a report that her

who wanted probation, or a lighter sentence, was apt to have his hopes dashed.

To be sure, not everybody went along with the mania for eugenics. In 1918, a federal district judge declared unconstitutional the Nevada law on sterilization. The law gave courts power to order an "operation . . . for the prevention of procreation" for defendants who were "habitual criminals" or were guilty "of carnal abuse of a female person under the age of ten years, or of rape."[54] The court called vasectomy "mutilation," a "brand of infamy," "ignominious and degrading."[55] The Indiana law ran afoul of the state's supreme court in 1921. The prisoner, said the court, had no "opportunity to cross-examine the experts who decide that this operation should be performed upon him"; he had no "chance to controvert the scientific question" whether he was a member of the class "designated" in the statute. It was "very plain" that such a law denied "due process."[56] Indiana, nothing daunted, passed new laws in 1927 and 1931, setting up new procedures for sterilizing the "feeble-minded."[57]

The Supreme Court did not share the skepticism of state courts and lower federal courts. It put its imprimatur on the eugenics movement, in the famous, or notorious, case of *Buck v. Bell*, decided in 1927.[58] This was not a criminal case, but it was directly relevant to the question of sterilizing prisoners. The case turned on the fate of Carrie Buck, described as a "feeble minded white woman," eighteen years old, in the State Colony for Epileptics and Feeble Minded in Virginia. Carrie was supposedly "the daughter of a feeble minded mother in the same institution, and the mother of an illegitimate feeble minded child." The question is whether she was to be sterilized.

The decision was written by Oliver Wendell Holmes, Jr. He gave the law a ringing endorsement. It is better for society not to wait "to execute degenerate offspring for crime" or "let them starve for their imbecility"; instead, society should prevent those who are "manifestly unfit" from "continuing their kind." If the state can order vaccination, it can order "cutting the Fallopian tubes. . . . Three generations of imbeciles are enough."[†]

Down the years, these words have more and more given off a cold, hollow, callous echo. But the attitudes that Holmes expressed were a long time dying. There was a burning faith in glandular tinkering. Leo

"mental age" was eleven, that she had a feebleminded son, and two other sons in jail. If a "eugenics expert" had found out the "history of this whole family at the time one moron was discovered," said Judge Olson, it would have been possible to keep an eye on this woman, and perhaps avert the tragedy that occurred.[53]

† In the event, Carrie Buck's child, a girl who later died of measles, was not retarded at all but "bright." Whether Carrie herself was retarded is also open to doubt. Her sister, who was also sterilized (without her knowledge), was apparently not.[59]

Stanley, chief surgeon at San Quentin, was a devotee of "testicular implantations"; the prisoners were, of course, a fine group of available guinea pigs. The staff of San Quentin performed over ten thousand "implantations" between 1918 and 1940, with excellent results. After all, "goldfish, fed on a diet of ground testicular substance from the ram, increased their activity by four hundred per cent over those fed on the ordinary dried shrimp." Human goldfish, too, found themselves significantly "toned up" by the treatment; they slept better, had an improved appetite, and were "more active and energetic."[60]* Around 1910, a certain Dr. H. J. H. Hoeve, of Chicago, did an autopsy on a "colored murderer" named Junkins, and found incontrovertible evidence that Junkins was a "born criminal"; he had "an enormous mandible, beef-like neck," and "long upper extremities to which the hands were fitted like the blade of a spade."[62] As late as 1939, the anthropologist E. A. Hooton was arguing vigorously that the born criminal was a scientific reality. Hooton meticulously analyzed the height, weight, noses, ears, and bodies of criminals—"old American" criminals as well as foreigners of various sorts, Italians, "Alpines," Irish-Americans, and "East Baltic criminals," capping it off with a study of "Negro and Negroid Criminals." Hooton was absolutely sure that the criminal betrayed itself physically: for example, with "low and sloping foreheads" (although, somewhat to his embarrassment, Hooton himself had this kind of forehead). The "nose of the criminal tends to be higher in the root and in the bridge, and more frequently undulating or concavo-convex than in our sample of civilians." It was, moreover, an amazing fact that "bootleggers persistently have broad noses and short faces with flaring jaw angles, while rapists monotonously display narrow foreheads and elongated, pinched noses."[63]

All along, to be sure, some voices in the scientific community protested against this quackery, and against sterilizing criminals. Eugenics had a wide racist streak in its makeup. World War II, fought against the racist Third Reich, dealt a severe political blow to the emotional roots of sterilization. In 1942, in the midst of the war, the Supreme Court handed down the case of *Skinner v. Oklahoma*.[64] Skinner had been convicted in 1926 of stealing chickens; in 1929 and 1934, he was convicted of armed robbery. Under the Oklahoma Habitual Criminal Sterilization Act, if a person was convicted three or more times of

---

* Stanley also felt that sterilization would "do much to stamp out crime. The right to bear children" should be "reserved to the fit." But he also reported that the California statute on sterilization of criminals had not been enforced, and that he knew of no such operations "as punishment" in all the many years he had served. Stanley did report, however, that there were many voluntary vasectomies; over six hundred prisoners asked for and got a vasectomy, including "Bluebeard" Watson, who "had murdered many of his twenty-two wives."[61]

"felonies involving moral turpitude," he could be sterilized. The state ordered a vasectomy for Skinner.

The Supreme Court struck down the statute. Legally speaking, what was wrong with it was that it violated (said the Court) the equal protection clause of the Fourteenth Amendment, in that it drew irrational, unjustifiable distinctions. For example, an embezzler or someone convicted of violating the Prohibition laws could not be sterilized, though a robber could. But Justice Douglas, writing for the majority, also voiced extreme skepticism about eugenics; and sounded a new note in constitutional doctrine. The right to marriage and procreation, he said, were "basic civil rights." The power to sterilize, in "evil or reckless hands," could "cause races or types which are inimical to the dominant group to wither and disappear."[65] Over the years, however, it was eugenic sterilization that withered away.*

National Prohibition

But beyond a doubt, the jewel in the crown of the morals revolution was national Prohibition. The temperance movement had won many local victories in the nineteenth century—and suffered, too, a fair number of defeats—but it came roaring into the twentieth century with a strength that could not be denied. The Eighteenth Amendment to the Constitution was adopted in 1919, and went into effect on January 29, 1920. Under it, making, shipping, importing, or selling liquor was prohibited. Congress also passed a strong enforcement law, the Volstead Act, over President Wilson's veto.

Prohibition had a profound effect on the system of criminal justice. Violations of the Volstead Act were, of course, federal crimes, but many states also passed their own "little Volsteads." In California, the local law was called the Wright Act. It was a short statute, which simply swallowed the Volstead Act into state law.[67] "Wets" in the legislature demanded, and got a referendum; California voters said yes to the Wright Act, but by a razor-thin margin. It went into effect in 1922.

Prohibition had a short, stormy, unhappy life. Millions of people never wanted it, never accepted it. Yet, in the ranks of the "dries" were many true believers. When Prohibition ran into trouble, as it became obvious that hordes of sinners were breaking the law, the dries cried out for more muscle, more teeth, more enforcement, more rigor. They got their wish in the Jones Act (1929), which stiffened federal penalties.[68] It

---

* There are, to this day, a handful of survivors: for example, Washington, which permits a court to order sterilization for anyone "adjudged guilty of carnal abuse of a female person under the age of ten, or of rape," or who was "adjudged to be an habitual criminal."[66]

did not, however, get at the roots of the problems that plagued the "noble experiment."

It is taken for granted today that Prohibition was a ghastly failure, indeed, that Prohibition was unenforced and unenforceable. But this has to be taken with a grain of salt. This "unenforceable" law put thousands of people in jail. In Columbus, Ohio, in 1929, there were 1,958 arrests for violations of liquor laws, which was ten times the rate of arrest for auto theft, and almost twenty times the rate of arrest for robbery.[69] Courts in many states were positively jammed with Prohibition cases. In Virginia, in 1917 (before the Volstead Act), there were 1.8 liquor-law felony charges per 100,000 population; in 1928 the figure was 63.9, and liquor felonies dominated all other forms of felony.[70] To be sure, most felony liquor charges did not stick: they were often downgraded to misdemeanor charges. Still, all this activity is a far cry from "nonenforcement"; the law was in vigorous use.

It is not easy to tell exactly what impact Prohibition had on law and society. People probably, in fact, drank less. Prohibition certainly affected the time, place, and manner of drinking. But it failed to get rid of the liquor problem; and many people thought it led to a general breakdown of law and order. Prohibition, as one Virginia judge put it, was enacted by "hypocritical representatives" who were "publicly dry and privately wet," and it brought about "contempt for all law."[71]

Worst of all, Prohibition fed the growth of organized crime: the gangsters, the "overlords of vice," flourished in its shadow. The phrase quoted is from E. W. Burgess, writing in the pages of the *Illinois Crime Survey* (1929). Burgess thought there was no "blinking the fact that *liquor prohibition* has introduced the most difficult problems of law enforcement in the field of organized crime. The enormous revenues derived from bootlegging have purchased protection for all forms of criminal activities and have demoralized law enforcing agencies."[72]

This charge against Prohibition somehow stuck; one hears it repeated, to this day. It is part of the enduring legend of Prohibition. No doubt there was something to it. Prohibition was the age of Johnny Torrio, the boss of Chicago, and his more famous successor, Al Capone, the boss of bosses in Chicago after 1925. Capone ruthlessly slaughtered and suppressed rivals; he controlled bootlegging, gambling, and other "rackets." In 1927, by one estimate, his organization pulled in some $60 million a year in ill-gotten gains.[73] To men like Capone, Prohibition was like a pot of honey to a bear.

Ultimately, Capone went to jail, for tax evasion; and Prohibition ended (in 1933). But the gangs went on. The forces that led to the rise of "organized crime" surely went deeper than the Prohibition laws. And liquor was not, and is not, the only illegal commodity people want to buy. Gambling and prostitution are two others; another is drugs; these supported a criminal culture long before Prohibition—and long, long after.

In retrospect, Prohibition was a last-ditch defense against powerful and primitive forces that had been somehow unleashed in the country. What "respectable society" labeled vice, a substantial minority (or majority?) labeled pleasure. Drinking was only one example. Drugs were another; gambling a third. In the case of "inverts" and "perverts," the letter of the law demanded that they utterly repress behavior that flowed out of basic human desires, that they deny a vital aspect of their selves. This was an extreme case, but there was always a large, though largely secret, opposition to all the laws about sex—people who held their tongues, or lived secret lives, or banished their impulses to some hidden corner of their psyche, burying naked feeling under layers of silt and guilt. Even inside the "moral majority" there were many traitors and moles—double agents, or simply tortured, conflicted human beings.

Prohibition itself ran counter to very deep cultural patterns. Millions of people saw nothing wrong with a drink or two—or three or four, for that matter. Others drank but voted dry. Again, it is not exactly right to call this hypocrisy. There was, no doubt, plenty of hypocrisy; but there was also an honest belief in what we have called the Victorian compromise, here displaced onto the liquor problem. This was, in essence, a theory of social control; it was an attempt by some people to find a balance between legitimation (which would lead to too much vice) and prohibition (which was bound to fall flat on its face). The compromise had broken down after 1870, when the moral side pressed for unconditional surrender. The compromise broke down even more rapidly later in the twentieth century, when permissiveness went on the offensive; and the repeal of Prohibition, in utter disgrace, was the first great victory in the next phase of this war.

The Great Counterattack:
Lifestyle Wars

The second half of the twentieth century, roughly speaking, was the period of the great counterattack. Very notably, much of the criminal fabric of the sex laws rotted away. Some aspects of vice laws remained almost intact—prostitution was and is still against the law, although much of the fervor has gone out of enforcement. The picture is mixed; and complicated. The motivating forces are various. But the general line of development seems perfectly plain.

With gambling, for example, there has been a definite turn of the wheel—though not everywhere. Decriminalization began in Nevada, the "great rotten borough."[74] Nevada had actually once outlawed gambling, in 1909.[75] The law was liberalized, then tightened; loosened again; finally, in 1931, the state made gambling legal, partly as a way to make jobs and bring money into Nevada.[76] Like every other state, Nevada was suffering from the Depression. Nothing much grows in Nevada, and it is hardly the place to build a factory. Instead, the state decided to make a living by legalizing what was illegal next door, in California. Gambling was the most obvious example.

It proved to be an excellent decision—for Nevada. In the forties, the gambling business boomed; and in 1945, the state reformed the licensing system, which had been strictly local, and gave authority over gambling to the State Tax Commission. Gambling became the big industry of Nevada, the keystone of its economy. By the fifties, an "incredible abundance of suckers" poured through "Nevada's gigantic cream separators twenty-four hours a day."[77] Las Vegas became the capital city of casino gambling,[78] perhaps the capital of American vulgarity as well. Like Sodom and Gomorrah, it was a desert city, but an angry God never swept it away. On the contrary, its economic power led to imitation, the most sincere form of flattery, in Atlantic City. Moreover, state after state, in the seventies and eighties, tried to make hay out of gambling, usually in the form of a state lottery. The voices of respectability protested; but they seemed to be talking to the wind.

Out of the Closet: Deregulating Sex

More dramatic, and much more significant, was the movement to deregulate the varieties of sex. The period after 1945 was a period of rapid social change, which meant, inevitably, rapid legal change as well. Most of the change was in one direction: away from prudery, repression, and the Victorian compromise. Some states wiped off the books all laws against *any* form of sexual behavior, so long as it was between those two (or more) randy partners, consenting adults.

The change did not come overnight. Obviously, adultery, fornication, sodomy, and the like, were as common as dandelions. In most cities, arrests did occur, but usually in small numbers. For the people involved, of course, it was a serious matter. As late as 1953, the Municipal Court of Philadelphia tried sixty-four cases of fornication and bastardy (2 percent of the total number of cases in that court), along with ten cases of adultery, seven of indecent assault, five of simple fornication, four of indecent exposure, three of sodomy, and one for contributing to the sex delinquency of a minor; eleven offenders were charged with possession or sale of obscene pictures.[79]

The *federal* campaign against "debauchery" became, as it were, much more flaccid. From 1940 on, the Mann Act entered, as one author put it, a period of "twilight."[80] During the Second World War, there was at least one notorious case: the great comedian Charlie Chaplin was arrested in 1944. A woman named Joan Berry claimed Chaplin gave her money for a trip to New York (from Los Angeles). In New York, they had sexual relations. J. Edgar Hoover, who considered Chaplin a dangerous red, was the driving force behind this bizarre trial, which provided sensational copy for the gentlemen and ladies of the press. The jury acquitted Chaplin, but he later left the country in disgust.[81]

By now it was, in fact, deep twilight. The Mann Act had come to seem—archaic. The conviction rate dropped dramatically in the sixties. In *U.S. v. McClung* (1960), a district court case out of Louisiana, Clarence C. McClung was indicted for transporting Lula Belle and Barbara Raub from Huntington, West Virginia, to La Place, Louisiana, "for the purpose of engaging in sexual intercourse." The district court threw the case out. Isolated acts of sexual dalliance did not violate the act, said the court; what was needed was some "sordid commercial scheme."[82] There were 157 convictions in 1961, but only 36 at the end of the decade. The last splashy prosecution resulted in the conviction, in 1962, of Chuck Berry, the rock-and-roll celebrity.[83]

The Mann Act was not quite dead. But it was dying. Word went out to U.S. attorneys: use the Mann Act sparingly, and only for commercialized vice. As a blunt federal weapon against immorality, the act passed into a state of suspended animation.[84] In 1978, the law became a bit more unisex; Congress outlawed the "commercial exploitation" of minors in the sex industry, adding minor boys to the protected class.[85] Finally, in 1986, Congress overhauled the whole bloody business. It dropped from the law the obnoxious and racist term "white slavery."[86] The pungent and evocative old word "debauchery" also departed, along with the reference to "immoral purposes." The act was now firmly gender-neutral. The crime consisted of transporting any "individual" with the "intent that such individual engage in prostitution, or in any sexual activity for which any person can be charged with a criminal offense."[87] Plain interstate lust was no longer illegal. The ghost of *Caminetti* was at rest at last.

The Well of Loneliness

Homosexual behavior was a crime throughout American history. In the colonial period, as we have seen, a few men found guilty of sodomy swung from the gallows. In the nineteenth century, the wages of sodomy was no longer death, but the "crime against nature" was very much a crime, and it carried, potentially, heavy penalties. It is hard to say much about enforcement. There was never any systematic crack-down. Fear of the police, and of scandal, made gay men and women out-laws and drove their behavior underground. There were times and places where arrest and prosecution were genuine risks. Police reports every-where record at least small numbers of arrests. Thus, in 1908, there were 73 felony arrests (out of 7,721) in Chicago for the "crime against nature"; in 1909, there were 31 (out of 6,460).[88]

The morality revolution of the late nineteenth and early twentieth centuries probably had an impact on the law of same-sex behavior as well. The total number of reported *appellate* cases on sodomy and re-lated matters increased. There were only six cases recorded before 1870, twenty-three between 1870 and 1900; and almost two hundred in the first half of the twentieth century—sixty-eight reported cases in the decade of the forties alone.[89] The cases of the twentieth century broad-ened the meaning of "sodomy" to include any sex except the kind that makes babies. There was, for example, the delicate question of oral sex. Was this a crime—"sodomy" or the "crime against nature"? Most courts thought it fell under the ban. In *State v. Start*, an Oregon case of 1913, one Rodby accused Harry Start of the "disgusting act" of "taking into his mouth the penis of Rodby and sucking the same until a seminal emission ensued."[90] The (rather vague) Oregon statute covered this act, said the court. In "the order of nature," the human body gets its "nour-ishment" by virtue of the "alimentary canal"; food enters at one "open-ing, the mouth," and wastes go out "through the nether opening of the rectum." Either end of the body, then, was equally off limits to sex; and both ends were included in the ban against "moral filthiness and iniq-uity."[91] It was iniquitous, of course, even when oral sex came into play between man and woman; this, too, was held unlawful.[92]

Legal change was, at first, exceedingly slow. Public attitudes began to change rather noticeably after World War II. The famous "Kinsey re-port," *Sexual Behavior in the Human Male*, appeared in 1948. This re-port, an empirical study of the sex lives of American men, created a sen-sation in its day. Its main author, Alfred C. Kinsey, had at one time been an expert on gall wasps. This may seem an obscure subject, but human sex life was so taboo that it was just as obscure, if not more so. Kinsey set about to rectify this situation.

He and his associates wrote their report in a dry, objective tone, liber-ally larded with charts, graphs, and figures. Even so, the book carried a distinctive, startling, and radical message. The message was this: illegal sexual behavior was as common as rain. Kinsey claimed that 85 percent of the men in this country who were sexually mature had gone in for some form of premarital intercourse, 59 percent had "some experience in mouth-genital contacts," 70 percent had "relations with prostitutes," and between 30 and 45 percent had "extra-marital intercourse." There were even worse shocks for conventional morality. As many as 37 percent of his subjects had had "some homosexual experience," and 17 percent of the "farm boys" had experimented with "animal intercourse."

All these activities, of course, were quite "illicit"; the vast majority of the behaviors were listed in penal codes as crimes. "Mouth-genital contacts" were a form of sexuality that a clear majority of the population had tried on for size; yet judges on the bench had called this behavior unspeakable, too disgusting for words, and totally beyond the pale. Kinsey was eager to draw policy conclusions from his figures. The men "involved in these activities, taken as a whole," amounted to "more than 95 per cent of the total male population." They were all technically "sex offenders." Taken literally, the idea of sweeping the community clear of "sex offenders" was, in effect, a "proposal that 5 per cent of the population should support the other 95 per cent in penal institutions."[93]

Kinsey followed up his report with a book about the sex lives of American women, which was less shocking only because the book about men had prepared the way.[94] There were plenty of differences between men's and women's sex lives, to be sure, both big and small (women, for example, did not seem to write sexual graffiti on toilet walls).[95] But the bottom line was the same: there was a lot of sex going on, and a lot of it would be a crime if we took the laws literally. So, for example, almost one woman out of five in Kinsey's sample had had a homosexual experience by age forty.[96] There was—and is—a great deal of controversy over Kinsey's methods, figures, and results. But for the public at the time, these books were bombshells. And, beyond a doubt, the Kinsey reports delivered a plain, simple, and powerful message: sex laws were cruel, unfair, and absurd, and should be purged from the books.

Liberalization, however, was neither easy nor automatic. In the fifties and sixties, despite the Kinsey reports, police continued to make arrests for homosexual behavior, at least in certain cities—more than a thousand a year in the District of Columbia in the early fifties. There were sudden sweeps of police enforcement in the fifties and raids on gay bars in New York, New Orleans, Miami, San Francisco, Baltimore, and Dallas.[97] A major scandal in Boise, Idaho (of all places), led to a crackdown on homosexuals in that city, vigorous police action, a wave of hysteria, and some extremely punitive sentences.[98]

A definite tide, nonetheless, was running in favor of sexual freedom. A number of states quietly dropped some or all of the punitive laws from their books. Fornication is, generally speaking, no longer a crime. Connecticut repealed its law in 1967. In New Jersey, in 1977, the state supreme court declared its fornication law unconstitutional.[99] Adultery hung on as a crime in a few states; the high court of Massachusetts upheld its law in 1983. Texas allowed a kind of private death sentence into the seventies: homicide was "justifiable" and no crime if a husband killed a man "taken in the act of adultery" with his wife.[100] But adultery itself was on its last legs, penally speaking, in the age of the sexual revolution. In April 1990, when a district attorney in northern Wisconsin actually brought a prosecution for adultery, the story made the front page of the *New York Times*.[101]

The changes in the penal laws of sexual behavior were dramatic, even though plenty of men and women thought they did not go far enough and there were also many who thought, to the contrary, that Satan was having a field day. The question naturally arises: Where did the changes come from? The obvious answer is: from the power of the sexual revolution itself, and its influence on legal culture. And where did the revolution come from? Why had attitudes toward sex changed so radically?

In the nineteenth century, doctors told people, as we have seen, that heavy sex was a danger to body and mind. They preached "moderation," that is, sexual discipline and repression. A man (or woman) who went in for too much sex (a point easily reached), risked disease, debilitation, delirium, and death. The twentieth century turned these ideas on their heads. New knowledge played a role. The Kinsey reports told "deviant" people that they were not alone. The emperor was not the only one without clothes; there were naked people under every bush. A certain dosage of Sigmund Freud trickled down into public consciousness.[102]

But basic changes in character, in personality, in social norms, were far more important; it was these that made the era receptive to Freud in the first place. The age of individuality, of "self-realization," meant an open door for sex, along with other aspects of the self. It was in consequence that sex attitudes turned turtle. The finger of doom now pointed at *repression*, not moderation. "The sexual impulse," after all, was an "insistent force demanding expression." Overindulgence in sex, if there was such a thing, was not what caused physical and psychological damage. On the contrary: it was unhealthy repression that curdled the psyche. It was dangerous to bottle up or squash natural instincts. Sex was healthy; self-denial was not.

In the 1977 New Jersey case that struck down fornication laws,[103]* Dr. Richard Green testified solemnly as an expert witness that the sex

---

* The defendant and a friend had been arrested for rape, after an incident in a deserted parking lot in Newark. The state's case was weak; the men denied using force, and the women were perhaps prostitutes. The judge then told counsel he intended to charge the jury that fornication was a "lesser included offense of rape." Defense counsel objected, "pointing out that the statute was in 'disrepute' and rarely applied."[104]

drive was "a central factor . . . in personality development." If you re-press it, "guilt and anxiety problems can arise." In the male, these prob-lems could be devastating: "inability to achieve erection," or "prema-ture ejaculation," among other horrors. In the female, one result could be "frigidity," the product of "years of guilt and taboo," leading to "painful intercourse, or if not painful, just not pleasurable to the point of sexual climax."[105] In the case itself, the court referred to fornication as an "intimate personal activity between consenting adults"; it would be a gross intrusion on "personal autonomy" if such behavior could be "dragged into court and 'exposed.'" The court admitted that fornication was "abhorrent to the morals and deeply held beliefs of many persons." But the justices hinted strongly that *they* were not among these "many persons." "Surely," the court said, "police have more pressing duties than to search out adults who live a so-called 'wayward' life."

For obvious reasons, same-sex issues were particularly touchy and less amenable to bloodless revolution. Nevertheless, homosexual con-duct, among adults, was decriminalized in a number of important states. A California law of 1975 legalized "sexual acts in private between con-senting adults"; a number of classic "victimless crimes" departed from the criminal code, probably forever: "adulterous cohabitation, sodomy, and oral copulation."[106] A number of states enacted similar reforms. But there are pockets of major resistance; and a good deal of backlash, all over the country.

The Supreme Court had a chance in 1986 to push all the remaining sodomy laws into extinction (*Bowers v. Hardwick*); but the Court re-fused to do so.[107] The "privacy" cases had kindled hopes of a different re-sult; a majority of the justices, however, delivered themselves of a par-ticularly mean-spirited and retrograde opinion. Justice White intoned that antisodomy measures had "ancient roots." He was "unwilling," as he put it, to find in the Constitution a "fundamental right to engage in homosexual sodomy," as if this was really the issue in the case. Chief Justice Burger was in no mood to "cast aside millennia of moral teach-ing." Four of the justices disagreed with Burger and White, and Powell (one of the five-justice majority) later recanted.[108] But still, the damage had been done. A number of *state* courts have struck down sodomy statutes—Kentucky joined the list in September 1992;[109] but as of this writing (1993) it seems most unlikely that the Supreme Court will soon change its mind and join this crowd.

Privacy

An important line of cases sounded an important theme in twentieth-century law—a theme that goes by the somewhat misleading name of

"privacy." The "right of privacy" has, very notably, contributed to startling changes in the law relating to sexual behavior, contraception, and
abortion. Any catalogue of causes would have to list changing attitudes
toward sex, the invention of the contraceptive pill, the growth of the
women's movement, and, perhaps most fundamentally, the spread of a
particularly potent form of expressive individualism in the United
States.[110]

The mind behind such emanations as the Comstock law rejected
even *talking* about contraception and abortion. But in the twentieth
century, freer sexual behavior, and (very important) peoples' desires for
small families, destroyed the power of Comstock's position. The old, restrictive laws against contraception, and contraceptive information, fell
by the wayside. Restrictiveness made a last stand in Connecticut, where
it suffered a mighty defeat in 1965 in *Griswold v. Connecticut*.[111] Connecticut law made it a crime to use "any drug, medicinal article or instrument for the purpose of preventing conception"; it was also a crime
to aid, counsel, or abet anyone to this nefarious end. The Supreme Court
struck down the statute, and, in the process, discovered for itself a
"right of privacy" mysteriously secreted somewhere in the Constitution—none of the justices were quite sure where.

The *Griswold* case talked about privacy, but it was never clear exactly what was private, or why it was protected. Of course, married
people using contraception usually did the dirty deed in the dark of
night, and in the "sacred" precincts of their bedrooms. Would we allow
the police, asked Justice Douglas, to search those "sacred precincts" for
"telltale signs" of contraception? A good question; but no one even pretended that this was much of a danger.[112]

In *Eisenstadt v. Baird* (1972)[113] the Supreme Court went one step further. Baird lived in Massachusetts. Under Massachusetts law, only doctors or druggists could distribute contraceptives, and only to married
people. Baird gave a lecture about contraception; and when he finished,
he gave out a "package of Emko vaginal foam to a woman in the audience."[114] He was arrested and convicted, but on appeal the Supreme
Court threw out his conviction; the Court held the statute was unconstitutional. In this case, the Court quietly dissolved the line between
married and unmarried people; and the "right of privacy," excavated
from its shadowy textual tomb, was clearly on the move.

The next step, which was the boldest, extended the right of privacy to
the case of abortion. Abortion, as we have seen, was first criminalized in
the late nineteenth century. In many states, the laws remained extremely restrictive in the twentieth century. Thousands of women got
abortions, one way or another; back-alley abortions were common but
dangerous. A study published in 1936 estimated that half a million abor-

tions were performed per year in the United States.[115] But there were not many arrests; and juries, in general, tended not to convict abortionists. Prosecutions were more likely to be successful where there was a "victim," that is, where the woman died.[116] And this, alas, was not so rare an occurrence.

In 1962, the thalidomide tragedy burst on the world: women who had taken this drug during pregnancy gave birth to children who were pitifully and horribly deformed. The drug, a sedative, was not generally marketed in this country, but Sherry Finkbine of Phoenix, Arizona, had taken it. When she learned what the drug could do, she tried to get an abortion at her local hospital, but the county medical society said no. Her search for a legal abortion—in the end she ran away to Sweden— was headline news and focused attention on the human dimensions of abortion.[117]

With *Roe v. Wade* (1973), the Court stepped into the abortion quagmire.[118] *Roe v. Wade* struck down all the state laws that made abortion a crime—at least as far as abortion in the early months of pregnancy was concerned. It would be hard to think of a more controversial decision in this century. Almost immediately, the case became intensely political; it has remained that way. It galvanized opposition groups into action; equally fervid groups sprang to its defense.

One charge leveled against the case was that it created a new constitutional right out of whole cloth, that the Founding Fathers would whirl in their graves if they saw how far the Supreme Court had gone in usurping power. But *Roe v. Wade* grew out of a specific background, legal and social. Its legal background was, as we have seen, the line of cases that led from *Griswold*. The social background (which underpinned *Griswold* as well) was, of course, more crucial and complex.

The *Griswold* case, for all its quirky language, seems to be snugly secure in the pantheon of legal doctrine; no one dares attack it, if only because the idea of making contraception a crime seems so out of the question in the 1990s. *Roe v. Wade* is another story. Its later history, too, has been highly complex. The Court's decision in the case was a solid seven to two. But the controversy refused to die down. In the years after *Roe v. Wade*, abortion moved, surprisingly, into the very center of the political stage. The decision was denounced and defended in terms that became more and more strident over the years. Republican Party platforms from 1980 on promised to amend the Constitution "to restore protection of the right to life for unborn children." In the event, the Republicans, though they won three presidential elections, could not deliver on this promise.

The Supreme Court was a different matter. As old justices dropped off and Reagan and Bush appointees took their place, the Court moved to the right on this issue. In the eighties, the Court chipped steadily away at *Roe v. Wade* without actually overruling it, until the fate of the decision hung by a hair. Some states passed repressive statutes, and challenges to these cases climbed inexorably toward the Court. In 1992, by the slimmest of margins, the Court reaffirmed the core idea of *Roe* and refused to overrule it.[119] Pro-choice forces breathed a sigh of relief. Bush's defeat in November 1992 made *Roe* seem, for the moment, unassailable.

Obscenity and Pornography

How much control should law and authorities exercise over obscenity and pornography—that is, over "dirty" books, pictures, and language? This is another old and thorny issue. It has a rather convoluted history, but, on the whole, twentieth-century law has followed one pretty clear trajectory: the law has gotten less and less harsh, more and more permissive. First soft core and then hard core have come leering out of the closet. But there have been countermovements, and a backlash—some of it from a fairly unexpected source.

In the nineteenth century, it was taken for granted that states and cities could put pornography under the ban and punish people who made it or sold it. What passed for obscene or pornographic was a far cry from what would pass as such today. Works were banned that would not bring a blush to the cheek of the most delicate plant in our times. There were, in fact, few decided cases, perhaps because pornography, though common enough, hardly dared show its face in public. Pornography was strictly underground. Like bodies, it was best kept under wraps.*

Victorian prudery and modesty made it impossible to discuss or portray many serious social issues. Literary quality or high purpose did not protect a book or play if it was "offensive." In 1905, George Bernard Shaw's play *Mrs. Warren's Profession* was banned in New Haven. When the play opened in New York, the police commissioner bought himself a box seat. After the curtain fell, he arrested the producer, the manager, and two actresses. In this instance, prudery lost its case; the New York

---

* The same general attitude cropped up in laws and cases that seem to have as their goal hiding sex, banishing it to the periphery, forcing it indoors and underground. There was, for example, the celebrated case of Jo Carol LaFleur, a junior-high teacher in Cleveland, Ohio. She successfully challenged a rule that prevented women from teaching after their fourth month of pregnancy; the school board gave a lot of reasons for the rule, but surely one of them was that it was indecent for students to see a swollen belly.[120] There were also rules in many high schools (later challenged) that excluded married students, perhaps because they knew too much about sex or were having too much of it legitimately.[121]

Court of Special Sessions acquitted the defendants. The play, the court thought, was simply not obscene.[122]*

James Joyce's *Ulysses* was the subject of a landmark decision in 1933. Random House wanted to publish an American edition of this twentieth-century masterpiece, but Joyce was pretty strong medicine for the delicate sensibilities of official America. The publisher tested the waters by importing a copy, which was seized by customs; the issue of obscenity was then tried in a federal court in New York. Judge John M. Woolsey gave the novel a clean bill of (legal) health. The book contained words generally considered "dirty words" and had graphic descriptions of sex. But it was not written with "the leer of the sensualist," and it had no "dirt for dirt's sake."[124] The Court of Appeals affirmed this decision.†

The *Ulysses* case was ahead of its time. The smut police were still in the saddle in Massachusetts. In 1930, the Supreme Judicial Court of Massachusetts upheld the conviction of a bookseller in Cambridge who sold a copy of *Lady Chatterley's Lover* to an investigator from the Watch and Ward Society.[125] At least *Lady Chatterley* was a shocker in its day. What, however, can be said about the conviction—same court, same year—of one Friede?[126] Friede had sold a book to Daniel J. Hines, a lieutenant of the Boston Police Department (we can only guess at his literary tastes), which was "obscene" and "indecent" and might corrupt the young. The book in question was Theodore Dreiser's *An American Tragedy*, a novel that would be rated, today, PG at worst. Until the thirties, the U.S. Customs Department, ever vigilant, banned works by such pornographers as Aristophanes, Balzac, Defoe (*Moll Flanders* and *Roxana*), Flaubert, and Voltaire (*Candide*).[127]

The venerable First Amendment protects freedom of speech.‡ It does not protect "obscenity," but where should we draw the line? In fact, until well into the twentieth century, there was very little decisional

---

* Self-censorship was a powerful force, even when no police or court were involved. In 1913, Lee Schubert reluctantly withdrew a play, *The Lure*, from Broadway; it dealt with white slavery. He acted under the shadow of a grand jury investigation. Schubert felt the play belonged on Broadway; that it performed an "important public purpose"; but he refused, in his words, "to be placed in the position of offending the sense of propriety of even a small minority of serious people who take a different view." After he acted, the grand jury dropped its inquiry, and public morality (but not the play) was saved.[123]

† Woolsey's opinion was *United States v. One Book Called "Ulysses,"* 5 F. Supp. 182 (S.D. N.Y., 1933). The dirty words, said Woolsey, were "old Saxon words known to almost all men and, I venture, to many women." True, the book paid a great deal of attention to the "theme of sex," but "it must always be remembered that his locale was Celtic and his season spring." The Court of Appeals' decision was *United States v. One Book Entitled Ulysses by James Joyce,* 72 Fed. 2d 705 (C.A. 2, 1934). Augustus Hand, who wrote the decision, praised the book; at times, it was "coarse, blasphemous, and obscene," but it did not "tend to promote lust."

‡ The First Amendment as such applies only to the federal government; the Supreme Court has decided that the Fourteenth Amendment has "incorporated" it, thus mak-

law on this question. No case reached the Supreme Court before the end of the Second World War.

In fact, there was no definite ruling on obscenity until 1957, in *Roth v. United States*.[128]* Defendant Roth had been convicted of violating the federal law against mailing "obscene" material. The Supreme Court affirmed his conviction. But the opinion of the Court left the issue unresolved, to say the least. The case pointed in two directions at once. On the one hand, it upheld the right to punish makers and sellers of obscene literature. Free speech had limits, and obscenity was outside the boundaries. But the Court did not do much of a job of *defining* obscenity. The best test Justice Brennan could come up with was this: Would "the average person" think that the "dominant theme of the material" was its appeal "to prurient interest"?

In 1966, the Supreme Court faced that formidable woman, Fanny Hill, heroine of John Cleland's pornographic classic, *Memoirs of a Woman of Pleasure*. This famous book was written in 1750, which makes it somewhat older than the First Amendment itself. For more than two hundred years, it had an underground or semiunderground existence, circulating from clammy hand to clammy hand. Now, in the 1960s, it emerged into the sunshine, published by a reputable publishing house, endorsed as serious literature (of a minor sort) by various professors of English—but banned as obscene in Massachusetts. The Supreme Court disagreed with Massachusetts. Justice Brennan now came up with a stricter test: a "book cannot be proscribed unless it is found to be *utterly* without redeeming social value," even if it is "patently offensive."[130] Whatever the formula, the times were definitely changing. This was not a book like *An American Tragedy*, or even *Ulysses*; it was written precisely to stir up "prurient interests," and its main defense was good English and two hundred years under its belt. Respectable opinion had changed since Fanny Hill first saw the light of day. The record showed, according to Justice Douglas, that when the book appeared boldly in public, in 1963, there was "an unusually large number of orders . . . placed by universities and libraries," and that the "Library of Congress requested the right to translate the book into Braille."[131]

Fanny Hill's victory was definitely a straw in the wind. The Supreme Court has been, on the whole, quite hostile to censorship disguised as

---

ing it applicable to the states as well. Also, each state has its own bill of rights and its own clause about freedom of speech.
* The first case to come before the Supreme Court was *Doubleday & Co. v. New York*.[129] The book was *Memoirs of Hecate County*, written by Edmund Wilson, the famous critic and writer. The state's sensibilities were offended by this novel, a judgment that, needless to say, would seem ludicrous today. The Supreme Court, however, divided four to four on the issue, and when that occurs, the lower court decision stands and the Supreme Court does not publish an opinion of its own.

antipornography. The day is past when bluenoses can freely use obscenity laws to suppress serious books. But the main source of change is not the courts, but society itself, which has become vastly more tolerant of sexual expression. Sex and the body are not secret subjects anymore. People say and do things on stage, in the movies, and in literature that would have been unthinkable a century ago—even a generation ago. Indeed today's "normal" Hollywood movie has love scenes and "dirty" words that were taboo as recently as the fifties. An occasional skirmish between parents and teachers in a high school library is about all that remains of the Watch and Ward mentality. There are rumblings about TV and rock lyrics, and puffs of smoke from the Bible Belt, but (formal) censorship of anything but triple-X, hard-core pornography is completely dead.*

Today, there are tons of books, magazines, plays, and movies that *nobody* would claim any value for as literature or anything else. Their value is that they are sexually exciting, period. Does *anything* go? In general, courts still find the issue of out-and-out hard-core pornography somewhat troubling. Judges and justices have gone this way and that, searching for the elusive "bright line," the magic formula, or even a halfway, wishy-washy formulation, to serve as a legal "test" for what can or cannot be banned. They have never found one. Legal arguments have marched up one side of the hill, so to speak, and down the other. All one can say is that there is something called "obscenity," but what it is, legally speaking, nobody really knows.

Does it depend on community standards? If so, prudery is in deep trouble. The public, not the courts, has set the trends. The reality is, sex magazines are on sale in drugstores and bookstores; they lie around on coffee tables and in barbershops. The normal fare goes beyond anything the Victorians dared think of in their most fevered erotic fantasies. In every major city (and some minor ones), there are theaters that show X-rated movies—movies that leave nothing to the imagination, and which show every conceivable permutation and combination of sex in mind-boggling detail and repetition. In most cities, the police do nothing about adult bookshops, adult movie houses (both gay and straight), and assorted sex shops. In smaller cities and towns, there are occasional crackdowns, but the general atmosphere is inescapably permissive.

The fight against "filth" has never abated, of course, although these have been lean years for upholders of the faith. In the most recent generation, religious and conservative opposition to pornography has gained what seems an unlikely ally. One wing of the feminist movement joined in the battle against pornography. The real problem of pornography, ac-

---

* Public funding, however, is quite another matter, as the fuss over grants from the National Endowment for the Arts to "obscene" and "blasphemous" artists and works shows quite graphically.

cording to Catherine MacKinnon and others, is that it is part of a system of gender oppression: pornography displays, and produces, the sexual subordination of women. MacKinnon and Andrea Dworkin drafted a model ordinance that attacked pornography on this basis. The ordinance defined pornography as the "graphic sexually explicit subordination of women, whether in pictures or in words." "Pornography," to be subject to the ordinance, had to contain one or more of certain elements: for example, women "are presented as sexual objects who enjoy pain or humiliation," or who like to be raped, or are shown as sexual objects "tied up or cut up or mutilated," or "penetrated by objects or animals," or in "scenarios of degradation, injury, abasement, torture, shown as filthy or inferior, bleeding, bruised, or hurt in a context that makes these conditions sexual," or presented "as sexual objects for domination, conquest, violation, exploitation, possession, or use, or through postures or positions of servility or submission or display."[132]

Minneapolis adopted the ordinance, but its mayor vetoed it. The proponents had more luck in Indianapolis, but the ordinance was promptly challenged in the courts. In 1985, the Court of Appeals for the Seventh Circuit found the Indianapolis ordinance unconstitutional. Judge Easterbrook, writing for the court, called the ordinance a form of "thought control." It establishes, he said, an "approved" view of women, "of how they may react to sexual encounters, of how the sexes may relate to each other." Those who "espouse the approved view may use sexual images"; others may not. This, said the judge, could not be constitutionally done.[133]

The battlers on behalf of the ordinance have not, of course, given up. But prospects for success, in this country, do not seem very bright. This is because the climate of opinion is essentially unfavorable. Whatever the merits of the feminist case against pornography, *any* significant move to repress "dirty" books, movies, and pictures just does not seem to be in the cards in the nineties. This is surely true of big cities—small towns and suburbs may be a different matter. It is not easy to disentangle the kind of pornography MacKinnon opposes from the freedom of sexual expression in general. Nor does it seem likely that the country as a whole will turn back to the way things were in the past. The era of the self, the antirepressive era, is not minded to go in for banning movies and books. Obscenity and pornography, it seems, are here to stay.

Drug Laws: The Great Exception

The counterrevolution we have described has taken its time in some fields, gone rapidly in others, zigged a bit and zagged a bit; but the general trend has been crystal clear. The great exception to the trend concerns narcotics—drugs. In the nineteenth century, as we saw, drug laws hardly mattered. There were scattered bits of legislation here and there, aimed at "opium dens" and the like, but, in general, addiction was not a crime, nor was the plain, unvarnished sale or use of narcotics. This situation changed radically in the twentieth century.

The first rumblings were in the state legislatures. A New York law of 1905 declared cocaine, morphine, and opium to be "poisons," not to be sold at retail without a warning label.[134] Congress passed an Opium Exclusion Act in 1909.[135] But the first major landmark of the drug wars was the Harrison Narcotic Drug Act, a federal statute passed in 1914.[136] This was, in form, a tax statute, but the aim was to put an end to the drug traffic. It applied to opium and its derivatives, and also, very notably, to "coca leaves" and *their* derivatives. This was a significant step; it put cocaine in the same pariah class as heroin and morphine.

The Harrison Act was not in itself particularly controversial. Rather, as one scholar has put it, it seemed like a "routine slap at a moral evil." Nobody *defended* drug use. The road of addiction seemed to lead downward, almost inevitably, to crime and insanity. Moreover, drugs were associated with unpopular subgroups. As David Musto observes, "Cocaine raised the specter of the wild Negro, opium the devious Chinese, morphine the tramps in the slums." These drugs were like infectious pestilences; they were liable to burst out of their dens and hovels and spread among respectable people unless they were firmly dealt with.[137]

Webb v. United States (1919) was a test case. Webb was a practicing physician in Memphis, Tennessee; Goldbaum was a retail druggist in that city. Webb prescribed morphine for habitual users; Goldbaum filled these prescriptions. Was this acceptable under the Harrison Act? The Supreme Court, in a brief opinion, said flatly no. To prescribe drugs not as a "cure" but to keep the user "comfortable by maintaining his customary use" was a "perversion" of the meaning of the act.[138]

This was not entirely unreasonable, as a reading of the statute. There were certainly abuses. One reads accounts of "dope doctors" who, for a trivial fee, were pleased to write out prescriptions for drugs.[139] The Minnesota drug statute, passed in 1915, made it unlawful to "prescribe for the use of any habitual user."[140] Still, the net effect of *Webb* was to make addiction itself a crime; to put the drug trade, and drug use, completely beyond the pale, and on a national level.

At first, to be sure, the drug problem did not loom very large in national consciousness. The Columbus, Ohio, police, who arrested almost two thousand people for liquor violations in 1929, made exactly nine arrests for "violation of narcotic laws."[141] The federal government was somewhat more active. More than half of the women inmates of the Federal Industrial Institution for Women, in Alderson, West Virginia, in October 1935, were in prison on narcotics charges (264 out of 505).[142] Congress established a Federal Bureau of Narcotics in 1930. Harry Anslinger directed the Bureau. He believed, quite passionately, that the drug trade was a massive national threat.[143] The Bureau was a tireless source of propaganda against marijuana and the way it destroyed young minds. The Marijuana Tax Act of 1937 added this substance to the list of the damned.[144]

Since then, the federal government, and most state governments, have never looked back, never wavered, always stuck like glue to a single policy of prohibition, prohibition, and more prohibition: interdiction at the source, the arrest of users and pushers, draconian punishments, and, on the official level, no understanding, no mercy, no letup in the war. In the sixties, marijuana and harder drugs burst out of the ethnic enclaves; they became part of the lifestyle of young rebels and would-be rebels. This generated still more panic.

Because of this national panic (some of it justified) and because any major problem in our day is a *federal* problem, the federal government was sucked further and further into the pit of drug-law enforcement. In 1973, Congress created a Drug Enforcement Administration. The size of this agency has swollen in the last two decades. The "war on drugs" now consumes billions of dollars every year; it is fought in the streets, in the air, along the coasts, and even in foreign countries.

The public hysteria over drugs is not, of course, totally wrongheaded; drug addiction and its criminal consequences are worth worrying about. But perhaps the question to ask is: Why, in an age that has relaxed so noticeably its attitudes on sex, vice, and gambling, does drug prohibition still stand so firm? The average person seems to associate drugs with certain enormous evils: the corruption of the young (their own children, perhaps); the wasted, impure lives of the urban underclass, much of it black or Hispanic; and the explosion of violent crime, mostly in the cities. Nothing would be worse than condoning the evils of drugs.

Of course, the programs, state and federal, have been largely exercises in futility. Sane voices speak out from time to time for a more rational course of action.[145] But nobody listens. There is political capital in fighting a war on drugs. A number of states have relaxed their sanctions against use of marijuana.[146] But few public figures dare speak out for legalization of hard drugs, or even for a healthy debate on the subject. Draconian force is the only language the drug enforcers speak. Mothers who smoke crack are arrested. Dealers and users by the thousands are swept up off the streets. Many people sincerely believe that addicts are responsible for most of our violent crime: they rob to get money for a high; and on this high they rape and rob and kill, wantonly, cruelly. Certainly, turf wars and drug deals add hundreds of victims to urban slaughter. Force generates force; war breeds counterwar. The prisons are jammed top to bottom with men and women convicted under drug laws.* Is this really the only way?

---

* Between 1947 and 1950, an average of 115 prisoners entered California prisons annually on drug charges; the figure for 1985 was 3,609; for 1990, 13,741.[147]

16

THE MECHANICS OF POWER: SOME TWENTIETH-CENTURY ASPECTS

The Modern Police

The master trend in police history has been toward what we have called, somewhat loosely, professionalization. It is no longer the case that anybody who knows an alderman and is young and reasonably healthy can become a police officer. Even in the nineteenth century, there was a trend toward upgrading police work, training the men, and holding them to certain standards. This trend continued in the twentieth century. Police work has also become far more specialized.

The job itself got harder, more complex. For one thing, as time went on, there was more to it than strolling around the streets with a billy club. The old-time policeman or detective did not have to know much of anything about crime-fighting devices. There was no such thing as forensic science. There were no radios, no telephones, no equipment of any kind. Scientific detection was, essentially, a twentieth-century invention. The Bertillon system (as we have seen in chapter 10) came in toward the end of the nineteenth century in Europe; and fingerprinting followed close on its heels. A detective from Scotland Yard demonstrated the technique at the St. Louis World's Fair, in 1904. St. Louis established the first fingerprint bureau in America.[1]

The automobile also had an important impact on the policeman. The ordinary cop had once simply trudged his way through his "beat"; by the 1960s, he (or she) was far more likely to be sitting in a patrol car—so much so, that in the eighties there was a move to get the police out of their cars and back onto the sidewalks. Radios, telephones, and walkie-talkies became standard equipment for police. In the early thirties, systems of radio communications were set up in cities all over the country. In 1934, Cincinnati established a modern crime laboratory, with ballistics equipment, X ray, and a polygraph, among other things. In 1935, the police department of Kansas City, Missouri, put two-way radios into patrol cars.[2]

Inevitably, such "improvements" changed the nature of police work. A cop on foot was a familiar cop, a neighborhood cop; he knew his beat, and the beat knew him. He was also pretty much on his own. Headquarters was far away; he was beyond its beck and call. But now a ton or more of steel separated the motorized officer from the community; police cruising in patrol cars were strangers to the dark, dangerous streets; these police tended to feel alien, beleaguered; the locals, for their part, thought of them as an outside, occupying force.

A policeman in a car, moreover, was, for the most part, a "reactive" patroller. He went where he was "dispatched." Mr. and Ms. Public called the police, perhaps on an emergency line. Headquarters radioed to officers in cars, telling them where they were needed. Consequently, the police spent less time "trawling" for drunks, disorderly persons, and the like.[3] At the same time, the new communications technology made it easier for headquarters to control and to monitor patrolmen from a distance. Rank and file police drew closer to headquarters, but further psychologically and socially from the men, women, and children in the area they were supposed to patrol.[4]

This increase in social distance was in a way inevitable. Technology should not get all the blame. Americans have always been rolling stones. In the twentieth century, more and more, they tended to roll from the countryside into the big cities; and from neighborhood to neighborhood, and city to city. It was a transient population, more and more suspicious of authority. Police were especially distant, socially speaking, from the folks who lived in the most crime-ridden and problematic areas. They were also likely to be a different race.

This social distance was magnified by other ways in which the police became more professional: police had to be better educated, and they had to pass tests, like other civil servants. They had to know something about their jobs. In the first decades of the century, August Vollmer, Po-

lice Chief of Berkeley, California, was a leader in the movement to up-
grade the quality of the police. In 1916, Vollmer developed the "first formal academic law-enforcement program," at the University of California at Berkeley. The program began to turn out "college cops" for
Vollmer at a time when most policemen did not even have a high school
diploma.[5]

One of Vollmer's most notable disciples was O. W. Wilson. He embodied the mixture of practical experience and university training that
Vollmer pioneered. Wilson, the son of a Norwegian-American lawyer,
started out as a patrolman in Berkeley. In 1928, he took over the police
department of Wichita, Kansas, where he battled against corruption and
preached the gospel of motorized patrol cars. At various times in his career he taught at Berkeley and Harvard, and served as a consultant to a
flock of police forces.[6] In 1960, in the wake of a police scandal that was
sordid even by Chicago standards, Mayor Richard Daley appointed Wilson superintendent of police with the mandate to clean out the Augean
stables of Chicago's force.[7]

Professionalizing did not come easily; or at one great gulp. An important aspect of the process was to cut the cords that tied the police to
local politicians. The days when aldermen simply signed men up passed
into history. The police became part of the civil service in New York in
1883, in Chicago in 1895. By 1915, 122 of the nation's 204 largest police
departments were under civil service.[8] Of course, the requirements of
the job were not that onerous. In Boston, in 1930, a budding policeman
had to be not less than twenty-five nor more than thirty-five years old,
"not less than 5 feet 8 inches in height in bare feet," and "not less than
135 pounds without clothing." Boston also required at least an elemen-
tary school education, with extra points for anything beyond that. Of
course, the policeman also had to pass a civil service exam.[9]

Despite these trends, the old problems still haunted the police: problems of discipline, graft, and corruption—and of police brutality. The
Wickersham Commission, in its report on the police, more than thirty
years after the Lexow Commission (see chapter 7), recommended an end
to the "corrupting influence of politics"—a pious recommendation unlikely ever to be fully realized. The commission called for better training, advanced technology, good record-keeping, and state bureaus of
criminal investigation and information.[10] A lot was done over the years
along these lines, but politics, graft, and corruption could not be exor-
cised with incantations, nor even with moderate reforms.

Some of the reasons are hardly mysterious. There is a deep hunger for
the illegal, and a lot of money chasing illegality—the most obvious case
is drugs; and there are whole communities where support for official
norms, and for what the police *have* to do, is shallow or downright nega-

tive. Under such conditions, a department of the pure and uncorrupt cannot exist.

Another issue is the norms of the police themselves. The police are a tight, beleaguered group. They develop their own subculture, and it is a subculture of tough, macho conservatism. There are few card-carrying members of the American Civil Liberties Union among the police. The police do dirty, dangerous work, and they can hardly be expected to smother their "enemies" with empathy. They see human beings at their worst, and that certainly colors their philosophy of life.

They also believe in fighting fire with fire. Police brutality was part of a more general system of police power. It rested on a simple credo: the battalions of law and order had the right, if not the duty, to be tough as nails with criminals. Force was the only language the criminal understood. Force was also necessary in self-defense, when "dealing with thugs and gunmen," as the mayor of New York put it in December 1914. How this worked out in practice is suggested by a minor incident that month: Patrolman McCloy, in Brooklyn, ran up against an eighteen-year old no-good, Peter Gaimano, who struck at him with a blackjack and ran. McCloy caught up with Gaimano and his cronies, and wielded his nightstick to "good advantage." He "dragged Gaimano to the street, and was on his way to the station house when the gangsters seemed to swarm from all directions. He used his night stick so efficiently that the ruffians fled." But all this time Gaimano was "unconscious" and had to be hospitalized.[11] An outside observer might wonder whether McCloy hadn't used a bit more force than was called for. The police also carried guns, and were not afraid to use them on "thugs."

Police brutality has a long, dishonorable history, not only on the street, but also in the station house. Here was the domain of the "third degree"—various ways of getting information out of suspects by inflicting "suffering, physical or mental."[12] This rather bland phrase conceals a whole world of torture and abuse—beatings with nightsticks and rubber hoses, and sometimes worse. Perhaps one of the most gruesome examples, if the account can be trusted, comes from the twenties in New York City. The police had before them a burly man, a Polish-American, strongly suspected of beating another man to within an inch of his life. The rubber hoses were getting the police exactly nowhere. So they called in a dentist, a "police buff," who "carefully selected an old dull drilling burr and began slowly drilling into the pulp chamber of a lower rear molar in the region of a nerve." This technique did the trick; the accused began to sing.[13]

Commission followed commission, investigation followed investigation; but brutality always managed to survive. The Wickersham Commission devoted one of its reports ("Lawlessness in Law Enforcement") to the problem of brutality and the third degree. The commission documented and exposed many horrible examples. But it was not easy to attack the police ethos, to puncture the subculture, or to convince the police that force was unnecessary. Moreover, the police enjoyed an enormous amount of discretion as far as the lower levels of society were concerned. Southern blacks were always fair game. And what the police did to drunks, hoboes, and the poor in general was largely invisible. It happened in the back alleys, in the station houses, on the streets, out of sight of the bright lights and boulevards of due process. In the realm that was theirs, the police *were* the law; they beat, they harassed, they hounded drunks, prostitutes, bums. And they arrested thousands of men and women every year for vagrancy, loitering, and similar "crimes"; or simply hauled them in "on suspicion."

Often, there was no legal basis for these dragnet and residual arrests. In 1930, a New York businessman, a Mr. Turner, went to Dallas on business. He tried to make a phone call from a public phone booth; the line was busy. He went to a second booth, then a third—still busy. A policeman watched him go from booth to booth and decided the man was a thief: he "had entered three booths—he must have been pilfering nickels." Turner was arrested—over his protest, of course—and held incommunicado for forty-eight hours. He was, "to all intents and purposes," simply "kidnapped."[14]

After this unpleasantness, the police let Turner go; but unlike the thousands of drunks and vagrants, he screamed bloody murder. It turned out that the Dallas police had arrested 8,526 people in 1929 "on suspicion"; less than 5 percent of them were charged with a crime. There was something of a public scandal over this "trial-and-error" style of crime control, but the police chief of Dallas was baffled by the uproar. What was all the fuss about? The practice, he admitted, "is not legal. But," he added, apparently without any sense of irony, "illegality is necessary to preserve legality."[15]

At the turn of the century, a police captain told young Cornelius Willemse, new on the New York City police force, that his job was to "protect the good people and treat the crooks rough." The nightstick was not to be used on "inoffensive citizens," but rather on "thieves and crooks." As to "real bad crooks," any force was justified: "They're enemies of society and our common foe."[16] The rules of restraint, in short, did not apply to these "crooks"; or, for that matter, to scum of all sorts. There seems little doubt that most of the white, middle-class public agreed with this (and still does). It is what one might call the "sausage theory" of law and order: so long as the taste is good and the results are right, we would just as soon stay out of the kitchen and not know what went into the sausage.*

Or perhaps it is another example of the double standard in criminal justice. But this two-faced system was not a historical accident, and to call it "hypocrisy" is no help in understanding it. It is a system of social control, a system that demands high ideals; but at the same time demands deviations from those very same ideals—for a good reason of course. It also assumes (unconsciously) that the criminal justice system is better off with a double system, than at either alternative pole: the pole of pure due process, that is, the pole of the bleeding hearts; and the pole of the raw and brutal "police state."

The double standard was at work in many, though not all, police functions. It was very noticeable in the "trawling" function—keeping order in public places. There was less of a double standard for traffic crimes and traffic control—that staple of twentieth-century police work—partly because drivers of cars were, on the whole, the better class of citizen. Even when dealing with drunks, the police were often careful to distinguish between respectable drunks, middle-class men on a binge; and the dirty common drunk.

Police work was thus drenched through and through with class consciousness. Leonhard Fuld, writing in 1909, deplored the fact that even "the most highly respectable member of the community, of exemplary character, habits, and associations," ran the danger of arrest on a misdemeanor charge, which meant placement in a "station-house cell together with felons, drunkards, and men guilty of every vice. A night spent in such surroundings will inflict more hardship and suffering upon an honest man than almost any indignity to which he might be subjected."[17] In fact, police departments (and police courts) tried to avoid undue discomfort to the comfortable classes. One example illustrates this point. In San Diego, California, in 1915, when drunks were arrested, and held overnight, they went to "Sunrise Court." Here, if they had no police record or prior convictions, and if they had a job and family, they were released. The rest, of course, were tramps or bums or drunkards, and they got quite different treatment.[18]

Personnel

In the twentieth century, there were major changes in police organization and personnel. We have already noted that police were put under civil service and made to pass tests and get training. For their part, the police

---

* Lynne Henderson suggested this very apt metaphor to me.

began to form unions in some cities. In the late nineteenth century, there had been a certain number of "benevolent societies" and fraternal organizations among the police. But only in 1919 did the American Federation of Labor (AFL), under "grassroots pressure," endorse the idea of actual unions for police. The AFL quickly chartered some thirty locals.[19]

But the course of police unionism did not run smooth. In Boston, the police, to the disgust of city officials, went over to the union. On September 9, 1919, most of the men walked off the job.[20] This was the famous Boston Police Strike. It caused a tremendous furor. While the cat was away, some mice went in for looting and violence. Newspapers all over the country hysterically magnified what was happening in Boston. The *San Francisco Examiner* cried out "Gangs Range Streets, Women Are Attacked, Stores Are Robbed"; the *Wall Street Journal* went so far as to predict that "Lenin and Trotsky [were] on their way."[21] In Boston, a volunteer force, including students and faculty from Harvard, tried to fill the gap, and Governor Calvin Coolidge called out the militia. The strike was smashed, the strikers lost their jobs, and Coolidge went on to the White House, where he compiled an enviable record of torpor. The union movement suffered a setback it took decades to recover from.[22]

In one important regard, police in the twentieth century did draw closer to local communities and the general population. For a long time, the stereotype of a policeman had been the Irish cop: very male, very white. In the nineteenth century, a certain number of "matrons" had been attached to the police; but women on the regular force were out of the question. Mrs. Lola Baldwin, of Portland, Oregon, early in the twentieth century, was apparently the first non-male to serve as a regular member of a police force. In 1910, Los Angeles took the plunge: Mrs. Alice Stebbins Wells joined the department. Mrs. Wells took an active role in the national movement to add women to the ranks of the police.[23] By 1914, the Los Angeles department had eight policewomen.[24]

Many other cities hired women after 1910, but the numbers were typically very small, and nowhere were they accepted as equals of men. Mostly they worked with young offenders, or with women in trouble; sometimes they patrolled dance halls and penny arcades—places where young people might congregate. Mary Hamilton, the first policewoman in New York, wrote that "Danger lurks in parks, playgrounds, beaches, piers, and baths unless there is someone to watch over these pleasure haunts experienced enough in recognizing a devastating evil."[25] Women had "peculiar value . . . as preventive agents in working with women and girls."[26] With such an attitude, of course, the movement stagnated. A survey in 1946 found that only 141 out of 417 key cities had any policewomen at all.[27] In 1968, however, Indianapolis broke the final taboo: it assigned two women to regular patrol duty.[28] Since then, there has been steady progress, but policing remains essentially a man's job, and the world of the police remains a man's world.

It was a slow process, too, to open up the force to blacks and members of other minorities. In 1930, blacks made up about 4 percent of the force in Philadelphia, 2 percent in Pittsburgh and Chicago, 1 percent or less in a number of cities, including Cleveland, Detroit, and New York.[29] This situation seemed glaringly out of tune in the period after *Brown v. Board of Education.* The combination of a strong civil rights movement and the mass migration of blacks from the rural South finally brought about change in the composition of police forces, as we shall see.

Hiring women and blacks—and Hispanics, Chinese, and even openly gay officers—was more than a sop to demography. It was at least potentially a minor coup d'état within the police. The police entered the twentieth century as an army against crime and the criminal class; they took their norms and values in part from the respectable elites, in part from the macho, working-class white culture of which they were a part. A mere sprinkling of blacks and women here and there probably had little effect on the normative world of the police. Corruption and brutality remained, along with racism and a ragbag of social prejudices. But personnel changes in the seventies and eighties carried at least the *promise* of a more accountable, more heterogeneous force. Unfortunately, as the police got (somewhat) better, the criminals got worse; and this no doubt had a curdling effect on the norms and culture of the people in blue.

Political Crime

In one stretched-out sense, many or most crimes are political: they are conscious or unconscious acts of rebellion against the duly constituted order. A few crimes have deliberately political motives, although the crime itself is not what people usually call political. An occasional revolutionary or terrorist might want to blow up a government office, or rob a bank to pay for the expenses of terror. There has been less of this in the United States than in most countries—certainly less than the hysteria over "reds" or "anarchists" or "Wobblies" would suggest. On the whole, though, few crimes are meant to be deliberate attacks on the political or economic system, or on some piece of it, or on the rules and norms that undergird that system.

There is another kind of political crime. All governments, alas, seem tempted to make it a crime to be part of the opposition. In many societies, to criticize the government is to sign one's own death warrant. The United States has a far better record than most countries at putting up with dissenters, but the record is far from perfect.

Wars and national crises are particularly bad times for freedom of speech and the right to protest. Toleration wears thin during emergencies; civil liberties go out the window. During the Civil War, Abraham Lincoln's record was hardly ideal. He suspended the writ of habeas corpus, and there was far too much military justice (or injustice).[30] To a degree, this was understandable. After all, the Civil War was a massive rebellion: half the country consisted of traitors (from the northern standpoint), and the fighting raged on American soil. It was a uniquely dangerous war.

The first World War should have been much better. Yet in June 1917, Congress passed an elaborate Espionage Act; an amendment to the act, in 1918, outlawed sedition—it was a crime to "incite or attempt to incite" insubordination or disloyalty among soldiers and sailors; or to utter, print, or publish "any disloyal, profane, scurrilous or abusive language about the form of government of the United States; or the Constitution;" or to come out with any "language intended to incite, provoke, or encourage resistance to the United States or to promote the cause of its enemies."[31]

The excuse was the war; and the war certainly legitimized a campaign against internal enemies. The statutes were, in a real sense, merely part of a longer campaign against radicals, especially the "Wobblies," members of the Industrial Workers of the World.[32] The first notable cases on freedom of speech before the U.S. Supreme Court grew out of the purge of leftists that followed passage of these laws. In *Schenck v. United States* (1919)[33], Socialists had been tried for mailing circulars to men about to join the army. The circulars passionately argued that the draft violated the Constitution, and that the war was a conspiracy of capitalists and politicians. The defendants were charged under the Espionage Act and convicted. They appealed, and lost; as a consolation prize, Oliver Wendell Holmes, Jr., enunciated one of the most famous phrases in Supreme Court history. Freedom of speech, he said, does not encompass "words . . . used in such circumstances and . . . of such a nature as to create *a clear and present danger* that they will bring about . . . substantive evils that Congress has a right to prevent" (emphasis added).[34]

Abrams v. United States (1919)[35] was an appeal brought by Jacob Abrams and some associates who had been arrested for distributing leaflets (in English and Yiddish) that attacked President Wilson as a hypocrite and argued that "allied capitalism" wanted to "crush" the Russian Revolution. The Supreme Court affirmed their conviction. Only Holmes and Brandeis dissented; Holmes, in his opinion, reminded the majority that "time has upset many fighting faiths" and that "the best test of truth is the power of the thought to get itself accepted in the competition of the market." But Abrams and his friends went to prison because of their "fighting faiths."[36]

Paranoia swept the country during the war; dissent was simply not tolerated. In 1918, John Fontana, a Lutheran minister in Salem, North Dakota, was indicted under the Espionage Act. He stood accused of interfering with the military and naval forces of the country, causing mutiny, and obstructing the draft. All this in darkest North Dakota. Fontana, it seems, was pro-German; he thought the sinking of the *Lusitania* was justified, prayed for the success of the German armies, and told people not to buy Liberty Bonds. Or so it was alleged. Moreover, in his church, people said, "Old Glory" was "not to be seen nor . . . the Star Spangled Banner heard." A federal district court jury found Fontana guilty. The judge thundered at him that Fontana had "cherished foreign ideals. . . . That is the basic wrong of these thousands of little islands of foreigners that have been formed through our whole limits. . . . They have striven . . . to make foreignness perpetual. That is disloyalty." Fontana got three years in the federal prison at Leavenworth.[37]

After the war, the struggle against radicals continued, but with a somewhat different excuse. Bolshevism replaced Kaiser Wilhelm as the main target. This was the period of the infamous "red scare" and the so-called Palmer raids. On January 2 and 6, 1920, agents of the Department of Justice, under orders from Attorney General A. Mitchell Palmer, arrested thousands of members of the Communist and Communist Labor parties in raids across the country.[38] There was hardly a shred of justification for these raids, and nothing about the raids even remotely resembled due process. But millions of Americans seemed to support the plan to get rid of filthy, bomb-throwing, dangerous, alien reds.

It was an age of ultra-Americanism, not to say jingoism; an age of flag-waving. The flag, of course, had to be the American flag; in fact, any other flag was legally suspect. Only the Stars and Stripes, and flags of the state, could be carried in a parade or "publicly displayed," according to an Arizona law of 1919. It was, in fact, a crime to display other, offensive flags, or parade around with them; specifically *verboten* was any "red or black flag, or banner, with or without any letters, inscription or design thereon."[39] Arizona was not alone; twenty-four states passed red-flag laws in 1919, and another flock of eight followed suit in 1920.[40]

But flag laws were small potatoes. Many states passed more stringent and far-reaching laws against radicals, Bolsheviks, and the like. Idaho began a trend in 1917 when it enacted a law against "criminal syndicalism." This, according to the statute, was the "doctrine which advocates crime, sabotage, violence, or unlawful methods of terrorism as a means of accomplishing industrial or political reform." Anyone who advocated such things, "by word of mouth or writing," or justified such acts, or organized "any society, group or assemblage of persons formed to teach or advocate ... criminal syndicalism," was guilty of a felony. The punishment could be as much as ten years in prison.[41] Within a year, six states passed similar legislation. And in 1919, California, egged on by the rabid propaganda of Harrison Gray Otis of the *Los Angeles Times*—and even more so by the fallout from a bomb that went off on the governor's back porch—passed its own version, so that any attempt to justify "criminal syndicalism ... by spoken or written words," or to put out any book, pamphlet, or poster advocating or abetting this dreaded doctrine, was a crime.[42]

The *Oakland Tribune* applauded this law, because it allowed a "summary policy ... toward dynamiters, Bolshevists, I.W.W. and the whole brood of anarchists. It should be enough to know of their general tendency and sentiments without having to fasten specific crimes upon them." So much for due process. In fact, the statute did not sit rusting on the shelf. During its years of vigor, 531 men and women were charged with violating this law, and 264 were actually tried. Of these, 164 defendants were convicted and 31 acquitted; sixty-nine trials resulted in a hung jury. No less than 52 of the convictions, however, were reversed by the Court of Appeal, and 2 by the California Supreme Court.[43]

The most notorious case, and the only one to reach the U.S. Supreme Court, was *Whitney v. California.*[44] This was an appeal brought by Charlotte Anita Whitney, a strong, outspoken woman active in "progressive" political circles in California. Ms. Whitney had been at a convention in Oakland, which aimed to organize a California branch of the Communist Labor Party. The convention adopted a rather militant platform; ironically, Ms. Whitney was opposed to this platform. But she stuck with the party nonetheless. She was arrested—and convicted—for violating the syndicalism act. She appealed all the way to the Supreme Court; but lost again. A state, said the Supreme Court, had the power to punish those who "abused" the rights of free speech, assembly, and association "by joining and furthering an organization" that menaced the "peace and welfare of the State."

The state of Georgia, for its part, dusted off an old statute (dating from the late 1860s), which made it a crime punishable by death (!) to incite "insurrection" against Georgia. "Circulating insurrectionary literature" was also a serious crime under this law and carried a long prison term. The assistant solicitor general of the state, John H. Hudson, a rabid red-baiter, unearthed this draconian gem, and from 1930 on used it to arrest and try members of the Communist Party and other such menaces to Georgia. In 1932, Angelo Herndon, a nineteen-year-old black man, who was indeed a member of the party, was arrested and tried. Hudson, with tears in his eyes, demanded the death penalty. He begged the jury to "send this damnable anarchistic Bolsheviki to his death by electrocution."[45] Herndon was convicted, and thrown into prison. Only after a long and tortuous legal struggle did the U.S. Supreme Court strike down the Georgia statute, in a five-to-four decision.*

The Herndon case had a double aspect. Yes, Herndon was a "red"; but in some ways the more important color was black. The white South was particularly fierce and unyielding toward those who dissented from the code of white supremacy. Herndon called on the black masses to rise up against white domination—with the help of the Communists, of course. This call to blacks was his real sin, or, at any rate, his worst sin; and it was this that got him to prison.

Political Justice and "Ordinary" Crime

So far we have discussed mostly cases in which political action was it-self the offense. Yet perhaps the most famous "political" trial of the twentieth century, the Sacco-Vanzetti case, was of a somewhat different nature. On April 15, 1920, a holdup took place in Braintree, Massachu-setts. A paymaster and his guard were robbed and shot to death. The brutal killers made their getaway by car. According to witnesses, there were two gunmen, and five men all told in the car. All but one were dark and looked Italian.[47]

Nicola Sacco, and Bartolomeo Vanzetti, Italian anarchists—a shoe-maker and a fish peddler by trade—were arrested and charged with the crime. The sensational trial ended in conviction and a sentence of death for both men. Felix Frankfurter (then a professor at Harvard Law School) took up their cause, and leftists the world over lionized Sacco and Vanzetti. The case became the American equivalent of the Dreyfus case.† The governor of Massachusetts appointed an advisory committee, headed by Abbott Lowell, president of Harvard, to review the evidence. The Lowell Committee endorsed the work of the trial court and pro-claimed that Sacco and Vanzetti were guilty. The two men were put to death. That was, however, hardly the end of the affair. Their "linked names have continued to echo across the years," as a kind of "symbol of man's injustice to man."[48] But were Sacco and Vanzetti actually guilty? If not, then American justice was guilty—of prejudice, of political bias, and of executing two innocent men. The question has never been fully

---

* The statute interfered with freedom of speech, among other things. As construed, it was a "dragnet which may enmesh anyone who agitates for a change of government"; and it was too "vague and indeterminate" in setting boundaries to freedom of speech.[46]

† This was, of course, the celebrated case that tore France apart politically at the end of the nineteenth century. Dreyfus was an army officer, and a Jew; he was (falsely) ac-cused of treason, convicted, and eventually exonerated.

and totally resolved; it may be that at least one of them *was* guilty; perhaps we will never know.

Political Justice: World War II
and Beyond

The hysteria level during the Second World War seemed to be considerably lower than during the first. There were no roundups of American Bolsheviks—the Bolsheviks, after all, were America's allies. The worst blot on the country's record was the shameful treatment of the Japanese on the West Coast. President Roosevelt signed an executive order authorizing the roundup of more than 100,000 Japanese-Americans (most of them citizens) for internment in camps in the desert. The justification was, to say the least, flimsy. These citizens and residents never faced trial, never had hearings on charges of disloyalty, and were nonetheless severely punished without a shred of due process. A racist odor hung over the whole business: General John DeWitt, head of the West Defense Command and the main architect of the program, felt that "a Jap is a Jap"; he was not inclined to make fine distinctions between spies and loyal citizens.[49] In *Korematsu v. United States*,[50] a supine Supreme Court, citing (baseless) fears of "an invasion of our West Coast," upheld the detention of the West Coast Japanese on grounds of military necessity, or, more accurately, the Court's unwillingness to overrule or second-guess "the war-making branches of the Government."

The war was also the excuse for declaring martial law in Hawaii. On December 7, 1941, the army suspended the regular courts and provided for a "military commission" to try cases of treason, sabotage, murder, and other major crimes. The commission tried only a few cases, but the "provost courts," also dominated by army officers, enforced "the whole range of military regulations" as well as "trials for felonies and misdemeanors under territorial and federal laws, which were continued in effect by military orders."[51] There were no jury trials. The average trial took five minutes or less, and the verdict was guilty in 99 percent of the cases. Many of the sentences were, by legal standards, bizarre: compulsory purchase of war bonds in lieu of a fine, or mandatory donation of blood.[52]

During the war itself, there were relatively few trials for treason, espionage, or sabotage. Afterwards, there were a certain number of arrests and trials for treason and treasonlike behavior. The poet Ezra Pound was indicted, but found incompetent to stand trial. Iva d'Aquino was tried for treason in 1949; she was, supposedly, the legendary "Tokyo Rose," who broadcast propaganda in English, from Radio Tokyo, to American troops in the Far East. The evidence against her was rather flimsy, but a jury convicted her of one count of treason, and she was sentenced to ten years in prison and fined $10,000.[53]

At the end of the war, there was no red scare—at first. But the honeymoon did not last. The Cold War broke out only a few years after the hot war ended, and it ushered in an era of loyalty oaths, witch-hunting, and a general purge of radicals and rumored radicals. In the overheated atmosphere, charges and countercharges were flung about. Senator Joseph McCarthy made a career out of reckless, lying accusations of disloyalty and treason; McCarthyism poisoned the air in politics, in the universities, and in the arts with its mindless paranoia. The attorney general drew up a list of subversive organizations. Communists and fellow-travelers, or alleged ones, were hounded out of their jobs; state and federal governments tried to destroy the power of any institution that they labeled leftist, or leftist-run.[54] It became a replay of the hyper-American jingoism of the original "red scare."

The Smith Act of 1940 made it a crime to preach or teach in favor of overthrowing the government by force. In 1948, the government pressed for indictments against leaders of the American Communist Party. A federal grand jury handed down twelve indictments. A bitter, heated trial in Foley Square (New York City) dragged on for nine months.[55] The jury convicted all twelve defendants, and the judge, Harold Medina, added insult to injury by ordering the defense lawyers to prison for contempt of court. Whatever the merits of Medina's action, it certainly did nothing to abate the atmosphere of political intimidation; the bar, after the judge's contempt action, started disciplinary proceedings of its own against the lawyers. All of this sent out a clear message: in repressive times, a lawyer who represented "subversives" and other unpopular defendants would be tarred by the very same brush.[56]

The Smith Act defendants, naturally, appealed their convictions. They claimed (among other things) that the Smith Act was unconstitutional. In a split decision, *Dennis v. United States*, the Supreme Court ruled against them. "We reject," said Chief Justice Vinson, "any principle of governmental helplessness in the face of preparation for revolution."[57]

The Smith Act convictions, the vendetta against leftist lawyers, the McCarthyite purges, no doubt had a chilling effect on radical thought and action. Indeed, that was the point. How much of an effect is impossible to tell; but it was certainly risky to come out with ideas that were too far to the left, or which challenged the anticommunist orthodoxy. Indeed, it was unpopular to espouse radical ideas of any sort. The crusade against communism was a convenient weapon against other social movements—movements for racial equality, for example.

The *Dennis* case was not the only political trial of the period. But in retrospect, it was, legally speaking, something of a climax (or nadir).

Prosecutions against left-wing groups had decidedly mixed results. The government lost quite a few of them. The red scare gradually lost its virulence. The Warren Court, not surprisingly, had no taste for *Dennis*-like cases. In *Yates v. United States* (1957),[58] the Court reversed the Smith Act convictions of a flock of leaders of the Communist Party of California. The court did not overrule *Dennis*; it claimed *Dennis* was distinguishable. But subtle differences in doctrine hardly mattered; the tone and the politics did. In *Brandenburg v. Ohio* (1969),[59] the Court overruled the *Whitney* case and got rid of the laws against criminal syndicalism. These laws punished "mere advocacy"—and were thus unconstitutional.

There were also a handful of actual prosecutions for espionage, or arising out of espionage-like charges. There was the headline-grabbing trial (really, trials) of Alger Hiss (1949–1950), who either was or was not a Soviet agent; and who stood accused of perjury.[60] The most notorious of all was the trial of Julius and Ethel Rosenberg, arrested in 1950 and accused of conspiracy to commit espionage—specifically, that they passed nuclear secrets on to the Soviet Union. The trial took place in March of 1951; the jury found the Rosenbergs guilty, and on April 5, 1951, Judge Irving R. Kaufman sentenced them to death. The harsh sentence escalated what had already been a sensational case to the rank of worldwide controversy. Battle was joined on both sides; there were motions, writs, petitions, appeals, pleas for clemency—still, in a swirling storm of controversy, the Rosenbergs, husband and wife, died in the electric chair on June 19, 1953. The debate over their guilt or innocence goes on—perhaps it will never end—but the punishment, in retrospect, seems grossly disproportionate to what the Rosenbergs did, if they did anything, or to the harm their actions may have caused. Judge and jury were in the grip of Cold War hysteria; and to a great extent, so too was the population at large. They were the victim, too, of the American search for scapegoats. We "lost" China to communism; *somebody* must be responsible. We lost our nuclear monopoly; there must be some treachery afoot.

The war in Vietnam, in the 1960s, was, or became, the most unpopular war in American history. There was a vast protest movement, and defiance of military and civilian authorities reached epidemic proportions. This was the first war since the Civil War in which countless thousands of young men tried to wriggle out of the draft, or defied it, or burned draft cards, or fled to Canada, or fathered babies, or went to school—anything not to serve. The administrations of Lyndon Johnson and Richard Nixon fought back, with propaganda and criminal justice. A fair number of draft-dodgers and draft-card burners went on trial, along with protesters who blocked induction centers, destroyed draft records, and otherwise interfered with the conduct of the war and the raising of armies.[61]

These trials reaped meager results. In some cases, defendants were acquitted; some judges handed out very light sentences. Some of the trials were blatantly political—often because of the antics of the defendants themselves. Usually, it was the government that wanted legalism and formalism; many defendants were only too eager to make guerrilla theater out of their trials. The "Catonsville Nine," radical Catholics who had destroyed draft files, converted their trial—in Baltimore, in October 1968—into an inquisition on the war itself. They considered their trial "a victory of sorts," even though they were convicted, because they had made publicity for their cause and evoked discussion about the meaning of the war.[62]

Political Justice Today

Throughout American history, there has never been a time without political crimes and political trials. Yet after the Vietnam War, a kind of lull set in. In the nineties, it would be hard to find solid, undisputed examples of American political prisoners. Few if any people are in jail for sedition, revolutionary propaganda, or similar crimes against the authority of the state. Of course, zealots with political motives who break the law do suffer the consequences; a person who lobs a firebomb at an abortion clinic, or trashes a laboratory in the name of animal rights, is committing a *kind* of political crime; but it is a crime, after all, to throw a firebomb at anything or anybody, or to trash a store, whatever the motive. Fringe leftists and radical rightists who hole up in the hills with stocks of heavy ammunition; KKK members who harass blacks; "Aryans" who paint swastikas on Jewish gravestones—these are all political criminals, but their crimes fall within the ordinary scope of the criminal code.

Has the state learned, at long last, to tolerate dissent? Hard to say. The state is an abstraction; government is made up of men and women. The FBI and CIA appear to have calmed down somewhat, lately; the Soviet Union has shattered into pieces; no *major* movements on the right or the left are agitating for radical change. At the moment, all seems calm. But nobody knows what would happen if crisis stretched the fabric of legitimacy. There are no reds to touch off a new red scare; but history is very inventive. Who knows what devil may be at work, this very moment, manufacturing new agents down below? Another unpopular war; a wave of race-hate crimes; ethnic unrest; riots in the cities; massive unemployment—new dangers are certainly thinkable. And in every period of danger there emerges a bogeyman, and perhaps some real enemies of the state.

Society *has* changed, of course, and in a particular way. American society recognizes—has been forced to recognize—diversity, multiplicity of cultures, religions, ways of life, habits, behaviors, points of view. This weakens the whole notion of sedition. *Tolerance* is not the right word to describe the modern form of coexistence. *Tolerance* implies a kind of benign, saintlike patience and respect. The reality is far more tumultuous: submerged and dissident groups have grabbed for their place at the national trough, kicking and shoving and demanding. Older, weaker hegemonies get pushed to the side. New powers and new groups elbow their way into the limelight. This, at any rate, is the tendency. It is one more aspect of the massive cultural revolution of the twentieth century, one more aspect of the radical redefinition of the self. This tendency seems to be fatal to traditional forms of political crime and political criminalization.

Of course, criminal justice is and remains intensely political, in many senses of the word—perhaps even more so than in the past. A small but significant number of trials crackle with political electricity. Victim groups pack the courtroom and howl for blood. Adverse decisions lead to riots. The trial of Dan White, in San Francisco, was a good example. White had gunned down the mayor of San Francisco and also Harvey Milk, the city's first gay supervisor. He mounted a vigorous defense, and the jury bought into it—partly, at any rate. When White received a light sentence, San Francisco's gay community exploded; crowds rampaged through the city.[63] More recently, on April 29, 1992, a jury in Simi Valley, California, acquitted four Los Angeles police officers who had brutally beaten a black motorist, Rodney King. A "storm of anger" engulfed south-central Los Angeles; dozens of people died in the burning, looting, and wholesale vandalism that swept over the city in the next few days.[64] The politics of criminal justice was never more visible than in those nights of carnage.

Race and Criminal Justice

I have touched on the relationship between race and criminal justice at a number of points in this chapter. Race figures prominently in political justice: for example, in the *Herndon* and *Korematsu* cases, and certainly in what has come to be called "the Rodney King trial."

At the beginning of the twentieth century, most American blacks still lived in the southern states. These states were white-supremacy territory. The early years of the century were the high point of American apartheid. Black Americans did not and could not vote, and they were suppressed and oppressed in countless ways. The criminal justice system in the South was no friend of the southern black; the most that could be said for it is that extralegal "justice" (lynch law, for example) was even worse.

Gerard C. Brandon, of Natchez, Mississippi, was a rarity among white southern lawyers: he told the truth about southern justice. Addressing the Mississippi Bar Association in 1910, Brandon said that even slaves got more out of the courts than Mississippi blacks in his day. "It is next to an impossibility," he said, "to convict even upon the strongest evidence any white man of a crime of violence upon the person of a negro. . . . I have even heard attorneys make the appeal to a jury that no white man should be punished for killing a negro." The converse was equally true: "It is next to an impossibility to acquit a negro of any crime of violence where a white man is concerned."[65] A Southern chief of police put it even more bluntly around 1920: "We have three classes of homicide," he said. "If a nigger kills a white man, that's murder. If a white man kills a nigger, that's justifiable homicide. If a nigger kills another nigger, that's one less nigger."[66]

Apologists for the South insisted that southern courts were honest and fair, that there was equal justice for all in the South. This was, of course, a lie. These were white people's courts; they served white interests and white interests only. Blacks could have justice only when they did not threaten those interests; and white supremacy was the highest interest of all.[67] The *ideology* of equal justice seemed to be worth something to white southerners. But white supremacy was worth far more.

Change came about very slowly. There were campaigns against lynching, some based in the South itself, but these campaigns achieved little or nothing in the first half of the century.[68] Lynchers were never punished. And when lynching itself slid somewhat into decline, it was certainly not because of anything the criminal justice system did. In May, 1930, for example, a mob in Sherman, Texas, lynched George Hughes, a black farm laborer accused of raping the wife of his boss. This charge was probably baseless, but a mob set fire to the jail, and burned George Hughes to death. Afterward, his corpse was dragged to a cottonwood tree in the black section of town and burned again. And the police? They helped out by directing traffic.[69]

Lynching was outside the law, although the law did almost nothing about it. *Inside* the law was little better. It was the southern way of life to beat and brutalize black defendants. (The North was, of course, not blameless either.) In *Brown v. Mississippi* (1936),[70] the Supreme Court confronted a case in which black defendants, arrested on a charge of murder, confessed after deputy sheriffs beat them repeatedly with leather straps. The transcript of the case read "more like pages torn from some medieval account, than a record made within the confines of a modern civilization." In one revealing bit of testimony, a deputy sheriff, asked how severely he had whipped one defendant, answered, "Not too much for a negro." The Court reversed the convictions.

The notorious Scottsboro case (see chapter 14) was a sensation of the 1930s. Nine young black men were arrested and accused of raping two white women on a freight train rolling slowly between Chattanooga, Tennessee, and Huntsville, Alabama. The two "victims," Victoria Price and Ruby Bates, were portrayed as the flower of southern womanhood, in propaganda about the case, after it became notorious. (In fact, they were prostitutes.) More to the point, their stories were out-and-out lies. Ruby Bates later recanted. Victoria never did, but her story was a tissue of contradictions. It was obvious she was lying. In the event, that hardly mattered. After a brief trial, with the most feeble sort of defense, the "Scottsboro boys" were sentenced to death.[71]

This time, the case refused to die. Perhaps it was too blatant an example of Alabama justice. The Communist Party seized on the case, and rode it for all it was worth. Blacks and a few white liberals also joined the battle. The original judge, a fair-minded man, became convinced that the defendants were innocent. He ordered a new trial. A virulently racist judge replaced him. The second trial was grossly unfair. The defendants were convicted and sentenced to death—again. This case was appealed to the Supreme Court, which ordered a new trial. The defendants, said the Court, had never had effective counsel. This was, as we have seen, a landmark in constitutional law; but it did not end the defendants' ordeal.

On retrial, Samuel Leibowitz, the most famous criminal lawyer of the day (except perhaps for Clarence Darrow), came down to Alabama to fight for the lives of the defendants.[72] He was sure he could win; after all, he had an ironclad case. But he did not understand the code of the South. The jury convicted again. By now, the case had the status of legend; it was larger than life. The battle dragged on for years. Jury after jury convicted and sentenced to death. Every man on every jury was white, since no blacks were allowed on Alabama juries (this was not the law, but it was certainly the practice). Eventually, the state gave up on four of the defendants; and, in the end, all the "Scottsboro boys" went free. By that time, they had served, in the aggregate, more than a hundred years in jail for a crime they did not commit.

Why did the state of Alabama fight like a bulldog to put these young black men to death? There was a perverse kind of principle at stake. Many white southerners hardly cared whether the defendants were guilty or not. That was a secondary issue. The real issue for them was the southern caste system. They somehow believed it would fall apart like a house of cards if *any* black accused of assaulting *any* white (and especially a white woman) escaped extreme punishment.

Only since the fifties has the situation changed in substantial ways. The civil rights movement raised the national consciousness, or at least enough of it to make a difference. Black defiance and black insistence made an impact, South and North. There was, of course, no stampede toward racial justice. Thousands of blacks were arrested for marching, protesting, sitting in at segregated lunch counters; Martin Luther King, Jr., wrote his most famous letter to a group of white ministers from inside the Birmingham jail. Civil rights workers were harassed, and in a few cases, murdered. Their killers invariably went free.

But a second emancipation *did* come. Segregation fell; Congress passed important civil rights laws—and, what is more, there was public and private muscle to enforce these laws and to ensure the right of black people to vote. The Voting Rights Act of 1965 did make a difference. In the South in particular, blacks began to vote in sufficient numbers to put some black officials in office and a few black judges on the bench. Equally important, black voters made it costly for whites to run for office themselves on a race-baiting basis. As a result of the civil rights movement, and civil rights laws, blacks began to enter the courthouse through the front door, so to speak—that is, not just as victims and defendants, but as real players in the game: jurors, lawyers, police officers, and even judges. For the first time in American history, blacks had a say in running the system, a voice, though perhaps not loud enough—and a decent chance at race-blind, or race-neutral, justice.

The entry of blacks into the system, however, was hardly a mass movement. As noted above, black police were a small band, a handful, in northern cities in the 1930s, and there were none at all in the South. By the late sixties, their showing had improved, but not by very much: blacks made up only 11 percent of the police force in St. Louis, 10 percent in Newark, 5 percent in New York, 4 percent or less in Oakland, Boston, and Buffalo, and less than 1 percent in Birmingham, Alabama. Even in Washington, D.C., after a vigorous campaign to recruit black police in a city with a black majority, only about one-fifth of the force was black.[73] Even in the nineties, the numbers of black police in the cities fell far short of the numbers population figures would suggest.

Moreover, throughout the twentieth century, both before and after developments in civil rights, blacks have been arrested, convicted, and jailed entirely out of proportion to their share of the population. Southern chain gangs, as we have seen, were, to all intents and purposes, gangs of black semislaves. The chain gangs came and went, and blacks still constitute far more than their share of the prison population; they have done so for decades. Since 1933, the federal government's *Uniform Crime Reports* have kept track each year of the race of men and women arrested for serious crime. Blacks were arrested at a higher rate than whites even at the start; in 1940, 17 blacks per 1,000 were arrested, and only 6 whites. Arrest rates for both races have skyrocketed since 1933, but the gap remains, and it gets if anything wider. The figures for blacks are, indeed, staggering. (The white rates are also staggering; they seem small only by comparison.) In 1978, 35 whites out of every 1,000 were arrested; and almost 100 out of every 1,000 blacks—nearly one out of ten.[74]

Since few women get arrested, and since senior citizens also perform poorly in this department, it is no surprise that the rates of arrest, trial, conviction, and imprisonment among young black men are astronomical. In 1939, 26 percent of the prison population was black; in 1985, 46 percent.[75] In 1990, according to one report, nearly one out of every four men in this group (ages twenty to twenty-nine) was "under the control of the criminal-justice system on any given day"—23 percent of this age cohort were either actually in prison or jail, or on probation or parole.[76] Worse yet, a study of Washington, D.C., made public in 1992, found that in 1991, of the black men in that city between the ages of eighteen and thirty-five, no less than 42 percent were "enmeshed in the criminal justice system on any given day": 15 percent actually in prison, 21 percent on probation or parole, and 6 percent out on bond or "sought by the police." Seventy percent of the black men in the capitol city of the United States had been arrested by age thirty-five; about 85 percent "are arrested at some point in their lives."[77]

Does race discrimination, plain and simple, explain these horrific figures? In the years before the civil rights revolution, there was an enormous amount of discrimination, in the crudest, most obvious sense, especially in the South. Today, *overt* forms of discrimination have been wiped from the books. But slavery and oppression have left their mark; poverty and social disorganization hang like yokes of stone around the necks of the urban black poor. Draconian drug laws punish thousands of blacks who are trapped in the drug world or bent on self-destruction. These facts explain a good deal of the disparity; do they explain it all?

Are prosecutors and courts biased against blacks? This is not quite so easy to puzzle out. Dozens of studies have looked at sentencing practices, for example. Do blacks get worse treatment than whites, all other things being equal? The results of these studies have been mysteriously inconclusive. A fair number of scholars, searching for prejudice in the jungles of data, never find it. Other scholars do. Some researchers think that "discrimination has not gone away," that the legal system has simply "caused discrimination to undergo cosmetic surgery, with its new face deemed more appealing," that discrimination against blacks is pervasive but "subtle rather than overt."[78] But plenty of scholars can be found who disagree.

It is not easy to answer the question, not even easy to know what to measure, or how. Blacks tend to be poor; the middle class has grown nicely since the end of segregation, but a good third or more of the black population is stuck at the bottom of the economic and social heap. Criminal justice has always been biased against the underclass, the unattached, the unrespectable. What this may mean is that bias tends to be systemic, organic; not the crude race-hate of older days. Moreover, the general weakness in authority structures, the enthronement of the self, the glorification of the celebrity, the mass media culture—all these features of modern society are bound to create unrest, disorganization, and pathology in those who are stuck at the base of the social ladder.

It is less often recognized that blacks are disproportionately *victims* of crime as well. Most crime is neighborhood crime; blacks trapped by poverty in ghetttos are the most vulnerable people in society. Two blacks are likely to fall victim to robbery, vehicle theft, or aggravated assault for every white; the black homicide rate is more than six times as great as the white rate, and has been so for over fifty years.[79]

Blacks need police protection more than any other group, but do they get it? Police forces are integrated, more or less. Yet blacks are more dissatisfied with the police than whites. On the one hand, police persecute and brutalize blacks; and on the other hand, they ignore black complaints about crime. They let black communities stew in their own juices, essentially unprotected. These, at any rate, are common charges and they may well have substance. Certainly, studies of white policemen turn up substantial evidence of prejudice. And in 1991, the Rodney King episode exploded onto television screens. The public was shocked to see a group of police officers savagely beating and kicking a black man who had been stopped for speeding and who seemed to be supine and helpless.* Blacks were not surprised.[80]

In the last decade, there have been a number of serious examples of race-hate crimes. One of the most troubling was the Howard Beach incident in New York City in December 1986. Michael Griffith, a twenty-three-year-old black man, was unlucky: his car broke down in a white section of Queens. Griffith and his two passengers, also black, went to a pizzeria to phone for help. When they left, they were set on by a gang of whites, who beat Griffith with a baseball bat. Trying to get away, Griffith ran onto a busy highway; a car struck and killed him. Twelve white men were put on trial: three were acquitted; two pleaded guilty to riot charges; one pleaded guilty to assault; and five were convicted of various crimes—two of them of second-degree murder.[81]

The contemporary system of criminal justice does not satisfy either blacks or whites, though for different reasons. The huge black ghettos

---

* The police officers were unaware that someone in the neighborhood happened to catch the incident on his home video recorder.

seethe with rage and disaffection. Until fairly recently, "race riots" were riots *against* blacks; blacks were the victims, beaten, persecuted, sometimes hunted down and slaughtered. As late as 1943, twenty-five blacks (and nine whites) died in a race riot in Detroit.[82] Now the ghettos produce their own riots, riots of rage and desperation—for example, after the death of Martin Luther King, Jr., and following the acquittal of the men who beat Rodney King. Each time, the police (and perhaps the National Guard) moves in; peace is restored; the ruins smolder for a while; newspapers run long stories; yet somehow, in the end, the situation returns to what it was.* Whether the country will have the will and the skill to face up to the problems of crime, poverty, disorganization, and race remains to be seen.

A Rainbow of Minorities

In the period since the Second World War, there has probably been a general decline in the United States in outright prejudice against Asians—Chinese, Japanese, Koreans, Vietnamese, and others. Immigration laws no longer exclude Asians, and immigration from Asia has increased rapidly. The states no longer pass discriminatory laws. True, the Japanese economic miracle has evoked envy, and there have been some ugly incidents against Korean shopkeepers and Vietnamese shrimp fishers. It seems amazing now that, within living memory, a group of Asians was singled out in this country and thrown into camps—which happened, of course, to the Japanese during World War II.

In the United States, acceptance brings with it a measure of assimilation, and perhaps also an affection for certain specific American social ills. In the sixties and seventies, juvenile delinquency emerged as a serious problem in Chinatown. The Chinese were famous for the strength of family ties, but these bonds did not prevent teenage gangs from forming—gangs that terrorized the community and fought bitterly against each other. In September 1977, a Chinese gang shot up the Golden Dragon Restaurant in San Francisco; at least five customers, innocently having their meal, were slaughtered for being in the wrong place at the wrong time.† In Seattle, two Hong Kong immigrants killed thirteen older Chinese in 1983.[83]

American experience with its own indigenous populations has fol-

---

* Even the notorious Tawana Brawley episode, in 1987, underscores the point. Tawana Brawley, a young black woman, claimed she was the victim of white violence in Wappingers Falls, New York. She was almost certainly lying, but many blacks were ready to believe her because she told a story that could well have been true and all too often *was* true. On the case, see Robert B. McFadden et al., *Outrage: The Story Behind the Tawana Brawley Hoax* (1990).

† The intended targets were members of another gang, eating in the same restaurant.

lowed a jagged, unhappy course over the years. In the twentieth century, incidents of outright slaughter stopped; the native tribes had long since been defeated and herded onto remote reservations. But native peoples continue to suffer from a massive amount of social disorganization, and a massive degree of desperate poverty. As far as criminal justice is concerned, Native Americans who live among the Anglos are disproportionately arrested, tried, convicted, and jailed—just like blacks.

On the reservations, the situation is somewhat more complicated. The native peoples are separate "nations," and they have a certain amount of autonomy, although Congress has felt free at all times to encroach on it. Since the late nineteenth century, there have been Courts of Indian Offenses on the reservations; these were not "native" courts as such, but very much under the thumb of the Bureau of Indian Affairs. After the 1930s, more emphasis was placed on "tribal" courts; and the Courts of Indian Offenses were phased out.[84] These various courts dealt with minor crimes.[85] The exact boundaries between tribal law and general law remain indistinct, and somewhat controversial. The Indian Civil Rights Act of 1968 extended much of the Bill of Rights to the tribes: the privilege against self-incrimination and the rules about bail, cruel and unusual punishment, and double jeopardy. The writ of habeas corpus was also extended to persons detained "by order of an Indian tribe."[86] Unquestionably, the tribes today have more control over their own criminal affairs, and the upsurge of Indian nationalism has led some of them to explore their past in search of a lost or faded tradition of indigenous law.

The Spanish-speaking minority is large, getting larger, and developing an increasingly distinct sense of self. After the Mexican War (1848), the United States acquired a compact block of Spanish-speaking people, mostly in the Southwest. They were of a different race and culture from the white Americans living in the region, and they suffered a good deal of discrimination.[87] Their great-grandchildren, along with millions more who have poured over the border, form the Chicanos, that is, Americans of Mexican ancestry, clustered primarily in California and the Southwest. Chicanos are not the only Hispanics. There is a solid contingent of (mainland) Puerto Ricans, centered in New York City; Cubans, heavily concentrated in southern Florida; and an increasing number of immigrants from Honduras, Guatemala, the Dominican Republic, and other countries of Latin America. Hispanics are, on the whole, poorer than Anglos; some speak little or no English; they are, in many parts of the country, no strangers to severe disadvantage and outright discrimination.

A large bloc of Hispanics live in Los Angeles. There, as elsewhere, the police department has been overwhelmingly Anglo. Many people in the

Chicano community, like many in the black community, look on the police more as an alien or occupying army than as protectors of the peace. Indeed, the whole legal system is deeply suspect in the community. Prejudice burst into the open in 1942, in the so-called "Sleepy Lagoon case."[88] Twenty-two young Mexican men were arrested (and seventeen were convicted) on charges of conspiring to murder a man named Jose Diaz. The incident supposedly took place on August 2, 1942, near a reservoir whose nickname was Sleepy Lagoon. There is some question of what actually happened there. The trial was blatantly unfair; newspapers ran stories about "zoot-suit gangsters" and "pachuco killers." A captain in the Los Angeles Sheriff's Office solemnly reported to the grand jury that Mexicans had a "biological" tendency to violence. They were the descendants of "tribes of Indians" who were "given over to human sacrifice", in which bodies were "opened by stone knives and their hearts torn out while still beating." Mexicans had "total disregard for human life"; the Mexican, in a fight, will always use a knife; he feels "a desire . . . to kill."

The District Court of Appeals overturned the convictions, though not before the defendants had spent almost two years in San Quentin. The so-called zoot-suit riots began in June 1943, one year after the Sleepy Lagoon affair. "Zoot-suits," with peg bottoms, long coats, and exaggerated shoulder pads, were a fad among young Chicano men, though others wore them too. The riots were touched off in part by rumors that "zoot-suiters" had stabbed a sailor. Servicemen and off-duty policemen chased, beat, and stripped "zoot-suiters" in four consecutive nights of rioting.[89]

How much has changed since the 1940s? The city of Los Angeles, along with other large cities, has made an effort to hire more Spanish-speaking police, and to be more sensitive to the needs and wants of Hispanic communities. Two somewhat contradictory impulses underlie the change. On the one hand, Hispanic victim groups are disaffected, rights-conscious, despairing and defiant at one and the same time. Their anger is a potent source of unrest, sometimes boiling over into violence. But behind the rage is a burst of pluralist energy. Americans more and more recognize themselves—or are forced to recognize themselves—as a colorburst of race and ethnicity and culture; not so much a rainbow as a wild Jackson Pollock oil, a dazzling and confusing storm of elements. The result is a political and cultural balance that is volatile and dangerous. Yet the energy trapped within cultures is more than a source of rage: it also channels the rage, forces it into political directions, and, perhaps, helps to keep it from exploding.

17

THE CONTEMPORARY CRIMINAL TRIAL

IN THE TWENTIETH CENTURY, AS ENORMOUS CHANGE SWEPT OVER THE LEGAL system (and society), the organization of the criminal trial did not remain untouched. In many ways, however, the contours of an actual trial remained familiar. Rip van Winkle, waking up after a century asleep, might recognize the criminal trial more easily than most other situations, events, and institutions in society. He would be surprised, of course, to see women serving in novel roles. He would also be surprised at the rainbow of races he would see in many courtroom.

What he would *not* see is the non-trials. Most cases today never get to trial; they are shunted onto various sidetracks—usually plea bargaining. Proceedings in the twentieth century became even more sharply bifurcated than in the past: full-blown trials for the few, bargained justice for the many.

The Basement of Criminal Justice

It was still true in the twentieth century that there was no criminal justice *system* to speak of. Criminal justice was, rather, a hulking, headless creature, uncoordinated, with nobody really in charge. Each of its several layers had its own way of working, its own procedures, its own goals and strategies. At the bottom were, as before, the petty courts, processing cases by the thousands. Many defendants here were what Justice William N. Gemmill of the Municipal Court of Chicago, speaking in 1914, called "the army of defeat." These were "not men and women, but the remnants of them only"—people without "hope, pride, ambition, courage, self-sacrifice and all those qualities which distinguish the human from the animal world." Gemmill spoke of them with contempt, as an "army of derelicts," an "appalling menace"; they were shiftless, were "constantly on the move. . . . In the summer they sleep in parks, under sidewalks and along the wharfs. In the winter they hibernate in cheap lodging houses . . . upon beds of filth, vermin and disease, and from which they . . . carry contagion and death to the whole community." They were "driftwood cast upon a turbulent sea."*

Not everyone who was tried in petty courts was "driftwood." There were also plenty of weak reeds: people who got dead drunk or involved in a brawl, but who had social roots, a family, a job. These tended to be treated with a lot more indulgence. We have alluded to the San Diego "Sunrise Court" (chapter 16). Los Angeles, too, had a "Sunrise Court" between 1915 and 1918. It convened itself at 5:30 A.M., to process last night's drunks. There were many of these: in the year ending June 30, 1915, 185 men and women were arrested for intoxication—over one-third of all the arrests in the city. The "court" aimed to warn men about the "the evil of overindulgence and to release them, if they have work, so that they will not lose their jobs through their weakness." The "court" was, in the judgment of the police department, a great success: most people found "the humiliation of arrest and confinement in jail for a few hours" quite enough punishment; and the court "saved the job of many men and prevented their dependents being thrown on public charity."†

The petty courts pulled in what the nets of the police yielded, as they trawled public spaces, keeping order and punishing those who violated

---

* These people, "burned out with drugs and liquor, . . . friendless and homeless and hopeless," are sent to the Bridewell "because we have no other place to send them." They are not "criminal" by nature; but few of them "can ever be regenerated or restored, for no foundation is left upon which to build."[1]

† The Chief Jailer was in charge. In its first year, the Sunrise Court processed 15,797 men; about two-thirds of them were released. The procedure was simple: each man was "given a cup of black coffee and made to sign a book which [was] kept as a record." "Repeaters" and parole violators were kept in jail until the regular police court opened. Cases of "Mexicans" were "disposed of by officers who [spoke] their language." The "Sunrise Court" was in fact not a court at all; it was an institution run by Tom Murphy "of the Murphy family of temperance fame." Murphy, at his own expense, installed two "distinct features" in "Sunrise Court." One was a "sanitary fountain, that the men may reach immediately upon their release in the morning." The other was "hot black coffee," served up just before release.[2]

norms of decency and respectable behavior. These courts separated the wheat from the chaff—the "real" criminals, the worthless, the dregs of society, from those who had a passing weakness, or who got in trouble from drink. Basically, the petty courts were places of tawdry squalor. In big cities, there was a general air of corruption, decay, and dispirit. What newspapers once described with condescending humor could also be described with bitterness and disgust. In the 1950s, the Harrison Street branch of the Chicago Municipal Court was a kind of scene out of hell:

> The clamor is nerve racking. The section before the bench is jammed with policemen, lawyers, bondsmen, reporters, detectives, visitors. . . . During the entire session the bailiffs constantly rap for order and plead with the mob to move back from the bench. . . .
>
> The smoke is always thick, the noise deafening. People are whispering, laughing, talking, spitting. . . . Many cases are dismissed for want of prosecution because the complaining witness fails to hear the case called. . . .
>
> In the course of a year approximately twenty-five hundred felony cases pass through this court, along with panhandlers, vagrants, dope victims and dope peddlers, exhibitionists and sensitive and refined persons who have violated traffic laws. . . . The professional yeggman who is a grave menace to society is given as cursory treatment as the comparatively harmless vagrant picked up when the first snow falls. . . .
>
> Everyone seems to be trying to "get it over with. . . ." The judge seems harrowed beyond endurance. . . . The prosecutor . . . is the most casual person in the room. . . . Occasionally he barks out an impatient question, usually indicating irritation with the police officer. The latter, . . . cynical because he knows that nobody cares whether his case is dismissed or not, is as anxious as the judge to hurry through the formality of a public hearing.[3]

Yet these courts played an important social role. They handled a volume of cases. They were also the first stop on the road to felony justice. If they were corrupt and neglected, dirty and underfinanced, it was because that was the state of criminal justice in American society: a ramshackle house for the dregs of society. Judging from more recent descriptions—including such novels as *The Bonfire of the Vanities*—not much has changed since the fifties.

The petty courts have always operated well below the klieg lights of due process. Light began to shine into a few of the chinks of the system during the period of the Great Reform, which reached its highest *legal* expression in the days of the Warren Court. For years, vagrancy laws had been used to control deviants and undesirables; the general revolt of the underdogs, in the civil rights period, included an attack on these vague and offensive laws. In *Wheeler v. Goodman* (1969), for example, a federal case out of North Carolina, twelve young people of the type "commonly called 'hippies,'" who were living together in Charlotte, complained about police harassment. The police used vagrancy laws to arrest and persecute these undesirables. In general, the police used vagrancy laws for dragnet purposes; this was standard practice. But the court struck the law down; it was so vague that it gave no real notice of what the law required; and, what was more, it impinged on human freedom. To be forced to "conform to community behavior patterns is not liberty," said the court, "but state regimentation."[4*]

The Felony Trial

Trial, especially trial by jury, is what all of us think of when we think of felony procedures. But, in fact, the trial is the residue of a residue: it is a mechanism for handling survivors of a long filtering process. Not all serious criminals are caught; not all those who are caught are arrested; not all those who are arrested are charged; and most of those who are charged never reach trial—their cases are dropped, or they plead guilty.

The Illinois Crime Survey (1929) examined 16,812 cases that entered the system in 1926, in Chicago and a group of Illinois counties. Of those, 43.66 percent were eliminated in preliminary hearings; another 12 percent at the grand jury stage; another 23.66 percent fell by the wayside in the trial court itself—that is, they were dismissed or reduced to misdemeanors. Of the surviving cases, the vast majority turned into guilty pleas.[5] The New York Crime Commission reported in 1928 that "Of all felony cases originating in arrest in New York City, about two per cent are eliminated by the police, 57 per cent in the preliminary hearing, 12 per cent in the grand jury, 8 per cent in the trial court, and 5 per cent after guilt is established."[6]

In trials themselves, there have been some technical changes. I will mention one, which is symptomatic of broader streams of change. In a famous speech made in 1906, the legal scholar Roscoe Pound castigated the "sporting theory" of trial—a battle of wits between two lawyers who treat the "rules of law and procedure exactly as the professional foot ball coach [treats] . . . the rules of the sport."[7] This was before the appearance of a device called "discovery." The root idea of discovery is simple. Each side, in a civil case, is forced to tip its hand before the trial begins—through depositions and the exchange of documents and other information. The theory is to discourage surprise, save time for judges, litigants, and lawyers, and encourage settlements. From the 1930s on, the states and the federal government radically extended pretrial discovery.

---

* Vagrants included people "wandering or strolling about in idleness," and people who led "an idle, immoral or profligate life, who have no property to support them and who are able to work and do not work."

But what about criminal cases? Nobody seriously suggested giving the right of discovery to the prosecution. Should defendants and their lawyers have the right? Learned Hand, in 1923, expressed a conventional view: the defendant already had enough, or too much, "advantage." He already is "immune from question or comment on his silence" and could not be convicted "where there is the least fair doubt in the minds of any one of the twelve [jurors]." Procedure had always been "haunted by the ghost of the innocent man convicted. It is an unreal dream." The real enemy of justice, according to Hand, was "watery sentiment" and "archaic formalism" that defeats "the prosecution of crime."[8]

Not surprisingly, then, discovery made its way into criminal trials rather slowly. The right was embodied in Rule 16 of the Federal Rules of Criminal Procedure (1940): defendants had substantial rights to discover and inspect "books, papers, documents or tangible objects," gotten from the defendant or from others, if the items were "material to the preparation" of a defense. (The present Rule 16 is more comprehensive and elaborate.) Over time, other states joined the parade. The main push came in the 1950s, in the era of the Warren Court, a high point of sensitivity to the rights of defendants.*

Discovery was, in theory, a step away from "archaic formalism" and the extremes of the adversary system. It was also a symptom of the long-term, secular shift in power away from the lay jury and the trial itself toward an administered, bureaucratic, professional system of justice. In this sense, discovery was, to a degree, a blood brother of plea bargaining and the decline of trial by jury.

On the surface, other changes in trials themselves seem more, rather than less, formalistic. As we will see, criminal appeals became more common. Because of this fact, lawyers may have become more prone to shout out "Objection!" at point after point in the trial, and to preserve "exceptions" to rulings of the judge, so as to register grounds for appeal. Systematic evidence, however, is hard to come by. But fear of appeals lay behind curbs on the judge's power to make sensible (or nonsensible) comments on the evidence, which most states did not allow.[10] Judges themselves probably had a horror of committing "error" and getting themselves reversed by higher courts. In the sixties, most of the states permitted the judge neither to summarize nor to comment on the evidence; a fair number, seventeen, allowed summary without comment; eleven states, and the federal courts, allowed both summary and com-

---

* Many of the cases involved confessions: defendants wanted to know exactly what they had confessed to or admitted doing. This was certainly the thrust of the 1950s version of Rule 16. In a leading California case, John Dyson Powell, who had been accused of embezzling public funds, wanted copies of a signed statement he had made in the office of a chief of police, as well as a transcript of a tape recording made in that same office.[9]

ment. Kalven and Zeisel, who studied jury trials, have figures showing that even in states that allowed comment, not all judges did so. In Pennsylvania and New Jersey, judges used their right to comment in the bulk of their cases. But in Vermont, it was the practice in only about half of all trials; in California and Utah, in just a few trials; and in New Hampshire, absolutely never.[11]

Instructions, too, tended to be dull, dry, and legalistic. In some states, in fact, there are standard or "pattern" instructions, officially approved. In 1961, the Illinois Supreme Court appointed a special committee to draft standard instructions for criminal cases. The committee found that a quarter or more of the criminal appeals from the forties and fifties involved "questions of instructions," and that "error" in instructions was the basis for a quarter of all reversals. The committee set about to draft instructions that would be "free of error, and in simple, concise, unslanted, non-partisan language." In 1968, the "pattern instructions" received the imprimatur of the Illinois Supreme Court. The court's Rule 451 made the pattern instructions mandatory, to all intents and purposes.[12] In state after state, these dreary, arcane formulations are the only "instructions" that the poor jury gets to hear.

The Twilight of Trial by Jury

One of the major secular trends in criminal justice since the early nineteenth century has been the decline of trial by jury. This was already well advanced by the late nineteenth century, as we have seen, and it only accelerated in the twentieth. In 1920 or so, slightly less than a quarter of the cases in the Cleveland Court of Common Pleas were decided through trial by jury (591 out of 2,539 cases disposed of). A fair chunk were dismissed, and almost half ended abruptly with a guilty plea.[13] Out of some 48,856 criminal cases in federal court, in the fiscal year ending June 30, 1940, there were only 4,941 jury trials. Another 1,390 cases were disposed of by "bench trial"—that is, a trial without jury run and decided entirely by the judge. The vast majority were simply "not tried"; they ended with a guilty plea.[14] Some sort of record was set in Rhode Island; in 1938 and 1939, not a single felony defendant went to trial at all. In 1939, this noble state reported 632 defendants charged with major offenses. The court dismissed exactly seven of these; and the other 625 pleaded guilty. Not a single citizen of Rhode Island, if these figures are correct, served on a criminal jury in a felony case or was convicted or acquitted by a jury of her peers during the entire year.[15]

The bench trial is an innovation of the twentieth century. One state, Maryland, had a form of bench trial in the nineteenth century; and in some states, toward the end of the century, a defendant who faced a misdemeanor charge before a justice of the peace or other low-level judge could, if he wished, dispense with a jury.[16] Most states, however, stood firm. Trial by jury meant trial by jury; a defendant could plead guilty, but otherwise, it was a jury or nothing.

As late as 1930, it was an open question whether a defendant in federal court could waive his right to a jury. In that year, the Supreme Court said yes, so long as the defendant's consent was "express and intelligent," and the judge and the government agreed.* Rule 23 of the Federal Rules of Criminal Procedure allowed a defendant to waive a jury trial "in writing with the approval of the court and the consent of the government." By 1938, twenty-one states and the federal government allowed bench trials. In some of these states, indeed, the bench trial became quite popular: in New Jersey, 54 percent of all defendants went this route; in California, 36.1 percent. Statistics for a group of eight states showed that the accused waived the jury least often in homicide cases (21.9 percent). It was waived in 45 percent of the sex-offense cases, and in 58 percent of the larceny cases.[18]

By 1960, it was possible to waive the jury in every single state; New York was apparently the last holdout, and it capitulated by 1957. There was, however, a good deal of variation, state by state, in the *use* of bench trial in the 1960s. According to Kalven and Zeisel's figures, in Wisconsin the jury was waived in 79 percent of the cases of major crimes; in California, 74 percent. But in Utah only 5 percent of the defendants waived; in the District of Columbia, 3 percent, and in Montana, a resounding zero. The average in a selected group of states was 40 percent.[19] Variation is still the case today: in Cook County, Illinois (Chicago and surroundings), bench trials are over seven times more common than jury trials,[20] while in other states, it is much less usual. It is not easy to explain these local variations.

Bench trial was part of the evolution away from "lay" justice, toward more "professional" justice. It is clear why the prosecution might prefer a bench trial. It was cheaper and faster—no fuss about picking a jury, or about admission of evidence. Bench trial was presumably more predictable than a jury trial. The judge was not an automaton, but he was a professional, something the jury most certainly was not. There were fewer risks of surprise. For his part, an unpopular defendant might prefer judge to jury; he might also hope for a "bonus" in the form of a lesser sentence for saving the taxpayers' money.[21] A defendant (or his lawyer)

---

* In the actual case, the defendants had been tried for "conspiring to bribe a federal prohibition agent." The trial began with a jury, but a juror became ill. All hands agreed to proceed with eleven jurors. These eleven found the defendants guilty. The Supreme Court held that a "constitutional jury" meant *twelve* not eleven, and went on to discuss the case as if a jury had been completely waived.[17]

will tote up his chances; if the judge seems a better bet, then this will be the choice.*

Pleading Guilty

The most serious rival of the jury trial, however, was not the bench trial; rather, it was (and is) the guilty plea. A guilty plea is even better than a confession at ending a case; and the law has always dearly loved confessions. Common law systems have long allowed the defendant to admit guilt and short-circuit the trial. There were always some defendants who did just that; but the percentage grew steadily over the course of the nineteenth century and into the twentieth. Friedman and Percival's sample of felony cases, from Alameda County, California, 1870–1910, showed, as we have seen, the popularity of guilty pleas: one-third of the defendants pleaded guilty.[23]

Why was the guilty plea so popular? A few defendants, no doubt, were smitten with remorse; in some instances, the prosecution had such a tight case that the battle seemed hopeless. But most defendants who pleaded guilty, or changed their pleas to guilty, did this because they had, or hoped to have, a deal.

The term *plea bargaining* as we noted (chapter 11), covers a number of practices. In all of them, defendant "cops a plea"—that is, he makes a deal; he promises to plead guilty, and in exchange the prosecutor or some other official agrees to drop some charges, or allow probation, or knock down a charge (reduce it from, say, murder to manslaughter). As we have seen, plea bargaining can be traced back to the nineteenth century. But there is no doubt about its marvelous career in the twentieth century. In Chicago in 1926, 78.9 percent of the defendants who pleaded guilty were pleading to a lesser offense than the original charge—an almost certain sign of plea bargaining.[24]

Chicago was no exception. Plea bargaining was common in state after state in the twenties.† In the federal courts, plea bargaining apparently became standard practice in or around 1916; by the years 1927 through 1930, it had swept everything before it. In the Northern District of California, 93.5 percent of all convictions in non-liquor cases

---

* Of course, it is hard to psyche out these matters in advance; but Kalven and Zeisel's figures do suggest that defendants are roughly on target. They rarely waived a jury in a murder case, where juries seemed to acquit more often than judges did; in certain other cases—drug-law violations (this was the 1960s) or auto theft—where there was not much difference between judge and jury, they waived quite often.[22]

† Out of 678 cases tried in Multnomah County, Oregon, for 1927–28, about one-quarter of the defendants (166) changed their plea from not guilty to guilty of the offense charged—many of these were surely the result of a plea bargain; and 12.4 percent (84) changed their plea from not guilty to guilty of a lesser offense, an almost invariable sign of a plea bargain.[25]

and 98.3 percent of all convictions in liquor cases came from a guilty plea. In Connecticut, too, in a sample of districts, the guilty-plea rate was over 90 percent. The "guilty plea technique," in the judgment of the American Law Institute, was "responsible for the prompt and efficient disposition of business," and it was "doubtful if the system could operate without it."[26]

Was it worthwhile for defendants? Prosecutors were sometimes callous and overreaching; but most defendants probably did get something out of the bargain. In some places, the carrot was probation. In New York in the twenties, a defendant had twice the chance of a suspended sentence if he pleaded guilty, compared to a defendant who went to trial and lost.[27] In Alameda County, in 1909–10, forty-one out of forty-two men put on probation had pleaded guilty.[28] No doubt word of this sort of thing got around. And in thousands of other cases, the deal meant fewer years in prison, or no prison at all.

The rise of plea bargaining was surely a significant development, but it has to be understood for what it was. Plea bargaining did not *cause* hasty, routine, assembly-line justice. That had long existed. "Trials" in many places, and for most defendants, had been quick and dirty affairs, without lawyers and without much of the trappings of due process. In some places in the twentieth century, the quick and dirty trial was hardly extinct. Here is Arthur Train, lawyer and author, and former assistant district attorney, writing in 1906 about felony trials in New York City: "Ordinarily in a full court day there will occur from two to four complete trials, while an equal number of pleas may be taken. Sometimes a hundred and fifty cases will be got rid of by trial or plea in a single term in one part of the General Sessions alone."[29]

Train did not regard these trials as unfair. He felt that even ordinary trials for pickpockets or streetcorner brawlers were allotted "plenty of time." Juries sat for a whole term or session of court, and the district attorney soon found out who were the "anarchists or idiots." These jurors were then excused and the D.A. could "rely pretty safely on the others rendering a fair verdict."[30] What the pickpockets or streetcorner brawlers thought is not recorded.

It is mainly this sort of "trial" that plea bargaining replaced. Plea bargaining was, after all, more professional. It was quick and it was cheap. It did not depend on the wild, unpredictable notions of twelve men or women off the streets. For routine trials, "bargain justice" became totally standard, in some places, all but universal.* Only a stubborn handful of cases went to trial.

---

* In the District of Columbia in 1966, the guilty plea accounted for nearly 80 percent of the convictions for serious crime in the General Sessions Court.[31]

In the current generation, then, plea bargaining had become a pervasive aspect of the criminal justice system. Pervasive, yes, but for most of the century, fairly invisible, and certainly not the stuff of controversy; its rapid rise was hardly noticed by the general public, or even by high courts and legal scholars. In 1970, in *North Carolina v. Alford*,[32] plea bargaining won a kind of stamp of approval from the U.S. Supreme Court. In any event, it survived constitutional challenge. Alford had been accused of first-degree murder, a charge that put him in the shadow of the gas chamber. He entered a plea of guilty to second-degree murder, but later insisted he was innocent: "I ain't shot no man, but . . . I just pleaded guilty because they said if I didn't they would gas me for it." Could he be convicted on this kind of plea—could a man who claimed to be *free* of guilt be convicted on a *plea* of guilt, entered out of fear and on a lawyer's advice? The Supreme Court said yes: a man accused of crime "may voluntarily . . . consent to the imposition of a prison sentence even if he is unwilling . . . to admit his participation in the . . . crime." In any event, there was "overwhelming" evidence against Alford, the Court felt, and hence his choice was quite sensible.

In 1971, in *Santobello v. New York*,[33] Chief Justice Burger went so far as to call plea bargaining "an essential component of the administration of justice.* Properly administered, it is to be encouraged." Why? Because otherwise, the courts would be swamped; plea bargaining is cost-effective—it "leads to prompt and largely final disposition of most criminal cases." Burger was not alone. Quite a few judges, prosecutors, and legal scholars have given at least a qualified nod to the practice.

But despite this fact, and the chief justice's kind words, plea bargaining became quite controversial in the seventies. The storm of anger and controversy that engulfed the whole criminal justice system did not leave this part of it untouched. The "bleeding-heart" wing of national opinion considered the system barbaric: a defendant's fate was decided by haggling, not by an honest trial. The "law-and-order" wing felt plea bargaining was defective for exactly the opposite reason: hardened criminals, adept at playing the game, bargained for a "slap on the wrist." Defendants themselves probably saw the whole ceremony—the "cop-out ceremony"—as a game, a cynical charade. This was especially true be-

---

* Santobello thought he had a deal with the prosecutor, but at the sentencing stage, a new prosecutor recommended the maximum sentence. The judge threw the book at Santobello (claiming, however, that he was not influenced by the prosecutor's recommendation). Santobello, naturally, tried to withdraw his guilty plea, but was told it was too late. On appeal, the Supreme Court insisted that the prosecution had to stick to its bargain. The Court vacated the judgment against Santobello and sent it back for "further consideration." What that consideration would be, the Court did not specify; but Chief Justice Burger, who wrote the majority opinion, did say that "when a plea rests in any significant degree on a promise or agreement of the prosecutor . . . such promise must be fulfilled."

cause some judges insisted on hearing, from the defendant's mouth, that there was no deal—which was, of course, an out-and-out lie.[34]

In July 1975, the attorney general of Alaska, Avrum Gross, issued instructions to all district attorneys and staff in that state: no more plea bargaining at all.[35] Plea bargaining is often explained as a response to crowded urban courts. But Alaska? This is a land mass twice the size of Texas, rich in scenery, home to grizzly bears, bald eagles, and caribou, but relatively few members of the human species. Its whole crop of mortals could fit comfortably in a single neighborhood in New York City. Yet plea bargaining was alive and well in Alaska; and it looked like a problem—a corruption of justice—even there.

Still, there *are* such things as "crowded urban courts," and what may work in the vastnesses of Alaska[36] is not necessarily practical for Miami or Chicago. But Alaska was not alone in its aspirations. In state after state, there were attempts to reform the system: to get rid of plea bargaining, either entirely, or for certain classes of cases (drug dealers, for example). The results were decidedly mixed. Plea bargaining, like a cat, seemed to have nine lives.

The basic problem is the problem of routine. There are never enough resources to go around; it is possible to whip up enthusiasm for building new prisons and perhaps for hiring more policemen (although this is not easy); but there is very little political sex appeal in scraping together money for judges, prosecutors, and (above all) public defenders, not to mention courtrooms and similar facilities. Plea bargaining was a method for dealing with the problem of routine; it may have done the job badly or unethically, but it did the job.

In any event, it is not at all clear that plea bargaining *can* be "abolished," at least in the present situation. In fact, it is plain that it *cannot*—at least not without something to replace it. The something must be a device or institution or procedure that deals with the routine but serious case. A two-time loser, twenty-two years old, is caught in the act of robbing a liquor store at gunpoint. Society does not want to spend a fortune on a full, grand trial; and, indeed, such a trial would be a waste of money. But what then? How shall we handle his case? If not plea bargaining, what else? Here, as in so many aspects of criminal justice, the system was adrift, blown this way and that by purely political winds.

Defending

It is not a job for amateurs to maneuver through the corridors of justice. Of course, habitual defendants, three-time losers, and "street smart" people have a certain amount of savvy; but on the whole, a solid defense requires a lawyer. Most people accused of crime do not *have* a solid defense, but they still need a lawyer, if only to drive a decent bargain.

Crime, in general, does not pay—or pay well. Routine felons are poor. The vast majority of them have no money to get a good lawyer. In modern times, the state will provide.* The older system was to use assigned counsel: the court would appoint some member of the bar to handle the case. A twentieth-century innovation was the public defender. This was a lawyer on the public payroll whose job was to defend criminals, and thus, in effect, to bite the hand that wrote the salary check.[37] Usually, Los Angeles gets credit for the first public defender system, in 1913; Cook County, Illinois (Chicago), got its system in 1930. The system was supposed to be more efficient, more professional than the old system of assigned counsel. It would save money; the public defender would avoid "unnecessary trials."[38] Thus the rise of the public defender is, in fact, tied in with plea bargaining, and the search for meaningful routine.

Public defenders dominate criminal defense today. Typically, they are overworked; burnout and cynicism are serious occupational diseases. Their salaries tend to be low, and there is a numbing volume of work: "rotten case after rotten case. It drives you crazy."[39] Defenders feel they get no respect from anyone. They are considered "crummy lawyers . . . dreck . . . an inferior breed."[40] Many clients share this view. One defendant, asked if he had had a lawyer in court, said: "No. I had a public defender."[41] Yet the life attracts young lawyers with ideals, hard-working men and women who love trial work, who are committed to the noble goal of defending *anybody*, good or bad, rich or poor; and who are then trapped by the deep ambivalence of a society that believes in fair trials, but also (and more so?) in punishment.

On Trial

Plea bargaining is the way the twentieth century has handled its routine (but serious) cases. A handful of cases still go to trial, and these tend to be the most serious, the most dramatic and sensitive cases. Men accused of murder and other heinous crimes often thought they had a better chance with a jury than with a judge—a man or woman who had heard all the excuses and was hardened, presumably, by long years on the bench. If life was at stake, why not try a jury? Who knows what might happen? In some notable cases, too, it was the prosecution that would not bargain, for one reason or another—perhaps to avoid bad publicity.

In steamy, difficult, or sensational cases, choosing a jury could be a

---

* Since *Gideon* (see chapter 14) all states are obliged to do this, in felony cases at least; but most states had much earlier moved to this position as we saw.

protracted struggle; and literally hundreds of prospects might be sifted before the two sides settled down to a panel of twelve. In Williamson County, Illinois, in 1922, eight union men were put on trial for their part in the "Herrin massacre," in which sixteen scabs were murdered. It took a full month to pick a jury.[42] The juror's lot in major cases is not a happy one; weeks or months of sitting in the courtroom listening to evidence (not always fascinating). Worst of all is sequestration—locking the jury up and treating jurors as virtual prisoners. This happens, on the whole, only in murder or capital cases. In one case in 1934, in Dedham, Massachusetts, an "unused courtroom was converted into a dormitory, and meals were eaten in a nearby restaurant." Jurors took a bath once a week at the YMCA. Deputy sheriffs guarded them constantly, and no one was allowed to see or communicate with them.[43]

Once in a while, jury duty was worse than unpleasant; it was downright dangerous. Not many people have ever been happy to serve as jurors in trials of well-connected gangsters. In 1927, Harry J. ("Lefty") Lewis was charged with murder in Cook County, Illinois. He was allegedly one of a group of union thugs who beat and choked junk men who refused to join the union. One of the junk men died after a bout of persuasion.

The trial was a sensation, not least because witnesses were told they might not live to tell the tale; the home of one witness was bombed. This was certainly not encouraging to jurors. In September 1926, over a thousand jurymen were summoned; 646 were questioned before twelve were actually selected. It took four weeks to pick the jury. Most of the men were excused because they claimed they had a fixed opinion about guilt or innocence; 163 claimed scruples against the death penalty. There were also thirty-two peremptory challenges, sixteen on each side. The trial lasted until November 18, 1927. At the trial, eight eyewitnesses testified that Lewis shot the junk man in the back while he was running away. Yet the jury, after six hours of deliberations, set Lefty Lewis free. The verdict produced "general indignation." The jury, it was said, was not at all representative; it was the dregs left over after the long, wearying process of selection. Perhaps the jury was simply too frightened to convict.[44]*

Who served on juries? Sam B. Warner and Henry Cabot of Harvard Law School, writing in 1936, complained about the quality of Boston ju-

---

* In the 1927 trial of Harry Sinclair, which arose out of the famous Teapot Dome scandal, Sinclair hired detectives to shadow the members of the jury—to find out what they did between the time the trial let out until they were safely in bed. The point was to gather material for a possible mistrial. But one of the detectives snitched; the plan became public knowledge, and Sinclair faced a sentence for contempt of court.[45]

rors. Jurors came out of lists of voters. But many professionals were excused, and others wormed their way out of duty. In federal court there seemed to be a higher class of juror; they were "more skilled occupationally than those in the state court."[46] Obviously, for Warner and Cabot, the jury did not have to be "representative" in any *literal* sense (when they wrote, for example, women were still excluded in Massachusetts). Jurors, ideally, were of the better sort: high-class men.

But as the years passed, there was a subtle, unconscious change in attitude. The legal culture in America in the late twentieth century was, as we have argued, strongly influenced by a form of expressive individualism. This meant, among other things, a commitment to shapes of pluralism beyond anything earlier periods had been willing to recognize. A jury of one's "peers," then, in the view of many people—and some judges—had to *be* a jury of peers—of people *like* the defendant, rather than the results of a lottery, randomly pulled from the general community; least of all a "blue ribbon" panel, a panel of elites.

Already, in the nineteenth century, the Supreme Court told the states they could not exclude blacks from the jury.* Now, in the late twentieth century, came attacks on other kinds of exclusion, and demands for new forms of *inclusion.*† Modern pluralism involves, among other things, a rejection of the idea that there is a single moral norm, a single hierarchy of values, a single standard—just as there is no longer a single race, religion, sex, or group that can claim *official* status (actual dominance is another story). Hence it is not surprising to hear demands for a jury that is "representative" in some deeper sense than the law has required. In a few cases, defendants have attacked juries because not enough young people, or poor people, or blue-collar workers, or the like, were among the jurors. A jury must represent a "fair" cross section of the community; isn't that the law?

Most of these challenges have failed, but it is significant that they were made at all. In *People v. Pinnell* (1975), a group of defendants, indicted for very serious crimes, argued that the grand jury that indicted them was "improperly chosen."[48] The pool from which these jurors was picked, they argued, was not a good cross section; there was no "fair" sample of the "group" to which defendants said they belonged: black, Latin American, "blue collar working class and . . . young." The Court

---

* This fell on deaf ears; the southern states continued to exclude blacks from their juries, although they were careful to repeal any actual *laws* that said so.
† In 1968 the Supreme Court put an end to what had been called the "death qualified" jury, which was standard practice before. The prosecution could not systematically exclude, "for cause," jurors who were against the death penalty. This would produce a jury "uncommonly willing to condemn a man to die." Justice Stewart referred to those who favored capital punishment as a "dwindling minority," words that seem ironic today.[47]

turned down the claim, but only because the selectors had made "substantial efforts to secure larger numbers of both youth and labor groups," and because the Court found no evidence of race discrimination.*

The Big Show: Major Trials and Their Discontents

Who were the men and women who passed up plea bargaining and went to trial? All kinds; but, as before, among them were defendants in a few great show trials—cases that stood out from the thousands of instances of aggravated assault, burglary, arson, rape, and manslaughter. Statistically, these trials were insignificant; but they made a deep impression on the public mind, they sold tons of newsprint, and occasionally they shaped the course of the law.

There was a sensation of sorts, probably, in every city, in every year. A few cases were super-sensations. In 1907, for example, there was the trial of Harry K. Thaw, charged with the murder of Stanford White the year before.[50] White came from an old, distinguished family; he mingled with the rich and famous of New York; he was a leading architect of the firm McKim, Mead and White. Thaw was the somewhat degenerate offspring of an old and extremely wealthy family. He had married a ravishing young beauty, Evelyn Nesbit Thaw, one of the famous "Floradora girls" of the Broadway stage. Harry Thaw shot White to death in front of thousands of horrified spectators in Madison Square Garden. As the journalist Irvin S. Cobb, who covered the trial, put it, this was

> the most spectacular criminal case . . . that ever sucked dry the descriptive reservoirs of the American press. You see, it had in it wealth, degeneracy, rich old wasters; delectable young chorus girls and adolescent artists' models; the behind-the-scenes of Theaterdom and the Underworld, and the Great White Way . . . the abnormal pastimes and weird orgies of overly aesthetic artists and jaded debauchees. In the cast of the motley show were Bowery toughs, Harlem gangsters, Tenderloin panders, Broadway leading men, Fifth Avenue clubmen, Wall Street manipulators, uptown voluptuaries and downtown thugs.

And it had Evelyn Nesbit Thaw—"the most exquisitely lovely human being I ever looked at—the slim, quick grace of a fawn, a head that sat

---

* In recent years, a "science" of jury selection has developed. The jury is sifted through the use of the most modern tools of demography and psychology. The object is not to ensure fairness, but to replace lawyers' hunches and rules of thumb about good jurors and bad jurors (from the defense or prosecution points of view), with something more solidly grounded. The process is extremely expensive; consequently, it is used only in very special cases. Whether it works or not has never satisfactorily been proven.[49]

on her flawless throat as a lily on its stem . . . a mouth made of rumpled rose petals."[51]

Since Thaw could hardly claim somebody else shot White, he had to dream up some other defense. He claimed "temporary insanity," but the real defense was something quite different. White, he claimed, was a cad who had defiled his wife (long before Thaw met her, by the way). The trial was a carnival of scandal mixed with psychiatric mumbo jumbo. It was interrupted while a "lunacy commission," on the prosecution's motion, debated whether Thaw was mentally fit to stand trial. In hindsight, Thaw seems clearly deranged, and not only temporarily. But the commission said yes, he was fit; and the trial went on. It lasted three months. The jury spent forty-seven hours wrangling fruitlessly over the verdict. At a second trial, the jury found Thaw not guilty by reason of insanity. Thaw was shipped off to the State Asylum for the Criminal Insane, at Matteawan, in New York State. (In 1913, after some judicious bribery by the Thaw family, the defendant escaped from Matteawan and fled to Canada. He was extradited and returned to his asylum; in 1915, he was declared sane and released from prison.)[52]

The Thaw-White case gave the public a vicarious thrill: a glimpse at the lifestyles of the rich and famous. Unlike Lizzie Borden's case, and all the other nineteenth-century cases of repressed anger and sexual frustration, this was a case of wild celebrities and their unbridled lusts. The man in the dock, and his victim, were both more or less celebrities. In other instances, the crimes were so lurid or extreme, that the *criminals* became celebrities. The 1924 murder of Bobby Franks, in Chicago, by Richard Loeb and Nathan Leopold—the "crime of the century"—presented just such a case: two rich, brilliant young men, who killed a young boy in cold blood, just for the thrill of it. Oddly enough, this "trial" was not a trial at all. Loeb and Leopold had confessed; the sole issue was punishment. Would they live or die? Clarence Darrow, the most famous lawyer of the day, argued for the defense. There was, of course, no jury. The courtroom, where the judge sat, had room for three hundred people; the judge issued "200 pink tickets to local newsmen and correspondents for news agencies and out-of-town papers."[53] Darrow argued brilliantly that the boys were not normal; they were emotionally immature, poisoned by reading Nietzsche, prisoners of forces beyond their control.[54] Whether the speech had an impact on the judge is, of course, unknown; but Leopold and Loeb did not get the death penalty; the judge sent them instead to prison for life. Loeb was stabbed to death in prison; Leopold was eventually released, a middle-aged man.

Another case that attracted swarms of reporters was the sensational Hall-Mills case of the twenties.[55] It began with the discovery, in September 1922, of the bodies of a man and a woman in a field, near a crab apple tree, in the vicinity of New Brunswick, New Jersey. The man, who had been shot, was the Reverend Edward W. Hall, pastor of an Episcopal church in New Brunswick. The dead woman, whose throat had been slashed, and her tongue cut out, was Mrs. Eleanor Mills, a choir singer active in the church, and the minister's lover.

For four years, the investigation simmered; then, in 1926, came a break. A certain Mrs. Jane Gibson, a farmer and local character (the "pig woman") came forward and claimed she had witnessed the murder. Partly on the basis of what the "pig woman" said, the minister's wife, Frances Hall, and two of her brothers, were put on trial for the murders. The trial was headline news, day in and day out. At the end, the defendants were acquitted. The mystery of the "minister and the choir singer" has never been resolved.[56]

Sexual misconduct and jealousy were at the root of Hall-Mills, or seemed to be; thus, like so many of the show cases, the trial was a kind of morality play. The audience was the courtroom public and the wider world of newspaper readers. In such cases, the great trial lawyers pulled out all the stops, as they had in earlier times. In 1918, Elmer Hupp of Cleveland shot Charles Joyce, a salesman, in Hupp's home. This was a "love triangle." Hupp supposedly shot Joyce, his wife's lover, in a "red rage" to protect the sanctity of his home. The Hupps had a daughter, Consuelo, a "winsome, cream and pink blonde girl," fourteen years old. When the attorneys made their "impassioned plea" to the jury, Consuelo "sobbed convulsively," her "arms about the neck of her father." The lawyers begged the jury to put "sunshine in the little girl's heart." One of the lawyers cried out, "We can't have people ask this little girl, 'Where is your Daddy?' and have her answer 'He's in the penitentiary.'"[57] The jury acquitted Hupp on March 7, 1918, after two hours and two ballots.[58]

The most sensational trial of 1927 was the trial of Ruth Snyder and Judd Gray for the murder of Ruth's husband, Albert. The two defendants, who seemed obviously guilty, were tried together. The only hope for Ruth was to put all the blame on Judd, while the only hope for Judd was to do likewise to Ruth. Judd's lawyer called Ruth "a poisonous snake," a "serpent" who "drew Judd Gray into her glistening coils. . . . This woman . . . was abnormal; possessed of an all-consuming, all-absorbing sexual passion, animal lust, which seemingly was never satisfied." Poor Judd was "enslaved . . . like a human mannikin, like a human dummy. Whatever she wanted he did."[59] Ruth Snyder's lawyer paid him back in kind, and the jury convicted both of them. They went to the chair in 1928.

But hardly any case of the century could match, for sheer notoriety, the kidnap-murder of Charles Lindbergh's baby, and the trial of Bruno

Hauptmann for this crime in 1935. Lindbergh was a national hero; and to steal and kill a baby was a crime guaranteed to horrify every parent in the country. The trial was a media circus. It hit Flemington, New Jersey, like a "tornado." There was an "avalanche" of spectators, who tried to squeeze in to see a trial that was, according to H. L. Mencken, the greatest story since the Resurrection. There were over three hundred newspeople and more than one hundred cameramen; a tangle of forty-five direct lines carried the news to places as far off as Sydney, Australia, and Buenos Aires. At a local airstrip, a dozen planes a day brought film to New York to feed the insatiable appetites of the press. Hauptmann was convicted, and died in the electric chair. The media tumult at the trial was such that, in 1937, two years after it was over, the American Bar Association (ABA) adopted a judicial "canon" (ethical rule) that banned courtroom photography or radio coverage of trials. In 1952, the ABA amended the ban to include television. (The ban disintegrated in the 1970s, when over twenty states came to allow cameras in the courtroom.)[60]

Could a trial be so sensational, the publicity so inflated, that the defendant's rights were compromised? The issue came to a head in two Supreme Court cases. In *Estes v. Texas* (1965),[61] Billie Sol Estes had been convicted of swindling in a federal court in Texas. He was accused of a scam involving the sale of fertilizer tanks and equipment to farmers. The case gained intense national attention, and it was standing-room-only in the courtroom. Initial hearings were carried live on radio and television. There were more than a dozen cameramen in the courtroom: "Cables and wires were snaked across the courtroom floor, three microphones were on the judge's bench and others were beamed at the jury box and the counsel table."[62] At the trial itself, the cameramen were more restrained: they worked out of a booth at the back of the courtroom. But the Supreme Court reversed the conviction. In its opinion, this kind of media carnival deprived Estes of his right to a fair trial.

Sheppard v. Maxwell (1966)[63] arose out of a notorious murder case. Marilyn Sheppard, the pregnant wife of Dr. Sam Sheppard, was beaten to death on July 4, 1954, in her home in suburban Cleveland. Dr. Sam claimed a bushy-haired stranger had done the foul deed; but the police never bought his story. They suspected Dr. Sheppard himself, who had been carrying on a love affair with a woman named Susan Hayes. The case had what it takes to match Thaw, Hall-Mills, Leopold and Loeb, and the other great lip-smacking scandal cases of the century. Representatives of the news media jammed the courtroom. Nobody except a cloistered nun could have escaped hearing about the case; certainly no juror or potential juror. The trial was not televised; but the Supreme Court found, nonetheless, that "bedlam reigned at the courthouse";

newsmen "took over practically the entire courtroom, hounding most of the participants." The news media "inflamed and prejudiced the public." One Ohio judge referred to the "atmosphere of a 'Roman holiday.'" On top of everything else, the jury was not sequestered. The Court felt that under these circumstances, Sheppard had not received a fair trial. Sheppard's conviction was vacated.*

The issue in these two cases was whether television and the feeding frenzy of reporters can make a trial inherently unfair; the Supreme Court clearly answered yes. The legal issues are complex and remain highly controverted. The root question, in a sense, is an old one. The press—television news most especially—has vastly increased the sensation-power of these cases. Moreover, as we have seen, the theory of jury function too has changed; while the media now reach into every home, legal theory has refined the concept of a virginal jury to *its* highest point. These two social facts, quite obviously, can collide; and in cases like Sam Sheppard's, they did. In 1981, in *Chandler v. Florida*,[65] the Supreme Court put a fence around *Estes* and similar cases: The "risk of juror prejudice in some cases does not justify an absolute ban on news coverage of trials," including coverage by the "broadcast" media.[66] Thus television won a place, even though a bit grudgingly, in the courtroom; and there it remains, feeding on celebrity trials (and trials it makes *into* celebrity trials), to this day.

The Insanity Defense

In the twentieth century, the insanity defense underwent important changes. Throughout the first half of the century, psychiatrists and jurists kept up a drumbeat of criticism against the standard "tests," especially the McNaghten rules. These rules, it was said, were narrow and unscientific; they ignored the progress of psychiatric medicine. In New York, where the McNaghten rules were embalmed in statute, the court of appeals, in 1928, affirmed the conviction of Moran, a cop-killer, even though he was a "psychopathic inferior," a "man of low and unstable mentality, and, in all probability, a sufferer from epilepsy." After all, he "knew the nature and quality of the act, and knew that the act was wrong"; that was all that the law of New York required.[67]

The insanity defense is and has been controversial. The noise of the arguments would lead one to think that the defense was an everyday affair, that shocking numbers of dangerous psychopaths were let loose on

---

* The case came up on a writ of habeas corpus. The Supreme Court remanded the case to the District Court, "with instructions to issue the writ and order that Sheppard be released from custody unless the State puts him to its charges again within a reasonable time."[64]

the street, or put in hospitals, instead of jails (where they presumably belonged). In fact, the defense was rarely used, and was rarely successful. In Illinois, in the years 1924 through 1927, there were forty findings of insanity among 14,690 defendants accused of murder, assault with intent to murder, rape, assault with intent to rape, and other crimes. In three additional cases, the defendant was insane at the time of the crime, sane at the time of trial. In only *four* of these forty-three cases did the prosecution oppose the verdict of insanity; presumably the other thirty-nine defendants were so obviously crazy that the prosecution saw no point in arguing.[68]

In some states, courts (as they often do) simply nibbled away at the rules, changing them without admitting change. A number of halfway measures emerged; one was the concept of diminished capacity or diminished responsibility. It emerged gradually; in some ways, the old cases on drunkenness were its intellectual ancestors; but it crystallized, perhaps, in the 1950s. *

There was certainly a sensible idea behind the concept. The law seemed to assume insanity was something either/or, black or white: you are or you are not. But this seems wrong, both logically and as a matter of experience. There are all sorts of shades of gray between normal (whatever that means) and a state of complete, hopeless, obvious insanity. A defendant, of course, ends up either guilty or not guilty, a kind of all-or-nothing fate. But, in fact, there *are* all sorts of way stations between the two poles: conviction on a lesser charge, for example. Murder is murder and not manslaughter because, among other things, the murderer has a certain frame of mind—"malice aforethought" is the technical phrase. It is certainly possible for a person to have some weakness or defect of mind that affects his ability to *form* that intent, even if he is not actually "insane" in the clinical sense.

In *State v. Padilla*, a New Mexico case of 1959,[69] the charge was first-degree murder. Padilla's lawyer tried to get the trial judge to instruct the jury on diminished capacity. He wanted the judge to tell the jury that they might consider second-degree murder (instead of first-degree) if the defendant was "incapable of thinking over the fatal act beforehand with a calm and reflective mind (or with a fixed and settled deliberation and coolness of mind)" because of a "disease or defect of the mind," even if he was not technically insane. The judge refused, and the jury convicted.

The Supreme Court of New Mexico reversed the trial court decision. The judge should have given the instruction. Under New Mexico law, a

* Darrow argued, as we saw, for a *kind* of "diminished responsibility" in the Leopold-Loeb case.

defendant could be so drunk or so befuddled with drugs as to be unable to "premeditate" a first-degree murder (this was a familiar doctrine; see Chapter 6). If so, said the Court, why not provide the same rule for "mental disorders"? A substantial number of courts agreed. A rule of this type, however, was a kind of back-door attack on the "right or wrong" test.

A frontal attack came in 1954, in the District of Columbia. Judge David Bazelon, dissatisfied with the state of the law, boldly struck out in a new direction. The case concerned a certain Monte Durham, convicted of housebreaking. Durham had a long history of instability; in fact, he spent his whole adult life in and out of jails and mental hospitals—a revolving-door life of "lunacy inquiries," suicide attempts, convictions for crime, commitments to St. Elizabeth's Hospital, releases. The trial judge, sitting without a jury, had applied the standard "right or wrong" test and convicted Durham. The circuit court, speaking through Bazelon, reversed. Bazelon had harsh words for the McNaghten rules, which did not "take sufficient account of psychic realities and scientific knowledge." His opinion in *Durham* was peppered with citations to psychiatric literature. Bazelon laid down a new "test" for insanity cases, presumably more scientific and enlightened than the older ones: "an accused is not criminally responsible if his unlawful act was the product of mental disease or mental defect."[70]

The *Durham* rule was controversial from the day it was born. It was supposed to be clearer, more modern, more scientific than what preceded it. But in practice it proved troublesome and confusing. Its critics also blasted it because it put too much power in the hands of psychiatrists; it turned a moral and legal judgment into what seemed to be a medical judgment. Perhaps this was unfair to the impulses behind the *Durham* case, but history and evolution have nothing to do with fairness. Many judges became convinced that the "insanity defense was going haywire" and was leading to a "psychiatric dictatorship combined with procedural anarchy."[71]

Statistical evidence does suggest that something was going awry. In 1954, the year of *Durham*, verdicts of "not guilty by reason of insanity" were rare in the District of Columbia—0.4 percent of all cases tried resulted in that verdict, a pretty standard percentage. This figure mushroomed to 3.3 percent in 1958, to 6.1 percent in 1960, and in 1961, to 14.4 percent—a staggering figure.[72] The D.C. Circuit Court of Appeals was itself alarmed and began to backtrack; finally, in 1972, this court junked the *Durham* rule, only eighteen years after it had so hopefully adopted it.[73] The new rule was based on language drafted by the American Law Institute as part of a proposed Model Penal Code. Under this rule, a person "is not responsible for criminal conduct if at the time of such conduct as a result of mental disease or defect he lacks substantial capacity either to appreciate the criminality of his conduct or to conform his conduct to the requirements of the law."

Whether this rule actually *says* anything meaningful about what constitutes insanity (or anything much different from the *Durham* rule, and other "tests"), it has a curiously soothing effect on conservatives, who despise the insanity defense, and anything that smacks of "excuses" for criminals. A large segment of the population positively lusts to believe that criminality is raw, naked evil, the devil in human form; that criminals are people who have sold their souls, who have brazenly, openly broken the rules we live by. At the same time, millions of people also seem to think that criminals are perhaps born that way; crime is in the blood, the genes, the bones. These two beliefs are, in several ways, inconsistent. They do have a common core. In both cases, rehabilitation, coddling, excuses, psychiatric treatment, and the like seem like a dangerous waste of time. The insanity defense, it would follow, is a trick to get people off the hook, a way to make mincemeat of morality and society's working norms.

The Age of Backlash

In retrospect, the 1950s and 1960s represented a peak or high point in the movement to make criminal justice more humane, and to tilt the balance away from the police and prosecution. A backlash or reaction then set in. A wave of conservatism swept over the country. It had its roots in the great fear: the fear and hatred of crime. This wave led to the collapse of the campaign against the death penalty; it brought about a reaction against parole and the indeterminate sentence; it engulfed the *Durham* rule, and put an end to "progress" in the insanity defense.

In November 1978, Dan White, a former member of the Board of Supervisors of San Francisco, ran amok in City Hall. He shot the mayor, George Moscone, to death, along with Supervisor Harvey Milk, a leader of the gay community. White was arrested and charged, and his trial took place, quite naturally, under the klieg lights of publicity. White's basic defense was diminished capacity; after all, White could hardly deny that he pulled the trigger. A straight-out insanity plea also seemed quite out of the question. The trial was notorious for what came to be known as the "Twinkie defense." There was testimony that White sometimes stuffed himself with junk food, and this kind of diet tended to unbalance him mentally. (Twinkies were mentioned at the trial, as one of the junk foods White ate when under stress.) The press went to town on this very minor point in the case, blowing it up out of all proportion. The "Twinkie defense" probably played little or no role in the actual result.

In any event, the jury found White guilty, but of voluntary manslaughter, not murder. The verdict, as we mentioned (in chapter 16, above), touched off riots in San Francisco. Howls of outrage were heard in Sacramento and reverberated all over the state. California then simply abolished the defenses of diminished capacity and irresistible impulse.[74] The voters of California liked the time-tested words of the McNaghten rule better than more modern alternatives.

On March 30, 1981, John Hinckley, Jr., stood outside the Hilton Hotel, in Washington, D.C., and shot six bullets at the president, Ronald Reagan, as the president was leaving the hotel for his limousine. The president was seriously wounded, and his press secretary, James Brady, struck by one of the bullets, suffered severe brain damage. Hinckley was peculiar and unbalanced, to say the least; he had shot the president not, apparently, for any political reason, but to impress a young movie star, Jodie Foster, whom he had never met. At the trial in federal district court, his defense (of course) was insanity. This was the only real issue, and consequently, the whole affair became a battle between psychiatric witnesses. The trial lasted eight weeks; the jury deliberated for three and a half days, and then returned with a verdict: not guilty by reason of insanity.

It was a plausible outcome, but it, too, evoked a storm of protest. A news poll the very next day found that three-fourths of the public disapproved of the verdict; 70 percent wanted to get rid of the insanity plea. In a Delaware poll a week later, 80 percent of the sample considered the insanity defense a "loophole." The president himself complained that the defense was "used more and more in murder trials." These people are "found innocent by reason of insanity," are put in a mental hospital, later to be "turned loose" as "cured"; then "they go right out in the street and commit the same crime over again."[75]

All this was nonsense, of course, but Congress heard the thunder and saw the lightning very clearly. In 1984, Congress reconstituted the insanity defense for federal cases; the new rules harked back to the old McNaghten rules, with changes. A defendant can use the defense only if "at the time of the commission of the act" he or she, "as a result of a severe mental disease or defect," is "unable to appreciate the nature and quality or the wrongfulness of the act."[76] "Insanity" does not include psychopathic and sociopathic behavior. A few states have gone so far as to abolish, or try to abolish, the insanity defense altogether.[77]

This legislative activity, to be sure, is based on half-facts, non-facts, or on plain prejudice. But the underlying rage is also, in a way, understandable. We have discussed the 1959 New Mexico case of *State v. Padilla* (see above, this chapter).[78] Here are the facts of the case, as set out rather drily by the Supreme Court of New Mexico. Padilla was a

Mexican-American, twenty-five years old when the crime was committed. He had a second-grade education and worked "as an itinerant farm laborer all of his life." His intelligence rating was "dull normal."

On October 5, 1957, Padilla drank beer in a bar in Roswell, New Mexico, from noon until midnight and smoked at least two marijuana cigarettes. He left the bar with a half-case of beer, went to the home of the victim, a five-year-old child, and "took her into his car. He then drove approximately fourteen miles. . . . [Then] he raped the child and thereafter killed her by stabbing her with a screwdriver." He took a seat cover from the car, put it over her body, and covered it with sand. Then he fled to Mexico. He was arrested and returned to New Mexico on October 12, 1957. He confessed soon afterwards. Padilla was, of course, convicted; his appeal turned on the question of diminished responsibility. As we have seen, he won the case.

There is a lot to be said for the court's decision in the light of Padilla's background and his mental profile. There is a lot to be said—that is, *if* you believe that a trial is for weighing and judging the fate of *this* particular person. But the crime itself was cruel, wanton, pointless. Padilla brutally snuffed out the life of a little child. He plunged her family into the darkest pool of grief. A crime so horrible evokes rage, not understanding; it is the kind of crime that gives the system its sorest, most difficult test. It does not always pass the test.

In the years after 1950, there seemed to be no end of senseless, vicious, wanton crimes; and the media played them for all they were worth. Public opinion froze solid. The wheel turned, and criminal justice became, relatively speaking, *offense*-minded; it focused more on the acts themselves, less on the actor. But in an offense-minded system, there is not much room for a doctrine of diminished capacity, and even the insanity defense itself moved into the danger zone.

After the Verdict: Probation

A jury's verdict of guilty, or a guilty plea, or a judge's decision, is not the end of the trial. The sentencing stage remains. And this is crucial. Here life or death may weigh in the balance; or, for far greater numbers, a prison term, or jail—or another chance. This "other chance" is probation.

Adult probation entered the system, for the most part, in the early years of the twentieth century. New Jersey enacted a probation law in 1900, New York in 1901, California in 1903.[79] If the defendant asked for probation and seemed to have a reasonable shot, the judge would turn the case over to a probation officer. The probation officer would investigate the prisoner, then file a report, either recommending probation or not. Usually, the judge did what the report recommended, though he had the discretion to ignore it.

Probation was another step toward a more professional system of criminal justice. Not that early probation officers had any special training; they learned on the job. As late as 1932, Charles Chute wrote that the states had no prerequisites at all.[80] Some did—in a minimal way. New York passed a law in 1928 saying that probation officers should be mentally, physically, and morally fit; over twenty-one; and have at least a high school education.[81] Probation at least gave the judge the help of a person whose specific job it was to look into the defendant's situation and character. Probation was also a move toward a more humane system of criminal justice. A poor wretch, a first offender caught in the tangles of justice, had a chance to escape the horrors of Sing Sing or San Quentin. But the probation system also gave probation officers and judges vast power, and vast discretion. They used this power to bend the system—consciously or otherwise.

The price of probation, to begin with, was a guilty plea and a humble attitude. Judges in many places demanded true confession and true atonement. Probation was the power to separate good people from bad. The good were more moral, moderate in habit, attached to work, family, and church—people who had slipped a bit but deserved another chance. The bad were the opposite of all this.

Early probation reports in California reveal a jumble of popular theories about crime and criminal personalities, and a jumble of popular prejudices about the morals of men (few women appeared in the records). The reports favored married men or men with family support. Jobs were a plus. And men who did not masturbate or go to brothels, and who stayed away from liquor and tobacco, were prime candidates. Drifters, the unattached, the vice-ridden, drug addicts—these never had a chance. Probation officers poked and rummaged in family histories. They examined character, habits, inheritance; they listened to gossip, they talked to neighbors. We read of one offender who had "masturbated since about fourteen" and was still (in 1914) not in full control of himself. He had gone to brothels ("three times") and was "fond of theatre." He had "no library card"—a sign, no doubt, of unregenerate ignorance. Probation was, of course, denied.[82] In Chicago, in 1931, eighteen-year-old Emil C. was arrested for burglary. The probation office wrote a damning report. Emil's brother Albert had been "Delinquent from the age of 8 years. Mother could do nothing with him. Loafed and stole at night." Albert himself had a criminal record: "I simply mention this to show a family trait." Emil's parents lived above the "cheap little store" that they ran. It was just "a very poor little home, scantily furnished, and the neighborhood is as poor as the home."[83]

Those who won probation were expected to toe the line. Young Albert Banks, of San Diego, who had written a bad check for $16.50 and defrauded a Mrs. Del Rey in 1908, pleaded guilty. Judge Lewis of Superior Court sentenced him to three years in prison, but Banks was spared this fate—on condition. "I think cigarette smoking is a bad habit," said the judge; so, of course, Banks was not to smoke. He was also supposed to avoid "all places of evil repute," which included saloons. He was to "shun all evil associates," pay back the woman he defrauded, and to send his earnings to his mother "to support his wife and two children." Lastly, he was to "abstain from liquor altogether."[84]*

Charles Coons of Santa Clara County, California, convicted of selling intoxicating liquor in 1925, was also lucky. But for him, too, probation was not exactly freedom. Six standard conditions were printed on the probation form the county used. The probationer had to "accept the first honorable employment" offered; he had to get written consent from the probation officer if he moved or changed jobs; he had to report to the probation office once a month; "in all respects" he had to "conduct himself honestly, avoid all evil associations, obey the law, and abstain from the use of all intoxicating liquors, opium in any form, cocaine or other noxious drugs"; under no circumstances was he to "enter a saloon, where liquor is either sold or given away." Judges could, and often did, add other conditions. Coons, for example, was not to "visit . . . pool rooms, or prize fights, or other improper places."[85] A young offender in 1922, Lawrence Narvaez, was to "remain at home at night for a term of six months; except when accompanied by his father he cannot go down town. At all times during his probation he shall obey his father and be under his control."[86]

Still, probation was a good deal; defendants were certainly more than willing to take it, whatever the conditions; and many judges made free use of it. In January of 1917 in the Common Pleas Court of Cleveland, 135 men out of 254 found guilty of felony got probation (which in Cleveland was called, somewhat confusingly, "parole"). Not everyone approved. Reginald Heber Smith and Herbert B. Ehrmann, who participated in the Cleveland crime survey, were bitterly critical. These defendants, they wrote, "were a selected bad lot," the dregs of the process; those who had "anything in their favor" had been filtered out *before* trial, or by pleading down to a misdemeanor. Yet this "dangerous group went practically unpunished." They compared the judge's behavior to the "old game of 'Donkey'" where the "blindfolded player often relies upon the cheers of the onlookers to guide him to the spot where he can pin the animal's tail in its proper place." The judges "follow the clamor

---

* Judge Lewis remarked, in court, that "state prisons are not suitable places for the reformation of young men" who go wrong. This was true enough; but the system's sympathies were heavily influenced by class considerations: Banks's father was a "prominent contractor of San Francisco," and he came from a good family. This surely was a factor in his lenient disposition.

of the press and public." The fault also lay, in part, in the weak, under-staffed probation department. Defendants were paroled to "relatives, detectives, clerks, and even stenographers in the prosecutors office." As a result, probation was a "joke."[87]

Probation survived such critiques, and flourished. In fiscal year 1970, in the federal district courts, 28,178 defendants were convicted; of these, 12,771 were put on probation, slightly more than the 11,071 who were imprisoned.[88] The backlash and cries for toughness that followed in the seventies, however, were bound to have an impact on probation. In 1988, in the federal district courts, imprisonment now outweighed probation, 22,473 to 16,057. And in the state courts in 1986, it was estimated that 28 percent of the male felony defendants got probation, while 70 percent went to prison or jail.[89]* Perhaps if the prison crush were not so great, probation would have shown even more signs of shriveling.

The Sentencing Process

Probation involved (ideally, at least) an individualizing process—weighing the man or woman in the balance to see what he or she deserved. This was at the heart, too, of the indeterminate sentence (see chapter 7). And it was at the heart of the whole sentencing process, which vested vast discretion in the judge.

In California, for example, in the first part of the century, "proceedings upon sentence" took place after conviction. Judge and district attorney would ask questions to find out if the defendant had remorse, whether he or she was human rubbish or was worth a crack at salvation. They asked about the crime, about the defendant's attitudes, family background, health, habits, and history. William McAlpin was convicted of bigamy in Santa Clara County, in 1922: Do you use liquor? he was asked. The answer was no. Drugs? No. Do you ever gamble? He said: "I never had time, and it takes too much money to gamble." Do you "play any musical instruments?" It seems he did: "Piano, violin and cornet. I play all by ear. I have had no lessons."[90]

This last strikes us as a bizarre question, but it was standard in the county. Sometimes the district attorney wanted to know if the defendant could sing. What he was really looking for were clues to middle-class respectability. These proceedings were little morality dramas. They tended to become routine, stereotyped, but not, of course, to the poor soul whose fate hung in the balance. The judge, after all, was going

---

* Interestingly, 47 percent of the women convicted of felonies in state courts were put on probation and 50 percent sent to prison or jail.

to recommend to the prison authority how to handle prisoner X; and that was of vast importance to his fate, and to the length of his term. But all the judge had to go on were bits and fragments of data that the two sides served up, and the pieces of conventional morality that rattled about in his head. Somehow, these produced decisions.

A case from 1921, in the same county, neatly illustrates the process. The defendant, Andrew Clark, was young, poor, and black. He pleaded guilty to robbery but begged the judge for another chance. The assistant district attorney, a Mr. Bridges, came down hard on Clark: he "is a wanderer upon the earth and tramps all over. You have got no ties on him, no strings on him and he simply leaves here and what is the result"; he will simply prey "upon some other community." The judge, at first, felt some sympathy: Clark was black and the judge knew all about "the characteristics of his race. . . . I know their disposition—they go and commit a crime and they are the first always to acknowledge it." But Bridges demurred: in fact, Clark was the "last one to acknowledge it. He has always denied it until he pleaded guilty here. He claimed that he bought the [stolen] watches from the other fellows." This obstinacy turned the tide. The judge sent Clark to San Quentin.[91]

Clark was a loner, a rolling stone, without social connections; his repentance and confession came too late; and he was black. All this doomed him to a tough sentence. The search for good eggs and bad eggs pervaded the system. It affected sentencing to the core. It also led to more and more savage statutes on habitual criminals, since these were, of course, the worst of the worst, the incorrigibles. New York's law, the so-called "Baumes law" (1926) was absolutely draconian. It called for life imprisonment after a fourth conviction for a felony.[92] The law showed the good citizens that New York could be, when it wished, exceedingly tough on crime.

The vice of such laws came out clearly in *People ex rel. Marcley v. Lawes*, decided by the New York Court of Appeals in 1930.[93] The *Marcley* case also shows, in a particularly vivid way, how the court's power to "interpret" law can mean the power to twist law like taffy. Marcley was a fourth offender. On June 27, 1921, he pleaded guilty to a felony: attempted theft of a motorcycle. Sentence was suspended. A year later, he pleaded guilty to burglary in the third degree: he broke into a chicken house and stole some chickens. Another suspended sentence. On the same day, he pleaded guilty to a third crime: burglarizing a garage and stealing "automobile accessories." This got him three years and six months in Sing Sing. The fourth offense was stealing an automobile; Marcley pleaded guilty and was sentenced to life imprisonment in Sing Sing.

A bare majority of the court (four judges) set the sentence aside.

These judges were clearly horrified at the thought that a man of twenty-five, "because he had previously stolen chickens, certain automobile parts, and a motorcycle, must spend the remainder of his days in a state's prison." To avoid this dreadful result, the court decided that a suspended sentence should not count as a conviction. This was almost certainly not what the legislature intended. But then, too, the legislature had not had poor Marcley in mind.

The case also illustrates how dangerous it is to *remove* discretion from sentencing. After 1950, as the crime rate escalated and fear of crime became the dominant force pushing policy in criminal justice, there were many attempts to impose stiff, mandatory sentences: use a gun, go to jail; sell a drug, go to jail, and so on. The most extreme, perhaps, was the New York drug law, which Governor Nelson Rockefeller pushed through in 1973. It called for very stiff, and mandatory, minimum sentences for drug offenses; the maximum was life imprisonment. Some restrictions on plea bargaining were built into the law. It was so harsh that even prosecutors and the police were aghast and opposed the bill; but to no avail. In practice, the law was an expensive and dismal failure. It did not solve the drug problem; it led to major injustices (extreme sentences imposed on small fry); and it nearly wrecked the system of criminal justice—or would have, if it had been carried out as designed. The law turned into an embarrassment, and the legislature, in essence, got rid of it in 1979.[94] But the very fact that such a law could be passed, and touted as a cure of the ills of the system, was a definite sign of the times.

The movement to reform sentencing was connected, politically and ideologically, with the movement that blasted away at indeterminate sentencing and parole. Nobody seemed to like the American sentencing system. It was, on the one hand, too flabby, and on the other hand, awfully unjust. Sentencing seemed to be totally irrational. It depended on the whims of the judge. Two people who had committed the "same crime" could receive wildly different sentences. The judge had "blank-check powers"; these powers, according to Judge Marvin Frankel, formed the "central evil" of the system—a "wild array of sentencing judgments without any semblance of the consistency demanded by the ideal of equal justice."[95] Some felt that this situation "fostered undue optimism among offenders who hoped to 'beat the rap,'" or that it "undermined deterrence and crime control objectives." Meanwhile, the "disparities fed prisoner resentment and impeded rehabilitation."[96] Evidence could be mustered to support some of these propositions, but it was hardly overwhelming.

Certainly, sentencing reform did not respond to any deep *public* yearning for justice; there was no outcry from the masses against disparities in sentencing; no major interest group stood foursquare for the principle that like must be treated like. The precise reforms came out of the academy and the profession. A good deal of the academic impulse was benign—part of the search for fairness, for due process. But it seems clear that the success of the academic efforts depended on something deeper, more subterranean. General dismay over crime, and the (apparent) failure of criminal justice, lent force to any change that promised to toughen up the system. In any event, firm, immovable sentences *seemed* like a step in the direction of "law and order," as well as a step toward justice. This was a potent political combination.

Minnesota established a special sentencing commission in 1978, charged with producing "guidelines."[97] In due course, the guidelines appeared and the state gave them its stamp of approval. Under the Minnesota scheme, the judge consulted a complex grid, or matrix, in order to figure out a defendant's "score." One dimension of the grid was the nature of the crime itself, ranked from the truly awful, like murder, down to less serious crimes. Another dimension of the grid was the defendant's "criminal history score," which meant, essentially, whether or not he was a repeater. Once the judge shoved the defendant into the right cell of the matrix, she could either give him the "presumptive sentence" or vary it a bit—that is, make it a shade tougher or more lenient. But these variations were small, and if a judge chose *not* to use the "presumptive sentence," she had to provide some sort of written defense of her action.[98]

Minnesota's experiment reverberated in other states. On the federal level, Congress did away with the U.S. Parole Commission in 1984 and set up a Sentencing Commission. This was an independent agency inside the judicial branch; its job was to draft sentencing guidelines for federal judges. The guidelines went into effect in 1987. Here too crimes were ranked on a scale. Murder got a top score of 43; blackmail got a 9. The judge could add and subtract from the basic score, according to formulas that gave values to this or that factor.

These guidelines, however, were not the last word. There have been amendments, and amendments of amendments; the whole process has become hideously complex. As of April 1992, there were 434 of these amendments, and the guidelines were well on their way to a level of convolution and intricacy hardly matched by any other laws—*maybe* the Internal Revenue Code.

The complexity was probably inevitable. To be fair, or even try to be fair, the guidelines would have to embrace all sorts of factors and make all sorts of fine distinctions. Robbery, for example, had a base score of 20; if you rob a bank, add two points; if you shoot a gun, add seven; but if you only "brandish" the gun, add a mere five.[99] All this goes to create a patchwork of complexity.

No surprise, then, that by 1992, there were rumblings of discontent among federal judges. Naturally, they resented the straitjacket effect. But they also considered the guidelines much too harsh. From academia, Albert W. Alschuler suggested scrapping them altogether, relegating the guidelines "to a place near the Edsel in a museum of 20th-century bad ideas."[100] There were also signs of outright rebellion: some judges simply ignored what the guidelines told them to do. This was an old, familiar story in the criminal justice non-system: one head of the Hydra frustrating another, or actually biting it. The law-and-order backlash collided here with the culture and politics of judges; and this led, as so often, to stalemate and slippage. Whether the guideline system can redeem itself remains to be seen.

Juvenile Justice

In the nineteenth century, a number of steps were taken to separate young offenders from grown-up criminals—before, during, and after trial (see chapter 7). At the very end of the century, the first juvenile court was established, in Cook County, Illinois. In the twentieth century, juvenile courts and a special brand of juvenile justice became the national norm. Colorado passed a juvenile court act in 1903. Like the Illinois law, it lumped together children who committed crimes, those who were simply "incorrigible," and a miscellaneous lot of difficult or troubled young people: those who were "growing up in idleness or crime," or who associated with "vicious or immoral persons," or who wandered about the streets at night, or who "habitually" wandered about "railroad yards," jumping or hooking on to "any moving train," or who used bad language or were "guilty of immoral conduct in any public place or about any school house."[101] Colorado also had a dynamic juvenile court judge, Ben Lindsey, who ran a charismatic, highly personal court in Denver, ruling it as a kind of "benevolent judicial despot."[102] In any event, in a relatively short span of time, almost every state had juvenile courts of its own.

The juvenile court, and juvenile justice generally, grew out of a movement of "child savers." Many leaders of this movement were women; in Illinois, one important group was centered around the famous reformer, Jane Addams, and Hull House, which she ran. There is some dispute about what moved these movers and what the juvenile courts actually accomplished. In a book that ruffled some academic feathers, Anthony Platt, a criminologist at Berkeley, took a fairly cynical (and leftist) view. These reformers, he argued, "invented" delinquency. Most casual observers (and practitioners) thought the juvenile court meant progress, humanity, and a retreat from barbarism; but not Platt. In his view, the laws only "consolidated the inferior social status and dependency of lower-class youth."[103] They were simply more bricks in the house of oppression—the oppression of poor children and their parents.[104]

What lends some credence to Platt's thesis is the fact that juvenile justice lumped together children of very different stripes and patterns: truants, kids who acted out, young hoodlums, abused and neglected children. It extended state control over children—mostly poor children—who were in trouble. But this seemed necessary at the time. As Judge Ben Lindsey put it, "all children are delinquent at some time or other." Delinquency was a "state, condition, or environment into which the child enters"; if something were not done to change the situation, the child might "eventually" grow up to *be* a criminal.[105] The juvenile court was supposed to bend the twig the other way. Hence the need for loose, flexible, humane, therapeutic procedures. In theory, proceedings in juvenile court were not criminal proceedings at all. Boys and girls sent to detention homes and reform schools were not going to prison, but to places where they would be nurtured and trained.

No doubt there was a good deal of middle-class snobbery and condescension in these attitudes—not to mention blindness to some obvious facts of life. No doubt, too, the reformers (and judges) really did not understand the kids and their families. These were mostly working-class families, many of them immigrants who spoke broken English and found American ways bewildering. The reformers believed that delinquency came from disrupted home life, a weak or vicious environment, immoral habits, and evil companions. A century later, their views may seem like Victorian or Edwardian hogwash. Thomas Travis, writing in 1908, mentions "bad literature" as one source of the problem. In the Waukesha Reformatory, "only twenty-four out of two hundred and fifty-five boys . . . had read a single good book. 'Diamond Dick' was the usual type. It is not unknown to find counterfeiting and even murder springing from bad reading." Many boys read "newspaper details of such criminals as 'Jack the Ripper.'" Another source was "bad theatres." Children see a "Buffalo Bill" drama or some "strikingly melodramatic piece" and the crime rate soars. The theaters contribute to delinquency because of two factors: "uncontrolled excitement and a craving induced in the poorer children which leads them to steal in order to get the entrance fee."[106] Judge Lindsey, writing in 1925, warned about the automobile and "unchaperoned rides"; about movies, which "have visualized in a dramatic way the activities of sex"; about jazz, and such modern conveniences as electric lights, all of which were "enormously stimulating." Youth's problems resulted from its confrontation with this sort of modernity.[107]

The modern reader smiles smugly at all of this, but the point becomes a bit less absurd if we try to translate it into contemporary terms. We can hardly laugh off the idea of "stimulation" and "craving," or the impact of the mass media. This is nothing less than the theory that one source of social pathology is the so-called revolution of rising expectations. The child in the twentieth century is no longer cocooned within the family. (The family itself is not what it used to be.) The child is exposed to the outside world, through books, newspapers, movies, the radio—and TV. The child looks hungrily through the screen at the glittering images of a consumer society. On this side of the screen is a drab, stunted, pinch-penny life. Traditional morality was once a wall of protection and insulation; but now these walls are moldy and decayed, crumbling, ineffectual.

In essays and reports appearing in the first decades of the century, there was mostly fulsome praise of the juvenile courts. What the children thought about it is something we hardly know at all. We have plenty of bland descriptions and studies of jurisdiction, procedures, outcomes,[108] but it is not so easy to peel the outer rind and see what the courts were really like—their smell, their look, how they felt from the bottom up.

What we do know does not quite jibe with Anthony Platt's diatribe. In the early years, in particular, the children were not, by and large, dragged into court by social workers, policemen, upper-class snoops and hegemonists. More often than not they were brought in by their very own parents. This comes out clearly in the files of the juvenile court of Alameda County from 1903 to 1910, which Friedman and Percival studied. Louise Rolland's mother complained that her thirteen-year-old daughter was "incorrigible." She kept company with "bad and dissolute characters" and stayed out all night. Minnie Young, the mother of George Oscar Young (seventeen years old), was a widow. Her son, she said, was "vicious" and paid her "no respect whatsoever." Bartolomeo Comella was a widower; his son, Salvatorio, kept late hours and "upon his return he does not explain to his father where he has been." He also stole $100 from his father's trunk.[109]

The evidence from this and other studies suggests that the juvenile courts were popular courts. Working-class and immigrant parents *used* the courts, as a club over rebellious children. It was a weapon in a culture clash—a clash of generations, especially between old world parents, at sea in America, confused about values, horrified at the mobility, the laxity, the narcissism, the "fatal liberty" that swallowed up their children and destroyed a nexus between parent and child that they had thought to be as sacred as a worshipped sun.

It all seems, in a way, terribly distant and somewhat innocent: kids who stole peaches, or went joy riding, or smoked and drank a bit, or had a taste for sex. Most delinquents were boys—in Cleveland, in 1920, there were 2,524 of them, and only 584 delinquent girls, according to the Cleveland Crime Survey of 1922.[110] Nonetheless, the double standard was in full flower. Girls were dragged into court for sexual activity that never troubled the parents of boys. Nobody dreamt then of fifteen-year-olds with submachine guns, or the hard-core delinquents and toughs who would appear after 1950. But as the years went on, the police role in juvenile justice got larger and larger, and the parental role diminished accordingly. As early as 1919, in Boston and St. Louis, the police referred to the court more than 80 percent of the delinquency cases in these cities; in Los Angeles, the police brought in 61 percent, parents only 21 percent.[111]

The system of juvenile justice was part of the general system of criminal justice, and it went through the same cycles of ebb and flow. There was the Warren Court era, with its emphasis on rights and due process, followed by the post-Warren backlash. The landmark juvenile case of the Warren Court was *In re Gault* (1967).[112] Gerald Francis Gault was fifteen years old. He got in trouble in 1964 "in the company of another boy who had stolen a wallet from a lady's purse." Gault was put on six months' probation. Before that period expired, the police picked Gault up again: a neighbor had complained about indecent phone calls. Process in the Juvenile Court of Gila County, Arizona, was informal, perfunctory; in the end, the judge declared Gault a delinquent, and committed him to the State Industrial School.

The Supreme Court cast a sharp, beady eye on the system of juvenile justice. It cut through the cant that had encrusted the system—the idea that the courts were motherly, caring places, dedicated to helping young people, not to punishing them; that there was no need for lawyers or due process because everything that went on was only for the child's own good. The system had committed Gault to an "institution where he may be restrained of liberty for years." This was punishment, whatever one called it. Naming the institution an "industrial school" instead of a prison did not change the realities. If this was a kind of punishment, then the informality and discretion would not do. Proceedings in juvenile court had to recognize the constitutional rights, the "due process" rights, of young people caught in this web.

The *Gault* decision left an important mark on the system. Since this case was decided, state and federal governments alike have had to reform juvenile justice. Everywhere, proceedings in juvenile court have become more like proceedings in adult criminal courts—though never *exactly* the same. The *Gault* decision today seems unassailable; there is no turning back to the early days before *Gault*.

But there have been other changes in the world, which also affect juvenile justice. Criminals have been getting younger and younger in the post–World War II era. Young crime, like older crime, has become tougher, more violent, more dangerous—and more prevalent. The processing of juveniles is thus more serious, more of a social problem—and more like *adult* criminal justice. Backlash, moreover, has set in here, too. So, in New York, after a juvenile murdered two subway passengers in 1978, a cry went up for some action against underage hoodlums. The action turned out to be a statute that allowed juveniles who committed certain crimes to be tried as an adult—as young as thirteen for murder, fourteen and fifteen for other serious offenses.[113] Similar statutes have been passed in other states.

Criminal Appeals

The last stage in the process, if a defendant lost, was the right of criminal appeal. It was, as we have seen (chapter 11), a right rarely exercised before the twentieth century. Few defendants appealed in the nineteenth century, and even fewer made use of constitutional arguments. This trend reversed itself in the twentieth century on both accounts, and the number of appeals grew tremendously. There was, however, considerable variation from state to state. In the twenties and thirties, for example, criminal appeals were a much higher percentage of the total load of high courts in the South than in the North. In New Mexico, Alabama, Tennessee, Georgia, and Mississippi, more than a fourth of all appeals were criminal appeals in 1912; in Kansas, in 1937, criminal appeals were 11.7 percent; in Rhode Island, in the late twenties, they were only 3 percent.[114]

Appeals were not usually successful; defendants generally beat against the doors of appellate courts in vain. In Kansas, in the decade ending in 1937, the high court affirmed over 80 percent of the cases appealed; in California, the affirmance rate in the 1930s approached 90 percent; and even in death penalty appeals, only one case out of fifty-eight was actually reversed.[115] A study of criminal appeals in California showed, in fact, that the reversal rate had been dropping steadily between 1850 and 1926 (the last year studied). In the decade of the 1850s, half of all the cases were reversed; in the last decade of the nineteenth century, 38.9 percent; in 1910–19, 15.9 percent; in the 1920s, 14.7 percent.[116]*

In the course of the century, criminal appeals seemed to show fewer

---

* Defendants did do somewhat better in some states. In Missouri, in the decade 1915–1924, the supreme court decided 745 criminal cases. Of these, 420 were affirmed, 279 reversed and remanded, and 46 reversed outright. (The affirmance rate was 56.4 percent.) It should be noted, though, that another 342 appeals by defendants during this decade were simply dismissed by the Missouri court because the defendant had "failed to take the steps necessary to perfect his appeal.[117]

and fewer horrible examples of "hypertrophy." Texas, to be sure, continued to produce some amazing instances. In *Gragg v. State* (1945),[118] the indictment had charged that Chesley Gragg killed his wife Flora "by . . . drowning the said Flora Gragg." Gragg had been in a boat with his wife and stepson. They died by drowning, and the question was, did Gragg drown them or did they die by accident? Gragg was convicted; but the Court of Criminal Appeals of Texas reversed the decision. The indictment had been defective; it did not say Flora Gragg was drowned in *water*; and, after all, there is "more than one means by which . . . drowning may be accomplished." (As an irate commentator put it, the indictment did not allege, according to the motion to quash, *"whether the deceased was drown [sic] in water, coffee, tea or what."*)[119] This, it seems, was a fatal flaw.*

But the tide was running the other way. In some states, statutes introduced the concept of "harmless error." An appeals court could affirm the trial court, even if that court had committed "errors," so long as the errors were "harmless," that is, they were unlikely actually to prejudice a jury. New rules of procedure—simpler, less technical, more streamlined—helped avoid trouble in the upper stories of the building. Most criminal appeals are affirmed, not reversed, as has long been the case. This is only to be expected. The flood of criminal appeals is not a historical accident. It is easy to find the causes. More free attorneys is one source. Another is the rapid expansions, especially in the 1950s, of due process rights. A third is the rights culture, which affects men in prison as well as the rest of society. If appeal is free, why not try it? There is little or nothing to lose. Hence, more marginal cases get appealed than, say, contract or tort cases; affirmances are thus exactly what one would expect.

To be sure, some situations are special. One is death-penalty cases. In many states, these are automatically appealed.[121] In many states, too, they are particularly liable to get reversed, as we have seen (chapter 14). For a judge horrified at the thought of putting a fellow creature to death, even a fly speck on the record is enough to send the case back down.

---

* On rehearing, the court stuck to its decision, though it did backtrack a bit. The problem (the court now said) was that the indictment did not say *how* Flora was drowned—did he push her into the water, or hold her head under, or what? There "should be an averment of some overt act of the accused which brought about the drowning of his wife, if such act is known."[120]

18

GENDER AND JUSTICE

CRIMINAL JUSTICE IN THE TWENTIETH CENTURY HAS COME TO RECKON WITH women in new and different ways. We have already touched on some of the points. Women arrived on police forces, for example. We also traced changes in some crimes that had special impact on women, statutory rape and seduction, for example. In this chapter, we look at gender and justice more directly.

Women in the Courtroom

In the nineteenth century, women were in the courtroom as onlookers, victims, witnesses, or defendants. They ran no trials, served on no juries. Even a western state like Wyoming, where women had the right to vote for state officers *before* the Nineteenth Amendment, balked at putting women on juries.*

---

* In 1892 a convicted defendant (male) tried out an argument that was novel for its day. His jury was invalid, he claimed, because it was "exclusively composed of male persons." The state high court declared flatly that no *man* had the right to raise this point, to begin with, and the custom in Wyoming was against using women on juries anyway.[1]

In the twentieth century, the situation slowly, and somewhat grudgingly, changed. The Nineteenth Amendment (1920) gave women the right to vote; it did not automatically put them in the jury box, let alone at counsel's table, or on the bench. A few states did move quickly to implement women's rights. But others dawdled and lagged. To put women on juries meant that men had to rethink, to a degree, their notions of the nature and role of women. Some men were fearful of disruption in the home: "baby . . . in a fury" with "mama . . . on the jury."[2] Some states let women serve on juries but made it easy for them to wriggle out of the duty—much easier than for men. Among these states was Oregon (1921); the Oregon statute made it the "duty" of the person who served a jury summons "to inform every female person so served" of her right to beg off.[3]* Early accounts often gave women jurors high marks. But male judges were still uncomfortable with the idea. One Pennsylvania court went to the heart of the matter: there was "no waiting-room for the women," inadequate toilets, "no separate rooms to which women could retire," and no beds except cots to sleep on.[4]

The bed problem was an obstacle because juries were sometimes sequestered, and, horror of horrors, what was to be done with a mixed jury under such circumstances? One writer suggested handling the overnight problem by putting "a woman bailiff in charge of the women, and a man bailiff in charge of the men," with "partitions between members of the two sexes, while still keeping them together in the same room."[5] One California county came up with an ingenious, though rather questionable, solution in a case where a woman, Anna Manuel, went on trial for forgery. The court produced a jury made up *entirely* of women; after all, a mixed jury "would not be nice" if night sessions proved necessary.[6] Another problem was that some cases were quite unsuitable for ladies. In Minnesota in 1927, local authorities, aware that cases of "carnal knowledge" were coming up, decided to exclude women; ladies, after all, would be deeply offended if they were forced to hear such things. An appeals court agreed.[7]

Some states simply made women exempt. In 1921, after the Nineteenth Amendment was ratified, South Carolina amended its jury law to excuse "female electors," along with the governor and a list of others, including "licensed embalmers."[8] The Louisiana Constitution of 1921 specified that no woman could serve on a jury unless she filed with the clerk of the district court "a written declaration of her desire to be subject to such service."[9] Naturally, under a rule like this, women were ex-

---

* The Oregon statute also provided, however, that in criminal cases "in which a minor under the age of eighteen years is involved," as defendant or complaining witness, "at least one-half the jury shall be women."

ceedingly scarce on Louisiana juries. But the provision was in full force until the U.S. Supreme Court finally struck it down in 1975. The Constitution, said the Court, required every state to guarantee a "fair cross section" of the community, and this was impossible if no women were allowed to serve.[10]* Today, women are as common as men on juries; and they have a reasonable chance of hearing women lawyers argue, or hear the gavel pounded by a woman judge.

"More Terrible Than Any Man": Women in Crime

When the "science" of "criminal anthropology" reached its dubious heights in the late nineteenth and early twentieth centuries, quite a few thinkers were intoxicated with the idea of the "born criminal." The Italian scholar Cesare Lombroso, leading light of the biological school, did the same number on women that he had already done on men when he published *The Female Offender* in 1894, in collaboration with Guglielmo Ferrero. Long passages in the book catalogued "facial and cephalic anomalies" or compared, for example, the skulls of female criminals with skulls of "normal" and "fallen" women.

Lombroso, of course, had to confront the obvious fact that women were sparse in the ranks of serious crime. Women, he thought, were "conservative . . . in all questions of social order." It was the "immobility of the ovule compared with the zoosperm" that brought about this conservatism. Sexual selection also operated to weed out potential women criminals. "Man not only refused to *marry* a deformed female, but ate her while preserving for his enjoyment the handsome woman."[13]

Women were also more "primitive" than men, and more "sedentary," less "subject to transformation and deformation." They were basically childlike, with a "deficient" moral sense. Ordinarily, "piety, maternity, want of passion, . . . weakness and an undeveloped intelligence" kept their vices in check. But watch out: if these traits failed, or if powerful counterdrives overwhelmed them, then "the innocuous semicriminal present in the normal woman must be transformed into a born criminal more terrible than any man." The female "born criminal," then, though rarer than the male, was "often much more ferocious."[14]

Ferocious or not, women were and are radically underrepresented among the ranks of those arrested, charged, and tried for crime. To this

---

* The Supreme Court had earlier ordered *federal* courts to avoid systematically excluding women in *Ballard v. United States*.[11] In *Duren v. Missouri* the issue was a Missouri statute that made it extremely easy for women to avoid jury duty. As a result, only 15 percent of the panels were composed of women. This, said the Court, violated the principle of a fair cross section.[12]

day, they make a rather feeble contribution to the criminal nation. Statistics can lie, or show bias, but the chasm between men and women in criminal statistics is so vast that no bias could possibly explain it away. No serious student of crime or criminal justice has the slightest doubt that women, in general, just do not go in for serious crimes, especially crimes of bodily harm, of violence, of bloodshed.

In the last generation or so, there has been considerable movement in gender relations. There has been a boom in women lawyers, doctors, politicians, accountants, even women clergy (in *some* religions)—nothing remotely approaching parity in most fields, but the trend is clear. Yet robbery, burglary, arson, and assault are still most definitely not equal-opportunity careers; and prison is still, by and large, a man's world. In 1950, 3.5 percent of the adult prisoners in state and federal prisons were women. In 1975, the figure had risen—to 3.6 percent. Between 1930 and 1973, 3,827 men were put to death; the figure for women—exactly 32—is less than 1 percent of that.*

Further down the scale of criminality, women do somewhat better— but only somewhat. In 1970, 5.7 percent of the prisoners in local jails were women. There is more balance among juveniles. In correctional facilities for young people, in 1950, there were 14,098 girls and 42,566 boys—about a quarter of the total number, in other words, were female. This did not change much in the next generation; the percentage of girls, in fact, declined somewhat. In 1974, 10,139 girls and 34,783 boys were in custody—the proportion of girls, in other words, had dropped to 22.6 percent of the total.[16]

To be sure, the *absolute* number of women arrested and tried is quite large. In 1905, the New York City police made 198,356 arrests; women made up one out of five of this group (39,886). There were 2,026 women vagrants (as against 6,307 men); 10,080 women were hauled in for "intoxication" (as compared to 34,005 men); and 13,114 for "disorderly conduct" (almost half of the figure for men, which was 26,858). But only 32 women were arrested for burglary, as against 2,247 men; 16 men were arrested for murder, but not a single woman. Women outnumbered men in only a handful of crimes: "keeping a disorderly house" (958 arrests of women to 511 of men), "soliciting" (for prostitution), and, interestingly, for violations of the Tenement House Law.[17] In Omaha, Nebraska, 9,277 women were arrested in the years 1930 through 1934; almost 20 percent were charged with "vagrancy and prostitution"; there were substantial numbers charged with drunkenness, disturbing the peace, liquor of-

---

* As of July 1992, there were 315 men and 5 women on death row in Florida. Nationally, there were 40 women condemned to die. One woman, Velma Barfield, has been executed since 1976 (she died in North Carolina in 1984), as against 175 men.[15]

fenses, and similar offenses—but only 1.24 percent for "assault and battery"; no other crime of violence amounted to even 1 percent of arrests.[18]

In 1966, women represented only 12 percent of the total arrests reported in the FBI's Uniform Crime Reports; they accounted for only 5 percent of the arrests for robbery, 4 percent for burglary, and 9 percent for violent crimes in general. However, some 16 percent of the arrests for homicides were laid at the doorstep of women. A decade later, in 1976, the women's figure had crept up to 16 percent of total arrests, and 10 percent of the violent crimes; they were dominant only in arrests for "prostitution and commercialized vice" (71 percent).[19] By 1987, women were making a game showing in crimes against property and white-collar crimes: they accounted for 31 percent of the larceny arrests, 44 percent of the fraud arrests, 34 percent of the forgery arrests, and 38 percent of the arrests for embezzlement. Women had entered the work force in droves, which put them in a position to commit these property and white-collar crimes—housewives, after all, have nothing to embezzle.[20] There were also definite but small increases in robbery and burglary figures—the woman's share had crept up to 8 percent of the total. But in 1987, women still accounted for only 11.1 percent of violent crime.[21] There are, as is obvious, oddities and quirks in the figures, as well as some bewildering variations. But the overall picture remains basically the same.

The drug wars that have swelled the jail populations have swept many women into their nets. In recent years, women (like men) have been arrested, convicted, and sent to prison in the thousands for drug offenses. A study published in 1977 showed that over 20 percent of the women in prison had been sent there for this reason; and for some population groups the percentage was even higher. More than 40 percent of the Hispanic women in prison had been convicted of drug offenses.[22]

Criminologists, on the whole, do not pay much attention to women's crimes; theories of criminality are mostly or entirely theories about men.[23] Yet, at the very least, what women do (and do not do) provides a magnificent control group for testing assumptions about men and their crimes. There are those, of course, who think genetics, plain and simple, explains the differences. Women, in other words, are not born criminals at all, but born *non*-criminals. Some sort of gene for aggression is missing; or, to put it the other way around, men have too much of one. Other theories are more social or psychological; they turn on gender roles, on the way women are raised, and so on. It remains to be seen what the halting steps toward gender equality will bring. Will women change the world, or will the world change women? Will there be an outburst in violence *by* women—along with more heart attacks and ulcers? Somehow one doubts it.

The Oldest Profession

Some criminal laws, of course, target women—especially laws against prostitution and disorderly houses. Men, to be sure, can also be arrested for prostitution, and, under many laws, for buying what prostitutes sell. But nobody *enforces* the laws against male customers; it is overwhelmingly women who pay the price. In a few states, this bias was quite overt and official. Under an Indiana statute, for example, dating back to the time of the First World War, it was a crime for a "female" to offer her body for sale; the law said nothing about male prostitutes, and certainly nothing about customers.[24]* Once in a while, a city tried to crack down on "johns." In New York City in 1921, in a test case, police officers arrested a man found in "certain premises," lying "in bed between two girls who were entirely nude." The defendant "was in his union suit" (there was disagreement "as to whether such union suit consisted of B.V.D.'s or underwear of another make"). This hapless soul was dragged into court; but the judge dismissed the case. In the judge's opinion, the male customer, who "had come for a good time," violated no known law of the state of New York. A few magistrates actually convicted male customers, but so few that the police were discouraged from making such arrests for fear of civil suits for false arrest, in case the defendant is discharged."[25]

Generally speaking, when men were arrested along with women, they escaped free, or, at worst, with a small fine and a healthy dose of embarrassment. In Philadelphia, during one "illustrative" instance in 1920, a "colored vice squad officer" watched a black streetwalker pick up a middle-aged white man (he turned out to be a shipyard worker with a wife and three children). The officer followed the couple, who entered a house; he waited outside for fifteen minutes (giving the couple enough time to get through the preliminaries), then burst in and arrested the two of them as they lay in bed. The woman had no record, but the judge sentenced her to six months in the house of correction. The shipyard worker paid ten dollars and court costs, and went sheepishly home.[26]

The destruction of the red-light districts, in the teens, closed down houses and drove many women into the streets. This crusade (see chapter 15) replaced madams with (often brutal) male pimps, and in many cities simply made the women's lives more degraded and more dangerous.[27] In New York, a special Women's Court was set up in 1918 to deal

---

* The Indiana law defined a prostitute as a female who "commits adultery or fornication for hire." Interestingly, a "female" was also declared a prostitute if she lived in a "house . . . of ill-fame" or "associated" with women of "bad character for chastity, either in public or at a house which men of bad character frequent or visit."

with "women sex delinquents." This court commonly processed large numbers of prostitutes after "jump-raids." The vice police followed the usual technique: after a pickup, they shadowed the couple to the scene of the crime, waited ten or fifteen minutes ("sufficient time," as one account rather delicately put it, "for incriminating evidence to be obtained"), and then made the raid. Most women defendants were, of course, convicted; first offenders often got probation, but repeaters (and there were many of these) were sent either to "reformative institutions" or to the Workhouse.[28] Of course, the people who worked in and around this court thought of themselves as humanitarians: they were helping to save society from disease and depravity while giving fallen women a second chance. In retrospect, however, it is clear where the burdens fell: on the poorest and most unfortunate of the women who sold their bodies on the street.

In 1922, Betty Carey, a San Francisco prostitute, was sentenced to the California Industrial Farm for Women. A California law, passed in 1919, allowed women found guilty of "prostitution . . . or of vagrancy because of being a common prostitute" to be sent to the farm (whose purpose, according to the law, was to provide "custody, care, protection, industrial and other training and reformatory help for delinquent women").[29] Ms. Carey did not want that sort of "help," and she protested on a number of grounds, among them the fact that only women were liable under the statute.

The court brushed aside her objections. For one thing, only women could commit the crime of prostitution (apparently, California high court judges in 1922 could not conceive of a male prostitute at all). In any event, "fallen women" represented "a greater single element of economic, social, moral, and hygienic loss than is the case with any other single criminal class." From the standpoint of public health, they were "pestilential, . . . a common pathological danger." The state, "realizing" that the fallen woman cannot escape from her "life of shame," had "undertaken to take forcible charge of this class of unfortunates and extend to them a home, education, assistance, and encouragement." In so doing, the state combined "both altruism and self-preservation."[30]

The rise of a strong feminist movement in the 1960s and 1970s focused attention on prostitution once more. In 1971, the National Organization for Women (NOW), after condemning the social conditions that permitted the exploitation of women, came out foursquare for the decriminalization of prostitution.[31] By this time, "working women" had even formed an organization, a kind of prostitutes' union. But society was apparently not ready for decriminalization. No other state seemed eager to follow the example of Nevada, which made prostitution legal by "local option," that is, county by county.* Elsewhere, prostitution remained illegal, though the laws were only gingerly enforced. This is one area where the Victorian compromise has apparently never died.

Sexual Justice

It is no surprise to find that the double standard, so deeply embedded in men's minds, found its way into criminal codes. The chastity of wives and daughters was very precious to the law. The Texas law that allowed a man to kill his wife's lover if he caught the pair in the act survived until only just yesterday (1973).[33] In a number of states, there were variations on this general theme. In Delaware, for example, manslaughter was a felony, but it dropped to a misdemeanor if "committed by a husband on a person found in the act of adultery with his wife."[34] Needless to say, a woman who caught her *husband* in the act was given no such license to kill. As we have seen, the double standard operated in delinquency law as well; girls were declared delinquent for sexual behavior that would not raise an eyebrow if committed by boys. What was "wild oats" for him was delinquency for her.

Paul W. Tappan, writing in the 1940s about New York's Wayward Minor Court, was one of the few who spoke out against the double standard. By what right, he asked, does a court impose penalties "for the nonprostitutional (and frequently nonpromiscuous) sex behavior of girls from sixteen to twenty-one"? What authorized it to punish "filial insubordination"? Tappan's case material was full of horror stories. An eighteen-year-old, the daughter of Greek parents, fell in love with a "dark-skinned Puerto Rican." The parents tried to get the Wayward Minor Court to commit her to Bellevue Hospital; they insisted she was "backward" and demanded that she be "put away." She escaped the grips of the court (and her family) only by marrying a different man.[35]

Mary Odem researched the cases of delinquent girls in the custody of the Los Angeles County Juvenile Court in 1920—220 cases in all. Most were working-class girls. They were charged primarily (90 percent) with status offenses: running away, violation of curfew, incorrigibility, and, above all (81 percent) with sex or morals offenses. In one case, a school principal turned a girl over to the authorities because she wore "tight skirts, high-heeled shoes, and silk stockings." A vice-principal turned in a twelve-year-old girl because she was "idle and in conversation with

---

* Curiously enough, prostitution is not legal in Las Vegas and its county; under the statute, a county license board cannot grant any license "for the purpose of operating a house of ill fame or repute" in any county "whose population is 400,000 or more."[32] There is only one such county in the state—Clark County, in which Las Vegas is located. Is Las Vegas worried that men will wander too far from the slot machines?

boys on Main St. and various places and finally I thought for the good of the other girls something must be done." These were perhaps extreme cases; mostly, girls got in trouble for sex, plain and simple—a typical case was Rose Lafitte, who worked at the Jewel City Cafe, arrested in a hotel room, naked, with her boyfriend, Eddie Morgan. Two policemen who had followed them to the hotel (and saw them register as man and wife) put their ears to the door and listened. They heard enough to justify barging in—and enough to send Rose to juvenile court.[36] Only in the days of the "sexual revolution" did the double standard start to weaken; it took a massive dose of social change, and the women's movement, to break down some of the taboos about women, young women, and sex.

These were the special crimes of women. When women were accused of ordinary crimes, how did they do? Were they treated the same as men, or worse, or better? Were they less likely to be arrested, tried, and convicted, or more? Less likely or more to get lenient sentences? The evidence for the sixties and seventies seemed to suggest a certain amount of "chivalry" among judges (who were still overwhelmingly male). The differences were not dramatic, but they were consistent. Women in grand larceny cases, for example, were more likely than men to be released on bail, or to get probation or a suspended sentence. One judge in the Washington, D.C. area, who allowed he was, in fact, more lenient to women, could not explain why, except to say that "I love my mother very much." Some judges thought jail was too degrading for women; some were particularly loath to lock up mothers of small children. The "chivalry effect" held up into the eighties as well.[37]

Women's Prisons

Chivalry extended to and beyond the prison gates. Women's jails and institutions tended to be more benign than the ones men were thrown into. In *State v. Heitman*, an interesting Kansas case of 1919, the defendant, a woman, was convicted of "keeping a liquor nuisance."[38] The judge imposed a fine of $100 and committed her to the state industrial farm for women, under an indeterminate sentence; this was in accordance with a statute of 1917. A man convicted of the same offense would have been treated differently; he would have gone to county jail, for a definite term. For both sexes, the maximum "jolt" (farm or jail) was six months. But Ms. Heitman, on appeal, insisted the statute violated her rights—why should men and women have different, and unequal, punishment, for one and the same kind of behavior?

The court saw no merit in her argument. The 1917 statute was not discrimination; rather, it was a sign of "progress." The county jail was (justifiably) unpopular: men in the county jail were in a demoralizing, idle cage. Moreover, the definite sentence was a "relic of the stone age of penological theory and practice." Ms. Heitman, to her good fortune, was going to an institution in which she would work "in the sunshine and wind and free air, . . . away from barred cells and frowning, guard-mounted walls." The poor woman did not know when she was well off. Appeal dismissed.

The court, of course, had a point. To be sure, some states were exceptionally slow to build prisons for women, and in these states, conditions for women were as bad as conditions for men (which was very bad), or even worse. California at the beginning of the century was a blatant example. Women were confined to the "bear pit" at San Quentin, a space sixty by ninety feet, in the middle of it a cell building forty by twenty feet. Here between twenty and thirty women were confined. They were not allowed out to take the air or get exercise. There was no heat; rats scurried about; and the system of "slop buckets" was in full use. A separate women's building was not built at San Quentin until 1927, and the California Institution for Women, at Tehachapi, did not function until the thirties.[39]

The first federal prison for women opened for business in 1927. This was at Alderson, West Virginia; the director was Dr. Mary B. Harris; its official title was the Federal Industrial Institute for Women. All women who were sentenced to a year or more were to be sent there. Three women from Vermont were the first arrivals, on April 30, 1927. On November 24, 1928, the institute mounted a formal opening ceremony, with the attorney general himself in attendance. By this time, the Institute for Women was a going concern.[40] As prisons went, it was benign and reformatory; it was "cottage-style," and occupied a campus of some five hundred acres. A skeptical judge sneered at the institute as a "fashionable boarding school." But Dr. Harris insisted it was a place of discipline and efficiency.[41] The women worked and learned, indoors and out; the buildings were named after social reformers like Jane Addams.[42] Despite the name, there was nothing particularly industrial about the place. The women worked at home skills, office work, and farming; they raised and canned vegetables, cooked and made candy, typed and filed and learned business English.[43]

In many states, women's prisons approached the reformatory ideal. Bedford Hills, in New York State, which opened in 1900, had no fences around it; it, too, was built on the "cottage plan." Each cottage had a flower garden, kitchens, and twenty-eight rooms, which the inmates could decorate if they liked. The women could take classes; there were even singing lessons and gymnastics.[44] In general, women's prisons were more "benign" than men's—but then, this was also true of most of the women in prison. Of the 505 women at Alderson in October 1935, more than half (264) had been convicted of narcotics charges; there were 80 on liquor charges, 58 for counterfeiting and forgery, 18 for violating the Motor Vehicle Theft Act—and only one for homicide.[45] All these women had broken the law; almost none had broken bodies and bones.

The Woman Victim: Violence and Rape

Only recently have the cries of victims of domestic violence broken through the apathy and downright callousness of institutions of criminal justice. Historically, police were extremely reluctant to intervene in "domestic disturbances." They often refused to make arrests; police manuals frequently told police to do nothing more than calm down the parties and mediate the dispute. A policy of this kind is really "tacit approval of the husband's right to beat his wife." Mediation, though it seems neutral, or benevolent, actually "serves the husband's interest by decriminalizing his behavior." Moreover, there can be grave risks in forcing a battered woman to go home and live with the man who battered her. A study of Kansas City homicides in 1971 found that 40 percent of them arose out of domestic violence; in about half of these cases, police had been called five or more times in the two years just before the murder.[46] In a world where men do the beating, and women get beaten, cool neutrality may be an invitation to murder.

In extreme cases, of course, there was criminal liability; but only extreme cases came to the courts. It is clear that the law did not take wife-beating very seriously. A Maryland statute, for example, made it a misdemeanor for any person to "brutally assault and beat his wife." The addition of the word "brutally" certainly implies that plain old assault was not really criminal.[47] As Linda Gordon has pointed out, social agencies in the twentieth century have long been active in the fight against child abuse, but the battered woman was not on the agenda.[48] Change came only with the most recent surge of feminist consciousness, and the recognition that the underlying problem is power. The basis of wife-beating, as Linda Gordon argues, "is male dominance—not superior physical strength or violent temperament." She describes wife-beating as the "chronic battering of a person of inferior power who for that reason cannot effectively resist."[49] The subordination of women puts them at the mercy of men who are callous or brutal or vicious or deranged. There are all too many of these. The first shelters for battered women appeared in the cities in the 1970s. The old excuses—she must have been a nag; he only does it when he's drunk—were no longer acceptable. Publicity about the problem encouraged the police to take the problem more seriously.

The dilemma of women trapped in abusive relationships comes out even more dramatically in cases where a woman goes on trial for murdering a cruel or battering husband or lover. Can a woman who lived in terror claim she killed the man in self-defense? The traditional answer was no: not unless she was in danger at that very moment. In recent years, courts have begun to relent. The "battered-wife syndrome" works its way into evidence. In some cases, juries have acquitted women who killed brutal men; in other cases, they have convicted women, but of lesser charges (manslaughter, for example).

In *State v. Lynch*, a Louisiana case (1983), the defendant, Sheral Lynch, was nineteen; she had been living for three years with Jimmy Dyess, a big, strong logger in his forties. He once beat Sheral "with a bat to the point where she was unable to walk for a couple of weeks." Another time, he knocked out one of her teeth. One night in 1977, he hit her and threatened her—and she shot him to death. A jury convicted her of manslaughter, but the appeals court was willing to stretch the conventional meaning of self-defense and set her free.[50] In another highly publicized case, two men beat and assaulted Inez Garcia sexually. They threatened to come back and do it again. She got a shotgun, and several hours later, she went looking for the men, and killed one of them. There were two trials; in the end she was acquitted on the grounds of self-defense.[51]

In fact, some form of self-defense underlies many—perhaps most—of the cases where a wife kills her husband. One study, conducted in the seventies, claimed that 40 percent of the women doing time for murder or manslaughter had killed abusive husbands or lovers. A survey of women in a California prison, published in 1978, found that twenty-nine out of thirty women who killed a mate had been abused.[52] The new consciousness of the eighties brought about a definite change: Angela Browne interviewed forty-two women charged with the death or serious injury of their male partners. One case was dropped; when the rest went to trial, nine were acquitted and twelve received probation or a suspended sentence; twenty did time, ranging from six months to fifty years.[53] These results were probably much more lenient than they would have been ten, twenty, or a hundred years before.

The Law of Rape

Here is another branch of law where change—reform—can be laid explicitly at the doorstep of a revived and militant women's movement. Rape, of course, had always been a crime, and a serious one; but the definition of rape, and the enforcement of the laws, had been warped by the interests of men, not women, consciously or unconsciously. There was no dialogue over rape, between men and women; nice women did not talk about such things, and women who were not nice were more or less outside the pale.

As Susan Estrich has put it, rape is a crime "which is defined more by the actions, reactions, motives and inadequacies of the victim than by those of the defendant." The rules themselves were unsettling. As Estrich observes,

> We do not require people to resist a mugger, even if the mugger was once a friend. We do not insist on witnesses to robbery. We rarely question the virtue of the robbed store clerk or even the defrauded company owner. We do not downgrade larceny if the victim wore an expensive suit or walked on a dangerous street, or even if he contributed to panhandlers in the past.

But victims of rape, to the contrary, historically had been asked to "prove their virtue," and the law imposed on them "obligations of actual resistance."[54]

Nothing in the formal law said it was all right to force sex on a woman who was divorced, or sexually experienced, or not-so-nice, or who drank and was chummy with men in bars; but the law in practice was another thing (see chapter 10). Kalven and Zeisel, in their jury study (published in 1966), found that jurors tended to convict only in cases of "aggravated rape," that is, cases of gang-rape, or where there was "evidence of extrinsic violence," or where defendant and victim were complete strangers. Anything else was "simple rape," and the jury had a habit of letting the defendant go—or convicting him of something less than rape. In one case, the woman drank "several beers," got into a car with the defendant and three other men, and was driven to a cemetery where she was raped. The jury acquitted. Another case involved a "group of young people on a beer drinking party. The jury, according to the presiding judge, probably figured the girl asked for what she got."[55]

Well into the 1980s, there is evidence that male jurors judged women harshly if they wore "provocative" clothing, or were "promiscuous," and even if they happened to be divorced rather than married or single.[56] In one Virginia case in 1980, a seventeen-year-old woman fell asleep in the back seat of a car, after riding around and drinking beer with some (male) friends. She accused one of the men (a nineteen-year-old) of rape. The jury acquitted, and the foreman told a reporter: "We reached a quick consensus that there was sexual intercourse and that there was not consent." Then why did the jury acquit? Because, he explained, there was no evidence of resistance, screams, threats of death, or the like.[57]

A woman victim was thus still caught in a deadly trap. She was both victim and accused. Her case depended on chastity, or respectability—and extreme resistance. This may be one reason why so many victims of rape never reported the crime to police. Victim studies suggest that rape and other forms of sexual assault are alarmingly common crimes. But many women apparently prefer, or have preferred, to keep their mouths tightly shut.* There *were* arrests for rape—and trials, and convictions—but the numbers were small, so small as to suggest that they must be the tip of the iceberg. There were only eighty-four rape cases in the Chicago criminal courts in 1926 (twenty-seven men went to prison); and, if we can believe the police report, only seventeen instances of rape in Honolulu in 1935, one of them "unfounded."[59] As late as 1969, there were 2,415 complaints of rape in New York, 1,085 arrests—and eighteen convictions.[60]

After 1970, however, there was a kind of revolution in the law of rape. The women's movement was largely responsible. Women focused attention on men's violence against them; they demanded changes in the law. They wanted to get rid of barriers to prosecution. They wanted women victims to be better treated. They wanted recognition that most rapists were not strangers, but friends, lovers, dates—even husbands. They wanted to abolish the flat rule of the law that no husband could be legally guilty of raping his wife.

What made women militant was nothing less than changes in the whole legal culture. It was a culture of rampant individualism, of a consciousness of self, and of rights to the self. The civil rights movement was a striking and successful model. What many women demanded, more or less openly, was equality of rights, of opportunity—and eventually, equality of power. This meant dismantling a social structure, and a family structure, that put men on top, a structure that almost all men, and probably most women, had once accepted without question as a natural, God-given plan.

The key word, perhaps, was *choice.* Coercion was the absence of choice, the opposite of choice; and rape was the epitome of coercion—the dark shadow that hung over women in the streets, in the workplace, even in their homes. Cracks in the legal structure began to appear in the sixties. Courts began to relax the doctrine that a woman had to offer extreme resistance. Many states passed what became known as "rape shield" laws, which barred evidence of prior sexual activity. Many of the reform laws were fairly comprehensive. Perhaps the most significant was the Michigan statute of 1974. It mentioned four types of "criminal sexual conduct" (the language was gender-neutral).[61] Under this law, the victim did not have the duty to resist heroically; the victim's testimony did not have to be corroborated; and the victims sex life was not to be paraded before judge and jury, except in rare circumstances. Not all

---

* According to a victimization survey, in 1983, there was one rape for every six hundred women in the United States; this is nearly twice the rate of rapes reported to police.[58]

states went as far as Michigan, but rape reform won many legal victo-ries—in the legislatures, at any rate.*

A dramatic change was the decline and fall of the rule that a husband could not be guilty of raping his own wife. Since a woman "promised to love, honor and obey," she was "obligated to submit." Also, it was said, men rarely raped their wives; and the state had no business meddling in the intimacies of marriage.[63] But the reality was that some marriages were a coercive hell; many wives were raped by sadistic or drunken boors; other wives, by the thousands, found themselves forced or browbeaten into sex-ual acts they had never really said yes to. Nothing better illustrated male power than the zone of male immunity inside the family.

In 1977, Oregon dropped the husband's immunity from its rape law; a year later, the first case under the statute appeared. It was a sordid and ambiguous affair, and John Rideout, the defendant, husband of Greta Rideout, was acquitted. By 1980, only three states—Oregon, Nebraska, and New Jersey—had entirely gotten rid of the husband's license to rape; five other states had reformed their laws in part. But the tide was run-ning fast: by 1989, only eight states still clung resolutely to the old rule. All the rest had either completely abolished it, or abolished it with some exemptions.[64] Between 1978 and 1985, 210 husbands were arrested for rape; 118 went to trial, and in 104 of these cases (88 percent), there was a conviction. The high rate of conviction suggests, according to one authority, that only the most aggravated cases end up in court: the "thousands of women who are raped by their husbands in more 'ordi-nary' ways, without the employment of tire irons, dogs, strangulation, or death threats, are simply not reporting their experiences to the police."[65]

The new women's consciousness has focused attention also on "date rape." It forced recognition of an uncomfortable fact: most men who push unwanted sex on women are not psychopathic or brutal strangers: they are not strangers at all. Date-rape prosecutions were not common; but the problem was widely discussed on college campuses; and what was arguably an instance of date rape burst into national prominence in 1991, when a woman accused William Kennedy Smith, a nephew of the late John F. Kennedy, of rape. The couple met at a bar in Palm Beach, Florida, and went from there to the Kennedy estate, where they had sex—willingly, in Smith's account; violently, in hers. Millions saw the

---

* Generally speaking, evidence of the victim's "sexual conduct," and "reputation evi-dence" about that conduct, was not to be admitted. But the judge, if convinced that evidence of the victim's "past sexual conduct" with the accused or of "specific in-stances of sexual activity showing the source or origin of semen, pregnancy, or dis-ease" was "material to a fact at issue in the case," and that "its inflammatory or prej-udicial nature does not outweigh its probative value," had the power to make an exception.[62]

trial on television (the victim's face was reduced to an electronic blur). The six-person jury (four members were women) acquitted Smith, on December 11, 1991.[66]

Did reform of rape laws make a difference? It is difficult to tell. Two scholars who recently studied rape-law reforms of various types found, to their surprise, little evidence of an impact on practice; and it mattered very little whether reform laws were strong or weak.[67] This was so for a number of reasons, some of which seem to contradict each other. On the one hand, the criminal justice system tends to resist change; it is so gangly, so obstreperous, so riddled with discretionary detours. Then, too, the reforms did not come out of the blue; they were effects as much as causes. Courts had already felt the moral and political pressure generated by the women's movement. When the reform laws finally came, they merely put a cap on a process that was already taking place. For example, there had been a rule that the woman's testimony had to be "corroborated." But even before the reform of the *statutes*, the courts had acted on their own; they reduced the need for "corroboration" down to the merest sliver of its former self.

Changes, both gross and subtle, *had* taken place, and will continue to do so. There is no returning to the dark ages. But law is a fairly crude instrument. It can hardly capture all the nuances and gradations in the tournament of sex, all the steps of the staircase that lead down from melting love to the crudest, darkest acts of violation. What is clear is that women have a voice in the system in a way that they never did before. Their interests and demands now make a difference. They raise questions about the meaning of consent; they shout in men's ears that *no* means *no*, and not *maybe*, or *yes*, or *try me*.* They challenge power, and the manipulations of power, in the relationship between women and men. As a result, the criminal justice system is no longer a band that plays a single tune. The rape reform laws are a symbolic victory for women. Are they anything more? The answer may be yes—if not now, then eventually. When a symbol is strong enough, strident enough, persuasive enough, it stops being a "mere" symbol, and translates into actual behavior.

---

* Today, says Susan Estrich, "more women do feel free to say yes," but that "provides more reason—not less—to credit the word of those who say no. The issue is not chastity or unchastity, but freedom and respect."[68]

19

CRIMES OF THE SELF: TWENTIETH-CENTURY LEGAL CULTURE

ONE MAJOR PURPOSE OF THIS BOOK HAS BEEN TO SHOW OR SUGGEST CONNECtions between criminal justice and the larger society. We took a close look at the face of nineteenth-century legal culture, especially at the way social and spatial mobility affected the system. This chapter, in turn, is about some aspects of twentieth-century legal culture, the legal culture of our own century, and how *it* reverberated in the world of crime and criminal justice.

Of course, the shouting and partying that brought in the twentieth century, the wild celebrations when the clock struck midnight, did not produce a new legal culture. January 1, 1900, was a special day of a special year, with the special magic of big, round numbers. But social life is a river that flows broad and deep; the river does not always flow at the same speed; it has calm spots, and areas of turbulence. Certainly, we cannot measure and mark off social change by the ticking of a clock or the banging of a drum.

The turn of the century was more than a lifetime ago. By now, in its closing years, we see more clearly how the world has turned in this, our own century. Above all, it has been a century of amazing change. In some senses, change has been disastrous; this has been a century of deadly wars and catastrophes and upheavals and revolutions. In other senses, it has been a time of wondrous, remarkable, fairy-tale change. Technology tore society up by the roots and put it together again. This is the century of the automobile, the jet airplane, television, air-conditioning, antibiotics, and, very notably, the computer. It is the century of gene splicing and *in vitro* fertilization; the century of the pill and surrogate mothers. It is also the century of the hydrogen bomb, the greenhouse effect, and mass toxic pollution. It is a century in which nothing has stood still, in which social change has been as radical as anything that went before, and incomparably more rapid.

I want to begin by describing a case that straddles the turn of the century. The villain of the piece is a certain Miller, convicted of grand larceny in New York.[1] Miller was, to put it plainly, a swindler. In 1899, he had put out the word to friends and neighbors that he had important inside information of the financial type—he knew how to make a killing in the stock markets. Miller was the manager of something he called the Franklin Syndicate. A picture of wise old Ben Franklin appeared in all his ads, together with the motto "The way to wealth is as plain as the road to market." Miller invited investors to deposit their money with him, promising to pay them at the astonishing rate of 10 percent a week on their money. The deposit could be withdrawn whenever the "investor" wanted to, and the principal was "guaranteed against loss."

As P. T. Barnum put it, there's a sucker born every minute. The money rolled in. At first, Miller ran his business out of a candy store; later he rented part of a two-story house; still later his "syndicate" had so swollen in size that he needed the entire building. "The house was filled with clerks, all working from nine in the morning until ten at night, drawing dividend checks, receiving money, and sending out circulars and newspapers." People stood in line to get in, to deposit and withdraw. "Money was piled in heaps about the place, upon the counter and the floor." It took twenty clerks, working with a rubber stamp, to write all the dividend checks.[2]

Of course, it was all a scam, a "transparent swindle." Miller had no connection with any stock exchange, and he never invested a penny of the money in securities. He paid the dividends, very promptly, out of new money that flowed in from the "ignorant and credulous." Naturally, this scheme could not go on indefinitely; at some point, the bubble was bound to burst. And burst it did. One day, Miller bought $100,000 in United States bonds and fled to Canada. Somehow, he was later returned to New York State, where he stood trial on the complaint of one of his many victims, a woman named Catherine Moser, who had given him $1,000 of her hard-earned cash. Miller was convicted, and appealed in 1902.

The precise *legal* question on appeal was how to label this crime. No one disputed that Miller had been up to no good; but law is law. The state had convicted him of larceny; but, legally speaking, had he actually *stolen* the money? The court thought yes. "Had the defendant actually used the money in speculation, however improvident or reckless, and lost, his act would not amount to larceny." But this was not the case: he was lying and cheating from the outset. He never intended to use the money in speculation at all. He got the money through a "trick, device, or artifice," with the intention right then and there of appropriating it "to his own use."[3] And this, the court said, was most certainly larceny; hence the conviction would stand.

The legal question is not uninteresting; but what attracts attention here is the crime itself. It was, in one sense, a fine example of a nineteenth-century crime of mobility. The victim, Catherine Moser, had aspirations; she saw no reason of class or caste or skill why she, too, could not be rich and famous. She testified: "I read something in the papers somewhere, I do not know where, that Vanderbilt, Gould and all of them made money in Wall Street. I knew this was true and I thought this money was to be used for the same purpose and I would get the benefit of it."[4] If Vanderbilt could make money speculating, and become filthy rich, why not Catherine Moser?

Moser and Miller were thus both products of a culture of mobility, bound together in knots of mutual greed and deception. Of course, he was the predator, and she was his prey. He was neither the first nor the last to try to bilk the gullible in this particular way. But Miller's crime was somewhat different from the crimes of *most* nineteenth-century swindlers. He did not use a disguise. He lied about many things, but he did not hide. A typical con man cheats and steals and then disappears. He finds a new neighborhood, a new city, a new mark; here he begins to cheat and steal again. If he is lucky, the chain is never broken. Miller's scheme was more daring and more dangerous. It was open and notorious.

And it was, of course, a house of cards. Miller, of course, must have known that. When he felt the end coming, he grabbed a pile of money and ran to Canada. Perhaps this was his plan all along. It is hard to know. But, in an important sense, this fact is not relevant. Unlike most confidence games and swindles, the biggest payoff came *during* the scam, not after: the excitement, the success, the adulation of the investors, the power, the high living. In Miller's crime there seemed to be an element of desperate narcissism. It was a wild, intoxicating party; and someday it was going to end. With luck, there was Canada to run to;

and money besides. Without luck, prison stared him in the face. But while it lasted it was a great game, a marvelous game; and perhaps the game was worth it for itself.

Much later in the century, Andy Warhol, the artist, made a famous comment that, in the future, everybody would be a celebrity—world famous—for fifteen minutes. Miller may have had a similar dream: a year or two of enormous wealth and luxury, and after that, well, all things come to an end. Crimes of mobility merged, then, into another form of crime, which we can call crimes of the self. These are crimes that rest, in some way, on the exaggerated individualism of twentieth-century Americans, which has been called expressive individualism. It is the notion that one's main task in life is to forge a separate, unique self; to develop one's potentialities. It is the idea that we pass this way only once, must make the best of it, and must make the trip, each of us, our own special way.[5]

Miller's crime was what would be called in the trade, today, a Ponzi scheme. Carlo Ponzi, who gave his name to the scheme, was a swindler of the 1920s. He operated his scam out of Boston. He lured investors into his web with the promise of a 50 percent return on their money in three months; the scheme had to do (he said) with international postal exchange coupons, exchange rates, and other black boxes that were total mysteries to his gullible victims. At the end of three months, investors could either cash in or leave the money with Ponzi for further investment and profits. People flocked to Ponzi, as they had flocked to Miller; millions of dollars flowed into his pockets. Of course, like Miller, he paid "dividends" to early suckers with money raised from later suckers. And of course, as usual, the house of cards collapsed. Ponzi ended up in prison.[6]

Ponzi and his victims, too, were locked into a single system; they were all pursuing the same goal: quick money, easy money, bonanza money. This in itself was nothing new. There had been no shortage of schemes in the nineteenth century for getting rich quick—it was, after all, the century of land speculation, robber barons, and innumerable Wall Street frauds (none of these are extinct in the twentieth century). But there was also a standard picture of the way up the ladder of success. It was Ben Franklin's way: hard work and patience, early to bed and early to rise, moderation, frugality, business acumen, self-discipline, and so on. There were few "bonanzas," few ways to vast sudden wealth, and many long and successful careers to emulate.

The mobility that made these dreams into *facts*, and which also shaped the dreams, ended up by creating a new personality as well; and it is this personality that lies behind crimes of the self. In the twentieth century, particularly in the second half of the century, Ben Franklin had powerful competition. The new theme was a theme of quick, young, early, sensational success. Radio, TV, the movies, and popular magazines all promote the kingship of celebrities: sports heroes, movie stars, popular rock-and-roll singers, the gliterati of popular entertainment. Careers that fascinate the public are not the careers of nuclear physicists or CEOs or Wall Street lawyers; they are careers that rise and fall in a single glamorous trajectory, streaking like rockets across the sky. This is a trajectory, interestingly, that criminal careers also describe. In fact, one way to become an instant celebrity is to commit a vivid or daring or horrible crime. Mobsters and gangsters are themselves celebrities. A criminal career is a young man's game. Crime also seems brief, youthful, glamorous, and exciting, thrilling to insiders and outsiders—and (so far) predominantly male.[7]

Probably nobody in the nineteenth century spoke about "role models"; this is a distinctly modern phrase. There were, of course, heroes, people one looked up to. They may have been members of the family, local notables, people one knew personally, religious leaders. Modern American culture, as we noted, makes idols out of sports heroes and rock stars—in any event, celebrities. In fact, baseball players or rock singers probably work like Trojans to achieve their success; and they have to start out with a certain amount of native talent. But in the end, it all looks rather effortless. It is, in any event, at least conceptually within the reach of the ordinary person, or so it seems. A kid from the slums can hardly conceive of what it takes to be a nuclear physicist, or the CEO of a Fortune 500 corporation, or the managing partner of a Wall Street firm. But if he could only shoot baskets a *little* better, or play his guitar with a slightly snappier twang, he, too, might be launched into the ranks of the rich and famous.

Social and technological changes, snowballing for a century, stronger and faster and bigger all the time, have undoubtedly imprinted themselves on American culture and personality. Warren Susman argues that the "modal type" of personality has been transformed over time: from a culture of "character," which emphasized order and discipline, to a culture of "personality," which emphasizes the idiosyncratic self.[8] Daniel Bell draws a distinction between the "techno-economic order," the world of "efficiency and functional rationality," and those elements of modern culture where the "self is taken as the touchstone of cultural judgment." In this newer domain, old "bourgeois values" get thrown out the window—values such as "self-discipline, delayed gratification, and restraint."[9] The world of the self is a world of the Ponzi scheme, of quick, glamorous money—the world of the cheat and the sucker alike.

Perhaps, then, it is "crimes of the self" that in some way distinguish this century from the one that went before. Mobility, the motor force in transforming criminality and criminal justice in the nineteenth century, was, in a way, a structural factor. It opened new opportunities for crime, and provided the soil in which certain kinds of crime (and certain criminal personalities) were especially apt to grow. Crimes of mobility—swindling, confidence games, market frauds, crimes that rest on simulated identities—are still very much with us; they have not been superseded. Moreover, most people were not and are not criminals. There are still millions of hardworking, disciplined, traditional human beings, millions who are "modern" without narcissism or fundamentalism. We are talking about changes at the margin. At the margin, shifts in personality and culture do affect the *kind* of crimes people commit, and their reasons for committing them.

Sensational crimes *and* banal crimes both show the impact of the culture of the self. The whole country was shocked, in 1924, when Nathan Leopold and Richard Loeb murdered Bobbie Franks in Chicago; that was "the crime of the century" (see chapter 17).[10] What was appalling about this crime was that Leopold and Loeb had no real motive, in the classic sense. They were college students, extremely bright, members of rich Jewish families; Bobbie Franks was a neighbor, a mere boy, also from a rich Jewish family. Loeb and Leopold kidnapped Franks and left a ransom note. But money was hardly their aim; they had plenty of money themselves. The two friends were worlds away from the conventional image of the criminal—feebleminded and lower class. Leopold, in particular, was a brilliant scholar. Sex did not appear to be a motive, either. Why, then, did they kill? No one knows for sure; apparently for the thrill of it, the high, the expressive, orgiastic rush that came from the sensation of crime.

Some sixty-seven years later, on November 16, 1991, Patricia Lexie was riding with her husband along the eastern edge of Washington, D.C., on the interstate highway. A car drew alongside. A man leaned out of the window and fired a shot, hitting Patricia in the head. She died almost immediately. She was twenty-nine years old, recently married. A few days later, the police arrested a high school dropout, nineteen years old, and charged him with the crime. He had a long record of criminal violence. But what was his motive? Patricia was a stranger; there was no robbery, no rape. Before the shooting, he had told some friends, "I feel like killing someone."[11] Essentially, this was a replay of the killing of Bobbie Franks, only more impulsive—and, by 1991, much more banal.

Crime certainly feeds on poverty; but for many young men, as Mercer L. Sullivan of the Vera Institute has argued, it has meaning "beyond its monetary returns." In the neighborhoods Sullivan studied, the young men who do crime call success in crime "getting paid" and "getting over," terms that "convey a sense of triumph and of irony." These young men steal not only to gain money, but to fulfill a sense of (male) self. Of course, they use the money to buy things; but what they buy is not food or shelter. Fancy clothes are their "first consumption priority. Next comes recreation, including ... drugs and alcohol ... sports ... movies and dances." They participate in crime "to share in the youth culture that is advertised in the mass media," a culture that middle-class kids can afford to buy on their own, *without* stealing.[12]

Crime, supposedly, does not pay; but this is not obvious to the naked eye. Many crimes, in fact, look like they do pay—and quickly, too. Drug dealing is one; robbery is another. Theft produces money which, if not effortless, is at least not earned by hard work in the usual sense. Theft is a way for young kids (males, almost exclusively) to make quick money, instant money. In 1990, a group of young men in New York tried to rob a family of tourists from Utah; in the scuffle that followed, they killed one family member, a twenty-two year-old man, who was trying to protect his mother. The point of the crime was to get money to go dancing. Which is exactly what they did after the crime. They went dancing.[13]

The twentieth-century world *is*, after all, the world of mass media. It is the world of radio, the movies, and, most strikingly, TV. It is self-centered, fast, glitzy, a world of instant communication. Crime in the United States (and elsewhere in the West) may be, in a sense, the price society pays for an open society, a mass-communication society, a society that stresses individualism and choice.[14] The outburst of crime in the twentieth century tracks, suspiciously, the apparent shift at the margin that Susman and Bell have noticed: away from emphasis on self-control, toward emphasis on expressive individualism. The effect on criminal justice is pervasive. It is certainly not all bad. It has paved the way, for example, to reform in crimes of morality, to a decrease in legally-enforced repression; we have noted its impact at many points in preceding chapters.

Cultural and personality change has an impact on crime and criminal justice that goes beyond the examples mentioned. For one thing, the culture simply does not encourage people to be modest, self-effacing, to submerge their egos, to sacrifice their personal desires on the altar of some higher cause. The culture exalts the self. It exalts personal success. But not everybody can *have* success, however you define it. There are millions of failed, stunted, poverty-stricken selves. Many of these are people who cannot swallow failure.

Failure, like success, is culturally and psychologically defined. In the nineteenth century, a poor but "respectable" person was presumably no failure. An immigrant dishwasher, escaped from some war-torn, starving country, may think of himself, or herself, lucky to be alive, lucky to be working, lucky to be on the way to a better life. A middle-class

American would regard this job and this life as absolute failure. A sense of failure can breed radical discontent; in some instances, crime. At least this seems plausible. In any event, crime may seem like a better or easier way to "get paid," to lay in a stock of gratification, than any of the obvious alternatives. Education, professional training, talent, and skill pay off; but not everybody can even dream of going these routes, and poverty weighs the swimmer down with stones. For truncated, dead-end lives, lives at the bottom of the barrel, there seems to be no real alternative to crime, except low-paid, low-status jobs (if you can get them). When the choice is between selling hamburgers at McDonald's for minimum wage and running errands for drug dealers or stealing, the illegal options may seem a lot more attractive. The temptations are great—in this culture.

"Crime" is a label attached to certain ways people act; but people are trained, or socialized, as children how to think and how to act and how to feel. We can reject the idea of born criminals without rejecting the idea that crime begins, as it were, in the cradle; certainly, in the home, or the neighborhood environment. There has been, in contemporary society, a dramatic shift in the nature of *authority*.[15] Authority was once vertical; it was above you and beyond you; it was what you looked up to. Authority gave you orders and rules. It worked slowly and carefully, within the family, the neighborhood, the village, the whole local ambience. It was the adult voice of the community. Authority was organized in the shape of a pyramid; the higher up one went in society, the greater the authority. But the base of the pyramid—your family, your teachers, the adults in your life—probably had the most powerful impact on your own personality and culture.

Authority is still a pyramid; but, relatively speaking, it has somewhat flattened out; it is no longer so sharp and so steep, certainly not in the United States. Today, one might speak of authority as rather more horizontal. There are criminal families, but most families do not teach children crime. The vertical authority of families and other adult groups is not what it used to be. What has grown stronger in the twentieth century is the horizontal power of the peer group, and the power of a culture that disdains authority and glorifies the individual self. The mass media—radio, movies, and above all, television—have to shoulder a good deal of the blame. The modern personality, practically from day one of life, is exposed to powerful influences that compete with family authority. The outside world, with all its power, its incredible wealth of images and colors, its infinitude of models and suggestions, breaks in electronically from distant places to overwhelm the child—and its parents.

It is a cliché to talk about the crumbling of the family. The family *is* crumbling, in all sorts of senses. Traditionalists worry about the decay of the nuclear family. But probably the *form* of the family is not so important; it probably does not really matter whether a child has one mother and no father, or two fathers and no mother, or three mothers and no father, or lives in a commune, or is raised by wolves. It is the authority of the family, the values, the love, and the discipline, that matters. Disintegration of family *authority*, if that is what is happening, is much more serious than disintegration of forms. It is hard to tell whether horizontal authority and the media are *causes* of this disintegration, or whether their powers are effects. Maybe both.

The Self and Its Limits

The novelty and impact of modern individualism on crime and criminal justice should not, of course, be exaggerated. The American system of criminal justice has always professed a deep concern for the self, for individual responsibility. The system makes the claim that every person accused of crime is a unique individual, uniquely treated; guilt, innocence, and desert are cut to the order of the individual. A criminal trial is by and large tailored to this end. The ideology of individual justice is quite old; so is the yawning chasm between ideal and reality. Every chapter of this book has tried to show, one way or another, how this ideal is violated, disregarded, compromised.

But changes in the twentieth century, particularly in the late twentieth century, show a consistent pattern. To take one example, the nineteenth-century penitentiary was highly regimented and disciplined; the twentieth-century prison is much more anarchic; indeed, by some accounts, groups of inmates *run* the prison; internally, the prison has become much more "horizontal."

Horizontal, yes, but individualistic? The prisoners are organized, after all, into cliques, gangs, race groups, ethnic groups. Outside, in the crime world, too, peer groups are everywhere. In many ways, this, too, is not new. Nineteenth-century writers complained about gangs, especially the tough gangs of the young who ruled the city streets. Sheldon and Eleanor Glueck of Harvard Law School, studying delinquents in the late 1920s, remarked on the power of the group. A young crime-committer was liable more than half the time to be "associated with one or more companions in the commission of the offense."[16] Frederick M. Thrasher carried out a classic study of gangs in Chicago in the twenties. Gangs, Thrasher wrote, "represent the spontaneous efforts of boys to create a society for themselves where none adequate to their needs exists." He adds that boys in the gang get something out of gang life that society cannot give them: "the thrill and zest of participation in common interests, more especially in corporate action, in hunting, capture, conflict, flight, and escape." For gang members, conflicts with other gangs and with "the world about them" are "exciting group activities" that add zest and spice and meaning to life.[17]

Bland theories of "differential association" or the rather arid statistical demonstrations of how crime intersects with poverty and the like, hardly convey this "thrill" or "zest." Jack Katz, a sociologist, writes that the closer one looks at crime, "the more vividly relevant become the moral emotions." People do not commit crimes because they want or need money, Katz argues. There have been times, of course, when people stole just to stay alive. But today, for many people who steal and ravage, crime is a "way of life." Violent or criminal acts can produce a real high; there are "emotional processes" going on that "seduce people to deviance."[18]

No theory of crime can ignore the social background of criminals; crime is the statistical and social companion of poverty, unemployment, social disorganization. But these factors cannot explain *individual* behavior; this is one reason why Katz's thesis has a certain dark attractiveness. It also fits in with the notion of crimes of the self. The exaltation of the self does not conflict with the idea of the gang. The self is horizontally organized; it rejects, in whole or in part, the vertical authority of family, law, elites. It seeks out the like-minded. "Conformity" is *not*, paradoxically, inconsistent with the idea of radical individualism. To the contrary, it is part of its essence. What people conform to is fashions and fads. Traditional societies never talked about conformity; it was taken for granted. The concept is distinctly modern. It implies the possibility of *not* conforming. Conformity recognizes choice: choice is inherent in selecting the group, the gang, the peers. When the conformist sees everybody around him wearing a certain style of sneakers, or certain cuts or colors of clothes, he is seized with a passion to do the same. The conformist is a sheep; but he chooses (or thinks he chooses) his flock.[19]

Against crimes of the self, the criminal justice system may be singularly impotent. The creaky machinery of justice assumes two things: a strong system of socialization, which does most of the work, leaving only some odds and ends and bits and pieces to be taken care of by criminal process; and a stern, efficient system of punishment to teach a lesson to those few who have not gotten the point. A narcissistic, rootless social order, in which even a small fraction of the population does not swallow and embody traditions of morality, is more than it can handle. Such a social order overwhelms the loose, disjointed system of criminal justice whose development this book has tried to describe.

American society exalts the individual; but human beings are inherently social. People are animals that live in families, packs, and clans. They are not solitary hunters—they are wolves, not panthers on the prowl. Wolf packs produce a good deal of modern crime. As the family weakens, as horizontal authority replaces vertical authority, some people, especially young males, detach from the larger society and reattach to wolf packs—to groups much more prone to that behavior which the rest of us label as crime. Crime and antisocial behavior also come from the packless wolves, from the loners, the unattached, the drifters and grifters of society. These, too, as we have seen, are particularly liable to be victims of the system as well.

Criminal Justice and Popular Culture

Crime is endlessly fascinating to the public. The rise of "yellow journalism" fed the reader's desire for sensational, scandalous, absorbing events. The twentieth century was, if anything, even more obsessed with crime and news of crime.

Executions are no longer public in this century. But the press is public, and newspapers continued to recount every gruesome detail. Twentieth-century executions took place in the bowels of the big house. The newspapers followed them there. When Ruth Snyder was electrocuted at Sing Sing in 1928, it was front-page news in the New York newspapers. Here was one account: "Tomb-like silence. Ruth Snyder in the electric chair. The crunching sound of the executioner cramming down a lever. A sinister whine and a crackling, sputtering sound like a Fourth of July sparkler. Silence. . . . Then the prison physician breaking the silence with these words: 'I declare this woman dead.'"[20] Thomas Howard, a reporter on special assignment for the *New York Daily News*, sat in the front row, with a concealed camera on his ankle. As the first jolt of electricity surged through Ruth Snyder's body, Howard took a sensational photograph, which the newspaper printed. People gasped in horror—but they bought, and they looked. No need, in this case, to rely on "artist's conceptions." The camera was there.

The fascination with crime and criminal justice never flags. The hero is not always the cop or the detective. There is a certain tendency to glorify the outlaw as well, or at least certain outlaws. This is an old strain in American literature, and in stories people tell and retell.[21] An enormous literature, and an enormous mythology, surrounds outlaws and gunmen of the Old West—Billy the Kid, Jesse James, Wyatt Earp. In the twentieth century, there was Bonnie and Clyde, who were, among other things, the subjects of an extremely successful movie; in the Hollywood of the thirties and forties, there was a rash of gangster movies; they cleaned up at the box office. The censors insisted that crime could not look as if it paid in the movies; still, crime had an awfully good run for its money.

Later on, in the seventies and eighties, *The Godfather* and its two sequels were even more successful in making money. *The Godfather* was a glossy, Technicolor update of the gangster movies. It, along with many other movies about crime families, carried a disturbing message hidden in the folds of the narrative. The message was this: members of criminal gangs are really ordinary businessmen who just happen to do crime (including murder) for a living, and a very good living at that. The flickering screen invests these men with that peculiar combination of glamor and banality that are the essence of a celebrity culture.

The celebrity criminal, like the celebrity outlaw, did not spring up overnight in the twentieth century. The twentieth century simply stepped up the pace. Defendants in the great trials are, of course, celebrities par excellence. Harry K. Thaw, tried for the murder of Stanford White in the early years of the century, was a celebrity defendant. When Thaw escaped (from an insane asylum), fled to Canada, and was arrested there and held, crowds of Canadians gathered to catch a glimpse of him in his place of confinement: "Men and women almost trampled upon each other in a mad rush to shake his hand. When he went to the courtroom he rode in an open carriage, acclaimed by the populace, lifting his hat and bowing right and left like an emperor."[22] There always seems to be at least one woman ready to throw herself at the feet of a famous murderer (or alleged murderer) or to marry a convict on death row. Few women are on death row, but Ruth Snyder, waiting to die at Sing Sing, got "many offers of marriage."[23] After all, a celebrity is a celebrity.

Ultimately, it is impossible to tell what impact movies and stories about gangsters have on the public; after all, outlaw themes are popular in many cultures, even those where crime rates are low and people do not tremble in fear of muggers and burglars. There is, I think, a distinction between outlaw themes in older cultures and those we find in modern America. The gangsters are not *heroes*, but celebrities; and it is worth saying a word or two about celebrity culture, which seems particularly strong in the United States. It seems less in character for Japan or Finland to put Elvis Presley on a postage stamp.

To begin with, a "celebrity" is not the same as an "authority." The celebrity is an object of envy and wonder, but not of deference. Of course, people fawn on celebrities—disgustingly so—but in the hope that some of it will rub off on them, not because of the kind of charisma that surrounded the ancient offices of king or chief. The celebrity is, psychologically speaking, close to the man or woman on the street. Celebrities are mostly people who have special talent at doing what many of us do ourselves; only they do it better. A Nobel prize–winning physicist is not a celebrity; a rock star or basketball player is. They are heightened forms of the popular, commonplace selves, the man and woman on the street. Thus celebrity culture rests on a paradox: being different means being just like us.[24]

The celebrity, then, is the idealized modern self. It is what we want to be, and what we *might* be with luck or skill. The celebrity, as a model, is morally neutral—a movie star, the president, a great criminal. It would be wrong to say that people admire or model themselves on, say, serial killers; but a celebrity culture weakens ideas of deference and respect, it erodes standards of inherited morality, all of which are the sunken piles that hold up the system of criminal justice.

It should come as no surprise, then, that the criminal justice system cannot compete with the culture, cannot go against the grain. In the battle of norms and goals, it is distinctly marginal; more than a spear-carrier, but very much less than a star. It cannot—in our society—even hope to crush crime. Crime is far too complicated; its roots are too deep. Thus the eternal sense of frustration, the smell of failure that surrounds the system.

I cannot repeat often enough that I am talking about *marginal* changes, tendencies and shifts, which may be quite slight. After all, as we said, most people are not criminals, no matter where they stand in society, or what they do. They live out their lives without *major* violations of law (everybody breaks a rule or two now and then). But it takes only a few thousand burglars, out of the millions of people who live in Philadelphia or Los Angeles, to turn the city topsy-turvy. A tiny band of armed robbers is enough to generate the need to spend millions of dollars on police, security guards, locks, burglar alarms, safes, and so on—and even so, nobody is safe. One reason it is so hard to craft social devices to "solve" the crime problem is that criminals *are* a small minority. Trying to prevent crime, or "cure" crime, is like trying to track down some rare disease. The criminal justice system is far too blunt an instrument. There must be other ways—but what are they?

In the next chapter, we will discuss whether criminal justice actually deters crime. This is, in a way, a raw economic issue: Does the system deliver a big enough electric shock to tell potential criminals, "Hands off"? It is, in part, a matter of benefits and cost. Here we raise (and do not answer) the other question: What has happened to the criminal justice system as a moral teacher and preacher? The system has always been dramaturgic, giving lessons, showing and telling. The colonial system leaned heavily on open trials and public executions. Show trials still exist, but exactly what message do they deliver?

I have the impression—and it is only an impression—that whatever else it does, the criminal justice system does *not* deliver a strong moral lesson. It delivers, primarily, entertainment. Perhaps it never *did* deliver an effective moral lesson. Perhaps the penologists and the judges and others were fooling themselves. Maybe Beaumont and De Tocqueville and the men who ran the prisons deluded themselves about what they were accomplishing. Very likely they did. But whatever was true of the past, it seems most unlikely that the messengers of the news, the TV shows, the movies, the magazine articles, obsessed though they are with crime and punishment, really deliver a sermon worth mentioning to the national congregation—or that, if they do, it is greeted with anything other than a yawn. Of course, there *is* a message, but one shudders to think what it is.

20

A NATION BESIEGED

EARLY IN THE 1950S, THE CRIME PROBLEM EMERGED FROM THE SHADOWS AND took its place at center stage. Crime, of course, had always been a theme in American political and social life. In almost every period, some writers bewailed (usually without much in the way of evidence) the terrible increase in crime. But there is not much doubt about a few central facts in the second half of the century. The "crime problem" has gotten more intense in people's minds, and in their lives. Politically, too, crime has become a central issue.

The postwar crime problem did not burst like a bombshell on the public; it crept up gradually. In the 1950s, there was an uproar over juvenile delinquency. One heard a lot of excited talk about the young and the wild, about adolescents mad for vice and violence. The sense of crisis probably peaked between 1953 and 1956.[1] Less is heard about juvenile delinquency these days, but not because delinquency has gone away. On the contrary. Today, the whole idea of "juvenile delinquency" seems somehow soft and flabby; it conjures up joyriding, stealing apples, truancy. "Youth crime" is another matter. People today are petrified of young toughs who swagger about the cities, speaking the language of rage and contempt with their clothes, voices, and bodies. These are not (we think) "delinquents," not "wayward youth"; they are just plain criminals, adult in their violence and menace, if not in their years. Middle-class parents are also deathly afraid that their own children will turn sour, and, more especially, that they may fall into the bottomless pit of addiction.

After the fifties, fear of crime became more general. Fear of violent, explosive crime has engulfed our huge, decaying urban centers, and gradually, over the years, spread into the suburbs, and even into small towns and villages. The Gallup poll, for what it is worth, records a feeling among people that crime is going up, up, and away. In 1990, 51 percent of respondents said there was "more crime" in their area than "a year ago"; only 17 percent said "less." No less than 84 percent thought there was "more crime in the United States than there was a year ago."[2] Earlier polls showed similar opinions.

In the sixties, there were cries of anguish all over the political map. A massive governmental crime report, issued in the 1960s, warned that violent crime, and the fear it spawned, was disfiguring American society and damaging the social order. Crime had "impoverished" the life of many Americans, especially Americans in big cities. People lived in a fortresslike atmosphere: they "stay behind the locked doors of their homes rather than risk walking in the streets at night."[3] Two specific types of violence lay behind these grim words. The first was overtly political—urban riots, especially race riots in the cities; and unrest over the unpopular war in Vietnam. The second was ordinary crime: violence and theft on city streets.

In retrospect, the political fear seems somewhat exaggerated. Since they had no crystal balls, no one could know that when the Vietnam War ended, the rioting would end with it. Certainly, there was no reason to be optimistic about race violence, or to suppose that the urban barrios and ghettos would simmer down. In 1968, an assassin's bullet struck down Martin Luther King, Jr., and the cities exploded. People talked about "long hot summers." Yet riots of the same magnitude did not break out again until the "Rodney King" riots of 1992. Political violence has been (so far) sporadic and limited. Even terrorism has not made much of a dent on the American scene (praise be). Fear of terrorists slows up check-in at airports, but terrorist attacks *inside* this country are exceedingly rare.

Of course, all this might change; race relations in the United States, for example, are hardly smooth, and the anger in black communities, together with the backlash in white communities, seems toughly resistant to change. Terrorism might well flare up, with some turn in the wheel of international politics. It certainly affects the texture of society. Security at airports, in public places, courtrooms, government offices, becomes a kind of tax of millions of dollars imposed on the public. But on the whole, political violence is not a major factor in American society.

Street crime is another matter altogether. Some people will always jump at the thought of ghosts and shadows; but in this case, there is something real to be afraid of. The crime rate itself skyrocketed after 1950. Crime and its consequences became a terrible blight on the landscape. There is some dispute about crime statistics, about the significance of a peak here or a trough there. Occasionally in the 1980s, a federal, state, or city government would announce with fanfare a leveling off, or even some slight reduction, but the ordinary citizen was probably not impressed. Crime remained high, streets were dangerous; no statistics could do much about the loathing and the fear.

There is also little doubt that there was and is a great deal to loathe and to fear. The period after the Second World War has been an age of crime; every category of serious crime has risen drastically from a base that was already high.[4] In 1990, 2.3 million Americans were victims of "violent crime," according to figures compiled by the Bureau of Justice Statistics. These numbers came from surveys in which people were asked about their own experiences as victims. It did not include victims of the 23,000 homicides, whose mouths had been permanently and violently shut. The total number of crimes, including thefts, was something on the order of 34.8 million.[5] In 1987, according to research done at the National Center for Health Statistics, 4,223 American men between the ages of fifteen and twenty-four died a violent death. This was a rate of 21.9 per 100,000, in that age group. The rate for black men in that same age group was 85.6 per 100,000. These were appalling statistics. The homicide rate for the United States was more than seven times as great as Finland or Canada, more than twenty times as great as Germany, more than forty times as great as Japan.[6]

The President's Commission had said in its report that crime was ruining the texture of urban life. Some people reacted to danger with a fortress mentality. They avoided dangerous situations, they kept out of parks and other shadowy places at night, and avoided suspicious places except in the blaze of daylight; sometimes they took cabs to avoid walking on questionable streets. They also bought guns by the hundreds of thousands; they locked and bolted and barred their houses and stores; they made burglar alarms big business. In 1977, an obsessed mother and daughter in the Philadelphia area barricaded themselves in their bedroom, a room with three locks on the door, and demanded a full time policeman.[7] This was a gross caricature of the "normal" reaction to crime; but fear of violence bent the lives of millions, and distorted their normalcy, day in and day out. The fear has not abated over time. On

February 18, 1993, the *New York Times* reported that sales of Mace in December, 1992, were ten times higher than one year before; that burglar-alarm companies were flourishing; that self-defense seminars were springing up like weeds; and that thousands of people were buying car phones so they could dial 911 in case of sudden predation.[8]

Because people were not satisfied with the protection of the state and its law, they privatized protection and created a private regime of law. Private police and the security industry grew dramatically—another reaction to the surge in crime. This trend seems likely to continue. The crime state is also the bodyguard state, the locked-door state, the tight-security state, the state in which there is a major boom in watchmen, guards, security people of every stamp.

Fear of crime also became a *political* fact in the postwar period; politics, as always, translated itself into law. We have already noted some of the results. One was an increased *federal* presence in the criminal justice system (see chapter 12). On the state and local levels there were louder and louder outcries that something had to be done; and politicians responded, at least at some symbolic or rhetorical level. Cities spent more on police and jails. Whether anything much came of all this, in the fragmented and chaotic conditions of American local governance, is an open question.[9]

Throughout the country, newspapers, movies, and TV spread the word about crime and violence—a misleading word, perhaps, but a powerful one. Even people who live in quiet suburban enclaves, or rural backwaters, are aware of what they consider the crime problem. They, too, may feel fearful and besieged: safe where they are perhaps, but conscious of a dangerous world beyond their doorsteps. As Franklin E. Zimring and Gordon Hawkins have pointed out, the level of violent crime is unlikely "in the real world," to go low enough "to abate the public's fear of assault or criminals." Indeed, South Dakota, "with crime rates about one-tenth that of, say, New York or North Carolina," felt impelled to enact death penalty legislation in the 1970s.[10]

There are, of course, still many people who plead for a more humane system, and who believe that criminals can be rehabilitated. But the predominant call is for tougher laws, more and longer sentences, more and bigger prisons. In the 1980s, "advances" in humanizing criminal justice, in the style of the Warren Court, became difficult or perhaps impossible. The prison population rose; it doubled and tripled.[11] Whenever voters got a chance to express themselves, they almost invariably cast ballots for law and order, toughness, stringency—not for due process or reform. In earlier chapters, we have seen sign after sign of this backlash.

The Question of Violence

Why is the United States such a violent country? Why is there so much serious crime? Why are there so many violators—men (and a few women) who take other people's property, intrude on their homes, assault their bodies, and even take their lives? What is it about our society that breeds this epidemic of violent crime?

Is American history, tradition, experience to blame? There is a lot of talk about the legacy of frontier violence. Does violence stem from these primal conditions? This was a new, raw, macho country; traditional authority was weak; conditions favored the violent and the strong. In fact, the question is a complicated one. There is some doubt whether the frontier was violent at all—or if it was, whether this was the same kind of violence as modern violence.

This question is raised by Roger McGrath, in his study of two towns of the old Wild West, Bodie, California, and Aurora, Nevada (see chapter 8). There was a good deal of shooting, fighting, and hell-raising in these towns, but it was confined to "men fighting men." Anybody outside the circle of macho fighters was more or less safe.[12] It was, in short, patterned violence, restricted violence; this kind of violence sends no chills of fear down the spine of the average person. Most people can buy immunity, just by staying on the sidelines or opting out.

But if this was, in fact, the case, it is no longer true. It is also worth pointing out that there is another historical pattern: domestic violence—crimes of passion and hatred, and family brutality. These account for most homicides, even today. In Marvin Wolfgang's classic study of violent deaths in Philadelphia, for the period 1948 through 1952, only 12.2 percent of the 550 homicides for which the killer was known were committed against "strangers," and 1.1 percent against "innocent bystanders." The big categories of victims included "close friends" (28.2 percent), members of the family (24.7 percent), and substantial numbers of "acquaintances," "paramours," "sex rivals," and the like.[13]* Some thirty years later, the situation had not changed very much. A study of eight cities for the years 1976 through 1978 found that about 20 percent of the homicides were in the family; about 40 percent were classified as "acquaintance homicide," with only about 13 percent as "stranger homicide." But since over a quarter were listed as "type unknown," it seems likely that the percentage of stranger homicides had risen modestly.[14] In absolute numbers, however, homicide was booming, which translated into a lot more murders in all categories.

One striking fact in Wolfgang's study was how few murderers used

---

* In thirty-eight cases the identity of the killer was unknown.

guns. Only a third of the victims in his study had been shot, and 38.8 percent had been stabbed. (Women who killed showed a preference for the kitchen knife—some 40 percent of them.) Another 21.8 percent of the victims had been beaten to death.[15] But in the later study, the gun emerges clearly as the weapon of choice (65 percent); knives were used in only 21 percent of the instances.[16] Is it possible that the population has not gotten more violent in the last thirty years, but simply more heavily armed, and therefore more lethal? A gun is more likely to kill than a knife, or a punch in the jaw. Of course, guns are only part of the story. One can ask, for example, *why* we are so heavily armed.

The raw figures on homicide, appalling and revealing as they are, raise as many questions as they answer. Domestic violence and stranger violence may be related; they may be two sides of the same coin. The blot of violence has spread over more and more of our social space. People in the late twentieth century have lost a sense of safety, of immunity against sudden, unprovoked attack. They feel themselves surrounded and trapped in a jungle of ruthless, hidden predators. Danger is everywhere, and comes from everywhere. Perhaps the ultimate nightmare is the drive-by shooting—random bullets sprayed from a car, ricocheting off walls and sidewalks, endangering us in our cars, at home, in our yards, putting at risk even children at play.

The rules of the game seem to have changed; indeed, now there were no rules at all, only a black hole, an anarchy in the very heart of the polity. Violence had been a macho sport, and it remained that way; but suddenly the norms had gone haywire; it was like some tremendous boxing match, where the boxers, instead of pounding each other inside the ring, suddenly jump through the ropes and begin mauling and maiming the screaming audience.

I have no solution to offer to the question of origins. Modern violent crime may or may not be the bastard child of frontier violence, or American machismo, or domestic violence, or the like. Even if there is a connection, the connection does not explain very much. Modern violence is *different* from frontier violence, or historic American violence. There have been plenty of outbursts of violence in the past—the New York draft riots of the Civil War period; vigilantism; race riots. Lynch law was an appalling aspect of our history. Brutality runs through our history. The bloodstained past may have something to do with it; yet our past is much *less* bloody than the pasts of other countries, which today are lambs to our wolves. The samurai code, unlike the Wild West, does not seem to have left Japanese streets littered with corpses. The French Revolution and the Terror do not seem to make Paris as raw and untamed as New York. Something has to be rotten in the *modern* state of affairs—

some sickness that is peculiarly our own, the child of our period, our customs, our times.

In short, there *may* be some continuity between the swaggering gun-fighter, the southern duellist, the lynch mob, the young gang members of the past, and the violent criminals of the present; but on the whole we have to look deeper and further. Violent crime is a product, by and large, of male aggression. But that aggression can take many forms, and seek all sorts of outlets, many of them quite benign. Somehow, macho honor and swagger have generalized; they have worked their way down the social ladder. They take forms that are, at times, violent, vicious, and perverse. A gang member has to be tough, has to be a man, has to be willing to fight, to shoot, to avenge. In neighborhoods without exit or hope, this terrible code mixes with drugs, drug money, the weakness of the family, the decline of traditional authority, the exaltation of individualism and choice, the vulgarity of media messages, the rampant narcissism and consumerism of American society, and the easy, cheap arsenal of guns, to form a witch's brew of crime, social pathology, and violence.

This book is about criminal justice, not crime; but at many points we have had to deal with theories of criminal behavior, popular or otherwise. Few modern scholars believe in "born criminals" anymore. "Criminal anthropology" is dead as a doornail. Some part of the public probably still thinks "bad blood" is passed down from father to son. Some professionals are still looking for a biological key—a crooked chromosome, for example. Most experts, however, search for the answer in personality, family, and social context. A criminal is a "misraised, mistrained person, unsuccessfully socialized."[17] Even the social scientists James Q. Wilson and Richard J. Herrnstein, who flirt with body type as one co-cause of crime, put the basic blame on child-rearing practices. They feel that parents are no longer interested in "inculcating moral and religious principles." Nowadays, if parents care about anything at all, it is personality development. The nineteenth-century stressed "impulse control," discipline, in short; and this put a damper on crime. Contemporary society has forgotten about impulse control; the main theme of modern life, on the contrary, is "self-expression."[18]

This sounds a bit nostalgic for a family life that perhaps never was—but let that pass. In the previous chapter, I argued along lines that are not too far from Wilson and Herrnstein's theme. But I would not put the blame entirely on parents and child-rearing. The whole society, including TV and popular music, has turned its back on "inculcating." Certainly, a good deal of crime flows out of indiscipline, anomie, normlessless, imperfect morality, inability to delay gratification. The culture certainly stresses the self, the individual; it does not invite people to submerge themselves in some higher cause or entity. It invites them, on the contrary, to be *themselves;* it is individualistic with a vengeance. We have referred to the result as "crimes of the self" (see chapter 19). We mentioned the impact of a celebrity culture—a culture that exalts people who succeed young, who succeed fast, and who career through life in a dizzy aura of money and glamor. Mass culture, media culture, are success cultures; cultures of narcissism and consumerism, cultures of individualism run riot. None of this is particularly new in American society, but the traits are, I believe, more pronounced than in the past.

Some observers put the blame on soft, permissive parents. But in fact, violent, harsh families may be much more likely to breed criminals than soft, indulgent ones.[19] In fact, loving parents may do a better job in our times precisely because they are more in tune with a permissive, indulgent culture. And the culture of individualism, the culture of self, the permissive culture, is not all bad—perhaps it is not even *mostly* bad. American crime rates may be the side effects of a culture that has accomplished a great deal in making people happy and rich. Or, if this seems too Pollyannish, call it a culture that is at least trying to redress tyrannies of the thoughtless past.[20] After all, the era of the self has its positive side: more human freedom, less discrimination and intolerance, less racial and ethnic and sexual repression. Most people would not want to go back to the hierarchical, repressive, prudish, intolerant—*and* racist, *and* sexist—society of a century ago.

Moreover, the vast majority of our citizens—cradled in the same general culture, watching the same TV programs, bombarded by the same temptations and advertisements—never choose a life of crime. What we are trying to explain is a change in *marginal rates of criminality;* that, to be sure, is serious enough, but it has to be kept in perspective. If the number of burglars or rapists doubles over time, this can create a dangerous, alarming situation. As we pointed out in chapter 19, a few thousand burglars can pile up an awful lot of crime; add a few thousand more, and you have a ferocious "crime wave" in a metropolitan area of millions of people. How many potential skyjackers does it take to throw the airline industry into panic? Yet the overwhelming majority of people are neither burglars nor rapists nor skyjackers.

Criminal Justice and Crime

If the sources of crime lie deep in the wellsprings of culture, then they do not lie within the criminal justice system itself. The public, furious and bewildered about violent crime, thrashes about, looking for scapegoats; and one easy scapegoat is the criminal justice system. The media reflect this view, or foster it, perhaps. A study of crime reporting in the

1970s, which analyzed crime stories in the *Chicago Tribune*, found that more than one-third of these stories "indicated that the criminal justice system encourages crime by dealing improperly with criminals" and suffered from the vice of "excessive leniency." A panel of people living in the Midwest agreed. They rated courts and the correctional system poorly (they liked the police); many also complained about laxity in sentencing and parole, and about "legal technicalities": "Society gets no protection at all from the courts. All the marbles are on the criminal's side."[21]

The criminal justice system, to be sure, deserves a great deal of criticism. Hardly anyone has a good word to say for it. It is corrupt, torpid, inefficient, underfinanced, and often inhumane. The big-city criminal court buildings are tawdry; they are the sewers of the social order, and they stink accordingly. The very air in the corridors smells of cynicism and hopelessness. But this is atmosphere: Does the system actually work? Apparently not to anybody's satisfaction. The system sins in all directions. Sometimes it *does* let "criminals" slip through holes in the net. Yet often it can be vicious, discriminatory, and brutal. For the public, the real question is: Does it have an impact on the actual crime rate? The answer is far from clear. Many experts insist that its impact, in reality, is slight.[22]

How can this be? To the layman, the opposite seems completely obvious: the power, or potential power, of a strong, tough system. Nobody really wants to rot in jail, nobody wants to go to the gas chamber. Stiffen the backbone of the system, make it more certain that criminals pay for their crimes, and pay hard; surely crime will dwindle as a consequence. Deterrence—that is the key. Moreover, a burglar in jail can hardly break into your house. This effect is called "incapacitation." It, too, seems like plain common sense. If the crooks are all behind bars, they cannot rape and loot and pillage. The death penalty, of course, is the ultimate incapacitator.

Never mind, then (so the argument goes), soft-headed worry about causes of crime; forget poverty, unemployment, racism, and slums; forget personality and culture. Use the steel rod of criminal justice to stamp out crime, or to reduce it to an acceptable level. Get rid of sentimentality; take the rusty sword down from the wall; let deterrence and incapacitation do their job.[23]

Is anything wrong with the theory of deterrence and incapacitation? Nothing, really—as far as theory goes. But in the streets, station houses, courts, and jails, and in society at large, where theory meets practice, huge gaps appear. To put it bluntly: the criminal justice system cannot deliver a strong enough wallop of deterrence, *beyond the way it is now*, to justify a policy of toughening up. Hans Zeisel's study of New York

City in the 1970s makes the point brutally clear: of every 1,000 felonies committed, only 540 are reported to the police; these turn into 65 arrests and 36 convictions; exactly three of these felons are sentenced to prison for a year or more.[24] If the system were three times as tough, it might put *nine* men in jail. If it were four times as tough, the number might be *twelve*. Even a *tremendous* increase in conviction rates, without something more, would hardly make a dent in the problem of crime.

Why does the criminal justice system deliver so little punch? There are many reasons. The courts can hardly convict somebody if the police do not catch him. It is not that easy to catch a robber or burglar in a vast, anonymous, complex society. Courts also cannot convict without strong evidence—which they often do not have. Whatever the reasons, not very much can be realistically changed, in the short run at least. The American system of criminal justice did not appear out of nowhere; it is a piece of American society, and it cannot be radically altered in ways that contradict the basic ground rules of society. We tolerate corruption and brutality so long as *we* are not the victims. But there are limits to our tolerance; and victims are more and more likely to fight back. Almost everybody seems to want more muscle in the system; but where can the muscle come from? A system that is surgically swift and ruthlessly efficient is simply not in the cards. A Hitler can arrest, try, sentence, and kill in days, and never worry about making a mistake or two along the way. Our system (to its credit) does not have this kind of steel.

Deterrence is a fact, not a mere theory; there is no reason to doubt that deterrence works. But the question is, *how* does it work—and on whom, and to what effect? What the public wants is *more* deterrence, deterrence at the margins; and it is hard to make that happen. Most people start out already deterred; they do not rob, rape, and kill because they think it is dead wrong to rob, rape, and kill. They may also be afraid of punishment, *any* punishment. Potential punishment is already pretty severe, despite the complaints of the law-and-order people. People imagine that the system mollycoddles criminals; but in fact, for those crimes that police, prosecutors, and judges consider really serious (and not "garbage" or "bullshit" cases), the system is and can be extremely tough—right now.[25] Adding a year or two to the average sentence makes the punishment in theory more severe; and, presumably, brings about a reduction in crime. But how much? If, say, a yacht dealer raises his price from $100,000 to $101,000, it is doubtful that the dealer will sell fewer yachts, although, in theory, all else being equal, that should be the tendency. Roughly the same can be said of deterrence through punishment.

The relationship between punishment and behavior is not a straight line but a curve; it flattens out as more and more people are, in fact, deterred. The few that are left become harder and harder to influence.[26] If the punishment for armed robbery (assuming we catch the robbers) goes up from seven to ten years (assuming, too, we can make the judges do this), will there be less armed robbery? In theory, yes. But in practice, who knows? *Most* of us are already deterred—by conscience, habit, fear. The few who are left are the toughest cases. And a *marginal* change in punishment is not likely to produce much more in the way of "incapacitation" than we have right now—even if the vacuum does not get filled with fresh crime recruits.

The criminal justice system has a way of reducing to the banal experiences that are among the most intense imaginable. A crime becomes a mere statistic, a tiny electronic shiver in a data base; but each crime is also an event, an eruption, a happening of great force and power on the individual level. Rage, hopelessness, desperation, anger, and fear accompany each act of murder, rape, robbery, or assault. For the most part, society depends not on cages and cops but on the inner iron of socialization to keep us in line. But if inner controls fade and weaken even slightly, then we have to face the bitter truth: socialization *as we know it now* cannot cope and contain the emotions that drive people to crime. Or, to be more accurate: it can for most of us, but not for all. And the uncontainable minority seem to be a growing group.

To be sure, there are other factors we have to take into account. Demographics make a difference. Most of the people we arrest are young males; when this age group bulges in the population, arrests and crimes go up, all else being equal; and when the age group shrinks, crime goes down. The drug epidemic—or, rather, the criminalization of drugs—also makes a big difference to many aspects of the system. The appalling number of guns loose in society must shoulder some of the blame—for the murder rate at least. Real progress in gun control seems politically impossible; some perverse streak in national politics, or national character, seems to guarantee that nothing much can be done, even when fourteen-year-olds "pack rods" in school and semiautomatic weapons are as common as microwave ovens.

The gun lobby does have a point (or a pointlet): *people* kill, not guns. The Swiss are armed to the teeth, and so are the Israelis; rates of violent crime in these countries are fairly low. But we are not either Swiss or Israeli. If we got rid of the guns, the murder rate might go down. Fewer children, certainly, would blow their brains out by accident. We would surely ameliorate the *effect* of assaults and the like. Of course, the murderous impulse would still be there, under the skin.

Race, too, is a factor in crime, but a mysterious and convoluted one. As we have seen, black men are accused, arrested, tried, and jailed out of all proportion to their numbers. There is no denying the corrosive impact of racism and the social position of the black underclass. To repeat a point made earlier: for many young men trapped in a black ghetto, crime offers an attractive route to money, fast cars, and some kind of comfort; the main alternative is the misery and humiliation of the welfare system, or a job at a taco joint or burger bar, or washing dishes, or scrubbing floors: hard work at minimum wage.

Yet, certainly, this is not the whole story. Racism is not *worse* than before; blacks were once enslaved. After emancipation, they were still little better than serfs in most parts of the country. Crime is obviously related, in some way, to oppression and repression; but, paradoxically, it seems to flourish most when the repression lifts somewhat. Moreover, crime rates in the United States are so high, compared to most other countries, that even if we excluded every arrest and conviction of a black, an astonishing, and abnormal amount of white crime would still remain, which can hardly be fobbed off on race. The crime explosion *must* mean the collapse of a system of restraining values, for whatever reason.

Thus there seems no way to avoid the message we began with: crime is imbedded in the culture—and in this particular culture, and at this particular time. The situation is organic to society; it is part of the very cell structure, the nucleus. It is like a virus that seizes control of some part of the organism and its genetic structure; and cannot be destroyed with any of our present instruments of cure.

Of course, there are great pressures on the criminal justice system— pressures to *do* something, to provide some relief. The frantic activity of the eighties, which continues into the nineties—the furious building of prisons, the stiff laws, the cries for more, more, more in the way of punishment—what has the upshot been? The effect on crime: imperceptible. On individual defendants, yes; there are, indisputably, results. Felony filings in state courts grew from 689,718 in 1984 to 1,032,053 in 1989. In the District of Columbia they more than doubled in this period. West Virginia was the only state with fewer felony filings in 1989 than in 1984. In large states such as California, New York, and Texas, filings grew by more than 50 percent in this five-year period.[27] The so-called war on drugs, of course, accounts for much of this growth. The prison population, too, has been rising dramatically. In 1880, according to the best data available, there were about 30,000 men and women in prisons and reformatories, about 61 per 100,000 in the population as a whole, and 170 per 100,000 of the population between the ages of twenty and forty-four. In 1983, the rate had risen to 179 per 100,000, 469 per 100,000 of the age group between twenty and forty-four. Some 419,000 men and women were imprisoned in that year. The prison population had more than doubled since 1970.[28] It is still rising rapidly. In 1986, there were 540,963 men and woman in state and federal prisons, and 277,271 in local jails.[29] In the state of California, in 1952, there were 13,169 men and women in correctional institutions; in 1990, there were 97,309.[30]

Yet if the new toughness has had any effect on crime rates, it is certainly hard to prove. Clear causal lines run the other way. High crime leads to high-stakes, high-profile politics, which leads to pressure on the law, and on the criminal justice system. The history of the death penalty, which we discussed earlier (see chapter 14), is a dramatic illustration of this point.

The agitation over crime triggered a general attack on every aspect of the criminal justice system that seemed too "soft" on crime. Supreme Court decisions in the days of the Warren Court, which seemed to "coddle" criminals, only fanned the flames of desire. Police expenditures went up; politicians scrambled to find the right reaction to the boiling, bubbling public rage.

Most of these reactions brought only temporary (political) relief, since the crime problem stubbornly refused to go away. In truth, local politicans could not really do much about crime. Crime, as Herbert Jacob, the political scientist, has pointed out, was a problem of the whole society rather than "one that had local roots" yet people tended to treat it *as if* it were local.[31] Conversely, although presidents have routinely thundered against crime and promised to attack it through their office, criminal justice was and is highly local; not much can be done about it on the level of the whole society. Not much, at any rate, that anybody is particularly willing to do.

There is, therefore, a major structural contradiction. The causes of crime, the reach of crime, the reality of crime—all these are national in scale and scope. Criminal justice, on the other hand, is as local as local gets.[32] Indeed, the criminal justice "system" is not a system at all. This particular mirror of society is a jigsaw puzzle with a thousand tiny pieces. No one is really in charge. Legislatures make rules; police and detectives carry them out (more or less). Prosecutors prosecute; defense attorneys defend; judges and juries go their own way. So do prison officials. Everybody seems to have veto power over everybody else. Juries can frustrate judges and the police; the police can make nonsense out of the legislature; prison officials can undo the work of judges; prosecutors can ignore the police and the judges. The system is like a leaky garden hose: you can try to turn up the pressure at one end, but more water does not come out at the other. All you get is more water squirting out of the holes.

Not that the system is static. It does, in fact, change; sometimes quite radically. But the changes are not smooth and neatly coordinated, traveling down a chain of command; they simply happen. The system is awkward, loose-joined, messy.[33] As a result, "reforms" dissipate into thin air, muscle turns to flab, innovation turns into shipwreck. The causes of these failures "are found at every stage of planned change," from conception to implementation.[34]

American criminal justice is organized (if you can call it organized at all) more or less along the lines of what Mirjan Damaska of Yale Law School has called the "coordinate" system. In such a system authority is extremely diffuse; there are many officials, none "clearly superior to others," and there is "essentially a single stratum of authority." The systems of continental Europe are more highly organized, more hierarchical, with clear lines of authority, tightly bound into a "strict network of super- and subordination." Coordinate systems are more anarchical: authority is "horizontal"; it is "a web without a spider sitting at its heart."[35] Damaska is surely right about the essential nature of the American system. Almost every aspect of American public life is this kind of spiderless web. Perhaps he overdoes the role of history and tradition in bringing this anarchy about. But whatever the cause, the result is likely to be frustration, a helpless flailing about in which experiments inevitably fail.

Not everybody in this country, of course, was and is in favor of more and tougher toughness. The due-process wing has never given up. Civil-liberty forces were never entirely silenced; they have always protested valiantly and continually against cruelty, callousness, and neglect in the criminal justice system, against what they consider the misuse of criminal justice.

Our criminal justice system—maybe *every* criminal justice system—includes an aspect that is downright oppressive. Criminal justice is, literally, state power. It is police, guns, prisons, the electric chair. Power corrupts; and power also has an itch to suppress. A strain of suppression runs through the whole of our story. The sufferers—burnt witches, whipped and brutalized slaves, helpless drunks thrown into fetid county jails, victims of lynch mobs—cry out to us across the centuries.

Nobody, of course, denies that there are bad people in the world; and, when all is said and done, most of us are only too eager to call on the criminal justice system when we need its help. The criminal justice system has always had two faces: devil and angel, good cop and bad cop. The right wing—the law-and-order crowd—tends to like *both* aspects of the system. They do not mind some suppression, to keep people down who deserve to be down. Southern whites, for example, used criminal process to crush rebellion among "their" blacks, to "keep them in their place." On the other hand, sporadic voices on the far left approve of *neither* aspect of the system. They consider even "ordinary" crime a form of protest against a rotten society. Most of the rest of the country is somewhere in the middle, or just plain confused. But the higher the crime rate, the more people lean toward "law and order."

Some groups have historically suffered more from the "bad cop," and these groups tend to lean the other way. Blacks and Hispanics, Native Americans, gays, and others have felt both ignored and oppressed. Police brutality has been a recurrent issue, one that flared up again in 1992 in the Rodney King incident (see chapter 16). The forces at play in the system are highly complex. There is a tendency for uneasy compromise—for example, in sentencing and correctional "reforms." Reforms often have curiously ambiguous roots, and curiously equivocal results. Neither side triumphs. There is a tendency, of course, in a high-crime, high-fear period, to switch attention from (helping) offenders, to (stamping out) offenses; but the switch is also resisted, and not always futilely. The picture is, and remains, extremely mixed.

A Concluding Word

This book has attempted to trace the history of criminal justice, its changes over the years, its successes and failures. There were plenty of failures to write about. Problems of criminal justice cannot be divorced from problems of crime. Crime, after all, is the main excuse for having such a system at all.

But, whatever the public may think, no solution to the problem of crime is in sight, not in the short run at least. The crime problem, of course, cannot be "solved" in the sense of wiping out crime entirely. What people really want is some way to contain crime; to reduce crime, especially violent crime, to more manageable proportions. Most of us— old and young, black and white, men and women— would settle for the rate of crime the Swiss or the Japanese enjoy. But that, too, does not seem to be in the cards.

If this is so—and I think it is—it is a bitter pill for the American public to swallow. Americans do not, on the whole, like to be told that problems are insoluble, just as they do not like to be told that some diseases cannot be cured. They live in a world in which miracles of medicine and technology happen all the time; they live in a world of rapid change, a world of novelty and adventure; they do not see limits to change; it would not surprise them if somebody invented a way for people to fly, or live underwater, or a cure for old age. Anything seems possible. So they keep searching for solutions, hoping for solutions, *expecting* solutions.

But the solutions do not come. What is the reason? It must be (people think) that the system is too flaccid. More police, more prisons, more iron fists: that is the ticket. Politicians, as we have seen, eagerly batten on these views. Cast your ballot for X and he will light a fire under the system. After election, disillusionment invariably sets in.

The sad fact is that no amount of tinkering, no amount of jail building or amendments to penal codes will do the trick, at least not in this society. This is so for a number of reasons. In the first place, we cannot and will not adopt truly savage, draconian measures. As we pointed out, the death penalty *might* be a good deterrent if we used it as Hitler or Stalin did, with utter ruthlessness and speed. If we routinely cut off the hands of thieves, this *might* stop thievery. But these measures are impossible in the United States; cutting off hands is out of the question, and as far as the death penalty is concerned, it takes years to drag each individual wretch from court to death row to appellate court to the place of execution; and I doubt that most people really regret this situation, whatever they may say.[36]

On the other hand, certain kinds of stern measures are impossible because the law-and-order crowd itself refuses to countenance them: gun control is an excellent example. Sixty percent of the people who were asked felt that "drugs" were the factor "most responsible for crime in the United States today."[37] Surely something should be done; or so people think. But drug policy has entered a state of pure paralysis. Legalization is apparently out of the question, politically, and so is *real* toughness (sealing the borders or beheading pushers).

In my view, the "crime problem" flows largely from changes in the culture itself; it is part of us, our evil twin, our shadow; our own society produced it. It has been a central theme of this book that criminal justice systems are organic, rooted in society. Crime is no different. It is part of the American story, the American fabric. Perhaps—just perhaps—the siege of crime may be the price we pay for a brash, self-loving, relatively free and open society.

Of course, this does not mean raising the flag of surrender—giving up the war against crime. There are certainly things we can do, and ought to do. Some people think a full-employment program for young men with nothing to do would do wonders in the fight against crime. This is probably a shade naïve, but it may not be a bad idea nonetheless. Surely *some* young men (and women) would choose a decent job over a life of crime if we gave them half a chance. We can think of other social remedies—education, training, social reforms. But, alas, very few measures we might imagine are likely to turn into reality. For one thing, nobody seems to want to put up the money.

For this reason, I fear, we are likely to bump along more or less as we are. The siege of crime and all the misery it brings, both to those who commit it and those who are victimized, is a high price to pay for our liberty. It is a cost that is badly and unfairly distributed. But for now, at least, there may be nothing to do but grit our teeth and pay the price.

BIBLIOGRAPHICAL ESSAY

THE HISTORY OF CRIMINAL JUSTICE IN THE UNITED STATES HAS BEEN RATHER badly neglected; it is not clear why. Legal history in general has also suffered from neglect, but this field has lately shown great signs of growth; the same is true of social history in general. Criminal justice lies at the intersection of these two, and consequently it has received a shot in the arm in recent years. The literature is still fairly small, and there are some gaping holes, but the amount of work is growing rather rapidly, and the quality of much of it is high.

Still, there are very few general treatments of the history of American criminal justice. In fact, that is one reason why I undertook to write this very book. Samuel Walker's *Popular Justice: A History of American Criminal Justice* (1980) comes the closest to filling the gap; this book, an excellent introduction to the subject in many ways, sets out some of the main lines of development clearly and concisely. Walker is particularly attentive to police history. Herbert A. Johnson's book, *History of Criminal Justice* (1988), was written to be used as a classroom text; Johnson put it together, he says, "in response to an acute pedagogical need." It too is brief, probably too brief, and many readers will find it a bit sketchy. David R. Johnson's book, *American Law Enforcement: A History* (1981), as the title suggests, concentrates on law enforcement, mostly on police forces and how they grew. Even shorter (and much less satisfactory all around) is William J. Bopp and Donald O. Schultz, *A*

Short History of American Law Enforcement (1972), but I have found this book useful in spots.

Criminal justice gets covered, of course, in general histories of American law. There are not too many of these, to be sure. I have to cite my own book here, *A History of American Law* (2d ed., 1985), which has several chapters on criminal justice; there is also material on criminal justice in the other general account, Kermit L. Hall, *The Magic Mirror: Law in American History* (1989). Melvin I. Urofsky's book, *A March of Liberty: A Constitutional History of the United States* (1988), is richly detailed, and much broader than the title suggests; it deals, at times comprehensively, with many other aspects of the American legal system, not merely with aspects that would be narrowly defined as "constitutional."

The literature on the colonial period is, in some ways, more voluminous than the literature on criminal justice in later periods. General accounts of the period often devote considerable space to crime and punishment. Mention must be made of the classic study by George Lee Haskins, *Law and Authority in Early Massachusetts: A Study in Tradition and Design* (1960), and David T. Konig's fine book, *Law and Society in Puritan Massachusetts: Essex County, 1629–1692* (1979). These two books, as their titles indicate, focus on Massachusetts; a recent, more general, and extremely lucid account is Peter C. Hoffer, *Law and People in Colonial America* (1992).

Among the many works dealing specifically with criminal justice in the colonial period, I list the following: Arthur P. Scott, *Criminal Law in Colonial Virginia* (1930); Douglas Greenberg, *Crime and Law Enforcement in the Colony of New York, 1691–1776* (1976); Donna J. Spindel, *Crime and Society in North Carolina, 1663–1776* (1989); Julius Goebel, Jr., and T. Raymond Naughton, *Law Enforcement in Colonial New York: A Study in Criminal Procedure* (1944); Bradley Chapin, *Criminal Justice in Colonial America, 1606–1660* (1983); and Gwenda Morgan, *The Hegemony of the Law: Richmond County, Virginia, 1692–1776* (1989). There is also a growing literature on more specialized topics; for example, N. E. H. Hull, *Female Felons: Women and Serious Crime in Colonial Massachusetts* (1987); Hugh F. Rankin, *Criminal Trial Proceedings in the General Court of Colonial Virginia* (1965); and, on infanticide, Peter C. Hoffer and N. E. H. Hull, *Murdering Mothers: Infanticide in England and New England, 1558–1803* (1981).

Some of the best work is not in book form at all, but in the form of essays and short pieces; these are scattered among legal and historical periodicals. Eric H. Monkkonen has done students a favor by collecting many of these essays and articles in *Crime and Justice in American History: 1. The Colonies and Early Republic* (1991), a two-volume set.

Scholars have also collected and published a considerable amount of primary material for the colonial period—court records, very notably. This is much less true for the nineteenth and twentieth centuries. Some scholarly editions of primary sources are especially valuable because of their notes and introductions. Various volumes of the *Archives of Maryland* might be mentioned; but probably the best of all is Peter C. Hoffer and William B. Scott, eds., *Criminal Proceedings in Colonial Virginia* (1984), which includes the records of trials in Richmond County, Virginia, for the period 1711 to 1754; almost as good is Joseph Smith, *Colonial Justice in Western Massachusetts (1639–1702): The Pynchon Court Record* (1961), another fine example of scholarly editing.

For the nineteenth century, there is precious little in the way of scholarly editions of legal records. Of course, for much of the century there are published case reports, in hundreds and hundreds of volumes—too much for anyone to digest. These are, of course, appellate cases. The trial courts are astonishingly obscure. On nineteenth-century criminal justice, there are two fascinating comparative studies, Michael S. Hindus, *Prison and Plantation: Crime, Justice, and Authority in Massachusetts and South Carolina, 1767–1878* (1980), and Edward L. Ayers, *Vengeance and Justice: Crime and Punishment in the Nineteenth-Century American South* (1984). For federal criminal law there is Dwight F. Henderson, *Congress, Courts, and Criminals: The Development of Federal Criminal Law, 1801–1829* (1985). An intensive and useful study of a single jurisdiction is Allen Steinberg, *The Transformation of Criminal Justice, Philadelphia, 1800–1880* (1989); there is also valuable material in David J. Bodenhamer, *The Pursuit of Justice: Crime and Law in Antebellum Indiana* (1986). Jack K. Williams, *Vogues in Villainy: Crime and Retribution in Ante-Bellum South Carolina* (1959), is lively and informative. On the later part of the century, see Lawrence M. Friedman and Robert V. Percival, *The Roots of Justice: Crime and Punishment in Alameda County, California, 1870–1910* (1981). The petty courts are pretty much neglected, which is no surprise; but there is a start on a literature: Theodore Ferdinand, *Boston's Lower Criminal Courts, 1814–1850* (1992); John R. Wunder, *Inferior Courts, Superior Justice: A History of the Justices of the Peace on the Northwest Frontier, 1853–1889* (1979). There is also some coverage of these courts in Friedman and Percival's *Roots of Justice*, and in Steinberg's book about Philadelphia.

On police history, there is a good deal to choose from, comparatively speaking. I have already mentioned David R. Johnson's book, *American Law Enforcement: A History*. Particularly noteworthy are Roger Lane, *Policing the City: Boston, 1822–1885* (1967); Wilbur R. Miller, *Cops and Bobbies: Police Authority in New York and London, 1830–1870* (1977);

Samuel Walker, *A Critical History of Police Reform: The Emergence of Professionalism* (1977); Robert M. Fogelson, *Big-City Police* (1977); James F. Richardson, *Urban Police in the United States* (1974); David R. Johnson, *Policing the Urban Underworld: The Impact of Crime on the Development of the American Police, 1860–1887* (1979); and Sidney L. Haring, *Policing a Class Society: The Experiences of American Cities, 1865–1915* (1983). Eric H. Monkkonen's book, *Police in Urban America, 1860–1920* (1981), is particularly thoughtful and insightful. There is also a literature on the FBI; for example, Sanford J. Ungar's study, called simply *FBI* (1975). There is not much on the history of detective forces; on private detectives, there is Frank Morn's study, *"The Eye That Never Sleeps": A History of the Pinkerton National Detective Agency* (1982). A fine study of a neglected subject is Gary T. Marx's book, *Undercover: Police Surveillance in America* (1988).

Prisons and penitentiaries have gotten their share of attention, too. On the origin of the penitentiary system, nobody should overlook David J. Rothman's interesting and controversial book, *The Discovery of the Asylum: Social Order and Disorder in the New Republic* (1971). An excellent recent treatment, which puts Rothman and others under a revisionist searchlight, is Adam J. Hirsch, *The Rise of the Penitentiary: Prisons and Punishment in Early America* (1992). There is a modern edition of Gustave de Beaumont and Alexis de Tocqueville, *On the Penitentiary System in the United States*, with a foreword by Thorsten Sellin (1964). The penitentiary also figures in Hindus's comparative study of Massachusetts and South Carolina, mentioned earlier; see also Shelley Bookspan, *A Germ of Goodness: The California State Prison System, 1851–1944* (1991); Donald R. Walker, *Penology for Profit: A History of the Texas Prison System, 1867–1912* (1988). For the twentieth century, there is James B. Jacobs, *Stateville: The Penitentiary in Mass Society* (1977); John J. DiIulio, Jr., has written a useful review essay, "Understanding Prisons: The New Old Penology," in *Law and Social Inquiry* 16:65 (1991). There are quite a few interesting firsthand accounts of prisons, prison life, and the like; see, for example, Lewis E. Lawes, *Twenty Thousand Years in Sing Sing* (1932), written by a warden at Sing Sing. A great deal of useful information is to be found in Margaret Werner Cahalan, *Historical Corrections Statistics in the United States, 1850–1984*, published by the Department of Justice in 1986. A very intelligent account of the social meaning of the recent rise in prison populations is Franklin E. Zimring and Gordon Hawkins, *The Scale of Imprisonment* (1991).

There is a sizable literature, too, on vigilantes and vigilante movements; and on law and order in the Wild West. It's a mixed bag at best. Richard Maxwell Brown, *Strain of Violence: Historical Studies of Ameri-*

can Violence and Vigilantism (1975), is the most comprehensive book on the subject. Among other works may be mentioned Robert M. Senkewicz, *Vigilantes in Gold Rush San Francisco* (1985); Philip D. Jordan, *Frontier Law and Order: Ten Essays* (1970); Glenn Shirley, *West of Hell's Fringe: Crime, Criminals and the Federal Peace Officer in Oklahoma Territory, 1889–1907* (1978); and Larry D. Ball, *Desert Lawmen: The High Sheriffs of New Mexico and Arizona, 1846–1912* (1992); Kevin J. Mullen, *Let Justice Be Done: Crime and Politics in Early San Francisco* (1989). Particularly interesting is the treatment of law and order in the West in Roger D. McGrath, *Gunfighters, Highwaymen and Vigilantes: Violence on the Frontier* (1984). A related matter is taken up in Wilbur R. Miller's *Revenuers and Moonshiners: Enforcing Federal Liquor Law in the Mountain South, 1865–1900* (1991). Another study worth reading is Stephen Cresswell, *Mormons, Cowboys, Moonshiners and Klansmen: Federal Law Enforcement in the South and West, 1870–1893* (1991). Paul Angle's book, *Bloody Williamson: A Chapter in American Lawlessness* (1952), which deals with a single American county (Williamson County, Illinois), is useful and very good reading, too.

Everybody (or almost everybody) loves a good mystery, and a good crime story; and there are many books dealing with this or that great American murder and the trials that ensued. I will mention only a few. For the nineteenth century, there is David Richard Kasserman, *Fall River Outrage: Life, Murder, and Justice in Early Industrial New England* (1986); and Raymond Paul, *Who Murdered Mary Rogers?* (1971). For later cases, see, for example, William M. Kunstler, *The Minister and the Choir Singer* (1964), on the famous Hall-Mills case; and Hal Higdon, *The Crime of the Century: The Leopold and Loeb Case* (1975). Some of these cases continue to fascinate generation after generation—the Lizzie Borden case most of all, it seems—and there are constantly new attempts to "solve" them (even those that do not seem to need to be solved). A good example of this genre is Robert Sullivan's book *The Disappearance of Dr. Parkman* (1971) on the sensational mid-nineteenth century murder at Harvard. Sullivan argues strenuously that Dr. Webster, who was executed for the crime, was innocent after all. I for one was not convinced.

In recent years, there has been increased interest, not surprisingly, in the intersection between race, gender, crime, and criminal justice. An important recent work on the criminal law of slavery is Philip J. Schwarz, *Twice Condemned: Slaves and the Criminal Laws of Virginia, 1705–1865* (1988); see also Arthur E. Howington, *What Sayeth the Law: The Treatment of Slaves and Free Blacks in the State and Local Courts of Tennessee* (1986); and Daniel J. Flanigan, *The Criminal Law of Slavery and Freedom, 1800–1868* (1973). Roger Lane, in *Roots of Violence in*

Black Philadelphia, 1860–1900 (1986), argues that discrimination separated the black population "uniquely" from the "experience of the urban industrial revolution" (p. 140) and tries to connect this fact with the criminality of black ghettos. Many studies of the civil rights movement have material on southern justice and the blacks. Dan T. Carter's fine book on the Scottsboro case, *Scottsboro: A Tragedy of the American South* (1969), is a rich case study of the problem.

Other minorities have gotten much shorter shrift. The Chicano experience is recounted in Alfredo Mirande, *Gringo Justice* (1987). Adequate accounts of Native American criminal justice, and the experience of Native Americans in Anglo courts, are yet to be written. Two books worth noting are John P. Reid, *A Law of Blood: The Primitive Law of the Cherokee Nation* (1970), and Yasuhide Kawashima, *Puritan Justice and the Indian: White Man's Law in Massachusetts, 1630–1763* (1986). On women and the criminal justice system, we have already mentioned N. E. H. Hull's *Female Felons* for the colonial period. Estelle B. Freedman, *Their Sisters' Keepers: Women's Prison Reform in America, 1830–1930* (1981), deals with women's prisons. Elizabeth Pleck, *Domestic Tyranny: The Making of Social Policy Against Family Violence from Colonial Times to the Present* (1987), covers wife-beating, child abuse, and related subjects; another good study is Linda Gordon, *Heroes of Their Own Lives: The Politics and History of Family Violence, Boston, 1880–1960* (1988). There is a lot of useful information on gender and law, including historical data, in Deborah Rhode's book, *Justice and Gender* (1989).

Political crimes, and political aspects of criminal justice, are mentioned or dealt with in a number of the studies already mentioned; for example, Haring's book on the police. For the twentieth century, there is Steven E. Barkan, *Protesters on Trial: Criminal Justice in the Southern Civil Rights and Vietnam Antiwar Movements* (1985), a thoughtful study, written by a social scientist with firsthand experience of political justice; Richard Polenberg, *Fighting Faiths: The Abrams Case, the Supreme Court, and Free Speech* (1987); and Stanley I. Kutler, *The American Inquisition: Justice and Injustice in the Cold War* (1982). Military justice is treated in Jonathan Lurie, *Arming Military Justice, Volume 1, The Origin of the United States Court of Military Appeals, 1775–1950* (1992).

The death penalty has been controversial for more than two centuries, and it has generated quite a bit of scholarly interest. Louis P. Masur, *Rites of Execution: Capital Punishment and the Transformation of American Culture, 1776–1865* (1989), is one of the most interesting and imaginative of these. Everybody seems interested in murder, too, and there are dozens of popular books about murders in this or that city or period; but if you want scholarly rigor, there is not much to recommend. One outstanding exception is Roger Lane's book, *Violent Death in the City: Suicide, Accident and Murder in Nineteenth-Century Philadelphia* (1979).

It is no surprise that criminal procedure has not produced a rich historical literature; and for most readers the legal literature will be tedious, to say the least. Duty requires me to mention two old but indispensable books by Lester B. Orfield, *Criminal Appeals in America* (1939) and *Criminal Procedure from Arrest to Appeal* (1947). These are the sort of books that nobody (including myself) could possibly have the stomach to actually *read* from cover to cover; still, we are all indebted to Orfield for his labors. A short and snappy account of the constitutional aspects of the subject may be found in David J. Bodenhamer, *Fair Trial: Rights of the Accused in American History* (1992). There is no good history of the jury system, but the classic study by Harry Kalven, Jr., and Hans Zeisel, *The American Jury* (1966), contains a good deal of historical material and is old enough by now to count as a primary source. On the grand jury, see Richard D. Younger, *The People's Panel: The Grand Jury in the United States, 1634–1941* (1963).

In one sense, there is much less of a literature on criminal justice in the twentieth century than is true of the nineteenth. I am referring to strictly *historical* studies. A number of the studies already mentioned, such as Friedman and Percival, do straddle the late nineteenth and early twentieth centuries. Moreover, the twentieth century is rich in studies and surveys that are not "historical" in themselves, but which have aged enough to count as documents of the past in their own right; for example, Hugh N. Fuller, *Criminal Justice in Virginia* (1931).

Particularly worthy of mention in this regard are the elaborate crime surveys of the 1920s and 1930s, notably *Criminal Justice in Cleveland*, (1922), directed and edited by Roscoe Pound and Felix Frankfurter; the *Missouri Crime Survey* was published in 1926, and the *Illinois Crime Survey* in 1929. All of these crime surveys are full of facts and figures, and they are extremely useful as guides to contemporary attitudes and ideas. The various vice-commission reports are also of enormous interest—for example, the report of the Vice Commission of Chicago, published in 1911 under the title *The Social Evil in Chicago*. There are also the various governmental crime reports, notably those of the Wickersham Committee. Some of the reports were published separately; for example, Ernest J. Hopkins, *Our Lawless Police* (1931). In this century, too, there are more and more firsthand accounts of experience with criminal justice—autobiographies or accounts of thieves, or life stories of detectives, policemen, or criminal lawyers. These were much rarer in the nineteenth century.

Some of the distinctive twentieth-century courts have their own literature, very notably, the juvenile court. Anthony Platt's *The Child Savers: The Invention of Delinquency* (1969) raised a lot of hackles and put forward some interesting and some dubious ideas. On juvenile justice in general, see Robert M. Mennel, *Thorns and Thistles: Juvenile Delinquents in the United States, 1825–1940* (1973); see also John R. Sutton, *Stubborn Children: Controlling Delinquency in the United States, 1640–1981* (1988); Steven L. Schlossman, *Love and the American Delinquent: The Theory and Practice of "Progressive" Juvenile Justice, 1825–1910* (1977). The juvenile court is one of the topics considered in David Rothman, *Conscience and Convenience: The Asylum and Its Alternatives in Progressive America* (1980). Paul W. Tappan's book, *Delinquent Girls in Court: A Study of the Wayward Minor Court of New York* (1947), is still quite valuable. Mention should be made of Mary Ellen Odem's fine doctoral dissertation, "Delinquent Daughters: The Sexual Regulation of Female Minors in the United States, 1880–1920" (University of California at Berkeley, 1989).

The campaigns against vice are dealt with, along with other topics, in the excellent study by Ruth Rosen, *The Lost Sisterhood: Prostitution in America, 1900–1918* (1982), as well as in the rather mordant and consistently interesting study by Frederick K. Grittner, *White Slavery: Myth, Ideology, and American Law* (1990). In general, the literature on victimless crime, prostitution, and the like, is growing; in addition to the books mentioned, see, for example, Mark Thomas Connelly, *The Response to Prostitution in the Progressive Era* (1980). (I have already noted the various vice-commission reports.) Drug regulation is treated in David Musto, *The American Disease: Origins of Narcotic Control* (1973), but this subject needs a lot more work. Henry Chafetz, *Play the Devil: A History of Gambling in the United States from 1492 to 1955* (1960), is, I hope, not the last word on the subject.

There is, of course, a large literature on organized crime and on the struggle against it. John Landesco's book, *Organized Crime in Chicago*, was originally part of the 1929 Illinois Crime Survey; it has been edited and republished (1968) with introductions by Mark H. Haller and Andrew A. Bruce. Some of the political aspects of the struggle against organized crime are deftly handled in William Howard Moore, *The Kefauver Committee and the Politics of Crime, 1950–1952* (1974). See also Francis A. J. Ianni, *A Family Business: Kinship and Social Control in Organized Crime* (1972).

The modern literature on the causes and cures for crime is absolutely immense; the same is true of the literature on the criminal justice system. There are at least half a dozen books, and probably more, on plea bargaining alone, and dozens of articles and books on the operation of courts of criminal justice, high and low. There are popular and scholarly dissections of the police and police behavior; hosts of "true crime" stories, and so forth and so on. I am loath to single out individual instances. Still, I would recommend Samuel Walker's sensible and well-written survey, *Sense and Nonsense About Crime: A Policy Guide* (2d ed., 1989), a masterpiece of debunking; and Charles E. Silberman, *Criminal Violence, Criminal Justice* (1978). Almost anything written by Marvin Wolfgang, Franklin E. Zimring, and Gordon Hawkins can be wholeheartedly endorsed. I also feel I must mention Hans Zeisel's fine study, *The Limits of Law Enforcement* (1982); this is social research at its best. David Simon's book, *Homicide: A Year on the Killing Streets* (1991), is another type altogether. This is an absolutely fascinating account of one year among the homicide detectives of Baltimore; it is journalism of the highest order. Another excellent study, more or less on the same subject, is Henry P. Lundsgaarde, *Murder in Space City: A Cultural Analysis of Houston Homicide Patterns* (1977)—another demonstration that social science training does not necessarily destroy one's ability to write good, clean English. And for a fresh, quirky look at some aspects of crime, there is Jack Katz's book *Seductions of Crime: Moral and Sensual Attractions in Doing Evil* (1988).

NOTES

INTRODUCTION

1. This account comes from Gail Sussman Marcus, "'Due Execution of the Generall Rules of Righteousnesse': Criminal Procedure in New Haven Town and Colony, 1638–1658," in David D. Hall, John M. Murrin, and Thad W. Tate, eds., *Saints and Revolutionaries: Essays in Early American History* (1984), pp. 99, 115.
2. Susan P. Shapiro, *Wayward Capitalists: Target of the Securities and Exchange Commission* (1984), p. 22.
3. *New York Times*, Jan. 3, 1901, p. 1; Jan. 29, 1901, p. 3.
4. Most criminologists, but not all, would agree with this general formulation; for an exception see Michael R. Gottfredson and Travis Hirschi, *A General Theory of Crime* (1990).
5. 4 Blackstone's Commentaries 7–8.
6. See the account in Johannes Andenaes, "The General Preventive Effects of Punishment," *University of Pennsylvania Law Review* 114:949, 962 (1966).
7. Lawrence M. Friedman, *The Legal System: A Social Science Perspective* (1975), p. 68. Apparently, whether there still exist societies that regularly practice cannibalism is in question; but the point remains, either way.
8. On this point, see Kai T. Erikson, *Wayward Puritans: A Study in the Sociology of Deviance* (1966), chap 1.

9. Gustave de Beaumont and Alexis de Tocqueville, *On the Penitentiary System in the United States and Its Application in France* (1833; reprint ed., 1964), p. 140.

CHAPTER 1.
THE SHAPE AND NATURE OF THE LAW

1. See, for example, John Phillip Reid, *A Law of Blood: The Primitive Law of the Cherokee Nation* (1970).
2. Yasuhide Kawashima, *Puritan Justice and the Indian* (1986), p. 15.
3. On the meaning and history of the grand jury, see Richard D. Younger, *The People's Panel: The Grand Jury in the United States, 1634–1941* (1963).
4. David T. Konig, "'Dale's Laws' and the Non-Common Law Origins of Criminal Justice in Virginia," *American Journal of Legal History* 26:354 (1982).
5. See Joseph H. Smith, *Appeals to the Privy Council from the American Plantations* (1950).
6. Joseph Smith, *Colonial Justice in Western Massachusetts (1639–1702): The Pynchon Court Record* (1961), p. 130. Instead, criminal proceedings began when a private victim brought a complaint, or when a town constable did so.
7. Younger, *People's Panel*, chap. 1.
8. John M. Murrin, "Magistrates, Sinners, and a Precarious Liberty: Trial by Jury in Seventeenth-Century New England," in David D. Hall, John M. Murrin, and Thad W. Tate, eds., *Saints and Revolutionaries: Essays in Early American History* (1984), pp. 152, 188–89; David J. Bodenhamer, *Fair Trial: Rights of the Accused in American History* (1992), p. 24.
9. Gail Sussman Marcus, "'Due Execution of the Generall Rules of Righteousnesse': Criminal Procedure in New Haven Town and Colony, 1638–1658," in Hall, Murrin, and Tate, *Saints and Revolutionaries*, pp. 99, 102ff.
10. Marcus, "'Due Execution,'" pp. 129–30.
11. Peter C. Hoffer and William B. Scott, eds., *Criminal Proceedings in Colonial Virginia, Richmond County, 1711–1754* (1984), p. xx.
12. Daniel E. Williams, "'Behold a Tragic Scene Strangely Changed into a Theater of Mercy': The Structure and Significance of Criminal Conversion Narratives in Early New England," *American Quarterly* 38:827 (1986).
13. Peter C. Hoffer, "Disorder and Deference: The Paradoxes of Criminal Justice in the Colonial Tidewater," in David J. Bodenhamer and James W. Ely, Jr., eds., *Ambivalent Legacy: A Legal History of the South* (1984), pp. 184, 196–97. Hoffer claims that a similar aversion to jury trials can be found in New York, Massachusetts, and Pennsylvania.
14. See, in general, Thomas Andrew Green, *Verdict According to Con-*

science: Perspectives on the English Criminal Trial Jury, 1200–1800 (1985).

15. A vivid picture of English criminal justice, and criminal procedure, chiefly in the eighteenth century, is found in John H. Langbein, "The Criminal Trial Before the Lawyers," *University of Chicago Law Review* 45:363 (1978).

16. Langbein, "The Criminal Trial," p. 307.

17. W. W. Hening, *Statutes at Large . . . of Virginia*, Vol. 2, p. 63.

18. William S. McAninch, "Criminal Procedure and the South Carolina Jury Act of 1731," in Herbert Johnson, ed., *South Carolina Legal History* (1980), p. 181.

19. David R. Johnson, *American Law Enforcement: A History* (1981), p. 5.

20. Douglas Greenberg, *Crime and Law Enforcement in the Colony of New York, 1691–1776* (1974), p. 156.

21. "An Act for Establishing the Method of Appointing Constables . . . ," Georgia, March 27, 1759.

22. Greenberg, *Crime and Law Enforcement*, p. 159.

23. Ibid., pp. 165–67.

24. Harry E. Barnes, *The Evolution of Penology in Pennsylvania: A Study in American Social History* (1927), pp. 65–66; Alexander J. Dallas, ed., *Laws of the Commonwealth of Pennsylvania, 1700–1781*, Vol. 1, pp. 265, 267–68.

25. Laws N.H. 1718, p. 127.

26. Pauline Maier, "Popular Uprisings and Civil Authority in Eighteenth-Century America," *William and Mary Quarterly*, 3d series 27:3, 19 (1970). On the "hue and cry" in colonial Virginia, see Arthur P. Scott, *Criminal Law in Colonial Virginia* (1930), p. 54. Fans of western movies are, of course, familiar with the "posse," which survived in a part of the country where criminal justice was not very professional and was chronically understaffed.

27. Maier, op. cit., p. 21.

28. Julius Goebel, Jr., and T. Raymond Naughton, *Law Enforcement in Colonial New York* (1944), p. 329.

29. A lot of research remains to be done; and the story is, on the whole, rather murky. See Albert J. Reiss, Jr., "Public Prosecutors and Criminal Prosecution in the United States of America," *Juridical Review* 20:1 (1975); [Comment:] "The District Attorney—a Historical Puzzle," *Wisconsin Law Review* 125 (1952); Jack M. Kress, "Progress and Prosecution," *Annals of the American Academy of Political and Social Science* 423:49 (1976).

CHAPTER 2.
THE LAW OF GOD AND MAN

1. Bradley Chapin, *Criminal Justice in Colonial America, 1606–1660* (1983), p. 88. Most slander and defamation cases were civil in form;

but the line between civil and criminal, for these actions, was pretty indistinct.

2. Chapin, *Criminal Justice in Colonial America,* pp. 104–5. Ledra died (in his view) "filled . . . with the joy of the Lord in the Beauty of Holiness," though the Puritans surely felt otherwise.

3. Laws N.H. 1718, p. 121. Under a Maryland law of 1723, if one dared to "blaspheme or curse God, or deny our Saviour . . . or . . . the Holy Trinity," the punishment, for the first offense, was to be "bored through the tongue"; for the second, to be "stigmatized by burning in the forehead with the letter B"; the punishment for the third was death. *Records of the States of the United States: A Microfilm Compilation* (1949), B. 2, Reel 1.2, Unit I, p. 598.

4. W. W Hening's *Statutes at Large . . . of Virginia,* Vol. 1, pp. 168–69. Interestingly, the statute applied specifically to "persons brought upp in the christian religion." For other blasphemy statutes, see Leonard W. Levy, *Treason Against God: A History of the Offense of Blasphemy* (1981), p. 333.

5. Leon DeValinger, Jr., ed., *Court Records of Kent County, Delaware, 1680–1705* (1959), pp. 328–29.

6. *Records and Files of the Quarterly Courts of Essex County, Massachusetts,* Vol. 4, 1667–1671 (1914), pp. 89–90.

7. Robert E. Moody, ed., *Province and Court Records of Maine,* Vol. 3, 1680–1692 (1947), p. 93.

8. Hening, *Statutes of Virginia* (1823), Vol. 2, p. 48 (act 9 of 14 Charles II, March 1661–2).

9. David T. Konig, ed., *Plymouth Court Records 1686–1859,* Vol. 3, General Sessions of the Peace, 1748–81, p. 203 (1978). The boy was acquitted.

10. Joseph L. Smith, ed., *Colonial Justice in Western Massachusetts (1639–1702): The Pynchon Court Record* (1961), entry of June 22, 1664, p. 268. On Captain Kemble, see John C. Miller, *The First Frontier: Life in Colonial America* (1966), p. 87.

11. Miller, *The First Frontier,* p. 89.

12. Kathryn Preyer, "Penal Measures in the American Colonies: An Overview," *American Journal of Legal History* 26:326, 333 (1982).

13. David Flaherty, "Law and the Enforcement of Morals in Early America," in Donald Fleming and Bernard Bailyn, eds., *Law in American History* (1971), p. 203.

14. See Robert F. Oaks, "'Things Fearful to Name': Sodomy and Buggery in Seventeeth-Century New England," *Journal of Social History* 12:268 (1978).

15. See, in general, Emil Oberholzer, Jr., *Delinquent Saints: Disciplinary Action in the Early Congregational Churches of Massachusetts* (1956).

16. Laws N.H. 1718, p. 121.

17. Oaks, "Things Fearful to Name," p. 275; 2 *Records of Plymouth* 44.

18. *Records of the Court of Assistants of the Colony of the Massachusetts Bay, 1630–1692,* Vol. 1 (1901), pp. 10–11.

19. H. Clay Reed and George J. Miller, eds., *The Burlington Court Book: A Record of Quaker Jurisprudence in West New Jersey, 1680–1709* (1944), pp. 142–43.

20. DeValinger, *Court Records of Kent County*, pp. 298–99.

21. *Records and Files of the Quarterly Courts of Essex County, Massachusetts*, Vol. 4, 1667–71 (1914), p. 270.

22. Roger Thompson, *Sex in Middlesex: Popular Mores in a Massachusetts County, 1649–1699* (1986), pp. 194–95.

23. Smith, *Colonial Justice in Western Massachusetts*, p. 289.

24. Ibid., p. 290.

25. Hening, *Statutes of Virginia*, Vol. 1, p. 433 (act II of March 1657–58).

26. Peter C. Hoffer and William B. Scott, eds., *Criminal Proceedings in Colonial Virginia, Richmond County, 1711–54* (1984), p. 19. This was on July 7, 1715; on the same day, Francis Williams, suspected of living in "Adultory with a Mulatto Woman," and John Champ, who allegedly was living with Mary Carter, were given very similar orders.

27. Thompson, *Sex in Middlesex*, p. 198.

28. Susie M. Ames, ed., *County Court Records of Accomack-Northhampton, Virginia, 1632–1640* (1954), p. 111.

29. Smith, *Colonial Justice in Western Massachusetts*, p. 231.

30. J. Hall Pleasants, ed., *Proceedings of the County Court of Charles County, 1658–1666* (Archives of Maryland, Vol. 53, 1936), p. 560.

31. Laws Gen'l. Ct. Mass. Bay, 1672, p. 6.

32. Charles T. Libby, ed., *Province and Court Records of Maine*, Vol. II (1931), p. 224.

33. Laws N.J. 1713, p. 57.

34. Court of Quarter Sessions of the Peace (Lancaster County), Quarter Session and Road Docket, 1729–41, p. 153 (May 4, 1736).

35. January Session, 1760, Mayor's Court of Philadelphia (microfilm, 1957, Temple University School of Law).

36. Julius Goebel, Jr., and T. Raymond Naughton, *Law Enforcement in Colonial New York* (1944), chap. 8, pp. 485–553.

37. Goebel and Naughton, *Law Enforcement in Colonial New York*, p. 517.

38. DeValinger, *Court Records of Kent County*, p. 298.

39. Hoffer and Scott, *Criminal Proceedings in Colonial Virginia*, p. 155.

40. Ibid., p. xxxii.

41. Ibid.

42. Joseph H. Smith and Philip A. Crowl, eds., *Court Records of Prince Georges County, Maryland, 1696–1699* (1964), p. 93.

43. Pleasants, *Proceedings of the County Court of Charles County*, p. 570.

44. *Laws of New Hampshire*, Vol. 1, Province Period, 1679–1702 (1904), p. 676 (law passed June 14, 1701).

45. Laws R.I. and Providence Plantation, 1749, p. 53.

46. John T. Farrell, ed., *The Superior Court Diary of William Samuel Johnson, 1772–1773* (1942), pp. 91–92.

47. Hoffer and Scott, *Criminal Proceedings in Colonial Virginia*, p. 121.

48. See Hening, *Statutes at Large . . . of Virginia*, Vol. 2, p. 510 (1670).

49. Douglas Greenberg, *Crime and Law Enforcement in the Colony of New York, 1691–1776* (1974), pp. 113–14.

50. Natalie E. H. Hull, *Female Felons: Women and Serious Crime in Colonial Massachusetts* (1987), p. 31.

51. John M. Murrin, "Magistrates, Sinners, and Precarious Liberty: Trial by Jury in Seventeeth-Century New England," in David D. Hall, John M. Murrin, and Thad W. Tate, *Saints and Revolutionaries, Essays on Early American History* (1984), pp. 152, 191.

52. Hull, *Female Felons*, p. 31.

53. Oaks, "Things Fearful to Name," p. 277–78.

54. This account is from David T. Konig, *Law and Society in Puritan Massachusetts, Essex County, 1629–1692* (1979), pp. 175–76. Richard Martyn, of Essex County in Massachusetts (1669), was another bad seed; he was convicted of "abusing his father and throwing him down, taking away his clothes and holding up an axe against him." For this he earned, not the gallows, but a whipping of "ten stripes." *Records and Files of the Quarterly Courts of Essex County, Massachusetts*, Vol. IV, 1667–1671 (1914), pp. 186–87.

55. Chapin, *Criminal Justice in Colonial America*, p. 58.

56. Negley K. Teeters, "Public Executions in Pennsylvania: 1682–1834," in Eric H. Monkkonen, *Crime and Justice in American History: The Colonial and Early Republic*, Vol. 2 (1991), pp. 756, 790, 831–32.

57. Arthur P. Scott, *Criminal Law in Colonial Virginia* (1930), p. 119.

58. Greenberg, *Crime . . . in the Colony of New York*, p. 130.

59. Ibid.

60. Goebel and Naughton, *Law Enforcement in Colonial New York*, pp. 755–56.

61. George Lee Haskins, *Law and Authority in Early Massachusetts: A Study in Tradition and Design* (1960), p. 150.

62. Hening, *Statutes of Virginia*, Vol. 6 (1819), p. 121 (act of Oct. 1748).

63. On the rule, see Haskins, op. cit., pp. 152–53; Marcus, op. cit., pp. 116–18.

64. Jeffrey K. Sawyer, "'Benefit of Clergy' in Maryland and Virginia," *American Journal of Legal History* 33:49 (1990); George W. Dalzell, *Benefit of Clergy in America* (1955).

65. J. Hall Pleasants, ed., *Proceedings of the Provincial Court of Maryland, 1663–1666* (Archives of Maryland, xlix, 1932), pp. 298–99. Later, Pope Alvey was in trouble again: he was indicted for stealing and killing a "Certaine Cow of black Culler" belonging to William Evans. Convicted, Alvey claimed benefit of clergy, but it was denied him, "the Record makeing it manefest that he have had it allready allowed him in this same Court." He was sentenced to death, but his sentence was commuted by the Governor. Ibid., pp. 150–52.

66. William S. Price, Jr., ed., *North Carolina Higher-Court Records, 1702–1708* (Colonial Records of North Carolina, Vol. 4, 1974), pp. 33–34.

67. Chapin, *Criminal Justice in Colonial America*, pp. 48–50.

68. There is some evidence that in seventeenth-century Maryland the courts still took seriously the notion that a defendant had to be actually able to read. Peter G. Yackel, "Benefit of Clergy in Colonial Maryland," *Maryland Historical Magazine* 69:383 (1974).

69. George W. Dalzell, *Benefit of Clergy in America and Related Matters* (1955), p. 98.

70. Quoted in Hugh F. Rankin, *Criminal Trial Proceedings in the General Court of Colonial Virginia* (1965), p. 108.

71. Hoffer and Scott, *Criminal Proceedings in Colonial Virgina*, p. lxxii.

72. Hening, *Statutes of Virginia*, Vol. 4, p. 271, pp. 324–25.

73. David H. Flaherty, "Criminal Practice in Provincial Massachusetts," in *Law in Colonial Massachusetts, 1630–1800* (Vol. 62, Publications of the Colonial Society of Massachusetts, 1984), pp. 191, 236–39.

74. *Laws and Liberties*, at pp. 4–5.

75. Philip Schwarz, *Twice Condemned: Slaves and the Criminal Laws of Virginia, 1705–1865* (1989), p. 15.

76. See Daniel Horsmanden, *The New York Conspiracy* (ed., Thomas J. Davis, 1971; the original was published in 1744).

77. See, for example, Kai Erikson, *Wayward Puritans: A Study in the Sociology of Deviance* (1966), pp. 141–59; Paul Boyer and Stephen Nissenbaum, *Salem Possessed: The Social Origins of Witchcraft* (1974). On witchcraft in the colonies more generally, see John P. Demos, *Entertaining Satan: Withcraft in the Culture of Early New England* (1982); Carol F. Karlsen, *The Devil in the Shape of a Woman: Witchcraft in Colonial New England* (1987).

78. I am indebted to Darryl L. Peterkin, a graduate student in history at Princeton University, for the material on Grace Sherwood and on witchcraft in North Carolina in general.

79. Demos, *Entertaining Satan*, pp. 179, 181.

80. Quoted in George Lincoln Burr, ed., *Narratives of the Witchcraft Cases, 1648–1706* (1914), p. 413.

81. Paul Boyer and Stephen Nissenbaum, *Salem-Village Witchcraft: A Documentary Record of Local Conflict in Colonial New England* (1972), pp. 9–12.

82. Burr, *Narratives* (letter of Governor William Phips), p. 196.

83. David T. Konig, *Law and Society in Puritan Massachusetts: Essex County, 1629–1692* (1979), pp. 171–72.

84. Ibid., pp. 173–74.

85. Erikson, *Wayward Puritans*, p. 149.

86. Karlsen, *The Devil in the Shape of a Woman*, p. 181.

87. Horsmanden, *The New York Conspiracy*, pp. 273–74. When Hughson was on the way to the gallows, he was seen "to have a red spot on each cheek, about the bigness of a shilling, which at that time [was] thought very remarkable, for he was always pale of visage" (p. 165).

88. Pleasants, *Proceedings of the County Court of Charles County*, pp. 163–64.

89. Greenberg, *Crime . . . in the Colony of New York,* p. 125. On the colonial background of imprisonment in general, see Adam J. Hirsch, *The Rise of the Penitentiary: Prisons and Punishment in Early America* (1992).

90. H. Clay Reed and George J. Miller, *The Burlington Court Book: A Record of Quaker Jurisprudence in West New Jersey, 1680–1705* (1944), pp. 79–80.

91. There is abundant material on imprisonment for debt during the colonial period in Peter J. Coleman, *Debtors and Creditors in America: Insolvency, Imprisonment for Debt and Bankruptcy, 1607–1900* (1974).

92. Laws N.H. 1718, pp. 254–55.

93. Coleman, *Debtors and Creditors,* p. 75.

94. Staughton George et al., eds., *Charter to William Penn and the Laws of the Province of Pennsylvania passed between the years 1682 and 1700* (1879), p. 121 ("Great Law or The Body of Laws" of 1682, chap. 53, 54).

95. Laws N.H. 1718, pp. 73–74.

96. Laws Gen'l. Ct., Massachusetts Bay, 1673, p. 8.

97. Quoted in Philip D. Jordan, *Frontier Law and Order* (1970), p. 140.

98. Greenberg, *Crime . . . in the Colony of New York,* p. 50.

99. Hull, *Female Felons,* p. 61.

100. Ibid., p. 53.

101. Hull, *Female Felons,* p. 115.

102. Acts and Laws, General Court of Massachusetts Bay, 1692, p. 186; see Hull, *Female Felons,* p. 27. Apparently, however, no woman was ever, in fact, executed for concealing a birth.

103. Peter C. Hoffer and Natalie E. H. Hull, *Murdering Mothers: Infanticide in England and New England, 1558–1803* (1981), p. 74. On similar leniency in Pennsylvania, despite a fair number of convictions, and eight executions, see G. S. Rowe, "Infanticide, Its Judicial Resolution, and Criminal Code Revision in Early Pennsylvania," *Proceedings of the American Philosophical Society* 135:200 (1991).

104. Eli Faber, "Puritan Criminals: The Economic, Social, and Intellectual Background to Crime in Seventeenth-Century Massachusetts," *Perspectives in American History* 11:81 (1977–78).

105. Peter C. Hoffer, "Disorder and Deference: The Paradoxes of Criminal Justice in the Colonial Tidewater," in David J. Bodenhamer and James W. Ely, Jr., eds., *Ambivalent Legacy: A Legal History of the South* (1984), pp. 187, 193–94.

106. William S. Price, ed., *North Carolina Higher-Court Records, 1702–1708* (Colonial Records of No. Car., 2d Ser., Vol. 4, 1974), pp. 351–52.

107. Faber, *Puritan Criminals,* pp. 138–43.

108. Hoffer, "Disorder and Deference," p. 193.

109. Louis B. Wright and Marion Tinling, *The Secret Diary of William Byrd of Westover, 1709–1712* (1941), pp. 112, 113, 119, 585.

110. William W. Hening, ed., *Statutes at Large . . . of Virginia,* Vol. III (1812), p. 459.

111. Scott, *Criminal Law in Colonial Virginia*, pp. 202–3.

112. Richard Gaskins, "Changes in the Criminal Law in Eighteenth-Century Connecticut," *American Journal of Legal History* 25:309, 319 (1981).

113. William E. Nelson, *Americanization of the Common Law: The Impact of Legal Change on Massachusetts Society, 1760–1830* (1975), p. 39.

114. Hendrik Hartog, "The Public Law of a County Court: Judicial Government in Eighteenth-Century Massachusetts," *American Journal of Legal History* 20:282, 302–3 (1976).

115. Hoffer and Scott, *Criminal Proceedings in Colonial Virginia*, p. lvi (table 5).

116. For the trial, see Stanley N. Katz, ed., *A Brief Narrative of the Case and Trial of John Peter Zenger* (1963).

117. See Leonard W. Levy, *Emergence of a Free Press* (1985), pp. 125–33.

118. David J. Bodenhamer, *Fair Trial: Rights of the Accused in American History* (1992), p. 28.

119. Thomas Barnes, ed., *The Book of the General Lawes and Libertyes Concerning the Inhabitants of Massachusetts* (facsimile ed., 1975), p. 50.

120. See John Langbein, "Criminal Law Before the Lawyers," *University of Chicago Law Review* 45:263 (1976).

121. For Massachusetts, see Gerard W. Gawalt, *The Promise of Power: The Emergence of the Legal Profession in Massachusetts, 1760–1840* (1979).

122. Goebel and Naughton, *Law Enforcement in Colonial New York*, p. 574.

123. William S. McAninch, "Criminal Procedure and the South Carolina Jury Act of 1731," in Herbert Johnson, ed., *South Carolina Legal History* (1980), pp. 181, 182–83. The act also recited that judges in the colony, who "ought to assist the prisoner in matters of law, cannot be presumed to have so great knowledge and experience as the great judges and sages of the law, sitting . . . at Westminster."

124. Rankin, *Criminal Trial Proceedings*, pp. 89–90.

CHAPTER 3. THE MECHANICS OF POWER: THE REPUBLICAN PERIOD

1. Samuel Walker, *Popular Justice: A History of American Criminal Justice* (1980), pp. 35–45.

2. On the social revolution, and its relationship to the political revolution, see the important study by Gordon S. Wood, *The Radicalism of the American Revolution* (1992).

3. Douglas Hay, "Property, Authority and the Criminal Law," in Douglas Hay et al., *Albion's Fatal Tree: Crime and Society in Eighteenth-Century England* (1975).

4. Edward Livingston, *Complete Works of Edward Livingston on Criminal Jurisprudence* (1873), Vol. 1, p. 148.

5. 7 Cranch 32 (1812).

6. Kanavan's Case, 1 Greenleaf (Me.) 226 (1821). The underlying crime was concealment of the birth of a bastard. Kanavan was indicted in "that he counselled and advised M. E., then pregnant with a bastard child, to bring it forth alone and in secret," as well as for throwing the dead child in the river. He was sentenced to eight months' imprisonment.

7. Commonwealth v. McHale, 97 Pa. St. 407 (1881).

8. Vanvalkenburg v. Ohio, 11 Ohio 405 (1842).

9. Rev. Stats. Ind., chap. 61, sec. 2, p. 352.

10. Similarly, there was a maxim that criminal laws were supposed to be "construed strictly." Joel P. Bishop, *Commentaries on the Criminal Law* (2d ed., Vol. 1, 1858), p. 114.

11. Jeffrey K. Sawyer, "'Benefit of Clergy' in Maryland and Virginia," *American Journal of Legal History* 34:49, 66–67 (1990).

12. On the law of treason, see James Willard Hurst, *The Law of Treason in the United States: Collected Essays* (1971), chap. 3.

13. Ibid., pp. 83–84. On the English law, see 4 Blackstone's Commentaries, 81–83.

14. Hurst, *The Law of Treason*, pp. 102, 104.

15. *Laws of the State of New York . . . since the Revolution*, Vol. 1, p. 26 (1792), act of Oct. 22, 1779.

16. Quoted in Negley K. Teeters, "Public Executions in Pennsylvania: 1682–1834," in Eric Monkkonen, ed., *Crime and Justice in American History: The Colonies and Early Republic* (Vol. 2, 1991), pp. 756, 764.

17. See 4 Blackstone's Commentaries 84.

18. *Laws of the State of New York . . . since the Revolution*, Vol. 1, pp. 335–36 (1792), act of Feb. 14, 1787.

19. Quoted in Edward H. Savage, *Police Records and Recollections* (1873; reprint ed., 1971), p. 42.

20. Wilbur R. Miller, *Cops and Bobbies: Police Authority in New York and London, 1830–1870* (1977), p. 5.

21. Walker, *Popular Justice*, p. 57.

22. David R. Johnson, *American Law Enforcement: A History* (1981), p. 41.

23. On this point, see Paul A. Gilje, "The Baltimore Riots of 1812 and the Breakdown of the Anglo-American Mob Tradition," *Journal of Social History* 13:547 (1980).

24. Allen Steinberg, *The Transformation of Criminal Justice: Philadelphia, 1800–1880* (1989), pp. 140–49.

25. Savage, *Police Records*, pp 95–96.

26. Johnson, *American Law Enforcement*, p. 27.

27. David R. Johnson, *Policing the Urban Underworld: The Impact of Crime on the Development of the American Police, 1800–1887* (1979), pp. 96, 97.

28. Ibid., p. 94; see below, chapter 7.

29. Miller, *Cops and Bobbies*, p. 43.

30. Ibid.

31. Savage, *Police Records*, p. 91.

32. Roger Lane, *Policing the City: Boston, 1822–1885* (1967), pp. 60, 64, 66.

33. Lane, *Policing the City*, p. 103, 187, 203.

34. Johnson, *Policing the Urban Underworld*, p. 139.

35. Miller, *Cops and Bobbies*, p. 51.

36. The federal crimes law was 1 Stats. 112 (act of April 30, 1790). On the general subject, see Dwight F. Henderson, *Congress, Courts, and Criminals: The Development of Federal Criminal Law, 1801–1829* (1985).

37. Barron v. Baltimore, 32 U.S. (7 Pet.) 243 (1833).

38. See Robert A. Rutland, *The Birth of the Bill of Rights, 1776–1791* (1962), p. 236.

39. Alexander J. Dallas, ed., *Laws of the Commonwealth of Pennsylvania*, Vol. 2, 1781–90, p. 802. The punishment for these crimes was forfeiture of property ("all and singular the lands and tenements, goods and chattels") and imprisonment for up to ten years.

40. Dallas, *Laws of the Commonwealth of Pennsylvania*, Vol. 3, pp. 599–600.

41. Edwin R. Keedy, "History of the Pennsylvania Statute Creating Degrees of Murder," *Unversity of Pennsylvania Law Review* 97:759 (1949).

42. Rev. Laws N.Y. 1829, Vol. 2, p. 657.

43. Kathryn Preyer, "Crime, the Criminal Law and Reform in Post-Revolutionary Virginia," *Law and History Review* 1:53, 58–59 (1983). In the same year, New Jersey struck a number of capital crimes off the books; see John E. O'Connor, "Legal Reform in the Early Republic: The New Jersey Experience," *American Journal of Legal History* 22:95, 100 (1978). See also, in general, Bradley Chapin, "Felony Law Reform in the Early Republic," *Pennsylvania Magazine of History and Biography* 113:164 (1989).

44. Quoted in Philip E. Mackey, *Hanging in the Balance: The Anti–Capital Punishment Movement in New York State, 1776–1861* (1982), p. 155.

45. Quoted in Louis P. Masur, *Rites of Execution: Capital Punishment and the Transformation of American Culture, 1776–1865* (1989), p. 65.

46. Livingston, *Complete Works*, Vol. 1, p. 43. Livingston, a New Yorker transplanted to Louisiana, drafted for his new state a penal code in which the death penalty did not appear. Louisiana never adopted the code.

47. Mackey, *Hanging in the Balance*, p. 127.

48. Rev. Stats. N.Y. 1829, Vol. 2, p. 656.

49. Masur, *Rites of Execution*, p. 157.

50. Michael S. Hindus, *Prison and Plantation: Crime, Justice, and Au-*

thority in Massachusetts and South Carolina, 1767–1878 (1980), p. 100.

51. David J. Bodenhamer, *The Pursuit of Justice: Crime and Law in Antebellum Indiana* (1986), pp. 13–14. According to Bodenhamer, local courts and juries, even before this, refused to allow whipping in some instances; and in one case, where a local court in southwest Indiana ordered it, the citizens (so it was reported in the press) were "shocked by the shameful spectacle of a fellow citizen tied to a sign post and flogged like a dog."

52. See, in general, Myra C. Glenn, *Campaigns Against Corporal Punishment: Prisoners, Sailors, Women, and Children in Antebellum America* (1984).

53. Glenn, *Campaigns*, p. 117.

54. Ibid., pp. 144–45.

55. Laws Del. 1820–1826, pp. 719, 720, 722.

56. John D. Lawson, ed., *American State Trials*, Vol. 2 (1914), p. 199.

57. Mackey, *Hanging in the Balance*, pp. 108–9.

58. Laws N.Y. 1835, chap. 258, p. 299.

59. Masur, *Rites of Executions*, p. 96.

60. Ibid., p. 100.

61. In one sense, executions did not go private at all. Later in the century, they were covered blow-by-blow by such organs as the *National Police Gazette*; and later still, by the "yellow journals." On capital punishment toward the end of the century, see chapter 7.

62. Livingston, *Complete Works*, p. 34.

63. See Adam J. Hirsch, "From Pillory to Penitentiary: The Rise of Penal Incarceration in Early Massachusetts," *Michigan Law Review* 80:1179 (1982); and *The Rise of the Penitentiary: Prisons and Punishment in Early America* (1992), especially chapter 3.

64. Code Va. 1849, Title 56, chap. 213, sec. 22, pp. 792–93.

65. David J. Rothman, *The Discovery of the Asylum: Social Order and Disorder in the New Republic* (1971), p. 71. For an account of the English experience, which was parallel to the American experience, see the fine study by Michael Ignatieff, *A Just Measure of Pain: The Penitentiary in the Industrial Revolution, 1750–1850* (1978).

66. Hirsch, *The Rise of the Penitentiary*, p. 66.

67. Hindus, *Prison and Plantation*, p. 101; Massachusetts had abolished whipping, branding, the stocks, and the pillory in 1804. Recidivists were tattooed in prison; but this pratice was eliminated in 1829.

68. Quoted in Zebulon R. Brockway, *Fifty Years of Prison Service: An Autobiography* (1912; reprint ed., 1969), pp. 24–25.

69. Walker, *Popular Justice*, p. 49.

70. Dallas, *Laws of the Commonwealth of Pennsylvania*, Vol. 2, 1781–1790, p. 802 (act of April 5, 1790); Bradley Chapin, "Felony Law Reform," at 178.

71. Dallas, *Laws of the Commonwealth of Pennsylvania*, Vol. 3, p. 773.

72. Hindus, *Prison and Plantation*, p. 163.

73. See Negley K. Teeters and John D. Shearer, *The Prison at Philadelphia: Cherry Hill* (1957).

74. Ibid., pp. 76–79

75. Gustave de Beaumont and Alexis de Tocqueville, *On the Penitentiary System in the United States and Its Application in France* (1833; reprint ed., 1964), p. 65.

76. Quoted in Francis C. Gray, *Prison Discipline in America* (1847; reprint ed., 1973), p. 40.

77. *Report of William Crawford, Esq., on the Penitentiaries of the United States* (1834; reprint ed., 1968), appendix, p. 2. This report was delivered to the House of Commons in England.

78. *Report of William Crawford*, appendix, p. 31.

79. Ibid., appendix, p. 24.

80. Laws Mass. 1828, chap. 118, sec. 14, 15.

81. *Report of William Crawford*, appendix, p. 31.

82. Charles Dickens, *American Notes* (1842; Penguin ed., 1972), pp. 146, 148.

83. Beaumont and De Tocqueville, *On the Penitentiary System*, pp. 48–49.

84. *Report of William Crawford*, appendix, p. 126.

85. Edward L. Ayers, *Vengeance and Justice: Crime and Punishment in the Nineteenth-Century American South* (1984), chap. 2.

86. Jack K. Williams, *Vogues in Villainy* (1959), p. 118; Acts So. Car., 1828, chap. 10, p. 22; 1831, chap. 21, p. 45.

87. Hindus, *Prison and Plantation*, p. 101.

88. On this point, see Ayers, *Vengeance and Justice*, chap. 1.

89. Ibid., p. 73.

90. Hindus, *Prison and Plantation*, p. 203.

91. Ibid., 169.

92. Dickens, *American Notes*, p. 150.

CHAPTER 4. POWER AND ITS VICTIMS

1. See Arthur Zilversmit, *The First Emancipation: The Abolition of Slavery in the North* (1967); Vt. Const. 1777, chap. 1, sec. 244; Alexander Dallas, *Laws of the Commonwealth of Pennsylvania*, Vol. 2, pp. 838–43.

2. George Fitzhugh, *Sociology for the South* (1854), pp. 46, 247–48.

3. Drew Gilpin Faust, *James Henry Hammond and the Old South: A Design for Mastery* (1982), pp. 73, 100.

4. Frederick Law Olmsted, *The Cotton Kingdom*, Vol. 2 (1862), pp. 202–6.

5. Frances Anne Kemble, *Journal of a Residence on a Georgian Plantation in 1838–1839* (ed., John A. Scott, 1984), pp. 79–80.

6. Public Acts of the Territory of Florida (1839), p. 225.

7. Daniel J. Flanigan, *The Criminal Law of Slavery and Freedom, 1800–1868* (1987), pp. 74, 78; English's Dig. Stats. Ark. (1848), chap. 51, part 12, sec. 4, p. 379.

8. See Lawrence M. Friedman, *A History of American Law* (2d ed., 1985), p. 222.

9. Stats. Miss. 1840, pp. 170–72.

10. Philip J. Schwarz, *Twice Condemned: Slaves and the Criminal Laws of Virginia, 1705–1865* (1988), p. 13.

11. Flanigan, *Criminal Law of Slavery*, pp. 86–88.

12. Michael S. Hindus, *Prison and Plantation: Crime, Justice, and Authority in Massachusetts and South Carolina, 1767–1878* (1980), pp. 139, 141–42.

13. Public Acts of the Terr. of Florida (1839), p. 224.

14. Hindus, *Prison and Plantation*, p. 145. Imprisonment, according to Hindus, was "unpopular," because it deprived the owner of the slave's valuable services and "forced owners to endanger the health of their slaves in the notorious, overcrowded, and decrepit local jails."

15. Quoted in Edward L. Ayers, *Vengeance and Justice: Crime and Punishment in the Nineteenth-Century American South* (1984), p. 61. After 1818, according to Ayers, "only Louisiana consistently admitted slaves to its prison as an alternative to hanging."

16. Schwarz, *Twice Condemned*, pp. 209–10.

17. Ayers, *Vengeance and Justice*, p. 136.

18. Laws La. 1854, Act. No. 215, p. 149.

19. See, for instance, Acts and Resolutions of the General Assembly of the State of South Carolina, 1830, p. 17.

20. Code of Va. 1849, Title 54, chap. 199, sec. 8, p. 754.

21. Hotchkiss's Ga. Stats. (1845), pp. 810, 811.

22. Ibid., pp. 812–14.

23. Stats. Miss. 1840, chap. xi, sec. 34, p. 163.

24. Rev. Stats. Ky, 1852, chap. 28, Art. 3, sec. 3, p. 248. The jury could provide, in its discretion, for confinement to the penitentiary for a minimum of six or a maximum of ten years as an alternative to the death penalty.

25. Code Va. 1849, Tit. 54, chap. 198, sec. 22, pp. 745–46. The offender "may be arrested, and carried before a justice, by any white person."

26. Lumpkin, J., in Bryan v. Walton, 14 Ga. 185 (1853).

27. Rev. Code No. Car. 1855, chap. 107, pp. 576–77.

28. Code Va. 1849, Title 54, chap. 200, sec. 8, p. 754.

29. Rev. Code No. Car. 1854, chap. 107, sec. 63, sec. 75. Whites were not to gamble with slaves either, Laws. No. Car. 1851, chap. 186.

30. Tenn. Code 1858, sec. 2726.

31. John Hope Franklin, *From Slavery to Freedom: A History of American Negroes* (1947), p. 213.

32. Laws No. Car. 1774, chap. 31; Laws No. Car. 1791, chap. 4; the laws are quoted in Paul Finkelman, ed., *The Law of Freedom and Bondage: A Casebook* (1986), pp. 200–201.

33. Ark. Const., 1836, Art. 4, sec. 25 (the same section provided that courts had to assign counsel to slaves in capital cases); Stats. Miss. 1840, chap. xi, sec. 28, p. 162.
34. See, for example, A. E. Keir Nash, "A More Equitable Past? Southern Supreme Courts and the Protection of the Antebellum Negro," *North Carolina Law Review* 48:197 (1970); "Reason of Slavery: Understanding the Judicial Role in the Peculiar Institution," *Vanderbilt Law Review* 32:7 (1979).
35. See, for example, Dig. Laws Miss. 1839, p. 749: "Any negro or mulatto, bond or free, shall be a good witness in pleas of the state [that is, criminal cases] for or against negroes or mulattoes, or in civil cases where free negroes or mulattoes shall alone be parties, and in no other cases whatsoever."
36. Hindus, *Prison and Plantation*, p. 134.
37. Ayers, *Vengeance and Justice*, pp. 134–35.
38. State v. Tackett, 8 No. Car. 210 (1820).
39. State v. Abram, a Slave, 10 Ala. 928 (1847).
40. Ibid., 930–31. The slave was tried under a statute that made it a capital crime for a slave to maim a white person "or bite off the lip, ear, or nose." The court felt that "the biting off a small piece of the ear, not destroying the body of it, was not mayhem"; that crime required a "disfigurement of the person."
41. Flanigan, *The Criminal Law of Slavery and Freedom*, p. 165.
42. Hindus, *Prison and Plantation*, pp. 153–54.
43. George (a Slave) v. State, 37 Miss. 316 (1859).
44. Laws. Miss. 1860, chap. 62, p. 102. The convicted defendant could receive up to a hundred lashes for five successive days, or be sentenced to death, as the jury might determine.
45. Rev. Code Miss. 1857, p. 578.
46. Eric Foner, *Reconstruction: America's Unfinished Revolution, 1863–1877* (1988), p. 198.
47. Laws Miss. 1865, chap. 6.
48. See, in particular, 16 U.S. Stats. 141, sec. 6 (act of May 31, 1870).
49. See Daniel A. Novak, *The Wheel of Servitude: Black Forced Labor After Slavery* (1978); William Cohen, "Negro Involuntary Servitude in the South, 1865–1940: A Preliminary Analysis," *Journal of Southern History*, 42:31 (1976).
50. See, for example, Gen'l. Stats Ky. 1873, pp. 902–4.
51. Cohen, "Negro Involuntary Servitude," p. 56.
52. Charles A. Lofgren, *The Plessy Case: A Legal-Historical Interpretation* (1987), p. 18.
53. The history of segregation is much disputed; any discussion has to start, however, with C. Vann Woodward's path-breaking book, *The Strange Career of Jim Crow* (2d revised ed., 1966).
54. 163 U.S. 537 (1896). In general, see Lofgren, *The Plessy Case.*
55. Lofgren, *The Plessy Case*, pp. 54–58.
56. Plessy v. Ferguson, 163 U.S. at 551–52.

57. Ayers, *Vengeance and Justice*, p. 176.

58. For the colonial period, see Yasuhide Kawashima, *Puritan Justice and the Indian: White Man's Law in Massachusetts, 1630–1763* (1986), chap. 6.

59. For example, a law of Kansas that made it a misdemeanor to "sell, barter, or give to any Indian intoxicating liquor" (Compiled Laws Kansas, 1862, pp. 601–2).

60. See Carol Chomsky, "The United States-Dakota War Trials: A Study in Military Injustice," *Stanford Law Review* 43:13 (1990).

61. Ex parte Crow Dog, 109 U.S. 556 (1883).

62. Ibid., pp. 569, 571.

63. 23 Stats. 362, 385; sec. 9 (act of March 3, 1885).

64. Shih-Shan Henry Tsai, *The Chinese Experience in America* (1986), pp. 67–72.

65. See Lawrence M. Friedman and Robert V. Percival, *The Roots of Justice: Crime and Punishment in Alameda County, California, 1870–1910* (1981), p. 89.

66. William J. Courtney, *San Francisco's Anti-Chinese Ordinances, 1850–1900* (1956), p. 56.

67. Ho Ah Kow v. Nunan, 12 Fed. Cas. 252 (1879). See also Courtney, *San Francisco's Anti-Chinese Ordinances*, pp. 62–65.

68. 118 U.S. 356 (1886). On the Chinese in California in general, see Robert F. Heizer and Alan J. Almquist, *The Other Californians* (1971), chap. 7.

69. For example, the item in the *National Police Gazette* for May 2, 1891 (headlined: "Girls in Chinese Dens"); the site was New York's Chinatown, the subject a raid on opium "joints" and "dives" on Mott and Pell streets; in Gene Smith and Jayne B. Smith, *The Police Gazette* (1972), p. 136.

70. *San Diego Union*, Oct. 26, 1891, p. 5. Whether the Chinese were discriminated against in actual court proceedings is not so obvious. See, for example, John R. Wunder, "Law and the Chinese on the Southwest Frontier, 1850s–1902," *Western Legal History* 2:139 (1989).

71. State v. Chandler, 2 Del. (2 Harr.) 553 (1837). In People v. Ruggles, 8 Johns. 290 (N.Y., 1811), however, Chancellor Kent stated that "we are a christian people, and the morality of the country is deeply ingrafted upon christianity."

72. See, in general, Edwin Brown Firmage and Richard Collin Mangrum, *Zion in the Courts: A Legal History of the Church of Jesus Christ of Latter-day Saints, 1830–1900* (1988).

73. Reynolds v. United States, 98 U.S. 145 (1878).

74. Stephen Cresswell, *Mormons, Cowboys, Moonshiners, and Klansmen: Federal Law Enforcement in the South and West, 1870–1893* (1991), p. 100.

75. 24 Stats. 635 (act of March 3, 1887). The law made husbands and wives of people accused of polygamy competent witnesses when a spouse

was prosecuted for this crime (sec. 1); it also directed the attorney general to institute proceedings to seize church property (sec. 13); and it dissolved the incorporation of the Church itself (sec. 17).

76. Eric H. Monkkonen, *The Dangerous Class: Crime and Poverty in Columbus, Ohio, 1860–1885* (1975), p. 73. The term "dangerous classes" was coined by Charles Loring Brace in his book *The Dangerous Classes of New York*, published in 1872.

77. David J. Rothman, *The Discovery of the Asylum: Social Order and Disorder in the New Republic* (1971), pp. 161–62.

78. There are many vivid descriptions of hobo life; see, for example, Josiah Flynt, *Tramping with Tramps: Studies and Sketches of Vagabond Life* (1899); Jack London, *The Road* (1907).

79. Christopher Tiedeman, *The Limitations of Police Power* (1886), pp. 116–17.

80. Charles Sutton, *The New York Tombs: Its Secrets and Its Mysteries* (1874), pp. 81–82.

81. Eric H. Monkkonen, "A Disorderly People? Urban Order in the Nineteenth and Twentieth Centuries," *Journal of American History* 68:539, 546 (1981).

82. Francis S. Philbrick, ed., *The Laws of Indiana Territory, 1801–1809* (1930), pp. 566–68.

83. Laws Cal. 1855, chap. 62 (act of April 30, 1855). The act also applied to "lewd and dissolute persons who live in and about houses of ill fame," as well as "common prostitutes and common drunkards."

84. David R. Johnson, *Policing the Urban Underworld: The Impact of Crime on the Development of the American Police, 1860–1887* (1979), p. 131.

85. John C. Schneider, *Detroit and the Problem of Order, 1830–1880* (1980), p. 110.

86. Sidney L. Harring, *Policing a Class Society: The Experience of American Cities, 1865–1915* (1983), pp. 119–20.

87. Helen Campbell, Thomas W. Knox, and Thomas Byrnes, *Darkness and Daylight; or Lights and Shadows of New York Life* (1896), pp. 512–13.

88. On the background of this case, and for excerpts from it, see Stephen B. Presser and Jamil S. Zainaldin, *Law and Jurisprudence in American History, Cases and Materials* (2d ed., 1989), pp. 600–619.

89. Commonwealth v. Hunt, 45 Mass. (4 Metc.) 111 (1842).

   A conspiracy, according to Shaw, meant getting together with others either to do something illegal, or to use "criminal or unlawful means" to do something not illegal in itself (ibid., at 123). It followed, for Shaw, that a labor association was not a criminal conspiracy unless it used unlawful means; merely adopting "measures that may have a tendency to impoverish another" was not criminal or unlawful.

90. Laws Ill. 1893, p. 98.

91. For example, Laws Minn. 1895, chap. 174.

92. William E. Forbath, *Law and the Shaping of the American Labor Movement* (1991), p. 61.

93. Felix Frankfurther and Nathan Greene, *The Labor Injunction* (1930), p. 21.

94. In re Debs, 158 U.S. 564 (1895).

CHAPTER 5. SETTING THE PRICE: CRIMINAL JUSTICE AND THE ECONOMY

1. William Francis Kuntz II, *Criminal Sentencing in Three Nineteenth-Century Cities* (1988), pp. 114, 129, 155. In New York, robbery (not as common a charge in Boston or Philadelphia) accounted for another 28 percent of the cases in 1830.

2. The definition is drawn from Stats. N.H. 1815, p. 317, but is quite typical.

3. State v. Henry, 31 N.C. (9 Ired.) 463 (1849).

4. State v. Willis, 52 N.C. (7 Jones) 190 (1859).

5. Rev. Stats. Ill. 1845, p. 161.

6. George Clark, ed., *The Criminal Laws of Texas* (1881), pp. 262–67.

7. 1 Stats. 115 (act of April 30, 1790), chap. 9, sec. 14; 1 Stats. 573 (act of June 27, 1798).

8. Stats. N.H. 1815, p. 321. See also, for example, the elaborate statute on forgery in Stats. Ohio 1841, p. 233.

9. See Spencer L. Kimball, *Insurance and Public Policy* (1960), a case study of Wisconsin insurance regulation.

10. Lawrence M. Friedman, "The Wisconsin Usury Laws: A Study in Legal and Social History," *Wisconsin Law Review* 515 (1963).

11. Ill. Rev. Stats. 1845, chap. 54, sec. 4, p. 295.

12. 4 Stats. 390, 392, sec. 4 (act of March 31, 1830). The fifth section of the statute voided any contract or "secret understanding" to buy land at a premium from someone who was to acquire the land at a public land sale.

13. Mo. Rev. Stats. 1845, chap. 147, sec. 20, p. 932.

14. See Wilbur R. Miller, *Revenuers and Moonshiners: Enforcing Federal Liquor Law in the Mountain South, 1865–1900* (1991); Stephen Cresswell, *Mormons, Cowboys, Moonshiners, and Klansmen: Federal Law Enforcement in the South and West, 1870–1893* (1991).

15. Code Tenn. 1858, secs. 1936, 1938, 1941; 3823, 4824; pp. 396–97, 864.

16. R.I. Stats., 1882, chap. 129, p. 319.

17. Rev. Code Md., 1878, Art. 72, secs. 93, 94, p. 805.

18. Julius Goebel, Jr., and T. Raymond Naughton, *Law Enforcement in Colonial New York: A Study in Criminal Procedure* (1944), pp. 131–32.

19. See, in general, Vertrees J. Wyckoff, *Tobacco Regulation in Colonial Maryland* (1936).

20. Stats. at Large, Pa., 1682–1801, Vol. 4 (1897), p. 5 (act of March 20, 1725.)

21. W. W. Hening, *Statutes at Large . . . of Virginia*, Vol. 3, p. 180 (act of 1699).

22. *Colonial Laws of New York*, Vol. 1 (1894), p. 845 (law of May 19, 1715). Under the act, no "Negro, Indian or Maletto [sic] Slave" could sell Oysters in New York City "any time whatsoever."

23. Acts, General Court of Mass. Bay, 1675, p. 20. The General Court also prohibited the export of sheeps' wool (ibid., p. 19).

24. Rev. Code Miss. 1857, p. 584.

25. Rev. Laws R.I., 1857, Title XVI, chap. 96, "Of Free and Common Oyster Fisheries," chap. 97, "Of Private and Several Oyster Fisheries."

26. Stats. Minn. 1866, pp. 247–48.

27. Ibid., pp. 268–72.

28. Rev. Code Md., 1878, Art. 72, sec. 73, 78, pp. 800–801.

29. This is the famous phrase used by J. Willard Hurst, in *Law and the Conditions of Freedom in the Nineteenth Century United States* (1956), as the title of chapter 1, describing the main thrust of the law in the first half of the nineteenth century.

30. Stats. Ohio 1841, chaps. 12, 23, 53, 61.

31. Laws Mass. 1855, chap. 121, pp. 567–68.

32. These examples are taken from: *City Charter of the City of Oakland, Cal., also General Municipal Ordinances of said City* (1898).

33. Frederick H. Wines, *Report on the Defective, Dependent, and Delinquent Classes of the Population of the United States, as Returned at the Tenth Census (June 1, 1880)* (1888), pp. 504, 508. Regulatory offenses do not appear as such in this report; they are, no doubt, hidden under the headings "violating city ordinance" (669 prisoners) and "offense not stated" (3,409).

34. Code Iowa 1873, title 24, secs. 4055–62, pp. 633–34.

35. 23 U.S. Stats. 31 (act of May 29, 1884).

36. Laws Mich. 1889, p. 331.

37. Laws No. Car. 1889, chap. 374, p. 372.

38. Cong. Rec. 20:1457 (50th Cong., 2d Sess., Feb. 4, 1889).

39. 26 Stats. 209 (act of July 2, 1890); for background, see William Letwin, *Law and Economic Policy in America: The Evolution of the Sherman Antitrust Act* (1965).

40. On the early administration of the law, see Letwin, *Law and Economic Policy*, pp. 100–137.

41. United States v. Nelson, 52 Fed. 646 (D.C. Minn., 1892); U.S. v. Patterson, 55 Fed. 605, 59 Fed. 280 (C.C. Mass., 1893).

42. 156 U.S. 2 (1895).

43. The case was United States v. Debs, 64 Fed. 724 (C.C.N.D. Ill., 1894).

44. Joel P. Bishop, *Commentaries on the Criminal Law* (3d ed., 1865), Vol. 1, p. 502.

45. Laws Illinois, 1891, pp. 212–13. The company-store law applied to any

"scheme for the furnishing of supplies, tools, clothing, provisions, or groceries" to employees.

46. Laws Kans. 1893, chap. 187.

47. Commonwealth v. Wentworth, 118 Mass. 441 (1875).

48. Joel P. Bishop, *Commentaries on the Criminal Law* (2d ed., 1858), p. 373.

49. Code of Virginia, 1849, Title 25, chap. 86, sec. 16, 17, p. 399.

50. Ashbrook v. Commonwealth, 64 Ky. (1 Bush) 139 (1866).

51. See, for example, Del. Const. 1897, Art. 12, establishing a state board of health, and local boards of health. See also Barbara G. Rosenkrantz, *Public Health and the State: Changing Views in Massachusetts, 1842–1936* (1972).

52. Laws N.J. 1895, p. 262.

53. Laws N.J. 1895, pp. 279, 473.

54. On this issue, see Arnold Paul, *Conservative Crisis and the Rule of Law: Attitudes of Bar and Bench, 1887–1895* (1960).

55. In re Jacobs, 98 N.Y. 98 (1885).

56. Johnson v. Goodyear Mining Co., 127 Cal. 4, 59 Pac. 304 (1899).

57. Laws Ill. 1893, p. 99.

58. Ritchie v. People, 155 Ill. 98, 40 N.E. 454 (1895).

59. N.J. Rev. Stats. 1874, p. 749.

60. Neb. Compiled Stats. 1885, pp. 537, 538.

61. N.H. Rev. Stats. 1851, chap. 127, pp. 240–41.

62. Laws N.J. 1884, p. 221.

63. Neb. General Stats., 1873, chap. 11, sec. 83, p. 738.

64. Rev. Stats. Wyo. 1899, pp. 599–603.

CHAPTER 6. MORALS, MORALITY, AND CRIMINAL JUSTICE

1. Ohio Stats. 1841 (act of Feb. 17, 1831).

2. Lawrence M. Friedman, *A History of American Law* (2d ed., 1985), p. 585.

3. Rev. Stats. Maine, 1847, pp. 685–86.

4. Rev. Stats. Ohio, 1890, sec. 7038–1, p. 1734.

5. Ill. Code 1833, p. 199. As we will see, these references to "the public" were significant.

6. On this point, see Hendrik Hartog, "The Public Law of a County Court: Judicial Government in Eighteenth-Century Massachusetts," *American Journal of Legal History* 20:282, 299–308 (1976).

7. Linda Kealey, "Patterns of Punishment: Massachusetts in the Eighteenth Century," *American Journal of Legal History* 30:163, 169 (1986). In Plymouth, however, a number of women were fined for fornication in the same period; see, for example, David T. Konig, ed., *Plymouth Court Records 1686–1859*, Vol. 4, *General Sessions of the*

Peace, 1782–1827 (1979), p. 37 (Rebecca Keen and Martha Keen, both fined twelve shillings for fornication in 1786.)

8. Edward M. Steel, "Criminality in Jeffersonian America—A Sample," *Crime and Delinquency* (1983), p. 154.

9. David J. Bodenhamer, *The Pursuit of Justice: Crime and Law in Antebellum Indiana* (1986), p. 140.

10. Quoted in Stephen Nissenbaum, *Sex, Diet and Debility in Jacksonian America: Sylvester Graham and Health Reform* (1980), p. 113.

11. Charles E. Rosenberg, "Sexuality, Class and Role in Nineteenth-Century America," *American Quarterly* 25:131 (1973).

12. See Lawrence M. Friedman, *The Republic of Choice: Law, Authority and Culture* (1990), p. 35. Needless to say, the notions in the text apply mostly to men; women's self-control was another matter. On this point, see chapter 9.

13. Rosenberg, "Sexuality, Class and Role," p. 140.

14. Cal. Penal Code, 1872, sec. 266a, for example.

15. Quoted in Allan Keller, *Scandalous Lady* (1981), p. 178.

16. Rev. Stats. Mich. 1846, chap. 158, sec. 6, p. 681.

17. Collins v. State, 14 Ala. 608 (1848).

18. On this point, see Peter C. Hoffer and N. E. H. Hull, *Murdering Mothers: Infanticide in England and New England, 1558–1803* (1984), pp. 50–53.

19. Edwin R. A. Seligman, ed., *The Social Evil: With Special Reference to Conditions Existing in the City of New York* (2d ed., 1912), pp. 124–25.

20. Rev. Stats. Mich. 1846, chap. 158, sec. 13, p. 682.

21. Anthony Comstock, *Traps for the Young* (ed., Robert Bremner, 1967), p. 240. The book was originally published in 1883.

22. Commonwealth v. Tarbox, 55 Mass. (1 Cush.) 66 (1848).

23. Quoted in Philip D. Jordan, *Frontier Law and Order* (1970), p. 46.

24. Idaho Code 1887, sec. 6850, p. 738.

25. Code Ill. 1833, p. 199.

26. Jordan, *Frontier Law and Order*, pp. 55–57.

27. Henry Chafetz, *Play the Devil: A History of Gambling in the United States from 1492 to 1955* (1960), p. 228.

28. James D. McCabe, Jr., *Lights and Shadows of New York Life; or the Sights and Sensations of the Great City* (1872; reprint ed., 1970), p. 715.

29. Chafetz, *Play the Devil*, p. 228.

30. McCabe, *Lights and Shadows*, pp. 715, 716, 730.

31. Jordan, *Frontier Law and Order*, pp. 40–42.

32. *Proceedings and Debates of the Convention of 1821, assembled for the purpose of amending the Constitution of the State of New York* (Nathaniel H. Carter and William L. Stone, reporters) (1821), pp. 569–70.

33. Quoted in Joseph Gusfield's important book on the temperance move-

ment, *Symbolic Crusade: Status Politics and the American Temperance Movement* (1963), p. 43.

34. Ibid., p. 51.

35. Public Laws Me. 1851, chap. 211, p. 210. This complex act did allow cities and towns to appoint a "suitable person" to sell liquor "for medicinal and mechanical purposes."

36. See David J. Pivar, *Purity Crusade: Sexual Morality and Social Control, 1868–1900* (1973); on legal aspects of the late nineteenth-century crusade against vice, see Lawrence M. Friedman, "History, Social Policy, and Criminal Justice," in David J. Rothman and Stanton Wheeler, eds., *Social History and Social Policy* (1981).

37. Paul S. Boyer, *Purity in Print: The Vice-Society Movement and Book Censorship in America* (1968), p. 7.

38. John D'Emilio and Estelle B. Freedman, *Intimate Matters: A History of Sexuality in America* (1988), p. 159.

39. 17 Stats. 598 (act of March 3, 1873). On the criminalization of abortion, see chapter 10, below.

40. Hill's Ann. Laws Oregon, 1887, Vol. 1, p. 949; Laws Ohio 1885, p. 184, passed April 30, 1885.

41. Laws Cal. 1889, chap. 191, p. 223; Laws Cal. 1897, chap. 139, p. 201.

42. McCabe, *Lights and Shadows*, p. 727.

43. John S. Ezell, *Fortune's Merry Wheel: The Lottery in America* (1960); the law was 28 Stats. 963, chap. 191 (act of March 2, 1895). The Supreme Court upheld the statute in the Lottery Case, 188 U.S. 321 (1903), against attack on various constitutional grounds.

44. Frederick H. Wines, *Report on the Defective, Dependent, and Delinquent Classes of the Population of the United States, as Returned at the Tenth Census (June 1, 1880)* (1888), p. 506.

45. The constitution also prohibited "Lotteries and the sale of lottery tickets" [sec. 3]. The Kansas legislature passed a drastic law to carry the constitutional provision into effect, Laws Kans. 1881, chap. 128, p. 233.

46. See Delaware Const. 1897, Art. 13 (local county option on prohibiton); South Dakota Const. 1889, Art. 24 (prohibition); an amendment to the Rhode Island constitution of 1842, Art. 5, adopted in 1886, prohibited the manufacture and sale of intoxicating liquors.

47. Minn. Stats. 1894, secs. 1999, 2002, 2006, 2008.

48. See Ga. Laws 1884–85, p. 121 (Sept. 18, 1885). (One-tenth of voters in any county can petition for an election to determine whether or not the sale of intoxicating liquor should be banned.) Kentucky and Florida were also local option states.

49. Laws Miss. 1872, chaps. 108, 109, 111, 112, 114.

50. Mass. Laws 1880, chap. 239.

51. Gen'l. Laws Tex., 1887, chap. 79, p. 58.

52. On the history of drug laws, see Troy Duster, *The Legislation of Morality* (1970); David F. Musto, *The American Disease: Origins of Narcotics Control* (1973).

53. *Oakland Tribune,* July 2, 1883, p. 3.

54. Idaho Code, 1887, secs. 6830, 6832, pp. 736–37. A Missouri law of 1887 outlawed "opium dens"; the statute also covered "hasheesh." Laws. Mo. 1887, p. 175.

55. Ord. City of Oakland no. 1214, Oct. 30, 1890, *City Charter and General Municipal Ordinances,* city of Oakland, 1898, p. 230. In 1887, the Supreme Court of California struck down a Stockton ordinance (In re sic, 73 Cal. 149, 14 Pac 405, [1887]) aimed at opium dens. The court felt that the ordinance conflicted with (general) state law. The Oakland ordinance on the same subject, apparently, was never challenged.

56. Laws Ill. 1897, p. 138.

57. Joseph Gusfield put this idea forward, with regard to temperance and Prohibition, in "Moral Passage: The Symbolic Process of Public Designations of Deviance," *Social Problems* 15:175 (1967); and in *Symbolic Crusade: Status Politics and the American Temperance Movement* (1963).

58. Friedman, "History, Social Policy, and Criminal Justice," pp. 203, 231.

59. These figures are from the annual reports of the Secretary of State of Ohio. I am indebted to Steve Johnson for the reference.

60. *National Police Gazette,* Feb. 21, 1885, p. 7.

61. Lawrence M. Friedman and Robert V. Percival, *The Roots of Justice: Crime and Punishment in Alameda County, California, 1870–1910* (1981), pp. 144–45.

62. *City Charter of the City of Oakland, Cal.;* also *General Municipal Ordinances* (1898), pp. 322, 352.

63. Wines, *Delinquent Classes, Census of 1880,* p. 506.

64. *San Diego Union,* Sept. 18, 1891, p. 5.

65. Samuel Walker, *A Critical History of Police Reform* (1977), p. 25.

66. A similar tale could be told about gambling: crackdowns, arrests, sweeps; and in between, corruption and toleration. See David R. Johnson, *Policing the Urban Underworld: The Impact of Crime on the Development of the American Police, 1880–1887* (1979), pp. 158–76.

67. Quoted in Ysabel Rennie, *The Search for Criminal Man: A Conceptual History of the Dangerous Offender* (1978), p. 67.

68. R. L. Dugdale, *"The Jukes": A Study in Crime, Pauperism, Disease, and Heredity* (1877), p. 7.

69. Rennie, *The Search for Criminal Man,* p. 79.

70. Dugdale, *"The Jukes,"* p. 13.

71. Ibid., p. 47.

72. Henry M. Boies, *Prisoners and Paupers* (1893), p. 266.

73. Ibid., pp. 267, 270.

74. Mark H. Haller, *Eugenics: Hereditarian Attitudes in American Thought* (1963), pp. 48–49.

75. See, in general, Thomas Maeder, *Crime and Madness: The Origins and Evolution of the Insanity Defense* (1985).

76. 4 Blackstone's Commentaries 24.

77. Daniel M'Naghten's Case, 10 Cl. and Fin. 200, 210, 8 Eng. Rep. 718

(H.L., 1843). See R. Moran, *Knowing Right from Wrong: The Insanity Defense of Daniel McNaughtan* (1981). (There are about a dozen ways to spell the name of the defendant, and none of them is totally canonical. This leaves an author free to take his pick.)

78. *The New York Judicial Repository* (1818), pp. 14, 34.

79. 3 Laws N.Y. 1881, p. 5; Penal Code, Title 1, secs. 20, 21, 23.

80. This skeptical account comes from the *San Diego Union*, Feb. 7, 1896, p. 5.

81. Ronald White, "The Trial of Abner Baker, Jr., M.D.: Monomania and McNaughtan Rules in Antebellum America," *Bulletin of the American Academy of Psychiatry and the Law*, 18:223 (1990).

82. Joel P. Bishop, *Commentaries on the Criminal Law* (Vol. 1, 2d ed., 1858), p. 335.

83. State v. Felter, 25 Iowa 67 (1868).

84. State v. Pike, 49 N.H. 399 (1869).

85. State v. Pike, at 402; Maeder, op. cit., p. 46.

86. State v. Pike, at 435, 438.

87. The trial is recounted in Charles E. Rosenberg, *The Trial of the Assassin Guiteau* (1968).

88. Ibid., pp. 237, 244–48.

89. For an account of the trial, see John D. Lawson, ed., *American State Trials*, Vol. 12 (1919), p. 494. On Sickles, see Nat Brandt, *The Congressman Who Got Away with Murder* (1991).

90. Kenneth Lamott, *Who Killed Mr. Crittenden?* (1963), pp. 214–22. Laura Fair's trial became a feminist issue; she was a woman, victimized by a man and facing trial before an all-male jury in an all-male system. See Barbara A. Babcock, "Clara Shortridge Foltz: 'First Woman,'" *Arizona Law Review* 30:673, 679, n. 25 (1988).

91. Friedman and Percival, *Roots of Justice*, pp. 239–44.

92. Joel P. Bishop, *Commentaries on the Criminal Law* (2d ed., Boston, 1858), p. 341; see also the note, "Insanity Produced by Intemperance," in *American Jurist and Law Magazine*, Vol. 3, no. 5, pp. 5–19 (Jan. 1830).

93. People v. Hammill, 2 Park. Crim. Rep. 243 (N.Y., 1855).

94. The New York penal code of 1881 codified this general doctrine. No act committed by a person "in a state of voluntary intoxication" was to be considered "less criminal" because of this condition. But if the "actual existence of any particular purpose, motive, or intent is a necessary element to constitute a particular species or degree of crime," then the jury may take into consideration the "fact that the accused was intoxicated . . . in determining the purpose, motive or intent with which he committed the act." (3 Laws N.Y. 1881, p. 5; Penal Code, Title 1, sec. 22.)

95. Commonweath v. French, *Reports of Criminal Cases tried in the Municipal Court of the City of Boston, before Peter Oxenbridge Thacher* (ed. Horatio Woodman; Boston, 1845), p. 163 (March Term, 1827).

Thacher told the jury that the case was different from one in which an adult, "by a free indulgence of strong liquors," voluntarily deprives himself of his reason. It was, he said, certainly true that "but few crimes are committed by persons who are habitually temperate in the use of ardent spirits."

96. Ibid.

CHAPTER 7. THE MECHANICS OF POWER II: PROFESSIONALIZATION AND REFORM IN THE LATE NINETEENTH CENTURY

1. Frederick H. Wines, *Report on the Defective, Dependent, and Delinquent Classes of the Population of the United States, as Returned at the Tenth Census (June 1, 1880)* (1888), p. 569.

2. Ibid., p. 566.

3. Samuel Walker, *Popular Justice: A History of American Criminal Justice* (1980), p. 61.

4. Robert M. Fogelson, *Big-City Police* (1977), pp. 14–15.

5. David R. Johnson, *Policing the Urban Underworld: The Impact of Crime on the Development of the American Police, 1800–1887* (1979), p. 94.

6. Eric H. Monkkonen, *Police in Urban America, 1860–1920* (1981), pp. 164–68.

7. *Evening News* (Detroit), Feb. 12, 1880, p. 4.

8. Sidney L. Harring, *Policing a Class Society: The Experience of American Cities, 1865–1915* (1983), p. 244.

9. Lawrence M. Friedman and Robert V. Percival, *The Roots of Justice: Crime and Punishment in Alameda County, California, 1870–1910* (1981), p. 88.

10. Friedman and Percival, *Roots of Justice*, p. 101.

11. Address by Charles E. Felton, to the National Prison Association, in *Proceedings of the Annual Congress, National Prison Assocation* (1888), pp. 195, 198–99.

12. Monkkonen, *Police in Urban America*, pp. 86–128.

13. Wines, *Delinquent Classes, 1880 Census*, p. 566.

14. Monkkonen, *Police in Urban America*, p. 90.

15. Samuel Walker, *A Critical History of Police Reform* (1977), pp. 18–19.

16. Monkkonen, *Police in Urban America*, pp. 31, 142.

17. Walker, *Police Reform*, p. 63.

18. The actual term was used, for example, in George W. Walling's *Recollections of a New York Chief of Police* (1887), p. 189.

19. Z. Chafee, Jr., W. H. Pollak, and Carl S. Stern, *The Third Degree* (1931; reprint ed., 1969), pp. 38–39.

20. Walling, *Recollections*, p. 194. George S. McWatters, who wrote about the "hidden life of American detectives" in New York in the 1870s,

made a somewhat similar point about detectives: with their "crafts and hypocrisies" they were "constantly breaking in upon common law and . . . statute law." But this illegality was absolutely essential in a "corrupt civilization." These tactics were the "silent, secret and effective Avenger of the outraged Majesty of the Law when everything else fails." *Knots Untied: or Ways and By-ways in the Hidden Life of American Detectives* (1873), p. 664. See chapter 9.

21. See Dennis C. Rousey, "Cops and Guns: Police Use of Deadly Force in Nineteenth-Century New Orleans," *American Journal of Legal History* 28:41(1984).

22. John C. Schneider, *Detroit and the Problem of Order, 1830–1880* (1980), p. 118.

23. *Report, Special Committee appointed to investigate the Police Department of the City of New York* (1895), pp. 15–17.

24. Ibid., pp. 21–33.

25. Ibid., pp. 27–44.

26. See Perry R. Duis, *The Saloon: Public Drinking in Chicago and Boston, 1880–1920* (1983), pp. 240–41.

27. Walker, *Police Reform*, p. 24.

28. Blake McKelvey, *American Prisons: A Study in American Social History Prior to 1915* (1936), p. 34.

29. See, for example, Paul W. Keve, *The History of Corrections in Virginia* (1986).

30. Michael S. Hindus, *Prison and Plantation: Crime, Justice, and Authority in Massachusetts and South Carolina, 1767–1878* (1980), p. 169. In 1863, another facet of the Massachusetts prison was consigned to oblivion: the admission of visitors on payment of a twenty-five-cent fee.

31. McKelvey, *American Prisons*, p. 32.

32. Hutchins Hapgood, *The Autobiography of a Thief* (1903), p. 141.

33. Laws Ill. 1845, pp. 105–7; Laws Ill. 1871–72, p. 294; Andrew A. Bruce et al., *The Workings of the Indeterminate-Sentence Law and the Parole System in Illinois* (1928; reprint ed., 1968), p. 26.

34. Shelley Bookspan, *A Germ of Goodness: The California State Prison System, 1851–1944* (1991), p. 2.

35. Keve, *The History of Corrections in Virginia*, p. 90.

36. 2d Ann. Rpt., Prison Comm. of Ga. (1899), p. 21.

37. On the ages of prisoners: ibid., p. 22. The data on literacy are from the year before: 1st Annual Report, Prison Commission of Georgia, 1898, p. 31. In that year, of 2,228 prisoners, 1,290 were single; the rest were married. (Ibid., p. 30.)

38. Edward L. Ayers, *Vengeance and Justice: Crime and Punishment in the Nineteenth-Century American South* (1984), p. 186.

39. Keve, *The History of Corrections in Virginia*, p. 74.

40. Ayers, *Vengeance and Justice*, pp. 178–79.

41. Ibid., p. 226.

42. So. Dak. Stats. 1899, Vol. 2, secs. 8964, 8966, 8970.

43. General Laws R.I. 1896, pp. 1049, 1050.

44. Lawrence M. Friedman, *A History of American Law* (2d ed., 1985), pp. 600–601.

45. James Leiby, *Charity and Correction in New Jersey* (1967), pp. 126–28.

46. Glen A. Gildemeister, *Prison Labor and Convict Competition with Free Workers in Industrializing America, 1840–1890* (1987), pp. 115–16.

47. Laws Pa. 1883, chap. 110, sec. 2.

48. See, in general, *Twentieth Annual Report of the Commissioner of Labor, Convict Labor* (1905).

49. Gildemeister, *Prison Labor*, pp. 168–75.

50. Zebulon Brockway, *Fifty Years of Prison Service: An Autobiography* (1912; reprint ed., 1969), p. 166.

51. Samuel Walker, *Popular Justice*, pp. 94–95.

52. The law was passed March 19, 1872. Laws Ill., 1871–72, p. 294.

53. E. C. Wines, "The Present Outlook of Prison Discipline in the United States," in Wines, ed., *Transactions of the National Congress on Penitentiary and Reformatory Discipline, Held at Cincinnati, Ohio, October 12–18, 1870* (1871), pp. 15, 19.

54. "The Indeterminate Sentence" by "A Prisoner," *Atlantic Monthly*, 108:330 (1911).

55. Frederick H. Wines, *Punishment and Reformation: A Study of the Penitentiary System* (rev. ed., 1910), p. 221.

56. Richard L. Dugdale, *"The Jukes;" A Study in Crime, Pauperism, Disease and Heredity* (6th ed., 1900), pp. 114–15.

57. Laws N.Y. 1877, chap. 173, p. 186.

58. Laws Ill. 1899, p. 142.

59. Laws N.Y. 1901, Vol. 2, chap. 428, pp. 115–16.

60. Laws Ohio 1885, pp. 236–37 (May 4, 1885). This law also established a parole system; the "habitual criminal" was eligible for parole after serving the regular term of imprisonment.

61. Rev. Stat. N.Y. 1881, Vol. 3, pp. 2536–37.

62. See, for example, State v. Moore, 121 Mo. 514, 26 S.W. 548 (1894).

63. On parole, see Samuel Walker, *Popular Justice* (1980), pp. 92–98.

64. Laws Ohio 1885, p. 236 (May 4, 1885).

65. See Sheldon L. Messinger et al., "The Foundations of Parole in California," *Law and Society Review* 19:69 (1985).

66. Quoted in "Operation and Effect of the Ohio Parole Law," a paper read by Warden E. C. Coffin of Ohio, printed in *Proceedings of the Annual Congress of the National Prison Ass'n.* (held in Austin, Texas, December 1897) (1898), pp. 164–66.

67. William F. Kuntz II, *Criminal Sentencing in Three Nineteenth-Century Cities* (1988), p. 150.

68. Kuntz, *Criminal Sentencing*, p. 151 (quoting Gershom Powers, agent and keeper of Auburn Prison).

69. Lawrence M. Friedman, *A History of American Law* (2d ed., 1985), p. 596.

70. The Massachusetts laws are Laws Mass. 1878, chap. 198, p. 146; Laws Mass. 1891, chap. 356, p. 920. The California law is Cal. Penal Code, secs. 1203, 1215, Laws Cal. 1903, chap. 34, pp. 34–35.

71. Joel P. Bishop, *Commentaries on the Criminal Law*, Vol. 1 (2d ed., 1858), pp. 323–24.

72. Margaret W. Cahalan, *Historical Corrections Statistics in the United States, 1850–1984* (1986), p. 113, table 5.7.

73. Cited in Robert H. Bremner, ed., *Children and Youth in America: A Documentary History*, Vol. 2, 1866–1932 (1971), p. 444.

74. James L. Hunt, "Law and Society in a New South Community: Durham County, North Carolina, 1898–1899," *North Carolina Historical Review* 67:427, 449 (1991).

75. Laws N.Y. 1824, chap. 126 (act of March 29, 1824), see Steven L. Schlossman, *Love and the American Delinquent: The Theory and Practice of "Progressive" Juvenile Justice, 1825–1920* (1977), pp. 22–32.

76. Robert M. Mennel, *Thorns and Thistles: Juvenile Delinquents in the United States, 1825–1940* (1973), p. 12. Mennel is the source of much of the following text. For a firsthand account of the New York House of Refuge, through rather rose-colored glasses, see Bradford Kinney Peirce, *A Half Century with Juvenile Delinquents* (1869; reprint ed., 1969).

77. Gustave de Beaumont and Alexis de Tocqueville, *On the Penitentiary System in the United States and Its Application in France* (1833; reprint ed., 1964), pp. 139–40. The two Frenchmen felt that the alternatives were worse. In an actual prison, young people would be thrown together with men "whom age has hardened in crime." Left alone, on the outside, their "impunity" would encourage them to "give themselves up to new disorders." (Ibid., p. 138.)

78. Hapgood, *Autobiography of a Thief*, pp. 71–72.

79. Laws Mass. 1847, chap. 165, p. 405.

80. Laws Mass. 1855, chap. 442, p. 837.

81. Laws N.Y. 1875, chap. 464, p. 531. In the same year, New York authorized the incorporation of "societies for the prevention of cruelty to children" (chap. 130, p. 114).

82. Mennell, *Thorns and Thistles*, p. 128.

83. 125 Ill. 540 18 N.E. 183 (1888).

84. *San Francisco Municipal Reports for the Fiscal Year 1888–1889, ending June 30, 1889* (1889), p. 457.

85. Anthony Platt, *The Child Savers: The Invention of Delinquency* (1969), p. 120.

86. Laws Ill. 1899, p. 131.

87. Quoted in Mennel, *Thorns and Thistles*, p. 132.

88. Frederick H. Wines, "American Prisons in the Tenth Census," in *Pro-*

ceedings of the Annual Congress of the National Prison Association, (1888), pp. 251, 254.

89. Enoch C. Wines, *The State of Prisons and of Child-Saving Institutions in the Civilized World* (1880), p. 162.

90. Lois A. Buyon and Helen Fay Green, "Calaboose: Small-Town Lockup," *Federal Probation,* 54:58 (June 1990).

91. George W. Walling, *Recollections of a New York Chief of Police* (1887), pp. 388–89.

92. Ibid., p. 390.

93. Ibid., p. 392.

94. Matthew Hale Smith, *Sunshine and Shadow in New York* (1880), p. 166.

95. Walling, *Recollections,* pp. 396–98.

96. *First Annual Report, Board of Public Charities of North Carolina, Feb. 1870* (1870), p. 43.

97. Hugo Adam Bedau, *The Death Penalty in America* (1982), pp. 21, 23.

98. The account is taken from the *New York Times,* April 20, 1878, pp. 1–2.

99. *New York Times,* April 19, 1878, p. 1.

100. Ibid.

101. Quoted in August Mencken, *By the Neck: A Book of Hangings* (1942), pp. 83–84.

102. Friedman and Percival, *Roots of Justice,* pp. 304–5.

103. James D. McCabe, Jr., *Lights and Shadows of New York Life; or, the Sights and Sensations of the Great City* (1872; reprint ed., 1970), pp. 233–34.

104. Quoted in Friedman and Percival, *Roots of Justice,* pp. 305–6.

105. Bedau, *The Death Penalty,* p. 15.

106. Quoted in In re Kemmler, 136 U.S. 436 (1890); this case upheld the system of death by electrocution, which had been attacked as unconstitutional (specifically, as cruel and unusual punishment).

107. Laws N.Y. 1888, chap. 489, p. 778.

108. *National Police Gazette,* April 8, 1899, p. 6.

CHAPTER 8. LAWFUL LAW AND LAWLESS LAW: FORMS OF AMERICAN VIOLENCE

1. Pauline Maier, "Popular Uprisings and Civil Authority in Eighteenth-Century America," *William and Mary Quarterly,* 3d series, 27:3 (1970).

2. On this point, see Ted R. Gurr, Peter N. Grabosky, and Richard C. Hula, *The Politics of Crime and Conflict: A Comparative History of Four Cities* (1977); Roger Lane, "Urbanization and Criminal Violence in the Twentieth Century: Massachusetts as a Test Case," in H. D.

Graham and Ted R. Gurr, eds., *Violence in America: Historical and Comparative Perspectives* (1969); Lawrence M. Friedman and Robert V. Percival, *The Roots of Justice: Crime and Punishment in Alameda County, California, 1870–1910* (1981), pp. 31–35.

3. David B. Davis, *Homicide in American Fiction, 1798–1860* (1957), pp. 240–42.

4. For an account of this bloody affair, see Iver Bernstein, *The New York City Draft Riots* (1990).

5. Roger Lane, *Violent Death in the City: Suicide, Accident and Murder in Nineteenth-Century Philadelphia* (1979), p. 53.

6. John Philip Reid, *Law for the Elephant: Property and Social Behavior on the Overland Trail* (1980).

7. Richard White, *"It's Your Misfortune and None of My Own"; A New History of the American West* (1992), p. 329.

8. Roger D. McGrath, *Gunfighters, Highwaymen and Vigilantes: Violence on the Frontier* (1984), p. 247. See also Kevin J. Mullen, *Let Justice be Done: Crime and Politics in Early San Francisco* (1989), chap. 26.

9. Ibid., pp. 253, 255.

10. For their career, see Robert M. Coates, *The Outlaw Years: The History of the Land Pirates of the Natchez Trace* (1930; reprint ed., 1986).

11. *Laws of the Commonwealth of Massachusetts, 1780–1800,* Vol. 1, (1801), pp. 193–95 (act of June 30, 1784).

12. George F. Norton's Case, *City Hall Recorder* 3:90 (New York, 1818).

13. Quoted in Edward L. Ayers, *Vengeance and Justice: Crime and Punishment in the Nineteenth-Century American South* (1984), p. 18; Michael Paul Rogin, *Fathers and Children: Andrew Jackson and the Subjugation of the American Indian* (1975), p. 58.

14. Jack K. Williams, *Dueling in the Old South: Vignettes of Social History* (1980), pp. 66–67.

15. J. Winston Coleman, *Famous Kentucky Duels* (1969), pp. 32–42.

16. Williams, *Dueling,* pp. 77–78. See also Kenneth S. Greenberg, "The Nose, the Lie, and the Duel in the Antebellum South," *American Historical Review* 95:57 (1990).

17. Elliott J. Gorn, "'Good-Bye Boys, I Die a True American': Homicide, Nativism, and Working-Class Culture in Antebellum New York City," *Journal of American History* 74:388, 406–9 (1987).

18. Milo Erwin, *History of Williamson County, Illinois* (1876), p. 152. See also Paul M. Angle, *Bloody Williamson: A Chapter in American Lawlessness* (1952), chap. 5.

19. Ayers, *Vengeance and Justice,* pp. 263–74.

20. Richard Maxwell Brown, *Strain of Violence: Historical Studies of American Violence and Vigilantism* (1975), pp. 95–96.

21. Jack K. Williams, "Crime and Punishment in Alabama, 1819–1840," *Alabama Review* 6:14 (1953).

22. Kevin J. Mullen, *Let Justice Be Done: Crime and Politics in Early San Francisco* (1989), p. 10.

23. Robert M. Senkewicz, *Vigilantes in Gold Rush San Francisco* (1985), pp. 2–3.

24. Ibid., p. 4.

25. Wayne Gard, *Frontier Justice* (1949), pp. 155–56.

26. There is a large literature on the San Francisco vigilante movements. The classic account is Hubert Bancroft, *Popular Tribunals* (1887), but this has to be taken with a grain of salt; Bancroft was extremely biased in favor of the vigilantes. Among recent works (in addition to Mullen, *Let Justice Be Done*), see Senkewicz, *Vigilantes in Gold Rush San Francisco*.

27. Doyce Blackman Nunis, ed., *The San Francisco Vigilance Committee of 1856: Three Views* (1971), p. 31.

28. William J. McConnell and James S. Reynolds, *Idaho's Vigilantes* (ed. Joyce Lindstrom, 1984), p. 42. This account was originally published in 1913.

29. See Joseph M. Kelly, "Shifting Interpretations of the San Francisco Vigilantes," *Journal of the West* 24:39 (1985).

30. Hubert H. Bancroft, *Popular Tribunals* (1887), Vol. 1, pp. 10, 11, 16.

31. Thomas J. Dimsdale, *The Vigilantes of Montana* (1866; new edition, 1953), pp. 13, 15–16.

32. Dimsdale, *Vigilantes of Montana*, pp. 194–205. For another version of the "arrest and execution of Captain J. A. Slade," see Nathaniel Pitt Langford, *Vigilante Days and Ways: The Pioneers of the Rockies* (1890), pp. 460–61.

33. John Clay, *My Life on the Range* (1924; ed. Donald R. Ornduff, 1962), pp. 265–66.

34. William S. Greever, *The Bonanza West: The Story of the Western Mining Rushes, 1848–1900* (1963), pp. 344–46.

35. Patrick B. Nolan, *Vigilantes on the Middle Border: A Study of Self-Appointed Law Enforcement in the States of the Upper Mississippi from 1840 to 1880* (1987), pp. 109–10.

36. *National Police Gazette*, March 18, 1885, p. 7.

37. Governor Thomas Ford, *A History of Illinois from Its Commencement as a State in 1818 to 1847* (2 vols., ed. Milo M. Quaife, 1945), Vol. 2, p. 354.

38. Senkewicz, *Vigilantes*, p. 86.

39. Dimsdale, *Vigilantes of Montana*, p. 13.

40. Bancroft, *Popular Tribunals*, Vol. 1, pp. 129–30. Bancroft was just as harsh on politicians: "Murderers were our congressmen, and shameless debauchees our senators. Our legislators were representatives of the sediment of society" (ibid.).

41. Clay, *My Life on the Range*, pp. 267–68.

42. Brown, *Strain of Violence*, p. 108.

43. McConnell and Reynolds, *Idaho's Vigilantes*, editor's preface, p. 1.

44. Brown, *Strain of Violence*, p. 155.

45. Lew L. Callay, *Montana's Righteous Hangmen: The Vigilantes in Action* (1982), p. 218.

46. Anthony Comstock, *Traps for the Young* (ed. Robert Bremner, 1967), p. 114. The book was originally published in 1883.

47. Brown, *Strain of Violence*, pp. 150–51.

48. On the whitecaps in this area, see Wilbur R. Miller, *Revenuers and Moonshiners: Enforcing Federal Liquor Law in the Mountain South, 1865–1900* (1991); see also Stephen Cresswell, *Mormons, Cowboys, Moonshiners, and Klansmen: Federal Law Enforcement in the South and West, 1870–1893* (1991); and William J. Holmes, "Moonshining and Collective Violence: Georgia, 1889–1895," *Journal of American History* 67:589 (1980).

49. *National Police Gazette*, Nov. 11, 1893, p. 6.

50. Eric Foner, *Reconstruction: America's Unfinished Revolution, 1863–1877* (1988), p. 425; on the origins of the Klan, see William Peirce Randel, *The Ku Klux Klan: A Century of Infamy* (1965), chap. 1; Albion W. Tourgee, "The Invisible Empire," Part II of Tourgee's *A Fool's Errand* (1880).

51. Randel, *The Klan*, p. 266.

52. Foner, *Reconstruction*, p. 426.

53. Ibid., p. 429.

54. Cresswell, *Mormons*, pp. 20–21.

55. Robert J. Kaczorowski, *The Politics of Judicial Interpretation: The Federal Courts, Department of Justice, and Civil Rights, 1866–1876* (1985), pp. 56–57.

56. Cresswell, *Mormons*, pp. 26–27, 62.

57. See, in general, Miller, *Revenuers and Moonshiners*; and Cresswell, *Mormons*.

58. Cresswell, *Mormons*, p. 158.

59. Brown, *Strain of Violence*, pp. 59–60.

60. Larry D. Ball, *Desert Lawmen: The High Sheriffs of New Mexico and Arizona, 1846–1912* (1992), pp. 133–34.

61. Robert P. Ingalls, *Urban Vigilantes in the New South: Tampa, 1882–1936* (1988), pp. 2–3.

62. Ibid., p. 4.

63. Francis A. J. Ianni, *A Family Business: Kinship and Social Control in Organized Crime* (1972), pp. 1–2.

64. Brown, *Strain of Violence*, pp. 214–15.

65. National Association for the Advancement of Colored People, *Thirty Years of Lynching in the United States, 1889–1918* (1919), pp. 7–8. Of the grand total of 3,224 victims, only 61 were women: 50 black women, 11 white (Ibid.).

66. *Kissimmee Valley Gazette* (Florida), April 28, 1899, reprinted in Ralph Ginzburg, ed., *One Hundred Years of Lynching* (1962), pp. 10–11.

67. Brown, *Strain of Violence*, p. 218.

68. E. M. Beck, James L. Massey, and Stewart E. Tolnay, "The Gallows, the Mob, and the Vote: Lethal Sanctioning of Blacks in North Carolina

and Georgia, 1882 to 1930," *Law and Society Review* 23:317, 329 (1989).

69. See Nancy MacLean, "The Leo Frank Case Reconsidered: Gender and Sexual Politics in the Making of Reactionary Populism," *Journal of American History* 78:917 (1991).

CHAPTER 9. LEGAL CULTURE:
CRIMES OF MOBILITY

1. On the themes of this chapter, see also my article, "Crimes of Mobility," *Stanford Law Review* 43:637 (1991).
2. Alexis de Toqueville, *Democracy in America* (ed., J. P. Mayer; 1969), p. 582.
3. I am indebted to Professor Adam Hirsch for this observation.
4. A typical example from the Compiled Laws of Kans., 1862, chap. 33, sec. 88: a person who "with intent to cheat or defraud another, shall, designedly, by color of any false token or writing, or by any other false pretence . . . obtain from any person any money, personal property . . . or other valuable thing," is to be treated as if he or she had stolen the "money, property, or thing so obtained." Under chap. 33, sec. 91, similar treatment is mandated for a person who "shall falsely represent or personate another, and, in such assumed character, shall receive any money . . . or property . . . intended to be delivered to the individual so personated."
5. So. Dak. Stats. (1899), Vol. 2, chap. 47, sec. 8082, p. 1976.
6. Anthony Comstock, *Frauds Exposed, or How the People Are Deceived and Robbed, and Youth Corrupted* (1880), p. 14.
7. James D. McCabe, Jr., *Lights and Shadows of New York Life: or, The Sights and Sensations of the Great City* (1872; reprint ed., 1970), p. 751.
8. McCabe, *Lights and Shadows*, p. 319. McCabe thought there was "no city in the Union in which impostors of all kinds flourish so well as in New York," because of the "immense size of the city, the heterogeneous character of its population, and the great variety of the interests and pursuits of the people" (ibid., p. 316).
9. *New York Times*, Dec. 13, 1902, p. 6; Dec. 21, 1902, p. 19.
10. McCabe, *Lights and Shadows*, p. 319.
11. *New York Times*, March 21, 1894, p. 1.
12. George W. Walling, *Recollections of a New York Chief of Police* (1887; reprint ed., 1972), pp. 335–37.
13. See T. F. Byrnes, *Professional Criminals of America* (1886), pp. 405–6.
14. See "Clever Swindlers Specialize in Victimizing Lawyers," *American Bar Association Journal* 12:132–33 (1926).
15. *New York Times*, March 10, 1888, p. 6.

16. Raphael Semmes, *Crime and Punishment in Early Maryland* (1938), pp. 205–6.

17. N. E. H. Hull, *Female Felons: Women and Serious Crime in Colonial Massachusetts* (1987), p. 114.

18. Code of Tenn. 1858, sec. 4839, p. 867. A person who had "good reason to believe such former husband or wife to be dead" was not guilty of the crime (sec. 4840, p. 868). It was also a crime for an "unmarried person" to marry, "knowingly," the "husband or wife of another" (sec. 4842, p. 868).

19. *Third Annual Message of Charles F. Warwick, Mayor of . . . Philadelphia, with Annual Reports . . . Superintendent of the Bureau of Police* (1898), p. 42; *Annual Report, Police Department of the City of New York* (1913), p. 17; *Annual Report, Police Department of the City of Los Angeles, 1924–25*, p. 18. There were over 62,000 arrests in Philadelphia in 1897, and over 35,000 in Los Angeles in 1924–25, so that bigamy, whatever its importance as a social indicator, did not loom large in police affairs.

20. *New York Times*, July 3, 1888, p. 2.

21. *National Intelligencer* (Washington, D.C.), Sept. 20, 1869, p. 1. The first wife, according to the newspapers, was so distraught when she learned the bad news that she swallowed a "quantity of corrosive sublimate" and was said to be "slowly dying."

22. *New York Times*, Sept. 11, 1888, p. 1.

23. *New York Times*, Sept. 27, 1897, p. 5.

24. John D. Lawson, ed., *American State Trials*, Vol. 2 (1914), p. 714.

25. *New York Times*, Sept. 27, 1897, p. 5.

26. Nancy F. Cott, *The Bonds of Womanhood: "Woman's Sphere" in New England, 1780–1835* (1977), pp. 64–74.

27. See Delger Trowbridge, "Criminal Intent and Bigamy," *California Law Review* 7:1 (1918).

28. *New York Times*, Sept. 21, 1896, p. 5.

29. *New York Times*, Oct. 6, 1896, p. 12. Foens may have honestly thought he was divorced.

30. On this case, see Craig Brandon, *Murder in the Adirondacks: "An American Tragedy" Revisited* (1986).

31. David R. Johnson, *Policing the Urban Underworld: The Impact of Crime on the Development of the American Police, 1800–1887* (1979), p. 65.

32. Carl B. Klockars, *The Professional Fence* (1974), pp. 1–28.

33. Johnson, *Policing the Urban Underworld*, pp. 47–49.

34. Matthew Hale Smith, *Sunshine and Shadow in New York* (1880), p. 150.

35. Roger Lane, *Policing the City: Boston, 1822–1885* (1967), pp. 146–47.

36. Walling, *Recollections*, pp. 519–20.

37. Gary T. Marx, *Undercover: Police Surveillance in America* (1988), p. 34.

38. George S. McWatters, *Knots Untied, or Ways and By-Ways in the*

Hidden Life of American Detectives (1873), pp. 648–49. On detective writings in the late nineteenth century in general, see David R. Papke, *Framing the Criminal: Crime, Cultural Work and the Loss of Critical Perspective, 1830–1900* (1987).

39. McWatters, *Knots Untied*, pp. 104, 649–50.

40. Ibid., pp. 104–6.

41. George W. Walling, *Recollections of a New York Chief of Police* (1887), pp. 519–20.

42. Matthew Hale Smith, *Sunshine and Shadow in New York* (1880), p. 162.

43. See Frank Morn, *"The Eye That Never Sleeps": A History of the Pinkerton National Detective Agency* (1982).

44. On this genre, see Papke, *Framing the Criminal*, chap. 6; see also Maxwell Bloomfield, "Creative Writers and Criminal Justice: Confronting the System (1890–1920)," *Criminal Justice Review* 15:208 (1990).

45. See Papke, *Framing the Criminal*, chap. 5. There is, of course, a vast literature on the history of this branch of literature; see, among others, Howard Haycraft, *Murder for Pleasure* (enlarged edition, 1968); David Lehman, *The Perfect Murder: A Study in Detection* (1989).

46. See, in general, Ian Ousby, *Bloodhounds of Heaven: The Detective in English Fiction from Godwin to Doyle* (1976).

47. I will behave ethically and not mention the name of the person who "did it." I would point out, though, that *The Moonstone*, unlike most mysteries, is such a wonderful novel that little harm is actually done by revealing the ending.

48. Allan Pinkerton, *Thirty Years a Detective* (1884; reprint ed., 1975), p. 17.

49. McCabe, *Lights and Shadows*, pp. 353–54.

50. Juergen Thorwald, *The Century of the Detective* (1964), p. 6.

51. David R. Johnson, *American Law Enforcement: A History* (1981), pp. 107, 110.

52. [Note:] "Medico-Legal Duties of Coroners," *American Law Register* 6:385, 395 (1858).

53. Acts and Resolves, Gen'l. Court of Mass., 1877, chap. 200, p. 580. In Suffolk County, the medical examiner was to be paid a salary of $3,000; in other counties, pay was on a piecework basis: "for a view without an autopsy, four dollars; for a view and autopsy, thirty dollars," plus travel expenses at the rate of five cents a mile "to and from the place of the view" (ibid., sec. 2).

54. See Charles H. Johnson, "The Wisconsin Coroner System," *Wisconsin Law Review* 529, 536 (1951).

55. See, in general, Carl B. Klockars, *The Professional Fence* (1974); Jerome Hall, *Theft, Law and Society* (1935).

56. The best analysis of the data is in Eric H. Monkkonen, *Police in Urban America, 1860–1920* (1981), chap. 2, pp. 65–85.

57. Ibid., pp. 76–77.

CHAPTER 10. WOMEN AND CRIMINAL JUSTICE TO THE END OF THE NINETEENTH CENTURY

1. George W. Walling, *Recollections of a New York Chief of Police* (1887), pp. 280–82.
2. James C. Mohr, *Abortion in America* (1978), pp. 48–50. Her colorful career has attracted a good deal of attention: see also Allan Keller, *Scandalous Lady: The Life and Times of Madame Restell* (1981); Clifford Browder, *The Wickedest Woman in New York: Madame Restell, the Abortionist* (1988).
3. Glenn Shirley, *West of Hell's Fringe: Crime, Criminals and the Federal Peace Officer in Oklahoma Territory, 1889–1907* (1978), pp. 242–50.
4. George Ellington, *The Women of New York: or the Under-World of the Great City* (1869; reprint ed., 1972), p. 441.
5. *National Police Gazette,* Nov. 28, 1896, p. 6.
6. *National Police Gazette,* Dec. 6, 1884, p. 6.
7. James D. McCabe, Jr., *Lights and Shadows of New York Life; or the Sights and Sensations of the Great City* (1872; reprint ed., 1970), p. 660; Edward Crapsey, *The Nether Side of New York; or the Vice, Crime and Poverty of the Great Metropolis* (1872; reprint ed., 1969), p. 122.
8. Allan Nevins and Milton H. Thomas, eds., *The Diary of George Templeton Strong,* Vol. 2 (1952), p. 57 (entry of July 7, 1851).
9. William Francis Kuntz, *Criminal Sentencing in Three Nineteenth-Century Cities* (1988), p. 370.
10. 1 Blackstone's Commentaries 28.
11. Charles Dickens, *Oliver Twist* (ed. Tilloston, 1966), p. 354.
12. Joel P. Bishop, *Commentaries on the Criminal Law,* Vol. 1 (2d ed., 1858), sec. 277, p. 316.
13. G. S. Rowe, "*Femes Covert* and Criminal Prosecution in Eighteenth-Century Pennsylvania," *American Journal of Legal History* 32:138, 151–52 (1988).
14. See Laws Ga. 1811, No. 377, sec. 7, for example.
15. Freel v. State, 21 Ark. 212 (1860). Technically, the issue was whether the judge's instructions to the jury on this point were correct or not. Presumably, the defendant had no evidence that her husband coerced her; and she was banking on a presumption of law: that is, that his mere presence implied coercion.
16. 43 Ala. 316 (1869).
17. Commonwealth v. Reynolds, 114 Mass. 306 (1873).
18. Commonwealth v. Samantha Hutchinson, 3 Am. Law Reg. 113, 115 (Pa., 6th Jud. Dist., 1854). The indictment was also defective because the "crime" was not part of the penal code; on the demise of common-law crimes, see chapter 3.
19. See, for example, Gen. Stats. Ky., 1887, chap. 29, art. 4, sec. 5 (rape of a

female over the age of twelve carries the death penalty, at the discretion of the jury). The most severe statutes were in the South and had distinctly racial overtones.

20. Laura F. Edwards, "Sexual Violence, Gender, Reconstruction, and the Extension of Patriarchy in Granville County, North Carolina," *North Carolina Historical Review* 58:237 (1991).

21. *Laws of the State of New York . . . since the Revolution,* Vol. 1 (1792), p. 338 (act of Feb. 14, 1787).

22. The Revised Statutes of New York of 1829 no longer punished rape with death; and its language had been cleaned up; but it was still a crime to "take any woman unlawfully, against her will, and by force, menace or duress, compel her to marry him, or to marry any other person, or to be defiled." Laws N.Y. 1829, Vol. 2, p. 663.

23. Code of Alabama, 1886, Vol. 2, p. 12, secs. 3736, 3737.

24. 42 Tex. 226 (1875).

25. Tenn. Code 1858, sec. 4610.

26. *New York Times,* July 15, 1894, p. 8; Oct. 31, 1891, p. 1. I am indebted to Deborah Castler for these references.

27. People v. Dohring, 59 N.Y. 374 (1874).

28. Ibid., at 375.

29. 45 Conn. 256 (1877).

30. Camp v. State, 3 Ga. (3 Kelly) 417, 433 (1847).

31. Ibid.

32. Tenn. Code 1858, secs. 4612, 4613. These provisions can be found much earlier: for example, Laws N.Y. 1829, Vol. 2, p. 663, in quite similar language.

33. Don Moran v. People, 25 Mich. 356, 357 (1872).

34. Commonwealth v. Stratton, 114 Mass. 303 (1873). Stratton was convicted of assault and battery.

35. N.Y. Laws 1848, chap. 111.

36. Ga. Code 1882, sec. 4371, p. 1148. Milder versions of the law were in force in some states. Thus, in Nebraska, the crime could be committed only if the "female of good repute" was "under the age of 18 years." Gen'l. stats. Neb. 1873, chap. 20, sec. 207, p. 771.

37. People v. Walter Clark, 33 Mich. 112 (1876).

38. Laws Ohio 1886, p. 92 (passed April 22, 1886).

39. *National Police Gazette,* Oct. 5, 1867, p. 4.

40. People v. Gould, 70 Mich. 240, 38 N.W. 232 (1888). See also Wright v. State, 31 Tex. Cr. R. 354, 20 S.W. 756 (1892). Edward H. Savage in *Police Records and Recollections* (1873; reprint ed., 1971), pp. 280–82, reports a marriage in 1861 in the Boston "Tombs." The defendant said "he *was* ready *to marry*" his pregnant girlfriend, the wedding was duly performed, and he was released.

41. Code of Alabama, 1887, Vol. 2, secs. 4031, 4032, p. 77.

42. Weaver v. State, 79 Ala. 279 (1885).

43. 41 Ga. 278 (1870).

44. *National Police Gazette,* July 13, 1878, p. 7.

45. On the Sickles case and "temporary insanity," see above, chapter 6; see also Nat Brandt, *The Congressman Who Got Away With Murder* (1991).

46. See Robert M. Ireland, "The Libertine Must Die: Sexual Dishonor and the Unwritten Law in the Nineteenth-Century United States," *Journal of Social History* 23:27 (1992).

47. See Robert M. Ireland, "Frenzied and Fallen Females: Women and Sexual Dishonor in the Nineteenth-Century United States," *Journal of Women's History* 3:95 (1992).

48. Ireland, "The Libertine Must Die," p. 34. The sentence was later commuted to ten years in prison.

49. Edward H. Savage, *Police Records and Recollections* (1873; reprint ed., 1971), pp. 221–22.

50. Crim. Laws of Texas 1881, art. 567, p. 191. The killing had to "take place before the parties to the act of adultery have separated."

51. It was repealed in 1973. Acts Texas 1973, chap. 399.

52. Deborah L. Rhode, *Justice and Gender* (1989), p. 238.

53. *American Jurist and Law Magazine,* October 1838, p. 243.

54. Ball Fenner, *Raising the Veil: or, Scenes in the Courts* (1856), p. 253.

55. See Elizabeth Pleck, "Wife Beating in Nineteenth-Century America," *Victimology* 4:60 (1979).

56. Laws Nev. 1877, chap. 43, p. 82. On the movement to bring back the whipping post, see Elizabeth Pleck, *Domestic Tyranny: The Making of Social Policy Against Family Violence from Colonial Times to the Present* (1987), pp. 108–21.

57. Maryland passed a law authorizing flogging for wife-beating in 1882. Laws Md. 1882, Chap. 120, p. 172; see also Laws Ore. 1905, chap. 203, p. 335; Laws Del. 1901, chap 204, p. 493.

58. Pleck, *Domestic Tyranny,* p. 65.

59. Linda Gordon, *Heroes of Their Own Lives: The Politics and History of Family Violence: Boston, 1880–1960* (1988), p. 251.

60. Douglas Greenberg, *Crime and Law Enforcement in the Colony of New York, 1691–1776* (1974), pp. 113–14; see chapter 3.

61. Braddy v. City of Milledgeville, 74 Ga. 516 (1884).

62. On the St. Louis experiment, I have drawn on James Wunsch, "Prostitution and Public Policy: From Regulation to Suppression, 1858–1920" (Ph.D. dissertation, Department of History, University of Chicago, 1976), pp. 38–59.

63. Ibid., pp. 39–40.

64. Ibid., p. 42.

65. Ibid., p. 54.

66. John H. Warren, Jr., *Thirty Years' Battle with Crime* (1875; reprint ed., 1970), pp. 37–38.

67. Barbara M. Hobson, *Uneasy Virtue: The Politics of Prostitution and the American Reform Tradition* (1987), pp. 11, 23.

68. Laws Mich. 1869, No. 145, sec. 4, pp. 264, 265. The act applied to "every person more than fifteen years of age who is a common prostitute." The inspectors of the Detroit House of Correction were empowered to establish "rules and regulations" under which these women might be "absolutely discharged from imprisonment," if they underwent "reformation." Ibid., sec. 5, p. 266.

69. Hobson, *Uneasy Virtue*, p. 32.

70. Quoted in Ruth Rosen, *The Lost Sisterhood: Prostitution in America, 1900–1918* (1982), p. 5.

71. These nice women, of course, were white, middle-class women. Black women in the deep South, both before and after slavery, were "an outlet for male sexual drives that would otherwise pollute white womanhood" (Rosen, *Lost Sisterhood*, p. 6).

72. John C. Schneider, *Detroit and the Problem of Order, 1830–1880* (1980), pp. 103–4.

73. Matthew Hale Smith, *Sunshine and Shadow in New York* (1880), pp. 371–72; see also George T. Kneeland, *Commercialized Prostitution in New York City* (1913; reprint ed., 1969), especially chap. 7.

74. L'Hote v. New Orleans, 177 U.S. 587 (1900).

75. Wunsch, "Prostitution and Public Policy," pp. 91–93.

76. See, in general, James C. Mohr, *Abortion in America: The Origins and Evolution of National Policy* (1978), on which much of this account is based; see also Reva Siegel, "Reasoning from the Body: A Historical Perspective on Abortion Regulation and Questions of Equal Protection," *Stanford Law Review* 44:261 (1992).

77. Mohr, *Abortion in America*, p. 21; Conn. Rev. Stats. 1821, Title 22, sec. 14, p. 152.

78. Rev. Stats. N.Y. 1829, Vol. 2, p. 694; see also the similar provision (p. 661) that specifically speaks of a "woman pregnant with a quick child."

79. Ellington, *Women of New York*, pp. 408–9.

80. Mohr, *Abortion in America*, chap. 6.

81. Quoted in Ellington, *Women of New York*, p. 411; the minister went on to cry out: "O women of America! . . . are you to see foreigners rear up large families . . . while you . . . refuse to meet the high responsibilities and the holy joys which God lays at your feet?" Ellington himself grumbled that "It is not considered fashionable to have children. It intereferes with the round of dissipation of the stylish woman" (p. 410).

82. Charles Sutton, *The New York Tombs: Its Secrets and Its Mysteries* (1874), pp. 359–60.

83. Quoted in Siegel, "Reasoning from the Body," p. 298.

84. Sutton, *The Tombs*, pp. 364–65.

85. *Brooklyn Daily Eagle*, Dec. 6, 1918, p. 5.

86. Katherine K. Christoffel and Kiang Liu, "Homicide Death Rates in Childhood in Twenty-Three Developed Countries: U.S. Rates Atypically High," *Journal of Child Abuse and Neglect* 7:339 (1983).

87. See, in general, Lionel Rose, *The Massacre of the Innocents: Infanticide in Britain, 1800–1939* (1986).

88. Digest Laws N.J., 2d ed., 1855, p. 163.

89. Mary Gardner's Case, 5 City-Hall Recorder 70 (1819). The judge thought that "wilful violence from the mother" was the real cause of death; but the jury went its own way.

90. Edward Crapsey, *The Nether Side of New York: or the Vice, Crime and Poverty of the Great Metropolis* (1872), p. 123. After 1870, according to Crapsey, the situation changed, because of the new "Foundling Asylum," where "a larger proportion . . . survive to become public burdens."

91. Warren, *Thirty Years' Battle*, pp. 167–68.

92. Gordon, *Heroes of Their Own Lives*, p. 44.

93. George Ellington devotes a chapter of his book to "infanticide in the great metropolis," but what he is talking about is abortion. He does, however, mention the baby farms, "temples of the innocents," where babies are either given out for adoption, or (if not adopted) starved to death or otherwise gotten rid of. Ellington, *Women of New York*, chaps. 33, 39.

94. Roger Lane, *Roots of Violence in Black Philadelphia, 1860–1900* (1986), pp. 129–30. Lane reports that the "official cases were only a small fraction of the number which really occurred"; as in London, hundreds of infants "were found dead every year in the streets, lots, and cesspools."

95. Lawrence M. Friedman and Robert V. Percival, *The Roots of Justice: Crime and Punishment in Alameda County, California, 1870—1910* (1981).

96. Edward L. Ayers, *Vengeance and Justice: Crime and Punishment in the Nineteenth-Century American South* (1984), p. 62.

97. Estelle B. Freedman, *Their Sisters' Keepers: Women's Prison Reform in America, 1830–1930* (1981), p. 11.

98. William Francis Kuntz II, *Criminal Sentencing in Three Nineteenth-Century Cities* (1988), p. 413.

99. Nicole H. Rafter, *Partial Justice: Women in State Prisons, 1800–1935* (1985), pp. 16–21.

100. Freedman, *Their Sisters' Keepers*, pp. 51–52; see also Laws Mass. 1875, chap. 385.

101. Massachusetts Public Documents, 1895, Vol. 10, Public Doc. No. 13, *25th Annual Report, Commissioners of Prisons of Mass.*, "Report Concerning the Reformatory Prison for Women," p. 70.

102. See Mass. Rev. Stats. 1881, chap. 207, sec. 29.

103. Laws Mass. 1875, chap. 385, sec. 21.

104. "Report Concerning the Massachusetts Reformatory," Public Doc. No. 13, *25th Annual Report, Commissioners of Prisons of Mass.*, 1895, p. 101.

105. Isabel C. Barrows, "The Massachusetts Reformatory Prison for

Women," in S. J. Barrows, *The Reformatory System in the United States* (report prepared for the International Prison Commission, 1900), pp. 101, 112.

106. "Report Concerning the Reformatory Prison for Women," Public Doc. no. 13, *25th Annual Report, Commissioner of Prisons of Mass.*, 1895, p. 82.

CHAPTER 11. THE EVOLUTION OF CRIMINAL PROCESS: TRIALS AND ERRORS

1. See Lawrence M. Friedman and Robert V. Percival, *The Roots of Justice: Crime and Punishment in Alameda County, California, 1870–1910* (1981), chap. 7.

2. Samuel Walker, *Sense and Nonsense About Crime: A Policy Guide*, (2d ed., 1989), pp. 19–34.

3. The printed version of the trial, and some valuable commentary, can be found in Julius Goebel, Jr., ed., *The Law Practice of Alexander Hamilton, Documents and Commentary*, Vol. 1 (1964), pp. 693–774.

4. See David R. Kasserman, *Fall River Outrage: Life, Murder, and Justice in Early Industrial New England* (1986), p. 136, which is about the sensational 1832 trial of the Reverend Ephraim Avery for murder.

5. Jack K. Williams, *Vogues in Villainy: Crime and Retribution in Ante-Bellum South Carolina* (1959), pp. 75–76.

6. Thomas Ford, *A History of Illinois from Its Commencement as a State in 1818 to 1847* (1854), p. 29.

7. Goebel, *Practice of Alexander Hamilton*, p. 771. The sessions court in South Carolina often heard cases well into the night. The practice was to swear in forty-eight men, from which two juries would be carved. While one jury was deliberating, the second would be hearing another case. Williams, *Vogues in Villainy*, p. 82.

8. 1 *City Hall Recorder* (New York, 1816), p. 6.

9. See Max Rheinstein, ed., *Max Weber on Law in Economy and Society* (1954), p. 213n.

10. Allen Steinberg, *The Transformation of Criminal Justice: Philadelphia, 1800–1880* (1989), pp. 1–2.

11. No settlement was possible if the victim of the misdemeanor was an "officer or minister of justice, whilst in the execution of the duties of his office," or if the crime was committed "riotously" or "with an intent to commit a felony." N.Y. Rev. Stats. 1829, Vol. 2, p. 730.

12. Steinberg, *Transformation*, pp. 46–49.

13. Ibid., p. 227.

14. Friedman and Percival, *Roots of Justice*, p. 120.

15. Ibid., p. 123.

16. *Oakland Tribune*, Sept. 17, 1884, p. 3.

17. *Oakland Tribune*, Oct. 23, 1895, p. 3.

18. John R. Wunder, *Inferior Courts, Superior Justice: A History of the Justices of the Peace on the Northwest Frontier, 1853–1889* (1979), p. 170. On the fees of the justices, see ibid., pp. 100–101. For another example, see Rev. Laws Ind. 1824, chap. 41, pp. 196, 203–4.

19. Horatio Woodman, ed., *Reports of Criminal Cases Tried in the Municipal Court of the City of Boston Before Peter Oxenbridge Thacher* (1845), p. vi.

20. Wunder, *Inferior Courts*, p. 121 provides an example of this punishment.

21. Police courts and justice-of-the-peace courts, on the whole, did not leave records behind. Nineteenth-century newspapers help fill in the gap. For an account of one case in justice court, see Zigurds L. Zile, "Vosburg v. Putney: A Centennial Story," *Wisconsin Law Review* 877 (1992).

22. Arthur Train, *The Prisoner at the Bar* (1926; originally published, 1906), p. 111.

23. Hurtalo v. California, 110 U.S. 516 (1884). On the operation of the California system in the late nineteenth century, see Friedman and Percival, *Roots of Justice*, pp. 166–68.

24. Ala. Const. 1875, Art. 1, sec. 17.

25. For the nineteenth-century law, see Seymour D. Thompson, "Bail in Criminal Cases," *Criminal Law Magazine* 6:1–49 (Jan. 1885); see also Friedman and Percival, *Roots of Justice*, pp. 161–66.

26. Friedman and Percival, *Roots of Justice*, pp. 164–65.

27. 100 U.S. 303 (1879).

28. Peter O. Thacher, *Observations on Some of the Methods Known in the Law of Massachusetts to Secure the Selection and Appointment of an Impartial Jury* (1834), p. 9.

29. Rev. Stats. Fla., 1892, p. 407, chap. 16, sec. 1150. This statute applied both to civil and criminal juries.

30. In some states it was less; in Florida, six would do, except in capital cases. Rev. Stats. Fla. 1892, p. 886, sec. 2854.

31. Cal. Penal Code (1886), sec. 1070; Colo. Ann. Stats. 1891, chap. 73, sec. 2596.

32. Rev. Stats. Ohio, 1890, sec. 7278, pp. 1783–4.

33. *Oakland Tribune*, Feb. 18, 1875, p. 3; Friedman and Percival, *Roots of Justice*, p. 184.

34. On the Haymarket affair, see Paul Avrich, *The Haymarket Tragedy* (1984); on the selection of the jury, see pp. 264–65.

35. John D. Lawson, ed., *American State Trials*, Vol. 5 (1916), pp. 369, 409, 432, 475, 503.

36. Francis Wharton, *A Treatise on the Law of Evidence in Criminal Issues* (8th ed., 1880), p. 338, sec. 428.

37. Lester B. Orfield, *Criminal Procedure from Arrest to Appeal* (1947), p. 459. An act of Congress, passed in 1878, provided that the defendant "shall, at his own request, but not otherwise, be a competent wit-

ness." And his failure to make the request "shall not create any presumption against him." 20 Stat. 30, chap. 37 (act of March 16, 1878).

38. See Friedman and Percival, *Roots of Justice*, p. 185.

39. The quote, dating from 1897, is found in John M. Maguire, *The Lance of Justice: A Semi-Centennial History of the Legal Aid Society, 1876–1926* (1928), pp. 261–62.

40. Friedman and Percival, *Roots of Justice*, p. 185.

41. This observation is based on my examination of Volume 10 of the Minutes Books of Leon County, Florida.

42. The charge is reprinted in Edmund Pearson, ed., *Trial of Lizzie Borden* (1937), pp. 377–92.

43. Lawson, *American State Trials*, Vol. 5, pp. 508, 509, 511.

44. "No judge, in any cause, civil or criminal, shall sum up or comment on the testimony, or charge the jury as to the weight of evidence; but it shall be lawful ... to charge the jury upon ... principles of law ... *Provided*, That all instructions ... shall be in writing." Rev. Code. Miss. 1857, p. 504.

45. See, for example, Dixon v. Florida, 13 Fla. 636 (1871).

46. In California, by agreement of both parties, the judge could give instructions orally. On instructions in California, see Friedman and Percival, *Roots of Justice*, pp. 186–88; on the Butts case, ibid., p. 187.

47. In our times, to be sure, there has been a great deal of research on what juries do and how they do it. See, for example, Valerie P. Hans and Neil Vidmar, *Judging the Jury* (1986). No such research exists, of course, for the nineteenth-century jury.

48. 35 Tenn. 302 (1855).

49. Joyce v. State, 66 Tenn. 273 (1874).

50. Glidewell v. State, 83 Tenn. 123 (1885).

51. Francis Wharton, *A Treatise on the Law of Evidence in Criminal Issues* (8th ed., 1880), pp. 1–2.

52. Mark Twain, *Roughing It* (1972; original ed. 1871), pp. 308–9.

53. See Robert M. Ireland, "The Nineteenth-Century Criminal Jury: Kentucky in the Context of the American Experience," *Kentucky Review* 4:52 (Spring 1983).

54. Shaffner v. Commonwealth, 72 Pa. 60 (1872).

55. Carter v. State, 77 Tenn. 440 (1882).

56. Spier v. State, 89 Ga. 737 (1892).

57. A bailiff was to be available to the jurors at all times, though never in the actual jury room. Dig. Laws Texas, 1873, Articles 3070–74, pp. 527–28.

58. Gen. Stats. Conn., 1887, chap. 100, sec. 1629.

59. Wunder, *Inferior Courts*, p. 75.

60. Kenneth Lamott, *Who Killed Mr. Crittenden?* (1963), pp. 248–49.

61. Twain, *Roughing It*, p. 316.

62. George Dargo, *Jefferson's Louisiana: Politics and the Clash of Legal Traditions* (1975), p. 108.

63. Arthur Train, *The Prisoner at the Bar* (1906), p. 226.

64. Theodore Ferdinand, *Boston's Lower Criminal Courts, 1814–1850* (1992), pp. 89–97.

65. Friedman and Percival, *Roots of Justice*, p. 177.

66. The phrase is from Milton Heumann, "A Note on Plea Bargaining and Case Pressure," *Law and Society Review* 9:515 (1975).

67. Another 112 said they pleaded guilty because they "had neither money nor friends"; 36 said "ignorance of the law" was their reason; 40 pleaded guilty "because of prior convictions"; and 19 were eager "to avoid prosecution for other crimes." *Eighth Annual Report, State Board of Prison Directors, 1887*, p. 88.

68. On this case, see Lamott, *Who Killed Mr. Crittenden?*

69. Charles E. Rosenberg, *The Trial of the Assassin Guiteau* (1968).

70. There is a large literature on the case; and every once in a while, some enterprising author dreams up a new "solution." Robert Sullivan, in *Goodbye Lizzie Borden* (1974), argues strongly that Lizzie was guilty. This account is especially valuable for its careful and full picture of the legal proceedings. For a transcript of the trial, there is Edmund L. Pearson, ed., *The Trial of Lizzie Borden* (1937); see also, Victoria Lincoln, *A Private Disgrace: Lizzie Borden by Daylight* (1967).

71. For this line of thought, see Mary Hartman, *Victorian Murderesses* (1977); Friedman and Percival, *Roots of Justice*, chap. 7.

72. Friedman and Percival, *Roots of Justice*, pp. 239–44.

73. Ibid., p. 260.

74. On the historical development of the law of appeals, Lester B. Orfield's, *Criminal Appeals in America* (1939) is still the most comprehensive account, and I have made liberal use of it in this section of the chapter.

75. Commonwealth v. Clare, 89 Mass. 525 (1863).

76. Shaw v. State, 2 Tex. App. 487 (1877).

77. Harwell v. State, 22 Tex. App. 251, 2 S.W. 606 (1886).

78. Curry v. State, 7 Tex. App. 92 (1879).

79. "Overruled Their Judicial Superiors," *American Law Review* 21:610 (1887).

80. 23 Tex. Ct. App. 639 (1887).

81. I am indebted to Reid Schar for these figures.

82. State v. Campbell, 210 Mo. 202, 224, 199 S.W. 706 (1908).

CHAPTER 12. A NATIONAL SYSTEM

1. See Mary H. Oakey, *Journey from the Gallows: Historical Evolution of the Penal Philosophies and Practices in the Nation's Capital* (ed. Belinda Swanson; 1988).

2. The formal system as of the beginning of the century is described in George B. Davis, *A Treatise on the Military Law of the United States* (1909); a recent comprehensive treatment is Jonathan Lurie, *Arming Military Justice*, Vol. 1 (1992).

3. See 30 Stats. 717 (act of July 7, 1898); 35 Stats. 1142, 1145, chap. 321, subchap. 11 (act of March 4, 1909). The statutes, however, provided that if the crime occurred "within the territorial limits of any State," and if there was no special *federal* law covering the crime but the act would be a crime under state law, then the person who committed the act on a federal enclave would be "deemed guilty of a like offense."

4. Christian G. Fritz, *Federal Justice in California: The Court of Ogden Hoffman, 1851–1891* (1991), pp. 259–62.

5. *Annual Report, Attorney General of the United States, 1889*, pp. 6–7. On the liquor violations of the period, and the struggle to enforce the laws, see Wilbur R. Miller, *Revenuers and Moonshiners: Enforcing Federal Liquor Law in the Mountain South, 1865–1900* (1991).

6. 38 Stats. 166, 171 (act of October 3, 1913). Tax fraud was not a major issue in the nineteenth century, except for moonshiners and the alcohol tax. There were prior income tax laws, before the act of 1913, but none lasted very long. In 1895, the Supreme Court struck down an income tax law, in Pollock v. Farmers' Loan and Trust Company 157 U.S. 429, 158 U.S. 601 (1895). A constitutional amendment undid this case.

7. There were 679 arrests for this offense in 1966, and 1,214 in 1985. Administrative Office of the U.S. Courts, *Federal Offenders in the United States Courts 1985*, table H-2, p. 30.

8. 38 Stats. 692 (act of Aug. 15, 1914) (sponges); 38 Stats. 693, 697 (act of Aug. 18, 1914) (cotton futures).

9. 36 Stats. 825 (act of June 25, 1910). This act is discussed in more detail in chapter 15.

10. 41 Stats. 324 (act of Oct. 29, 1919).

11. Brooks v. United States, 267 U.S. 432 (1925).

12. 40 Stats. 443 (act of March 8, 1918).

13. *Annual Report, Attorney General of the United States, Fiscal Year 1924*, p. 79. This was about a third of all the criminal cases; selective service cases made up another third (ibid., p. 124).

14. 277 U.S. 438 (1928).

15. Ibid., at 470.

16. 47 Stats. 326 (act of June 22, 1932); Horace L. Bomar, Jr., "The Lindbergh Law," *Law and Contemporary Problems* 1:435 (1934).

17. Quoted in Sanford J. Ungar, *FBI* (1976), p. 72.

18. Ibid., p. 74.

19. Mark H. Haller, "Urban Crime and Criminal Justice: The Chicago Case," *Journal of American History* 57:619, 623 (1970).

20. 48 Stats. 783, chap. 304 (act of May 18, 1934); 48 Stats. 781, chap. 300 (act of May 18, 1934); 48 Stats. 794, chap. 333 (act of May 22, 1934).

21. 48 Stats. 782, chap. 302 (act of May 18, 1934).

22. 48 Stats. 1236, chap. 757 (act of June 26, 1934).

23. *Annual Report, Attorney General of the United States, 1915*, pp. 31–33.

24. *Annual Report, Attorney General of the United States, 1924,* pp. 89–90.

25. *Annual Report, Director of Administrative Office of the U.S. Courts, 1940,* pp. 90–91. The IRS, aside from the liquor cases, had only 187 cases to show. For another study of the growth of federal prosecutions, see Edward Rubin, "A Statistical Study of Federal Criminal Proceedings," *Law and Contemporary Problems* 1:494 (1934).

26. *Annual Report, Director of the Administrative Office of the U.S. Courts, 1973,* p. 189.

27. Administrative Office of the U.S. Courts, *Federal Offenders in the United States Courts, 1985,* p. 7.

28. Administrative Office of the U.S. Courts, *Federal Offenders in the United States Courts, 1986–1990,* p. 7.

29. Yale Kamisar, Wayne LaFave, Jerold Israel, *Modern Criminal Procedure: Cases, Comments and Questions* (6th ed., 1986), p. 21n.

30. National Center for State Courts, *State Court Caseload Statistics: Annual Report 1990,* p. 27.

31. There were, however, jails in the District of Columbia. The "United States jail" was built in the district in the 1870s—an "imposing-looking edifice" of stone. See Mary H. Oakey, *Journey from the Gallows,* p. 55.

32. 24 Stats. 411, chap. 213 (act of Feb. 23, 1887).

33. *Annual Report, Attorney General of the United States, 1889,* p. xi.

34. Friedman and Percival, *Roots of Justice,* p. 300. The federal prisoners in 1905 were better off than the county prisoners, whose daily allowance was a mere twenty-five cents and who got only two meals a day instead of three.

35. Harry F. Barnes and Neglect K. Teeters, *New Horizons in Criminology* (1943), pp. 675–76.

36. 46 Stats. 325, chap. 274 (act of May 14, 1930).

37. Blake McKelvey, *American Prisons* (1936), p. 228.

38. *Attorney General's Survey of Release Procedures: Prisons, U.S. Department of Justice, 1940,* p. 309.

39. U.S. Department of Justice, Federal Bureau of Prisons, *Statistical Report: Fiscal Year 1986,* p. 16.

40. U.S. Department of Justice, Federal Bureau of Prisons, *1989 State of the Bureau,* p. 54.

41. Richard Hawkins and Geoffrey P. Alpert, *American Prison Systems* (1989), p. 55.

42. Margaret Werner Cahalan, *Historical Corrections Statistics in the United States, 1850–1984* (1986), table 3.2, p. 29. The state figures do not include prisoners in local jails, which is a sizeable population on its own. The prison figures, of course, reflect the more serious crimes.

43. David R. Johnson, *American Law Enforcement: A History* (1981), p. 168.

44. Ungar, *FBI,* p. 40.

45. Fred J. Cook, *The FBI Nobody Knows* (1964), p. 420.
46. Johnson, *American Law Enforcement*, p. 174.
47. Samuel Walker, *Popular Justice: A History of American Criminal Justice* (1980), p. 184.
48. Ungar, *FBI*, p. 57.
49. See Taylor Branch, *Parting the Waters: America in the King Years, 1954–63* (1989).
50. William W. Keller, *The Liberals and J. Edgar Hoover: Rise and Fall of a Domestic Intelligence State* (1989), p. 6.
51. Walker, *Popular Justice*, pp. 186–87.
52. Victoria W. Schneider and Brian Wiersema, "Limits and Use of the Uniform Crime Reports," in D. MacKenzie, P. Baunach, and R. Roberg, eds., *Measuring Crime: Large-Scale, Long-Range Efforts* (1990), pp. 21–23.
53. Richard Maxwell Brown, *Strain of Violence: Historical Studies of American Violence and Vigilantism* (1975), pp. 160–61.
54. See William H. Moore, *The Kefauver Committee and the Politics of Crime 1950–1952* (1974); another account, equally disparaging, is in Michael Woodiwiss, *Crime, Crusades and Corruption: Prohibitions in the United States, 1900–1987* (1988), chaps. 10, 11.
55. Moore, *The Kefauver Committee*, p. 189.
56. Walker, *Popular Justice*, pp. 206–8.
57. Thomas E. Cronin, Tania Z. Cronin, and Michael E. Milakovich, *U.S. v. Crime in the Streets* (1981), p. 28.
58. Walker, *Political Justice*, pp. 173–77.
59. Morris Ploscowe, "Some Causative Factors in Criminality," in National Commission on Law Observance and Enforcement, *Report on the Causes of Crime*, Vol. 1 (1931), p. 137.
60. Quoted in Malcolm M. Feeley and Austin D. Sarat, *The Policy Dilemma: Federal Crime Policy and the Law Enforcement Assistance Administration* (1980), p. 35.
61. Ibid., pp. 36–37.
62. 82 Stats. 197 (act of June 19, 1968).
63. On the history of the rise and fall of LEAA, see Walker, *Popular Justice*, pp. 232–38; and Feeley and Sarat, *The Policy Dilemma*.
64. Feeley and Sarat, *The Policy Dilemma*, p. 91.
65. *New York Times*, Jan. 29, 1992 (national ed.), p. A14.

CHAPTER 13. CRIME ON THE STREETS; CRIME IN THE SUITES

1. *Annual Report, Police Commissioner of the City of New York, year ending Dec. 31, 1906* (1907), p. 19.
2. Laws Cal. 1925, p. 396.
3. Laws Cal. 1931, chap. 1026, p. 2108.

4. Laws N.Y. 1910, Vol. 1, chap. 374, sec. 287, p. 681.

5. Any driver who knows he has caused injury to person or property, and who leaves the scene "without stopping and giving his name, residence, including street and street number" and his license number, could get up to two years in prison in addition to revocation of license. Ibid., sec. 290(3), p. 685.

6. George Warren, *Traffic Courts* (1942), p. 9.

7. *Supplemental Report, Senate Interim Committee on Traffic and Motor Vehicle Violations*, State of California (1950), p. 24.

8. John A. Gardiner, *Traffic and the Police: Variations in Law-Enforcement Policy* (1969), pp. 27–28.

9. Annual Report, Administrative Office of the Courts, *North Carolina Courts, 1989–1990*, p. 237.

10. *Michigan State Courts, Annual Report, 1988*, p. 47. The felony cases in this court were preliminary examinations only.

11. See, in general, Warren, *Traffic Courts*, for a picture of these courts in operation in the period of the Second World War; on the traffic bureau of the Columbus, Ohio, municipal court in the 1930s, see William J. Blackburn Jr., *The Administration of Criminal Justice in Franklin County, Ohio* (1935), pp. 198–203.

12. Warren, *Traffic Courts*, pp. 81–82.

13. American Bar Association, *A Report on South Carolina Traffic Courts* (1968), p. 145.

14. Warren, *Traffic Courts*, p. 114.

15. Ibid., p. 112.

16. American Bar Association, *A Report to the State of Oklahoma on the System of Courts Which Adjudicate Traffic Cases* (1958), p. 99.

17. Laws N.Y. 1910, Vol. 1, chap. 374, sec. 290(3).

18. Josephine Y. King and Mark Tipperman, "The Offense of Driving While Intoxicated: The Development of Statutory and Case Law in New York," *Hofstra Law Review* 3:541 (1975); Laws N.Y. 1926, chap. 732, p. 1369; Laws N.Y. 1941, chap. 726, p. 1623.

19. Laws N.Y. 1953, chap. 854, p. 1876. The police, however, had to have "reasonable grounds to suspect such person of driving in an intoxicated condition."

20. This was apparently a common practice in Missouri; see the empirical study reported in Edward H. Hunvald, Jr., and Franklin E. Zimring, "Whatever Happened to Implied Consent? A Sounding," *Missouri Law Review* 33: 323 (1968).

21. Harry Kalven, Jr., and Hans Zeisel, *The American Jury* (1966), pp. 293–97.

22. Joseph W. Little, *Administration of Justice in Drunk Driving Cases* (1975), pp. 192–93.

23. James B. Jacobs, *Drunk Driving: An American Dilemma* (1989), pp. xiv, xv.

24. Ibid., p. 60. See also Joseph R. Gusfield, *The Culture of Public Problems: Drinking-Driving and the Symbolic Order* (1981).

25. H. Laurence Ross and Robert B. Voas, "The New Philadelphia Story: The Effects of Severe Punishment for Drunk Driving," *Law and Policy* 12:51 (1990).

26. 34 Stats. 768, chap. 3915 (act of June 30, 1906).

27. 49 Stats. 449, chap. 372 (act of July 5, 1935), sec. 12. Violation of this section exposed the violator to a fine of up to $5,000, or a prison sentence of up to one year.

28. Sam B. Warner and Henry B. Cabot, "Changes in the Administration of Criminal Justice During the Past Fifty Years," *Harvard Law Review* 50: 583, 614–15 (1937).

29. Laws Ohio, 1911, pp. 53, 56, 127, 427.

30. Laws Ohio, 1911, p. 586.

31. *Annual Report, Police Commissioner of the City of New York, year ending Dec. 31, 1907* (1908), pp. 162–63. The total number of arrests was over 200,000.

32. See Marshall B. Clinard, *The Black Market; A Study of White Collar Crime* (1952).

33. Clinard, *Black Market*, pp. 238–40.

34. Ibid., p. 149.

35. Judy L. Whalley, "Crime and Punishment—Criminal Antitrust Enforcement in the 1990s," *Antitrust Law Journal* 59:151 (1990). I am indebted to Jack Szczepanowski for this reference.

36. The Federal Trade Commission Act is 38 Stats. 717, chap. 311 (act of Sept. 26, 1914); the Clayton Act is 38 Stats. 730, chap. 323 (act of Oct. 15, 1914); the resale price maintenance law is 50 Stats. 693 (act of Aug. 17, 1937).

37. 467 Fed. 2d 1000 (C.A. 9, 1972; cert. den. 93 S.Ct. 938, 1973).

38. 467 Fed. 2d at 1004.

39. La. Acts 1910, No. 150; the earlier laws were Laws La. 1880, no. 20; Laws La. 1882, no. 82; Laws La. 1914, no. 282.

40. La. Acts 1898, Act 68, p. 93.

41. Laws N.H. 1885, chap. 68, sec. 1. The material on oleomargarine regulation is drawn from Geoffrey P. Miller, "Public Choice at the Dawn of the Special Interest State: The Story of Butter and Margarine," *California Law Review* 77:83 (1979).

42. 24 Stats. 209 (act of Aug. 2, 1886).

43. 46 Stats. 1549 (act of March 4, 1931).

44. Laws Wis. 1967, chap. 42, p. 44.

45. Upton Sinclair, *American Outpost: A Book of Reminiscences* (1932), p. 154.

46. Peter Temin, "The Origin of Compulsory Drug Prescriptions," *Journal of Law and Economics* 22:91 (1979).

47. Ralph P. Schipa, "The Desirability of Uniform Food Laws," *Food, Drug, Cosmetic Law Quarterly* 3:518, 522 (1948).

48. Laws Ind. 1939, chap. 38, p. 140.

49. Laws Wyo. 1929, chap. 103, secs. 1, 6, pp. 172, 174. It is something of a disappointment to learn that selling these disgusting eggs was a

mere misdemeanor, carrying a fine of between $25 and $100.

50. Richard Curtis Litman and Donald Saunders Litman, "Protection of the American Consumer: The Muckrakers and the Enactment of the First Federal Food and Drug Law in the United States," *Food, Drug, Cosmetic Law Journal* 36:641, 651–52 (1981).

51. Sutherland had been using the term for more than a decade before his monograph appeared. See Gil Geis and Colin Goff, "Edwin H. Sutherland's 'White Collar Crime in America': An Essay in Historical Criminology," in *Criminal Justice History*, Vol. 7 (1986), p. 1.

52. Stanton Wheeler, Kenneth Mann, and Austin Sarat, *Sitting in Judgment: The Sentencing of White-Collar Criminals* (1988), p. 5.

53. See Stanton Wheeler and Mitchell L. Rothman, "The Organization as Weapon in White-Collar Crime," *Michigan Law Review* 80:1403 (1982).

54. On the Teapot Dome scandal, see Francis X. Busch, *Enemies of the State* (1954); and Morris R. Werner, *Teapot Dome* (1959).

55. Geis and Goff, "Edwin H. Sutherland's White Collar Crime," p. 5.

56. 48 Stats. 881 (act of June 6, 1934). On the history and early enforcement of the SEC act, see Michael E. Parrish, *Securities Regulation and the New Deal* (1970).

57. Susan P. Shapiro, *Wayward Capitalists* (1984), p. 5.

58. See Kitty Calavita and Henry N. Pontell, "'Heads I Win, Tails You Lose': Deregulation, Crime, and Crisis in the Savings and Loan Industry," *Crime and Delinquency* 36:309 (1990).

59. David Weisburd et al., *Crimes of the Middle Classes: White-Collar Offenders in the Federal Courts* (1991), p. 4.

60. Weisburd et al., *Crimes of the Middle Classes*, p. 131.

61. Despite "frantic appeals," Leona Helmsley was sentenced to four years in prison (*New York Times*, Dec. 13, 1989, p. B1). On Boesky, see, for example, *Washington Post*, May 10, 1987, p. A1.

62. *New York Times*, Feb. 6, 1992, pp. A1, C4.

CHAPTER 14. REALIGNMENT AND REFORM

1. The rules were not to take effect until reported to Congress by the attorney general. 54 Stats. 688 (act of June 29, 1940). On the history and development of the rules, see George H. Dession, "The New Federal Rules of Criminal Procedure: I," *Yale Law Journal* 55:694 (1946).

2. The terms, of course, are derived from the classic work by Herbert Packer, *The Limits of the Criminal Sanction* (1968).

3. On the imagery and social meaning of the Constitution, see Michael Kammen, *A Machine That Would Go of Itself: The Constitution in American Culture* (1986).

4. See Lawrence M. Friedman and Robert V. Percival, *The Roots of Justice: Crime and Punishment in Alameda County, California 1870–1910* (1981), pp. 283–84.

5. Albert J. Harno, "The Supreme Court in Felony Cases," *Illinois Crime Survey* (1929), p. 117.

6. Robert A. Kagan et al., "The Business of State Supreme Courts, 1870–1970," *Stanford Law Review* 30:121, 148 (1977). This was a study of sixteen state supreme courts; in these sixteen courts, 18.2 percent of the cases between 1940 and 1970 were criminal, and 30.8 percent of these raised issues of procedural due process. Criminal cases had become more important in general to appellate courts. In 1965, no less than 6 percent of *all* appeals heard by the same group of sixteen state supreme courts derived from murder trials. (Ibid., p. 146.)

7. 32 U.S. (7 Pet.) 243 (1833).

8. 149 U.S. 60 (1893).

9. Ibid., at 67.

10. 168 U.S. 532 (1897).

11. 318 U.S. 332 (1943).

12. 211 U.S. 78 (1908).

13. Ibid., at 99.

14. In the first part of his opinion, Justice Moody, speaking for the majority, dealt with another question: whether or not the privilege against self-incrimination was one of the "privileges and immunities" of American citizens, protected under the Fourteenth Amendment. He held that it was not.

15. 287 U.S. 45 (1932); see David J. Bodenhamer, *Fair Trial: Rights of the Accused in American History* (1992), pp. 92–94; on the Scottsboro case generally, see Dan T. Carter, *Scottsboro: A Tragedy of the American South* (1969).

16. Powell v. Alabama, 287 U.S. 45, 71 (1932).

17. For the whole story, see Carter, *Scottsboro*.

18. For this thesis, see Lawrence M. Friedman, *Total Justice* (1985).

19. 232 U.S. 383 (1914).

20. 338 U.S. 25 (1949).

21. 367 U.S. 643 (1961).

22. 380 U.S. 609 (1965).

23. The case, as we saw, was Wilson v. U.S., 149 U.S. 60 (1893).

24. Miranda v. Arizona, 384 U.S. 436 (1966). For the story of this famous case, see Liva Baker, *Miranda: Crime, Law and Politics* (1983).

25. Baker, *Miranda*, pp. 408–9.

26. 372 U.S. 335 (1963). For an account of this fascinating and important case, and the human story behind it, see Anthony Lewis, *Gideon's Trumpet* (1964).

27. Bruce Allen Murphy, *Fortas: The Rise and Ruin of a Supreme Court Justice* (1988), pp. 87–89; Laura Kalman, *Abe Fortas* (1990), pp. 180–93.

28. Sam B. Warner and Henry B. Cabot, "Changes in the Administration of Criminal Justice During the Past Fifty Years," *Harvard Law Review* 50:583, 589 (1937).

29. See Lawrence M. Friedman, *The Republic of Choice* (1981); and the discussion in chapter 19.

30. Some commentators at the time thought the case would be "received with rejoicing by every thug in the land." See *U.S. News and World Report*, June 27, 1966, p. 34. This, of course, was a wild exaggeration, but did the decision do anything to *tame* the police? Most of the studies do not find dramatic changes, which is not surprising. "Interrogations in New Haven: The Impact of *Miranda*," *Yale Law Journal* 76:1519 (1967), was an early, and thorough, study; another was Neal A. Milner, *The Court and Local Law Enforcement: The Impact of Miranda* (1971), a study of police practice in Wisconsin. A more recent and gloomy assessment is that the *Miranda* warnings "are almost wholly ineffective"; Matthew Lippman, "Miranda v. Arizona: Twenty Years Later," *Criminal Justice Journal* 9:285 (1987). But the case, and others like it, may have had fairly subtle ripple effects, or provided a bit of reinforcement to a trend already under way.

31. David Simon, *Homicide: A Year on the Killing Streets* (1991), pp. 199–200.

32. The description is drawn from Sheldon Glueck and Eleanor T. Glueck, *Five Hundred Criminal Careers* (1930), pp. 31–32.

33. Andrew A. Bruce et al., *The Workings of the Indeterminate-Sentence Law and the Parole System in Illinois* (1928; reprint ed., 1968), p. 48.

34. Va. Stats. 1942, Tit. 40, chap. 1883; Code Miss., 1942, sec. 40004.

35. Bruce et al., *Indeterminate-Sentence Law*, p. 49.

36. Ibid., p. 56.

37. These are listed in Hans von Hentig, "Degrees of Parole Violation and Graded Remedial Measures," *Journal of Criminal Law and Criminology* 33:363 (1943).

38. See Samuel Walker, *Popular Justice: A History of American Criminal Justice* (1980), pp. 248–49; Lynne Goodstein and John Hepburn, *Determinate Sentencing and Imprisonment: A Failure of Reform* (1985).

39. Pamala L. Griset, *Determinate Sentencing* (1991), p. 39.

40. Ibid., pp. 30–31; see also Jessica Mitford, *Kind and Usual Punishment: The Prison Business* (1973), pp. 79–94.

41. In re Lynch, 8 Cal. 3d 410, 105 Cal. Rptr. 217, 503 P. 2d 921 (1972).

42. Ibid., 105 Cal. Rptr. at 235–36.

43. In re Foss, 10 Cal. 3d, 910, 112 Cal. R. 649, 519 P. 2d 1073 (1974).

44. Ill. Rev. Stats. (1983), Tit. 38, sec. 1003-3-3(c).

45. Goodstein and Hepburn, *Determinate Sentencing*, pp. 58–60.

46. Ibid., pp. 157, 169.

47. Ill. Rev. Stats. (1983), Tit. 38, sec. 1003-3-3(b).

48. For a critical assessment, see Lynne N. Henderson, "The Wrongs of Victim's Rights," *Stanford Law Review* 37:937 (1985).

49. Ibid., p. 951.

50. Laws Cal. 1965, Vol. 2, chap. 1549, p. 3641.

51. 98 Stats. 2170 (act of October 12, 1984); federal grants to state programs as well.

52. Friedman, *Total Justice*.

53. Quoted in Frank Tannenbaum, *Osborne of Sing Sing* (1933), pp. 6–7.

54. Lewis E. Lawes, *Twenty Thousand Years in Sing Sing* (1932), pp. 23, 24, 33, 34.

55. Tannenbaum, *Osborne*, pp. 326, 328, 329–30.

56. Joseph F. Fishman, *Crucibles of Crime: The Shocking Story of the American Jail* (1923; reprint ed., 1969), pp. 21, 42, 81, 168.

57. Harvey R. Hougen, "Kate Barnard and the Kansas Penitentiary Scandal, 1908–1909," in *Journal of the West* 17, 1:9 (Jan. 1978).

58. A prisoner who was sent to Pontiac (Illinois) in the 1920s described the prison as "very clean and sanitary." But "the way of the transgressor of the prison rules was hard." Guards delighted in sending prisoners to the "hole" (solitary confinement), which was "dark, absolutely barren. . . . The odor is awful." Although prisoners were "allowed out in the yard," and the prisoners played "lively ball games," the monotony was maddening. Clifford R. Shaw, *The Jack-Roller: A Delinquent Boy's Own Story* (1930), pp. 104, 110–11.

59. Robert E. Burns, *I Am a Fugitive from a Georgia Chain Gang* (1932), p. 47.

60. Oscar Dowling, "The Hygiene of Jails, Lock-ups and Police Stations," *Journal of the American Institute of Criminal Law and Criminology* 5:695, 697 (1915).

61. Johnson v. Dye, Warden, 175 Fed. 2d 250 (C.A. 3, 1949).

62. Dye v. Johnson, 338 U.S. 864 (1949); apparently, the Court reversed on the grounds that Johnson had not exhausted state remedies. The case is discussed in [Note:] "Prisoners' Remedies for Mistreatment," *Yale Law Journal* 59:800 (1950).

63. Laws Ga. 1946, p. 46, secs. 7, 12, 13.

64. Osborne wrote a book about his experiences in the prison, *Within Prison Walls* (1914). He dedicated his book to "our brothers in gray," who had won his "lasting gratitude and affection by their courtesy, sympathy, and understanding." He was *not* incognito during his week in prison; the prisoners knew who he was, but respected him anyway (he says) for choosing to share their life. Needless to say, his somewhat romantic account has to be taken with a grain of salt. On Osborne's career, see Tannenbaum, *Osborne*; and Samuel Walker, *Popular Justice*, pp. 150–53.

65. Quoted in Hougen, "Kate Barnard," p. 11.

66. The Ragen era and the history of Stateville up to the mid-seventies are described in James B. Jacobs, *Stateville: The Penitentiary in Mass Society* (1977).

67. Mitford, *Kind and Usual Punishment*, pp. 244–45.

68. Merrick v. Lewis, 22 Pa. D. 55 (1912).

69. Ruffin v. Commonwealth, 62 Va. (21 Gratt.) 790 (1871). The prisoner, said the court, "as a consequence of his crime, not only forfeited his liberty, but all his personal rights except those which the law in its humanity accords to him. He is for the time being the slave of the state."

70. 247 F. Supp. 683 (E.D. Ark., 1965).

71. Ibid., at 689.

72. 309 F. Supp. 362 (E.D. Ark., 1970).

73. Ibid., at 373; see Susan Sturm, "Resolving the Remedial Dilemma: Strategies of Judicial Intervention in Prisons," *University of Pennsylvania Law Review* 138:805 (1990).

74. See Erving Goffman, *Asylums: Essays on the Social Situation of Mental Patients and Other Inmates* (1962).

75. Leo D. Stanley, the chief surgeon of San Quentin, wrote, in *Men at Their Worst* (1940), about a surly "malcontent" with a long history of "petty violations of the law" who wrote a long letter "berating and sneering at his mother." Stanley was proud to report that the "long-suffering mother never received that letter. The aroused censor saw to that" (pp. 102–3).

76. 416 U.S. 396 (1974).

77. Ibid., at 419.

78. 393 U.S. 483 (1969).

79. Richard Hawkins and Geoffrey P. Alpert, *American Prison Systems: Punishment and Justice* (1989), p. 325.

80. Charles E. Silberman, *Criminal Violence, Criminal Justice* (1978), p. 390.

81. Fishman, *Crucibles of Crimes*, pp. 73–74.

82. Clifford R. Shaw, *The Jack-roller: A Delinquent Boy's Own Story* (1930), p. 38.

83. Ibid., p. 153.

84. Osborne, *Within Prison Walls*, p. 323.

85. See, in general, Franklin E. Zimring and Gordon Hawkins, *The Scale of Imprisonment* (1991).

86. U.S. Department of Justice, *Sourcebook of Criminal Justice Statistics, 1989*, p. 582. This increase is, of course, completely out of proportion to population growth. In the fifties and sixties, the numbers were stable, and even declining.

87. Franklin E. Zimring and Gordon Hawkins, *Prison Population and Criminal Justice Policy in California* (1992), pp. 1, 3.

88. On the Attica riot, see Tom Wicker, *A Time to Die* (1975). Prison riots seem to break out on a regular basis. For example, the *Los Angeles Times* reported on October 30, 1989, that the Pennsylvania prison system was "rocked" by its fourth riot in one week. Officials clamped a lock-down on Holmesburg Prison near Philadelphia after a four-hour riot that injured 150 inmates and guards. *Los Angeles Times*, October 29, 1989, Part A, p. 25. See also Bert Useem and Peter Kimball, *States of Siege: U.S. Prison Riots, 1971–1986* (1991).

89. 408 U.S. 238 (1972). On the background of this case, see Michael Meltsner, *Cruel and Unusual: The Supreme Court and Capital Punishment* (1973). For a perceptive study of *Furman* and what followed, see Robert Weisberg, "Deregulating Death," *Supreme Court Review* (1983), p. 305.

90. Between 1930 and 1984, 3,891 prisoners were executed in the United States. Of these, 53.1 percent (2,067) were black. Of the 455 individuals executed for rape, almost 90 percent (405) were black, virtually all of them in the South. Adalberto Aguirre, Jr., and David V. Baker, "Empirical Research on Racial Discrimination in the Imposition of the Death Penalty," *Criminal Justice Abstracts* 22:135 (1990).

91. Neil Vidmar and Phoebe C. Ellsworth, "Public Opinion and the Death Penalty," *Stanford Law Review* 26:1245–70 (1974).

92. Walker, *Popular Justice*, p. 250.

93. Weisberg, "Deregulating Death," p. 315.

94. Woodson v. North Carolina, 428 U.S. 280 (1976).

95. 431 U.S. 633 (1977).

96. 428 U.S. 153 (1976).

97. Cal. Penal Code, sec. 190.2.

98. 31 Cal. 3d 797, 647 Pac. 2d 76 (1982).

99. U.S. Department of Justice, *Sourcebook of Criminal Justice Statistics, 1989*, pp. 168–69.

100. 433 U.S. 584 (1977).

101. Ibid., at 592.

102. 481 U.S. 281 (1987).

103. Ibid., at 312.

104. More appeals were brought on behalf of McCleskey, all of which failed. On September 25, 1991, he was put to death.

105. 109 S. Ct. 2969 (1989).

106. So, for example, the Supreme Court in the Bush years tried to cut back on the writ of habeas corpus in death cases. See McCleskey v. Zant, 111 S. Ct. 1454 (1991), (Warren McClesky again); Coleman v. Thomas, 111 S. Ct. 2546 (1991).

107. Discussed in Charles F. Bostwick, "Proposed Reforms in Criminal Procedure," *Journal of Criminal Law* 2:216, 227 (1911). The writer contrasted this case with the contemporary English case of Dr. Crippen, who was executed five weeks after his trial began.

108. *New York Times*, Feb. 16, 1933, p. 1; March 21, 1933, p. 1.

109. *New York Times*, June 18, 1991 (national ed.), p. A10. For a graphic account (as of 1990) of two men on death row for crimes committed sixteen years earlier, see *New York Times*, July 23, 1990, p. A1: "Two Lives Ended, but Two Convicts Survive." As of this writing (February 1993), both convicts were still alive.

110. *New York Times*, April 22, 1992 (national ed.), pp. A1, C23.

111. *New York Times*, April 21, 1992 (national ed.), p. A7.

112. *New York Times*, Aug. 9, 1991 (national ed.), p. A10.

113. *New York Times*, Jan. 16, 1992 (national ed.), p. A12.

114. See District Attorney of Suffolk v. Watson, 381 Mass. 648, 411 N.E. 2d 1274 (1980); Commonwealth v. O'Neal, 369 Mass. 242, 339 N.E. 2d 676 (1975); Opinion of the Justices, 372 Mass. 912, 364 N.E. 2d 1984 (1977).

115. The case was Commonwealth v. Colon-Cruz, 393 Mass. 150, 470 N.E. 2d 116 (1984).

116. Robert Weisberg, "Deregulating Death," p. 386.

117. *New York Times*, March 27, 1992, p. B16; for Arizona's execution, see *New York Times*, April 7, 1992, p. A25. The execution took place on April 6, 1992.

CHAPTER 15. LAW, MORALS, AND VICTIMLESS CRIME

1. *San Diego Union*, Nov. 22, 1908, p. 16; Nov. 25, 1908, p. 8.

2. Lawrence M. Friedman and Robert V. Percival, *The Roots of Justice: Crime and Punishment in Alameda County, California, 1870–1910* (1981), p. 93.

3. Ibid.

4. 36 Stats. 825 (act of June 25, 1910). A major study of the background, meaning, and effect of this law is David Langum, *Crossing Over the Line: Interstate Immorality and the Mann Act, 1901–1986* (forthcoming).

5. Quoted in Frederick K. Grittner, *White Slavery: Myth, Ideology and American Law* (1990), p. 91.

6. 18 Stats. 477 (act of March 3, 1875).

7. 36 Stats. 825 (act of June 25, 1910), sec. 6.

8. Grittner, *White Slavery*, p. 96.

9. Sally Stanford, *The Lady of the House* (1966), p. 95.

10. See Ruth Rosen, *The Lost Sisterhood: Prostitution in America, 1900–1918* (1982), pp. 112–35.

11. Maude E. Miner, *Slavery of Prostitution: A Plea for Emancipation* (1916; reprint ed., 1987), pp. 88–89.

12. 242 U.S. 470 (1917). The full story of this case is told in Robert L. Anderson, *The Diggs-Caminetti Case, 1913–1917* (2 vols., 1990).

13. Marlene D. Beckman, "The White Slave Traffic Act: The Historical Impact of a Criminal Law Policy on Women," *Georgetown Law Journal* 72:1111, 1119 (1984).

14. State v. Reed, 53 Mont. 292, 163 P. 477 (1917); the statute was Laws Mont. 1911, chap 1.

15. James Wunsch, *Prostitution and Public Policy: From Regulation to Suppression, 1858–1920* (Ph.D. thesis, University of Chicago, 1976), p. 136.

16. Rosen, *Lost Sisterhood*, p. 118.

17. Beckman, "White Slave Traffic Act," pp. 1124–33.

18. The survey is described in *Vigilance* 24:5 (May 1911).

19. *Vigilance* 23:13 (Oct. 1910), p. 9.

20. Walter C. Reckless, *Vice in Chicago* (1933; reprint ed., 1969), pp. 1–3; Herbert Asbury, *Gem of the Prairie: An Informal History of the Chicago Underworld* (1940), pp. 281–308.

21. Rosen, *Lost Sisterhood*, pp. 14–15.

22. Vice Commission of Chicago, *The Social Evil in Chicago: A Study of Existing Conditions* (1911), p. 25.

23. Edward R. A. Seligman, ed., *The Social Evil, with Special Reference to Conditions Existing in the City of New York* (2d ed., 1912), pp. 72–74; this is a revision of a report originally published by the "Committee of Fifteen" in 1902. In a speech Seligman gave in 1910 he said: "Anything that tends to render vice innocuous tends to incite to debauch"; and if the state "whitewashes" the situation, "it tends to augment the . . . demand" (p. 250).

24. Rosen, *Lost Sisterhood,* pp. 28–29.

25. Laws. Mich. 1915, No. 272, p. 481.

26. Clare V. McKanna, Jr., "Prostitutes, Progressives, and Police: The Viability of Vice in San Diego, 1900–1930," *Journal of San Diego History* 35:44 (1989).

27. Described in Thomas C. Mackey, *Red Lights Out: A Legal History of Prostitution, Disorderly Houses, and Vice Districts, 1870–1917* (1987).

28. *Illinois Crime Survey* (1929), p. 852.

29. McKanna, "Prostitutes," p. 59.

30. Rosen, *Lost Sisterhood,* p. 33.

31. *Annual Report, Police Commissioner of the City of New York, year ending Dec. 31, 1910* (1911), pp. 12, 14.

32. *Annual Report, Police Department of the City of Chicago, year ending Dec. 31, 1926,* p. 19.

33. George E. Worthington and Ruth Topping, "The Second Sessions of the Municipal Court of the City of Boston," *Journal of Social Hygiene* 8:191, 200, 222 (1922).

34. *Second Annual Report, Municipal Court of Philadelphia (1915),* pp. 54, 72.

35. Laws. Ind. 1907, chap. 60. On the role of women's movements in the campaign to raise the age of consent, see Rosen, *Lost Sisterhood,* p. 55.

36. Laws Cal. 1913, chap. 122, p. 212 (amending Section 261 of the Penal Code).

37. See the table of ages in Mary Ellen Odem, "Delinquent Daughters: The Sexual Regulation of Female Minors in the United States, 1880–1920" (Ph.D. thesis, Department of History, University of California, Berkeley, 1989), pp. 73–74.

38. Friedman and Percival, *Roots of Justice,* p. 140.

39. *Columbus Dispatch,* June 17, 1891, p. 7.

40. Superior Court Records, Santa Clara County, California, Case No. 18661.5, June 5, 1925.

41. Odem, "Delinquent Daughters," pp. 87–88.

42. Jacob A. Goldberg and Rosamond W. Goldberg, *Girls on City Streets: A Study of 1,400 Cases of Rape* (1935; reprint ed., 1974), p. 300.

43. William J. Blackburn, *The Administration of Criminal Justice in Franklin County, Ohio* (1935), pp. 152–53.

44. Henry Herbert Goddard, *The Kallikak Family: A Study in the Heredity of Feeble-Mindedness* (1925).

45. Ibid., pp. 18–19, 110.

46. Ibid., p. 108.

47. Laws Ind. 1907, chap. 215. See also, in general, J. H. Landman, "The History of Human Sterilization in the United States—Theory, Statute, Adjudication," *Illinois Law Review* 23:463 (1929); Philip R. Reilly, *The Surgical Solution: A History of Involuntary Sterilization in the United States* (1991).

48. Laws Cal. 1909, chap. 720, p. 1093.

49. Mark H. Haller, *Eugenics: Hereditarian Attitudes in American Thought* (1963), pp. 49, 136.

50. Ibid., p. 123.

51. Quoted in Donald K. Pickens, *Eugenics and the Progressives* (1968), p. 90.

52. W. D. Funkhouser, "Eugenical Sterilization," *Kentucky Law Journal* 23:511, 513 (1935).

53. See Pickens, *Eugenics and the Progressives*, (1968), p. 90.

54. Rev. Stats. Nev. 1912, sec. 6293, Vol. 2, p. 1812.

55. Mickle v. Henrichs, 262 Fed. 687 (D.C. Nev., 1918).

56. Williams et al. v. Smith, 190 Ind. 526, 131 N.E. 2 (1921).

57. Acts Ind. 1927, chap. 50, p. 116; Acts Ind. 1931, chap. 241, p. 713.

58. 274 U.S. 200 (1927).

59. *New York Times*, Feb. 23, 1980, p. 6; March 7, 1980, p. A16. See also Paul A Lombardo, "Three Generations, No Imbeciles: New Light on *Buck v. Bell*," *New York University Law Review* 60:30 (1985).

60. Leo Stanley, *Men at Their Worst* (1940), pp. 113–14.

61. Stanley, *Men at Their Worst*, pp. 157, 162–63.

62. Quoted in a review by Robert H. Gault, in *Journal of Criminal Law* 2:648 (1912). There were other anomalies, for example, the "thickness of the skull . . . the fusion of the two parietal bones in the sagittal line of the skull," and so on. Junkins had been a "tin-can tramp. His early habitat was as undesirable as could be imagined." He was hung for a brutal murder in 1910.

63. Earnest A. Hooton, *Crime and the Man* (1939), pp. 124, 367.

64. 316 U.S. 535 (1942).

65. Ibid., at 541.

66. Wash. Rev. Code Ann. sec. 9.92–100 (1961). The statute is apparently rarely, if ever, used.

67. The Volstead Act was established in 41 Stats. 305 (act of October 28, 1919), and the Wright Act in Laws Cal. 1921, p. 79.

68. 45 Stats. 1446 (act of March 2, 1929). The act recited the "intent of Congress" that courts should "discriminate between casual or slight violations and habitual sales of intoxicating liquor, or attempts to commercialize violations of the law."

69. William J. Blackburn, *The Administration of Criminal Justice in Franklin County, Ohio* (1935), p. 237. In that year, there were also 4,285 arrests for drunkenness, and 166 arrests for "driving while intoxicated," which are, in a way, measures of the obvious fact that Prohibi-

tion, whatever the enforcement level, did not stamp out drinking or drunkenness.

70. Hugh N. Fuller, *Criminal Justice in Virginia* (1931), p. 66.

71. Quoted in Fuller, *Criminal Justice in Virginia*, p. 136.

72. *Illinois Crime Survey* (1929), p. 1099.

73. Samuel Walker, *Popular Justice: A History of American Criminal Justice* (1980), p. 182.

74. Gilman M. Ostrander used this term in his book *Nevada: The Great Rotten Borough, 1859–1964* (1966).

75. Laws Nev. 1909, chap. 210.

76. Ostrander, *Nevada*, p. 207; see Laws Nev. 1913, chap. 149, p. 235; Laws Nev. 1931, chap. 99, p. 165.

77. Henry Chafetz, *Play the Devil: A History of Gambling in the United States from 1492 to 1955* (1960), pp. 452–53. The quote is from the columnist Red Smith.

78. See, in general, Jerome H. Skolnick, *House of Cards: The Legalization and Control of Casino Gambling* (1978).

79. *Fortieth Annual Report, Municipal Court of Philadelphia (1953)*, p. 245.

80. William Seagle, "The Twilight of the Mann Act," *American Bar Association Journal* 55:641 (1969).

81. Grittner, *White Slavery*, pp. 149–50.

82. U.S. v. McClung, 187 Fed. Supp. 254 (D.C.E.D. La., 1960). The judge, Skelly Wright, read the Mann Act as condemning only immorality that was "habitual . . . an immoral *status* of some duration." (Ibid., at 258.) He also tried, somewhat feebly, to distinguish the *Caminetti* case.

83. Grittner, *White Slavery*, p. 163.

84. Nevertheless, Beckman reports that 439 defendants were committed to prison between 1970 and 1982 for violating the Mann Act—presumably all for commercialized vice offenses. "White Slave Traffic Act," p. 1134.

85. 92 Stats. 7, 8–9 (act of Feb. 6, 1978); 18 U.S. C. A. 2423.

86. The new title of the law was Transportation for Illegal Sexual Activity and Related Crimes.

87. 100 Stats. 3511 (act of Nov. 7, 1986); 18 U.S. C.A. 2421.

88. *Third Annual Report, Municipal Court of Chicago (1908–1909)*, p. 80.

89. Lawrence R. Murphy, "Defining the Crime Against Nature: Sodomy in the United States Appeals Courts, 1810–1940," *Journal of Homosexuality* 19:49, 63 (1990).

90. State v. Start, 65 Ore. 178, 132 P. 512 (1913); for the statute, see Rev. Stats. Ore., 1909, Vol. 1, p. 929, simply referring to "sodomy or the crime against nature."

91. Start's conviction, however, was reversed on other grounds. For a similar reading of a statute, see State v. Guerin (51 Mont. 250, 152 P. 747 [1915]). The court said: "Every intelligent adult person understands

fully what the ordinary course of nature demands or permits for the purpose of procreation ... [and] any departure from this course is against nature."

92. Murphy, "Defining the Crime," p. 61. Apparently, there is no reported case before the Second World War in which a lesbian was convicted under a sodomy statute, according to Murphy. Some statutes plainly excluded this possibility, by referring exclusively to crimes against nature committed with men. The other sort of crime against nature was, apparently, totally unthinkable.

93. Alfred C. Kinsey, Wardell B. Pomeroy, and Clyde E. Martin, *Sexual Behavior in the Human Male* (1948), p. 392.

94. Alfred C. Kinsey et al., *Sexual Behavior in the Human Female* (1953).

95. Ibid., pp. 673–74.

96. Ibid., p. 453.

97. John D'Emilio and Estelle B. Freedman, *Intimate Matters: A History of Sexuality in America* (1988), p. 294.

98. See John Gerassi, *The Boys of Boise: Furor, Vice, and Folly in an American City* (1966).

99. State v. Saunders, 75 N.J. 200, 381 Atl. 2d 333 (1977). The Connecticut repeal is Laws Conn. 1967, p. 1618.

100. On Texas: See Jeremy D. Weinstein, "Adultery, Law and the State," *Hastings Law Journal* 38:195, 230–36 (1986); the Massachusetts case is Commonwealth v. Stowell, 389 Mass. 171, 449 N.E. 2d 357 (1983). The Texas statute was repealed in 1973 (Laws Tex. 1973, chap. 399), as part of a general reform and reenactment of the Penal Code.

101. *New York Times*, April 30, 1990, p. A1.

102. D'Emilio and Freedman, *Intimate Matters*, p. 223.

103. State v. Saunders, 75 N.J. 200, 381 Atl. 2d 333 (1977).

104. State v. Saunders, 75 N.J. 200, 381 Atl. 2d 333, 335 (1977).

105. Quoted in Richard Green, "Fornication: Common Law Legacy and American Sexual Privacy," *Anglo-American Law Review* 17:226 (1988).

106. See Andrew J. Cesare, "Updating California's Sex Code: The Consenting Adults Law," *Criminal Justice Journal* 1:65 (1976); the law is Laws Cal. 1975, chap 71, p. 131. Under this statute, sodomy remained illegal for anyone in jail or prison, despite consent. Ibid., at 133.

107. 478 U.S. 186, 106 S. Ct. 2841 (1986). The background of the case is discussed in Peter Irons, *The Courage of Their Convictions* (1988), chap. 16.

108. "I think I probably made a mistake in that one," said Justice Powell in a discussion with a group of students at New York University Law School, October 18, 1990. (*National Law Journal*, Nov. 5, 1990, p. 3.)

109. Commonwealth v. Jeffrey Wasson, 842 S.W. 2d 487 (Ky., 1992).

110. See Lawrence M. Friedman, *The Republic of Choice: Law, Authority, and Culture* (1990), pp. 152–53.

111. 381 U.S. 479 (1965). A number of states had recently joined the decriminalization parade, including Colorado, Indiana, and Kansas. Laws

Colo. 1961, p 327; Laws Ind. 1963, chap. 12, sec. 9; Laws Kans. 1963, chap. 222.

112. Ibid., at 485.

113. 405 U.S. 438 (1972).

114. Ibid., at 440.

115. James C. Mohr, *Abortion in America: The Origins and Evolution of National Policy* (1978), p. 254.

116. Leslie J. Reagan, "'About to Meet Her Maker': Women, Doctors, Dying Declarations, and the State's Investigation of Abortion, Chicago, 1867–1940," *Journal of American History*, 77:1240 (1991).

117. Mohr, *Abortion in America*, pp 252–53.

118. Roe v. Wade, 410 U.S. 113 (1973).

119. Planned Parenthood v. Casey, 112 S. Ct. 2791 (1992).

120. Cleveland Board of Education v. LaFleur, 414 U.S. 632 (1974); Peter Irons, *The Courage of Their Convictions* (1988), chap. 13.

121. See Lawrence M. Friedman, "Limited Monarchy: The Rise and Fall of Student Rights," in David L. Kirp and Donald N. Jensen, eds., *School Days, Rule Days: The Legalization and Regulation of Education* (1986), pp. 238, 244–45.

122. Felice F. Lewis, *Literature, Obscenity and Law* (1976), pp. 54–57.

123. *New York Times*, Sept. 17, 1913, p. 9.

124. Lewis, *Literature, Obscenity and Law*, pp. 125–31.

125. Commonwealth v. Delacey, 271 Mass. 327, 171 N.E. 455 (1930). The name of the book is not even mentioned in the case. The court agreed that the book was "obscene, indecent and impure", and utterly tended "to corrupt the morals of youth." Laurence H. Tribe, *American Constitutional Law* (1978, p. 659.)

126. Commonwealth v. Friede, 271 Mass. 318, 171 N.E. 472 (1930).

127. Lewis, *Literature, Obscenity and Law*, p. 44.

128. 354 U.S. 476 (1957).

129. 335 U.S. 848 (1948).

130. A Book Named "John Cleland's Memoirs of a Woman of Pleasure" et al. v. Attorney General of Massachusetts, 383 U.S. 413, 419 (1966).

131. Ibid., at 425–26. Justice Clark, dissenting, was less tolerant: "I have 'stomached' past cases for almost 10 years without much outcry. Though I am not known to be a purist—or a shrinking violet—this book is too much even for me" (Ibid., at 441).

132. Quoted in American Booksellers Association v. Hudnut, 771 F. 2d 323 (C.A. 7, 1985). The Indianapolis ordinance was in form *civil* rather than *criminal*, somewhat like the red-light abatement ordinances discussed earlier in this chapter.

133. American Booksellers Association v. Hudnut, at 328.

134. Laws N.Y. 1905, chap. 442, p. 977.

135. 35 Stats., Part 1, chap. 100, p. 614 (act of Feb. 9, 1909); it was unlawful under this act to import opium or any opium derivative except for "medicinal purposes."

136. 38 Stats. 785 (act of Dec. 17, 1914).

137. David F. Musto, *The American Disease: Origins of Narcotic Control* (1973), p. 65.

138. Webb v. United States, 249 U.S. 96 (1919).

139. See, for example, *Brooklyn Daily Eagle*, Dec. 1, 1918, p. 6.

140. Laws Minn. 1915, chap. 260. A doctor, however, could prescribe whatever he wished, "in good faith," for the "treatment of a drug habit." The Minnesota statute was upheld by the U.S. Supreme Court in Whipple v. Martinson 249 U.S. 86 (1921).

141. Blackburn, *Criminal Justice in Franklin County*, p. 237.

142. Mary B. Harris, *I Knew Them in Prison* (1936), p. 260; there were thirteen women in the institution for Mann Act violations.

143. On Anslinger, see Musto, *The American Disease*, pp. 210–14.

144. 50 Stats. 551 (act of Aug. 2, 1937).

145. See, for example, Franklin E. Zimring and Gordon Hawkins, *The Search for Rational Drug Control* (1992); John Kaplan, *Marijuana—the New Prohibition* (1970); John Kaplan, *The Hardest Drug: Heroin and Public Policy* (1983); Ethan A. Nadelmann, "Thinking Seriously About Alternatives to Drug Prohibition," *Daedalus* 121:85 (1992).

146. For example, Ore. Rev. Stats., sec. 135.907, offering "diversion"— sending a defendant to some program not involving jail—for defendants charged with possession of less than one ounce of marijuana.

147. See *California Prisoners, 1952* (1953), p. 11; *California Prisoners and Parolees, 1990* (1991), pp. 2–6.

CHAPTER 16. THE MECHANICS OF POWER: SOME TWENTIETH-CENTURY ASPECTS

1. David R. Johnson, *American Law Enforcement: A History* (1981), pp. 112–13.

2. William J. Bopp and Donald O. Schultz, *A Short History of American Law Enforcement* (1972), p. 110.

3. Eugene J. Watts, "Police Response to Crime and Disorder in Twentieth-Century St. Louis," *Journal of American History* 70:340, 356 (1983).

4. Samuel Walker, *Popular Justice: A History of American Criminal Justice* (1980), pp. 190–91.

5. Ibid., pp. 208–9.

6. Robert M. Fogelson, *Big-City Police* (1977), pp. 142–43.

7. Walker, *Popular Justice*, p. 211.

8. Samuel Walker, *A Critical History of Police Reform: The Emergence of Professionalism* (1977), p. 74.

9. Leonard V. Harrison, *Police Administration in Boston* (1934), pp. 31, 38.

10. Bopp and Schultz, *Short History*, pp. 108–9; Morris Ploscowe, "Some Causative Factors in Criminality," in vol 1. *Report of the U.S. National Commission on Law Observance and Enforcement* (1931).

11. *Brooklyn Daily Eagle*, Dec. 4, 1914, p. 3. The mayor's comment was reported in the paper on Dec. 3, p. 2.

12. Zechariah Chafee, Jr., Walter H. Pollak, and Carl S. Stern, *Mass Violence in America: The Third Degree* (1931; reprint ed., 1968), p. 19.

13. Emanuel H. Lavine, *The Third Degree: A Detailed and Appalling Exposé of Police Brutality* (1930), pp. 62–64.

14. The account is taken from Ernest J. Hopkins, *Our Lawless Police: A Study of the Unlawful Enforcement of the Law* (1931), pp. 61–64.

15. Ibid., p. 64.

16. Cornelius W. Willemse, *Behind the Green Lights* (1931), p. 30.

17. Leonard F. Fuld, *Police Administration: A Critical Study of Police Organisations in the United States and Abroad* (1909), pp. 136–37.

18. Indeed, the chief of police of San Diego suggested that the city create an "Inebriate Farm" for "common drunks, and persons who neglect their families." (San Diego Police Department, Annual Report, 1915 [Mss., San Diego Public Library].)

19. Walker, *Popular Justice*, p. 168.

20. See, in general, Francis Russell, *A City in Terror: 1919, the Boston Police Strike* (1975).

21. Ibid., p. 169.

22. Walker, *Police Reform*, pp. 110–20.

23. Ibid., pp. 84–94.

24. *Annual Report, Police Department of the City of Los Angeles (year ending June 30, 1915)*, p. 59.

25. Quoted in Walker, *Police Reform*, p. 90.

26. Raymond B. Fosdick, *American Police Systems* (1921), p. 376n.

27. Ibid., p. 94.

28. Walker, *Popular Justice*, p. 243.

29. Fogelson, *Big-City Police*, p. 124.

30. See, in general, Mark E. Neely, Jr., *The Fate of Liberty: Abraham Lincoln and Civil Liberties* (1991).

31. 40 Stats. 230 (act of June 16, 1917); 40 Stats. 553 (act of May 16, 1918).

32. See, in general, William Preston, Jr., *Aliens and Dissenters: Federal Suppression of Radicals, 1903–1933* (1963).

33. 249 U.S. 47 (1919).

34. Ibid., at 52.

35. 250 U.S. 616 (1919); the case, its background, and its aftermath are discussed in Richard Polenberg's fine study, *Fighting Faiths: The Abrams Case, the Supreme Court and Free Speech* (1987).

36. Abrams and others were later deported to the Soviet Union; Polenberg, *Fighting Faiths*, p. 341; still later, ironically, the Soviet Union itself deported them as subversives.

37. John D. Lawson, ed., *American State Trials*, Vol. 12 (1919), pp. 897, 960–61.

38. Robert K. Murray, *Red Scare: A Study in National Hysteria, 1919–1920* (1955), pp. 210–22; Preston, *Aliens and Dissenters*, pp. 220–21.

39. Laws Ariz. 1919, chap. 11, p. 11. The Espionage Act of 1918 had made it a crime to display the flag of "any foreign enemy." 40 Stats. 553 (act of May 16, 1918).

40. Murray, *Red Scare*, pp. 233–34.

41. Laws Idaho 1917, chap. 145, p. 459.

42. Laws Cal. 1919, chap. 188, p. 281; Stephen F. Rohde, "Criminal Syndicalism: The Repression of Radical Political Speech in California," *Western Legal History* 3:309 (1990).

43. Rohde, "Criminal Syndicalism," p. 316. It is estimated that about 1,400 people were arrested under syndicalist and related laws in 1919–20, in the United States; about 300 were convicted and sent to prison. Murray, *Red Scare*, p. 234.

44. 274 U.S. 357 (1927).

45. This account is based on Charles H. Martin, *The Angelo Herndon Case and Southern Justice* (1976). The Hudson quote is pp. 57–58; the statute struck down was Ga. Code 1933, sections 26–901 to 904.

46. Herndon v. Lowry, 301 U.S. 242, 263 (1937); Martin, *The Angelo Herndon Case*, p. 182.

47. Francis Russell, *Sacco and Vanzetti: The Case Resolved* (1986), p. 222.

48. Russell, *Sacco and Vanzetti*, p. 202. Russell argues that Sacco was guilty and Vanzetti innocent. The literature on the case is enormous and highly polemical. The weight of the writing, in sheer tonnage at least, comes down on the side of innocence and miscarriage of justice.

49. Melvin I. Urofsky, *A March of Liberty: A Constitutional History of the United States* (1988), p. 726.

50. 323 U.S. 214 (1944). The background and the cases are discussed in Peter Irons, *Justice at War* (1983).

51. Harry N. Scheiber and Jane L. Scheiber, "Constitutional Liberty in World War II: Army Rule and Martial Law in Hawaii, 1941–1946," *Western Legal History* 3:341–352 (1990).

52. Scheiber and Scheiber, "Constitutional Liberty," pp. 353–54.

53. On the trial, see Stanley I. Kutler, *The American Inquisition: Justice and Injustice in the Cold War* (1982), chap. 1.

54. For one example, the vendetta in New York against the International Workers Order, an insurance organization, see Arthur J. Sabin, *Red Scare in Court: New York versus The International Workers Order* (1993).

55. On the trial and other aspects of the McCarthy period, see Urofsky, *March of Liberty*, pp. 748–57.

56. Kutler, *The American Inquisition*, chap. 6.

57. Dennis v. United States, 341 U.S. 494 (1951).

58. 354 U.S. 298 (1957).

59. 395 U.S. 444 (1969).

60. On this trial, see, for example, Alistair Cooke, *A Generation on Trial: U.S.A. v. Alger Hiss* (1950).

61. On these trials, see Steven E. Barkan, *Protesters on Trial: Criminal*

Justice in the Southern Civil Rights and Vietnam Antiwar Movements (1985).

62. Barkan, *Protesters on Trial*, p. 127.

63. *Washington Post*, May 30, 1979, p. B1; "Night of Gay Rage," *Newsweek*, June 4, 1979, p. 30.

64. *New York Times*, April 30, 1992, p. 1; May 1, 1992, p. 1.

65. Gerard C. Brandon, "The Unequal Application of the Criminal Law," *Journal of Criminal Law* 1:893, 896–97 (1911).

66. Fosdick, *American Police Systems*, p. 45.

67. See Dan T. Carter, *Scottsboro: A Tragedy of the American South* (1969), pp. 110–11.

68. See, on the Association of Southern Women for the Prevention of Lynching (ASWPL), Jacquelyn Dowd Hall, *Revolt Against Chivalry: Jessie Daniel Ames and the Women's Campaign Against Lynching* (1979). Hall is particularly good at discussing the gender aspects of lynching, that is, the way it reinforced a particular view of southern womanhood.

69. Hall, *Revolt Against Chivalry*, pp. 129–30. This particular lynching was the impetus for the creation of the ASWPL.

70. 297 U.S. 278 (1936).

71. The full story of the case is beautifully told in Carter, *Scottsboro*.

72. On Leibowitz's role in the case, see Robert Leibowitz, *The Defender: The Life and Career of Samuel S. Leibowitz, 1893–1933* (1981), pp. 186–249.

73. Fogelson, *Big-City Police*, p. 248.

74. The data in this and the following paragraph are drawn from Gerald David Jaynes and Robin W. Williams, Jr., eds., *A Common Destiny: Blacks and American Society* (1989), chap. 9. Professor Joel F. Handler, of the UCLA Law School, was chair of the panel that produced this material.

75. Jaynes and Williams, *A Common Destiny*, p. 461.

76. *New York Times*, Oct. 4, 1990, p. B6.

77. *New York Times*, April 18, 1992, p. 1.

78. Marjorie S. Zatz, "The Changing Forms of Racial/Ethnic Biases in Sentencing," *Journal of Research in Crime and Criminology* 24:69, 87–88 (1987).

79. Jaynes and Williams, *A Common Destiny*, p. 464.

80. John Gregory Dunne, "Law and Disorder in Los Angeles," *New York Review of Books*, Oct. 10, 1991, p. 23.

81. For a chronology of the Howard Beach incident, see J. Clay Smith, Jr., "The 'Lynching' at Howard Beach: An Annotated Bibliographic Index," *National Black Law Journal* 12:29 (1990).

82. Richard Maxwell Brown, *Strain of Violence* (1975), p. 213.

83. Shih-Shan Henry Tsai, *The Chinese Experience in America* (1986), pp. 165–66. On the Golden Dragon affair, see *Washington Post*, Sept. 21, 1977, p. A6.

84. Paul S. Volk, "The Legal Trail of Tears: Supreme Court Removal of Tribal Court Jurisdiction Over Crimes by and Against Reservation Indians," *New England Law Review* 20:247 (1984–85).

85. A report published in 1932 found that the Indians were fairly law-abiding people. In tribal courts, about half of all prosecutions were for drunkenness, another 16 percent for such crimes as adultery and fornication. Indians committed felonies at rates far below that of whites. See Russel Lawrence Barsh and J. Youngblood Henderson, "Tribal Courts, the Model Code, and the Police Idea in American Indian Policy," in Lawrence Rosen, ed., *American Indians and the Law* (1976), pp. 25, 41.

86. 82 Stats. 77 (act of April 11, 1968). 25 U.S.C.A. secs. 1301, 1302. On this act, see Vine Deloria, Jr., and Clifford Lytle, *The Nations Within: The Past and Future of American Indian Sovereignty* (1984), chap. 14.

87. See, in general, Alfredo Mirande, *Gringo Justice* (1987).

88. The account is drawn from Mirande, *Gringo Justice*, pp. 156–66.

89. On the riots, see ibid., pp. 166–73.

CHAPTER 17. THE CONTEMPORARY CRIMINAL TRIAL

1. William N. Gemmill, "The Criminal, Who Is He, and What Shall We Do with Him," *Journal of the American Institute of Criminal Law and Criminology* 5:170, 174–75 (1914).

2. *Annual Report, Los Angeles Police Department 1916–1917*, p. 31; *Annual Report, Los Angeles Police Department, (year ending June 30, 1915)*, pp. 6–7. The Sunrise Court was discontinued in 1918. *Annual Report, 1917–1918*, p. 53.

3. I. P. Callison, *Courts of Injustice* (1956), pp. 419–21; the New York Magistrates' Courts, as Callison described them, were much the same. See also, on the Municipal Court of Chicago, Samuel Dash, "Cracks in the Foundation of Criminal Justice," *Illinois Law Review* 46:385 (1951).

4. Wheeler v. Goodman, 306 F. Supp. 58 (D.C.W.D. No. Car., 1969); Rev. Stats. No. Car. 1969, sec. 14–336.

5. *Illinois Crime Survey, 1929*, p. 35.

6. Quoted in Lester B. Orfield, *Criminal Procedure from Arrest to Appeal* (1947), p. 365.

7. Roscoe Pound, "The Causes of Popular Dissatisfaction with the Administration of Justice," *Reports of the American Bar Assocation* 29:395 (1906).

8. U.S. v. Garsson et al., 291 Fed. 646 (S.D. N.Y., 1923).

9. Powell v. Superior Court of Los Angeles 48 Cal. 2d. 704, 312 P. 2d 698 (1957); see also Robert L. Fletcher, "Pretrial Discovery in State Criminal Cases," *Stanford Law Review* 12:293 (1960).

10. Orfield, *Criminal Procedure*, p. 457.

11. Harry Kalven, Jr., and Hans Zeisel, *The American Jury* (1966), pp. 420–23.

12. Illinois Judicial Conference. *Illinois Pattern Jury Instructions: Criminal IPI* (1968), pp. v, vii.

13. Roscoe Pound and Felix Frankfurter, eds., *Criminal Justice in Cleveland* (1922), p. 306.

14. *Annual Report, Director of Administrative Office of the U.S. Courts, 1940*, p. 15.

15. [Note:] "R.I. Statistics," *Journal of the American Institute of Criminal Law and Criminology* 31:475 (1941).

16. See Susan C. Towne, "The Historical Origins of Bench Trial for Serious Crime," *American Journal of Legal History* 26:123 (1982). Trial without jury was, of course, the norm in some of the colonies (chapter 1).

17. Patton v. U.S. 281 U.S. 276, 312 (1930).

18. *Fifth Annual Report, Judicial Council of the State of New York (1939)*, pp. 160, 174–75.

19. Kalven and Zeisel, *American Jury*, p. 25.

20. Annual Report, *Administrative Office of the Illinois Courts* (1989), p. 204.

21. Kalven and Zeisel, *American Jury*, p. 26.

22. Ibid., pp. 28–29.

23. Lawrence M. Friedman and Robert V. Percival, *The Roots of Justice: Crime and Punishment in Alameda County, California, 1870–1910* (1981), p. 173.

24. *Illinois Crime Survey, 1929*, p. 82.

25. Wayne L. Morse and Ronald H. Beattie, *Survey of the Administration of Criminal Justice in Oregon* (1932), p. 138.

26. American Law Institute, *A Study of the Business of the Federal Courts, Part I: Criminal Cases* (1934), pp. 12, 117 (tables 8 and 9).

27. Albert W. Alschuler, "Plea Bargaining and Its History," *Law and Society Review* 13:211, 231 (1978).

28. Friedman and Percival, *Roots of Justice*, p. 226.

29. Arthur Train, *The Prisoner at the Bar: Sidelights on the Administration of Criminal Justice* (1906), pp. 156, 158.

30. Ibid., p. 159.

31. Harry I. Subin, *Criminal Justice in a Metropolitan Court: The Processing of Serious Criminal Cases in the District of Columbia Court of General Sessions* (1966), pp. 12–13.

32. 400 U.S. 25 (1970).

33. 404 U.S. 257 (1971).

34. Jonathan D. Casper, *American Criminal Justice: The Defendant's Perspective* (1972), pp. 83–84.

35. Michael L. Rubinstein and Teresa J. White, "Alaska's Ban on Plea Bargaining," *Law and Society Review* 13:367 (1979).

36. See the report of the Alaska Judicial Council, *Alaska's Plea Bargaining Ban Re-evaluated* (January 1991). The verdict is: the reform is not perfect, there is slippage, but it has had a definite and long-term impact.

37. See Raymond Moley, *Tribunes of the People: The Past and Future of the New York Magistrates' Courts* (1932), pp. 178–85.

38. Lisa J. McIntyre, *The Public Defender: The Practice of Law in the Shadows of Repute* (1987), p. 41.

39. Ibid., p. 162.

40. Ibid., p. 87.

41. Casper, *American Criminal Justice*, p. 101.

42. Paul M. Angle, *Bloody Williamson: A Chapter in American Lawlessness* (1952), p. 45. The eight defendants were acquitted.

43. Sam Bass Warner and Henry B. Cabot, *Judges and Law Reform* (1936), p. 133.

44. *Illinois Crime Survey*, 1929, pp. 234–35.

45. M. R. Werner and John Starr, *Teapot Dome* (1959), pp. 225–27.

46. Warner and Cabot, *Judges*, pp. 125–26.

47. Witherspoon v. Illinois, 391 U.S. 510, 520 (1968).

48. 43 Cal. App. 3d 627, 117 Cal. Rptr. 913 (1975).

49. See *Washington Post*, Jan. 5, 1987, p. B1; *Los Angeles Times*, Aug. 27, 1986, Part 1, p. 1.

50. On this case, see Richard O'Connor, *Courtroom Warrior: The Combative Career of William Travers Jerome* (1963), chaps. 7 and 8.

51. Irvin S. Cobb, *Exit Laughing* (1942), pp. 198–99.

52. O'Connor, *Courtroom Warrior*, p. 301.

53. Hal Higdon, *The Crime of the Century: The Leopold and Loeb Case* (1975), p. 169.

54. Kevin Tierney, *Darrow: A Biography* (1979), pp. 338–39.

55. The account here is taken from William M. Kunstler, *The Minister and the Choir Singer: The Hall-Mills Murder Case* (1964).

56. William Kunstler (*The Minister and the Choir Singer* [1964]) feels that the defendants were, in fact, innocent and that the killings were carried out by the Ku Klux Klan, as a kind of vigilante action against adulterers. This guess seems to be as good as any; but it is, of course, purely a guess.

57. Quoted in M. K. Wisehart, "Newspapers and Criminal Justice," in *Criminal Justice in Cleveland* (1922), pp. 533–36.

58. *Cleveland Plain Dealer*, March 8, 1918, p. 1.

59. John Kobler, ed., *The Trial of Ruth Snyder and Judd Gray* (1938), pp. 302–3.

60. On the Lindbergh case, see, for example, Ludovic Kennedy, *The Airman and the Carpenter: The Lindbergh Kidnapping and the Framing of Richard Hauptmann* (1985), pp. 255–56. As the title suggests, Kennedy is convinced that Bruno Richard Hauptmann was innocent, but this is decidedly a minority view. For another account, see Jim Fisher, *The Lindbergh Case* (1987). The Mencken reference is

Kennedy, p. 255. On the television ban, see *Ann. Rpt., American Bar Association* 62:1134 (1937); 77:110 (1952); 104:297 (1979).

61. 381 U.S. 532 (1965). The flamboyant career of Billie Sol Estes, the pious, churchgoing, Texas swindler whose misdoings were the subject of this case, is recounted in *Time*, May 11, 1962, p. 22; May 25, 1962, p. 24. I am indebted to David Himelfarb for these references.

62. 381 U.S. 532, 536 (1965).

63. 384 U.S. 333 (1966).

64. Sheppard v. Maxwell, 384 U.S. 333, 363 (1966).

65. 449 U.S. 560 (1981).

66. Ibid., at 575.

67. People v. Moran, 249 N.Y. 179, 163 N.E. 553 (1928).

68. H. Douglas Singer, "The Deranged and Defective Delinquent," in *Illinois Crime Survey* (1929), pp. 737, 757, 759.

69. 66 N.M. 289, 347 Pac. 2d 312 (1959).

70. Durham v. United States, 214 Fed. 2d 862 (D.C., 1954).

71. Thomas Maeder, *Crime and Madness, the Origins and Evolution of the Insanity Defense* (1985), p. 92.

72. Maeder, *Crime and Madness*, pp. 92–93.

73. United States v. Brawner, 471 Fed. 2d 969 (D.C. Cir., 1972).

74. Laws Cal. 1981, chap. 404, p. 1592; Penal Code section 28(b). White was paroled after five years, and then committed suicide; see *Los Angeles Daily Journal*, Nov. 5, 1985, p. 4.

75. William F. Lewis, "Power, Knowledge, and Insanity: The Trial of John W. Hinckley, Jr.," in Robert Hariman, ed., *Popular Trials: Rhetoric, Mass Media, and the Law* (1990), pp. 114, 117, 127.

76. 98 Stats. 2057 (act of Oct. 12, 1984); 18 U.S.C.A. sec. 17.

77. See General Laws Idaho (1979), sec. 18–207; also, Mont. Rev. Stats. (1991), sec. 46–14–102, which makes evidence of mental disease or defect admissable, however, to prove "state of mind" if this is an "element of the offense." Interestingly, there were a few precursors to these statutes. Laws Miss. 1928, chap. 75, p. 92, provided that "the insanity of the defendant" was not to be "a defense against indictments for murder"; but "evidence" of insanity could be offered "in mitigation of the crime." If the jury found the defendant guilty but insane, they were to say so, and the penalty would be life imprisonment. The trial judge had discretion to "certify to the governor" his view that "the mental condition of the prisoner is such that he should not be confined in the penitentiary," and the governor could then set a process in motion which might end with the prisoner's hospitalization.

78. 66 N.M. 289, 347 Pac. 2d 312 (1959).

79. Laws N.J. 1900, chap. 102, p. 289; Laws N.Y. 1901, chap. 372, p. 1029; Laws Cal. 1903, chap. 34, p. 34.

80. Charles L. Chute, "The Development of Probation in the United States," in Sheldon Glueck, ed., *Probation and Criminal Justice* (1933), pp. 225–35.

81. Laws N.Y. 1928, chap. 460, sec. 928, p. 1014.

82. Friedman and Percival, *Roots of Justice*, p. 233.

83. Criminal Court of Cook County, Case No. 59452, Jan. 13, 1931; Adult Probation Office, Investigation Report. Despite the tone of the report, the court put Emil on twelve months' probation.

84. *San Diego Union*, Sept. 3, 1908, p. 12.

85. Charles Coons, Superior Court of Santa Clara County, Calif., Criminal Case No. 18597.5 (1925).

86. Lawrence Narvaez, Superior Court of Santa Clara County, Criminal Case No. 17894.5 (Feb. 14, 1922).

87. *Criminal Justice in Cleveland* (1922), pp. 323, 324, 330.

88. Michael J. Hindelang et. al., *Sourcebook of Criminal Justice Statistics—1973* (1973), p. 297.

89. Timothy J. Flanagan and Kathleen Maguire, eds., *Sourcebook of Criminal Justice Statistics—1989* (1990), pp. 506–7, 513.

90. William McAlpin, Superior Court of Santa Clara County, Criminal Case No. 17893.5 (Feb. 3, 1922).

91. Superior Court of Santa Clara County, Criminal Case No. 17835.5 (Oct. 28, 1921).

92. Laws N.Y. 1926, chap. 457, p. 805, amending penal code section 1941.

93. 254 N.Y. 249, 172 N.E. 487 (1930).

94. Malcolm M. Feeley, *Court Reform on Trial: Why Simple Solutions Fail* (1983), pp. 118–28; the statutes in question were Laws N.Y. 1973, chap. 278, p. 402; Laws N.Y. 1979, chap. 410, p. 905.

95. Marvin E. Frankel, *Criminal Sentences: Law Without Order* (1973), pp. 7, 9, 69.

96. Stephen J. Schulhofer and Ilene H. Nagel, "Negotiated Pleas under the Federal Sentencing Guidelines: The First Fifteen Months," *American Criminal Law Review* 27:231, 238 (1989).

97. Laws Minn. 1978, chap. 723, p. 761.

98. Lynne Goodstein and John Hepburn, *Determinate Sentencing and Imprisonment: A Failure of Reform* (1985), pp. 76–80.

99. *New York Times*, April 12, 1992 (national ed.), p. 20.

100. *New York Times*, April 12, 1992 (national ed.), pp. 1, 20.

101. Laws Colo. 1903, chap. 85, p. 178.

102. Steven L. Schlossman, *Love and the American Delinquent: The Theory and Practice of "Progressive" Juvenile Justice, 1825–1920* (1977), p. 56.

103. Anthony M. Platt, *The Child Savers: The Invention of Delinquency* (1969), p. 77; on the rise of juvenile justice, see also John R. Sutton, *Stubborn Children: Controlling Delinquency in the United States, 1640–1981* (1988); Thomas J. Bernard, *The Cycles of Juvenile Justice* (1992).

104. At the same time they created juvenile courts, states often put a new crime on the statute books: "contributing to the delinquency" of a child; see Laws. Colo. 1903, chap. 94, p. 198, which may be the first of these. Such a law, of course, could be used against parents whose parenting did not meet middle-class standards.

105. Judge Ben B. Lindsey, introduction to Thomas Travis, *The Young Malefactor* (1908), p. x.

106. Travis, *The Young Malefactor*, pp. 160–62.

107. Ben B. Lindsey and Wainwright Evans, *The Revolt of Modern Youth* (1925), pp. 159, 160, 162.

108. For example, Katharine F. Lenroot and Emma O. Lundberg, *Juvenile Courts at Work: A Study of the Organization and Methods of Ten Courts* (1925).

109. Friedman and Percival, *Roots of Justice*, pp. 223–24.

110. *Criminal Justice in Cleveland* (1922), p. 329.

111. Lenroot and Lundberg, *Juvenile Courts at Work*, p. 40.

112. 387 U.S. 1 (1967).

113. Edmund F. McGarrell, *Juvenile Correctional Reform: Two Decades of Policy and Procedural Change* (1988), pp. 110–11. The statute was Laws N.Y. 1978, chap. 481.

114. Lester Orfield, *Criminal Appeals in America* (1939), pp. 225–27.

115. Ibid.

116. C. G. Vernier and Philip Selig, Jr., "The Reversal of Criminal Cases in the Supreme Court of California," *Southern California Law Review* 2:21, 24–25 (1928).

117. J. Hugo Grimm, "Ten Years of Supreme Court Decisions," in *Missouri Crime Survey* (1926), p. 221

118. 186 S.W. 2d 243 (Tex. Crim. App., 1945).

119. Quoted in A. R. Stout, "Criminal Procedure in Texas Should Be Revised: An Address," *Texas Law Review* 25:613, 618 (1947).

120. 186 S.W. 2d at 247.

121. So, for example, under the Utah Rules of Criminal Procedure, *Utah Court Rules, 1992*, p. 411, Rule 26, section 10, a death penalty case will be "automatically reviewed by the Supreme Court," even if the "defendant has chosen not to pursue this appeal."

CHAPTER 18. GENDER AND JUSTICE

1. McKinney v. State 3 Wyo. 719 (1892).

2. Deborah Rhode, *Justice and Gender* (1989), p. 49.

3. Laws Ore. 1921, chap. 273, pp. 513, 514; R. Justin Miller, "The Woman Juror," *Oregon Law Review* 2:30 (1922).

4. Commonwealth v. Garletts, 81 Pa. Super Ct. 271 (1923).

5. R. Justin Miller, "The Woman Juror"; at 42.

6. People v. Manuel, 41 Cal. App. 153, 182 P. 306 (1919). The appellate court affirmed Ms. Manuel's conviction; the all-woman jury was in no way prejudicial, the court thought.

7. State ex rel. Passer v. County Board, 171 Minn. 177, 213 N.W. 545 (1927).

8. Acts. So. Car. 1921, No. 184, pp. 269–70.

9. La. Const. 1921, Art. 7, sec. 41.

10. Taylor v. Louisiana, 419 U.S. 522 [1975].

11. 329 U.S. 187 (1946).

12. 439 U.S. 357 (1979).

13. Caesar [Cesare] Lombroso and William [Guglielmo] Ferrero, *The Female Offender* (1958; originally published in 1894), p. 109.

14. Ibid., pp. 150–51; Joy Pollock, "Early Theories of Female Criminality," in Lee H. Bowker, *Women, Crime, and the Criminal Justice System* (1978), pp. 25, 29.

15. *Los Angeles Times*, July 2, 1992, Part A, p. 5.

16. Bowker, *Women, Crime, and the Criminal Justice System*, pp. 225–26.

17. *Annual Report, Police Department of the City of New York, year ending Dec. 31, 1905* (1906), pp. 43–48.

18. T. Earl Sullenger, "Female Criminality in Omaha," *Journal of the American Institute of Criminal Law and Criminology* 27:706 (1937).

19. Bowker, *Women, Crime, and the Criminal Justice System* (1978), p. 5.

20. See Dorothy Zietz, *Women Who Embezzle or Defraud: A Study of Convicted Felons* (1981), which also contains interesting observations on differences between male and female embezzlers.

21. Rita J. Simon and Jean Landis, *The Crimes Women Commit, the Punishments They Receive* (1991), p. 103.

22. Coramae Richey Mann, *Female Crime and Delinquency* (1984), p. 196.

23. See the discussion in Mann, *Female Crime and Delinquency*, pp. 262–71.

24. Ind. Rev. Stats. 1914 (sec. 2372, p. 1180).

25. George E. Worthington and Ruth Topping, "The Women's Day Court of Manhattan and the Bronx, New York City," *Journal of Social Hygiene* 8:393, 420–21 (1922). Laws N.Y. 1965, chap. 1030, made it a specific crime to patronize a prostitute.

26. George E. Worthington and Ruth Topping, "The Misdemeanants' Division of the Philadelphia Municipal Court," *Journal of Social Hygiene* 8:23, 33 (1922).

27. See, in general, Ruth Rosen, *The Lost Sisterhood: Prostitution in America, 1900–1918* (1982).

28. Worthington and Topping, "Women's Day Court," pp. 418, 428–29; Laws N.Y. 1918, chap. 419, p. 1268.

29. Laws Cal. 1919, chap. 165, p. 246, sec. 2.

30. In re Betty Carey, 57 Cal. App. 297, 207 P. 271 (1922).

31. Deborah Rhode, *Justice and Gender*, p. 258.

32. Nev. Rev. Stats. (1986) sec. 244.345(8).

33. It was removed in the course of a general revision of the penal code Laws Tex. 1973, chap. 399.

34. Rev. Code Del. 1915, sec. 4701, p. 2059.

35. Paul W. Tappan, *Delinquent Girls in Court: A Study of the Wayward Minor Court of New York* (1947), pp. 35, 117.

36. Mary Ellen Odem, *Delinquent Daughters* (1992), pp. 228, 234, 244, 250.

37. Simon and Landis, *Crimes Women Commit*, pp. 60–61, 62, 104.

38. 105 Kans. 139, 181 P. 630 (1919).

39. Shelly Bookspan, *A Germ of Goodness: The California State Prison System, 1851–1944* (1991), pp. 75–92.

40. Mary B. Harris, *I Knew Them in Prison* (1936), pp. 245–381, describes her experience as director.

41. Ibid., pp. 290–91.

42. Estelle Freedman, *Their Sisters' Keepers* (1981), p. 146.

43. Ibid., p. 150; Harris, *I Knew Them in Prison*, pp. 339, 359.

44. Freedman, *Their Sisters' Keepers*, pp. 131–32; for a firsthand account of one woman's experiences in Bedford Prison (New York), see Edna V. O'Brien, *So I Went to Prison* (1938).

45. Harris, *I Knew Them in Prison*, p. 260.

46. Del Martin, "The Historical Roots of Domestic Violence," in Daniel Jay Sonkin, ed., *Domestic Violence on Trial: Psychological and Legal Dimensions of Family Violence* (1987), pp. 3, 6–7.

47. Ann. Code Md. (ed. Bagby, 1924) Vol. 1, pp. 973–74. The guilty party could be sentenced to prison for up to one year, but could (theoretically) also be "whipped, not exceeding forty lashes," the act to be carried out "within the walls of the city or county jail." This is a very late, rather surprising survival (see chapter 10).

48. Linda Gordon, *Heroes of Their Own Lives: The Politics and History of Family Violence: Boston, 1880–1960* (1988).

49. Gordon, *Heroes*, at 251.

50. State v. Lynch, 436 So. 2d 567 (La., 1983).

51. The case is discussed in Lenore E. Walker, Roberta K. Thyfault, and Angela Browne, "Beyond the Juror's Ken: Battered Women," *Vermont Law Review* 7:1, 4 (1982).

52. Angela Browne, *When Battered Women Kill* (1987), p. 10.

53. Ibid., p. 12. Governor Celeste of Ohio pardoned a group of such women when he left office. *New York Times*, Dec. 22, 1990, p. 1.

54. Susan Estrich, "Sex at Work," *Stanford Law Review* 43:813, 815 (1991). The point is a good one, although rape is not the only example of a crime where the defense strategy is to "try the victim." It is more or less true for many cases of aggravated assault and murder, where the defense tries to show, if not self-defense, at least some sort of moral justification.

55. Harry Kalven, Jr., and Hans Zeisel, *The American Jury* (1966), pp. 250–52.

56. Rhode, *Justice and Gender*, pp. 248–49.

57. The case, Commonwealth v. Pugh (unreported), is discussed in H. Lane Kneedler, "Sexual Assault Law Reform in Virginia—A Legislative History," *Virginia Law Review* 68:459–82 (1982).

58. Susan Estrich, *Real Rape* (1987), p. 11.

59. *Annual Report, Police Department of the City of Chicago, year ending Dec. 31, 1926*, p. 18; *Annual Report, Police Department of the City and County of Honolulu, Terr. of Hawaii, 1935*, p. 24.

60. Rhode, *Justice and Gender*, p. 246.

61. Laws Mich. 1974, no. 266, p. 1025.
62. Laws Mich. 1974, no. 266, at 1028–29.
63. Rhode, *Justice and Gender*, p. 250.
64. Diana E. H. Russell, *Rape in Marriage* (rev. ed., 1990), pp. 17–23. The Oregon statute which abolished spousal immunity was Laws Ore. 1977, chap. 844.
65. Russell, *Rape in Marriage*, pp. 24–25.
66. See *New York Times*, April 5, 1991, p. A13; the acquittal was noted in *New York Times*, Dec. 11, 1991, p. A1.
67. Julie Horney and Cassia Spohn, "Rape Law Reform and Instrumental Change in Six Urban Jurisdictions," *Law and Society Review* 15:117 (1991). For a before-and-after study in Washington State, see Wallace D. Loh, "The Impact of Common Law and Reform Rape Statutes on Prosecution: An Empirical Study," *Washington Law Review* 55:543 (1980).
68. Estrich, *Real Rape*, p. 102.

CHAPTER 19. CRIMES OF THE SELF: TWENTIETH-CENTURY LEGAL CULTURE

1. People v. Miller, 169 N.Y. 339, 62 N.E. 418 (1902).
2. Ibid., at 346, 347.
3. Ibid., at 356.
4. Ibid., at 349.
5. See Lawrence M. Friedman, *The Republic of Choice: Law, Authority, and Culture* (1990); on expressive individualism, see Robert Bellah et al., *Habits of the Heart: Individualism and Commitment in American Life* (1985).
6. Roger M. Olien and Diana Davids Olien, *Easy Money: Oil Promoters and Investors in the Jazz Age* (1990), pp. 2–3.
7. On this point, see the interesting book by Jack Katz, *Seductions of Crime: Moral and Sensual Attractions in Doing Evil* (1988).
8. Warren I. Susman, *Culture as History: The Transformation of American Society in the Twentieth Century* (1985), chap. 14.
9. Daniel Bell, *The Cultural Contradictions of Capitalism* (1976), p. 37.
10. For an account of the crime and the trial, see Hal Higdon, *The Crime of the Century: The Leopold and Loeb Case* (1975).
11. *New York Times*, Nov. 27, 1991 (national ed.), p. A6.
12. Mercer L. Sullivan, *"Getting Paid," Youth Crime and Work in the Inner City* (1989), pp. 247, 249; Michael R. Gottfredson and Travis Hirschi, in *A General Theory of Crime* (1990), put lack of self-control and desire for easy gratification at the center of their theory.
13. *New York Times*, Sept. 4, 1990, p. B7; Sept. 5, p. A1; Sept. 7, p. B4.
14. Friedman, *Republic of Choice*, p. 135.
15. Ibid., pp. 126–30.

16. Sheldon Glueck and Eleanor T. Glueck, *Five Hundred Criminal Careers* (1930), p. 152.
17. Frederick M. Thrasher, *The Gang: A Study of 1,313 Gangs in Chicago* (2d ed., 1936), p. 37.
18. Katz, *Seductions of Crime*, pp. 312, 321.
19. Friedman, *Republic of Choice*, p. 128.
20. Quoted in Joseph L. Holmes, "Crime and the Press," *Journal of the American Institute of Criminal Law and Criminology* 20:246, 254 (1929).
21. See, for example, Paul Kovistra, *Criminals as Heroes: Structure, Power and Identity* (1989).
22. Quoted in Richard O'Connor, *Courtroom Warrior: The Combative Career of William Travers Jerome* (1963), p. 295.
23. Lewis E. Lawes, *Twenty Thousand Years in Sing Sing* (1932), p. 312.
24. Friedman, *Republic of Choice*, p. 115.

CHAPTER 20. A NATION BESIEGED

1. James Gilbert, *A Cycle of Outrage: America's Reaction to the Juvenile Delinquent in the 1950s* (1986), p. 14.
2. George Gallup, Jr., *The Gallup Poll: Public Opinion, 1990* (1991), pp. 122–23.
3. President's Commission on Law Enforcement and the Administration of Justice, *The Challenge of Crime in a Free Society* (1967), p. 166.
4. Ibid., pp. 102–4, p. 110; see James Q. Wilson and Richard J. Herrnstein, *Crime and Human Nature* (1985), pp. 408–9, 416–17.
5. *New York Times*, March 25, 1991, p. A15.
6. *New York Times*, June 27, 1990 (national ed.), p. A12.
7. Wesley G. Skogan and Michael G. Maxfield, *Coping with Crime: Individual and Neighborhood Reactions* (1981), p. 189.
8. Barry Meier, "Reality and Anxiety; Lives Changed Not Just by Crime but by Fear," *New York Times*, February 18, 1993, p. A8. The consequences of this great fear, of course, reverberate through society in large and small ways. On the very same page of the *Times*, there is a tragic story about seven children, left alone in a frame house in Detroit, who died in a fire: "anti-burglar bars on the windows kept them from escaping."
9. See, in general, Herbert Jacob, *The Frustration of Policy: Responses to Crime by American Cities* (1984); Stuart A. Scheingold, *The Politics of Law and Order: Street Crime and Public Policy* (1984).
10. Franklin E. Zimring and Gordon Hawkins, *Capital Punishment and the American Agenda* (1986), p. 150.
11. See, in general, Franklin E. Zimring and Gordon Hawkins, *The Scale of Imprisonment* (1991).
12. Roger D. McGrath, *Gunfighters, Highwaymen, and Vigilantes: Violence on the Frontier* (1984), pp. 253, 255.

13. Marvin E. Wolfgang, *Patterns in Criminal Homicide* (1958), p. 207.

14. Marc Riedel and Margaret A. Zahn, *The Nature and Patterns of American Homicide* (1985), table 2.2, p. 13.

15. Wolfgang, *Patterns in Homicide*, pp. 84, 86.

16. Riedel and Zahn, *American Homicide*, p. 51.

17. Lawrence M. Friedman, *The Republic of Choice* (1990), p. 134.

18. James Q. Wilson and Richard Herrnstein, *Crime and Human Nature* (1985), pp. 420, 435; see also Warren Susman, *Culture as History* (1984), chaps. 13 and 14.

19. See Elliott Currie, *Confronting Crime* (1985), pp. 186–210.

20. On this theme, see Friedman, *Republic of Choice* (1990).

21. Doris A. Graber, *Crime News and the Public* (1980), pp. 70–71, 80–81.

22. See, very notably, Hans Zeisel, *The Limits of Law Enforcement* (1982); Samuel Walker, *Sense and Nonsense About Crime: A Policy Guide* (2d. ed., 1989).

23. There is a large literature on the theory of deterrence. See, for example, Jack Gibbs, *Crime, Punishment, and Deterrence* (1975); Franklin E. Zimring, *Deterrence: The Legal Threat in Crime Control* (1973). On incapacitation, see Zimring and Hawkins, *Scale of Imprisonment*, pp. 104–10.

24. Zeisel, *Limits of Law Enforcement*, p. 18.

25. This point is emphasized in Walker, *Sense and Nonsense About Crime*, pp. 27–28.

26. See, on this point, Lawrence M. Friedman, *The Legal System: A Social Science Perspective* (1975), pp. 75–76.

27. *State Court Caseload Statistics: Annual Report 1989*, pp. 39–41.

28. Margaret Werner Cahalan, *Historical Corrections Statistics in the United States, 1850–1984* (1986), p. 34.

29. Zimring and Hawkins, *Scale of Imprisonment*, p. 38.

30. Department of Corrections, State of California, *California Prisoners, 1952*, p. 3; *California Prisoners and Parolees, 1990* (1991), p. 1–1.

31. Jacob, *Frustration of Policy*, pp. 166–67.

32. On the national level, there are "structural capabilities," but few "incentives to act structurally." Locally, "there is more inclination to seek structural solutions, but there are virtually no capabilities to do so." Stuart A. Scheingold, *The Politics of Street Crime: Criminal Process and Cultural Obsession* (1991), p. 182.

33. Lawrence M. Friedman and Robert V. Percival, *The Roots of Justice: Crime and Punishment in Alameda County, California, 1870–1910* (1981), p. 324.

34. Malcolm M. Feeley, *Court Reform on Trial: Why Simple Solutions Fail* (1983), p. 205. Feeley's book contains many vivid examples of the process of failure and its causes.

35. Mirjan R. Damaska, *The Faces of Justice and State Authority: A Comparative Approach to the Legal Process* (1986), pp. 17, 25.

36. Of course, the U.S. Supreme Court, at this writing (1993), seems in the

mood to speed up the process (see chap. 14). But we do not know how far they are likely to go, and there is a limit to the control they have over the process.

37. Gallup, *Gallup Poll: 1990*, p. 123. Only 6 percent thought "breakdown of family, social values" was the main factor; and "courts too lenient" was selected by only 2 percent.

INDEX